BUSTED

WENDY RUDERMAN

BARBARA LAKER

A Tale of Corruption and Betrayal

BUSTED

in the City of Brotherly Love

HARPER

www.harpercollins.com

The names and identifying characteristics of some of the individuals featured throughout this book have been changed to protect their privacy.

HarperCollins books may be purchased for educational, business, or sales promotional use. For information, please e-mail the Special Markets Department at SPsales@harpercollins.com.

FIRST EDITION

Designed by Fritz Metsch

Library of Congress Cataloging-in-Publication Data has been applied for.

ISBN 978-0-06-208544-3

14 15 16 17 18 OV/RRD 10 9 8 7 6 5 4 3 2 1

For my boys, Brody and Sawyer,
who give me immeasurable joy. I love you.

In memory of my father, Stan Ruderman, my spiritual guide.
Thank you for always cheering me on and for inspiring me to
dream—and dream big. In memory of my nephew, Jake, a little
firecracker who died too young.

—WENDY RUDERMAN

For my children, Josh and Anna,
who make everything in life better and brighter.
I'll never love anyone more.

In memory of my mom, Etta Laker, who gave me strength and
love. She taught me to never give up—and to take time to
dance in the kitchen.

—BARBARA LAKER

BUSTED

1

VENTURA "BENNY" MARTINEZ HADN'T
SLEPT IN DAYS. THIS FRIGID DECEMBER
NIGHT, LIKE SO MANY OTHERS, HE SAT
AWAKE, STIFF-BACKED AND TENSE IN A
living room chair. His pudgy, sweaty fingers
gripped the handle of a .44 Ruger equipped
with an infrared laser to illuminate whoever
would be coming for him.

His wife, Sonia, and their two small children slept on a mattress in the dining room
behind him. There, they would be insulated
from any bullets that tore through the walls.

Benny locked his eyes on the front door
of his two-story brick Philadelphia row
house and waited. Maybe tonight he'd get
whacked. Maybe tomorrow. He didn't know
when. He just knew it would happen.

Even on those rare nights when he
could briefly doze off, slumped in a chair,
his chin hitting his chest, he'd bolt upright
in a cold sweat. He had a recurring nightmare in which Jeff Cujdik, the cop he had

worked for as a drug informant, blasted his face off with a shotgun.

Benny inched toward the living room windows. He split the plastic window blinds with his fingers and checked the front porch, then slowly moved his eyes up and down the block—over and over. A streetlight cast a dull, shadowy glow. No one was there. At least Benny couldn't spot anyone.

Benny stood stock-still.

"Babe, babe, what are you doing?" Sonia asked.

"Shhh," Benny whispered.

In the darkness, Benny listened to the sounds of the street: a far-off police siren, a dog's growl, a hip-hop pulse blaring from a car stereo, the buzz-saw whine of the El.

"I can't take this no more," Sonia said. "We've gotta leave up out of Philly."

"Nah. It will be okay," Benny told her. But Sonia knew Benny didn't believe his own words.

For three years, Benny had been happy and safe in this tan row house sandwiched into a narrow block of Pacific Street. It was a neighborhood where Latinos, blacks, and whites judged one another only by who went to work and who was on welfare.

Now he feared a silent sniper, maybe crouched behind a parked car or hidden in the shadow of a neighbor's porch.

Benny never thought it would come to this. Just a few months earlier, he'd considered Jeff a blood brother. Benny's kids called him Uncle Jeff.

They were an unlikely pair. Jeff, tall, muscular, and confident, with chiseled movie-star good looks, came from a family of cops; Benny, short, plump, and street-smart, was an ex–drug dealer. Yet they developed a bond, bitching about their wives, gushing over their kids. And they both got an adrenaline rush from danger.

Jeff was a narcotics cop who relied on Benny to bust drug dealers. Time and time again, Benny ticked off names for Jeff. He told Jeff what they sold, where they lived, and the places they stashed the drugs. Then Benny made drug buys, so Jeff could get a search warrant to raid the dealers' homes and make arrests. Benny was rewarded for each buy he made, and Jeff's arrest numbers skyrocketed. They stroked each other's egos. They rose together, mismatched allies, and both became stars of the game.

Benny was practically a lifer in the world of Philadelphia police informants. The tenure of the typical informant was short. Most ran out of people to roll on, and after they made lots of drug buys, dealers could figure out who had dimed them out. But Benny was the king. He had worked for Jeff for seven years. He was smooth and convincing, the perfect con man. Dealers believed Benny was part of their world because he had been for so long. That is, until something went terribly wrong.

Now Benny was convinced that Jeff wanted him dead. And maybe worse, so did Philly's drug dealers, who'd figured out Benny was a snitch. He had a target on his back. Too many people knew where to find him and how to gun him down.

Benny knew he couldn't live like this anymore.

He came up with a plan. Tomorrow was the day.

2

IT WAS A COLD BUT SUNNY DAY IN
EARLY DECEMBER 2008, AND MY WEEK-
DAY MORNING BEGAN IN A GROUND-
HOG DAY KIND OF WAY. AFTER I SLIPPED
into jeans, sweater, and sneakers for my job
as a reporter at the *Philadelphia Daily News*, I
served the kids Eggo waffles, submerged in
a lake of gooey syrup, on the black leather
couch. I turned on the TV. They always
complained when I turned on *Sesame Street*
or *Clifford the Big Red Dog*, so I put on *Sponge-
Bob*, or some other age-inappropriate cartoon, and went to fetch the newspaper.

We subscribed to both the *Philadelphia
Inquirer* and the *Daily News*, even though
I could get them for free at work. As fewer
and fewer people bought newspapers—let
alone had them delivered—I felt it was my
duty to support the dinosaur of an industry
that was mine. It was sad to me that ours was
the only house on the block to get a daily
newspaper. Seven days a week, a woman

drove up in a maroon minivan, rolled down the driver's-side window, and hurled the plastic-wrapped newspaper sleeve onto our front lawn, a grassy postage stamp dotted with weeds and bald patches. She barely slowed before banging a K-turn in the neighbor's driveway.

At 8:00 a.m., my husband, Karl, was still asleep. I had met Karl in a tae kwon do class back in the early 1990s. He was a second-degree black belt and taught classes three nights a week. I spent the entire class watching his firm butt as he demonstrated down block, center punch. I could see his navy-blue Fruit of the Loom briefs through his white uniform. He was lanky yet muscular, with a big, beaky nose, a sexy cleft chin, and doelike brown eyes that were so warm and gentle they caught me by surprise, and still do.

Most of the friction in our marriage centered on sleep—and who got more of it. At times, I resented that Karl could sleep in, but I told myself that he, as the stay-at-home parent, needed his sleep to handle Brody, five, and Sawyer, three. The boys had a way of pulling your nerves taut and snapping them over their little knees like kindling.

"Mom, I'm sticky. I need a wipe," Brody called from the couch.

"Okay." I kept reading the newspaper, over coffee, at the dining room table.

"Mommmm! I need a wipe!"

"Okay! Jesus! I'm coming!"

In my decade-long career as a reporter, I'd written stories that helped send a corrupt New Jersey state senator to jail, shamed a governor into firing a rotten state police superintendent, and prompted lawmakers to hold hearings on racial profiling by police, nearly jettisoning the career of an ambitious and powerful state attorney general. I'd earned my share of scalps. At work, I wasn't afraid to take on the law. At home, I was totally unable to lay down the law.

I had never put my kids in time-out. Not once. Not when Sawyer punched me in the back and barked, "Get me something to drink, little woman," or when he cleaned the television screen with a wet wipe and one of his many concoctions—a mixture of pancake syrup and body lotion.

I breast-fed Brody until he was two and a half. He'd walk up to me and say, "I want boob," and I'd lift my shirt and bring his curly blond head toward me. I couldn't say no. Ever.

If the kids wanted Popsicles for breakfast, fine. Though every so often, I got tough: "No Popsicle until you finish that whole bowl of Apple Jacks." Then I'd add, "I mean it."

If they wanted dinner in the bathtub, I spoon-fed them spaghetti while they played with a fleet of blue and yellow plastic boats. Chunks of tomato and strands of pasta drifted to the bottom of the sudsy water and left an oily slick on the white porcelain.

I allowed them to watch so much TV that they went around the house singing jingles to commercials for Nationwide insurance and electric wheelchairs for the elderly—"I want to go, Go, GO in my Hoveround."

When Brody woke up in the middle of the night and stumbled into our bedroom on his stick-figure legs, I held up the covers and nestled him close, even though I knew he kept Karl awake. Brody flopped around all night, kicking and jabbing Karl with his little toenails, until Karl fled to Brody's bed or squeezed into bed with Sawyer and his menagerie of stuffed animals. Karl was a nighttime nomad, condemned to wander the Land of Bad Parenting.

Karl liked to say that I was a great mom and a terrible parent. Part of it was guilt. A workaholic, I was never home during the week. The other part was fear. The responsibility of being a parent intimidated me. So I handed over the job to Karl. He stayed home with the kids while I went off to work and sank my teeth into the hide of some crooked or incompetent city official. This way, if the kids refused to eat veggies, if they were disrespectful to other adults, if they didn't do their homework, if they became social outcasts and landed in therapy, I could blame Karl.

Karl was good at the job, too. He had the mommy thing down. He was loving and stern all at once. Of course, I didn't help much. When Karl went out grocery shopping or to the store, chaos and mischief ruled. I became the third kid. On summer nights, I allowed Brody and Sawyer to catch fireflies in Tupperware containers and let them free in the house. We turned off the lights and watched them flit around the ceiling, giggling. Sawyer sometimes dumped entire bottles of bubble bath into the tub. He then jumped out of the water and did body slides across the hardwood floors in our living room. I quickly cleaned up the snail-trail of suds with a towel before Karl came home. Karl was annoyingly compulsive about water on the hardwood. In the mornings before work, I let them play with mounds of moldable Moon Sand at the dining room table or allow them to decorate the chairs with Lightning McQueen stickers. Or they turned our kitchen into a bowling alley, flinging ripe peaches into V-shaped lines of Dixie cups. The game left splats of sticky peach juice all over the tile floor. Then I scooted out the door, leaving Karl to mop up the mess and deal with two kids, hopped up on sugar, smacking each other with pillows and wrestling naked.

It took me less than ten minutes to get from my New Jersey house to the foot of the Ben Franklin Bridge. From there, it was a straight shot down the Vine Street Expressway, through Chinatown, to Broad Street, the city's north-south artery. Broad Street cut through Philadelphia, spilling down and around City Hall like an asphalt stream.

The *Daily News* was a white multitiered building that resembled a giant wedding cake topped with a clock tower and brass dome. We had shared 400 North Broad with the *Philadelphia Inquirer*, or *Inky*, since 1957, when *Inky* owner Walter Annenberg purchased the scrappy but near-bankrupt tabloid, but locals still referred to the eighteen-floor landmark as the Inquirer Building. The *Daily News* was the *Inquirer's* brassy little sister with flaming red hair and an attitude. The edifice stood alone on Broad Street, cut off from the city's other skyscrapers by the expressway. Inga Saffron, the *Inquirer's* acclaimed architecture critic, liked to say that the building's location was symbolic of an independent press, an unbiased government watchdog, "the noble, lone seeker of truth."

Around midafternoon, Benny walked through the front doors. He stood in the front lobby and reached into his jacket pocket to pull out a crumpled piece of paper with my name scrawled on it.

"I'm here to speak to Wendy Rudumam," Benny said, butchering my last name. The security guard nodded and dialed my extension.

That morning, Benny had put his plan to get help and protection in motion. He had gone to the Police Advisory Commission, a watchdog over the 6,600-member city police force. Benny talked to Wellington Stubbs, whose job was to investigate citizen complaints against police officers. The commission was supposed to be independent from the police department and the mayor's office, but it relied on city funding. It was so understaffed and underfunded that Wellington and a handful of other investigators struggled to keep up with complaints. The commission lacked the clout and resources to do much about rogue officers. Police corruption in Philly was like a recurring cancer that reared its ugly head every ten years or so, and the commission could do little to stop or expose it. This frustrated Wellington. So he fed me story tips.

Wellington called to let me know that he was sending Benny over. Although Wellington didn't feel like he could immediately help Benny, he felt urgency. Benny didn't come across like your run-of-the-mill disgruntled criminal who wanted to seek revenge on a cop and sue the city for money. In words and actions, Benny sounded and looked desperate. Wellington didn't give me any details about Benny's story. He just figured maybe I could help him and told me so—a decision that would later cost him his job.

I headed to the lobby. Odds were, this would be a waste of time. Most stories about police corruption or brutality were garbage. They often came from lowlifes who wanted either to have their criminal records wiped clean or a payout from city coffers. Or from people who had no proof, nothing to back up their story. But some stories were the real deal. I prided myself on knowing the difference. The fact that Benny came to me through Wellington would give his tale extra weight.

Benny and I greeted each other warily. We shook hands. His palm felt moist and meaty. Benny had the baleful look of a tired basset hound, a round face atop a short, plump body. His brown eyes sat afloat in bloodshot pools of white. He wore dark blue Dickies work pants and a puffy charcoal-gray jacket, embroidered with BENNY and GEGNAS CHRYSLER JEEP, the auto dealership where he cleaned and buffed cars.

I led him up the lobby's worn marble steps near the elevators. The lobby was a tomb of marble and gold-painted molding. The light fixture was a giant globe with blue oceans and white continents encircled by a brass Saturn-like ring. The *Inquirer* used to cover the world, but the paper had called home its reporters and shuttered its last foreign bureau, an outpost in Jerusalem, in 2006. The *Daily News* had never covered the world. It covered Philly. Period.

The ornate lobby was the magisterial curtain that hid the building's grimy—and desolate—innards. Brian Tierney, the new CEO and head of an investors group that purchased the *Inky* and *Daily News* in June 2006, now hoped to sell the building. The investors needed the cash. Layoffs and financial cutbacks had left the place half empty. The printing presses had been moved to a plant in the suburbs more than a decade ago. The building was so empty that randy staffers roamed its vacant floors looking for rooms where they could have sex.

I'd come to the *Daily News* about two years ago as an *Inquirer* refugee. After four years as an *Inquirer* reporter, I jumped ship and landed on the *Daily News* dinghy to avoid being laid off. At the time, I was one of some seventy *Inquirer* newsroom staffers on the chopping block. For the *Daily News*, this was an era of buttercream-frosted sheet cakes served at newsroom good-byes. So many staffers had taken buyouts that the *Daily News* was exempt from this round of cuts.

I led Benny through the lobby, then he followed me down a flight of steps that led to the *Daily News*. I heard the clack of Benny's industrial work boots on the tile floor, where a black, gooey gunk made its home in the crevices. The ceiling was all exposed water pipes and wires. A neon 1950s-style sign mounted outside the newsroom read "Philadelphia *Daily News*. The People Paper." I pushed opened the beige door to reveal a football field of empty desks separated by chest-high gray partitions. Fluorescent lights hung from the ceiling like suspended tanning beds. A stout metal filing cabinet doubled as a table, with a fax machine on each end. We walked past stacks of yellowed newspapers, dusty dictionaries, a broken typewriter, and an ancient unplugged TV set.

We sat down in the "penalty box," the reporters' nickname for the small meeting area enclosed by low glass walls, slightly bigger than the time-out box for hockey players.

"Do you want coffee? Or water?" I asked.

I hoped he'd say no. I wasn't sure we had cups, let alone fresh coffee.

"Nah. I'm OK."

Benny sat across from me, his hands folded on the table. He licked his lips, ran his tongue over a chipped top tooth, and began talking, his words a whispered cascade. I leaned in. I opened my reporter's notepad and started to scribble: "Ventura Martinez Perez. Confidential Informant. Jeffrey Cujdik, cop, Narcotics Field Unit."

Over the next forty-five minutes, Benny laid out a Shakespearean tale of trust, betrayal, and revenge. I felt stressed and overwhelmed, not certain how to proceed, but my gut told me there was something to his story.

"Benny, can you excuse me for a minute? I'll be right back."

Barbara Laker was at her desk. Of all the reporters in the room, she was the one I admired most. Like me, she lived the job. She'd been a reporter since 1979 and worked at the *Daily News* for more than sixteen years. When I came to the *Daily News*, she was my editor. At the time, her kids were away in college, she was mourning the dissolution of a twenty-five-year marriage, and she thought the editing gig might fill a void. Instead, it gave her migraines. During her three-year editing stint, she nurtured cub reporters so much that they pegged her "Mama Laker." She was known for baking gooey chocolate brownies for staff parties and mentoring rookies, helping them craft their stories.

Barbara walked them through how to master street reporting, sometimes even writing out questions for them. She knew she did too much hand-holding, but she wanted the best story possible and enjoyed seeing inexperienced reporters learn and get better. But as time went on, she grew frustrated with reporters who returned to the office with little in their notebooks. She couldn't understand how some reporters were satisfied with canned interviews that everyone else had. How could you be a reporter without any fire in your belly? Barbara wondered. She had to resist the urge to push them out of the way and just do the job herself.

Barbara was a sweetheart who, unlike me, never dropped the f-bomb or got crass about her sex life. Barbara was like no boss I'd had at the *Inquirer*. *Inquirer* editors came across as Ivy League intellectuals—cynical, self-important, stiff. The men resembled aging college professors, with disheveled, thinning hair, khaki pants, striped ties, and light blue or white dress shirts, usually with the sleeves rolled up. The women looked more like aging Flower Power hippies, with long flowing skirts, Birkenstock sandals, no makeup, and flat, graying hair that hadn't seen a box of Clairol in years. So when I first laid eyes on Barbara, I thought, Who is this bimbo?

Barbara was oblivious to her ability to make men's heads turn, even at our workplace cafeteria, where a horny *Inquirer* reporter once had the chutzpah to ask me if her boobs were real. At fifty, she was an avid runner, trim and shapely, with three marathons under her belt.

Barbara had long, wavy highlighted blond hair and a tangerine slice of a nose. Her big green eyes, flecked with caramel, reminded me of top-of-the-line granite kitchen counters.

She rimmed them with dark olive eyeliner and a hint of grayish blue eye shadow. With her coral lip gloss, silver hoop earrings, snug skirts, and candy-colored blouses, Barbara came off all bubble-gum—wifty and gee-whiz. But that was just her facade. She was a master at getting people to talk, using her charm, smarts, and girlish warmth to get into houses and get the story. She truly got people. She knew just what to say to convince anyone from criminal to victim that she was friend, not foe, and that they could let their guard down, she could be trusted. When she stood to leave with her full notebook, they would invariably say, "I can't believe I told you all this! I haven't told anyone."

Obsessive reporters often describe themselves with one phrase: "Journalism is in my blood." And Barbara and I had the same blood.

I grew up in a family of newspaper readers. A newspaper landed on my front porch every morning. Each week, a delivery boy showed up at my door for his $3.50. At night, I'd walk by my parents' bedroom and see them lying beside one another, each of their faces obscured by newsprint stretched between their hands. My parents loved newspapers. When I got busted in college for underage drinking and my arrest got written up in the local paper, my parents cut out the article and saved it in a scrapbook. They were thrilled to see my name in the paper, even for something criminal.

My dad, who grew up in Brooklyn and was short and balding, spent his entire career as an accountant for a car dealership. He dreamed of bigger things for himself and for me, my sister, and my brother. He took us as kids to Broadway shows, read us poems by A. E. Housman and Edwin Arlington Robinson, and recited—from memory—Ernest Thayer's "Casey at the Bat" from the top of the three steps leading from our kitchen to the living room. He took us to great restaurants every Friday night. "Eat slow. Eat slow," he'd tell us, wanting us to savor the meal. He planned family vacations to historic landmarks, like Colonial Williamsburg, where we complained of boredom while watching actors in eighteenth-century costume churn butter in the scorching August heat.

My dad, who died of cancer when I was twenty-eight, thought I was a superstar. He believed I could do anything and do it better than anyone else. When I graduated from Columbia University with a master's in journalism, he wanted to know why some other student—and not me—got an award at graduation: Didn't the professors recognize how great I was? A lot of my ambition as a reporter was tied to my need to live up to my father's galactic expectations.

Barbara came of age in journalism's heyday. With a gaggle of other teenage know-it-all Baby Boomer idealists, she decided she wanted to be a reporter in the 1970s when Watergate broke. She was fascinated by *Washington Post* reporters Bob Woodward and Carl Bernstein, and how they, with the help of a then-mysterious source known only as Deep Throat, uncovered the most notorious political scandal in American history.

She wanted to know step by step how Woodward and Bernstein had unearthed a trove of secrets, including sabotage, spying, and bribery, that in the end would topple a president. She still remembered huddling around the boxy black-and-white TV with her family to hear Richard Nixon resign in August 1974.

That year, applications to journalism schools reached an all-time high. Barbara's was among them. Since then, two of the five newspapers that Barbara worked for—the *Clearwater Sun* and the *Dallas Times-Herald*—have died. A third, the *Seattle Post-Intelligencer*, is now online only.

The afternoon when I first met Benny, I hoped that Barbara wanted in on his story. Truth be told, I was tired of being alone in the trenches battling police misdeeds. I'd already gained a reputation as the go-to reporter for people who had run-ins with cops. I'd written stories about a cop caught with a racist sticker in his locker, a cop who unleashed a testosterone-fueled beating on a group of women at a baby shower, and a swarm of cops who stomped on and kicked the heads of three shooting suspects while a TV news helicopter filmed overhead. I was sick of being called a "cop hater" and a "bitch" by anonymous callers. I needed reinforcements, someone to help steel up my backbone, an ally in the fight.

3

BARBARA JOINED US IN THE PENALTY
BOX, AND BENNY STARTED FROM THE
TOP. HE'D BEGUN WORKING WITH
JEFF CUJDIK IN LATE 2001, AFTER JEFF
caught him selling marijuana on a corner.
Benny was thirty-five years old and on probation for a prior drug conviction. He didn't
want to go to prison, so he accepted Jeff's
offer to turn informant.

"I knew I was gonna do some time,"
Benny told us. "So I said, 'Well, I gotta do
what I gotta do.' "

So Benny became Confidential Informant 103. Roughly three times a week, Jeff
picked up Benny in an unmarked police
car. They worked a list of suspected drug
homes. Benny's job was to knock on the
door and make a drug buy, while Jeff and
his partner watched from a hidden location. Benny used cash that Jeff had given
him, called prerecorded buy money, for the
drugs. Benny then handed over the drug
packets to Jeff, who put them into evidence.

Once the deal was done, Jeff prepared an application for a search warrant, which he would need to enter a home. In the warrant, he typically included why he was targeting a certain house, what drugs he saw Informant 103 buy, where he bought them, and from whom. Sometimes Jeff had a first and last name of the suspect; other times only a physical description and a street name like "Macho" or "Blackie."

A judge then issued a search warrant that Jeff would use when he and his squad members busted into the house.

The police department, through Jeff, paid Benny cash for the jobs. He usually got $20 for each drug buy and $150 to $250 for a big drug seizure, and if police found weapons, the department paid Benny an additional $100 for each gun. And Jeff nearly doubled his $55,400 salary in court overtime because each time he locked up a dealer, he had to testify in the case. More important, Jeff got attaboys from the "white shirts," sergeants and captains who had earned enough stripes to hang up their uniform blues.

Over the years, Benny emerged as one of the city's most prolific drug informants, and Jeff became one of the department's golden boys, a favorite son who brought home the stats and made his bosses look good. Jeff, perhaps more than other cops, needed informants like Benny. With his clean-cut looks and his I-own-this-town swagger, Jeff's appearance screamed cop. No dealer would be stupid enough to sell to him.

Benny told us that at first he and Jeff did things by the book, but then the lies began. If Benny couldn't score drugs from a house, Jeff sometimes told him to buy elsewhere. Then in the application for a search warrant, Jeff would say that the drugs came from the targeted house. Benny even set up some of his closest friends—people he considered family, people who trusted and loved him. But that wasn't the only secret Benny and Jeff shared.

About four years after they started working together, Jeff rented a house he had purchased for $30,000 to Benny and his family. The rent was $300 a month—a steal in Philly's rental market.

Some of the cash that Benny earned as a police informant flowed back to Jeff in the form of rent money. This was against police department rules, and Jeff knew he'd get in big trouble if internal affairs found out.

The beginning of the end of their friendship came in 2006, though Jeff and Benny didn't know it at the time. In November of that year, Benny tipped Jeff off to a drug dealer named Raul Nieves. Benny knew Raul from an auto-detailing shop where he had worked. Raul knew Benny as Benny Blanco, a reference to a character in the 1993 movie *Carlito's Way*. In the film, Al Pacino plays a Puerto Rican ex–drug dealer dogged by Benny Blanco, a pesky young gangster from the Bronx.

Benny got Raul's cell number and arranged to buy $125 worth of weed, enough to roll about fifty joints. After that, Benny hounded Raul for more pot, but Raul brushed him off. Something didn't feel right.

Jeff and his squad later tore apart Raul's Ford Expedition and found fifty-six orange-tinted crack baggies stashed behind the dashboard. Another twenty baggies were hidden behind a driver's-side door panel. They locked up Raul on felony drug charges.

Raul hired a meticulous, serious-minded veteran defense attorney named Stephen Patrizio. Right away, Raul suspected that Confidential Informant 103 was Benny. Patrizio hired a private investigator to tail Benny home from work.

Raul's case lingered in criminal court. Again and again,

hearing dates got scheduled, then postponed. Raul waited, coolly. Finally, on October 10, 2008—almost two years after Benny bought weed from Raul and two months before Benny came to the *Daily News*—the case leaped forward, exploding at Jeff's feet.

Jeff sat in the witness stand. Patrizio stood before him. He was short and stocky, with a fuzz of hair on a mostly bald head, his pants pulled up perhaps a bit too high, and belted over his paunch. Those who wrote him off as a mild-mannered, harmless geek would soon be proven wrong.

Patrizio took out a copy of Police Directive 15, the rules that officers should follow when dealing with informants, and showed it to Jeff.

Patrizio began to read aloud: " 'Police personnel will maintain professional objectivity in dealing with informants. No personal relationships will jeopardize the objectivity of the informant or the integrity of the department.' "

Patrizio paused and looked up at Jeff. "Correct?"

"Correct," Jeff replied.

Then Patrizio pounced. He stuck a photo under Jeff's nose. It was a snapshot of Benny walking out of Jeff's house.

"Without asking you anything about the person depicted in the picture, do you recognize that street?"

"Yes," Jeff said.

"And not only do you recognize the street, but you recognize the house that the informant is coming out of, correct?"

"I don't know exactly what house the individual came out of, but I can identify one house on that block," Jeff said.

"You can identify the house of 1939 East Pacific Street?"

"I own that house," Jeff said.

"That was my question. You can identify that house?"

"I answered the question," Jeff said, icily.

Patrizio told the judge that he planned to subpoena Informant 103. Defense attorneys often filed motions seeking to drag informants into court. Ninety-nine percent of the time, prosecutors and judges laugh at the request. Confidential informants were just that—confidential. For good reason. Judges protected their identity to prevent drug dealers from killing them. But this case was different. Raul already knew Benny's identity, and he hadn't touched him.

"He has known who he is for long periods of time, and nothing has happened to him," Patrizio argued.

The judge saw Patrizio's point, and the court issued a subpoena for "Benny Blanco," aka "Benny Martinez."

Jeff panicked. With their relationship exposed, he moved to cut all ties with Benny. Jeff put the rental property up for sale and told Benny that he had to leave. Benny wouldn't budge.

So in December 2008, Jeff filed a complaint in landlord-tenant court to evict Benny and Sonia, noting that he'd received no rent since October. Jeff then deactivated Benny as an informant.

By the time Benny came to Barbara and me, he was desperate. Benny, the woman he referred to as his wife, Sonia, and their two small children had nowhere to go.

He sat across from us, seemingly terrified, convinced that he'd soon be a dead man. Word had spread on the street that Benny was a snitch. He feared Raul wanted to kill him. If not Raul, some other drug dealer. He told us that he'd opened his door to find a chunk of cheese on the stoop. It was a street message: Benny was a rat.

He told us that, like prisoners, he, Sonia, and the kids spent nights in the upstairs middle bedroom, where his ten-month-old daughter Gianni slept. He pushed her crib against the wall and dragged a king-size mattress onto the pink carpet. He told his three-year-old son Giovanni to pretend they were camping. He figured they were safer there, holed away in a Benny-made bunker. But he still couldn't sleep. He sat saucer-eyed, fixated on the bedroom door, convinced the knob would turn and he'd see the barrel of a gun.

Jeff no longer had his back. In fact, Benny told us he feared him, that Jeff could patiently lie in wait for the perfect moment to put a bullet in his head, which we later learned was Benny being overdramatic.

"I was dreaming the other night that Jeff shot me in my face," Benny said. "Jeff is a hunter. He likes to hunt. . . . I could be sitting on my porch smoking a cigarette and I could get shot real easily."

Benny stopped talking. Barbara and I looked at each other. We sat back in our chairs. Quiet. Dubious.

"Look, it's true. I could call Jeff right now," Benny said.

Benny flipped open his cell. Jeff answered immediately. Barbara and I practically laid our upper bodies across the table. I kneeled on my chair seat, propped myself up on my elbows, and shoved my head next to Benny's cell phone. I was close enough to kiss his cheek. I could see every follicle of his scant pencil mustache and goatee and smell his cologne. Barbara did the same on the other side.

"You know I know a lot," Benny was saying.

"I don't know what you're talking about," Jeff said.

Benny tried to bait him, but Jeff gave up nothing. "Don't do anything stupid," he warned Benny.

The conversation was short, and Jeff sounded guarded, edgy. Could Jeff really kill Benny or find some street thug to do it for him? We didn't know. What we did know was that Jeff wanted Benny out of his life.

Before long, I'd want the same thing.

4

BENNY WAS ALL ABOUT BENNY, AND HE KNEW HOW TO PLAY PEOPLE TO GET WHAT HE WANTED. AFTER COPS BUSTED HIM FOR SELLING COCAINE IN 1994, Benny summoned tears during his sentencing hearing. He told the judge that he started dealing only because he had no money to buy a birthday present for a daughter from his first marriage, that jobs and opportunities were scarce in the hood, especially for a high school dropout like him. Sure, he knew it was wrong, but the drug trade was all there was, often the only means of survival in Philly's tar pit of hopelessness and poverty. Benny's wife and kids, who sat behind him in the courtroom, began to sob, and the judge cut him a break, meting out house arrest instead of prison time.

"I had the whole courtroom in tears," Benny boasted. "People came up to me afterwards and said, 'Good luck to you.'"

When Benny needed money to buy cocaine and crack, he concocted tales of personal tragedy so people would feel sorry for him and not be able to say no. He'd knock on doors of family friends and frantically recount how his wife, his father-in-law, whomever, had been in a serious car accident and he needed cash to get a cab to the hospital or to get the banged-up car out of the impound lot. He once weaseled money out of his oldest son's high school friends by telling them that his son had been injured in a car wreck. The friends were shocked to see Benny Jr.—unscathed—at school the next day.

One day Benny showed up at the bodega that his oldest daughter managed with a tale of woe. He mumbled, through half-paralyzed lips, cradling a limp arm, that he'd suffered a stroke.

Another time, he told me that he felt weak and was bleeding profusely from his rectum. A few days later, he told me he had colon cancer and needed chemotherapy but didn't have health insurance. Then he said doctors feared that the cancer had spread to his vocal cords because his voice sounded raspy. When I went to the store and told Benny's daughter about his cancer, she looked at me and said, "Yeah, he told me the same thing. I'm waiting to see paperwork."

Of course Barbara and I didn't realize that Benny was still a drug addict, who often told lies to feed his habit, until long after he first came to the *Daily News*. He told us that he had given up drugs years ago and wanted to be an informant to make things right and clean up the hood.

He was convincing. He was good, real good.

Benny was instantly likable. There was something about him—people always wanted to help him; they wanted to trust him. He cracked jokes at his own expense and was an expert on salsa music. Pick any song and Benny could name the artist, the producer, and the label. He saw himself as a tough guy, but actually he was mushy at the core, quick to tear up and say he loved you—"Youse like family," he'd say. He was a hard worker, known as one of the best auto detailers in Philadelphia. He won trophies in detailing competitions and specialized in exotics—Beamers, Mercedes, Escalades—the cars of drug dealers. He could hand-polish black cars without leaving a single swirl. Even after Benny stole chrome tire rims worth $2,200 from an auto-detail shop, the owner told Barbara that he liked Benny and would hire him back. Another shop owner swindled by Benny told me that he still loved Benny and would "cry at his funeral." Again and again, people told us that Benny had a good heart, but drugs made him do evil things.

Jeff, too, fell under his spell. Jeff, a decorated and seasoned cop who regularly dealt with some of Philly's seediest characters, let his guard down with Benny. He allowed Benny into his life and routinely helped him out. When Benny told Jeff that he needed money for child support, Jeff gave him the cash. When Benny said he was stressed out, Jeff gave him money for a trip to the Jersey Shore. When Benny needed a job, Jeff got him a gig working for a cop friend who owned an air-duct cleaning business.

And when Benny needed a place to live, Jeff told him that he could help him out. Jeff told Benny that he owned a house on Pacific Street, and Benny could rent it from him. This was something Barbara and I were able to confirm. We found court documents showing that Jeff did in fact own the house. And Benny gave us a copy of the rental agreement and other paperwork showing that Benny and Sonia lived there and paid rent to Jeff. This was just one part of Benny's story that checked out. The thing about Benny was, buried underneath his lies, there was truth.

Truth that Barbara and I would prove.

Benny told us that because Jeff had moved to evict Benny, both of them would show up at landlord-tenant court for a hearing before a judge. As the plaintiff, Jeff was expected to tell the judge that Benny had failed to pay rent, and he wanted him out.

Barbara and I knew one of us had to show up in court to see Jeff and witness the showdown between the two men. Benny assured us that Sonia would be there, too, so Barbara went to the house they had rented from Jeff to meet her a few days before the court hearing.

Sonia greeted Barbara warmly, but she was visibly scared; she knew Benny was terrified. Sonia was not the shy or skittish type. She was a tough ghetto girl who grew up in the bloody Badlands, an embattled section of Philly held hostage by gun-packing drug dealers who lorded over corners.

Sonia favored fake nails, long as daggers. She painted them hot pink or blood red. Her chubby body was inked with tattoos. One on her forearm read "Angel," a tribute to her first son, a stillborn. Two days before her due date, the doctor couldn't find a heartbeat. The umbilical cord had gotten tangled around Angel's neck. Sonia, then only twenty years old, chose to give birth to him without an epidural or sedatives. She wanted to feel Angel come into this world.

Sonia wasn't afraid to feel or fight. Not girlie fighting, with hair pulling and clawing at her opponent, but full-throttle punches. She went straight for the face. She could lock it up. Benny liked that about Sonia.

The day of the hearing, set to begin at 8:45 a.m., Barbara walked in the thirty-five-degree chill to municipal court on Eleventh Street in the shadow of City Hall. Her heart was pounding. She went through security, turned off her cell, and took the elevator to the fourth floor.

A court clerk approached. "Ma'am, are you a landlord?"

"No," Barbara answered.

"Are you a tenant?"

"No."

Barbara wanted to give as little information as possible.

"Then who are you?"

Barbara knew she couldn't lie. "I'm a reporter for the *Daily News*," she replied.

"Well, you can't be here," she said.

"Yes, I can," she said, trying to sound authoritative, not belligerent. "It's open court. It's not closed to the media." Barbara showed the clerk her business card.

The clerk ushered Barbara into an adjoining room. Barbara was panicked. She couldn't miss this hearing. She explained as politely as possible that she was allowed to observe the court proceedings.

"I'll be back," the clerk said, looking Barbara up and down, probably wondering why she seemed so desperate about a landlord-tenant dispute.

Barbara waited, tapping her foot nervously and twirling her hair. Finally, after about ten minutes, the clerk returned.

"Okay. I checked. You can go in," the clerk said. "Just no tape recorder."

"Thank you," Barbara said. "No tape. I promise."

When Jeff sauntered into the landlord-tenant courtroom, he had no idea that Barbara was seated, watching. Jeff plopped down next to his attorney near the front. He looked straight ahead and appeared calm as he propped his right ankle on top of his left knee.

Benny and Sonia took seats far from Barbara, on the other side of the room. Barbara glanced over at Benny. His face and ears were beet-red.

He leaned over and whispered in Sonia's ear: "Jeff thinks he's Mr. Big Shot. I wanna get up and smack him."

"Calm down," Sonia said, patting him on the knee.

Judge Bradley Moss called Jeff's case, and Sonia and Benny approached the witness table. Moss pointed out that Benny and Sonia hadn't paid rent for three months. Benny tried to explain that he'd stopped paying rent when Jeff put the house up for sale, but Moss, who couldn't understand why that mattered, started to calculate how much they owed Jeff in rent and attorney fees.

"May I say something?" Benny asked.

"Absolutely," Moss said.

"The reason my lease was never renewed was because me and him are real good friends, all right. We are real good friends. Every time I paid him, he never gave me rent receipts because we were good friends. . . . Until the beginning of October, then I went through a little something with him because I worked for him as a CI. I'm his CI. Okay. I'm living in his property."

Benny's voice started to shake. "I had a defendant named Raul Nieves," he began. "When I told Jeff I had the subpoena right here, he automatically wanted me out of the house. That's the reason why I'm here today. And I don't think it's right that after I put a lot of people away and took guns off the street, I'm getting treated like this. My life is in danger right now, and no one is helping me."

"Well, that's a different issue," Moss began.

Benny's voice became shrill. "Right now they are looking for me to kill me and my family and nobody is there to help me. And he's supposed to be a good friend, Jeff!"

He turned sideways to look at Jeff. But Jeff looked stone-faced, his eyes fixed on Moss.

"You were a good friend to me, man. I do anything," Benny quavered.

Benny was on the verge of tears. It seemed as if every time Barbara and I saw Benny, he cried, spigot-like.

"Sheriff! Sheriff! Sir, you're in a court of law," said Moss, summoning backup, sensing that things could turn ugly or, worse yet, explosive.

"I'm getting treated . . . ," Benny said, his voice trailing off.

"You are in a court of law. I'm not Judge Judy. This is a real court," Moss said sternly.

Benny apologized. Moss told him to address him, not Jeff.

Benny hung his head. He wiped his eyes and cheeks with his palms.

"We'll take a break," Moss said.

"Can I use your bathroom?" Benny asked, sounding like a little kid.

Benny and Sonia looked beaten down as they walked to the hallway. Barbara saw Sonia slip into the ladies' room and followed her in.

"Benny's doin' bad. I hate to see him like this," Sonia whispered, leaning against the sink.

Sonia and Benny went way back. She'd fallen for him in the late 1990s. She was just seventeen when she saw him hanging on the corner of Howard and Cambria, the heart of Philly's open-air drug market. She was walking to the corner store, a half block from the row house where she lived with her mom.

"You have nice hair," she told him in her coarse, seductive way. He smiled impishly and slowly stroked his right hand over coarse black hair that he swept back and gelled to a sticky sheen.

Back then, Benny was thirty-four and living with Susette, his first love and mother of his three children. But Benny was smitten with Sonia, and he'd run around on Susette before. Benny was thick and chunky, yet saw himself as a sculpted stud. He said that he would have started messing around with Sonia that day, only she was too young. Never mind that he was with Susette.

Then one night, Benny went to a bar alone and ran into Sonia. He couldn't help but notice her. She was in the middle of one of her vicious all-out cat fights. Some woman had made her mad, and Sonia went off, going for the woman's hair and earrings.

"I gripped her up because I had to break up the fight," Benny told us. "She was like, 'Get the fuck off.' I was like, 'Yo. It's me.' She couldn't believe it. I dragged her outside. From then on, we just started messing around," Benny recalled.

The romance began. Susette found out and told Benny she was done with him once and for all.

Barbara and I often wondered why Sonia stuck by Benny, putting up with all his drama and bullshit. Benny once pulled his shirt collar down in the newsroom to show us a tattoo on the left side of his chest. The tattoo was of a heart with the name "Sue" for Susette in the middle. He refused to remove it. "She's my first love," he'd tell Sonia. Benny called Susette his wife; he called Sonia his wife. He never married either. Now, convinced that he was going to get popped in the head, mob-style, he persuaded Sonia to stick with him, that they were a team.

Sonia stood in the court bathroom and dried her hands, over and over, until the paper towel fell apart.

"When he gets out the car, I always be watching him," she told Barbara. "He knows all these people out to kill him."

Barbara told Sonia to go ahead of her back into the courtroom so nobody saw them together.

Moss gave Benny time to compose himself, then tried to keep him on point. Moss explained that Benny and Sonia owed $1,200 in unpaid rent, $350 in attorney's fees, and $62 in court costs. If they paid up, they could stay for twenty-one days. After that, Jeff could kick them out.

Benny said he understood. Moss asked a clerk if the sheriff was around.

"I don't want any problems in the elevator, so I don't care who leaves first. But I want the other party, the other side, to sit in the courtroom for five, ten minutes so that we don't have any problems in the elevator or outside, okay?" Moss asked.

"Okay. No problem," Benny said.

Benny volunteered to leave first. Barbara hung back as he and Sonia left the courtroom, then she followed Jeff to the elevator.

"Hi, Officer Cujdik," she said, holding out her hand. "I'm Barbara Laker, a reporter for the *Daily News*, and I just wanted to ask you a few questions."

Jeff looked puzzled but smiled and shook her hand. "About what?"

He wore blue jeans, brown work boots, and a blue T-shirt under a black North Face sweatshirt. At thirty-five, Jeff Cujdik (pronounced Chud-ick) stood six-foot-two with an athletic build, broad shoulders, and piercing blue eyes. His thick brown hair was neatly moussed into rows of tiny spikes. Jeff was practically groomed to be a cop. He grew up in the city's northeast section, a mostly safe white working-class neighborhood—Philly's version of Cop Land. Jeff's dad, Louis Cujdik, was a near-legendary narcotics officer, a cop's cop who mentored rookies. Drug dealers knew him by name, and some feared him. His older brother, Richard, was also a cop, married to a city assistant district attorney.

Jeff's younger brother, Gregory, was the splinter in this family of wooden lawmen. Gregory was twenty-nine when he pleaded guilty to felony drug charges after he sold pot to an undercover cop in a suburban town far from Philly.

Jeff graduated from an all-boys Catholic high school, where he wasn't a standout among his 215 classmates. He didn't participate in a single club or sport, and few classmates, even those who had sat near him in homeroom, could remember much about him. After graduation in 1992, Jeff got a job in maintenance for the Southeastern Pennsylvania Transportation Authority, or SEPTA, the city's rail and bus system. He married Jeanette, an attractive and kindhearted woman who'd graduated from an all-girls Catholic high school and stayed at home with their two young daughters.

Jeff joined the police force in 1997 and quickly landed a coveted spot on the narcotics field unit, where plainclothes officers cultivated tips on drug houses and used informants to bust them. Jeff's dad and brother also worked in the same unit.

Based on how Benny had described Jeff to us, Barbara thought he would look cold, be dismissive, and have an edge, an attitude. He wasn't at all what Barbara expected. He seemed approachable, with no hint of a don't-you-dare-come-near-me look.

When Barbara introduced herself to Jeff near the elevator, he didn't dismiss her curtly. Instead Jeff was polite, almost soft-spoken.

Barbara asked him about renting his house to an informant.

Jeff didn't hesitate to answer. "I'm Jeff Cujdik, the landlord," he said calmly. "I'm not here as a police officer." He knew that it would be a mistake to tell Barbara that he, as an officer, was collecting rent from his informant.

So he had to tell Barbara that he, like any other landlord, was renting a house to Benny and his family, and he was trying to evict them because they hadn't paid rent. Nothing more.

Barbara asked him for his phone number in case she had any more questions. Without hesitation, he gave her his cell number.

Even though Jeff didn't seem rattled, he was. He was desperate.

He had to boot Benny out of his house for good, before he could make even more trouble. Trying to evict Benny and Sonia in landlord-tenant court hadn't worked. Benny could still pay him to stay another twenty-one days, and Jeff couldn't wait any longer.

Jeff was going to try another tactic. Two weeks after the landlord-tenant court hearing, on a cold Friday afternoon, Jeff showed up at the rental house. Sonia opened the white aluminum screen door with an emblem of a black horse-drawn carriage on the front. Jeff handed her a letter: "I'm giving you $1,000.00 cash to vacate the property. . . . By accepting the $1,000.00 cash, you agree to vacate . . . by no later than January 31, 2009."

Sonia signed the letter and took the money.

5

BENNY HAD COME TO THE *DAILY NEWS* AND CONTINUED TO TALK TO US BE- CAUSE HE WANTED SOMETHING—TWO THINGS, REALLY. IN EXCHANGE FOR HIS story, he insisted on being anonymous. And he wanted us to put him up in a hotel or pay for housing, like some kind of witness protection program.

Barbara and I said no to both. Benny didn't get it—he was a convicted drug dealer with questionable credibility. And Benny wanted to be anonymous? This was a time of increasing public mistrust of the news media. Journalists had come under attack for using anonymous sources too liberally, à la Judith Miller, the *New York Times* reporter who was criticized for her stories about whether Iraq had weapons of mass destruction based largely on unnamed "American officials" and "American intelligence experts."

Of course we weren't the *New York Times*,

the great gray lady. We were the bawdy broad, a tabloid that lived—or died—off street sales. We never apologized for showing a little leg, in the form of a salacious sex story or a rubberneck tragedy—"grief porn," as some reporters called it—on our front page.

Still, we had our standards. There was no way we would agree to allow Benny, a convicted drug dealer, to accuse a decorated cop of wrongdoing without using his name. Benny had to go on the record.

When we told Benny this, he balked and left the newsroom. A few days later, he was back. "You're all I got," he told us.

Benny had gone to the Philadelphia Police Department's Internal Affairs Division, but he didn't think investigators took him seriously, nor did he trust them. He also shopped his story to Fox 29, but he didn't even get past the television station's front lobby.

We explained to Benny that the *Daily News* doesn't have a witness protection program, and certainly doesn't pay people for stories. We thought the FBI might be interested in Benny's story. We also knew that once the FBI started digging around, they wouldn't want Benny talking to us. So we milked Benny dry, talking to him for hours, with a tape recorder running.

When we were done, we steered Benny to the feds. We gave him the name and telephone number of John Roberts, the supervisory special agent of the FBI's Public Corruption Squad.

Roberts had a record of tackling police corruption. He was one of the FBI agents who investigated the Thirty-Ninth District police corruption scandal in the mid-1990s. In that probe, the feds charged five rogue narcotics cops with stealing money from drug suspects and covering up the thefts with phony arrests and search warrants.

History had a way of repeating itself in Philadelphia. And

Barbara and I suspected that what Benny was telling us could prove that those who fail to learn from history are doomed to repeat it.

To tell Benny's story, Barbara and I needed access to police search warrants.

Each search warrant would be a road map: it would list the address of the drug dealer, the dealer's name or street name, the amount and type of drugs purchased by the informant and how the deal went down, the badge number of every officer who participated in the raid, and what, if anything, police found in the house.

The warrants would show us what Jeff said he and other officers had witnessed to persuade a judge to authorize a raid. The paperwork would tell us whether Jeff used Benny as an informant, and what Jeff said Benny had bought in each house. These warrants would give us Jeff's version of events. Then we could ask Benny for his version of what happened. Finally, we could track down the arrested drug dealer or his relatives for their story.

But Barbara and I hit a roadblock. The city lawyer in charge of records requests was stonewalling us. We needed some legal muscle. The *Daily News* and *Philadelphia Inquirer* had just one full-time lawyer on staff. Scott Baker was an ambitious thirty-nine-year-old corporate lawyer when he joined our company as general counsel. Brian Tierney, the charismatic and peacockish CEO of the *Daily News*, the *Philadelphia Inquirer*, and Philly.com, wanted to grow readership and expand the business through acquisitions. Baker saw the job as a good opportunity.

But no one, including Tierney, could predict the crippling recession that put the newspaper industry on its knees. Lehman Brothers collapsed, and the economy tanked. The newspapers lost millions in advertising sales, and Tierney struggled to pay off the creditors who had lent him $350 million to buy the newspapers back in 2006.

Baker became mired in an effort to reach a deal with the lenders. Barbara and I would see him zipping through our newsroom, his eyes locked on his BlackBerry. He'd rush by and nod hello—a tall and trim blur in an Italian suit with salt-and-pepper hair. We e-mailed him: How can we get those search warrants? We called and left messages with his assistant: It's about the search warrants. Then e-mailed again.

Baker was working on our problem—ours and twenty others. The foundation of the newspaper industry was caving in, and all Barbara and I could think about were those damn search warrants.

Obsessive and antsy, we looked up the law pertaining to warrants. We printed out a copy of Pennsylvania's Rules of Criminal Procedure, which clearly stated that warrants, after police executed the search, were available for public inspection. The search warrants were stored in a dusty room on the fourth floor of the city's criminal court.

On Christmas Eve, just two weeks before Barbara went to landlord-tenant court, we walked over to the Criminal Justice Center with a copy of the rule on search warrants. The court staff was in the holiday spirit, eating cookies, drinking nonalcoholic eggnog, and getting ready to go home early. We found Marc Gaillard, the court's second deputy, and showed him the paper.

"Yeah, I know. I just talked to the city solicitor's office," he said.

"Woo-hoo!" Barbara yelped.

"Yaaay!" I said.

We sprang forward like two jack-in-the-boxes and grabbed Gaillard in a hug. Surprised, he took a step back, then smiled at us, probably thinking, These crazy *Daily News* ladies.

After Christmas, Barbara and I spent hours, days, in that dingy room, which was crammed with cardboard boxes, stacked floor to ceiling on metal shelves. Inside the boxes were yellow search warrants, thin as onionskin, crinkled and stuffed haphazardly into brown accordion folders. Written on each box in black permanent marker was the year, dating back to the early 1990s.

"Holy shit," I said as I sat cross-legged in jeans and sneakers on the dirty, school-cafeteria-like tile floor and looked through a box marked "Search Warrants 2006." Barbara paged through the wisps of yellow paper, periodically wetting her index finger with the tip of her tongue, while seated on a black milk crate in an electric-blue skirt and knee-high leather boots. My back ached as I flipped through hundreds of warrants.

We pulled three years' worth of search warrants, every one with Jeff's name and Benny's informant number. We ended up with stack a foot high—at least. We knew it would have cost the newspaper hundreds of dollars to order copies of all the search warrants, so we did it the *Daily News* way. We lugged reams of white copy paper from our office to the courthouse and befriended court employees on every floor. We charmed our way to their Xerox machines, and like a two-person army of leaf-cutter ants, we skittered in and out of the room to make copies, one search warrant at a time.

I had learned the art of getting something for nothing from my parents. At restaurants, my mom always asked the waitress for a plate of lemon wedges so she could make lemonade using water and sugar packets. My parents required me, my sister, and my brother to go to synagogue twice a year—on Rosh Hashanah and Yom Kippur, two holidays in which Jews sought repentance and atonement for past wrongs—but my dad refused to pay for tickets to attend services, so we snuck in through the synagogue's basement. As a teen, I sat in the pew, arms crossed, wearing a petulant scowl and an ugly floral dress, and rolled my eyes at my dad as the rabbi urged the congregation to start off the Jewish New Year with honest intentions. Later, when my rabbi, Fred Neulander, hired two hit men to bludgeon his wife to death in their Cherry Hill, New Jersey, home, my dad finally relented: Okay, we're done with synagogue.

When Barbara and I finished copying search warrants free of charge, we divvied up the stack and hit the streets.

Barbara and I went door to door, following MapQuest directions from one dealer's house to the next. Many of the homes were in West Kensington, a largely Puerto Rican neighborhood stricken by poverty and drug sales. It contained Philadelphia's most dangerous streets where bloodshed was so common it wasn't considered news.

Benny had told us which jobs were bogus, meaning that Jeff wrote in the search warrant application that he watched Benny make a buy at a certain house, but Benny told us he hadn't. He'd bought the drugs elsewhere—or not at all. Those search warrants, Benny told us, were lies.

We hit those homes first. We wanted to ask the dealers if they recalled anything unusual or fishy about the police raid. We thought we'd be less intimidating and have a better chance of getting people to talk to us if we went alone. So we split up and canvassed dangerous Philly streets taken over by drug dealers.

Snarling pit bulls, baring teeth and spewing saliva, lunged

at us. Wild-eyed, well-meaning crack addicts offered advice: "Honey, hope you gotta gun on youse, or at least some Mace." Drug dealers, wearing their version of business casual—tan Timberland boots, low-slung baggy jeans, and crisp white oversize T-shirts—told us to watch our backs.

"You know, you're in a bad neighborhood," drug dealers would tell us, as if we were naive adventurers who had wandered off across a border in search of designer knockoffs and good, cheap ethnic food.

Barbara chatted up drug dealers the same way she did her mail carrier. "You know I own this block," one drug dealer warned Barbara as she walked up the sidewalk.

"Well, that means you got my back, right?" she replied with a smile. Taken aback, he shook his head in amusement and chuckled.

At four-foot-eleven and ninety pounds, I took full advantage of my kidlike stature, even though I was pushing forty. I came across all pixie, with my Little Lord Fauntleroy haircut, flashing a puckish smile, but that was my secret weapon, perfect for disarming anyone from the career criminal to the corrupt politician. When I was out on the street reporting a story, I felt all badass—a legend in my own mind.

I had once picked up a just-freed convicted murderer and secreted him away in my house so I'd have an exclusive. At the time, I worked for the *Bergen Record* as a statehouse reporter based in Trenton. Another reporter got a tip that Thomas Trantino, dubbed New Jersey's most notorious cop killer, was about to be paroled.

Trantino spent almost forty years in prison for the execution-style murder of two police officers. In the early hours of August 25, 1963, Trantino and a friend, Frank Falco, raged out of control at a North Jersey bar. Lodi Borough police sergeant Peter Voto and police trainee Gary Tedesco arrived to investigate complaints of rowdiness. Trantino beat Voto on the head with a gun, and then ordered him to strip. When Voto disrobed too slowly, Trantino pumped him full of bullets while shouting, "We are going for broke! We are burning all the way! We are going for broke." Falco fatally shot Tedesco. New York police officers later shot and killed Falco while he was resisting arrest, and Trantino was sentenced to die in the electric chair. The US Supreme Court overturned the death penalty in 1972, however, and Trantino escaped execution. The state parole board, succumbing to public outrage, denied his parole nine times, making Trantino the longest-serving prisoner in New Jersey history.

Trantino's release in 2002, on his sixty-fourth birthday, was a big story for the *Bergen Record*. The slain cops had been from our region, and their relatives and friends still lived in our coverage area. The story was very competitive. Every news outlet in and around Manhattan wanted an interview with Trantino, the face of evil. Every editor wanted him first.

My editors picked me for the task. I was the newspaper's teeth-baring Chihuahua, but that's not entirely why they picked me. Trantino was being freed from a halfway house in Camden—less than two miles from my house.

My plan was to get to the halfway house ahead of the media horde. I set the alarm for 2:00 a.m., stopped at a WaWa for a large coffee, then parked my Honda Civic alongside a vacant lot across the street from the halfway house. The two-story brick building, surrounded by a tall metal fence, looked like a small jail. I sat in darkness, my coffee quickly cooling in the February air, and checked to make sure the car doors were locked. Camden had been ranked—yet again—among the top ten most dangerous cities in America.

Pretty soon, I had to pee. Damn it. I unlocked the door, stepped out of the car, and looked around. My best bet was the abandoned lot. I tiptoed around the clumps of knee-high weeds and nearly slipped on an empty beer bottle. I yanked down my jeans and underwear and squatted, then sprinted back to the car.

The sky turned from dark to pale gray, and by 9:00 a.m., I started to think the tip was bad. I didn't see any other reporters or TV news vans. I felt frustrated. Tired. Hungry. Bored.

Then I heard a rap on the car window. I looked up. An old man stood there. He had neatly trimmed white hair, a slim build, and a wrinkled face, and wore a gray sweatshirt and brown corduroy pants. I rolled down the window.

"I hear you're looking for me. The security guard told me you've been out here all night," he said.

Holy shit. It was Trantino.

"Yes. Yes," I said. "Get in. Get in!"

I leaned over and unlocked the passenger-side door. Trantino sank into the passenger seat, using his sneakered foot to move aside a crusty cereal bowl, flecked with dried oatmeal. Yesterday's breakfast. He dropped his black shoulder bag on the floor and eyed the dusty dashboard. A tangle of green, red, and black electrical wires hung from the car's busted mechanical sunroof. The windows leaked during rainstorms, and the seats stank of mold. The check-engine light, which reminded me of an orange throat lozenge, was on, as always.

"Man, your car's a mess," Trantino said.

Oh yeah, and you're a convicted cop killer, I thought.

I didn't want to piss him off. I also didn't want other reporters to get a hold of him. Where could I take him? Instinctively, I drove to my house. I lived just outside Philadelphia in a working-class, mostly white New Jersey town, a slice of Wonder Bread, where local cops worked hard to keep Camden's criminal element out. My Craftsman-style bungalow, with its leaky A-frame roof and faded yellow aluminum siding, sat under the flight path to the Philadelphia International Airport.

The house was quiet when Trantino and I walked in. Karl was at work; we didn't yet have kids. Trantino took in the living room, eyeing the black leather couch, hardwood floors, and shelves of art books. He noticed one of Karl's paintings, an abstract with red, orange, and yellow slashes, a depiction of a violent thunderstorm. Trantino sat at the dining room table. I made him a cup of hot chocolate and gave him a Jell-O pudding snack.

I asked the question I wanted to know most: Why?

"I can't believe that I did it. And that's the truth. I can't believe that I would kill anybody," he said.

We were wrapping up the interview when Karl came home from his job as an art director at an ad agency. Trantino stood and shook his hand.

"Tommy Trantino," he said.

I could tell that the name didn't register. Karl had no clue.

"Nice artwork," Trantino said, gesturing toward Karl's painting with a sweep of his hand.

While in prison, Trantino pursued an interest in poetry and art, particularly Asian art—Karl's favorite.

Karl and Trantino launched into a conversation about Khmer art, Buddha statues, Ganesha wall hangings. It wasn't long before the two men had their heads buried in one of Karl's many art history books. Trantino bragged that an art gallery owner in Tokyo wanted to present a show of his artworks.

"You should stay for dinner," Karl said.

Oh, crap, I thought.

"That's nice. Thank you. But I need to get going," Trantino said.

By then, another reporter, who had joined us, offered to drive Trantino back to Camden. Trantino said he had a line on an apartment there. He borrowed an art book from Karl. We never saw him or the book again. When I told Karl who Trantino was, he was miffed but not furious. We'd been married for three years, and he was used to my shenanigans. A year after Trantino's home visit, I signed up to cover the war in Iraq without first consulting Karl. It didn't occur to me that he'd be mad.

"C'mon, you know I would never volunteer to go to Iraq if we had kids. That'd be selfish," I argued.

Karl gave me a look, shaking his head. He wasn't buying my bullshit. He knew me too well. A good story was my drug.

Barbara drank from the same Kool-Aid.

She thought nothing of plunking down her credit card to buy a powder blue bulletproof vest for a ride-along with cops on drug raids. "Don't worry, honey," she told her husband at the time. "You'll see $795 on the Visa, but it's for a bulletproof vest, and the paper will reimburse me." She didn't get why the color drained from his face. He told her she had a serious problem.

Not long after that, Barbara had worn the vest as she shadowed narcotics cops into a crack den. Two little kids—one in diapers—sat on a soiled carpet, watching cartoons and eating Cheerios for dinner. A Phillies Blunt box filled with crack vials sat within reach. There was a filthy mattress strewn with lighters and matches. Barbara opened the refrigerator to find only ketchup, mustard, margarine, and wilted celery. She stood in the doorway as cops cuffed the glassy-eyed twenty-two-year-old mom. Her children sat just a foot away, with blank stares, their legs tucked under their tiny bodies. As cops led the mom outside, she walked by her kids, silent, not even looking at them. Barbara cried when she left the house.

The next morning, Barbara called the Philadelphia Department of Human Services to see if a social worker could check on the children. An intake worker told Barbara that parents who smoked and sold crack don't fit the city's definition of abuse or neglect. Barbara was incensed. She told Ed Moran, a reporter she had partnered with for the story, that she was going to check on the kids. He told her not to go, but she wouldn't listen, so he reluctantly went along.

The children were playing outside when they arrived. Their mom, released from jail six hours ago, sat on a stoop a few houses away. She shot Barbara a steely stare. Barbara knelt down and asked the kids, "How are you guys?" A cluster of drug dealers walked toward Barbara. To them, she was a busybody meddling with their business.

"Time to go, Barbara," Ed said, heading to the car.

"I'm not ready," she said, shooing him away with one hand.

"It's time," he shouted.

The young dealers closed in on Barbara. A few reached into the pockets of their baggy jeans.

"Barbara, NOW!" Ed bellowed in his thick Boston accent. Only then did she hop in the car.

So when friends and relatives asked Barbara and me if we were scared to knock on the doors of drug dealers, we didn't understand the question.

6

IN THE SEVEN YEARS THAT BENNY HAD WORKED WITH JEFF, THEY BEGAN TO LOCK UP SECOND GENERATIONS OF DRUG DEALERS. IN PHILLY, THERE were cop families and drug families. Children of cops wanted to wear the badge; children of drug dealers got sucked into an underworld of fast money.

The first house that Barbara visited belonged to Jorge Garcia and his family, whose names have all been changed in this book. Benny had told us that he'd never bought heroin from Jorge, even though the search warrant said otherwise. Jorge lived in the Badlands, a four-square-mile drug bazaar centered in West Kensington, home to the city's top three drug corners.

Drug dealers hung on corners while lookouts, teens on four-wheelers, sped around the block, looking for cops in uniform or street clothes. They yelled various codes as a warning:

Bomba! Aqua! Gloria! Five O!

This was corporate America of the streets, home to a multimillion-dollar business that had a finely tuned organizational structure. Above the corner boys were the holders, or guys who stashed the dope, and the caseworkers who picked up cash and delivered it to the drug bosses. Blood was spilled over turf wars. Little else.

By 2007, murder in the Badlands almost single-handedly gave Philly its nickname: "Killadelphia." That year there were 391 murders, the highest rate per 100,000 residents among the nation's ten largest cities, according to crime statistics compiled annually by the FBI. Gunshot wounds were so common that trauma surgeons from Sweden traveled to Philadelphia to learn lifesaving techniques they'd rarely need in their country. On average, one person was killed in the city every day. Many of these murders happened here in the Badlands.

When kids walked to school, they saw dealers pushing their brands. At Cambria and Hope Streets, the dope was known as Louis Vuitton. At Cambria and Master, Bart Simpson. At Cambria and Palethorpe, Seven-Up.

At Howard and Cambria there were two brands, Nike and Lucifer. This was the corner that never slept, one of the hottest drug spots in the city—and the most dangerous.

Most children at the elementary school on Cambria Street knew at least a few people who had been killed. Some were relatives. Kids as young as seven spoke of gunfire and blood on the street as if it were part of life; for them, it was. Every morning, school custodians swept up used condoms, needles, vials, and trash from the concrete play yard before children arrived.

Weathered memorials with teddy bears, balloons, and candles were scattered all over the Badlands. Sidewalks became street cemeteries. And these urban graves became part of the drug trade. Some dealers hid their heroin packets under worn stuffed animals.

A number of homes in the area were vacant or boarded up and reeked of pee and dead rats. Inside, addicts shot up, sitting on grungy mattresses or sofas with no springs. In the middle of some blocks, one or two houses had collapsed or been torn down to become weed-filled lots that looked like broken, missing teeth in a row of red brick. None of the battered homes on Jorge Garcia's block was worth more than a $15,000 used Chevy.

Barbara walked past the corner drug dealers and knocked on the door of the two-story redbrick row house with splotches of peeling cream paint. Jorge was still locked up, but his mom, Dolores Jimenez, was home. Dolores was suspicious of Barbara, almost hostile, but she was also curious about what Barbara had to say.

Family portraits in wood frames hung from the living room wall. A cross with Jesus on the crucifix was on the dining room wall, near a glass-top table with four chairs. Dolores's collection of black leather horses was inside an old wood cabinet. A playpen for her grandkids sat on the smudged linoleum floor. Two candles burned in clear glass. Her son Ricky's dusty basketball, baseball, and football trophies were scattered around.

Dolores's skin was sallow, and she moved slowly, as if her body hurt. That's because it did. Dolores suffered from high blood pressure, diabetes, asthma, a severe anxiety disorder, insomnia, and a ripped bowel duct. "They tried to take my gallstones out, but they messed up and now I have a stent in my stomach." She lifted her black T-shirt to show Barbara a dark, foot-long scar under her belly.

Dolores packed about 225 pounds on her four-foot-eleven frame. Her long black hair cascaded down to her waist, but most days she tied it back tightly in a ponytail, accentuating her full lips and large brown eyes that looked tired of the struggle. She wore no makeup, never did, except for a hint of black eyeliner every once in a while. Her nails were acrylic, perfectly rounded and finished in a natural shine, no color. She chose sweats in the winter, shorts in the summer, T-shirts always.

Dolores looked nothing like the other drug dealers that Barbara and I had met. When Barbara arrived, Dolores had just been released from prison on her own drug case. Eight years earlier, Jeff had busted her with Benny's help. Dolores was Benny's childhood friend, then a chunky, good-hearted, scruffy girl who went to church. Only a year apart in age, they rode the same school bus, and their moms were close friends. Later, she would become one of his drug suppliers.

Dolores didn't consider herself a drug dealer. In her mind, she was a thirty-six-year-old grandmom who dealt $20 bags of cocaine from her deep-pocketed black apron to make ends meet.

At the time of her arrest, she lived in a neighborhood on the cusp, just fifteen blocks from the Badlands. Her seven-room home was subsidized by the Philadelphia Housing Authority, and she got a welfare check. So did her twenty-year-old daughter Sofia, her firstborn. Problem was, Dolores told Barbara, there were so many children to feed and clothe. Dolores had four children. Sofia had her first baby at fourteen, followed by three more, all about a year apart.

Dolores had watched the mom across the street in disgust; the woman often left her seven kids alone with no heat so she could go "party."

"If you don't feed those kids, they'll take them away," Dolores warned her. Sure enough, she lost her children.

That would never happen to me, Dolores told herself. "I take care of my kids."

Dolores raked in about $1,000 or so a week, wads of twenties that gave her a taste of middle-class life. She bought a minivan. She had the house painted and fixed up because PHA seldom made repairs.

"I bought the kids designer clothes," she told Barbara with a proud smile. "Polo, Nautica, Nikes, Air Jordans."

At first Dolores was nervous about selling drugs. But then she shrugged; what the hell. It was easy, really. Her customers called her cell phone, said they'd stop by. She greeted them at the front door in her apron, the same one she wore to cook beans and rice or pan-fried chicken for her kids. She wiped her hands on the black cotton, then gave them ziplock bags of coke and folded their twenties into her apron pockets. Some buyers made small talk, but they never stayed long.

Business was brisk. Paydays were golden, like happy hour at five on a Friday. All kinds came—blacks, Puerto Ricans, whites from the Pennsylvania or New Jersey suburbs. In a snap, she switched from Spanish to English in dope speak. "No offense," she told Barbara, "but even Italians came," as if somehow they were considered the drug world's elite.

She had been selling cocaine about a year when Benny knocked on her door in 2001, while Jeff watched. It was Benny's first job as an informant.

Dolores wasn't suspicious, since she'd sold to Benny before. She pulled a $20 bag of cocaine from one pocket of her apron and put the cash in another. "It was like she had a little cash register," Benny said.

Benny felt a tinge of guilt, but nothing more. "Jeff was telling me, 'You're doing the right thing. You're cleaning up your hood.' I told Jeff I felt bad, but he said, 'They're sellin' in front of their kids. They're going to end up just like them.' "

Dolores didn't see it that way. "Yeah. We got in the game," Dolores told Barbara unapologetically. "You get in the game to survive. And that comes with it, getting booked."

She figured she wouldn't sell forever, just a year or so more to stay afloat.

Dolores's brother, Manuel, who lived with her, also helped with the drug business. Until Jeff busted them, neither had a criminal record. Dolores's biggest crime had been a parking ticket.

Manuel had worked for more than twenty years at Today's Man, where he was a supervisor of the shipping and receiving department, making sure slacks, jackets, and button-down shirts landed in the right place.

At home, Manuel's closet was a shipping and receiving center—for cocaine. Everything they needed, including a metal sifter, digital scale, cutting agent, staples, and bags, was stored in a black leather bag.

It was four days before Christmas 2001, around 6:30 at night, when Jeff and his squad knocked on Dolores's front door. She cracked the door open and saw men she immediately figured were cops behind the iron-gated, locked storm door. She slammed the front door shut, scurried upstairs and flushed packets of cocaine down the toilet. In seconds, cops pried the steel apart with a crowbar and burst in.

Dolores's three-year-old grandson started to scream, terrified by a cop wearing a thin, silky black ski mask over his face. All anyone could see were his eyes. Some undercover narcotics cops who made buys wore masks during raids to conceal their identity, but Dolores's grandson thought a monster was coming after him.

Dolores said she'd never forget the way Jeff looked at her, like she was scum, or worse, a murderer. "It's like his shit don't stink, like he's better than everyone," she said. "It was like I was a nobody."

In Dolores's living room, cops found 119 packets of cocaine at the base of a baby stroller. They were tucked inside a Christmas cookie tin with a picture of Santa Claus on the cover. There was more upstairs. All in all, cops found $10,000 worth of coke in Dolores's house.

Prosecutors called her house a drug "operation." To them, it was people like Dolores who sank neighborhoods, smothered them like kudzu, that noxious coiling weed that quickly spreads over trees and shrubs until they die.

Dolores and her brother were sentenced to three to six years in prison. Guilt ate at her. Not for selling drugs, but because she couldn't be with her kids. "They was all lost souls," she said. Her worst fear was realized; her three youngest were alone. Jorge was sixteen, Ricky, fourteen, and Elena, eleven. Dolores asked her mom to take care of them, but she doubted that would work. Her kids drifted. Jorge, the one she'd nicknamed Macho as a baby, got locked up for violating probation on a gun case. Jorge's urine came back dirty because he was getting high on weed. The system couldn't save kids like Jorge. When he was released, there was no one, and that, in part, sealed his fate.

Jorge roamed the Badlands, the place Dolores knew was trouble for her kids. But there was little other choice. After the raid, Dolores and the kids were evicted from the Philadelphia Housing Authority house. Ricky, ever resourceful, even at thirteen, made a few calls to find a place for which the landlord didn't require references or job history. He found a three-bedroom house in the Badlands. The rent was $500 a month.

Dolores was still behind bars when Jeff locked up Jorge. It was 2005, and Jeff was no longer a stickler for rules. Jeff was sure he'd find heroin in Jorge's house. He just needed to get in there, and Benny knew exactly where to score dope. Benny purchased heroin from a drug house not far from Jorge's place, and Jeff used that heroin as the basis for a search warrant.

When Jeff and his squad raided Jorge's house, they found three bundles of heroin on top of a china cabinet in the dining room. They were stamped GAME CRAZY. In the back of a black dresser drawer, in a rear second-floor bedroom, cops found six clear plastic baggies of cocaine. Just shy of his twentieth birthday, Jorge was sentenced to two to four years in prison.

People like Jorge and his family almost always expected cops to lie, to be dirty, like pigs. They understood corruption. What they didn't understand was snitching.

"I'd rather someone stab me and let me bleed out before I'd become a fuckin' snitch," said Jorge's brother, Ricky, hate blazing from his eyes.

"He's a rat. And a rat should get poison," Ricky said, his lip curled as he almost spat out the words.

Ricky lived with Dolores and on this day, as Barbara interviewed her, Ricky sat by his mother's side, listening intently, interjecting frequently, as if Barbara was taking Dolores's deposition and he was her legal advisor.

Benny knew that we were going to talk to Jorge and drug dealers like him. He knew we were going to print that he was an informant, an informant who helped lock up dealers based on lies. And after we heard the venom spewed at Benny, we were surprised no one had killed him yet. It was then that Barbara and I realized that if Benny ended up dead, we'd be to blame. By talking to the dealers whom Benny had set up, we were salting the wounds.

Barbara sat across from Ricky at his dining room table and wondered what, if anything, he'd do to Benny. Ricky was shirtless, with low-slung black pants. He had a goatee, combed his short hair forward, close to his scalp, and had a space between his two front teeth. His arms, chest, and back were adorned in tattoos. Stretched across the top of his back were the words ONLY GOD CAN JUDGE ME above an unfinished cross.

Ricky seemed more upset that Benny played a role in his mom's drug arrest than in Jorge's. At fourteen, Ricky went to Dolores's sentencing, prepared to beg the judge for leniency. "I would have told him she did what she had to do. I don't blame her. People may see it as she was introducing me to drugs, but she raised four kids on her own, and how you gonna pay for all that? DPA don't pay for that."

Ricky was fiercely protective of Dolores, and he took care of her. Late at night or early in the morning, he slipped into her room, careful not to wake her, and placed food, usually a fruit yogurt, by her bed.

Dolores's life was unlike lots of others in the Badlands. She was born in Puerto Rico in 1965 and lived in a wood house with her parents and seven brothers. She was the only girl— "Daddy's little girl." Life was hard for her dad, who delivered Coca-Cola by truck. The family moved to Paterson, New Jersey, when she was four or five. "We came for a better life."

As a girl, she bounced around with her family, mostly

back and forth from Camden and Philly. Dolores hooked up with a high school boy, got pregnant with Sofia at sixteen, and dropped out. She met another man, Diego, when she was studying to become a nursing assistant. They had three children together, but had a turbulent, violent relationship. In the beginning he worked at a body shop, but he lost his job because he smoked crack all the time. He never worked again.

"I wanted to go back to being a nurse, but he didn't want that, so I didn't," Dolores told Barbara.

When he got mad or hallucinated, he hit or punched her, threw lamps at her. Even as a young kid, Ricky was her protector.

"I got in the way once. He cracked my head open. Here, feel this," he told Barbara, as he bent down and put her finger on his thick black hair. He wanted her to feel the bumpy scar tissue on the back of his head.

Dolores mustered enough courage to leave Diego when her dad got sick. "Poppy" was a diabetic with high blood pressure who endured heart surgery and suffered from Alzheimer's. She slept on a cot beside him in the hospital. When he couldn't walk, she stayed with him in rehab. She was the only one who shaved his face to his satisfaction. "He said his face had to feel like a baby's bottom." When he came home, she cooked him anything he wanted—hot dogs, boiled eggs, oatmeal, rice, and chicken.

He died on May 3, 1998, a Sunday. He opened his eyes, smiled at Dolores, then took his last breath.

Barbara understood Dolores more than she knew. Barbara's mom died of pancreatic cancer in November 2000. After she was diagnosed, Barbara did everything to save her. She begged a Mount Sinai Hospital researcher to include her in

his coffee enema experiment. She knew it sounded ridiculous, but she was desperate. Her mom was seventy-three. She
wasn't a candidate for surgery, and she refused chemo, said it
would make her sicker. Barbara knew it wouldn't help anyway.

She wanted to die at home, even though she couldn't say
the word *die*. "I want to go home," she told Barbara. And Barbara knew. She took a leave of absence from the *Daily News*
and flew back and forth to Florida every week to sit beside
her in bed all day and help her dad. Then she came home to
take care of her two children because her husband needed to
travel for work.

Barbara cooked her mom's favorite meal of roast chicken,
boiled potatoes, and green peas. She spoon-fed her in bed
while they watched her favorite reruns of *Law & Order*. When
she could no longer chew, Barbara gave her broth, milkshakes,
and Ensure. She sponge-bathed her, washed and brushed her
thinning hair, and put lip gloss on her lips. As she slipped
away, weighing not more than seventy-five pounds, Barbara
stroked her cheek to trick her into opening her mouth so Barbara could slip in the painkiller Oxycontin. Barbara gave her
more when she moaned. She changed her diapers. When her
mom lost consciousness, she gave her Oxycontin in a dropper. Water in a dropper. Anything to keep her alive. Until the
day Barbara knelt on the floor, held her limp hand, and told
her it was okay to go. She'd take care of her brother and dad.
Barbara didn't know if she heard her.

"How can my heart still be beating when hers isn't?" Barbara cried when her mom died two days later.

Soon after Dolores's dad died, she started selling drugs.
When her mom died, Barbara fell into a deep depression that
she tried desperately and unsuccessfully to hide. It was the
beginning of the end of her marriage.

Death wasn't all Barbara shared with Dolores. Barbara's mom's mom was a four-foot-eleven Orthodox Jewish bootlegger who stashed cash under her mattress in her tenement at C and Eighth Streets on Manhattan's Lower East Side. Barbara's mom hid under the bed each time cops busted into their apartment and hauled her grandmother off to jail.

Her grandmom had a mission—her three sons and daughter would claw their way out of poverty and land careers to make her proud. When New York University had already filled their quota of Jewish medical students, her grandmom stormed down to the university with wads of cash in her purse.

"What does it take to get my son in?" she asked someone in the admissions office, in her Yiddish accent, plopping twenties on the counter. Barbara's uncle was accepted into med school and became a pediatrician. Another uncle became a rabbi; the other, an engineer.

Dolores and Ricky knew they came from a different world than Barbara. Ricky seemed curious about her home, her neighborhood. "When am I going to come see your land?" he asked her.

He told Barbara she must be comfortable. He thought Barbara lived in a mansion. She told him she lived in a three-bedroom home, nothing fancy.

"Don't bullshit me. Your three-bedroom home is different than my three-bedroom home," he said.

Ricky was right. She lived in a leafy, affluent Philly suburb just west of the city. The heart of her town was lined with trendy restaurants, with names like Plate and Verdad, and boutique shops that sold swimsuits year-round to rich housewives who went on winter cruises to tropical islands. Barbara's house, a three-bedroom brick colonial with blue shutters, sat on an ivy-manicured hill.

Unlike more than 90 percent of kids in Barbara's neighborhood, Ricky didn't have a high school diploma. "I didn't graduate, but I got brains like I did."

Ricky, who described himself as a "hard-core Christian," was cryptic about how he earned money, saying that he sometimes worked "off the books." He asked Barbara if she knew of any jobs.

Every so often, the conversation was interrupted by a knock on the door. Ricky would get up and furtively step outside for a minute or so. Dolores froze and lifted an eyebrow cautiously each time someone pounded on the door. The only person whom Ricky introduced to Barbara was "the Movie Man," an obese guy in a white T-shirt and jeans with a kind smile. Ricky sifted through his stack of pirated movies and chose some for himself and his mom—the street version of Netflix.

After the Movie Man left, Ricky brought the DVDs to Dolores and sat down at the dining room table. Barbara noticed he was staring at her hands.

"No ring?" he asked. "You're not married?"

"No. I'm not married."

"No?" he asked with a coy smile. "How could that be?"

"I'm divorced." Barbara still cringed when she said that word.

He asked about her children. She told him that her son, Josh, was in law school and her daughter, Anna, had just graduated from college and was working.

He stared at her, locking into her eyes. "You're still suffering from your divorce," he said.

The words took her aback. She didn't tell Ricky, but she still kept photos of her ex-husband in her wallet—one family portrait and one by himself.

"You need to get out more and live your life," he told Barbara. "You have your whole life ahead of you."

He paused. "You know what? We should go on a cruise."

"What?" she asked.

"You and me. A cruise."

In the span of an hour, Ricky asked Barbara to touch the back of his head, acted as her fortune-teller, gave her relationship advice, and asked her to sail away with him on the Love Boat. This was a typical day of street reporting for Barbara. On the other hand, when I went out on a story, people asked me if I came from a family of midgets or told me that I reminded them of Steve Urkel, the bespectacled nerdy character from the TV sitcom *Family Matters*. I'd think, Huh? But I'm white!

7

OF ALL THE PEOPLE BENNY BETRAYED,
HE FELT THE WORST ABOUT HECTOR
SOTO. HECTOR WAS LIKE A FATHER TO
BENNY, MORE SO THAN HIS OWN DAD.

Benny's dad, Ventura Martinez-Perez Sr.,
was a local celebrity. He made Philadelphia
history in 1971 when he became the first
Latino officer on the city's public housing
police force. He earned his FCC license at
Temple University in 1976 and moonlighted
as a Spanish-language radio announcer.
On the airwaves, he talked sports, music,
and politics. His on-air name was El Coqui,
a type of frog in Puerto Rico that makes a
racket.

Benny craved his father's affection and
approval but knew he was a disappointment,
even an embarrassment.

"My father always told me that I was a
loser," Benny said.

Benny said his father once chased him
down the street after he spotted him selling

drugs on the corner. He kicked Benny out of the house and tossed all Benny's designer clothes—the Sergio Valente and Jordache jeans, leather blazer, Adidas sneakers—because he knew that Benny had bought the high-end threads with drug money.

Benny went to middle school with Hector's son, Noel, and Benny spent a lot of time over at their house. Hector and his wife, Lucy, were fond of the boy they knew as Flash. Benny and Hector shared a love of salsa music. Hector was a record producer who worked with some of the biggest names in Latino music; Benny took up the timbales and got regular gigs as a DJ.

When Hector wasn't recording music, he dabbled in drug dealing. He drove nice cars, wore neatly pressed slacks and Panama-style hats, and raised tropical birds. He was everything Benny wanted to be, and Hector took him everywhere in his 1976 Cadillac Seville, a two-toned light and dark blue beauty. They cruised through the neighborhood, driving past row houses with aluminum awnings draped with Puerto Rican flags. Brassy salsa music bubbled from front stoops, where old men sat talking or playing dominoes, flyswatter in hand, on folding chairs on the sidewalk.

Benny brought his girlfriends around to meet Hector, whom he introduced as "my pop." When Benny needed money to take a girl to a hotel, Benny called Hector, sometimes waking him in the middle of the night. Hector often gave Benny money for a hotel room, a movie, whatever. Hector's own son grew jealous. Noel couldn't understand why Hector never gave him money. The reason, Hector told Noel, was that Benny pestered him and whined until Hector opened his wallet.

Benny always spent Christmas Eve with Hector and his

family. Lucy made her famous Puerto Rican soup, a stew of black beans and garlic, and her shrimp *pastelillos*. Benny got drunk and spent the night on Hector and Lucy's couch. Lucy adored Benny. She would have let him move in, if he had asked.

In 1990, around the time that Benny was hustling $10 bags of coke on the corner, the cops nabbed Hector for selling cocaine out of his house. They confiscated twenty-nine grams of coke, a grinder, pestle, heat sealer, and scale. Hector landed in jail on felony drug charges. He posted $50,000 bail. While awaiting trial, he jumped bail and became a fugitive. At forty-three, Hector went on about his life, lying low but not hiding. He probably would have avoided prosecution and remained free—if not for Benny and Jeff.

When Benny turned police informant after Jeff busted him for selling marijuana and threatened to lock him up if he didn't, he didn't just flip—he transformed. He grew to like the power and got a rush from knocking on doors and conning his way into drug houses. He emerged from houses, drugs in hand, and strutted over to Jeff, bragging, "Man, I got these guys. They were supposed to be untouchable." Benny began to see himself as a cop, and Jeff grew to rely on Benny and treated him like a brother, or so Benny thought.

Over time, Benny's loyalty and alliance shifted from family friends like Hector to Jeff. Nobody killed Benny, because they hadn't figured out yet that he was a snitch. Benny was smoother than smooth.

In 2006—almost fifteen years after Hector became a fugitive—Jeff got a tip that he was selling drugs out of his corner row house. The house was a fortress. The front porch was caged by black iron bars. A surveillance camera, rigged to a television in Hector and Lucy's second-floor bedroom, was pointed at the front gate. Hector and Lucy described the camera system as a safety precaution in a dicey neighborhood, but Jeff knew that drug dealers used video cameras for countersurveillance on the cops.

It was 6:20 a.m., still dark out, on a chilly October morning. Hector and Lucy were asleep in their upstairs bedroom. The air-conditioning unit, cranked on high to alleviate Lucy's hot flashes, hummed and gurgled in the window. Lucy stirred slightly. Her barely conscious brain registered a muffled noise outside. *Thud. Thud. Thud.* Maybe the neighbor, hammering something. She had no idea that Jeff and seven other cops were at the front gate. Again and again, they slammed a battering ram into the metal lock until the wrought-iron gate banged open.

The cops came in like a freight train, roaring up the narrow staircase, single file, guns drawn. As they reached the second floor, Lucy opened the bedroom door. She stood, terrified, in her nightgown, barefoot.

A cop yelled, "Come down right now!"

She hustled down the steps to the living room. The cops burst into the bedroom and handcuffed Hector.

A cop shoved Hector to the ground. Hector fell on knees creaky and swollen with arthritis; he was an old fifty-nine. The cop struck Hector on the side of the head with the butt of a rifle. Hector's right ear, which later turned black and purple, took the brunt of the rifle. His ear throbbed.

From downstairs, Lucy heard Hector howl. She began to cry.

"Bingo!" one cop blurted. They found a clear, knotted sandwich bag, secreted in a dresser drawer, with fifteen ziplock packets amounting to 37 grams of cocaine, worth about $3,700 on the street.

A few days later, Lucy sat crying on the porch. With Hector locked up, she felt lost and scared. As she wiped tears from her cheeks, Benny happened by.

"Ma? Ma? What's the matter?"

"You didn't hear? They took Hector away, the cops, they took him."

Benny acted stunned. "If you need anything from me, if you need anything . . ."

Hector pleaded guilty to two felony drug charges: possession with intent to distribute and conspiracy. With the 1990 case still open, Hector could have gone to prison for twenty years. In exchange for his guilty plea, the judge sentenced him to three to eight years. They shipped him to a prison two hours away from Philadelphia.

Hector had been in prison for almost a year when Benny first came to the *Daily News*. Benny began to sob when he told Barbara and me about Hector. We believed he felt bad, but we struggled to understand how Benny could help set up someone so close to him.

On a cold January day in 2009, while Barbara tracked down Jorge's family, I drove from the *Daily News* to Hector and Lucy's house on the corner of Seventh and Lycoming Street. I knew from court records that Hector was in prison, but hoped Lucy was home. A gangly teen straddling a bike on the corner watched as I struggled to parallel-park my shrimpy car in a spot big enough to fit two Hummers. I got it on my second try, not too bad on the embarrassment scale, though the back bumper of my car stuck out, all hokeypokey, more than a foot from the curb.

Standing on the icy sidewalk, I was stumped by the iron bars encasing Hector and Lucy's porch. The gate was locked, and there wasn't a way to reach the front door.

"She not home," the teen called out. "You lookin' for Miss Lucy, right? She not home."

"Oh. Okay." I pulled out my reporter's notebook and scribbled a note, asking her to call me. I folded the note around one of my business cards and stuffed it in the gate lock. A few hours later, Lucy called and arranged for me to come over the next morning.

She greeted me at the gate. Lucy was a petite woman with bleached blond hair tied up in a ponytail. A girlish fifty-three years old, her face was smooth, except for a few faint lines that crinkled around her brown eyes when she smiled. A single freckle sat just above her upper lip.

Her living room looked like a white-and-black checkerboard. The popcorn ceiling and the plaster walls were painted a crisp white. The couch and chairs were a velvety black. The thick carpet was a sea of black. Everything else—the china cabinet, coffee table, end tables, knickknacks—was glass. We sat down at her dining room table. I gingerly placed my tape recorder and notepad on the pearl-colored glass table.

Lucy was eager to talk about Hector. She showed me a handmade Christmas card that he'd sent her from prison. On one side, he drew a heart and a rose with the words JUST LOVE underneath. On the other, he inked a portrait of them together, both smiling, with Hector's arm around her waist.

"I love him so much. You'd never believe how much I love that man," she said.

I told her what I knew. That Benny and Jeff set up Hector. Benny said he didn't want to buy from Hector, so he bought a $20 bag of coke from a guy who sold out of a nearby bar.

"For real?"

She thought about it for a minute, quiet. She narrowed, then widened her eyes, her face a fan of expressions that

changed from puzzlement to dismay. Lucy's reaction reminded me of the plastic volcano that my son Brody got for
Christmas. We spooned baking soda into the shot-glass-size
base, screwed on the tepee-like cone, and poured vinegar
into the narrow opening at the top. We watched as the white
liquid fizzed from the volcano's mouth and then bubbled
over in an angry cascade. I don't think the depth of Benny's
deception sank in until long after I left Lucy's house.

Later that evening, Hector called Lucy from the prison.

"Poppy, you know who did this?"

"Who?" Hector said.

"Flash."

"Flash. Flash? No. No, I don't believe it. He's like my son,"
Hector said.

Hector and Lucy would later throw out all the photos of
them with Benny. A photograph of Benny hugging Lucy went
straight in the trash. Lucy told me that Benny was raised in a
family with no love.

"We gave him love, and look what he did. . . . If you see
him, tell him that we don't want to see his face."

8

AFTER BARBARA ASKED JEFF ABOUT
RENTING A HOUSE TO BENNY, JEFF
HIRED A PIT BULL OF A LAWYER TO
FEND OFF BARBARA AND ME. HIS SOLE
job was to kill the story. Our job was to hold
our ground.

On January 31, 2009, George Bochetto
launched the first salvo in the form of
a letter. The subject line read: "Urgent
Warnings Regarding News Story." Just to
make sure we got it, he sent the letter by
fax, e-mail, and first-class mail.

"Officer Jeff _____ is an undercover
narcotics officer with the Philadelphia
Police Department, and is married and
has two school-aged children living in Philadelphia. Any publication of Officer Jeff
_____'s name, address, photograph, or
any other facts which could lead to his identification or home address will place Officer
Jeff _____, his wife, and his children in extreme danger."

We thought this argument was ludicrous. Jeff routinely testified in open court. He took the witness box and not only said his last name, but spelled it. When the prosecutor asked Jeff if he recognized the person whom he arrested, Jeff pointed to the drug dealer seated at the defendant's table. Jeff often made this identification in front of a courtroom full of other criminal defendants awaiting their own cases.

Bochetto also wrote that Benny's rap sheet read like a "credibility horror story," and he urged us to meet with him immediately.

On a late February afternoon, as heavy wet snowflakes fell, leaving faint pinwheels that quickly melted on the slick streets, Barbara and I stepped out of a cab in front of Bochetto's downtown law office on Locust Street. With boutiquish French glass doors, hunter green awning, and white stone entranceway, it was nestled among trendy restaurants, shops, and theaters.

I dressed for war. I ditched my size three and a half sneakers for tan leather pumps that I'd had to special-order from a shoe company called Cinderella. I swapped my owlish eyeglasses for contact lenses, put on crimson lipstick, eye makeup, and blush. I wore a plaid wool skirt and a purple V-neck sweater, with a brown scarf looped around my neck. Barbara, who had a wardrobe with clothes dating back to the 1980s, sported a black pencil skirt that she'd recently hemmed just above the knee, bringing the style into this decade. She paired it with a fitted jacket and her signature black leather boots, with the broken zipper and glued-on left heel. The Jewish hillbillies from Philly had arrived.

Once inside the reception area, we took a seat on a chocolate brown leather couch, tufted with buttons, the kind we imagined could be found in an English riding club. The decor was brut masculine, heavy on soft leather and dark wood. We waited for what seemed like a good while, at least one *Sponge-Bob* episode, I figured, using my kids' measurement of time. We wondered if the wait was intentional, if Bochetto wanted to make us sweat.

A skinny guy, with pasty skin and slicked-back black hair, approached us. He looked like a boy who had dressed up in his dad's pin-striped suit, which he paired, thoughtfully, with a blood-red silk power tie. A cross between Pee-wee Herman, a child vampire, and a pimp wannabe. He led us up a flight of steep, narrow stairs and ushered us into Bochetto's office.

Bochetto stood up from his massive, polished wood desk and shook each of our hands with a confident grip. He wore a smirk, an expression of amusement and curiosity. Clearly, he intended to make quick work of us. Bochetto's minion sat off to the side in a corner, with a yellow legal pad and pen on his lap.

We sat down across from Bochetto in matching teal-green upholstered chairs with deep seats and wood trim. When I sat back, the chair swallowed me up, clamlike, and my feet didn't touch the floor. I felt like Lily Tomlin as her five-year-old Edith Ann persona in a giant rocking chair. So I scooted forward and perched myself on the edge.

"Do you mind if I use my tape recorder?" I asked, as I placed it on his desk.

"No. No. You can't," Bochetto huffed. "That's a violation of Pennsylvania's Wiretapping and Electronic Surveillance Control Act."

I started to protest, but he cut me off. "This conversation is off the record."

"No," I said, petulant and defiant.

He looked at me incredulously. We could see him begin to simmer.

"I'm sorry, but we can't agree to that," Barbara said.

Ding. Ding. We were in Bochetto's boxing ring, and round one had begun. The fiery attorney liked to fight. He was a fighter from the moment he was born.

As an infant, Bochetto was abandoned at a Brooklyn orphanage and spent the first seven years of his life without a last name. He cycled in and out of foster homes and fell prey to street punks who teased him and beat him up. A family from Rochester, New York—the Bochettos—adopted him. The scrawny teen found a second home in a nearby gym, where he taught himself to box, punching a weight bag to toughen himself up—inside and out. Bochetto became an amateur boxer and later graduated, cum laude, from Temple University School of Law in 1978. Then-governor Tom Ridge appointed Bochetto state boxing commissioner in 1995, and the Pennsylvania Veteran Boxers Association named him Man of the Year in 1997. As boxing commish, Bochetto raised money to open gyms and boxing leagues in neighborhoods battered by violence. He dug into his own pocket to pay gym fees for poor kids.

The fifty-six-year-old Bochetto oozed panache and power. Under other circumstances, we might have thought him handsome, in his stylish dark-framed eyeglasses and starched white dress shirt embroidered GEORGE near the breast pocket. He combed his thick graying hair back in a wavelike ripple.

His office was a shrine to boxing. The dark green walls were decorated with posters of legends like Muhammad Ali and Mike Tyson and photos of Bochetto with them. Silk boxing trunks autographed by Ali and Joe Frazier hung on the wall near oil paintings of fighters. Boxing gloves were displayed in an antique china cabinet with a glass door. On Bochetto's desk sat a 1936 bronze sculpture of clashing boxers.

The work, entitled *The Uppercut,* was created by boxer-turned-artist Joe Brown. A black T-shirt sold during the 1995 fight between Mike Tyson and Buster Mathis Jr. was preserved in a picture frame. As boxing commissioner, Bochetto had licensed Tyson to fight in Pennsylvania after Iron Mike got out of prison for rape, paving the way for the Philadelphia Tyson-Mathis matchup. On a side table was an original, unopened Wheaties cereal box with Ali on the front.

Bochetto, who specialized in libel law, began to lecture us, his voice laced with anger and frustration. He couldn't understand why we would even consider writing a story based on the word of a convicted drug dealer turned informant.

"What do you guys think you are going to do? Win a Pulitzer Prize?" he sneered.

Of course drug dealers arrested by Jeff, a decorated cop, would say that Benny never made the buy. They'd feed us any bullshit to beat the case, and Benny was a bottom-feeder, Bochetto told us.

"Being a confidential informant, those are spaces occupied in the main by scumbags," Bochetto said. "These are liars and thieves and snakes who will do anything and say anything for any reason. They never man up. They never face reality and accept the consequences. They are always looking for a crack to crawl in, a rock to crawl under."

Any reasonable person, anyone playing with a full deck, would have got Bochetto's point and probably dropped the story.

Not us. Maybe we were off our gourd, but we knew that Jeff had rented a house to Benny. I mean, Barbara had been at landlord-tenant court. We believed that Jeff had lied on some of the search warrants. They read alike, as if they were cookie-cutter form letters that Jeff filled in with different names and addresses, a kind of Mad Libs. And we weren't the only ones who thought that the search warrants smelled. Veteran and smart attorneys like Stephen Patrizio, who had represented Raul Nieves and figured out Jeff had rented a house to Benny, thought so, too.

And no one—not even Bochetto, this hardscrabble bully with his commonsense argument—could convince us otherwise. This was why Bochetto was worried. He knew we were trouble. We lacked the skepticism and doubt that Bochetto had seen in other seasoned reporters. He sensed our enthusiasm, our energy. He could tell we were enjoying this fight, though he was convinced we'd lose.

He leaned forward, his arm extended over a Civil War–era sword—a gift from a client—that sat in the middle of his desk. He jabbed his index finger, first at me, then at Barbara. "I'm going to sue you—and you—personally!"

We stood up to leave. I whipped my scarf over my left shoulder and shook his hand. "It's been a pleasure," I said, rolling my eyes. My sarcasm elicited a little snort, almost a chuckle, from Bochetto.

We climbed into a cab and looked at each other, wide-eyed.

"Do you think he can sue us? Personally?" I said.

"Geez, I hope not. We'd lose our houses. Wendy, we'd be homeless," Barbara said.

We began to giggle nervously.

"Nahhhhh!" I said.

Barbara and I did cede some ground to Bochetto. He had chastised us for not contacting officers and supervisors who could vouch for Jeff's character. We realized he was right. Bochetto agreed to e-mail us names and numbers of Jeff's colleagues, and we agreed to send him a list of our questions for Jeff.

Bochetto sent over the list of people he described as "more than willing and anxious to provide you with direct, firsthand knowledge of important facts relating to your article." We hit the phones the minute we got the list. Richard Eberhart was the first name. Eberhart was Jeff's former partner. He had retired a few years earlier and now, along with Jeff, owned J&R Dunk Tank Rentals, a company that rented moon bounces and carnival games for kiddie parties.

Barbara called Eberhart on his cell. Not surprisingly, Eberhart described Jeff as "an excellent police officer, a straight shooter, a hard worker, an all-around good guy." She asked Eberhart if he thought Benny was credible and reliable. When Eberhart said, "Yes," Barbara began to feel the endorphins of a reporter's high, a blend of panic attack, sugar rush, too much caffeine, and great sex.

"Did you know that Jeff rented a house to Benny?" she asked, and threw in, as if a casual afterthought, "What did you think of that?"

"Would I have done that? Probably not. But who am I to judge?" Eberhart said. "I thought he was helping him out. It didn't seem inappropriate at the time, but looking back, maybe it was."

Barbara hung up and zoomed over to my desk, flapping her arms like a seal just before the zookeeper tosses a fish. "You're never gonna believe this," she said.

"Get the fuck out!"

We sent Bochetto our questions, fourteen in all, and to tweak him further, we gave him a deadline—highlighted in bold—of 5:00 p.m. the following day. He must have wanted to box our ears.

Bochetto didn't answer a single question, but he gave us a colorful and snarky quote: "It is overwhelmingly clear that, when the hard facts are put on the table, your story falls apart and your questions become empty vessels of naïveté. What you have, and what you apparently want to rely upon, are nothing but a self-serving series of fictionalizations by professional liars, felons, and drug addicts, each of whom are looking to avoid more jail time by playing the *Daily News* for a patsy."

Barbara and I labored over writing the story. We spent hours together in front of the computer, surrounded by documents, interview notes, and empty coffee cups. The floor underneath my desk was littered with Rice Krispies Treats wrappers. At ninety calories apiece, the marshmallow sponges were the only junk food that Barbara allowed herself to eat. I bit my fingernails and gnawed at the cuticles until they bled. I would have salted myself and chewed off my fingers—if I didn't need them to type.

The story was a sprawling tale about how Jeff and Benny met, their rental arrangement, and Benny's allegations that Jeff fabricated evidence to get into drug homes.

9

OUR IRASCIBLE CITY EDITOR, GAR JOSEPH, WAS HOLED UP IN HIS CLOSET-SIZE OFFICE FOR WHAT SEEMED LIKE HOURS. WE WEREN'T SURE IF THAT WAS a good thing or bad; we just knew that he was in there reading a draft of our story. Actually, it was draft number four.

Gar had declared our first version "a fucking mess." He wasn't the type of editor to tiptoe around reporters' fragile egos. He got impatient, sometimes unapologetically rude, with reporters who couldn't pitch a story idea in one sentence or less.

"I have no idea what the fuck you're talking about," he'd say. "Can you tell me again—in English."

As city editor, Gar was the first stop for rough drafts, and often the last. "This story ain't gonna run, unless you can figure out a way to make it unboring." The sixty-year-old former City Hall reporter with a salt-and-pepper goatee had been around so long that he didn't think anything was story-worthy. Here's an e-mail he sent to editors assigned to work on Thanksgiving: "I don't give a shit about the [Thanksgiving] parade unless a small child is entangled in the ropes of the Mighty Mouse balloon and choked to death, so don't waste a reporter on it."

Gar walked toward Barbara and me with his trademark limp, the result of running too many marathons.

"I think you've got something really good here," he said, waving us into his office. A sticker that read "Easy Sucks" was taped to the glass panel beside the door. We sat on his ratty, gamy-smelling couch as he called up the story on his computer. His idea of a motivational poster hung on the wall: "Despair. It's always darkest just before it goes pitch black."

"The story's way, way, waaaaaay too long. This section here veers off a cliff," Gar said.

Gar despised long stories. He believed the Bible could be boiled down to six words. "Old Testament: 'God is great.' New Testament: 'God is love.' Bam, done. Of course, you lose some of the metaphors," Gar liked to say.

He also hated stories written in esoteric geek-speak.

"This part doesn't make any fuckin' sense," Gar told us, as we stared at the blinking cursor on his computer screen. "It's written in mumbo-jumbo police jargon that no reader's gonna understand.

"Other than that, it's pretty good. Fixable," he sniffed.

After a two-hour-long journalistic colonoscopy on a cold, rainy Friday night, Gar leaned back in his swivel chair, adjusted his eyeglasses, folded his arms across his chest, and said, "Now let's see what our lawyer has to say."

We weren't sure the story would ever run, or when the lawyer would read it.

Thinking we had done all we could do before the weekend,

Barbara left work at about 6:30 p.m. to go on yet another blind date.

She'd been divorced for more than three years and was tired of being alone or stuck in relationships that she knew, deep down, weren't quite right. She signed up for Match.com and spent hours crafting her profile. She began, "I'm the kind of woman who likes to pack a lot into each day so I can go to bed at night with a smile on my face, knowing I truly live."

When she showed me her profile, I blurted, "Oh, Barbara, that's soooo schmaltzy. You gotta change that."

She looked crushed and later went home and rewrote the top. Not surprisingly, Barbara's profile generated dozens of electronic "winks." She quickly realized that winkers fell into two camps: shy, insecure types who were interested but wanted her to return the wink before they wrote a note; or fishermen daters who cast a huge net and winked at hundreds of women to see who bit.

Some nights after work, we'd sit at Barbara's desk and she'd pull up the latest dating prospects. We scanned their photos and bios. Some made us laugh, others made us cringe, and a few went in the "not bad" category. One with a username something like "sexyfunsmart77QX" looked neither sexy, fun, or smart. Another resembled a wild-eyed Charlie Manson who might stuff her body in a trunk. He wanted to meet for a drink. She visualized her blood in a glass. Two more were not much older than her twenty-two-year-old son, Josh. "We'd be great together, gorgeous," one wrote. We knew where he wanted to be "great." The last one had an anger-management problem: "The LEAST you could do is write back. Your loss!"

The guy she planned to meet on that Friday night sounded promising. He had told her that he was a fifty-four-year-old manager for a computer company, had two adult kids, and loved to run. She met him at a coffee shop.

This couldn't be him, she thought, as she saw this man, mostly bald, with a few strands of gray hair swept to the right in a comb-over, walk toward her. With tense, slightly hunched shoulders and a slow gait, he looked close to Barbara's dad's age. Nothing like his Match photo. He said in his profile that he was six feet tall. Maybe thirty years ago, Barbara thought.

He stretched out his liver-spotted hand for her to shake, and they walked inside.

Within twenty minutes, he pulled out his wallet to show Barbara photos of his three grandkids. They were next to his AARP card. He told her he had retired from his job.

"So how old are you?" she asked curiously.

"Sixty-six," he said.

"But your profile says you're fifty-four."

"I know. I figured most women your age would dismiss me if I put my real age. And all they have to do is meet me."

"But that's a big age difference. That's like twelve years," she said.

"You know what?" he said, leaning toward her, clearly irritated. "Most women your age have no problem with it. I have a five-bedroom house, a pool. I drive a Mercedes, have a boat. The last woman I dated was forty-eight."

Barbara looked at her watch.

At about 7:30 p.m., I was just shutting down my computer when Gar came over to my desk and said that our attorney, Scott Baker, and Michael Days, the paper's top editor, wanted to go over the story. Right now.

I thought about calling Barbara but didn't want to interrupt her date. Loaded down with an armful of documents, I trailed Gar, beetle-like, into Michael's glass-front office.

Michael waved me in and I took a seat at the conference table. Scott had inked up a copy of our rough draft; he'd circled words and phrases that he deemed too loaded and scribbled notes and question marks in the margins. We went over the story, line by line. I slid documents—search warrants, interview notes, Bochetto correspondence, the rental agreement, and the landlord-tenant eviction notice—across the table for Scott's review.

"Do you think we are going to get sued?" I asked.

"There's a fifty-fifty chance," said Scott, who pointed to Benny's criminal record. "The guy is a convicted drug dealer."

"Yes, I know," Michael said, "but these are two fine reporters. Ultimately, you have to trust your reporters." He turned to me. "What does your gut tell you? Do you believe him?"

"I do," I said.

"To me, it passes the smell test," Michael said about Benny's story.

Fear of a libel lawsuit, said Scott, is not a good enough reason to kill a story. "This is a newspaper. You're a reporter. We're in the business of writing stories."

I felt the urge to hug this corporate lawyer, this unexpected ally and champion of journalism.

Barbara and I came into the office on Sunday to fact-check the story one more time. Barbara called Bochetto to let him know that the story was slated to run the next day. She asked if he had any additional comment. He had none. Gar gave the story a final read. Kevin Bevan, the editor in charge of the page-one design, who wore a down-on-the-farm plaid flannel shirt to work every day, showed us the headline he coined: "Tainted Justice?" The question mark was a hedge, the *Daily News* version of a wink, as if just askin'—"Hey, readers, do you think this cop is corrupt?"

"You can commit a lot of sins with a question mark," Bevan once said, half joking. The *Daily News* was famous for slapping question marks on headlines. "Trish's Killer?" on a story naming a homicide suspect. "Armed & Angry?" on a story about cops arresting NBA star Allen Iverson on gun and assault charges. "A Veteran Kidnapper?" "Devil in Blue?" "Highway Robbery?" It fit when we believed a criminal, politician, or public figure was guilty in the court of public opinion, but not yet charged.

The front-page mock-up that Kevin showed us featured a grainy silhouette of Benny, with a hoodie pulled tight around his face. The photograph, filmed against the backdrop of the paper's dimly lit loading dock, had a sinister feel. The headline blared, "A Cop and an Informant Got Too Close and Bent the Rules. Now, the Informant Fears for His Life. Tainted Justice? Page 3."

We believed Jeff was a dirty cop. No question. And every story we wrote after that first one carried the moniker "Tainted Justice." Fact.

The next morning, we came to work prepared to take some heat for the story. We never expected the hair-singeing, ass-burning thermonuclear fireball that would soon unfold.

10

BARBARA AND I IMMEDIATELY LANDED
ON THE FBI'S MOST DESPISED LIST.

"Our investigation is in the toilet," a
miffed FBI agent told me the day our story
ran.

The feds were mad that we had convinced
Benny to tell his story and then pointed
him in their direction. "I realize that you
guys have a job to do," the agent conceded,
adding that he wished Benny had gone to
the FBI first and not the other way around.

In the days before our story ran, Benny
sat down with the feds and they wired him
up in hopes of snagging Jeff on tape. They
wanted Jeff to admit that he had phonied
up arrest paperwork and perjured himself
in court. Benny told Barbara that the feds
had given him a keychain, rigged with a
miniature tape recorder. When Jeff arrived
at landlord-tenant court, Benny confronted
him in the hallway and tried to goad him
into a confession. Jeff was leery; he gave

up nothing, and we didn't help matters. When Barbara approached Jeff after the eviction hearing, he knew Benny had sicced us on him. He wasn't stupid.

The Internal Affairs Division was equally rankled. Police commissioner Charles Ramsey railed that we'd blown their cover, forcing investigators to abandon their undercover operation. Ramsey had no choice but to strip Jeff of his gun and police powers and put him on desk duty. Ramsey transferred Jeff to the Roundhouse—the hatbox-shaped police headquarters building, where Jeff spent all day taking fender-bender accident reports over the phone. Without the opportunity to use a wiretap, the probe would take months as investigators painstakingly dissected every job Jeff did with Benny.

As vexed as internal affairs was by us, they were even more furious at Benny for going over their heads.

When Benny went to the feds before giving the police department time to investigate, he might as well have flipped all of internal affairs the bird. But that was Benny. He worked all the angles until he got what he wanted, or in his mind, what he needed. His alliances were on spin cycle.

When Jeff told him that he had to get out of his house, Benny went to internal affairs. When internal affairs didn't whisk him into witness protection, he went to Wellington Stubbs at the Philadelphia Police Advisory Commission. When Barbara and I told him that we couldn't write his story without using his name, he went to Fox 29. When the FBI asked him why he went to the *Daily News*, he rolled Wellington under the bus.

"I only did what Wellington told me to do," Benny shrugged, as if he had no clue that the FBI and internal affairs wouldn't be happy with Wellington. When the city's deputy mayor learned that Benny got my name from

Wellington, he scolded Wellington for exercising poor judgment. The city later forced Wellington to resign. Wellington believed the city fired him in retaliation for sending Benny my way, but the city claimed Wellington had violated a rule requiring city employees to live within Philadelphia.

Benny was good at playing victim. Once, after FBI or internal affairs investigators picked him up in a car without tinted windows, Benny bitched to us that they didn't give a shit about his safety.

"Jeff might have been an asshole with me and jammed me up, but he always picked me up in a tinted car. He was protecting me," Benny complained to me.

When the FBI wouldn't help him out with money or housing, Benny claimed they were punishing him for talking to us. The guilt ate at us because we cared about Benny and his family. His kids were close in age to mine, and I agonized that the story had put them at more risk. For me, telling Benny's story came at a price—I would forever feel responsible for his safety, despite all his faults. I often found myself caring about people I wrote about, but usually they were sympathetic characters. Benny was not.

It didn't bother me and Barbara when FBI and police heaped blame on us. They had their job; we had ours. Our job was to shine a white-hot light on wrongdoing.

In the early 1980s, there was the One Squad scandal—a small circle of narcotics officers were convicted of selling drugs they stole from dealers. Then, in the late 1980s, came the Five Squad Scandal—four officers in an elite narcotics squad went to prison on federal racketeering charges for taking bribes from drug dealers. In the 1990s, there was the Thirty-Ninth District scandal—a half dozen narcotics cops pleaded guilty to framing and beating suspects, lying under oath, and robbing drug dealers. The Thirty-Ninth District scandal was an iceberg that ripped open the hull of the criminal justice system and sank the public's trust in narcotics cops. Hundreds of cases got tossed or overturned, and the city paid millions of dollars to settle federal civil rights lawsuits filed by people wrongly arrested and jailed.

Cops who worked narcotics were especially susceptible to corruption. For one thing, narcotics cops faced a Sisyphean task, an endless and hopeless battle to stem a tsunami of drugs. The dealers literally outgunned and outnumbered the cops, so why play fair? Why not cut some constitutional corners to gain the upper hand? Day in and day out, narcotics cops arrested gun-toting dealers who raked in thousands of dollars a week, drove luxury cars, and adorned themselves with fur coats, jewelry, and designer clothes, while the cops were risking their lives and slogging out a living on a $50,000-a-year cop's salary. If they helped themselves to some drug money or pocketed a diamond ring or framed suspects to boost their overtime pay, what did it matter? Didn't they deserve additional compensation? Corrupt cops were unapologetic.

After each scandal, police watchdogs and civil rights lawyers cited poor training, failure to discipline, and lax rules and oversight of cops who worked with drug informants. They made recommendations for reform—and the police department largely ignored their suggestions. The fact was, Benny didn't trust internal affairs because its investigators had a history of failing to police their own.

If police brass and internal affairs wanted to blame Barbara and me for blowing their investigation, fine. But if they had cleaned their own house years back, we wouldn't be here. That's how we saw it.

The Defender Association of Philadelphia, which represents

poor people in criminal cases, began to scrutinize scores of drug cases in which Jeff used Benny as an informant. In the wake of our first page-one story, civil rights attorneys clamored for more supervision of and better training for narcotics officers. The police inspector in charge of narcotics lamented that the allegations, if true, could free dozens of drug dealers, casting a black cloud over the entire narcotics field unit. And the city district attorney's office launched an investigation into Benny's allegations. A few days later, the mayor, the FBI, police internal affairs, and the Philadelphia Office of the Inspector General announced the formation of a joint task force. During an afternoon news conference, city mayor Michael Nutter, whose nasal voice reminded me of Kermit the Frog, especially when he was trying to sound firm, said he wouldn't hesitate to come down hard on Jeff if the investigation revealed wrongdoing.

"We think that high ethical standards matter in the entire city, but especially in the Philadelphia Police Department," said Nutter, grim-faced. "If any of these allegations are true, we will take, I'm sure, the swiftest action."

"Obviously, ensuring the safety of individuals involved in this investigation will be paramount," Janice Fedarcyk, FBI special agent in charge, said at the press conference when reporters asked about witness protection for Benny.

By now, the age-old *Daily News–Inquirer* rivalry was in full tilt. *Inquirer* editor Bill Marimow had won not one but two Pulitzer Prizes—in 1978 and 1985—for an investigative series that exposed police brutality and misconduct. This was his kind of story, and he wanted his paper to own it. The *Inky* reporters weren't going to follow us, they were going to beat us. Within two weeks, the *Inky* had seven reporters on the story. The sleeping giant was wide awake.

When *Inky* deputy managing editor Vernon Loeb thought

that his reporters did a better job than us on their follow-up story about the fallout from Benny's allegations, he dashed off a congratulatory e-mail from his BlackBerry and copied all the top editors:

"While I never liked getting beat on a story (and I'm not saying it was you two guys who got beat on the original *Daily News* piece about [Jeff and Benny]), I knew it was an occupational hazard, and you could never break every story. But I always vowed to myself that I'd never get beaten on a follow, and I always loved to take over the stories I was beaten on and mercilessly pound my competitors once I was on the case. And this is why I absolutely loved—loved!—this scoop you guys had this morning, significantly advancing this important story and announcing to the *Daily News*, with data analysis they can't possibly match, that we're not going to be beaten again, and that we in fact intend to own this story from here on out. Great work. Best, Vernon."

The e-mail became a running joke in our newsroom. *Daily News* columnist Howard Gensler, who wrote the paper's celebrity gossip du jour, slipped the phrase "mercilessly pound" into a column about how *Extra* beat out *Access Hollywood* and *Entertainment* as the first to report that Nicollette Sheridan was leaving *Desperate Housewives*.

It was ridiculous that reporters at the two newspapers—owned by the same company, operating out of the same building—regarded one another as competition, even enemies. Ridiculous, that is, to everyone but us.

When the *Daily News* scooped the *Inquirer* on a story, *Inky* editors dressed down their reporters. "You got beat, don't let it happen again." When they scooped us, our editors minimized their victory. "Well, you know, they have more people, more resources."

The *Daily News* harbored an inferiority complex, fueled by the fact that some of our reporters had applied for jobs at the *Inquirer* and didn't get hired and that *Inky* staffers made more money. When I parachuted down to the *Daily News* to avoid being laid off in late 2006, I got to keep my $76,648 *Inquirer* salary, which meant I made more than some *Daily News* reporters who had been with the company longer. Barbara, who was my editor at the time, made only $4,316 more than me, even though she had worked at the company a decade longer. The *Daily News* was a second-class citizen, and that made our victories somehow sweeter. The Goliath *Inquirer* looked down at us from its perch as we bobbed and weaved, swinging hard. Occasionally, we got our jabs in.

Some *Inky* reporters viewed our mangy troupe as a pest, a persistent termite problem within their stately institution. They secretly wanted us to close, and whenever company number crunchers talked about folding the *Daily News*, the *Inky* reporters wished it so, though they'd never say the words aloud.

At the venerable and cultured 180-year-old *Inquirer*, I was like a kazoo in a symphony. "I'm your bitch," I once told a reserved editor who asked me to help cover the deadly shooting of five Amish children at their Lancaster schoolhouse. There was silence on the other end of the phone. He didn't know how to take my comment, which was just my quirky and profane way of telling him, "Look, I'll do whatever you need." Once, when Karl came down with epididymitis, a painful inflammation of the testicles, I told my editors that I had to leave early because "my husband's balls are killing him." They shook their heads as I shut down my computer.

The "mercilessly pound" e-mail egged us on, feeding our desire to kick some *Inky* ass.

Barbara's will to win, the force within her that drove her

to cross the finish line in three marathons, was the fuel that made her a tenacious reporter.

She wasn't a natural athlete. Far from it. As a teen, she was klutzy, always among the last to be picked for a volleyball or basketball team. When she had to do a routine on the uneven bars in a high school gym class, she got stuck on the top bar, her feet and head dangling hopelessly as the bar cut into her stomach.

By the time she reached her twenties, she got out of breath walking up stairs and felt out of shape. She decided to start running. The first day she couldn't make it three blocks. It took her a month to build up to a mile. She ran at such a slow pace, walkers passed her. She stuck with it and even ran during the first six months of being pregnant with her son, Josh.

To train for a marathon, she got up before dawn and, donning a reflector vest, headed outside, whatever the weather. Some days she ran the same hill eight times over. She seemed to get a sick pleasure out of pushing her body to its limit. She ran the New York City Marathon with an overtraining injury. At mile 20, her legs and feet had turned to lead. Every step felt like daggers piercing through her calves and thighs, but she knew she'd get to the finish line, even if she had to crawl. In every marathon, the last 6.2 miles are killers, the ones where the body checks out and the mind takes over.

Barbara fed off the human chain of 2 million spectators who lined the 26.2-mile course—men, women, and children, three layers thick, who let out a deafening, thunderous roar for Barbara and other average joe runners as if they were Kenyans. They held out their hands for runners to high-five. Barbara slapped hand after hand, using that human connection to tell herself she would not, could not quit.

In the last mile, tears came to her eyes. She saw flashes of her life, but only the good parts, like the moments her children were born and she held them for the first time. All she heard was applause. "Keep going. I can't do what you're doing," yelled one man who caught her eye.

Then she saw the packed bleachers, the blue banner, and the time clock. The finish line.

Barbara would go for a run on frigid mornings, the cold air burning her nose and eyes. She flexed her stiff fingers, wrapped in gloves emblazoned with the words I KNOW I RUN LIKE A GIRL. TRY TO KEEP UP.

Barbara approached her job like a marathoner. Stuck to her computer, she kept a Winston Churchill quote: "Never Never Never Give Up."

We were the underdogs. The B team. The long shot. We weren't expected to win. The thing was, Barbara and I both hated to lose.

11

LESS THAN TWO WEEKS AFTER OUR
FIRST STORY RAN, BARBARA AND I
CAME INTO WORK TO FIND AN AVA-
LANCHE OF HATE E-MAILS.

"You fucking piece of shit!" one reader
wrote. "You are a disgrace to yourself and
your family and this city!" The reader continued, "It's a shame that you have an ability to get the word out about the positives of
this police department . . . and this is how
you earn your money."

We understood the root of their anger.
A North Philadelphia drug dealer, Thomas
Cooper, aka Thomas Smith, was poised to
walk free because Jeff and Benny were tied
to his case.

Jeff and Benny often targeted nickel-
and-dime drug peddlers. This case was different. Thomas Cooper—twice convicted
on felony drug charges—was big-time.
When Jeff and his squad raided his house,
they found a stash of drugs, including 155.6

grams of crack worth more than $12,000, an amount that bumped the case up to the federal level. This was Thomas's third strike, and if convicted, he would spend the rest of his life in prison.

Federal prosecutors were preparing the case for trial when our first Tainted Justice story hit. The story prompted them to reexamine what had led up to Thomas's arrest. The facts didn't add up.

In an application for a search warrant, Jeff said Benny had tipped him off to a guy named Pooh Bear who stored guns and sold marijuana and crack from his mother's row house. Jeff claimed that he and another cop watched Benny knock on the door and buy marijuana from Pooh Bear. Jeff described Pooh Bear as tall, about six-two, and thin, roughly 180 pounds.

"I never heard of a guy named Pooh Bear. I never made a buy at this place," Benny told us.

Thomas Cooper never went by the nickname Pooh Bear and wasn't exactly thin—he topped the scale at 350 pounds.

Federal prosecutors decided to drop the charges "in the interests of justice." It was the first case to be dismissed since Barbara and I had started the Tainted Justice series.

I called Cooper's public defender, Nina Carpinello Spizer, who told me she had always been troubled by the case because the warrant gave an inaccurate description and nickname for Cooper.

"We never suspected that this was all made up," she told me. "We didn't know until it came out in the newspaper," she said, referring to our first Tainted Justice story.

Thomas Cooper was set to walk free at any time. We wanted to talk to him, or at least find his relatives and see his house.

When Barbara walked up to his three-story brick row house with smudged cream paint and brown trim, she had a gnawing feeling in the pit of her stomach. The house, owned by the Philadelphia Housing Authority, sat across the street from an elementary school for children pre-K through eighth grade.

It was around 2:30 in the afternoon, and school had just let out. Children clamored outside in their winter coats, and Barbara knew that to get home, these kids had to walk past corner drug boys with dark hoodies pulled tight over their heads to shade their hard-boiled eyes.

Barbara and I knew that nothing tore down a neighborhood faster or harder than drug houses. They attracted desperate addicts who were unpredictable when they couldn't get a fix and potentially dangerous when they did. They took over abandoned houses and made them crack dens or shooting galleries. Many dealers were never far from a weapon and often shot each other over territory or nonsense—it didn't matter. Children, some of them toddlers, had been gunned down in the crossfire, even outside a school. Neighbors feared telling cops about the drug trade on their block, believing their homes would be firebombed.

Barbara knocked on Thomas Cooper's worn front door. Cooper's mother, a woman we'll call Helen, let Barbara into the gloomy, sparse living room, empty except for two chairs. Helen plopped down in one, and Barbara carefully perched herself on a wobbly metal folding chair with a bent, misshapen leg, knowing that with one wrong move, she would topple to the floor.

Helen was forty-nine but looked haggard and moved so precariously, she appeared more like a sickly sixty-year-old. A colostomy bag was attached to her hip. She blamed two recent surgeries on the stress of the raid and the "nasty" cops who threw her son in jail.

Barbara had no doubt that she was sitting in a drug house.

While Helen said she was angry that the cop had set up her son, she made no apologies for Thomas or his lifestyle. Drugs were a cottage industry, the one and only economic engine in her section of town.

Thomas mostly hung out on the third floor, and Helen said she seldom climbed the stairs to see his bedroom or look at what he kept inside. Against the backdrop of a bedroom window that overlooked the elementary school, Thomas cut, weighed, and packaged a potpourri of drugs with studious precision.

Helen told Barbara she suspected that the search warrant was bogus because her son never ran a knock-and-buy operation.

"This is not like you could come to my house, knock on my door, and come in and buy drugs," she said.

Barbara knew that Helen, without saying it, meant that her son didn't roll that way—he gave the drugs to street corner dealers, probably so he wouldn't risk getting his family booted out of public housing. This was home. The family had lived there ten years.

"I don't understand why the cops were here," Helen said with a shrug.

"Did you know your son was selling drugs?" Barbara asked flat-out.

"I kind of thought it, but I didn't see it myself," Helen said.

Some moms of drug dealers played dumb, telling us that they had no idea what cops had found in their homes. Not Helen. She told Barbara she knew cops had discovered crack cocaine, cocaine, and marijuana. She didn't talk specifics or mention that inside her son's bedroom, Jeff and his squad found marijuana in eighty-nine glass jars with pink lids and a digital scale.

Thomas didn't have a job because of a bad knee, yet police found almost $2,000 in his pocket when he was arrested.

"They tore the whole house up. They didn't find no guns," she proclaimed, punctuating the end of her sentence with a slight smile and an expectant pause, as if waiting for Barbara to respond, "You go, girl! Those pesky cops are always making a big deal out of nothing."

Helen cast herself in the role of victim. "It really makes me angry," she said. "Cops are supposed to help us, not to lock people up for nothing so they can make themselves feel better. I think they get off on making themselves feel better."

Barbara emerged from the house feeling like a hypocrite. She never intended to become a champion for the city's drug dealers. It's one thing to get all high and mighty about cops who piss all over the US Constitution, but she didn't have to live here. Her children never had to go to school across the street from a drug dealer's house.

Barbara could parachute into the city's blood-splattered neighborhoods to report on the latest murder, then go home to comfy suburbia, where she never awoke to the sound of gunfire at midnight.

On the first morning of Thomas's freedom, Barbara and I had a front-page story about how Pooh Bear was released from prison because the search warrant seemed to rely on fabricated evidence. The headline on the story: "Dismissed! People Paper Exposé Leads to Release of North Philly Man."

Barbara and I groaned when we saw the photo and headline. We knew that the average reader would take one look at the headline and conclude that we were gleeful that we had helped free the neighborhood crack vendor. Most readers don't know that reporters don't write headlines. To further make us appear that we were empathetic to Cooper's plight, the story featured a family photo of Thomas, this happy hulk of a man, grinning from ear to ear while holding his two small nephews, ages two and four months. The timing couldn't be worse.

The day the story ran, yet one more slain police officer was buried. This time it was John Pawlowski, just twenty-five years old, the fifth officer killed in the line of duty in the past twelve months.

It was a hellish period for a police department that felt under siege. In a city where cops were heroes, the number of police deaths in such a short span was unprecedented. Soccer moms displayed photos of fallen officers in the back windows of their minivans. Cops fastened black ribbons over their badges, and working-class guys with grease under their nails wore T-shirts or buttons to memorialize the latest fallen cop.

For each funeral, the city came to a virtual standstill to allow for the motorcades that stretched for miles. Thousands of mourners, some waving American flags, lined the streets outside the Cathedral Basilica of Saints Peter and Paul. Cops from as far away as Canada came to pay their respects. The sound of sobs, the wail of bagpipes, and the *tat-boom-tat* of drums rose from the crowd as each flag-draped coffin was loaded into the hearse.

Pawlowski, whose father and brother were also cops, was shot to death by a revolving-door criminal, a parolee with a decade-long arrest record for theft, robbery, and gun crimes. When Pawlowski responded to a 911 call from a cabbie who said Scruggs was threatening him, Pawlowski ordered Scruggs to raise his hands. Instead, Scruggs squeezed the trigger of a .357 Magnum that had been tucked inside his coat pocket. A bullet tore into Pawlowski's upper chest, just over the top of his bulletproof vest.

Police Commissioner Ramsey and Mayor Nutter spoke at Pawlowski's funeral, where the cries of Pawlowski's wife, Kimmy, his childhood sweetheart, echoed through the cavernous cathedral. Kimmy was five months pregnant with their first child, a son she would name after her husband. A grainy ultrasound photo was tucked into Pawlowski's folded hands before undertakers closed his brushed copper casket.

To some readers, Barbara and I were no better than killers like Scruggs. "It's people like you who are to blame for the unprecedented violence against the Philadelphia Police," one e-mailed us.

Barbara and I were targeted on Domelights.com, an Internet forum where cops, their supporters, and cop wannabes vented anonymously. The website's slogan—"The Voice of the Good Guys"—was a joke. Many of the postings were angry, racist rants. In one posting, the writer described black children as "a bunch of ghetto monkey faces." Cops and others who posted on the site dubbed us "Slime Sistas," some wished us dead, and a few wrote that they hoped we got raped and no one would respond when we called 911. I didn't tell Karl that cops had posted our home address on the site.

The verbal assault became so savage that our colleague Jill Porter felt compelled to write a column defending us. "You may be furious that a suspected drug dealer was freed—as well you should be. But don't aim your fury at Laker and Ruderman," she wrote.

Again and again, our critics argued, Who cares if cops cut corners or lie to take a drug dealer off the street? They believed that the ends justified the means.

The argument reminded Barbara and me of a famous scene from the 1992 movie *A Few Good Men*, a courtroom drama about two US Marines on trial for killing a fellow marine. When pressed by the prosecutor for the truth about the murder, Colonel Nathan Jessup, played by Jack Nicholson, barks, "You can't handle the truth!" meaning that national security comes at a price. "Son, we live in a world that has walls. And those walls have to be guarded by men with guns. Who's gonna do it? You?"

Yes, Barbara and I weren't cops. We didn't know how it felt to chase down an armed robber or deranged killer, only to find ourselves in a dark alley, staring into the barrel of a gun. But we did know that when reporters fabricated stories, when they invented people, facts, or quotes, they tarnished the entire industry and eroded trust. The same applied to cops, only more so. Martin Luther King Jr. put it this way: "Injustice anywhere is a threat to justice everywhere."

12

BARBARA AND I WERE HUDDLED OVER
MY COMPUTER WRITING OUR NEXT
TAINTED JUSTICE STORY. THE NEWS-
ROOM WAS UNUSUALLY LIVELY FOR
a Sunday evening. It was Oscar night, and
editors had ordered pizza, as they did for
all big events—election night, the Super
Bowl, the World Series. Reporters and copy
editors gathered, vulture-like, around a
white cardboard tower of pizza boxes. They
pulled apart the gooey slices, wiped their
greasy fingers on thin takeout napkins—or
on their jeans—and then zipped back to
their desks.

From my desk, I could see the Sunday-
night editor, Will Bunch, furiously typing
away at his computer behind stacks of yellowed newspapers. Will, the Ivy League–
educated, fifty-year-old mad scientist of
the *Daily News*, always looked like he'd just
jammed a metal fork into an electric outlet,
with his thin strands of hair zigzagging every

which way. Between bites of pizza, Will took generous swigs of Diet Coke straight from the two-liter bottle. By night's end, the bottle would be empty, left on a desk smeared with sticky brown crop circles of corn syrup and a dusting of dandruff.

Will, like everyone else in the newsroom, had just learned that the parent company of the *Daily News* and *Inquirer* had filed for Chapter 11 bankruptcy protection. As he worked on a piece about the filing, which he later posted on his liberal-infused blog *Attytood*, reporters began to Google "Chapter 11" to see if they'd still get paid.

Barbara and I barely looked up, deaf to the chatter of doom around us. We had come in on our day off to write a story about a woman named Lady Gonzalez. Gar, our editor, wanted the story for Monday's front cover. We could hear the thundering hooves of *Inquirer* reporters behind us, and we were determined to outrun them. That meant working double-time to get our story in the paper.

We'd spent most of the week chasing tips that Jeff wasn't the only blemished cop in his squad. A suburban narcotics cop who occasionally joined forces with Philly drug cops called Barbara with a tip that one cop in Jeff's squad was known as the Boob Man.

"Boob Man?"

"Yeah. You know. He fondles women. He's a perv. He goes up under their shirts and touches their breasts when he's on a raid," he told Barbara.

"Oh my God. You've got to be kidding me," Barbara said.

"I'm not fucking with you. He gets them alone in a room. All the other cops know it. I hear he likes large-breasted women—the bigger, the better."

Around the same time, I'd heard similar rumblings from Benny. It wasn't long before we discovered that the cop with the breast fetish wasn't an urban myth. In hunting down people who had been set up by Jeff, we met Lady Gonzalez, a soft-spoken, almost demure woman with almond-shaped brown eyes, smooth skin, high cheekbones, Angelina Jolie lips, and a small diamond stud in her nose. Her father named her Lady because he thought his tiny, delicate baby was deserving of such a regal name.

We met Lady on a Friday night in her tidy home with burgundy walls, CDs stacked in towers inside wood cabinets, comfy sofas, and family photos pinned to the fridge with magnets. She stood only five feet and had a curvy figure and a shy smile. Barbara and I could tell immediately from the moment we met her that she was not just skittish; she was frightened. She fiddled with the dark hair that swept over her shoulders and massaged her hands in an obsessive-compulsive way, and her sentences periodically drifted off as she tried to compose herself.

Jeff and his squad had raided this house where she lived with her husband, Albert Nunez, and her five young children. Jeff had written in a search warrant that Albert had sold a packet of cocaine to Benny, but Benny told us that was a lie—he'd never bought drugs from Albert.

When Jeff and eight other cops burst through the front door, Lady was home with the children. When Lady saw Jeff point a drawn gun at her, she froze. One cop took her children, crying and screaming, to a neighbor's house. While the other cops ripped the house apart in search of drugs, one cop, whom Lady described as husky and average height, led her into a small room off the kitchen.

Lady recounted how the barrel-bellied cop shifted his body, shuffling his feet closer to hers. She tried to back up, but there was nowhere to go. The wall was at her back.

"He asked me if I had any tattoos. I told him I had one on

my lower back," Lady told us. "He told me to show it to him. He pushed down my jeans so he could see the crack of my ass and where I have a tattoo of the Puerto Rican flag," she said, illustrating how low he pulled down her pants.

"Mmmm, a Puerto Rican," he said.

He spun her around, unzipped her blue jacket, hiked up her shirt and bra, and fondled her breasts.

"I was so scared," Lady told us, her voice shaking as she wiped a tear from the corner of her eye. "I was in a panic. I thought he was going to rape me."

The cop stopped and stepped away from Lady only when he heard the other cops stomp down the staircase and head toward the kitchen. At first, the cops found nothing more than Albert's dime bag of weed, but during one last sweep, Jeff emerged from the back room with a teddy bear with a small pouch secreted inside. The pouch contained forty-seven packets of cocaine. Albert claimed the drugs were planted. Maybe. Maybe not.

What shook up Lady most was that the cop who sexually assaulted her had then pocketed her house key and had warned that he'd be back. He promised that he'd return every day, every night. The night we met Lady, more than a year had passed since the cop had fondled her. He hadn't been back, but Lady couldn't get his face out of her head.

"I think of him. I dream of him," she told us. "Still, till this day, I think he's going to come back."

She hadn't reported the incident to internal affairs because she didn't think they'd believe her, and they might even retaliate.

"I'm sorry, but why am I going to report this to a police officer when a police officer stood in front of me and molested me?" she asked us.

She agreed to talk to Barbara and me only because she suspected she wasn't the first victim, and probably not the last.

We believed she was right.

In the story, we didn't identify the cop who fondled Lady by name. We didn't have the goods. Not yet.

Barbara and I finished writing our Lady story and were about to power down our computers when, at 11:38 p.m., Brian Tierney, our company's charismatic CEO, issued a staffwide call to arms. The e-mail subject line read, "Important Notice." It should have read, "Don't Panic."

"As a company, we have been hit with a perfect storm, including a dramatic decline in total revenue, the worst economic conditions since the Great Depression and a debt structure which is out of line with current economic reality," Tierney wrote. "Now more than ever, we need to continue the hard work that has already begun."

The company's bankruptcy filing was the number-three story on CNN, right after North Korea's suspected missile tests and President Obama's stimulus plan.

The *Daily News* and *Inquirer* were officially part of the Chapter 11 Club, joining the ranks of other major dailies on death watch. The *Los Angeles Times*, the *Chicago Tribune*, the *Minneapolis Star Tribune*, the *Baltimore Sun*, and the Journal Register Company, which owned twenty-two daily newspapers and three hundred nondaily publications—all were in bankruptcy protection.

The Big Fall for the *Daily News* and *Inquirer* had taken only three years. In 2006 Tierney had spearheaded a group of Philadelphia-area investors who purchased the *Daily News*, the *Inquirer*, and our website, Philly.com, for $562 million, which included pension liabilities. Tierney, a flamboyant advertising and public relations executive who put up $10 million of his own money, was supposed to be our savior, the hometown guy who freed us from "the cold dead hand of Knight Ridder," as *Inky* Metro columnist Tom Ferrick Jr. put it. Over the years, the publicly traded Knight Ridder Inc. had decimated our newsrooms with its slash-and-burn cost-cutting. Private local ownership was supposed to be the antidote to Wall Street's iron-fisted demands for high profit margins.

Tierney was a much-needed shot of energy and determination. He dreamed about flying. He really believed he could revive local and national advertising, reverse circulation losses, and beat back competition from the Internet.

We were leery at first. Tierney had been an archenemy of Philadelphia reporters for years. He was known for intimidating and browbeating reporters in defense of his clients. If he hated a story, he was quick to call editors and complain, railing that the reporters were biased, unethical, and incompetent.

Tierney grew up learning to fight for what he wanted. The fourth of five brothers, he spent his early childhood in a largely blue-collar Philly suburb, where his mom was a waitress and his father was a claims adjuster. He sucked his naysayers up with a straw and spat them out. He thrived on challenge, especially if the stakes were high. Philly was Tierney's home, and he fit perfectly in this town of scrappers.

Philadelphians were the stars of not one but two reality television shows: A&E TV's *Parking Wars*, which featured ticket writers and car booters in confrontations with Philly loudmouths; and the Discovery Channel's *Wreck Chasers*, in which the city is billed as "the Wild West of tow-trucking." Television producers needed only to roll the cameras, and they were guaranteed drama.

Philadelphia sports fans were famously obnoxious and

rowdy. Their notoriety could be traced all the way back to a December day in 1968 when the Eagles played horribly and fans booed Santa Claus, pelting the red-suited Saint Nick with snowballs during the game's halftime show. For a time, Lincoln Financial Field was the only NFL stadium in the country that housed a jail with four holding cells, for unruly Eagles fans.

Tierney was a gloves-off brawler, and he wouldn't have wanted to be a newspaper publisher in any other city. When he bought the *Inquirer* and *Daily News*, Tierney had put everything on the line—not only his personal wealth but his reputation. Tierney understood the importance of image and had an ego large enough to power every house in Philly. He wanted to go down in Philadelphia history as the local guy who single-handedly saved the city's newspapers.

In a sense, Tierney was our best hope. We knew to fail meant that Tierney had failed, and that wasn't how Tierney wanted the story written.

Tierney's caffeinated enthusiasm was infectious. On his first day on the job, Tierney gave a champagne send-off to a fleet of delivery trucks adorned with the company's new slogan: "Bringing Home the News." He danced at a pep rally, brought in Eagles cheerleaders, and boldly declared, "The next great era of Philadelphia journalism begins today."

I had learned I was going to be laid off from the *Inquirer* four months after Tierney took the helm. Suddenly, Tierney-land didn't seem so magical.

Tierney blamed the cuts on a "permanent" free fall in ad revenues. Classified advertising, too, took a beating, as ads for jobs, real estate, cars, pets, and personals migrated to Craigslist and other Internet sites. At the same time, newspaper circulation was in decline. We had trained a whole generation of readers to get their news for free on the Internet while drinking $4 lattes. Not even the smartest people in our industry could figure out how to close the Pandora's box that we had opened.

Tierney's group had overpaid for the papers, borrowed too much money, and now struggled to make debt payments. As they scrounged around for $20 million in savings, they discussed laying off as many as 150 of the 415 *Inquirer* newsroom jobs. Reporters who had worked at the *Inquirer* for almost a decade were in danger of losing their jobs. I had only been there four years. And I was number eleven on the *Inquirer* layoff list.

"Tierney should change the company's slogan to 'Bringing Home the Pink Slip,'" Karl snorted when I called home.

I tried to focus on work, but my bosses kept coming over to my desk. "Why aren't you looking for a job?" they'd ask. A huge swath of reporters—myself included—began to spend our workday writing cover letters and tweaking résumés.

I soon landed a job offer from the *New York Daily News*, but I wanted the *Inquirer* to lay me off so I could collect my severance. Bill Marimow, the *Inky* editor, was in his office when I got back from my interview in Manhattan. I summoned the balls to ask if he could finagle my severance pay, even though I'd be gone before the layoffs hit.

Marimow was an old-fashioned newspaper man. He'd circulate through the newsroom, shirtsleeves rolled up to the elbows. An avuncular champion of his reporters, especially those who hustled, he emitted a quiet strength. "And how are you today, Miss Ruderman," he'd say slowly, enunciating each word. When I told Marimow that I'd gotten a job at the *New York Daily News*, this soft-spoken, two-time Pulitzer winner sat back in his chair and smiled.

"I didn't know you'd be willing to work at a . . . tabloid," Marimow said. "Let me make a call."

The next day at work, I answered my phone to find Tierney on the other end. "Congratulations on your new job at *Philadelphia Daily News*," he said. I was saved.

On January 3, 2007, my first day at the *Daily News*, Tierney sent layoff notices to seventy-one *Inquirer* employees. I envisioned tears, anger, and despair two floors above in the *Inquirer* newsroom. "The guillotine has finally fallen," said one *Inky* reporter who got laid off. I had survivor's guilt.

But two years had passed, and now I was at the *Daily News* working on Tainted Justice, and the guilt had subsided—even vanished. Barbara and I were deep into the series, even though we knew that our industry, on journalistic hospice, appeared to be nearing the end, taking its last few labored breaths. Newspapers had become "quaint," like the milkman or the paperboy.

So on that Sunday night, when Barbara and I wrapped up the Lady story, we were relieved the paper was still alive, albeit barely.

At 11:00 p.m. or so, we walked out of the newsroom, tense, tired, hungry. Barbara turned to me.

"What if the paper closes before we've finished the Tainted Justice series?" she asked.

13

"YOU AND WENDY NEED TO BE CARE-
FUL," A COP SOURCE WARNED BARBARA
DURING A CONVERSATION FROM HIS
PERSONAL CELL. "THE STUFF YOU GUYS
are reporting is serious. A lot's at stake.
Cops could go down 'cause of this."

On top of the hate e-mails, Barbara and I
had started to get nasty voice-mail messages
and hang-up calls. The paper's top editor,
Michael Days, was concerned enough to ask
the company's telecommunications staff to
trace the calls. Denise Gallo, the scarily efficient *Daily News* den mom who served as
Michael's right arm, came over to us with a
printout of incoming calls to the newsroom.
She highlighted calls to our extensions in
yellow. "Girls, do you recognize any of these
numbers?" At fifty-seven, Denise always referred to us as the Girls, though Barbara was
fifty-one and I was thirty-nine. No number
looked familiar, except for one—a hang-up
from my home phone. Karl had a habit of

calling and hanging up when I didn't answer. The three of us erupted in giggles.

We tried to brush off the anger directed at us, but our imaginations sometimes led to our brains' dark crannies. I was afraid to get my morning newspaper. I'd open the front door and scan up and down my street before dashing to the lawn to snatch the paper. I'd quickly dead-bolt the door behind me.

"Why do you keep locking the door?" Karl asked after dropping Brody at school.

"I don't know," I said dumbly.

I wasn't a door-locker by nature, and Karl knew that I rarely bothered to lock the door when we left to go grocery shopping or out to dinner.

During a morning run, on a winding road without sidewalks, Barbara jumped into the bushes when a speeding pickup truck veered toward her. This is it, she thought. The pickup rocketed by, disappearing around a curve, and she breathed puffs of relief, uncertain whether to laugh at herself or hurry home.

Barbara's neighbor, Hutch, walked across the street to her house every night before she came home from work to flip on every overhead light and lamp. The past three years, Barbara and Hutch had had an on-again, off-again relationship. She'd met him three months after moving here with her teenage children, her divorce still raw. She gardened obsessively, thinking a manicured lawn, prettied up with flowers, could mask the chaos of an uprooted life. On a Saturday afternoon in May, Barbara kneeled in the dirt and planted yellow and purple pansies. She thought of her ex-husband, all the weekend afternoons, twenty-five years together, spent working on the lawn. She looked a mess in her mud-splotched running clothes, her eyes pink and puffy from crying, when Hutch yelled from across the street, "How about coming over for a get-to-know-your-neighbor drink?"

It took her three weeks to fall for him.

Hutch, a rugged, broad-shouldered, six-foot-tall man with a strong jaw, was like a teenager with a bad-boy edge. He had a bald spot and a nose that sported a bump and curved slightly to the right—the result of three bloody breaks sustained in ice hockey and wrestling dustups. He didn't walk; he swaggered, exuding self-confidence.

After the divorce, Barbara probably needed someone like Hutch. They spent evenings in his basement, dancing to Led Zeppelin and the Cure like high-schoolers. He wasn't guarded with his emotions and spoke without a filter. But over time, some of his raunchy, off-color remarks made Barbara cringe. They often had spats about race, politics, priorities, lifestyles, children. A gun lover, he kept a 9mm Glock in his bedroom dresser and stashed shotguns and hunting rifles in a locked safe. Barbara hated guns. The highs of the relationship were euphoric; the lows chipped away at her.

Barbara hadn't dated in over twenty-five years, and Hutch was the opposite of her ex-husband, Matt. Matt was reserved, reliable, predictable, and so steady that his emotional pendulum rarely budged. Those were some reasons she fell in love with him. He grounded her. Matt was the "Whoooa, Nellie" to her exuberant "Giddy up! Woo-hoo!"

The problem was, Hutch was a little too "Woo-hoo" and that scared Barbara. She pictured herself with a man whose personality was a blend of Matt and Hutch's. But dating was hell.

On one date, a guy pulled up his pant leg to show Barbara

his tattoos. On his calf, he had tattooed the name of his then-wife inside a heart. When he started dating after his divorce, his new girlfriend hated the tattoo, so he covered up his ex-wife's name with a rose and added the girlfriend's name in bigger print underneath. Barbara imagined her name, in even larger letters, scrawled underneath the ex-girlfriend's name, camouflaged with a giant pink chrysanthemum.

Another guy described himself as "athletic and toned" on his Match.com profile and looked about 180 pounds in his photo. Barbara didn't recognize him when they met. Somewhere along the way, he'd packed on an extra hundred pounds. He confessed that he first called Barbara from the family station wagon because he was still living with his ex-wife. He assured Barbara that he wasn't intimate with his ex and slept in the den on a broken La-Z-Boy chair.

Still another guy, who Barbara had really liked, turned out to be a pathological liar. He even spun a tale about making pot roast for his grown daughters, when he'd really ordered pizza.

"It was the pot roast," Barbara told me incredulously. "Why would he lie about pot roast? I mean, pot roast, Wendy. As if I care that he didn't cook."

Barbara shared her dating horror stories with Hutch. He had a few of his own.

"I keep telling you. I'm the one for you," said Hutch, who then smiled, threw his shoulders back, and swept his hands up and down his body, stopping at his crotch. "Look. I'm the full package."

Hutch liked to parody the line from *Jerry Maguire*, in which Tom Cruise tells Renée Zellweger, "You complete me."

"I," Hutch said with a theatrical pause, "complete myself."

Even when Barbara and Hutch weren't dating, they stayed

friends, and Hutch loved being her protector. After he lit up her house like the Griswold family's Christmas, he would poke his head into every closet and under all three beds. During the nightly patrol, he had a Glock holstered on his hip, just in case. Years ago, he'd been a cop and had a license to carry.

"Hutch can be soooo sweet sometimes," Barbara told me.

Around this time, George Bochetto, the hawkish attorney hired by Jeff, was readying a Laker-Ruderman smackdown. He assured Jeff that we were easy prey. He'd clobber us. On Jeff's dime, Bochetto hired a private investigator to blast holes in Benny's story and discredit our work.

The PI spent days interviewing Benny's relatives and former bosses, who characterized Benny as an unredeemable liar, con artist, drug addict, and thief, disowned by his own father. He pulled Benny's criminal record and interviewed cops who vouched for Jeff, casting him as the kind of cop they'd want beside them in a foxhole. Jeff's former partner, Richard Eberhart, denied knowing that Jeff rented a house to Benny. He claimed Barbara had twisted his words. The PI pulled Jeff's awards, commendations, and letters of praise from community leaders. He compiled the interviews and documents into a textbook-thick binder, which included exhibits A through K.

With the PI's report in hand, Bochetto set about organizing a news conference with the Fraternal Order of Police. In Philly, politicians tiptoed around the FOP. Lawmakers and judges who dared to poke the 14,600-member beehive with a stick felt their collective sting. The FOP relentlessly bashed municipal court judge Craig Washington when he refused to allow a memorial photo of slain officer John Pawlowski to rest on the bench during court proceedings. The police union

hung a huge banner reading "DUMP Judge Craig Washington" outside its headquarters.

Barbara and I had whacked the beehive with a baseball
bat. We'd taken on one of their own, and the cops were about
to unite in a swarm.

14

WE WALKED OVER TO FOP HEADQUAR-
TERS ON A FRIGID, WIND-WHIPPED AF-
TERNOON IN LATE FEBRUARY. A UNION
SECRETARY DIRECTED US TO A HALL,
no fancier than a grade school gymna-
sium, where the FOP held parties and fund-
raisers for families of fallen officers. Rows of
folding chairs sat before a stage. Reporters
from every news outlet in the city filed in.
Barbara and I took seats up front. We exchanged polite, nervous chatter with the
Inky reporter seated next to us. FOP president John McNesby took to the podium. A
semicircle of fifteen plainclothes cops lined
up behind McNesby. They stood shoulder to
shoulder, arms crossed, glaring at us.

Bring it on, I thought.

"At a time when we're burying police officers at an alarming rate," McNesby began,
"we have a newspaper that on the same day—
the same day—we're laying one of our fallen
heroes to rest, is persecuting another officer
for frivolous, mindless, baseless allegations."

McNesby was a former narcotics cop who had worked with Jeff. With his square head, rotund body, and triple-thick turkey neck, McNesby was a city icon. He was famous for his inappropriate, politically incorrect rants, which reporters considered a gift, a pinch of hot sauce to spice up an otherwise bland story.

McNesby swore that the FOP would "go to the wall" to defend Jeff. The attack turned personal. "You have to remember, you're dealing with a confidential informant here. A confidential informant in the city of Philadelphia is one step above a *Daily News* reporter."

The snarky remark drew laughter and applause from the roomful of cops. I could feel my cheeks redden in anger. I crossed my legs and began to furiously pump my foot. I was having a Napoleonic moment. I envisioned pulling all of McNesby's search warrants. He better watch it, or we'll investigate his fat ass, I thought.

Next came Bochetto's turn on the podium. He handed out copies of the binder compiled by his private investigator. The binder, Bochetto promised, offered proof that Jeff had rented the house to Sonia, not Benny. How was Jeff to know that Benny had struck up a romantic relationship with Sonia? The argument was so stupid that I bit the inside of my cheek to stifle a snicker.

The supremely confident Bochetto was spooling out a barn burner. He began to pontificate: Naturally Benny was scared. The guy set up scores of dangerous drug dealers who wouldn't hesitate to kill him. "His life was in danger and in order to save himself, he made up this fanciful story . . . that Jeff Cujdik made up all the facts in the affidavits and that it couldn't possibly be him. Why? To save his own skin!"

Bellowing from the podium with the fire of a preacher,

Bochetto claimed he had warned Barbara and me, weeks ago, that to print Jeff's name would put the cop and his family in danger, and we'd responded, "That's not our concern." It was like pouring gasoline on a flame; a disapproving gasp rippled from one cop to the next. I wanted to jump out of my seat and scream, as if it were the Salem witch trials, "He's lying!"

Bochetto said he'd been preparing a lawsuit against the *Daily News* when the company filed for bankruptcy protection. Now he wasn't sure if a suit would be feasible. The press conference, he said, would serve to put an end to the hysteria generated by a newspaper desperate to stave off its extinction.

McNesby and Bochetto vilified us for almost fifty minutes. The moment they finished, TV news crews swung around and trained their video cameras on Barbara and me. They trailed us out of the building; they needed b-roll of our stricken faces for the evening newscast. Two radio reporters and the *Inky*'s Joseph Slobodzian, whom reporters called Joe Slo because they couldn't pronounce his name, asked us for comment. Barbara and I didn't know what to do.

"Maybe you should call Michael Days for comment," I said.

Never before had the FOP orchestrated a press conference specifically to single out and intimidate individual reporters. The attack was unprecedented, and Michael Days, a journalist for more than thirty years, knew it. Looking back, he wished he'd sent another reporter, instead of Barbara and me, and fretted that he'd inadvertently subjected us to a public flogging.

Now he worried about our safety. Police officers were anguished and their emotions volatile over the deaths of so many of their brethren, and Michael feared they'd misplace their anger.

Philly cops and the *Daily News* had a long-standing adversarial relationship. To us, "the People Paper" wasn't just a slogan; it was a journalistic doctrine. That meant we didn't just regurgitate the police version of a controversial story, like a police shooting. We hit the streets to get the neighborhood's account.

Michael knew the Tainted Justice series would forge an even wider divide between the newspaper and the police department. But he didn't waver.

Michael, at fifty-five, had a glossy bald head and a compact, athletic build. He favored steel-gray suits, paired with a bold-colored tie and crisp shirt. He scanned the paper early every morning and tore out stories he liked, scribbling words of praise on Post-it notes. Denise Gallo trotted across the room in her sensible pumps and slipped the Mike-agrams into our mailboxes. Michael was so generous with accolades that sometimes we wanted to ask, Did you really like it? Or are you just being nice?

At news meetings he listened intently, his right palm pressed against his cheek, as editors describe the day's top stories. He never raised his voice. He wasn't the type of boss people feared. When he disapproved of something one of his editors said, he'd drop his chin to his chest and tilt his head to the side. He'd raise his brows and widen his eyes with a fixed stare.

"Oh reeeeally now," he'd say slowly, probably thinking, C'mon, are you for real?

And when something tickled him, he let out a loud, contagious chuckle that made his body shake so hard that he gripped his tie to keep it from swaying back and forth.

Michael became the first black editor in *Daily News* history in 2005. He loved stories that thrust the bullhorn into the hands of the little guys, people on the fringes who felt neglected, even punted to the curb, by the city's power elite. Michael understood the struggles of row-house people because he was one. He and his younger sister grew up in a hard-bitten part of North Philly with their mom, who didn't have a high school diploma and worked long hours making salads at the stately and grand Ben Franklin Hotel.

His mom, a strict, no-nonsense woman who stressed education, wouldn't allow Michael to use the word *can't*. She enrolled him in Catholic school, even though they were Baptists, because she believed public schools weren't good enough. They rarely ate in restaurants, didn't have money for a car, and his mom didn't have one credit card, but once a year, she took them to see Santa Claus at the Wanamaker Building, where they ate lunch in the elegant Crystal Tea Room with hand-carved columns, intricate crystal chandeliers, and crisp table linens.

Michael came of age when the civil rights movement was in full throttle. In 1967 Thurgood Marshall became the first black Supreme Court justice, but out on the streets, police were using tear gas, whips, and clubs to subdue civil rights marchers. Michael was a high school sophomore when Martin Luther King Jr. was assassinated. He boiled with anger.

In 1991 Michael and his wife did something few couples would even consider: they adopted four brothers, between the ages of four and nine, who had bounced from foster home to foster home. The boys had deep emotional scars from being born to a drug-addicted mom and a father they didn't know. Michael and his wife soon learned the youngest was autistic.

At home and at work, Michael dutifully played the role of quiet guardian. Barbara and I never doubted he would defend us. The quote he provided for the FOP story was so Michael—succinct and definitive:

"The stories are accurate and we will defend our reports and our reporters."

15

A FEW DAYS AFTER THE FRATERNAL
ORDER OF POLICE NEWS CONFERENCE,
IN EARLY MARCH 2009, *TIME* MAGAZINE
LISTED THE *DAILY NEWS* AS NUMBER
one on its list of "The 10 Most Endangered
Newspapers in America."

But Barbara and I had a plan that had
nothing to do with our newspaper's pre-
dicted demise. We had to track down every
drug informant who had ever worked
with Jeff. High on our list was Tiffany, a
hellcat and former stripper from the row-
house-lined streets of Philly's Kensington
neighborhood, home to a hodgepodge of
hustlers, from hookers and drug dealers to
minimum-wage workers juggling two jobs
and sorry souls eternally on the dole.

Tiffany's ex-boyfriend claimed that she
and Jeff had conspired to set him up in a
lover's revenge plot, and that Jeff lied on the
search warrant used to raid his house.

We wanted to hear what Tiffany had to

say about Jeff. We knew she wouldn't be happy to see us. But it never—not for a minute—occurred to us that it could be dangerous for us to pursue Tiffany, even though a year earlier, cops had arrested her for bashing a man in the head with a glass bottle and stealing $250 and a necklace.

On a cold gray afternoon in early March, with a snowstorm looming, Barbara knocked on the door at Tiffany's two-story redbrick row house. At twenty-eight, Tiffany was the mother of two kids by two different men and still lived with her parents. Her mom, Mickey, answered the door with a Marlboro Menthol wedged between two fingers. Mickey stood steely and stone-faced in the doorway. Barbara offered a sunny hello and thrust out her hand, which Mickey reluctantly shook. Still gripping Mickey's palm, Barbara stepped closer and wormed her way into the living room.

Mickey was a stout and sturdy woman who favored baggy T-shirts and sweats. She was fifty-one years old and had had the same job as a machine operator at a ribbon factory for nearly two decades, working the overnight shift from 2:30 a.m. to 1:00 p.m. On Fridays, she stopped by the liquor store to pick up her favorite—coconut vodka.

Barbara smiled as she plopped herself down on a velour couch the color of rotted red grapes and opened her notebook.

"I was just wondering," said Barbara, trying to sound casual. "Have you ever seen Jeff? Has he ever been over to the house?"

Mickey proceeded to tell Barbara that Jeff had showed up on her doorstep after Tiffany got arrested for aggravated assault and robbery. He handed her $300 in cash to bail Tiffany out of jail. Wow, this is good stuff, Barbara thought as she felt the first pinpricks of adrenaline, the rush that reporters feel when they get a juicy nugget. Barbara instinctively knew that Jeff had crossed the line when he footed Tiffany's bail. With her cheeks warm and head down, Barbara scribbled away. She flipped the blue-lined pages with her fingertips like paper somersaults as quickly as Mickey spoke. She was so focused and excited that she didn't pay any attention to the loud stomps from the top of the staircase leading to the second floor. Tiffany barreled down the steps, a she-devil with a pierced nose and long, dirty blond hair flaring out behind her, and charged toward Barbara.

"I'm gonna fuckin' kill you!"

When Barbara looked up, Tiffany loomed over her. The first strike came hard and fast, Tiffany's open hand slamming into Barbara's left cheek and knocking her head sideways. The second belt, to Barbara's right cheek, had even more force. Barbara felt the sting of something hard, maybe Tiffany's rings as they whacked into her cheekbone. Barbara let go of her notebook and crossed her arms over her head in an X shape to shield her face from more blows. Tiffany snatched the notebook and hurled it across the room. It landed near Mickey, who just sat there, on an adjacent couch, not saying a word, as Barbara cried out, "Please! No!"

Barbara stood up, the pen on her lap dropping to the floor, and quickly grabbed her brown leather purse. She crouched low, her back hunched, and darted across the room as if dodging gunfire. Her hand shook as she scooped up the notebook and sprinted out the front door.

As she ran, Barbara fished around in her bottomless, sack-like purse for her cell phone. She flipped open the phone and pressed my number. Her voice was a high-pitched squeak.

"Wendy! Wendy! She hit me!"

I was seated at my desk. I bolted up out of my chair and shouted, "What? What happened?" The reporters who sat near me looked up from their computers. The phone went dead. I dialed her back. No answer. I dialed and redialed, each time getting her voice mail. I began to panic.

Barbara, cheeks aflame, closed her phone when she heard fast footsteps behind her. Barbara glanced over her shoulder and saw Tiffany, a wild-eyed, fuel-raged bullet train, screaming bloody murder into a cell phone.

Tiffany had frantically called Jeff. At that moment, Jeff felt sick: he knew Barbara and I weren't going to stop with just Benny; we planned to track down all of his informants.

In a panic, Barbara finally found her car keys. She struggled to steady her hand as she unlocked the car door, jumped in, locked all the doors, and sped off. When she got a few blocks away, she pulled over and examined her face in the rearview mirror. She wanted to make sure she wasn't bleeding. Then she called me back.

"Tiffany hit me. Twice. Across the face. She threatened to kill me," Barbara said. "But don't worry, I got the notebook . . . but I lost . . . my pen."

It wasn't funny at the time but later, the lost pen would become a running joke between us. The *Daily News* supply closet only stocked cheap Bics, which tended to leak and smudge, so Barbara bought her own special ones: Paper Mate Profile retractable ballpoint pens in assorted colors in packs of four for $3.99 at the grocery store. To her, losing a pen was a big deal.

Barbara knew the city well, having been a Philly reporter for sixteen years, but this, her first assault, rattled her. Suddenly she couldn't figure out how to get back to the office. She asked me to stay on the phone until she found I-95 South, heading toward Center City.

By the time Barbara walked into the newsroom, Brian

Tierney had gathered the staff for a big announcement. Barbara joined the circle of about forty reporters, photographers, and editors gathered around Tierney near the sports desk. Because Tierney had filed for Chapter 11 bankruptcy protection just a week ago, the staff was extra jittery and abuzz with rumors that Tierney planned to merge our ragtag ranks with the restrained *Inquirer* staff and close the *Daily News.*

We'd been on journalism's endangered species list for decades, and a lot of the old-timers had become numb to death threats, like prisoners of war. They put out the paper each day with an attitude that said, *Either shoot me in the head or get out of my way.*

Tierney nervously swooped back his thick mane of chestnut hair, a cross between Donald Trump's and Shaun Cassidy's locks, and explained that starting March 30, the phrase "an edition of the *Philadelphia Inquirer*" would appear under the *Daily News* logo on the paper's front page. He assured us that the two papers would remain intact, with separate news staffs, and that the move was purely economic. Tierney hoped that making the two papers a single entity with combined circulation numbers would help boost ad sales, and save us money as a single subscriber to wire services.

"Instead of telling advertisers we have 330,000 circulation (at the *Inquirer*) plus the *Daily News*, it will help to say we have 440,000 daily circulation," Tierney explained to a roomful of journalists trained to expose and rail against any cooking of the books in city government who were suddenly resigned to accepting our own creative math.

But I barely heard what Tierney was saying. I kept looking at Barbara, who stood among the crowd, somewhat dazed, gingerly touching her cheeks, which sported angry red slap marks. I could actually see handprints parallel to her pearl earrings. She looked dainty in those earrings, with a long strand of fake pearls draped over a peach-and-cream-colored J.Crew sweater. What kind of person would hit Barbara Laker?

I could feel a nervous giggle creeping up my throat. My reaction was inappropriate and insensitive, but I couldn't help it. I kept thinking: What the fuck? Tiffany hauled off on Betty Crocker! It was funny in a horrible kind of way.

"You okay?" I asked after the meeting.

"Do you think it will bruise?" she said.

"I'm gonna get you ice for your face."

When I got back from the cafeteria with Styrofoam cups packed with ice, Barbara was talking to Gar, our editor, who wanted her to press criminal charges.

"If you get killed, it's a good one-day story, but long-term, it's bad for business," I overheard Gar telling Barbara.

She refused to file a police complaint against Tiffany, mostly because she didn't want to become part of the story.

The thing was, Tiffany came from a seamy world, one in which she could, if she wanted, find some lowlife to off Barbara for a price. And Jeff now knew that Tiffany had told us one more thing that could get him in trouble. Jeff and Bochetto wanted more than ever to shut us down. Bochetto got the private investigator right on it.

Tiffany soon found herself in a scene straight out of a film noir. She climbed into the gumshoe's Mercedes-Benz, and they sat in the Home Depot parking lot on Aramingo Avenue, a busy commercial artery lined with big-box stores.

Russell Kolins, a private investigator since 1969, was an old hat. With his weathered, pleasant face and classy business suit, Kolins came off as both grizzled and imperial. He was a marine who worked counterintelligence in Vietnam, and the former owner of a Jersey nightclub called Private Eyes.

The impeccably dressed Kolins began to pepper Tiffany with questions. What did the reporter ask? And what did Tiffany's mom tell her? He needed details, specifically any minefields surrounding Jeff.

Tiffany was spooked. In the mind of this hardened hood diva, Kolins was the embodiment of the Man. He might as well have been a state senator, judge, bank president, corporate CEO. It didn't matter. She had to get out of that car.

Once home, Tiffany wondered what the hell she'd gotten herself into. She called Barbara.

"I'm real sorry I hit you," Tiffany said.

"Tiffany, that's okay. I know you're sorry. I know you didn't mean it," Barbara replied.

I was standing by Barbara's desk when she picked up the phone. My ears perked up: Tiffany? The notorious bitch slapper? I turned to the reporters and editors around me and stage-whispered, "She's on the phone with Tiffany," woodpeckering my finger above Barbara's head. Everyone came over to eavesdrop.

"Wow, Barbara has a new BFF," joked hipster reporter Stephanie Farr.

Tiffany explained to Barbara that she felt confused. She'd thought Jeff was a good guy. If she got jammed up on a traffic ticket or got collared, Jeff helped her out, often with cash. He talked to her like a buddy, all chatty and warm.

"What's going on, kiddo?" Jeff asked, fishing for neighborhood intel that might lead to his next drug bust.

After talking to Kolins, Tiffany realized that Jeff had slapped her informant number on drug buys she never made. She was scared to venture out of her house. She felt like all the local dealers were giving her an accusatory stare-down.

"They think I'm a snitch," she told Barbara.

The informant job, at least under Jeff, came with perks. Jeff rewarded Tiffany and his other informants with cartons of cigarettes, prepaid phone minutes, candy bars, and snacks.

"Here, get your sugar up," he'd say, tossing Benny a Snickers bar.

Barbara and I didn't really think about where Jeff got the stuff. Until we got a phone call from a Center City lawyer.

16

OUR STORY ABOUT TIFFANY AND HOW JEFF HAD PAID HER BAIL MONEY UN-EARTHED ONE MORE EXAMPLE OF HOW JEFF HAD CROSSED THE LINE. A few days later, a Philadelphia attorney, Todd Henry, called me. Todd told me he represented a fifty-three-year-old Jordanian shop owner named Samir.

"You know those cops you're writing about?" Todd asked me. "Well, I have a client whose shop was raided by those cops, and he says they took thousands of dollars from him and other stuff like cigarettes," Todd told me.

My heart started to race.

"And you know what, those cops cut all his video surveillance wires. So what do you think? You want to talk to him?"

Absolutely. "Just tell me when and where," I said.

I darted over to Todd's office later that day. Todd's receptionist showed me into a conference room and shut the door. "He'll be with you in a moment."

I took out my notebook, tape recorder, and a pen, lining them up on the glossy wood table. The anticipation of an interview, especially one that held so much promise, was one of life's teeny pleasures, like that first sip of hot coffee in the morning or the gradual dim of lights at the start of a movie.

Todd came into the room and I shook his hand. I looked behind him, expecting to see Samir.

"I'm sorry. Samir changed his mind," Todd said.

Samir was too scared to talk. He feared retaliation from the cops and didn't want a story in the paper.

I walked the nine blocks back to the *Daily News* office, disheartened and anguished. Maybe if I went to Samir's house, I could convince him to tell his story. Wait. No. That might wig him out. Might be better to show up at his smoke shop. . . .

Barbara and I needed to brainstorm. We got something to eat from Gus and Joan, the Greek couple who operated a lunch truck parked outside our office. Barbara got her usual salad—romaine lettuce, tomatoes, egg, cucumbers, mushrooms, grilled chicken, and absolutely no cheese. I almost always ordered a BLT. Back at my desk, I opened a mayo packet with my teeth and squeezed creamy ribbons onto the bread.

"Wendy, I'm telling you this as your friend, if you don't eat more green leafy vegetables, you could get cancer," she said.

"I don't like salad. It's like eating grass." We'd had this conversation a zillion times.

As much as we were the same, Barbara and I were different. She was a frugal, coupon-clipping, to-the-penny bookkeeper; I never looked at my pay stubs and only learned how much money was in my checking account when I withdrew cash from an ATM and looked at the receipt. For breakfast, Barbara ate low-fat Greek yogurt, mixed with fresh berries and raw oatmeal; I ate a chocolate chip muffin. When Barbara's lower back ached, she did core-strengthening exercises; I popped two Aleve. She religiously got an oil change every 3,000 miles; I rarely checked my oil. Barbara obsessed over her throw pillows, which she meticulously arranged on couches and beds in a complex puzzle of patterns and colors; I never bothered to make the bed each morning. I didn't see the point.

Barbara stabbed a plastic fork into her salad, and I wiped grease and mayonnaise from the corners of my mouth with a napkin. We sat in silence, chewing. Then Barbara thought of something. "Wendy, what if there are more Samirs out there?" We remembered from combing through search warrants that Jeff's squad had raided a lot of corner stores. We didn't think much of it at the time, but now we wondered aloud why this elite narcotics squad had zeroed in on so many mom-and-pop stores.

The next morning, Barbara and I headed back to the search warrant room to pull every store raid done by Jeff's squad. We practically jogged to the criminal courthouse, and in a gust of excitement, we flew through the room's doorway—and then came to an abrupt halt, as if we'd careened into a concrete barrier. Two *Inky* reporters and an intern, perched on metal chairs, looked up at us. We exchanged polite yet leery hellos. They were methodically sifting through the onionskin-thin warrants. Barbara and I tried to appear unruffled and blasé, but on the inside, we seethed like territorial hornets. This was OUR secret chamber of buried treasures and it was being invaded by a battalion of *Inky* reporters.

We had learned about the search warrant room through

an attorney source, and for the first few stories about Jeff, Barbara and I had the place to ourselves. Not anymore.

There sat Andy Maykuth, a former foreign correspondent first dispatched to Nicaragua in 1985 and later sent to forty-eight other countries, mostly war-ravaged and dangerous, including Afghanistan, where he shadowed anti-Taliban forces in bullet-pocked Kabul. As the *Inquirer*'s correspondent in Africa from 1996 to 2002, Andy covered the blood feud between Ethiopia and Eritrea, genocide in Rwanda, apartheid in South Africa, and famine in Zimbabwe. But Andy was unassuming, not full of himself. I watched him flip through search warrants and wondered if he viewed the self-inflicted bloodlust between *Inquirer* and *Daily News* staff as absurd.

There was Joseph Slobodzian, or Joe Slo, an *Inquirer* reporter since 1982, who'd covered federal courts in Philadelphia for almost two decades.

On yet another day, we walked into the room to find Gail Shister, the *Inky*'s prickly former TV columnist. Gail had written about television for a quarter of a century, or, as she put it, since "God was a boy." She wasn't just a columnist; she was an *Inky* brand with her own link on the Drudge Report, a news website that got 2 million hits a day. Gail prided herself on unearthing celebrity dirt and knowing which TV shows were cued up for the morgue before the actors themselves. When CBS wanted to dump Katie Couric from the *Evening News*, Gail broke the story. On Gail's Facebook page, she posted a favorite quote (from Alice Roosevelt Longworth, the saucy daughter of Theodore Roosevelt): "If you haven't got anything good to say about anybody, come sit next to me."

Gail knew she could be caustic. She recognized herself in the best-selling novel *Good in Bed*, written by *Inquirer* colleague Jennifer Weiner. Though Weiner denied it, Gail suspected that the Gabby character, a sharp-tongued newsroom gossip, was modeled after her.

In 2007, Gail fell out of favor with *Inky* editors. They killed her TV column and booted her to the Metro desk. She was bitter about the reassignment, and the last place she wanted to be was the search warrant room.

Gail's editor, Rose Ciotta, expected Gail to pull and copy all of Jeff's search warrants. During a cell-phone call, Rose instructed Gail to use her own money to cover the copying costs—25 cents a page—and the *Inquirer* would reimburse her.

"You know how much this is going to cost?" Gail said, heatedly. "I'm not using my lunch money for this." She looked at us, all pissy, and threw open a hand in a gesture that conveyed, "Can you believe this bitch?"

Barbara and I smiled, simpatico, and Gail hung up with Rose. "Even if I had a million dollars in cash, I'm not going to use my own money," she spat. Gail was fifty-six and openly gay. She paired her foul mouth with a truck-stop wardrobe of oversize jeans and flannel shirts and sported a short and choppy hairdo that looked like she cut it herself.

Rose was a control freak with corkscrew curls that she dyed black using "a hair color called Snow Tire," an *Inky* reporter joked. Rose relentlessly rode reporters, but on this battle, she wasn't going to win. So she sent another reporter, cash in hand, to meet Gail at the courthouse. Gail and Rose were like two stag beetles, horns locked, each battling to flip the other over onto her back. They shared Buffalo roots and an upstate New York twang, but little else. When Jeff Greenfield, a senior political correspondent with CBS News, came to the *Inky* newsroom to interview Gail for a story, Gail introduced Rose: "This is Rose. Before she worked here, she was a guard at Auschwitz."

Barbara and I didn't know which was funnier—the fact that Gail was bickering with Rose over the search warrants, or that the *Inquirer* was scrounging up change to make copies, while Barbara and I had cooked up a system to Xerox for free.

On this day, we were twitchy. We couldn't let *Inky* reporters figure out that we had moved past Jeff and Benny and were now focused on bodegas raided by any cop in Jeff's squad. We pulled out a stack of search warrants, flipped through the pages, and set aside the ones we wanted to copy—facedown. Once they'd been copied, we reshuffled them like blackjack dealers into the stack.

We tried to hide our joy when we picked up a folder that *Inky* reporters had just scoured to find warrants they'd copied, lumped together, on top of a neat pile. They were all warrants we'd pulled weeks ago.

Back in the newsroom, Barbara and I spread out the search warrants on a conference table. We were amazed by how many stores Jeff and his squad had raided over a two-year period. Sometimes they hit two stores in one afternoon.

In six months alone, Jeff's squad and another squad, which included Jeff's brother, Richard, raided twenty-two bodegas, boutiques, tobacco shops, and other stores for drug paraphernalia. That number was seven times more than the unit's ten other squads combined. Those ten squads—made up of more than a hundred officers—had raided only three stores during the same period.

One of my best sources was a cop assigned to one of those ten other squads. I had met the cop, who we'll call Ray, in 2007 when I first joined the *Daily News* and was covering a story about a perv lawyer who got caught naked in a courthouse conference room with a fourteen-year-old girl. My job was to get reaction from people in the courthouse. I was outside a courtroom when I spotted Ray, his back resting against the wall as if he were seated on a comfy recliner instead of a stone bench. I walked by slowly, staring at him as I mulled over whether to approach him about the perv lawyer.

"Hey, how ya doing?" he asked.

Ray had a bright smile and a warm, casual way about him. He wore blue jeans and a neatly pressed pin-striped dress shirt. Turned out, Ray was an undercover narcotics cop like Jeff.

Yeah, he knew the perv lawyer or knew of him, but couldn't be quoted. The police department had strict rules about giving information or quotes to the news media. Ray could get in big trouble for talking to me.

I gave Ray my card, and he began to call me with story tips, like a big drug bust done by his squad or a cop who got caught with a racially offensive sticker in his locker. The sticker was a cartoon of a man, half as an officer in uniform and half as a Klansman, with the words BLUE BY DAY—WHITE BY NIGHT.

Ray was ballsy and almost cavalier about feeding me information. He'd meet me on a street corner near my office and slip me internal police documents. He'd make jokes about the clandestine handoff. "I should be wearing a trench coat and a fedora hat," he'd say.

We instantly hit it off, and he became not only a great source but a good friend. He sometimes called me just to talk, like when his ex-wife was acting nutty or his kid was doing poorly in school. He had an offbeat sense of humor and a reputation among other cops as a jokester who never let the job of chasing down drug dealers and dopers get to him. When I saw him in the courthouse, I pretended not to know him. He was often at the center of a cluster of cops, all laughing and talking and slapping each other's backs. Everyone seemed to like him.

I could rely on Ray to tell it to me straight. He believed that right was right and wrong was wrong. Even if he was the one doing the wrong, he'd own up to it. During the Tainted Justice series, I called him a lot to take his temperature, to get his perspective as a drug cop who managed informants. He once met me at a library and patiently detailed the anatomy of a drug bust, from the initial drug buy to the search-warrant application and the dos and don'ts of house raids. One day I asked Ray if female cops thought Jeff was good-looking.

"I think a lot of cops think Jeff has sugar in his tank," he said.

"What? Sugar in his tank? What does that mean?" I asked, laughing.

"Gay," he said, with his trademark bluntness.

When I called Ray to ask what he thought about all the store raids, I wasn't surprised to learn that he had only done a handful of baggie busts in his twelve years as a narcotics cop.

Jeff and Ray, though in different squads, were both part of the narcotics field unit. The elite unit was supposed to go after big fish—kingpins who headed violent drug organizations that packaged and distributed mounds of poison, bringing entire neighborhoods to their knees. Arresting shop owners on misdemeanor charges for selling tiny ziplock bags was like shooting fish in a barrel. Store-raid jobs were the smallest of small-time.

Barbara and I divvied up the search warrants. We knew there was something there, but we didn't want to prompt store owners. We decided to avoid leading questions like "Did the police dismantle your surveillance cameras?" or "Did the officers take any merchandise or money?"

"Agreed," Barbara said, and we went to work.

"Hi, I'm not sure I have the right number. I'm looking for the owner of Dominguez Grocery Store?" I heard Barbara say into her phone.

I got on the phone with another shop owner. "I'm a reporter with the *Daily News,* and I wanted to ask you about the police raid on your store," I said.

My eyes widened as I took notes. When I got off the phone, I jumped up and ran toward Barbara, who was already halfway to my desk.

"Wendy! You're never going to believe this!" she shouted.

"I know! I know," I said.

17

PHILADELPHIA WAS HOME TO ONE OF
THE LARGEST AND FASTEST-GROWING
IMMIGRANT POPULATIONS IN THE
NORTHEAST, PARTLY BECAUSE THE
cost of living was lower than in other cities
like New York. Between 2000 and 2006,
113,000 immigrants flocked to Philly, nearly
as many as had arrived in the entire decade
of the 1990s. The majority came from Asia,
Latin America, and the Caribbean. Some
came to reunite with relatives or work at the
city's numerous hospitals, tech firms, or uni-
versities. Others were entrepreneurs who
opened shops with the belief that if they
worked long and hard enough, they'd earn
a decent living.

Bodegas could be found on almost
every other block in all four corners of the
city. Immigrants ran them and patronized
them. At these shops, both the food and
the language were familiar. Without nearby
supermarkets or cars, the people in these
neighborhoods bought everything there.

Barbara and I had split up the search warrants, and we began to track down the merchants. Most spoke little to no English. I'd taken five years of Spanish in high school and college; Barbara had studied French just as long. But all we remembered were textbook-taught phrases like "Excuse me, sir, can you direct me to the toilet?" or "Do you know what time the train arrives from Madrid?"

None of that would help when we talked to store owners from the Dominican Republic or Haiti. Or Korea. So we overcame the language barrier by using their relatives, store clerks, and customers to translate. Sometimes we resorted to hand signs and gestures, almost like a humorless game of charades.

When Barbara walked into a cigar and tobacco shop, she was struck by the brittle and slight appearance of the owners. Almost birdlike, the Korean couple, Du Hyon "David" and Yun Lois "Eunice" Nam, stood behind a long pane of bulletproof glass. Eunice handed lottery tickets to a customer through an opening in the protective divide, just large enough for a hand.

The Nams earned a middle-class life the hard way. They didn't expect handouts and paid their taxes. They toiled away at their store ten hours a day, six days a week, and commuted two hours a day to and from their store. David had left Seoul for the Philadelphia area in 1981 with a master's degree in foreign trade. He first opened a deli, then the smoke shop. "America Dream," he told Barbara with a bashful smile.

Barbara empathized with the Nams. Barbara was born on a chicken farm in Kent, England, about fifty miles south of London. She came to the United States with her parents and younger brother by way of the storm-tossed Atlantic in the bowels of Cunard's *QE2*. She arrived as a homesick, gangly twelve-year-old with a thick British accent. They moved to the Chicago suburbs, where kids teased her, threw paint at her front door, and beat up her younger brother—once with fists, another time with a bag of dry cement that they smashed over his head. "Why can't you leave us alone? We're not hurting you," Barbara yelled.

As a teen, Barbara wanted so desperately to fit in that she used money, earned through chores and babysitting, to buy audiotapes of people speaking with American accents. Every night after homework, Barbara listened to the tapes and parroted the words until she'd purged her British accent.

Every once in a while, I'd catch Barbara using an English expression. When she didn't quite catch what someone was telling her, she'd politely say, "Pardon?" I was more inclined to say, in my brassy toot, "Huh? Hold on. Back up. What the hell are ya talkin' about?"

In broken English, the Nams recounted the sweltering July afternoon in 2007 when Jeff and four squad members raided their shop.

"I so scared," Eunice told Barbara.

Eunice was fifty-six years old, just under five-two, and didn't weigh more than a hundred pounds. She had a tiny sliver of a nose and smooth skin, with a few faint lines around her deep-set eyes and thin lips. She didn't wear a smidge of makeup. With short, thin, curly black hair and brown-framed eyeglasses, she favored loose-fitting black pants, simple, nondescript T-shirts, and sensible flats. She was all business, just like her sixty-two-year-old husband, who was only five-seven, had a receding hairline, and hiked his pants high above his waist with a thin black belt, making his 120-pound frame appear even smaller.

Jeff and his squad blazed into the shop, screaming words

the Nams didn't understand. The cops weren't wearing their dress blues, and the terrified couple thought they were being robbed.

"They put us on floor," Eunice told Barbara, pointing to the square vinyl tiles. "Handcuffs on me," she said, clasping her spindly fingers behind her back.

"They had guns. Gun on my head," she said. "Me on floor. Stand over with gun." Eunice curled her three fingers into her palm and used her index finger and thumb to form the shape of a gun.

"Then I, how do you say?" she said as she swept her right hand toward her crotch and moved it down her thigh. "I all wet."

Barbara looked to David, who spoke a bit more English. "She wet her pants?" Barbara asked.

"Yes. Yes!" he answered, nodding his head up and down frantically, his dark eyes widening.

"I so, so scared, I wet my pants," Eunice said, shaking her head in embarrassment.

The cops smashed their two surveillance cameras with a metal rod and yanked camera wires from the ceiling. David, who stood in front of a small radio playing Korean music, showed Barbara; he pulled his hands back as if he held a golf club and then took hard, ferocious swings into the air, toward his new surveillance camera.

"Over and over, they hit. They broke it," David said.

The officers rifled through drawers, dumped dozens of cigarette cartons on the floor, and swiped cash from the registers. Then they hauled the Nams to jail for selling the baggies. When David and Eunice later unlocked the store, they discovered that a case of lighter fluid and handfuls of Zippo lighters were missing. Cops wrote in paperwork that they seized $2,573 in the raid, but the Nams said they actually had between $3,800 and $4,000 in the store. Most of their cash came in lottery sales to customers who hoped they were one lucky number away from a Powerball jackpot in the millions.

No matter the language—Korean, Arabic, Spanish, Cantonese—the merchants' stories translated the same: the cops barreled into the stores, guns drawn, spewing curse words and slurs like *mama-san,* a derogatory term typically used for a woman who runs a brothel. They sometimes shoved or struck the merchants, tying their hands behind their backs in plasticuffs— plastic handcuffs that bit into their skin. They smashed video surveillance cameras with sledgehammers or metal rods, or cut camera wires with knives they took from the store deli.

When the cameras went dark, the cops stole thousands of dollars in cash and pillaged the stores, guzzling energy drinks and scarfing down Cheez-Its and Little Debbie fudge brownies. They inhaled bags of sunflower seeds, spitting the salty shells on the floor, and helped themselves to fresh turkey hoagies, not bothering to close the refrigerated deli case, leaving the meat and cheese to spoil. They left deep fryers filled with hot vegetable oil simmering on high, not caring if the store burned to the ground. Hopped up on power, the cops swiped the shelves bare, carting off brown boxes filled with cigarettes, batteries, and canned goods. A Hispanic woman who worked at a Dominican-owned store put it simply: "It was like they was shopping."

The merchants were financially ruined—robbed with a badge—but somehow they were the criminals. The cops arrested them on either misdemeanor charges or felony charges that the court then knocked down to misdemeanors. Immigrants with no criminal records—all living here legally—found themselves being dragged through Philly's archaic justice system. They shelled out thousands of dollars in bail and attorneys' fees. They lost thousands more because their stores were shuttered for days or weeks after the raids. Some were so shaken that they closed their stores for good. Their cases took months to weave through an overburdened criminal court, costing taxpayers money. In the end, a judge sentenced them to probation and fines or lesser penalties.

The drug paraphernalia laws in Pennsylvania were open to dubious interpretation. It was only a crime to sell the baggies if the merchant knew, or should have known, that the buyer intended to use them to package drugs. The merchant had to figure out whether the customer wanted to use the bags for drugs or for some legitimate reason, like preserving rare coins or jewelry. Cops were supposed to target stores, like tire or electronics shops, which would have no reason to sell baggies. Jeff's squad should have never raided merchants like the Nams and Samir, because they had smoke shops and they sold baggies to customers who bought loose tobacco.

To make their case, cops or informants had to walk into the store and specifically ask for "weed bags" or "rock bags." That's assuming merchants, particularly those who struggled with English, were schooled in drug lingo.

Granted, most baggie buyers weren't little old ladies who wanted to store sweater buttons, earrings, or high-blood-pressure medication. They were corner drug dealers who used the baggies to peddle street-size quantities of drugs. Tiny empty baggies were discarded everywhere— playgrounds, empty lots, alleys, sidewalks. Baggies were the conduit of the drug trade. "It's like selling bullets and saying, 'We're not selling the guns, we're only selling the bullets,' " a police detective explained to Barbara and me. Some shop owners disagreed: "It's the equivalent of getting locked up for selling knives, and police saying it's murder paraphernalia," countered one merchant.

Most store owners knew that the baggies were being used to package drugs. But this was Philly. It wasn't the kind of town where you chirpily asked, "What exactly do you need those little bags for?" That could get your head blown off.

These weren't the mom-and-pop stores of yesteryear, when merchants knew their customers by name and didn't worry if they were short on cash or left their wallets at home. Back then, they'd say, "No problem, we'll settle up next time."

Many merchants bought or rented corner stores in drug-sick neighborhoods devoid of big-chain supermarkets, and of law and order. They were often afraid of their clientele, barricading themselves behind thick, scratched-up walls of bulletproof plastic and exchanging money and goods through a small slit. At least once or twice a year, a merchant got gunned down during a robbery. They invested in video-surveillance systems with multiple cameras pointed at every corner of the store. It wasn't unusual for police to show the store's grainy footage at news conferences when asking the public for help identifying armed perps.

The stores were vulnerable to robberies because the merchants typically dealt in all cash. In one day, they'd take in thousands of dollars in lottery, cigarette, and phone card sales. They used cash to pay wholesale grocery vendors and store rent or mortgages.

Jenny Lu, a fifty-one-year-old Chinese immigrant who arrived here via Vietnam, where she and her husband were fishermen, was a prisoner in her own store. Though she owned a home in South Philadelphia, she rarely slept there. Most nights, she'd lock up the shop and head upstairs to a small apartment with a bed. Jenny's store had been burglarized six times. Break-ins usually happened when the building was empty. Jenny sat sentry over her store—and her money, which she stashed under the bed mattress—like a little hamster, Jenny's daughter, Anh, liked to say.

For Jenny, it seemed safer to keep the money hidden above her store. Walking to the bank with wads of cash in her purse was dangerous. When Jeff, his brother Richard, and three other cops raided Jenny's store, she had more than $10,000, mostly in small bills, stuffed in a plastic bag under the bed. The cops upended the mattress and took it all.

Jenny, like all the other merchants we'd found, never reported the theft to police. Why would they? They came from countries where cops were notoriously corrupt. "Back home, police get away with everything, including murder," explained Danilo Burgos, president of the city's Dominican Grocers Association. Besides, what if criminals without badges robbed their stores, and they called 911? They couldn't risk being blacklisted by district cops.

18

AT FIRST THE MERCHANTS WERE RE-
LUCTANT TO TRUST BARBARA AND
ME. THEY DIDN'T WANT THEIR NAMES,
STORE LOCATIONS, OR FACES PRINTED
in the newspaper. They were scared of retaliation. They were willing to eat the loss,
chalking up the cop robberies as a Philly
street tax.

But little by little, as the merchants realized they weren't alone, the tide shifted.
Every time Barbara got another merchant
on board, she euphorically zipped through
the newsroom looking for me, even hunting me down in the bathroom. She looked
under each stall until she spotted my kid-
size sneakers.

"Wendy, I just got another one!" Barbara
whooped.

We'd have entire strategy meetings in
the bathroom with Barbara yelling ideas at
me over the stall door.

I decided to try to circle around to Samir,

the Jordanian smoke shop owner who was a no-show at his lawyer's office. I knew his name and the location of his store, and I thought maybe I could persuade him to add his voice to our story.

I found Samir's son, Moe, at the store, and he agreed to meet me with his dad at his house later that day. Just from a brief conversation with Moe, I could tell the father and son were close and Moe was protective of his father.

That night Samir greeted me at the door, where I slipped off my sneakers before entering the living room. As soon as I sat down, his wife served me homemade Middle Eastern sweets and hot mint tea. Moe translated.

"We have other store owners who told us the same story," I said. "They are going to go on the record and let us use their names in the paper."

Samir and his wife looked at each other and nodded. Moe would speak on behalf of the family.

Though Samir had lived in America for about seven years, he struggled with English. Samir was a massive man, at least six feet tall, with a hulking frame, big droopy eyes, black as olives, and long ears on either side of a meaty bald head. He was taciturn and shy and kept within the half-mile between his tobacco and cigar shop and his South Philadelphia row house, where he and his family spoke mostly Arabic. He politely nodded and smiled at neighbors and customers, who by all accounts saw him as a gentle giant.

Samir spent all day and most of the night ringing up lottery and cigarette sales, crammed in the narrow aisle between the counter cash register and a wall of white shelves, lined with sea-green cartons of Newports and mahogany boxes of Mavericks. He sold loose tobacco, coffee, and trail mix. He also sold tiny ziplock bags—$5 for 100.

Two years ago, on a late December afternoon, Samir had just finished tallying about $14,000 in cash from the day's sales when Jeff and six other cops burst into the store. Samir's son, Moe, arrived a few minutes later. Samir had been waiting for his twenty-one-year-old son, who manned the register while Samir walked the half-block to the bank to deposit the money.

"What's going on?" Moe asked, as a cop blocked him from going inside.

"We'll tell ya later," the cop said gruffly.

Moe panicked when he looked through the store window and saw his dad in handcuffs.

"I would like to know why you guys are locking up my dad for no reason," he said. "I'm his son."

A cop shoved Moe away from the window, and another plainclothes cop came over and said, "We're arresting your dad because he's selling drug supplies."

"What kind of drug supplies are you talking about?"

"Little baggies," the cop said.

"Those baggies that we got, we got those bags from the cigarette wholesaler, they sell them. People came in and asked for them and we got them, we started selling them," Moe said, the words pouring out.

The cops tore apart the store, while Moe watched through the window. He grew angry and suspicious when he saw one narcotics cop with a pair of pliers in his hand. The cop reached up to a surveillance camera mounted high on the wall and clipped the wires. The cop, who wore a navy blue jacket and a baseball cap, was careful to keep his head down as he cut the wires; he didn't want the camera lens to capture his face. One by one, he sliced the wires to all four security cameras.

Samir had never been arrested before, and he sat in the jail cell, feeling like a scared child.

When Moe opened the shop a few days later, he couldn't see the floor because of the mounds of dumped coffee grinds, candy wrappers, and crushed cigarette cartons. Nearly 40 cartons of Newports were missing. A cigar box, which contained about $900 from the day's lottery ticket sales, was bare, tossed to the floor. The cash register drawer sat ajar and empty, except for a few quarters, pennies, and dimes. Fourteen thousand dollars. Gone.

Jeff left a property receipt on the store counter. Moe looked at the receipt and wanted to pound the wall with his fist: $7,888. That was the amount Jeff claimed police had seized in the raid.

Samir shook his head and looked at Moe with those dark, soulful eyes. In Arabic, Samir said, "There is no way, because I know how much money I had that day. I counted it all up so I could take it to the bank and pay the wholesaler."

Samir lost more than money in the raid. He lost his dignity. Moe, who moved to the United States from Jordan a decade earlier, had to give up his job as a satellite-dish technician to take over his dad's store. After the raid, Samir was too scared to be in the store. Moe was twenty-three, with thick black hair, slightly gelled back. He had dark eyes and long lashes and a swagger and confidence not inherited from his dad.

"If he sees cops now, he freaks out," Moe said. "My dad never been in jail. My dad never been in trouble. Now he's like a little kid that got bit by a dog. He won't go out."

Ultimately, all the merchants decided to break their silence. Telling us what happened was their way of taking back control, of feeling empowered.

19

WHEN BARBARA AND I SAT DOWN TO WRITE THE LATEST TAINTED JUSTICE INSTALLMENT, WE HAD SEVEN STORE OWNERS AND AN ATTORNEY REPRESENT-ing an eighth—all on the record. Some even agreed to be photographed. The number of victimized merchants would more than double in the next few weeks.

There was a collective catharsis among merchants across the city. They were angry and disillusioned. Once they started talking, they didn't want to stop.

Emilio Vargas was a teenager when he arrived in the US from the Dominican Republic. Now, at twenty-nine, he was jaded. Emilio was so rattled by the police raid that he walked away from his store. "I believed in the American dream. I still do. I believed that if you work hard, you get ahead. But everything changed after this. . . . I used to believe in justice in America. I don't know now. It makes me question the justice system."

The story seemed to write itself—a rarity for us. We always wrote at my desk, sitting so close that the wheels of our swivel chairs sometimes clanked together and our shoulders touched. When staffers saw us hunkered down, typing with an intense, coffee-infused hysteria, they'd remark, "Oh boy, the Girls are up to something. Can't wait to read it."

Barbara and I sometimes struggled in our writing. On those stories, we used all kinds of excuses to procrastinate. I'd get a cup of tea. Barbara checked in with her kids at college. We ran upstairs to get trail mix from the cafeteria and chatted up other reporters during bathroom breaks.

Not with this story. The words came fast, and I only stopped typing long enough to high-five Barbara. "I love it! Do you love it?"

"Yeah, I love it," Barbara said.

We were amped up. What the cops had done to these store owners was an outrage, and we couldn't understand how the cops got away with stealing from these merchants for so long. The looting went on for years at stores all across the city, and no one said a word. It was a story hiding in plain sight, and these merchants were easy pickings.

The raid on Jenny Lu's store left her saddled with debt. The cops took every nickel, between $10,000 and $12,000, which Jenny needed to pay two mortgages, one on the store, the other on her house. She owed money to soda and food vendors and utility companies. Jenny, whose husband had died of lung cancer, was forced to close the store and take a cashier's job at a Chinatown supermarket, where she worked twelve hours a day, six days a week, earning $1,200 to $1,400 a month.

The thing was, Jenny and her adult children, who helped run the store, had followed the rules. Jenny's twenty-five-year-old daughter, Anh, didn't take shit from anyone. When customers came in and asked for baggies, she'd question, point-blank, "What do you need them for?" If they muttered "Weed" or "Crack," she'd always say, "I'm sorry, we don't have any of those bags."

Prosecutors initially charged Jenny, who was barely over five feet tall and 110 pounds, with a felony because of the large number of baggies found in her store. The city district attorney's office moved to seize the store through drug forfeiture. Jenny called Anh collect from the jail at 3:00 a.m. and told her to post bail. "Are you serious?" Anh asked when she got to the police station. "A fifty-one-year-old lady in clogs committing a felony?"

Barbara and I were close to finishing the story about the merchants when we contacted Jeff's attorney, George Bochetto. We already knew that there was no reason for cops to smash the stores' video surveillance systems and yank the wires from the ceiling. I had passed it by Ray, and Barbara had done the same with a high-ranking police source. Both cops told us that destroying cameras wasn't part of any police protocol and was actually in violation of a directive that read, "Unnecessary damage or destruction of personal property by police during a search is strictly prohibited and WILL result in severe disciplinary action." We couldn't imagine how George was going to defend Jeff on this one.

George's response was quintessential George. "Now that the *Daily News* has created a mass hysteria concerning the Philadelphia Narcotics Unit, it comes as no surprise that every defendant ever arrested will now proclaim their innocence and bark about being mistreated," he e-mailed.

We filed the story to Gar and watched him disappear into his office to read it. He seemed gone for a long while. Then at 6:40 p.m., right around the time Barbara and I wondered whether we should grab dinner, an e-mail popped up on my computer. It was from Gar, with a single subject line: "This might be the best story I've edited in my entire career."

Barbara and I were stunned. Gar was the Ebenezer Scrooge of the compliment department. His e-mail was totally out of character, akin to planting sloppy wet kisses on our cheeks.

Gar's office was no bigger than a handicapped-bathroom stall and kind of smelled like one. Glue mouse traps, sprinkled with bait pellets, sat under his computer and behind the door. Mice had burrowed into the cushions of a small, faded black couch pushed against the wall. We sat down and caught a whiff of death. We suspected that at least one mouse was dead somewhere, a sofa coil wrapped around its tiny neck.

On the wall directly above Gar's computer, next to the "Despair" poster, was a reprint of a locomotive train emerging from the ornate and Gothic former Broad Street Station on the Pennsylvania Railroad. Gar, whose grandfather had worked as a railroad machinist, was one of those quirky adults who still loved trains. No one—and nothing—could beat the boy out of Gar, not even years of editing incomprehensible stories written by reporters with borderline personalities.

Gar had a love-hate relationship with his job. "It's very manic-depressive. I'm either so fuckin' depressed that I want to quit or I feel on top of the world because we've got a great story."

He was having an on-top-of-the-world kind of day.

"We got these sons of bitches, dead to rights! We got 'em. We got 'em!" Gar screeched gleefully after finishing the edit.

Gar wanted reporters to see him as a gruff and hardened editor. But he secretly teared up when he read a poignant story, one with heart. "This is not fuckin' brain surgery," he said about journalism. "It's simple. Write stories that evoke emotion, that make readers cry or laugh or get outraged or disgusted, and give them their money's worth."

That night, Gar went home and told his wife, Marty, "We have a great story coming out tomorrow." Marty knew not to ask for any details, including the general topic. As a longtime *Inquirer* reporter who covered the education beat, Marty was, technically, the enemy. Marty was the reporter who showed up at the search warrant room to give Gail money for copies. Of all the *Inky* reporters at Rose's whim, she chose to dispatch the wife of our editor. In all of their twenty-four years of marriage, Gar and Marty worked at Philly's rival papers. Staying married meant no shop talk.

Barbara got home around midnight. She was greeted by her dog, Seven, a name Barbara's daughter got from a *Seinfeld* episode in which George says he would name his firstborn child Seven after Mickey Mantle's jersey number. Seven was a rescue mutt with a pointy face and a mop of long, wavy brown, gold, and white hair over a Corgi-like sausage body. Barbara always felt guilty when she worked this late. Seven was crazed for attention and followed Barbara all around the house, her bushy tail sweeping the worn oak. With her three-inch legs, Seven had to angle her body to get down the steps.

Barbara ate like a single woman on a budget. She opened a can of fat-free vegetarian baked beans and grabbed a box of wheat crackers from a kitchen cabinet. As the beans heated in the microwave, she poured a glass of $8.99-a-bottle chardonnay and sat on the couch to watch *Nightline*. She capped off dinner with a Tylenol PM and went to bed.

I came home to find Karl, pajama-clad in plaid flannel, seated in his leather maroon recliner, rubbing Icy Hot into the arches of his bare feet. Karl, who jogged every other morning, liked to say that Icy Hot was the cologne of choice for middle-aged men who exercised. Karl was in front of the TV, watching one of his home-improvement shows. The entire living room reeked of menthol. He was in the throes of his make-your-own-furniture phase, having recently cobbled together a pair of faux-leather chairs. The cushions hung so far past the wooden frame that brave friends who sat down unexpectedly slid to the floor.

This was around the time that Karl started calling our Tainted Justice series "T'ain't Been Home in Weeks." As usual, Karl left my dinner in the fridge on a plate covered with Saran Wrap. And as usual, it was his usual: penne pasta sautéed in olive oil, fresh spinach, and garlic. I took two bites and buried the rest in the trash can.

The next morning, I ran out my front door to get the newspaper. My stomach fluttered with excitement. There was nothing like seeing your story on the front page, especially one this powerful and explosive. The headline trumpeted, "Smash & Grab: Shopkeepers say narcotics cops disabled security cameras, looted and trashed their stores." Underneath the headline was a photo of a bodega owner. He stood in front of his store with his arms crossed and a defiant scowl on his face. Bam.

The *Inquirer* had nothing. Yeah, we really got "mercilessly pounded" on that one, I thought.

Officer Jeffrey Cujdik, of the Philadelphia Police Department's Narcotics Field Unit. He recruited Benny Martinez as Confidential Informant 103. *(David Maialetti/Staff Photographer/*Philadelphia Daily News*)*

Raul Nieves's lawyer Stephen Patrizio was the first person to suspect something was amiss. *(Yong Kim/Staff Photographer/*Philadelphia Daily News*)*

The row house at 1939 East Pacific Street that Jeff Cujdik rented to Benny Martinez, below market rate, as part of their arrangement. *(Courtesy of the authors)*

Michael Days, editor of the *Philadelphia Daily News.* *(Jessica Griffin/Staff Photographer/*Philadelphia Daily News*)*

A COP AND AN INFORMANT
GOT TOO CLOSE AND
BENT THE RULES.
NOW, THE INFORMANT
FEARS FOR HIS LIFE.

TAINTED JUSTICE?

PAGE 3

The first article about Benny Martinez, featuring a silhouette photograph of him to conceal his identity, ran on the front page of the February 9, 2009, edition of the *Philadelphia Daily News* under a headline that would come to define the series. *(Courtesy of* Philadelphia Daily News*)*

Lady Gonzalez, the first woman to say that she was sexually assaulted by a Philadelphia Narcotics Field Unit officer during a raid. *(Sarah J. Glover/Staff Photographer/*Philadelphia Daily News*)*

Brian Tierney *(right)*, owner of the *Philadelphia Daily News*, after the first day of the 2009 bankruptcy hearing at Philadelphia's Federal Courthouse. *(Elizabeth Robertson/Staff Photographer/ Philadelphia Inquirer)*

From left: Philadelphia police commissione Charles Ramsey; Janice Fedarcyk, specia agent in charge of the FBI's Philadelphi field office; and Mayor Michael Nutter a a joint press conference held on Februar 13, 2009, to address Wendy and Barbara' story. *(Alejandro A. Alvarez/Staff Photogra pher/*Philadelphia Daily News*)*

John McNesby, president of the Philadelphia Fraternal Order of Police, speaks out against the *Philadelphia Daily News* at a February 25, 2009, press conference. George Bochetto, Jeff Cujdik's lawyer, is on the right. *(David Maialetti/Staff Photographer/*Philadelphia Daily News*)*

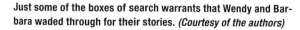

Just some of the boxes of search warrants that Wendy and Barbara waded through for their stories. *(Courtesy of the authors)*

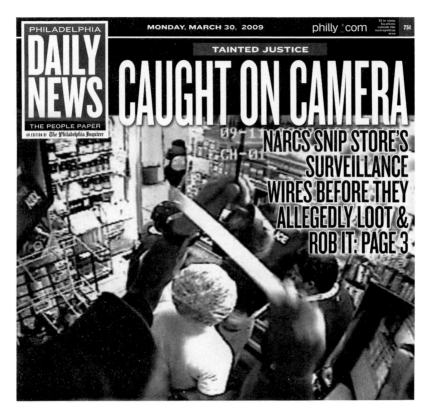

PHILADELPHIA

DAILY
NEWS

THE PEOPLE PAPER
AN EDITION OF The Philadelphia Inquirer

MONDAY, MARCH 30, 2009   philly com   75¢
$1 in some
locations
outside the
metropolitan
area

TAINTED JUSTICE

CAUGHT ON CAMERA

NARCS SNIP STORE'S
SURVEILLANCE
WIRES BEFORE THEY
ALLEGEDLY LOOT &
ROB IT: PAGE 3

This frame of surveillance video from Jose Duran's store shows Narcotics Field Unit officer Anthony Parrotti poised to cut the camera wires with a bread knife. The frame was run on the front page of the March 30, 2009, edition of the *Philadelphia Daily News*. *(Courtesy of Jose Duran and* Philadelphia Daily News*)*

Another still, which was published in the *Philadelphia Daily News* with faces blurred, shows Narcotics Field Unit officer Thomas Tolstoy *(foreground)* checking out the camera. Cujdik is directly behind him. Tolstoy was identified by at least three women as the officer who sexually assaulted them during raids. *(Courtesy of Jose Duran)*

The aftermath of the Philadelphia Narcotics Unit raid on Jose Duran's store. *(Courtesy of Jose Duran)*

Angel Castro hugs his Thayer Street neighbor Dagma Rodriguez, another woman who said she was assaulted by Officer Tolstoy. *(David Maialetti/Staff Photographer/*Philadelphia Daily News*)*

TAINTED JUSTICE

AFTER SHE REPORTED A DRUG COP'S INDECENT ASSAULT — SO ROUGH IT SENT HER TO THE HOSPITAL — THE TERRIFYING, ANONYMOUS PHONE CALLS BEGAN

'NAOMI' IN FEAR

PAGE 3

"Naomi," the third of Officer Tolstoy's alleged sexual assault victims to come forward, appears in silhouette on the cover of the June 17, 2009, edition of the *Philadelphia Daily News. (David Maialetti/Staff Photographer/*Philadelphia Daily News*, courtesy of* Philadelphia Daily News*)*

The photograph of Wendy with her father that Wendy slipped under her pillow for luck the night before the 2010 Pulitzer Prize announcements. *(Courtesy of Wendy Ruderman)*

Before the Pulitzer announcement, Barbara drew strength by praying to her mother. This photo of Barbara's mother sat on her desk. *(Courtesy of Barbara Laker)*

City editor Gar Joseph, Barbara *(center)*, and Wendy react to the news of their Pulitzer Prize win on April 12, 2010. *(Sarah J. Glover/Staff Photographer/*Philadelphia Daily News*)*

Brian Tierney, about to throw the ceremonial first pitch at a Phillies game, wears a shirt that captures the spirit of the *Philadelphia Daily News*. *(Yong Kim/Staff Photographer/*Philadelphia Daily News*)*

20

THE FBI AGENTS ON THE POLICE-
CORRUPTION CASE READ THE BODEGA
STORY AND FLIPPED OUT. THEY DIDN'T
KNOW ABOUT THE STORE ROBBERIES
because Benny didn't know about them. All
Benny knew was that Jeff sometimes gave
him cartons of cigarettes and other goods.
Now the FBI had to follow us. Agents imme-
diately fanned out to interview store owners.
This gave Barbara and me a little thrill, but
we doubted that the FBI was overjoyed.

We were "feeling our oats," as my mom
always said when I got all cocky and full of
my pint-size self, when my phone rang at
work.

"This Wendy? I have video. Backup," the
man on the other end said.

"What? Did you say video? Of a raid on
your store?"

"Yeah. Yeah. Video. I got computer hid.
They went crazy looking for computer," he
said. "I got copy."

"A copy? Of the video?" I said, practically yelling into my phone.

Jose Duran had come to the United States some thirteen years earlier, but his English was a nightmare. It's not that he didn't speak the language. He did. Only with an accent that smothered his words like a wet wool blanket. He had a high-pitched gravelly voice that reminded me of Tattoo, the midget who played Mr. Roarke's assistant on the TV series *Fantasy Island*. I asked Jose if I could get the tape that night. He gave me his address in New Jersey. He lived only five miles from my house.

I turned into his long driveway, and even in the dark, I could see that the house was a stately colonial with a wide front porch framed by ornate white columns. The three-story house, set back from the street, was parchment yellow with dark shutters. Oh shit, I thought, I hope he isn't some kind of big-time drug dealer.

Jose answered the door. He was stout, with a thick helmet of black hair and dark eyebrows, like two bushy caterpillars. He wore khaki pants, tan leather loafers, and a sweater with a dress shirt underneath. He had a long vertical scar on his forehead from when, as a thirteen-year-old in the Dominican Republic, he crashed a motorized dirt bike into a utility pole with a nail that ripped into his skin.

Jose was only twenty-eight, and at the time of the raid, he ran a bodega in Philly and a mini-mart in New Jersey. Turned out, Jose shared the house with a nest full of relatives, including his sister, her husband, and their kids. He handed me a copy of a CD containing ten minutes of footage, including audio. I knew from the search warrant that Jeff's squad had raided Jose's bodega, with Jeff's brother, Richard, in charge.

It was about 9:30 p.m., and I called Barbara from Jose's driveway, shrieking, "I got it. I got it!" Then I called Karl.

"I'm on my way home. I was gonna stop by the grocery store. Do you need anything?"

"Yeah, a wife," he said, and we both laughed.

I couldn't sleep that night, thinking about Jose's CD in my black vinyl work bag. When I got to work the next morning, the first thing I did was call my cop source, Ray. Barbara and I wanted him to see the tape. We knew what Jeff looked like, but we needed Ray to help identify the other cops and school us on what was police protocol—and more importantly, what wasn't. Ray was nearby at the criminal courthouse and said he'd be right over.

In the two years I'd known Ray, we'd never met in the newsroom. This was a big risk for him. What if another cop saw him going into the *Daily News* building? Ray's curiosity won out over good sense. There was nothing surreptitious about his entrance into the newsroom. He strutted down the center aisle with a toothy grin.

Barbara had put the CD in computers all over the newsroom, but couldn't get it to play on any of them. Everything at the *Daily News* was janky. The computers were bulky and sounded like jet planes taking off whenever we turned them on. Barbara, Ray, and I walked over to a graphic artist who was computer-savvy to see if he could get the tape to play. Still, no go. Damn it. Damn this washboard newspaper with its old-timey technology.

We knew we'd have to drive back to Jose's house to play the tape. To our surprise, Ray offered to go with us. Barbara checked out a company car and Ray stretched his legs out in the back of a PT Cruiser, one of about a dozen fleet cars shared by reporters at both newspapers. Barbara drove.

I told Ray that my driving scared Barbara because I was a nervous, brake-stomping wheel-jerker. I couldn't get my mind around the idea that we humans are really nothing more than souped-up monkeys who vroom down highways at eighty miles per hour, sometimes doing so while applying lipstick or texting or reading MapQuest directions. Even I was guilty of tweezing my mustache hairs while driving. I hated the idea of entrusting strangers to stay in their own lanes while driving and often thought how the only thing separating me and my car from a horrific crash, possibly death, was an imaginary barrier in the form of a white painted line. As I was explaining my driving phobia to Ray, I looked at Barbara, who gripped the steering wheel tighter and darted her head from left to right to check her side mirrors.

"You're freakin' me out," Barbara said as she changed lanes.

We arrived at Jose's house by late afternoon. Jose and Ray shook hands in the foyer. "Ray is a friend. He's helping us with the story," I offered with a shrug.

Jose was a savvy guy; he didn't ask too many questions. He led us to the dining room, where a computer sat at the head of a polished wood table with a glass chandelier overhead. Jose's wife flitted in and out of the kitchen, offering iced tea and snacks.

Jose told us he was a technology buff who loved to tinker with computers and electronic gadgets. After high school, he studied electronics at a trade school in the Bronx. He'd rigged his bodega with a sophisticated $15,000 surveillance system, which recorded video on a backup hard drive hidden behind a display of bobby pins in the store. The backup downloaded the footage to a secure Internet site that he could access from any computer.

"I record everything because sometimes I got to go out and I leave employees by themselves. That's how you find out who's doing right, who's doing wrong. Plus, the money. I got cameras watching the money," Jose explained.

The four of us huddled around Jose's computer. He slid the CD in. We instantly recognized Jose on the screen, wearing baggy knee-length jean shorts, a dark blue polo shirt, and black Adidas slider sandals with white ankle socks.

In the video, Jose paces back and forth in front of the store's ice-cream freezer, which sits in front of the cash register window. As he chats with his brother-in-law in Spanish on a cell phone, Jose's back is turned to the store's front door when the first cop bursts in. The cop, a pudgy frat-boy type, has his gun drawn. He points it at Jose's head.

Ray recognized the cop immediately. "That's Tom Tolstoy."

"The Boob Man?" Barbara asked, referring to the nickname for the cop who fondled Lady Gonzalez's breasts and was rumored to have sexually assaulted other women during raids. Barbara moved in closer to Jose's computer screen for a better look at Tolstoy's face. Tolstoy was a cross between Fred Flintstone and Bob's Big Boy, particularly with his doo-wop hairstyle. His bangs were moussed or jelled into a stiff point that swooped back, S-shaped.

"Hand me the phone! Gimme the phone," Tolstoy yells on the videotape.

"Hey, I work here," Jose says.

"Put your hands on your head!"

"I'm the owner."

"Put your hands behind your back!"

Tolstoy spins Jose around and cuffs him. Five other cops, all wearing jeans and vests or shirts emblazoned with the word POLICE, barrel into the store behind Tolstoy. At first the cops ask routine questions, presumably for their safety: Does Jose have a gun? Does anyone live on the second floor? Are there dogs in the basement?

Sergeant Joe Bologna, a beer-bellied bully with a baseball cap who supervised the raid, looks up and wags his finger toward the ceiling.

"Whaddya got, cameras over there? . . . Where are they hooked up to?" Bologna barks.

Every cop in Jose's store is fixated on the surveillance system.

"There's cameras all over the place," Jeff's brother, Richard, says. "Where's the video cameras? The cassette for it?"

"Does it record? Does it record?" Jeff quickly interjects. Standing next to Jeff, Richard appears much shorter and scrawny, lacking his brother's good looks.

Tolstoy glances up and scans the ceiling. "I got, like, seven or eight eyes."

"There's three right here," says Thomas Kuhn, a squat and chubby cop who is wearing shorts and a baseball cap on backward.

"Listen to me," Tolstoy says. "There's one outside. There is one, two, three, four in the aisles, and there's one right here somewhere."

Jose asks if he can call his wife, and Tolstoy gruffly tells him he can't call anyone. Then Tolstoy opens the cash register drawer and eyes the money, then looks up at the camera above the register, and back down at the money. His meaty frame stuffed in the narrow space behind the cash register, Tolstoy reaches up and swats at the camera lens. He can't get at it, so he walks away, comes back with a long serrated knife, and goes to work on the camera. There's a close-up of his wrist and the blade of the knife. Jeff is in the background, looking at the cash register. The camera eventually goes dark.

An outdoor camera, aimed at the street, catches Richard rummaging through Jose's white van without a search warrant.

Back inside the store, Kuhn on the other side of the counter steps up onto a blue milk crate and struggles to grab a camera above his head.

"I need to be fucking taller," Kuhn mumbles as another cop laughs.

"You got a ladder in here, cuz?" Kuhn asks Jose.

"Yo," Tolstoy calls out from behind the cash register. "Does this camera go home? Can you view this on your computer, too?"

"I can see, yeah, home, yeah," Duran replies.

"So your wife knows we're here, then?" Tolstoy asks.

"My wife? No. She not looking the computer right now."

"Hey, Sarge . . . Come 'ere," Tolstoy shouts.

Bologna waddles over to the front counter, and Jeff leans in and whispers, "There's one in the back corner right there."

Officer Anthony Parrotti, sporting a khaki military cap and a goatee, his forearms covered in tattoos, reaches up to a camera in front of the register, pulls a wire down, and slices it with a bread knife from the store's deli.

"It can be viewed at home," Tolstoy tells Bologna.

"Okay. We'll disconnect it. That's cool," Bologna assures Tolstoy.

One by one, the cops disarm and destroy all seven of Jose's cameras until the screen goes dark and the audio cuts out.

When the tape ended, we sat at Jose's table looking at each other. No one could watch that tape and not know that the cops were up to no good. We played it again, and Ray pointed out each cop by name.

"He no touch the money with the system looking at him. No, he touch the money after they destroy all the system," Jose said while watching Tolstoy behind the cash register.

"These cops are in so much fucking trouble," Ray said.

"Look at these i-d-i-o-t-s," Jose said.

"I know," Ray said, shaking his head. The two men busted out laughing, as if they were old friends.

It was a surreal scene, watching a narcotics cop and a merchant victimized by narcotics cops joking around together about the video. "He a good guy," Jose said about Ray.

After leaving Jose's, Barbara and I took Ray to Applebee's for dinner. We sat at a booth, surrounded by families with whiny toddlers in high chairs and old couples chewing their food in silence. The food was bad, the place was loud, and the service sucked. It was pure paradise. We had the goods on these cops, the video was gold—and all three of us knew it.

21

OVER THE NEXT FOUR DAYS, BARBARA
AND I WORKED LATE EACH NIGHT PUT-
TING THE STORY TOGETHER. THE MOST
LABORIOUS PART WAS TRANSCRIBING
the audio portion of the video. I spent close
to eighteen hours listening to, then pausing
and replaying, the audio. I worried that the
Daily News could get sued if I didn't get the
verbiage exact or I screwed up which cop
said what.

On one of those nights, at about 10:00
p.m., Barbara and I walked out the building's back door and got spooked when we
saw a pickup truck.

The truck was idling at the stop sign on
the narrow road that reporters crossed to
get to the parking garage. The truck had
a small flatbed and a Fraternal Order of
Police specialty license plate. Two men,
both white, glared at us from the truck's
front seat. Barbara and I froze. "Wendy,
they're cops," she said, grabbing my arm,

a gesture that grew out of Barbara's protective maternal instinct, not fear.

If they intended to hurt us, now was the time. At this hour, the area was desolate, with plenty of dimly lit crevices and alleys between closed office buildings. At least one editor had been mugged here. The corner bar, Westy's Tavern, was still open, but the place wasn't crowded on weeknights, except for Thursday karaoke nights.

The men, stone-faced, stared us down. We didn't recognize their faces from the video. Maybe they were friends of the cops on Jeff's squad. We didn't know. Barbara and I darted across the street, keeping an eye on the truck's reverse lights just in case the driver decided to flatten us. We got to our cars, parked close to one another.

"Wendy, they might follow one of us home. Make sure you lock your doors," Barbara said. "Call me as soon as you get home."

I spent the whole ride home checking my rearview window to see if the truck or some other car had followed me. Once home, I had to crawl over to the passenger door to get out because the driver's-side door, when locked, didn't open from the inside.

I checked in with Barbara; neither of us slept well that night, listening for the rumble of cars or any unusual house sounds.

By then, we'd practically memorized the store video. The cops' voices replayed in our heads. The cops unholstered their guns and stormed into Jose's store as if they were taking down Pablo Escobar or some other notorious kingpin. Not looking for a businessman selling ziplock baggies.

"You have any paraphernalia in here? Twelve-twelves," Richard says to Jose on the video.

"What you mean, twelve-twelves?" Jose asks, hands cuffed behind his back.

"The baggies. You got twelve-twelves? . . . You have some?"

"A little bit, yeah."

Jose tries to explain to Richard that he bought the store already stocked with merchandise, including baggies.

"Okay, it don't matter. You should know your business," Richard says.

Richard then inexplicably asks Jose, "You have cats in here, too?" As if he's about to get mauled by a killer tabby.

Jeff tells Jose that he has to seize the cameras as evidence. "So we gotta get rid of it. You got yourself on video selling drug paraphernalia."

"It's illegal, boss. It's illegal," Richard tells Jose.

Yeah, and it's also illegal to lie on search warrants, Barbara and I thought when we viewed the video. The fact was, Richard got captured on video selling bullshit.

In the application for the search warrant, Richard wrote that he watched as a confidential informant went into Jose's store and bought baggies at about 4:30 p.m. on a September afternoon, about two and a half hours before the store raid.

Jose's digital surveillance footage was time-stamped. Barbara and I studied the stretch of tape between 4:00 and 5:00 p.m. Not a single customer asked for or bought a ziplock bag. On top of that, the video shows Richard searching Jose's van without a warrant, which is illegal. Richard left it unlocked with the keys in the center console, so anyone could steal it.

The cops locked up Jose on misdemeanor charges, stole almost $10,000, and left his store in a shambles. Jose couldn't understand why the cops didn't just give him a warning or even a citation for having baggies in his store. "If it's illegal, okay, take it out . . . don't destroy my business and rob me," Jose said.

A judge sentenced Jose to nine months' probation.

I called Charles Ramsey, the city's police commissioner, to tell him about the video and get a comment. Ramsey couldn't think of any reason cops would destroy video surveillance cameras. "You wouldn't just cut and take it because that's somebody's private property," he said.

Ramsey wanted us to turn over the video to internal affairs and the FBI. "It's pretty serious, and I want to get to the bottom of it."

Ramsey thought that Barbara and I only cared about getting a big story. In his mind, we weren't interested in nabbing dirty cops, not really. "You're looking at something I've not seen. I've got a task force that's looking into this entire matter. They need to be informed of this and they need a chance to look at it," Ramsey said. "If we need a subpoena . . ."

"We'll give it to you. We're putting it up on our website tomorrow," I told him.

Michael Days asked me, Barbara, and Gar to come into his office.

"This video is great stuff. It's unbelievable. And when you see that cop cut those wires with the knife—wow, I mean wow," Michael said with a chortle.

Michael intended to put the entire ten-minute tape online, along with a transcript. He wanted to name names. The only question was whether we should blur the cops' faces. There wasn't any law or court opinion that forced us to do so. After all, these cops routinely testified in open court, where they faced drug dealers seated a few feet away at the defendants' table.

"You know what? I think we should take the high road on this one," Michael said. "I don't want anyone to accuse us of putting these cops' lives in danger, with them being undercover and all."

It took hours for the photo and online staff to fog the cops' faces with grayish circles and make sure the blur followed them as they moved through the bodega.

Barbara called George Bochetto, who by this point was almost crying uncle. The fight in his voice was gone. When Barbara told him about the video, he didn't ask any questions. He didn't even ask to see it.

"I stand by what I said before," he offered lamely.

Barbara and I recycled Bochetto's quote from the first bodega story in which he accused the *Daily News* of stirring up mass hysteria.

The front page was a freeze-frame of Officer Anthony Parrotti wielding a bread knife, seconds before he slices the camera wire. The headline was, "Caught on Camera: Narcs Snip Store's Surveillance Wires Before They Allegedly Loot & Rob It."

Allegedly. What a great word.

The next day, computers across the Philadelphia region kept crashing because so many people wanted to view the video. By 8:15 a.m., there were nearly a hundred reader comments posted online. That number would swell exponentially by day's end. Overwhelmingly, readers were disgusted with the cops:

Why would the *Daily News* blur the officers' faces in these shots? As members of the community, shouldn't we know what these dangerous men look like?

World's Most Stupidest Criminals.

Where's fat-neck [Fraternal Order of Police president] McNesby to defend to these scumbag heroes?

Now will someone get "Training Day" out of the Police Department Film Library? My hope is that the *Daily News* is watching out for these reporters. . . . There are too many armed thugs with badges running around masquerading as good cops.

Well, it's nice to know that the crackdown on ziplock baggies is in full swing in a city that records 300+ murders a year, and solves less than half.

Barbara and I wouldn't hear from Bochetto again.

22

AFTER SEEING THE VIDEO, COMMIS-
SIONER RAMSEY TOOK RICHARD
CUJDIK OFF THE STREET. RICHARD
JOINED HIS BROTHER AND JEFF'S PART-
ner, Robert "Bobby" McDonnell, on desk
duty, where they spent their days answering
phones and shuffling police paperwork,
their law enforcement powers virtually non-
existent. Bobby hadn't been part of the raid
on Jose's store, but he was linked to bogus
search warrants with Jeff.

Richard went around defending himself
to other cops, spinning his desk-duty stint
as a mere hiccup in his police career. He
believed he'd be back on the street soon
enough. For Richard, the months riding
a desk would stretch into years as the FBI-
led investigation crawled forward. Richard,
Jeff, and Bobby were stuck there, and Barbara and I were determined to land Officer
Thomas Tolstoy, the Boob Man, on the desk
with them.

Tolstoy's preoccupation with large-breasted women was an open secret among the cops in his squad. In fact, at least one narcotics cop from a neighboring town knew Tolstoy, a thirty-five-year-old married father of two little boys, as the Boob Man. Tolstoy was a predator, and we wanted him off the street.

Benny had told us early on that Tolstoy "fisted" a woman; at least, that's the story he heard from Jeff.

"What?" Barbara asked. She recoiled, not able to get her mind around it. "What do you mean?"

Benny blushed while explaining that Tolstoy supposedly shoved his hand up a woman's vagina during a drug raid. His words were peppered with nervous chuckles and awkward pauses.

The feds had told Benny not to talk to us. But he called constantly using throwaway Cricket Wireless phones. There were health dramas: a garage-bay door slammed down on his back at the auto dealership where he worked detailing cars. He tumbled down some steps and broke his foot. Sonia had a lump on her breast; she slipped on the sidewalk outside a doctor's office and smacked her head, which triggered a brain bleed. They made frequent trips to the hospital, mostly for painkillers, and to the offices of personal-injury lawyers.

There were Benny's I'm-gonna-die dramas: The cops were going to hire a hit man to make him "disappear." One of the drug dealers set up by Benny and Jeff got knifed in prison, and the guy's relatives wanted to retaliate against Benny. He regretted turning against Jeff and wanted to kill himself. The feds sent Benny to a therapist, but he didn't trust her.

There were money dramas: He couldn't afford the rent at his new place, and the feds weren't helping him. He didn't have money to buy his kids birthday presents. He had to sell

the family's wide-screen television. He couldn't afford a defense lawyer and feared the feds might charge him with theft
or fraud for accepting money for drug jobs he never did.

Behind all the drama, there was an unspoken message:
Barbara and I had ruined his life by writing his story. We were
to blame.

As journalists, Barbara and I couldn't give him money, but
we tried to help him in other ways. We went on Apartment
Finder.com to search for a cheaper place for Benny and his
family to live. We called criminal defense attorneys to see if
they would accept him as a client. I bought him groceries,
rushing over to his home with bags of vegetables, turkey,
and Dora the Explorer fruit snacks. I bought his son a Razor
scooter for his birthday and told Benny to say it was from him.
In retrospect, I wondered if Benny sold the scooter for drugs,
but at the time, I was so plagued with guilt that I couldn't see
through his manipulation and lies.

Barbara and I knew the things we did for Benny crossed
the line. But that line—the one between reporter and human
being—got blurry.

After we started writing about the bodegas, the FBI knew
Tainted Justice was much more than a case of fabricating evidence for search warrants. It was going to get big. The FBI
needed Benny to be safe, so they relocated him, Sonia, and
their two kids to a fully furnished two-bedroom suite near
Philadelphia International Airport. The rent was $2,600 a
month, which the feds agreed to pay—at least for now. The
suite, described in a brochure as a "chalet," was like no place
Benny and Sonia had ever lived. It was equipped with a washer
and dryer, a luxury for most people back in the hood. The
decor was simple and crisp, with a taupe couch, a glass coffee
table, and a dining set with high-backed chairs. Powder-blue

walls offset a spotless beige carpet. The suite's front door opened up to a courtyard with a manicured lawn bordered with shrubs and flowers.

Benny watched the store-raid video on a computer in his suite. "I couldn't believe it," Benny said excitedly. "And Tolstoy . . . I was like this motherfucker, he's just a fuckin' bastard."

The Hispanic community, particularly the Dominicans, was in a furor over the bodega raids. "None of these people should have spent half a day in jail over these bullshit charges," fumed Danilo Burgos, head of the three-hundred-member Dominican Grocers Association.

One week after the *Daily News* posted Jose's video online, the city's Hispanic leaders banded together and wrote a searing letter to Ramsey. The letter, which they copied to the district attorney, a city councilwoman, and the mayor's office, called on Ramsey to crack down on bad cops.

"The fact that many reluctant businesspeople have felt compelled to come forward with their complaints, risking their livelihoods and that of their families, indicates that the problem of police abuse has reached a boiling point," Danilo and five other Hispanic leaders wrote.

Jose's video forced Ramsey to do something that his predecessors had failed to do. He took a sledgehammer to the cliquish and chummy squads within the narcotics field unit, splitting up cops who had worked side by side for years.

Seven years earlier, a police watchdog had recommended regular reshuffling of narcotics officers and their supervisors to keep cops honest and prevent abuse. Police brass had ignored the recommendation—until now.

But Ramsey's move to break up the ten narcotic squads did nothing to appease angry Hispanic leaders. "That's just shuffling the deck. It's just window dressing," one said.

Ramsey's style was to tackle thorny issues and criticism head-on. Before coming to Philadelphia in 2008, Ramsey had served as chief of police in Washington, D.C. As an outsider, Ramsey didn't care whether he was popular among Philly's rank and file. He agreed to address irate residents and merchants at a nighttime community meeting. The meeting was held at a church, not far from some of the bodegas raided by Jeff's squad.

We didn't both have to attend the meeting. One of us could have gone and written the story on deadline for the next day's paper, but neither of us wanted to miss it. Ramsey had to appease an entire community because of our stories. Typically, Barbara and I wrestled with our own insecurities, fearing that we weren't good enough or smart enough. For me, those doubts stemmed from grade school, when my teacher wanted me to repeat fourth grade and labeled me a "late bloomer," which I thought meant I was destined for the tart cart, the short blue school bus that brought "slow" kids to special ed. Barbara's doubtfulness, in part, came from her mom, an advertising sales rep who pushed herself to be No. 1, and set the bar high for Barbara. Her mom often started sentences, "The problem with you, Barbara, is . . ."

Now, at the community meeting, our insecurities were on hiatus, temporarily banished by our egos.

Ramsey stood up at the podium, looking weary, as usual. Whenever Barbara and I saw Ramsey, he looked as if he had fifty problems on his mind. The boyish freckles smattered across his face didn't seem to mesh with his trademark stoicism. Ramsey had buried slain cops and fired dirty ones, each time finding just right the words to honor or scorn.

And here, before a contentious crowd of sixty or more, Ramsey again struck just the right note. "Corruption of any kind will not be tolerated in this department, period. And those who engage in it are going to face charges both from the department as well as criminal charges."

Immediately, loud applause broke out in the church.

When the meeting ended, merchants and community leaders came over to Barbara and me. They grasped our hands in theirs and thanked us for exposing a wrong, for caring about them. I looked at Barbara and saw her green eyes moisten. We fed off their emotion and left the church feeling good about the *Daily News* and the power of journalism. At that moment, the death knell of our industry seemed remote.

23

BRIAN TIERNEY, AS CEO AND PUB-
LISHER OF THE *DAILY NEWS* AND THE
INQUIRER, WAS IN THE FIGHT OF HIS
LIFE. THE COMPANY WAS NEARLY $400
million in debt, with the economy, advertising sales, and newspaper circulation in a
tailspin.

It wasn't just Tierney's money on the
line. It was his reputation, his image. What
Tierney had once visualized as a Hollywood
script about a champion of a man who saved
a dying business was turning into a story of
doom. His dream was just that—a dream,
almost a fantasy. Tierney loved the challenge of being the underdog in a business
brawl, but this appeared insurmountable.

Tierney's group failed to reach a deal
with senior lenders, led by Citizens Bank,
to restructure the debt load. And Tierney
emerged as the protagonist in a Greek tragedy, playing out in US bankruptcy court,
that would determine the fate of Philadelphia's two largest newspapers.

He was also under fire for taking a 37 percent raise, which boosted his pay from $618,000 to $850,000 just two months before the bankruptcy filing. Leaders of the Philadelphia Newspaper Guild, the union that represented reporters, were furious because they had convinced union members to give up a $25-a-week raise to help stem the company's financial hemorrhage. Tierney, who had put $10 million of his own money into buying the papers, argued he got the raise because he was doing two jobs—CEO and publisher—which effectively saved the company $1.25 million over two years. Still, Tierney rescinded the raise amid the outcry.

Barbara and I weren't worked up over the whole Tierney raise controversy. Tierney had saved my job, and I was grateful. As long as our paychecks covered the bills and mortgages, Barbara and I were happy. We didn't wish for Friday or watch the clock, willing it to 5:00 p.m. Journalism defined us. Our identities were so entwined with our work that when we were on a good story, everything else in our lives seemed rosy. My marriage was perfect, my kids were headed for Harvard, and Barbara went on dates with a confident zing and sang Rolling Stones tunes—off-key—while driving to work.

Even while home with the kids, I was still in work mode. I talked to Barbara so often that when my cell phone rang, Brody would say, "I hope that's not Barbara wanting a playdate." Each summer Karl and I took the kids to a weekend-long YMCA family camp on a lake dotted with cabins. When I told Brody that I wanted to be in the camp talent show, he said, "What's your talent? Work? Are you going to get up there and work?"

For the first time in her journalism career, Barbara could work twelve-hour days whenever she wanted. When Josh and Anna were younger, she often had to race out at 6:00 p.m.—literally sprinting to her car—to shuttle Josh to hockey practice or Anna to dance class, and pick up the slack at home when her husband left for one of his many business trips. She had more freedom now that her kids were in college, but she felt alone. She missed the chatter and chaos of family life, and work filled a void.

As syrupy as this sounds, on most days Barbara and I saw the job as a privilege, and the Tainted Justice series affirmed it. A tidal wave was cascading over the newspaper business, with Tierney atop the peak in Philadelphia, yet Barbara and I were still on a journalism high.

Under Tierney, the *Daily News* was a favorite child. Even on Tierney's darkest days, when his boyish, contagious enthusiasm was hard to muster, he walked through the *Daily News* newsroom, a flurry of energy, wisps of hair fluttering over his ears, to catch an elevator to his executive suite. He could have avoided reporters and taken the hallway to loop around the *Daily News*, but it seemed he needed to siphon the spirit, zeal, and zaniness of the newsroom. Barbara and I thought all the chatter about stories gave Tierney a daily reminder as to why the battle was worth it.

"Love that story today about . . . ," he shouted to reporters. If not too rushed, he stopped to chat about the big story of the day.

From the jump, Tierney and the *Daily News* staff got each other. Tierney was a "bare-knuckles player in a bare-knuckles town and the *Daily News* was a bare-knuckles kind of newspaper." That's how Zack Stalberg, a *Daily News* editor for twenty years before Michael Days took the helm, summed up the relationship. Tierney also liked the fact that the *Daily News* was able to do a lot more with a lot less than the *Inquirer*. We were like a cheap date; we were low-maintenance—content to grab a Bud Light at a dive bar.

When creditors wanted to shutter the *Daily News,* not because we were bleeding money but because they thought our demise would help the *Inquirer*'s bottom line, Tierney refused. "As long as I'm running the place, the *Daily News* will never be closed."

By spring 2009, media analysts were writing print journalism's obituary. "It's the end of the newspaper business right now, this point in time," pronounced longtime media watcher Michael Wolff.

Tierney wouldn't hear it.

"We," he told CBS News, "are the originators of the investigative work that needs to be done."

24

WE SPENT HOURS IN THE OFFICE, RE-
PLAYING THE JOSE VIDEO. WE PAUSED
IT ON A CLOSE-UP OF TOLSTOY'S FACE.
WE ALREADY HAD HIS BADGE NUMBER;
now we knew what he looked like.

Of all the cops in the video, Tolstoy came
across as the biggest asshole, a caricature
of a cop on a power trip, the self-important
type who gleefully puts people in handcuffs,
making them extra tight, and slams their
heads against the cruiser to show who's boss.

We wanted Lady Gonzalez to see Jose's
video, the version without the cops' faces
blurred. The cop who sexually assaulted her
had told her to call him Tom. When Barbara and I first met Lady three months earlier, we hadn't told her the cop's full name.
We wanted to play fair; we needed Lady to
identify him without prompts from us.

Lady had grown to trust Barbara and
me, so when we asked her to come to the
office to see the raw video, she immediately

agreed. We cued up the raw video on a computer in the newsroom and asked Lady to take a seat.

"Lady, we want you to look at this video and tell us if you recognize the cop who fondled you. I can't tell you if he's on here, and I can't say anything while you watch it," Barbara said.

She repeatedly said she was nervous and rubbed her palms up and down the front of her blue jeans.

"Okay. I'm ready," Lady said softly before taking a deep heave of air.. Barbara pulled up a chair and sat next to Lady. I leaned over and pressed play.

There's a few seconds of Jose talking on his cell phone, pacing back and forth in his store. Tolstoy hits the door first. He zooms in, gun drawn. "Hand me the phone. Gimme the phone," Tolstoy orders.

Lady immediately stiffened, and her brown velvet eyes widened.

"Oh my God, that's him," Lady said. Tears spilled down her cheeks faster than she could wipe them away.

"Are you okay?" Barbara asked, putting her hand across Lady's back.

"My heart is just racing right now," Lady said, starting to tremble. "Just to see him come through that door like that makes me shake all over. It brings back a lot of bad memories."

"Put your hands behind your back," Tolstoy barks to Jose.

"That's him talking right now. I know it," Lady said. His loud and pompous voice was unmistakable.

"You're sure?" Barbara asked. "You're really sure?"

There was no doubt. Shortly after leaving the *Daily News*, Lady contacted internal affairs and the special victims unit to identify Tolstoy as her attacker. "He doesn't deserve to wear the police badge. If he did it to me, he'll strike again," she said.

And yet Tolstoy remained on the street. Barbara and I thought this was mind boggling, indicative of a back-slapping good ol' boys culture in which a cop's word trumps a woman's damning and convincing accusation. At the time, we didn't know that internal affairs had a file on Tolstoy.

Barbara and I went back to the search warrant room. We had little to go on. No names or addresses, just a hunch that we'd find other victims.

We pulled search warrants for raids in which Tolstoy was present, combing through three years' worth. Out of thousands, we set aside at least 150 warrants that listed Tolstoy's badge number.

The warrants gave us the addresses and dates of the raids. To find people, Barbara and I typically used a database that culled information, like home mortgages, liens and bankruptcies, civil suits and voter records, creating thumbnail people profiles. All we had to do was type an address into the database, and names of occupants, both former and current, would pop up. But the women we were looking for lived off the grid. They didn't have landlines, their cell phone numbers changed constantly, and they moved every few months.

Barbara and I would have to rely on old-fashioned shoe leather to find potential Tolstoy victims. The method was inefficient, tedious, and tiresome. We'd often arrive at a house to find the tenants long gone. Other times we'd find the house abandoned, the windows and doors boarded with graffiti-marred plywood. We kept in touch via cell phone, updating each other on our progress—or lack thereof.

Occasionally we went out together, and of course Barbara drove. One afternoon, we turned down a narrow street and found ourselves in the middle of a feud. Two men, each surrounded by their own posse, stood on opposite sides of the street, cursing at each other. One of the men walked over to a parked car and popped the trunk. "I'm gonna get my piece," he said.

"Oh shit. Did he say he's getting his piece?" I said.

"Yeah, we need to get out of here," Barbara said.

That's all we need, to get killed in the crossfire, I thought.

Barbara hit the gas, the car lurched forward, and she sped through the stop sign. "Whoa, Slicey," I cautioned. Barbara stretched her right arm across my chest, like the protective bar on an amusement park ride, as I jammed my hands against the dashboard. We came to a dead stop, stuck behind an idling car parked in the middle of the one-way street. The driver was yapping to a guy on a stoop. This wasn't a part of town where you wanted to beep your horn. We had two choices: wait, or reverse down the street. We waited.

When we finally tracked down people who got raided, they told us a slew of horror stories about the cops. Tolstoy and his squad members splintered doors with battering rams, urinated in bathtubs, poured bleach on family photos, upended couches, and sliced open cushions. The cops ordered pizza or made a McDonald's run and then discarded empty boxes, Styrofoam containers, and food wrappers all over the house. They helped themselves to beer and vodka, drinking straight from the bottle. They spewed venom—"You people live like animals" and "This place stinks like shit." They swiped whatever caught their eye—PlayStations, video games, CDs, jewelry. They always took money and even smashed kids' piggy banks and pocketed coins.

Almost everyone Barbara and I talked to remembered Jeff, the cop they described as "the tall one with the blue eyes." They mostly remembered his lunatic rants. "Get the fuck on the floor. Shut the fuck up!"

Jeff's style was all gangbusters. "He started out with no re-spect," a narcotics cop told us. "He'd say, 'I have pictures of you, if you don't tell me where the drugs are, you'll lose your kids.' He'd lose control. He started with chaos."

But in Jose's video, Barbara and I saw a softer side to Jeff. When the cops raided the store, a boy, roughly twelve years old, was inside.

The cops usher the boy to the front of the store and tell him to put his hands up. He stands with his back to the camera, his hands cupped to the back of his head, elbows out. Dressed in khaki shorts and a lime green shirt, the boy is a statue as an officer searches his pockets for a gun. Jeff approaches the boy and gingerly questions him. "Where do you live at? In the hood?" Jeff asks his name and age, then lightly pats the boy's stomach and tells him to scram.

Barbara and I saw a tenderness there. It was like Jeff was two people.

We were getting a more complete picture of these cops. After each house we visited, Barbara and I made little nota-tions on the search warrant:

> This is a crack house. White girl (messed up) answered door. Didn't want to talk; Mary Lou says the cops found small amount of pot in her house, stole two PlayStations and money; Fat short white guy choked me. I had kid-ney and pancreas transplant, threw me on the floor; Broke ceiling fans, asked me where cash box was, took $1,500, no woman there; Big guy put gun in my face and said what will happen if I pull the trigger.

Between my sleep-deprived mommy brain and Barba-ra's early-onset senility, plus the sheer number of homes, we relied on these scribbled notes to keep track of which doors we'd knocked on and what people had to say about the raids.

At least a dozen women told us that Tolstoy and the other cops in his squad had degraded and demeaned them.

A forty-eight-year-old woman named Denise described Tolstoy's modus operandi. The cop, whom she described as white and stocky with brown hair, took her alone to an upstairs bedroom. "What's your chest size?" the officer asked, eyeing up Denise's generous breasts in her low-cut white summer dress. Denise gave him lip and more than a little attitude: "What has that got to do with anything?" With that, the cop backed down and didn't touch her.

In another summertime raid, a thirty-year-old woman was asleep, naked, when the cops whooshed into her bedroom. She sat up, startled, gripping the bedcovers to her chest.

"I'm not dressed. I'm not dressed," she shouted, but an officer, whom she described as white with a big belly, scruffy brown hair, and a small goatee, yanked the sheets from her fingers so viciously that she thought he was going to rape her. The woman reached for her clothes and turned to dress with her back to the cops, but the officer who pulled off the covers ordered her to face them. She stood naked before them. She was so terrified that she put her clothes on inside out. The cops sent her downstairs, and she heard them cackling in her bedroom. After they left, she found her personal items, including the couple's sex toys, strewn around the room. They removed a black leather teddy from a drawer and laid it out on top of her dresser. The whole scene frightened her. The cops arrested her thirty-five-year-old husband for giving a few of his prescription painkillers to a friend. The couple lived in Cop Land, a term Barbara and I used to refer to the section of Philadelphia that many police officers, firefighters, and other city employees called home. The woman and her husband weren't drug dealers; they were hardworking middle-class people, and the raid humiliated and wounded them. They felt such shame.

"I'll never get that day out of my head," the woman told me. "Ever since this happened, I don't sleep. I'm not comfortable in my house. . . . I felt like all my dignity had been stripped from me."

Barbara and I were disturbed and repulsed by the cops' behavior. Nothing pissed us off more than men in power who preyed on vulnerable women, and on a Friday night in May, Barbara would meet yet another Tolstoy victim.

25

BARBARA STOOD IN THE CENTER OF A WEARY BLOCK OF THAYER STREET IN WEST KENSINGTON, WHERE THE ACID OF THE DRUG TRADE HAD EATEN AWAY at its core. A pair of sneakers dangled from a utility wire that sagged from one side of the street to the other, probably a signpost, placed by dealers, to let junkies know that crack was sold here and to mark the block as theirs. Barbara could roll her foot over a drift of litter and find quarter-size drug baggies obscured by sticky soda cans, broken beer bottles, and Chinese takeout menus.

Tolstoy's squad had raided at least five homes on this block. Every single one was now boarded, some with plastic tarps covering glassless second-story windows.

Abandoned homes were a pox on neighborhoods like this. There were some 40,000 vacant homes or lots in Philadelphia, and the drug war nudged that number higher. Under state forfeiture laws, the city district attorney's office had the power to seize drug homes, which then sat empty for months, even years. Drug addicts weaseled through plywood to make crack dens or shooting galleries. Stray dogs and cats took refuge in basements with dirt floors and rodents burrowed into soggy drywall. Neighbors on either side struggled to keep the scourge at bay.

Barbara took in the decay around her—slumped roofs on the verge of collapse, crumbled brick facades, rotted wooden porches, and missing front steps. It was around seven on a Friday night, and Barbara, tired and beaten down, called me. I was at my desk, flipping through Tolstoy search warrants in a manila folder marked "cases w/potential."

"Wendy, I'm on Thayer, and these houses are boarded," she said. "I don't know how we're going to find these people."

"Just come on back. It's getting dark," I said.

For eight weeks now, Barbara and I had been out knocking on doors. Winter had given way to spring, and summer was almost here. Each night, we went home sweaty and dirty. Our clothes and hair reeked of cigarette smoke and household insecticide, and our legs were pocked with flea bites. One night, I tossed my work bag on the stone-tiled porch and a plump cockroach crawled out. I yelped and stomped it to death.

Barbara wasn't ready to give up on Thayer Street. "I'm already here. Let me try a couple more neighbors," she told me.

Barbara climbed the steps to a rickety and cluttered porch, haphazardly covered in green outdoor carpeting. The man who opened the door was short, with a pencil mustache and ink-black hair, slicked back into curls at the nape of his neck. His name was Angel Castro, and he warmed quickly to Barbara. He vividly recalled the raid at the house next door.

In a raid led by Tolstoy, the cops stormed into Angel's

neighbors' house looking for marijuana. Soon after the cops left, a woman emerged; she stood sobbing on her porch.

"Are you okay?" Angel asked softly from his adjoining porch.

"No," she said. Little by little, Angel coaxed details from her. "An officer touched my breasts. . . . He was feeling up on me. . . . He rubbed up on me."

Barbara got excited. "Oh, Angel. Do you know her name? Do you know where she lives now? Can you help me? Please, I have to find her."

Her name was Dagma Rodriguez, and Angel thought he might be able to trace her whereabouts through friends and relatives. "Let me make some calls," he said, and Barbara took a seat next to him on the porch. About an hour later, Angel had an address.

Barbara leaped up and hugged him, then bolted to the car, where she called to tell me, rapid-fire, what Angel had told her. "Can you believe it? I'm telling you, Wendy, we're going to find this woman." I gave Barbara directions to Dagma's house.

There was no way I was going home until I heard back from Barbara. I sat at my computer and gnawed at the jagged skin around my fingernails. Most everyone had gone home for the weekend, but the light was still on in Michael Days's office. I ran through the newsroom and breathlessly flew through his door. "Michael! I'm so excited . . ."

Barbara pulled up at Dagma's house ten minutes later. Dagma's cousin cracked open the door and said Dagma wasn't home; she was out with her fiancé and would be back later that night. Barbara explained why she wanted to talk to Dagma. "Do you mind if I wait for her? I'll just be out here. In my car."

Barbara sat in the dark and thought about Tolstoy. She felt for Dagma and knew what it was like to feel violated. When Barbara was in high school, a boyfriend had tried to force himself on her. She cried no and shoved him away. "You're cold. You're just a prude. No one will ever love you," he sneered.

Dagma arrived home in an old beat-up Chevy. "A reporter is here to talk to you," Dagma's cousin told her as she stepped out of the car. "She wants to know what happened during the raid."

Dagma walked slowly toward Barbara, as if in a trance. Barbara thought Dagma was tentative and leery; she wasn't sure the woman would want to talk about the raid. Then Dagma held out her arms and embraced Barbara. She clutched Barbara tightly for a few long seconds. Dagma stepped back, wiped a tear from her cheek, and said something that Barbara would never forget: "I've been praying for this day."

Dagma recounted the dinnertime raid. It was a tale that would make Barbara despise Tolstoy.

Dagma's fiancé, Armando, was cooking rice and beans and frying chicken drumsticks on the stove when Tolstoy and eight other cops slammed open the front door. "What are you doing—killing cats?" one cop said.

When a cop, whom Dagma would later identify as Jeff, saw the family's pit bull, Goldie, he yelled, "Get the fucking dog out of here before I shoot it."

The cops flipped over the futon couch, ripped a closet door off its metal hinges, and tossed clothes, CDs, everything they had, on the floor. "Where's the fucking gun? Where's the fucking drugs!"

Tolstoy almost immediately spied Dagma, who stood in the living room wearing a lime-green nightgown over a pair of gray sweatpants. He cornered her: "Do you have any tattoos? Let's talk."

Dagma's three kids—ages fifteen, nine, and eight—were outside on a porch of splintered wood planks. The cops had threatened to board her house, take her kids, and throw her out in the street.

Tolstoy led her upstairs. He told her everything would be all right. He just wanted to talk. Dagma inched away from the beefy cop. They were alone in a back bedroom. The room was dark, cavelike, with just a glint of light from a shattered windowpane.

She placed one foot behind her, then the other, and pressed her back against the faded blue wall. Her palms, slick with sweat, fluttered against the cracked plaster. He moved closer. She felt his breath on her face.

"You know you got some big tits," he said. "What size are you? Can I touch them?"

"Please, please, no," she whimpered.

Tolstoy stood cocksure, his bay window of a belly thrust out. She saw a rabid look in his brown eyes.

"Can you show them to me?"

"No. No."

The thirty-three-year-old woman began to cry, tears streaking her smooth brown face framed by coils of long dreadlocks. She folded her hands and clasped them over her breasts. Her heart felt jammed in her throat, choking her. She feared she'd vomit.

"Don't cry. Shhh. Sshhh. Shut up. Be quiet."

She fell to her knees.

"Get up."

"I'm nervous, and I got heart problems. I need my heart pills," she said.

"C'mon. Get up. Get up!" He yanked her up by the elbows and pinned her against the wall.

Oh my God, he's gonna rape me, she thought.

He plunged his hands into the top of her nightgown. His thick fingers slithered under her beige bra. He rubbed her nipples, thumbs moving in circles.

She grabbed his wrists, her hands trembling, and cried louder.

"Shut the fuck up!" Tolstoy yelled.

Now, as he forcefully groped her breasts, she had no way to escape.

"I'm scared. I'm so scared," she told him.

"You don't have to be scared. Scared of what?"

Downstairs, the other narcotics cops noticed he was missing. They knew the deal.

A cop, whom Dagma described as tall and handsome with blue eyes, came halfway up the steps. "Is everything all right?" he called out.

Tolstoy took his hands from Dagma's breasts.

"Yeah. Everything's all right. We're about done here."

He stepped back, a smirk on his face. She slid down the wall and crumpled to the floor, wheezing and gulping.

Tolstoy paused in the doorway and looked back at her.

"Take your shit pills."

26

DAGMA'S STORY WAS UNIMPEACH-
ABLE. FOR STARTERS, SHE'D TOLD HER
FIANCÉ WHAT TOLSTOY DID TO HER
DURING A PHONE CALL TO THE JAIL,
where Armando was locked up after the
cops found three marijuana joints in his
pockets and a rusty, unloaded hunting rifle
inside the Thayer Street house.

"I went off. I was in jail, and there was
nothing I could do but punch the walls. All
I could think of was that he could go back
and do something more," Armando told us.

Next, there was Angel, who consoled
Dagma as she cried on the porch.

Lastly, on the night of the raid, Dagma
went to the nearest police district. She was
hysterical and shaken. "I'm here to make a
complaint against this cop who came to my
house." An officer who spoke Spanish took a
statement.

An internal affairs investigator later
came to Dagma's house. He wanted to bag

her nightgown, bra, and sweatpants as evidence, but Angel advised her not to turn over the clothes. Angel thought it unwise for her to part with the only physical evidence she had. Angel and Dagma's guardedness was symptomatic of a pervasive lack of trust between the community and police. Of course, the police department didn't help mend the rift.

Internal affairs showed Dagma a photo array of some eighty cops. The photos were headshots of uniformed cops. Most dated back years, likely taken when they first joined the force, and Dagma didn't recognize Tolstoy among all those baby-faced cops. "I felt like they were hiding him," Dagma said.

Tolstoy had assaulted Lady four months earlier. But unlike Dagma, Lady didn't file a police complaint immediately after the raid; she went to internal affairs after Barbara and I knocked on her door. Dagma's single complaint, coupled with an inability to identify her attacker, wasn't enough for internal affairs to restrict Tolstoy to a desk.

That all changed on October 16, 2008, when internal affairs yanked Tolstoy off the street. In the six months between Dagma's complaint and October 16, Tolstoy did something that got him red-flagged.

Police sources told us that Tolstoy had engaged in "sexual misconduct," and Barbara and I were almost positive that the incident was connected to the woman Benny had told us about, the woman who'd been fisted.

Benny thought the assault had happened near Torresdale and Orthodox Streets. Barbara and I pulled out a map, zeroed in on the intersection, and pressed "enlarge" on the Xerox machine, tapping the button until it reached 150 percent. We printed out two copies on eleven-by-seventeen paper and drew a fifteen-square-block radius in yellow highlighter.

We circled the intersection with a navy blue Sharpie. We left the office with folders crammed with search warrants for raids on homes within the area's zip code—19124.

We went together; of course Barbara drove. Karl had bought me a GPS for Mother's Day, but Barbara, who sometimes got lost while jogging around her own neighborhood, still managed to get all turned around. "Recalculating route," the GPS girl crooned in a calm, robotic voice. We heard her voice so often that we gave her a name—Henrietta. I wanted to throw the thing out the window.

Torresdale and Orthodox was a wide intersection with bus lanes. There was a pizza shop on one corner and a bodega across the street, next to an appliance store, where each morning the employees dragged used washers and dryers and fridges and stoves out onto the sidewalk, lining them up at curb's edge. There were several car-repair shops and a seedy gentlemen's lounge.

We split up the search warrants and fanned out on foot. In between knocking on doors, we ran down every woman we saw on the street. We ambushed them as they stepped off the bus, emerged from a shop, or ambled along the sidewalk, some with kids in strollers. We asked them if a cop had ever touched them inappropriately, and we were surprised by the number of women who, without hesitation, started off, "Oh yeah. There was this time when . . ."

They recounted chilling stories about a vice squad cop or district cop, or a cop who didn't fit Tolstoy's description. They'd say his name was John or Bill. Some said they'd never been sexually assaulted, but they had a friend or an acquaintance . . .

We had so many tips that Barbara and I didn't know which ones to chase. Some led us miles outside of the 19124 zip code. Because the women weren't sure whether the victim they knew had been "fisted" by a cop, we thought we had to find out—so we could at the very least rule her out. We even asked the women who had supplied the tips to drive around with us while they scanned the streets for the victim they described.

One description was of a white woman with blond, dirty blond, or mousy brown hair and a butterfly tattoo on her shoulder—or maybe her wrist. Barbara and I chased tattooed women down the street, trying to get a closer look.

We began to question whether the incident was even connected to a raid. What if Tolstoy had assaulted this woman somewhere out on the streets? Maybe she was a prostitute. Torresdale and Orthodox was a short 2.3-mile drive from the ground zero of lost souls, an area known as K&A—short for Kensington and Allegheny Avenues, where blow jobs went for $20 and full-on sex in a car or alley was just $10 more.

We spent hours talking to drug-addicted prostitutes with rotten teeth and scabbed faces and arms, the result of obsessively picking at their skin while high on crack. They wobbled around on rail-thin legs, wearing rhinestone-studded stilettos and miniskirts or worn-out Chuck Taylors and low-rise jeans. All had glazed eyes and vacant expressions.

"Are you ladies from the church?" a waiflike woman came up and asked us. Candace had an angelic face—catlike blue eyes, high cheekbones, and dirty blond hair pulled up in a ponytail. She was almost twenty-eight, though she looked no more than twenty. She was drug-worn but beautiful. In her fist, she clutched a wad of bills. She told us she desperately wanted to get clean; she wanted to be able to care for her four-year-old son. I gave her my card. A cop arrested Candace for drug possession a few days later, and she wrote me a letter from jail. "Ms. Ruderman, I honestly need help once return-ing home. My mom reminds me her home is not my home, due to my addiction . . . I do not want to repeat that lifestyle of drugs and prostitution. I write to you with hope of direc-tion. I therefore have no one else to turn to." She included a postscript, "PS, one day maybe you can write a story of my success."

I wrote her back and contacted a social worker who met with Candace in jail. Four days after Candace got released, and two months after we met her, Candace was dead of an overdose. It was heartbreaking.

Barbara and I grew frustrated, yet not discouraged. We decided to track down pimps, thinking it would be an easier and more efficient method to find a hooker who'd been vic-timized. We guessed that a prostitute might confide in her pimp.

A lot of the pimps we met didn't fit the stereotype. One was toothless and frail, in his sixties, and suffering from diabetes-related foot ulcers; another was a former hooker turned mother hen in her fifties. She had large, saggy breasts and wiry, broomlike gray hair.

She suggested we find a pimp named Omar, who had a stable of hookers, but she warned us that he was violent, possi-bly dangerous, known to smack his girls around.

I took one side of Kensington Avenue; Barbara took the other. The El trains whistled and click-clacked overhead. Bar-bara found one of Omar's hookers outside a mini-mart. The girl was skittish and her eyes shifted around in the sockets, chameleon-like. She gestured with her head toward me. "See that short little woman with the glasses . . ."

I was on the other side of the street, talking to a black man wearing a white knit skullcap, even though the temperature was pushing eighty. He sat on a concrete step, his back against a reddish brown door.

"Hi, I'm looking for Omar," I said. "Do you know him?"

"Yeah, I know him."

He was friendly, a bit of a jokester, and we started to chit-chat. Somehow we got on the subject of our favorite movies. We both liked films about police corruption, like *Serpico*. Laughing, I handed him my card and asked him to pass it on to Omar.

Barbara rushed toward me, crossing the street against the light. "What did he say?"

I was puzzled by her excitement. "He said he'd tell Omar we were lookin' for him."

"Wendy. That was Omar. You were talking to Omar."

I looked back, and he was gone. He'd slipped behind the reddish door. We knocked, and no one answered. I tugged on the handle, but the door was locked.

I got home, and Karl was watching a home-remodeling show on the DIY Network. My escape was work; his was fantasizing about projects that never got done. He was adorable, with those damn Bambi eyes and heart-shaped lips that broke into a gigantic smile. I leaned in and kissed him.

"How was work?"

"I spent all day looking for a pimp named Omar."

Karl put his hand up. "Please, I don't want to know. Don't tell me."

Barbara and I could do crazy. We understood crazy.

We both came from zany Jewish families that instilled a strong, often obsessive and neurotic work ethic. Karl summed up the Ruderman motto as "Work till you drop, then go out to a restaurant." I was surprised Karl, who came from a reserved Catholic family, married me.

A few months before our wedding, Karl went with my family on a trip to Martha's Vineyard. It was my mom's idea to go to a bathing-suit-optional beach. She stripped naked, wearing only sneakers and white tube socks, and slathered sunscreen all over her body. Karl averted his eyes. "Take a good look," she told Karl. "See these raisin boobs—this is what Wendy will look like in thirty years."

Barbara's mom was a rebel. Instead of settling down with a nice Jewish boy, she fell in love with a smooth-talking British goy. When the couple married, Barbara's grandmother sat shivah and threatened suicide; she refused to meet her daughter's new husband, never even spoke his name. Years ago, Barbara's dad worked on a cruise line, entertaining elderly women. He later described his job title as "cruise ship gigolo." Barbara wasn't sure he was joking.

People like Omar had nothing on Barbara's dad and my mom. Now, *they* were scary; they were uncorked and unfiltered, and Barbara and I were sometimes more afraid of what would fly out of their mouths than of getting hurt—or killed—while in pursuit of this mystery woman. But we also feared failure—and at times, that fear blinded us.

"You're putting this story ahead of your own safety," Hutch told Barbara. "You're losing touch with reality. You're all consumed with this story, but you're gonna knock on a door and get assaulted, raped, or robbed."

Hutch worried constantly about Barbara and gave her unsolicited advice on how to stay safe. Some of his suggestions made sense—carry Mace and step back, out of reach, after knocking on a stranger's door. Of course she did neither. Hutch also doled out advice that made us chuckle. "Before you go out, call the district cops, tell them you're a reporter for the *Daily News* and let them know where you are and what you're doing, and see if they can send someone by to check on you."

I worked so much that when I headed out one morning, Brody smirked and said, "Mom, it was so nice having you for a visit." He knew how to twist the knife.

When Karl went shopping or out for a jog, Sawyer asked, "Mom, are you babysitting us?"

I had largely relinquished my parenting role to Karl, but I still wanted control. I left Karl notes on the refrigerator or front door: "Don't forget to give Brody and Sawyer fruit." "Brush their teeth." "Make them eat carrots." I often added, "I love you," so Karl wouldn't be too mad.

Karl began to talk about getting a vasectomy, and I suspected that he wanted to get snipped just so he could veg on the couch for a weekend and get a break from the kids.

Barbara and I realized we were driving the people in our lives nuts, but we just couldn't stop. We kept coming back to the same search warrant. A raid that took place on October 16, 2008—the exact date Tolstoy was pulled from the street.

27

IT WASN'T JUST THE DATE ON THE SEARCH WARRANT THAT DREW OUR ATTENTION; IT WAS THE ADDRESS. THE COPS RAIDED AN APARTMENT—ON OR-THODOX STREET.

The apartment wasn't anywhere close to Torresdale, but Barbara and I had a strong feeling that this particular raid was key to our search for the woman. We repeatedly swung by the apartment. Sometimes we went together, other times separately. Each time no one was home, and we left business cards and notes, only to find them still jammed in the door seam when we returned.

The search warrant offered scant details. The cops were looking for a drug dealer named Beamer, whom they believed sold crack out of the apartment. During the 7:45 p.m. raid at the apartment, the cops found a gun and drugs, but they couldn't arrest Beamer because he wasn't home and they didn't know his real name.

"Beamer." That was all we had to go on.

Beamer no longer lived there, so Barbara and I canvassed the blocks around his old apartment, asking if anyone knew where we could find him.

The neighborhood was in the heart of a once-robust retail mecca of family-owned pharmacies, hardware stores, diners, florists, and shoe and clothing shops. The shopping district started to lose its luster in the late 1990s, when dollar stores and cash-for-gold pawnshops elbowed out the charm.

Despite the area's decline, many of the homes, including Georgian-style structures built in the late 1700s, retained their grace. Most homes were boxy free-standing, three-story twins separated by alleys. From the street, Barbara and I could see the Philadelphia skyline in the distance.

By now, a lot of the people we approached on the street knew who we were. All we had to do was mention *Daily News* and police corruption and they'd say, "Ohhh! You're the ones doing Tainted Justice." They were eager to help and loaded us up with first names of women who had lived in Beamer's apartment building: Latifa, Kia, Keiana, Tonya, Dashay, and Nicole.

Barbara and I were convinced that Beamer had some kind of connection to this woman. To find him was to find her. But no one seemed to know where Beamer had moved.

Then on a warm, sunny afternoon, I met Shante. When I first approached her as she sat on a front stoop, I wasn't sure if she was a man or a woman. Her head was shaved, and she reminded me of a black Sinead O'Connor. She wore knee-length jean shorts, brown Timberland boots, and a wife-beater, or ribbed white tank top, that showed off her muscular biceps.

Shante was a twenty-one-year-old convicted drug dealer,

openly gay, with a sexy, raspy voice. She'd been locked up at least six times, beginning at age sixteen, when she was found guilty of attempted murder in a bloody shootout. Shante's street name was Pop, and Barbara and I wondered if the nickname sprang from the shooting, though Shante claimed Pop was a reference to her old soul ways. She was fiercely loyal to family and friends, a street lioness who protected and provided for her loved ones.

On her Facebook page, she posted photos of herself holding wads of cash, getting high, and wearing designer Air Jordans. Shante was proud of her plum-shaped lips and poked fun at her gut, calling herself "fatboy shit."

Tattoos covered Shante's neck, upper chest, arms, and hands. The designs were rudimentary, inked in one color, either black or navy. Some of Shante's tattoos were the work of a guy named Skinny who made house calls, like the Fuller Brush man. Shante wanted to get rid of a tattoo that read DANGER. "This is gone," Shante said, rubbing her neck. "It was a girl I used to mess with." Two teardrops, tattooed in black ink, were etched under her left eye, just above her cheekbone. On her right arm she sported a tattoo of comedy-tragedy theater masks, with the words GOOD GIRL BAD GIRL. That about summed her up.

Shante not only knew Beamer, they were close friends, and she had his cell number programmed into her phone. She wouldn't give me Beamer's number, but she promised that she'd tell him we were looking for him. When I didn't hear from Shante, I called her—a lot. "I'm so sorry. I know you must think I'm the biggest pest, but . . ."

A week or so later, late in the evening, I called Shante yet again. She picked up, and I could hear music and laughing in the background. She sounded giddy, and I wondered if she was high. I took a deep breath. "Shante, I haven't heard from Beamer yet. Can you please just give me his number?" To my amazement, she did.

Barbara offered to call Beamer, and I agreed that was a good idea. Barbara had a knack for cracking tough nuts. She could have broken Al Capone.

But each time she tried Beamer's number, no one answered, and Barbara decided to stop by Beamer's old apartment for the fourth time. A teenage girl answered the door, called her mom at work, and handed Barbara the phone. The girl's mom was furious. "Listen, I'm tired of you and that other reporter coming around here. I told the police the same thing—'The woman doesn't live here anymore. I don't know who she is, and I don't know where she went.' Just leave us alone."

Barbara zoomed back to the office. "Wendy, this has got to be the right place. The cops had been there. They were looking for a woman." We decided to play our last card. Barbara called a source on the FBI–internal affairs task force. Barbara knew to ask a narrow question, one with a yes or no answer. This way, the source wouldn't feel too exposed.

"I'm going to give you three addresses. All you have to do is tell me if the address is familiar to you. Okay," Barbara asked.

"Okay," the source said.

Barbara gave him the Orthodox Street address first. "Yes," he said, "that's familiar."

The task force was looking for the woman, too, and at this point, the source figured Barbara and I might have a better chance of finding her. He knew we were tenacious; he also knew that people on the street often felt more comfortable talking to us than to police investigators.

"If you find her, can you try to convince her to contact us?" the source asked, and Barbara agreed.

Beamer. Beamer. Beamer. We had to find him. I was giving up hope. It was about 8:30 on a Friday night. I rolled a chair next to Barbara, and she dialed Beamer's number. I heard a muffled hello, and Barbara stiffened and gripped my arm. I clenched both my fists and pumped them up and down, wearing an alligator smile. Go, go, go, go, Barbara. C'mon, c'mon, do it.

"I'm soooo happy to finally talk to you. You just don't know," Barbara cooed, her moss-colored eyes bulging as she glanced at me and nodded like a bobblehead.

Barbara explained that she was looking for a woman who'd been sexually assaulted by a cop during the raid at his apartment. "We know he's done this to other women. . . . This is your chance to do the right thing and see justice."

I rolled my eyes. Barbara stopped talking, and Beamer said he'd help us. He knew the woman and thought he might see her over the weekend. He promised to call Barbara back.

"Thank you. Thank you so much, Beamer," Barbara gushed. "You're my hero."

I gently punched Barbara in the arm. She was incorrigible. I later teased Barbara about her new hero after we learned that Beamer was a twenty-eight-year-old pimp who ran a brothel.

Because Barbara had been editor for a few years, the *Daily News* hadn't given her a work cell and she hadn't thought to ask for one. So she used her personal phone for the Tainted Justice series. But now this was becoming a problem. Unfamiliar numbers popped up on Barbara's cell at all hours. She was never sure whether the caller was a pimp, drug dealer, crackhead—or a suitor from Match.com.

Barbara kept her phone within earshot all weekend, even while gardening or bathing. At a dinner party, Barbara placed her phone in front of her on the table. "I'm really sorry. I'm expecting an important call from Beamer." Her friends just looked at her.

He never called. Early Monday morning, Barbara couldn't take it anymore. She paced around her back deck and dialed his number. "Yeah, I talked to her," Beamer said casually. "She's really scared, but . . ."

Beamer gave Barbara the woman's first name—we'll call her Naomi—and her number.

Barbara called me right away. "Wendy, Beamer came through. My hero came through," she said, tickled with delight.

28

NAOMI AGREED TO MEET WITH BAR-
BARA AND ME, BUT SHE WAS PETRI-
FIED OF THE COPS, TERRIFIED THAT
TOLSTOY AND HIS CRONIES WOULD
harm her if she talked. We picked her up
about a block from her new apartment. She
slipped into the backseat and slid down, ob-
scuring the side of her face with her right
palm. Barbara drove us out of the area.

Naomi was twenty-four and eight months
pregnant with her fourth child. She sup-
ported her kids—ages four, two, and one—
and her out-of-work father with a part-time
job at a child day care and help from
public assistance. Her black hair, which
she straightened, fell like a smooth, velvety
sheet down her back. A thick curtain of
bangs stopped just above her eyes, the color
of coffee beans. She was reticent by nature,
her emotions enclosed within eggshell-thin
walls. She had a regal air about her.

Naomi had been living on Orthodox

Street for about a month when the cops raided the apartment building. Beamer wasn't her pimp or her boyfriend; he was her landlord, or so she thought.

She had bumped into Beamer, an acquaintance, on the street while looking for a place to live. Beamer was a slickster who never missed an opportunity to make some extra cash. The tenants who had lived on the second floor got evicted, and the apartment sat empty. Beamer, who lived in the first-floor apartment, masqueraded as the building's landlord and duped Naomi into paying him $200-a-month rent for a room upstairs. She was essentially a squatter, though she didn't realize it at the time.

Barbara and I offered to take her to lunch. Naomi picked a hole-in-the-wall pizza joint where she ordered a single slice, eating only a few bites, and no drink.

She spoke in whispers, recounting in a flat, detached voice what Tolstoy had done to her, as if the assault had happened to a stranger.

The night of October 16 was unseasonably warm, and Naomi was getting ready for a night out with her live-in boyfriend, Raheem. Naomi's kids were spending the night at her mom's house. She stepped out of the tub and began to towel off. Suddenly, a loud boom from the downstairs apartment rattled the floor beneath her, and Naomi flinched. The sound startled her, and she quickly dressed, pairing a pink and white spaghetti-strap top with a mini jean skirt. Her skin still warm from soapy bathwater, Naomi walked to the stairwell and inched gingerly down the steps to see what was going on. One after the other, cops powered upstairs toward her.

The cops ordered Naomi and Raheem to go to the first floor, where they cuffed them with plastic restraints. The couple couldn't understand why the cops were there, and so many of them—ten in all.

"Where are the drugs?" one cop yelled.

"We don't have any drugs," Naomi replied.

"Where's this guy Beamer?" a cop asked.

"I don't know. We're just renting a room from him," she explained.

Naomi noticed Tolstoy eyeing her up and down. There was something sinister about him.

"I need to talk to you upstairs," Tolstoy told her.

Tolstoy directed her to the steps and she complied, with him following closely behind. Raheem, who stayed downstairs with the other cops, lost sight of her.

"Look. We're not doing anything wrong," she warily told Tolstoy, her hands restrained behind her back, as she treaded upstairs. "Really. We don't have any drugs."

"Be quiet," he said. She sensed frustration in his tone. "I just want to talk to you. I'm just going to ask you more questions, and then I'll take off the handcuffs."

They reached the landing, and Tolstoy freed her hands. They stood in the doorway of her apartment.

"You know anyone in the area who sells crack cocaine?"

"No, Officer."

"You sure you have nothing in your room?"

"I have nothing, Officer. I'm sure."

"Well, I have to see for myself."

She told him he could look all over the apartment; she had nothing to hide. She expected Tolstoy to ransack her room, but he didn't.

"I'm gonna need to see under your shirt."

"But I have no bra on."

"That's OK," Tolstoy said.

She asked if he could send up a female officer. Tolstoy ignored her request.

"You know I could lock you up for the drugs we found downstairs."

Naomi knew that made no sense, but she was too scared to argue. Her hands quivered as she slowly lifted up her pink and white top. Not saying a word, Tolstoy's meaty hands clasped her breasts with his fingers moving in a caressing squeeze.

"Lift up your skirt," he told her.

Naomi again asked for a female officer, and Tolstoy again threatened to lock her up for drugs that weren't hers.

Naomi gripped the denim and slowly lifted the skirt up.

"I have to see in your underwear."

Naomi tugged her panties down just slightly, just enough to show him she had nothing hidden there. Tolstoy lurched forward and yanked her panties down further.

"Please. I don't feel comfortable with that," she begged.

"Be quiet."

Tolstoy jammed his index and middle fingers into her vagina. He thrust them inside her with a violent jab. Naomi turned her head to the side, avoiding his face. If I don't look at him, I won't feel anything, she thought.

Naomi winced at the pain. She could feel the burn, the sting as she began to bleed.

She backed up, trying to pull away from him. She reached down and tried to pull up her panties with one hand and push down her skirt with the other.

"I don't want you touching me like that," she whimpered.

"I'll have to put you back in handcuffs."

"Stop," she cried. "Stop."

He grabbed her shoulders with such force that the spaghetti strap of her shirt broke off.

Tolstoy's expression changed instantly. His eyes became saucer-like. He looked flustered, almost fearful.

"If they ask you how your strap broke," he told her, "you tell them you always tie it, and it just came loose."

After the cops left, Raheem went upstairs to find Naomi. The first thing he noticed was her torn shirt, then the terror in her eyes. She told him she was bleeding, that the cop hurt her, maybe scratched her or caused internal damage.

They walked almost a mile to the nearest hospital where Naomi gave the staff a false name—Asia Johnson. Naomi was vague with the details.

"I just want to get myself checked out. I just feel funny down there," she told nurses. "I just want to make sure I'm okay." She was too embarrassed to say exactly what Tolstoy did, but nurses suspected immediately that she'd been sexually assaulted.

"I know there's something going on," a nurse gently told her.

The staff called uniformed cops to escort Naomi and Raheem to another hospital, where the special victims unit was located. Nurses ordered a rape kit and alerted SVU investigators, who bagged her ripped shirt and underwear as evidence, and told her they'd run DNA tests. Naomi pulled aside a female officer. "My name's not Asia Johnson," she whispered. "I made up the name because I was scared."

Naomi didn't know Tolstoy's name. But internal affairs had more than a hunch. Dagma had made a similar complaint six months earlier, and at the time she, too, couldn't identify Tolstoy by name. But in both cases, Tolstoy was the only cop who had been alone with the women.

So internal affairs took Tolstoy off the street the same night that Naomi showed up at the special victims unit.

Two days after the assault, Naomi was walking down the sidewalk near her apartment when two uniformed cops pulled their police car to the curb beside her. The cop on the passenger side rolled down his window and asked her what happened in her apartment.

"Nothing happened," she said, hoping they'd drive off and leave her alone.

"We've got some information . . . ," the cop began. She ignored him, turned around, and walked off. The cop leaped out of the car, thrust her arms behind her back, handcuffed her, and threw her in the back of the cruiser.

Naomi insisted that this cop was Tolstoy, but Barbara and I couldn't prove it. Tolstoy was on desk duty at the time, but there was a possibility that Tolstoy met up with a cop buddy after work. We knew Tolstoy's squad was chummy with the patrol cops in Naomi's neighborhood. Two district cops had given the squad the initial tip about Beamer dealing crack out of his apartment.

"Whatever you said, take it back," the cop said, all red-faced as he glared at her.

"I don't know what you're talking about," she said.

"You'll be seeing me around," he warned. Then he let her go.

Naomi ran to a pay phone and dialed her mom, who came to pick her up. Together they went to the police district to file a report. But the officers told Naomi they needed a name of the cop who stopped her.

"Listen. We have thousands of police officers."

Naomi and her mom left, disgusted and frustrated. Naomi moved from her apartment on Orthodox Street to her mom's house in New Jersey. Then the phone calls started. Naomi's cell rang at all hours from restricted or unavailable numbers.

"Drop it."

"Don't say nothing."

"I know where you're at."

"We'll find you."

Naomi suspected the callers were cops. She and her mother changed their phone numbers several times, but the calls continued, and Naomi grew afraid to leave home.

Then one day, roughly five weeks after the raid, two investigators showed up at Naomi's mom's house. They sat the two women down and explained they had some evidence linking an officer to the sexual assault. They wanted Naomi to press criminal charges. She just couldn't do it.

"I wouldn't mind going to court if I knew he was going to get locked up," she said. "I'd go to court, but it's not just him making the phone calls. It's not just him stopping me. I don't want to walk down the street and worry what will happen."

Naomi refused to cooperate, and then she disappeared, moving from her mom's house to another apartment. Internal affairs investigators lost track of her. Without Naomi, they decided they didn't have enough to keep Tolstoy on desk duty. So on January 12, 2009—three months after the assault—Tolstoy was put back on the street.

It wasn't until Lady, Dagma, and Naomi all told similar stories to internal affairs that police superiors felt they had no choice. They couldn't leave Tolstoy out there. On April 2, 2009, Lady went to the special victims unit and internal affairs to name Tolstoy as her attacker. The next month, on May 20, 2009, Tolstoy was put back on desk duty and had to relinquish his service weapon.

"Until we investigate further, we don't want him taking police action. We don't want to expose the city to other accusations or to any liability or risk," internal affairs chief inspector Anthony DiLacqua told us.

Barbara called Lady and Dagma to let them know that Tolstoy was off the street. They were grateful and relieved, though forever traumatized.

"I felt like a pig," Dagma told Barbara. "He made me feel so bad. I felt disgusting. I didn't even want to be touched no more from nobody. I was aggravated with myself. I hated myself that instant because I wish that never would have happened to me. I just wanted to run away where no one can find me and just run, run, and leave everything, everything behind, but it's something that I can't do. I can forgive, but I will never, ever forget."

Tolstoy targeted Dagma, Lady, and Naomi for a reason. Each was beautiful, with smooth skin, full sensual lips, and large brown eyes framed by curly lashes. They were pleasers— soft-spoken, slightly fearful of authority, with no arrest record, the type of women who put the needs of their men and their children before their own. They constantly doubted themselves, but beneath the insecurity, there was a sunniness, an optimism. Lady and Dagma shared an inner strength and resolve that propelled them to allow the *Daily News* to print their full names and photos. Dagma and Lady also agreed to do videos, which we posted online. Even now, when Barbara and I watch the videos, we're moved to tears—awed by their courage.

29

BARBARA AND I SPENT THE FALL
CHASING NEW TIPS ABOUT NARCOT-
ICS COPS GONE ROGUE. WE LOOKED
INTO CLAIMS OF MONEY LAUNDERING,
shady real-estate deals, a $50,000 theft of
drug money from a notorious motorcycle
club, and the blackmailing of prostitutes
who advertised on Craigslist. On each lead,
we ran smack into a dead end.

While we spun our wheels, exhausting
ourselves, the police department moved
forward with reforms. For the first time in
twenty-three years, police brass put out a
new directive that placed tighter controls on
narcotics officers and their confidential informants.

The new regulations spelled out what
narcotics cop could and could not do with
informants. Some of the dos and don'ts on
the list were so obvious they were almost
comical: No sexual relationships. No gifts.
No social, financial, or business dealings.

Police Commissioner Ramsey also appointed a chief integrity officer to scrutinize drug cases that used informants. The reforms recognized that the relationship between a cop and his informant was potentially toxic. Drug informants weren't trustworthy, and corruptible cops couldn't be trusted to work with them, not without close supervision. From now on, all contact between the two, including phone conversations and meetings, had to be documented and reviewed by higher-ups, and a supervisor had to witness all police payouts to informants.

The police department finally got what some of Benny's relatives had been saying all along: as Jeff and Benny grew more dependent on one another, their relationship was poisonous. Jeff earned about $100,000 a year, almost half from court overtime, and he won accolades and commendations for drug arrest numbers that soared—mostly on Benny's back. Benny used some of the money he earned helping to take down dealers to feed his own drug habit. They were addicted to each other.

Barbara and I only came to understand this after we spoke with Susette, the woman Benny called his first wife, and their three adult children—Susette Jr., Benny Jr., and Iesha.

"They were using each other," twenty-six-year-old Benny Jr. said. "But it was like my dad was going down, and Jeff was going up."

Barbara and I sat in Susette's living room, where the family explained that Benny was, and probably always would be, an addict. He liked it all—crack, cocaine, marijuana, and pills.

He'd been in and out of rehab at least four times, and even now, he would pawn almost anything for a fix.

When Susette was in Puerto Rico for her grandmother's funeral, Benny claimed someone broke into their house through a back window and stole a television and Benny Jr.'s

Nintendo, but Susette knew better. When Benny Jr. was fifteen, he bought a new bike with money he earned as a stock boy at a sneaker store, but his father snuck it out of the basement and sold it for crack. Benny Jr. asked his father what happened to his $250 GT bicycle. At first Benny denied knowing anything about it, then he just said, Yeah, I took it. "He didn't give a reason. I already knew," Benny Jr. said. When Susette realized her high school graduation ring and her grandmother's necklace were missing, she forced Benny to tell her what he'd done with them. Susette marched over to the drug dealer's house to try to buy the jewelry back.

Time after time, Benny called Susette from dark, fetid crack dens, where she'd find him sprawled out on a filthy mattress, immobilized by paranoia. "Don't let him back in here," Susette rebuked the dealer as she dragged Benny out to the car. She screamed at him the whole ride home.

"Sorry, Susette. I'll never do it again," he vowed.

She thought, Yeah, right. "Da, da, da . . . I'm not going to get you no more. That's on you."

When the kids were little, Susette covered for Benny. But when they grew older, she wanted them to understand the poison. She dug around in Benny's pockets and fished out a baggie of crack. She sat the kids down at the kitchen table and held the drugs out in her open palm. "This is what your father is doing," she told them. She walked stoically into the bathroom and flushed the drugs down the toilet.

Benny's habit only grew worse after he started working with Jeff. Benny sometimes sampled the drugs during a buy, claiming if he didn't, the dealer might suspect he was a snitch or an undercover cop. At the end of the night, Jeff handed Benny his informant pay and dropped him at a corner near his house, but Benny didn't go home. He disappeared for days.

Susette called Jeff to let him know. "Benny went out and did this for you, and now he didn't come back. He's doing his stuff out there. You know he's snorting coke and smoking crack," she said.

"Nah. Not Benny," Jeff said.

"He's always out there doing stuff with you, and then he gets caught up because he has to try it. He keeps on," she told him.

"He doesn't have to try nothing. Benny comes out and he's perfectly fine," Jeff said.

Jeff either didn't believe her or didn't want to listen.

Benny Jr. called Jeff five times, sometimes crying:

"My dad is on drugs heavy."

"My dad has problems. You have to help my dad."

"You're making my dad worse."

"He's gonna kill himself, or someone's gonna kill him."

Still, Jeff wouldn't listen. He couldn't quit Benny. It was a vicious cycle—Jeff gave Benny money. Benny bought dope and now had a new address to give Jeff. Jeff set up a raid. Benny again got paid. Then Benny scoped out his next crack house. And on it went.

When Benny was off on a binge, he'd sell his sneakers for crack. "It would be a miracle if he'd come back with his shoes on. He'd come back barefoot," Benny Jr. said.

One day, Susette couldn't take it anymore. She wanted him out, but he refused to leave unless she gave him $2,500. "I asked at work about borrowing from my 401k. He went with me to cash the check," said Susette, who worked as a social worker. "Then I started thinking if I gave him the whole thing, I'd be behind. I gave him two thousand dollars and kept five hundred." Benny, who was already running around with Sonia, moved in with her.

For the big moments in the lives of his oldest children,

Benny was a no-show. In 2007, he bought Iesha a $500 dress for her Sweet Sixteen party, but he didn't give her what she wanted most. In front of the some 250 guests, Benny, as her father, was expected to perform a coming-of-age ceremony. Benny was supposed to remove Iesha's flat shoes and replace them with strappy heels to symbolize that she'd become a lady. Iesha cried, her face streaked with mascara, as Benny Jr. stepped in for their dad. He didn't go to her high school graduation, nor did he show for his two oldest kids.

"He was always promising stuff," Benny Jr. told us. "Like 'I'm going to take you to the Phillies game. I'm going to do this. I'm going to do that.' Somehow I would expect it. But after a while, I knew not to expect it."

Benny Jr. tried to act like he didn't care, like he was over it, but he wasn't—clearly. None of them were. They were wounded.

For Benny, being an informant was like having a legal license to do drugs. The police department essentially became Benny's pusher. Cops like Jeff were curbing the drug trade— and at the same time feeding it. When Jeff evicted Benny and deactivated him as an informant, Benny lost a key pipeline to money and drugs.

Barbara and I thought that Jeff might not have known that Benny was an addict. We kept coming back to the fact that Jeff rented a house to Benny. "Would you rent a house to a known crackhead?" Barbara asked me when we wrestled with it in our heads. "You'd have to be crazy." Jeff also helped Benny get jobs with his friends, including current and former cops who had started their own businesses.

Benny never came across, at least not to Barbara and me, as a dope fiend. He was a master at hiding it. Up until Benny burned Jeff, Jeff probably thought he was a good judge of character and knew how to smell a con. I thought the same thing about myself.

Throughout the yearlong Tainted Justice series, Benny was my albatross. He would call me, not Barbara, whenever he had a problem. Barbara and I later speculated that Benny picked me because I had little kids. Brody and Sawyer were around the same age as Benny's two youngest, Giovanni and Gianni. On top of that, I was a pushover around kids, and Benny knew how to play me, knew just the right sob story to spin: he had no heat in the house and the kids got sick from the cold; he and Sonia couldn't afford to give the kids a Christmas; he'd spent what little money he had on Catholic school tuition for Gio.

Benny repeatedly told me, with slight variations, that his kids were suffering in the wake of the *Daily News* story about him. He said Gio didn't understand why the family had to keep moving. "I feel like we're running from place to place," Benny told me, crying. "I feel bad. I should be taking my son to Cub Scouts." Benny said he couldn't risk being seen with the kids. He couldn't walk them to school or take them trick-or-treating without putting their lives in danger. He painted himself as a good parent who was miserable because he couldn't give them a normal childhood or provide for them. He said that every time he tried to get a job, potential employers Googled him and got put off when they came across the *Daily News* story.

Other times Benny called and said he was being followed, convinced that this was the day his body would end up in a ditch. Sometimes Barbara and I believed that the day would come when we'd hear from Sonia, the police, whoever, that Benny was dead and we wondered how we'd live with the guilt. There were plenty of drug dealers who would get freed from prison and want street justice. Revenge and snitch murders were commonplace on Philly's streets.

But those who knew the rules of the hood told Barbara and me that anyone who wanted to off Benny would wait. They would make him sweat, for seven, eight years maybe, knowing that life on the run was no life. And time would protect his killer. Cops would be hard pressed to finger a suspect. There were too many to name, and the cases had grown rusty.

When Benny wasn't talking about his own murder, he claimed he'd kill himself, if not for the kids. "These little guys, they keep me going."

I was tortured by this. I spent hours talking to Benny on the phone, trying to console him while trying to console myself.

"Benny, I'm sorry. I feel like this is my fault."

"No. No. Noooo, Wendy," Benny said, before throwing in that FBI and internal affairs investigators always told him that Barbara and I didn't give a shit about him, we just wanted a story. "I tell them, noooo. Youse girls have been there for me."

Benny did a number on my head, and for the longest time, I couldn't disentangle myself from him. I bought Benny groceries for Thanksgiving and toys for his kids at Christmas and for Gio's birthday. At my weakest moments, Barbara stopped me from giving him money. "Wendy, don't do it." She reminded me that it would be unethical and would cross the line as a journalist; she saved me from myself. Jeff didn't have the same oversight. Jeff allowed himself to get sucked in by the drug trade's riptide, which separated him from his oath as a law enforcement officer.

When Barbara and I left Susette's house, we felt sick. I realized that we weren't to blame for the mess Benny had made of his life. I was done with Benny, done feeling responsible. I was free.

30

NOT SURPRISINGLY, BARBARA AND I
DIDN'T MAKE GEORGE BOCHETTO'S
CHRISTMAS CARD LIST.

That year Jeff's attorney sent out holiday
cards that could only have been dreamed
up by this contentious barrister. The card
featured a Photoshopped image of Bochetto
and his law partner swimming underwater,
surrounded by teeth-baring sharks and a
bosomy blonde in a skimpy bikini. In the
photo, Bochetto's wavy hair floats atop his
head and a plume of air bubbles rise up
from his nose. He's wearing a ferocious expression and his trademark pinstriped suit,
briefcase in hand. The card reads, "Liti-
gation is an ocean . . . full of sharks." The
words next to Bochetto and his law partner,
Gavin Lentz, say: "Man Eaters . . . George
and Gavin wish you an ocean of good fortune in 2010."

A *Daily News* reporter who had received Bochetto's card thought I'd find it

humorous and handed it to me. "I love it," I said, as I thrust a pushpin through Bochetto's forehead and tacked it up on the fabric-covered wall divider near my computer.

Barbara and I had moved past Tainted Justice to write stories on topics other than police corruption, and the *Daily News* was nearing the end of its fourteen-month slog through bankruptcy.

Philadelphia Media Holdings, which owned the *Daily News*, the *Inquirer*, and Philly.com, was more than $300 million in debt. Though the company cleared about $15 million in profit in 2009, that gain was gobbled up by $26.6 million in legal and professional fees associated with the bankruptcy. That expense included legal bills generated by the lenders, but paid for by Philadelphia Media Holdings.

The company was now slated for the auction block, where it would be sold to the highest bidder. For months, the auction was held up by a legal battle over credit bidding in federal court: company CEO Brian Tierney and his investment group wanted all the bids in cash; the senior lenders, who held the largest portion of the company's debt, wanted to use that debt as IOUs to bid on the company. Tierney wasn't expected to win the fight, but the US Court of Appeals for the Third Circuit handed him an improbable victory—and the auction was a go.

The victory meant Tierney stood a chance of holding on to the papers. Tierney ramped up his efforts to recruit investors who would go up against senior lenders. He approached every super-rich benefactor or businessman in the region and crisscrossed the country in search of civic-minded bidders. Tierney put it to them straight: This isn't an investment. It's philanthropy. We'd be saving a cultural gem, an institution with a community value that could never be measured in dollars.

This was a change in thinking for Tierney. Like a lot of publishers across the country, Tierney had believed that Internet advertising would save newspapers. He figured if he could drive up web traffic on Philly.com and increase the number of page views, he could charge more for online advertising. But even though the number of page views soared on Philly.com, the Internet became awash with competing websites, which drastically drove down the price of online advertising.

"This aspect of the business really scares the crap out of me," Tierney mused. "You look at it and you say to yourself, 'Online maybe isn't the future.' . . . That was the killer for the model."

Tierney finally realized that newspapers as a for-profit venture were a thing of the past. But that didn't stop him from fighting for his hometown papers, and he mounted a last stand against the lenders in the form of a "Keep It Local" advertising campaign that made them bristle.

"You're in Philadelphia, pal," Tierney said. "This is my town. . . . If this was a box-manufacturing company in Akron, I wouldn't be fighting like this. But I live here."

Tierney cast himself as the home-team backer, and the senior lenders, who included Angelo Gordon, a New York–based hedge fund that specialized in distressed debt, as vultures who would ruthlessly go after short-term dollars and erode the quality of journalism.

Tierney's sales pitch worked, and local investors—the very ones who had lost millions in the first 2006 go-around—once again agreed to put up money, this time sold on the notion that without their help, journalism in Philadelphia would die. The team assembled by Tierney also included new investors: benefactor David Haas, an heir to the Rohm & Haas chemical company fortune; Revlon chairman Ronald Perelman and his philanthropist father Raymond, who together threw in $27 million; and at the last minute, amid the heat of the auction, cable television mogul H. F. "Gerry" Lenfest, who went in for $10 million.

The reality of the impending auction didn't really hit Barbara and me. We were too focused on a fantasy. Barbara and I had already won two national awards for Tainted Justice. The *Daily News* had nominated Tainted Justice for a Pulitzer for investigative reporting, one of the hardest categories to win. Editors at big newspapers across the country nominate reporters every year. Being nominated was nothing more than a pat on the back by your colleagues. It had as much weight as a parent advocating that their kid deserved to be Student of the Year. The *Daily News* wasn't exactly a heavy hitter in Pulitzer world.

We couldn't bring ourselves to say the word, even though there was buzz that we had a shot. Almost every other day, Barbara scooched over to my desk, crouched down until her Cheshire Cat face was at eye level with mine, and began to sway, hands clasped, as if praying or gripped by a stomach cramp. "Wendy," she whispered, "can you imagine if we won the P? Imagine that?"

Any chance of winning would require a little divine intervention. I took out an old photo of my dad. In the photo, I'm no more than fifteen, wearing a sea-green sundress, my long bangs feathered back à la Farrah Fawcett. I'm smiling at the camera, and my dad is gazing at me adoringly. I kissed the image of my dad's face and tucked the photo under my pillow. While out for a jog, Barbara looked to the sky and talked to her mom. "Ma, please, please make this happen . . ."

My dad died in 1997; Barbara's mom died three years later, both of pancreatic cancer. Each was the parent who pushed us to achieve and understood what drove us. Barbara prayed to her mom when she was struggling and grieving over her divorce. I prayed to my dad for help when my three-year-old nephew developed a brain tumor. Barbara and I prayed to them when we wanted something really bad.

At exactly 3:00 p.m. on Monday, April 12, 2010, the winners would be posted on the Pulitzer website, and Barbara and I would know if our break-glass-in-an-emergency parents came through.

The Columbia University Graduate School of Journalism, which administered the Pulitzers, tried to keep the winners a secret until the announcement. A committee of top-tiered editors and journalists from across the country judged the Pulitzers. Committee members often had friends or colleagues at newspapers that submitted Pulitzer entries. Once the committee had whittled down the entries to a few finalists, leaks happened, and winners and finalists got a heads-up.

But on the Friday before the announcement, Barbara and I still hadn't heard anything. We lingered around until about 7:00 p.m., when Michael Days stopped by Barbara's desk on his way out. As the paper's top editor, he'd be the one to get tipped off.

"So I guess you haven't heard anything," Barbara said, looking at him, sullen, with her chin down and her head tilted to the side. Michael shook his head.

"You would have heard something by now, wouldn't you?" Barbara pressed.

"Probably," he said quietly. Michael promised to call her over the weekend if he got any news.

All weekend, Barbara waited for Michael to call. Nothing. By Sunday night, I was depressed. I turned off my cell and went to bed.

The next morning, I debated what to wear to work and whether to break out my contact lenses. I always felt more confident and less bookish without my eyeglasses. I settled on my beat-up ASICS sneakers, $2 black capris from Goodwill, a robin's-egg-blue granny sweater, and saggy cotton undies. I slipped on my glasses. It was my no-win-Pulitzer look, insurance against getting my hopes up. I gave Karl a long squeeze and a kiss.

"Good luck," he said.

"I know we didn't win."

Driving to work, I could barely see out the windshield, which was splattered with purplish white bird droppings, and I couldn't hear the radio over the rumble of my broken muffler. Barbara was just getting out of her car when I pulled into the parking lot. She wore fitted black slacks and a cotton-candy-pink sweater with a matching pink belt.

"I'm sooooo depressed," I said, as I hugged her.

"Me too."

For weeks Barbara and I had nurtured a tiny sprout of hope, and we didn't want that hope to die.

By 2:30 p.m. Barbara had a migraine, and I was holed up in Gar's office while he edited one of my stories. My phone rang.

"Any word?" Karl asked.

"Nope."

I hung up, releasing a puff of air through my lips. "Sorry, that was Karl. He wanted to know if we'd heard anything about the Pulitzer."

Gar seemed taken aback. The *Daily News* had won two Pulitzers in its eighty-five-year history—Richard Aregood won in 1985 for editorial writing, and Signe Wilkinson won for her editorial cartoons in 1992—and both times, Gar and the

rest of the newsroom had gotten word ahead of time. Gar
had plucked his sapling of hope and tossed it on the compost
pile days ago. He had no intention of replanting any seeds
until he checked with Michelle Bjork, the assistant managing
editor who'd entered our series in the Pulitzer contest.

Gar walked down the corridor to Michelle's office and
came back seconds later. "She hasn't heard a thing."

Staring us in the face was Gar's satirical poster, "Despair.
It's always darkest just before it goes pitch black." At that
moment, I didn't see any humor in it.

"It doesn't matter. This was a great series. These prizes are
all politics," Gar said, waving his arm dismissively.

At 2:55 p.m., Michael summoned Barbara and me to a
computer in the middle of the newsroom.

"Why does he want us to see that the *New York Times* or the
Washington Post won?" Barbara muttered in my ear.

"I'm not going over there," I told her.

"We have to. Michael wants us over there."

We walked over to the computer, feeling as if the entire
newsroom was about to witness our heartbreak.

31

AT 2:59 P.M., I CHEWED MY NAILS AND LOOKED DOWN AT THE FLOOR. BARBARA STOOD LIKE A STATUE, ARMS FOLDED, HER LIPS DRAWN TIGHT. MIchael seemed anxious, too. He pressed his right palm to his cheek. Michelle Bjork sat at the computer, the Pulitzer website already on the screen. She repeatedly tapped the refresh button, but the site had yet to be updated with the 2010 winners.

Then at 3:04 p.m., we heard shouts from across the room. "Yes! Yes! Yes!" It was Kevin Bevan, the burly lumberjack-like news editor who'd coined the phrase "Tainted Justice."

"Yes? Yes?" Michelle called out.

There it was on the computer screen. "2010 Pulitzer Prize winners: Investigative Reporting. Barbara Laker and Wendy Ruderman of the *Philadelphia Daily News.*"

The newsroom went bonkers. Gasps exploded into joyful shrieks and raucous cheers. Barbara and I sprang into the air like spastic crickets. Barbara's long, honey-colored hair flew upward into a tangled flame, and we bear-hugged Michael, who lifted us off the ground and spun us around. Much of the staff was crying.

Barbara called Josh and Anna, her voice high-pitched in a Minnie Mouse squeak. "I won. We won the Pulitzer."

"I knew it, Mom. I knew you'd do it. I'm so proud of you," Josh said.

I called Karl at home. "We won!"

"You won!"

"Yeah, we won! Get your ass down here!"

Bottles of champagne materialized, followed by the sound of popping corks. Someone handed me an opened bottle of champagne. I looked around for cups and didn't see any, so in a moment of lunacy, I took off my smelly sneaker and poured bubbly into the insole. I gripped the sneaker by the heel, tilted it to my mouth and took a giant swig. It was my tribute to shoe-leather journalism—in a newsroom with no cups.

When Karl arrived, gripping Brody's hand and holding Sawyer on his hip, everyone applauded, and Karl's eyes welled up. They were clapping for him. He had survived a year as a single dad, a year of feeding the kids dinner, giving them baths, putting them to bed, and waiting up for me—often past midnight. I couldn't have won a Pulitzer without his help, and everyone knew it.

Soon, *Inquirer* reporters and editors graciously came down to our newsroom to congratulate us. By then someone had found cups, and the champagne flowed.

The crowd pressed Barbara and me to say a few words, and the room fell quiet. In halting, half-finished sentences, we told everyone that this wasn't just our Pulitzer, it was theirs, too. They had picked up the slack, reporting and writing two or three stories a day so Barbara and I could chase Tainted Justice. "How many papers with thirty people . . . win a Pulitzer," Barbara said shyly, shrinking from the attention.

With that, Michael raised his glass. "It's a great day at the *Daily News.*"

Brian Tierney was at a Newspaper Association of America convention in Orlando when he got the call from Michael. He stood alone in an empty ballroom after a meeting had just broken up. He hung up the phone and stepped into the hallway, where bigwigs from the nation's most prestigious newspapers milled about. He wore a high-wattage grin.

"What's up?" asked a *Washington Post* executive.

"The *Daily News* just won a Pulitzer Prize for investigative journalism," Tierney blurted.

They gathered around, patting him on the back, "Way to go, Bri. Way to go, Brian!"

Tierney later laughed at himself when he realized that most of the newspaper executives congratulating him didn't mention that they, too, had snagged a Pulitzer, though in a different category.

But the *Daily News* was an underdog—the only paper in the country to win a Pulitzer while in bankruptcy. Tierney was on a roll.

"A while back, I was saying that I had this dream we would win at the Third Circuit, then win a Pulitzer, and then we had a good outcome on the auction. . . . Two out of three ain't bad, so, so far, so good," Tierney told *New York Times* media writer David Carr.

About two weeks after we won the Pulitzer, a tense, twenty-nine-hour auction of the newspapers played out at a midtown Manhattan law firm. Tierney and his investment team were holed up in one room, while the creditors were bunkered in another, each camp sleep-deprived, fueled by coffee and emotion, as the bidding war ratcheted up. Tierney's group hit $129 million, and the creditors topped that bid by $10 million. It was soon clear that no matter how much Tierney's group put in, the creditors were going to outbid them.

In the end, the creditors won control of the *Inquirer*, the *Daily News*, and Philly.com for $139 million—roughly one quarter of the $515 million sale price four years earlier. Tierney couldn't believe he'd lost. He turned to his group, his brown eyes and round face bewildered. "That's it? It's over? We're done?"

Tierney felt helpless, just like when he learned his parents had died. "When my mom and dad, both times, when I got a call that they had died, there's that sense when you put the phone down, and you realize there's not a darn thing I can do. There's nobody I can call, there's no, like, 'Oh, let me run there and I can help you.' There was nothing you could do, and this felt the same way."

Tierney boarded a train home from New York City and slumped into a seat. He stared out the window, nursing a Scotch. The train rolled into Philadelphia's Thirtieth Street Station, where Tierney was met by a throng of TV, radio, and print journalists—all looking for a quote to that rote reporter question, "How do you feel?"

"It's been a heck of a fight. . . . We didn't make it. I think I'll go home tonight and sleep like a baby, which means I'll wake up every hour crying," Tierney said, stealing John McCain's line when he lost the 2008 presidential election to Barack Obama.

On May 21, 2010, Tierney sat in his twelfth-floor office for the last time. Feeling spent, he removed his glasses and rubbed his eyes. He packed up his belongings and walked out of the ivory tower on Broad Street.

Three days later, on a drizzling Monday morning, Barbara and I, along with Karl, walked through the gates leading into Columbia University's majestic campus. We climbed the steps to the Low Library, an imposing neoclassical edifice, where the Pulitzers are awarded every year. We walked through the doors, greeted by bronze busts of Zeus and Apollo. Tables draped with white linen and adorned with china plates and wineglasses sat underneath the 106-foot ceiling of the library's rotunda, surrounded by solid green marble columns.

We sat at a table with Michael Days, Gar Joseph, Michelle Bjork—and Brian Tierney. After accepting the award at the podium, we came back to the table, and Tierney stood up. He hugged us and wiped tears from his eyes.

"A beautiful and poetic ending," he said.

The Pulitzer committee cited Barbara and me for "resourceful reporting."

On the cab ride to the train station, I looked over at Barbara and smiled. " 'Resourceful.' *Resourceful*—they got that right, Slime Sista," referring to the nickname bestowed upon us by our cop detractors.

"You think *resourceful* is another word for crazy?" Barbara asked.

We laughed and playfully swatted each other on the arm.

E PILOGUE

AS OF JULY 2013, FOUR YEARS AND FIVE
MONTHS AFTER OUR FIRST TAINTED
JUSTICE STORY, THE FIVE OFFICERS AT
THE CENTER OF THE INVESTIGATION,
including Jeff Cujdik And Tom Tolstoy, have
not been charged with a crime. All but one,
who retired, are still Philadelphia police officers, although they remain on desk duty.
They still earn paychecks, paid by taxpayers,
and are building up healthy pensions.

The city has paid out almost $2 million
to settle thirty-three lawsuits filed by bodega
owners and two women who claimed they
were victimized by these officers. In settling
the cases, the city did not admit any liability.

The FBI has refused to divulge the status
of the probe.

John McNesby, president of the Fraternal Order of Police, continues to staunchly
defend the officers. He is adamant that the
officers did nothing wrong and will be back
on the street soon. He wants the city to award
the officers hundreds of thousands of dollars

in lost overtime. In Philadelphia, cops can win back pay based on a hypothetical, arguing that they *would* have earned a certain amount of extra money had they not been placed on desk duty. In this case, the theoretical overtime owed to Jeff and the other officers could exceed $1 million.

George Bochetto, the bulldog attorney who defended Jeff and railed when we first met him, "What do you guys think you are going to do? Win a Pulitzer Prize?" still practices law in Philadelphia. About a month after winning the Pulitzer, Barbara and I bumped into him at a state awards banquet. He sheepishly congratulated us. He shook our hands while patting us on the back. He leaned in closer and in a half whisper, half mumble, said, "I didn't realize . . ." That moment was almost as satisfying as winning the Pulitzer. Not really, but you get the point.

Jose Duran, the bodega owner who captured the officers on video cutting surveillance camera wires in his store, lost his business shortly after the raid. He couldn't afford his mortgage and had to sell his large South Jersey colonial. He now rents a smaller rancher on a busy street. He works as a butcher in the meat department at a Costco.

Dagma Rodriguez and Lady Gonzalez struggle to get past what happened to them. They're angry and incensed that Tom Tolstoy remains an officer. "If it would have been any other citizen on the street, he would be in jail already," Lady said.

Tolstoy, who never met with or talked to us, does have a dream though: He plans to open a charter school for teenagers who want a career in law enforcement.

The feds stopped paying for Benny's housing. He had become too much of a handful. They wanted him to stay out of Philly, but he kept returning to the very streets where he had set up drug dealers. He felt compelled to apologize to them for what he had done. But that only made them more vengeful. Barbara spent more than an hour on the phone with one drug dealer, convincing him not to kill Benny. Eventually, we lost touch with Benny.

The hedge funds took control of the *Philadelphia Daily News* and *Philadelphia Inquirer* and got rid of the editors of both papers. A series of buyouts, budget cuts, pay cuts, and mandatory furloughs ensued. In 2011, the new overseers sold the iconic white tower that housed the papers. Morale plummeted.

Amid rumors that the hedge funds planned to close the *Daily News* and further slash the *Inquirer,* the papers were sold yet again in the spring of 2012—this time for $55 million, 11 percent of the $515 million Tierney's group had paid in 2006. It was the fourth time in six years that the papers had been flipped. The new owners were a group of local, high-profile businessmen, some of whom were entrenched in Democratic politics and fund-raising. They reinstalled Michael Days as editor of the *Daily News* and Bill Marimow as editor of the *Inquirer.* The owners promised to revive the papers, twenty-first-century style: online and behind paywalls. Time will tell.

Barbara and I continue to do investigative reporting for the *Daily News.*

In May 2012, I landed my dream job covering the New York City Police Department for the *New York Times*. A little less than a year after I started working for the *Times* as Police Bureau Chief, my marriage to Karl fell apart. We separated in May 2013 and agreed to get divorced. With my personal life in turmoil, I decided to leave the *Times* and return to the Philadelphia area, where most of my family and friends are anchored. It was an extraordinarily difficult decision, but I felt that it was the right one for me and my boys. As Barbara often says, "Women really can have it all—just not at the same time." I returned to the *Philadelphia Daily News* in late July 2013 and reclaimed a desk, right next to Barbara.

—Wendy Ruderman

ACKNOWLEDGMENTS

This book, which grew out of our *Philadelphia Daily News* series, Tainted Justice, would not have been possible without the support of the entire newspaper staff. The victory of the Pulitzer was not ours alone. It was shared with reporters and photographers who fueled us with energy and inspiration as they filled the paper every day with breaking news, freeing us up to chase leads. Just as there are too many people to thank, there are too many adjectives to describe our colleagues, but a few that immediately come to mind are quirky, self-deprecating, tenacious, and all heart.

We're thankful to *Daily News* staffers, including Denise Gallo, Howard Gensler, Jon Snyder, Kevin Bevan, Pat McLoone, Michelle Bjork, Vince Kasper, David Lee Preston, Bob "Boop" Vetrone, Will Bunch, Michael Mercanti, and staff attorney Scott Baker, who went the extra mile to provide help and advice. Former *Daily News* owner Brian Tierney and *Daily News* editor Michael Days were fearless advocates of our work and champions of journalism and its power to expose wrongs and effect change.

From start to finish, city editor Gar Joseph made this book his baby. He selflessly read every word of draft after draft, infusing the manuscript with a brand of giddiness that was un-Gar-like.

We thank *Inquirer* editor Bill Marimow for helping Wendy parachute into the *Daily News* so she could dodge the 2007 *Inquirer* layoffs. After we won the Pulitzer, Bill, who cultivated a fierce competitive spirit between the *Daily News* and *Inquirer,* would always say "Savor it" every time we bumped into him.

To our agent, the ever-dogged Larry Weissman, and his wife, Sascha Alper—a talented editor in her own right—we thank you for believing in this book from the jump. You shepherded this project from the beginning, prodding us up each mountain, with unwavering zeal and commitment. You are a dynamic team. To the staff at HarperCollins, you had us from "hello." We're thankful to our editor, Claire Wachtel, for her seasoned advice and clarity, which greatly improved the manuscript and kept the narrative moving. We are indebted to associate editor Hannah Wood for keeping the trains running and pushing us to the finish line. Fabio Bertoni, assistant general counsel, has a keen legal mind and was a huge help. We are forever appreciative to HarperCollins publisher Jonathan Burnham and Tina Andreadis, senior vice president and director of publicity, for enthusiastically embracing this project and giving it life.

We're grateful to Philadelphia lawyers and court staffers who helped us obtain criminal files and other documents and lent their expertise: Jeremy Ibrahim, Stephen Patrizio, Bradley Bridge, Guy Sciolla, Ralph Silvestro, Theresa Costello, Marc Gaillard, and Joanne Franchini.

We'd be remiss if we didn't single out Philadelphia attorney and former Pennsylvania boxing commissioner George Bochetto, a ferocious advocate for his clients who graciously agreed to be interviewed for the book and patiently described the history of collectibles in his office.

Police Commissioner Charles H. Ramsey always told it to us straight, even when the truth was an ugly stain on the department. We thank our police sources in narcotics and internal affairs who provided us with invaluable information. We would name them individually but cannot because they helped us under the condition that we would not reveal their identities and therefore put their jobs and lives at risk. We're particularly grateful to the cop we call "Ray," who is not only a great officer and salt-of-the-earth person, but who also became a friend.

We thank Wellington Stubbs, former investigator at the Police Advisory Commission, for literally risking his job to cast a light on corrupt police officers and for sending Benny Martinez our way. We are grateful to Benny, who gave us the first glimmer into the lies, deceit, and secrets of an elite narcotics squad.

We're in awe of bodega owner Jose Duran and all the other merchants who entrusted us with their horrific and heartbreaking stories. If not for their courage, we believe that store owners across Philadelphia would continue to be victimized to this day.

The word admiration falls short to describe how we feel about the three women who spoke out about their dark encounters with Officer Tom Tolstoy. In doing so, they gave voice to victimized women everywhere. Two of the women, Lady Gonzalez and Dagma Rodriguez, not only allowed us to use their names and photographs, but bravely agreed to go on camera. This resulted in poignant videos rendered by pros—*Daily News* photographers David Maialetti and Sarah J. Glover. Even now, years later, the videos move us to tears.

We couldn't have gotten through the nail-biting angst of writing our first book without great friends. Those who read parts or all of our early drafts provided candid input, sometimes painfully so, but saved us from ourselves—they are Yvonne Latty, Dave Davies, Lisa Breslin, Cullen Murray-Kemp,

Harry Green, Nicole Weisensee Egan, Kristen Graham, and Stephanie Farr.

A few friends stand out for being staunch advocates of us and this book. Monica Yant Kinney became our honorary Slime Sista. Her enthusiasm for this book was infectious. Her feedback, along with that of her husband, David Kinney, was invaluable. Once, when we needed a quiet place to write, we camped at their dining room table, drank their coffee, and swiped their pens (though not ones on par with Barbara's favorite Paper Mate Profile ballpoints).

Hutch Raymer always had our backs. Practically a bodyguard, he looked out for Barbara after we received angry and, in some cases, threatening e-mails and phone calls from cops while writing the Tainted Justice series. While holed up in Barbara's house, tired and stressed from writing various drafts of this book, Hutch came to the rescue. This time he brought levity—baked chicken and vegetables and Southern Comfort instead of his 9mm Glock.

—Wendy and Barbara

The love and support of my family and friends is boundless. To my Slime Sista, Barbara Laker, I am so grateful that you came into my life. It might sound whacky but I believe my dad's spirit brought us together. You are a one-of-a-kind, rare friend; a talented journalist; and a darn good person with a big heart and a fiery passion for life. You bring out the best in me—always.

I thank my mom, Isabel Ruderman Amenta, and dad, Stan Ruderman, for giving me the lifetime gift of a magical childhood and building a solid foundation upon which to launch my dreams and embrace adventure. My dad, who died in 1997, was my biggest fan and instilled in me a love of the arts and a belief in myself. My mom is a geyser of energy and strength—traits that have rubbed off on me and my sister and brother. She taught us how to dust ourselves off and start anew when life delivers a setback, or a major blow, and the ability to delight in butterflies and colorful flowers. I'm thankful to my mom's husband, Alan Amenta, for his unconditional support and for being a loving grandfather to my kids.

I cherish my sister, Amy Ruderman Plassio, and brother, David Ruderman, for always being there for me, for rooting me on with genuine pride, and for bolstering my spirits whenever I feel low. I admire their capacity to see the bright side of everything. They inspire me to be a better person. I thank David's husband, Juilliard voice teacher Robert White, for making my family's life more musical.

My life would be empty—and far less interesting—without my boys, Brody and Sawyer. I never tire of their hugs or the funny things they do and say. They surprise me every day with their astute observations and wonderment. I thank them for indulging my inner kid. I feel pure happiness when I am alongside them building sand castles, jumping in piles of leaves, and sledding under a clear night sky. Brody and Sawyer, you have my heart, forever.

—Wendy

Even though, Seven, my rescue dog, can't read that I know of, I want to thank her for patiently waiting for dinner that came too late, and for her wet kisses and tail wags every time I came home.

The Tainted Justice series and this book would have never come to be without Wendy, my Slime Sista, the best reporter I've ever known. Some people come into your life at just the right time for all the right reasons. Wendy, you are that person. I look up to you like no other. You're not only my best friend, you're like family to me and always will be.

I am grateful to my cousin, Rachel Goldberg, who has been like a sister I never had. I want to thank my brother, David Laker, who has always been my cheerleader and believed in me more than I did. My dad, Peter Laker, a rare bird in the truest sense, could always make me laugh, even when I felt like crying. He taught me obstacles were just that—and I could climb over them. Thank you, Dad, for telling me I was special and could make a mark in this world. Those words put fire in my belly.

None of my life adventures—and there have been many—would feel the same or mean as much without my children, Josh and Anna. They have grown into kind and driven young people who I would like and admire even if they weren't mine. Josh and Anna—you inspire me like no one else. You have taught me to let the little stuff go and make the big stuff count. My mom taught me the power of love. You taught me that in the end, nothing else matters.

—Barbara

ABOUT THE AUTHORS

WENDY RUDERMAN has a master's degree from the Columbia University Graduate School of Journalism. Before joining the *Philadelphia Daily News* in 2007, she worked at several media outlets, including the *Philadelphia Inquirer,* WHYY-TV and WHYY-FM, the *Trenton Times,* the Associated Press, and the *Bergen Record.*

BARBARA LAKER graduated from the University of Missouri Journalism School and worked for several newspapers, including the *Atlanta Journal-Constitution,* the *Dallas Times Herald,* and the *Seattle Post-Intelligencer.* She began working at the *Philadelphia Daily News* in 1993 and has been a general assignment reporter, an assistant city editor, and an investigative reporter.

SMOKESCREEN

ALSO BY IRIS JOHANSEN
(IN ORDER OF PUBLICATION)

EVE DUNCAN
SERIES
The Face of Deception
The Killing Game★
The Search
Body of Lies
Blind Alley★
Countdown★
Stalemate
Quicksand
Blood Game★
Eight Days to Live★
Chasing the Night
Eve
Quinn
Bonnie
Sleep No More
Taking Eve+
Hunting Eve+
Silencing Eve★+
Shadow Play+
Hide Away+
Night and Day
Mind Game★
Shattered Mirror
Dark Tribute
★Starring Jane MacGuire
+Featuring Margaret Douglas

KENDRA MICHAELS
SERIES
(written with Roy Johansen)
"With Open Eyes" (short story)
Close Your Eyes

Sight Unseen
The Naked Eye
Night Watch
Look Behind You
Double Blind

CATHERINE LING SERIES
Chasing the Night
What Doesn't Kill You
Live to See Tomorrow
Your Next Breath
STANDALONES
The Ugly Duckling
Long After Midnight
And Then You Die
Final Target
No One to Trust
Dead Aim
Fatal Tide
Firestorm
On the Run
Killer Dreams
Pandora's Daughter
Silent Thunder (Iris & Roy Johansen)
Dark Summer
Deadlock
Storm Cycle (Iris & Roy Johansen)
Shadow Zone (Iris & Roy Johansen)
The Perfect Witness
No Easy Target (featuring Margaret Douglas)
Vendetta

SMOKESCREEN

IRIS JOHANSEN

GRAND CENTRAL
PUBLISHING

NEW YORK   BOSTON

Copyright © 2019 by IJ Development

Cover design by Flag. Cover photograph by Getty / CoffeeeAndMilk
Cover copyright © 2019 by Hachette Book Group, Inc.

Grand Central Publishing
Hachette Book Group
1290 Avenue of the Americas, New York, NY 10104
grandcentralpublishing.com
twitter.com/grandcentralpub

First Edition: July 2019

Grand Central Publishing is a division of Hachette Book Group, Inc. The Grand Central Publishing name and logo is a trademark of Hachette Book Group, Inc.

The publisher is not responsible for websites (or their content) that are not owned by the publisher.

The Hachette Speakers Bureau provides a wide range of authors for speaking events. To find out more, go to www.hachettespeakersbureau.com or call (866) 376-6591.

Library of Congress Cataloging-in-Publication Data

Names: Johansen, Iris, author.
Title: Smokescreen / Iris Johansen.
Description: First Edition. | New York : Grand Central Publishing, 2019.
Identifiers: LCCN 2018048366| ISBN 9781538713082 (hardcover) | ISBN 9781538715543 (large print) | ISBN 9781549141409 (audio book) | ISBN 9781549141416 (audio download) | ISBN 9781538762974 (ebook)
Subjects: | GSAFD: Mystery fiction.
Classification: LCC PS3560.O275 S66 2019 | DDC 813/.54--dc23
LC record available at https://lccn.loc.gov/2018048366

ISBNs: 978-1-5387-1308-2 (hardcover), 978-1-5387-1554-3 (large print), 978-1-5387-5101-5 (Canadian trade), 978-1-5387-6297-4 (ebook)

Printed in the United States of America

LSC-C

10 9 8 7 6 5 4 3 2 1

SMOKESCREEN

PROLOGUE

Headlights!

Jill Cassidy's fingers stabbed into the mud as she saw the light spearing the darkness on the road ahead. The vehicle was going slowly, but they'd never see her on this side path. She had to get to the main road. But she had no shoes, and every muscle was aching, throbbing. She'd tried to get to her feet and walk as soon as she'd heard those bastards leave, but she was too weak. She had only managed to crawl slowly, painfully, through the jungle.

She could *do* this, she told herself desperately as she forced herself to propel her body through the mud on the path. The pain wasn't as bad as it had been when they'd first left her. Ignore it, think about the story. Always think about the story. It wasn't the pain, it was the shock that was causing her to shake and feel so weak.

The shock and this gentle, warm tropical rain that had started to fall just as she'd finally managed to pull herself together and force herself to move. Strange that warm rain could make her feel this cold. So gentle, she thought dazedly. Why on earth had that word occurred to her when there seemed to be no gentleness left in her world?

The headlights drew closer.

She had to get to the road before the car passed her.

She tried to move faster.

It was a jeep, she realized. The motor was so loud... Would they hear her if she called out? She *had* to catch their attention. She made a last effort and rolled out onto the road.

"Jill!" The jeep screeched to a halt. "Dammit to hell!"

Novak, Jill realized. It was Jed Novak, and he was angry... That was okay, let him be angry. All that mattered was that he had come, and nothing else could happen to her as long as he was here.

He jumped out of the jeep. "Jill." He was striding toward her. "I almost ran over you."

"You... wouldn't do... that. Spoil your... image. CIA to the... rescue."

"Shut up." Then he was kneeling beside her, the rain beading off the brim of his hat as he looked down at her. "Just look at you, Jill," he said hoarsely as he wrapped his jacket around her. "I told you to be careful. What happened? Why wasn't someone with you?" In spite of the roughness of his tone, his hands were gentle as he picked her up and set her inside the jeep. "How badly are you hurt?"

"I don't know. It... feels bad. But I made it through that jungle... so I guess it's not—" Jill struggled to keep her voice steady. It was over. Those bastards were gone. Don't let them *do* this to her. "I thought they—were going to—kill me. But it turned out they—only wanted to teach me a lesson and get me sent home."

"You have some nasty bruises." He stiffened as the dashboard lights fell on her torn blouse and upper body. "Blood. Shit. I shouldn't have moved you."

"Not—my blood. Hadfeld. They—wanted to show me—his head. They threw it at me... He's dead, Novak."

"You're not in good shape yourself. Those bruises are really bad, and they're all over you." He was carefully feeling her arms and body. "Here, too. Your head? Concussion?"

"I don't think so. I never totally blacked out." She'd wanted to black out, but she'd been afraid that if she stopped fighting, she'd never wake up. She started to shake again. Don't think about it. She'd made it this far, and she'd be fine. Just don't think about it.

But she couldn't stop *shaking*.

"Hey, it's okay. You're safe." Novak had pulled her into his arms and was holding her tight. "Breathe deep. Just take it easy. We'll talk about it later."

Safe. She lay there against him, letting his heat warm her, shut out the chill. He was so strong, and she felt as if his strength were pouring into her and shutting out that horrible weakness. Yet more than five minutes passed before she could stop shaking.

She finally sat up and pushed him away. "I'm sorry," she said unsteadily. "I fell apart. You asked me why—there wasn't someone—with me. I got the phone call from Hadfeld. But it was a trap. They were waiting for me."

"How many were there?"

"Four."

"Can you describe them?"

Describe the pain? Describe the smell of them? Describe the helplessness she'd felt? But she had to focus and try. She shook her head. "Scarves over the lower...half of their faces. One black man, three white. Two of the white men had dark hair, one was fair-haired. It felt like...straw. Most of the conversation was in a Maldara dialect."

She had to stop a minute before she could go on. "They...wanted to hurt me and...they did. The one who was fair-haired kept driving the others to hurt me more and more. He beat me himself, then he told the others what they had to do and how to do it. He said they'd been sent here to do a job, so do it." Say it. She had to tell him. She swallowed. "I have a little blood—down there, and I'll need a rape kit."

Silence. "They raped you?"

"Three of them did. The one with fair hair only seemed to want to beat me. He seemed...angry."

"Son of a *bitch*." Then Novak began to swear softly and viciously. "We'll get you to the local hospital in Jokan," he said. "Another fifteen minutes."

"No hospital. Not here," Jill said jerkily. "You're CIA, and I've seen you pull strings. You can get me anything—I need—without throwing me into the system. Do it, Novak."

"The system isn't all that bad when you've been savaged the way you've been, Jill. You're one of the best journalists I've ever come across, but not even a Pulitzer is worth this." He added harshly, "You should have done what I told you and stayed out of it. Would it have been too much to leave it up to me? You knew I'd follow up."

"Yes, I knew you would," Jill said wearily. "Because you're as obsessed as I am. But it was my story—you might have been—too late." She was getting weaker, she realized. That temporary adrenaline rush when she'd felt so safe with Novak was fading. And there was something she had to do, she remembered vaguely. "Do you have a first-aid kit in this jeep?"

"You don't have to do it yourself. I'll get you help right away, Jill."

"It's not for me. I need some medical gloves. I couldn't describe those men, but I—fought them. When they surprised me, they took away my gun, but they'll have scratches." She looked numbly down at her hands. "And I might have some DNA beneath my nails if it survived my trip—through—all that mud."

He muttered another curse, reached into the backseat for the first-aid kit, and handed it to her. The gloves were on top of the bandages, and she quickly pulled them on to protect her nails. She set the first-aid kit on the floor at her feet. Better. One more thing done to rid herself of that terrible feeling of helplessness. "You were driving slow. You were looking for me, weren't you? How did you know I was here?"

"My informant at the embassy intercepted an anonymous call to the secretary shouting about how U.S. journalists were to blame for the ruin of his country and claiming that he'd taken care of one tonight. Their directions were pretty damn accurate. They *wanted* you to be found. I was lucky to reach you before the soldiers from the embassy."

"No, I'm the lucky one." Though luck was a bittersweet concept tonight. But she could imagine how she would have felt if anyone but Novak had found her. "Now take me somewhere you can get those gloves off to a lab so I can get clean again. Then I'll try to figure out how to find out how they knew it was me Hadfeld had contacted."

He was silent. "It might be my fault."

Her gaze flew to his face. "You've got a lead?"

"Better. I think I might be able to get my hands on the skull. So go home and let me work on it," he said roughly. "You've gone through too much as it is."

"Yes, I have." Her hands clenched into fists. "And I'm not the only one. Do you actually believe I'd ever let those bastards get what they wanted? Can't you see? They knew the first thing that the embassy would do if they found out about this would be to notify my publisher. And then they'd send me back to the U.S. to some discreet hospital to go through debriefing and therapy. That's why that bastard told those other men that they had a job to do. That's why they kept beating me. That's why it was rape." Her eyes were suddenly blazing at him. "After all that's gone down here in Maldara, the last thing those diplomats would want would be to have a journalist injured and raped at this stage of the game. Six hundred thousand people were murdered here. Genocide. Now they think they've put Humpty Dumpty back together again. So they'd need to hush any disturbance and wrap me in tender loving care. Why else do you think this happened?" Her voice was shaking. "I told you, those men *knew* what they were doing. They *wanted* to hurt me. They had their orders. Well, I won't let them get away with it."

"Easy," Novak said quietly. "I'll take care of it. No one's going to let that happen."

And if he took care of it, it would mean anyone in Novak's way would be destroyed. She had seen it before. But she didn't want it to go down that way. "You bet they're not. Do you know how weak they made me feel? The pain kept coming and wouldn't stop, and I couldn't do anything about it. I'm never going to be that weak ever again." She wanted to close her eyes and just stop arguing with him. She needed to shut out the world, and maybe, for a little while, those four monsters would vanish with it. But she had to get Novak's promise first. "So this night never happened. Because you're going to let me see to it myself, aren't you? It will take a little while for me to get over this, but you're not going to let anyone sideline me. You're going to let me go after them. I *deserve* it, Novak."

"Do you think I don't know that?" he asked hoarsely. He looked away from her. "Okay, you don't go back to the U.S. I use you and let you help me take them down. And, if you get hurt again doing it, I just consider you collateral damage. Is that the plan?"

"That's the plan." She could close her eyes now. She could relax her body and attempt to block out the pain...and the memory. "Just get me fixed, and then you can tell me how you're going to get the skull."

"And just how am I supposed to fix you, Jill?"

She was getting so blurry she wasn't sure she understood. "You're right, I spoke without thinking. My responsibility...Just take me somewhere, and when I'm better, I'll take care of it."

He was cursing beneath his breath. "Never mind. You're not thinking straight enough to recognize monumental frustration when you hear it." He said slowly, clearly, "Listen. Stop trying to be strong. I know you're strong. You don't have to prove it to me. And I'm not leaving you until I know you're okay. We're in this together." He reached out, grasped her hand, and pressed it tightly. "Do you understand? I'll not let you go."

And, in spite of Novak's being one of the toughest men she'd ever met, he was having trouble with her being hurt and not being able to put her back together again. Strange...

But she couldn't help him now. Maybe later . . .

Right now, she could only cling desperately to his hand and take whatever comfort he could give her. Because she was starting to shake again, and he had said she didn't have to be strong. "That's very . . . kind. Do you mind if I—don't talk anymore, Novak?"

"Hell, no." His grip tightened. "Look, this is what we're going to do. I'm taking you to Baldar, the private airport we use near the border, and flying you to Nairobi. There's a hospital there where I send my men when I need absolute secrecy. No reports. No leaks. No one in Maldara will know where you are." He muttered a curse. "Even though I don't want to do it because it will take about an hour and a half to get you there."

"That doesn't matter." Yet she could see he was upset again, and she had to make one last effort. "None of this was your fault. Your decision. My—choice. Stop blaming yourself."

"That's right," he said bitterly. "Collateral damage."

She didn't reply. She was at the end of her strength, and she just wanted to crawl away somewhere until she could heal.

Collateral damage.

It wasn't an accurate description of her role in this nightmare. She had gone after the story with her usual drive and determination. Novak might have thought that the decision he had made caused this to happen to her, but she did not. She'd not been smart enough to read the signs of betrayal when Hadfeld had phoned her. She'd been too eager to get to him and obtain the proof she needed. Even if Novak had found a way to get the skull, things might still be on the verge of exploding.

And there might be true innocents on the horizon who could be hurt by what had happened here at Maldara.

Collateral damage . . .

CHAPTER

1

I thought you'd be finished with her by now." Michael was tilting his head and gazing in disappointment at the reconstruction of the skull on Eve's worktable. "I wanted to see Nora before I left today. Did you have trouble with her?"

"No." Eve made a face at her son as she wiped the clay off her hands with her work towel. "I had trouble with you. I was busy packing your bags and making arrangements for that summer camp your sister, Jane, is so set on taking you to. Nora had to wait."

"She won't mind." Michael wasn't taking his gaze off the skull of the six-year-old child who was Eve's current forensic sculpture. "She'll know you're trying to do what's best for her, that you're trying to bring her home, Mom."

His voice was gentle. Even as a toddler, he had never had a horror of these skulls of the victims that had appeared in her studio through the years. Now, though he was only ten years old, that understanding and gentleness seemed to have deepened. Eve had never had to explain to him about the monsters who had killed these children, then tried to burn them, bury them, toss them away as if they had never existed. Michael just accepted that Eve was trying to fix something that was broken, that those children were lost and had to go home. Lord, she was lucky.

She gave him a quick hug. "Well, Nora may understand, but the Chicago Police Department isn't that patient. I have to finish this reconstruction and get it back to them so that they can start sending out photos to the newspapers and TV shows. We have to see if anyone can identify her." She turned him around and pushed him toward the hall. "And you have to gather all the treasures you can't bear to leave behind for the next month and pack them in your duffel. Last chance. We have to be at the airport in four hours."

"Right." He smiled at her over his shoulder, his amber eyes shining with mischief. "You're first on the list. Can I take you, Mom?"

She wished he could. She didn't know what she was going to do without him and Joe for a month. "I wouldn't fit in your duffel. But we can Skype." She made a shooing gesture. "Get going."

He laughed and ran down the hall.

She turned back to the reconstruction with a sigh. Noise. Laughter. Family. She was going to miss all of it. She reached out and gently touched the reconstruction's cheekbone. "Sorry, Nora. You're important, too. I'm just having a few issues at the moment."

"Then come with us." Joe was standing in the doorway, looking at her. "A month is a long time." He crossed the room and took her in his arms. "Or let me come back to you." He kissed her. "Screw that seminar. I'll go next time."

"Scotland Yard doesn't offer them that often. And everything is cutting-edge when they do." Joe was a detective with ATLPD and was always interested in all the bells and whistles connected with crime fighting. "And the timing is just too good to miss. Jane is taking Michael to that dig in Wales, and you'll at least be close enough to keep an eye on them."

"Come on, Jane adores Michael. And she's introducing him to digging for ancient Roman treasure at that Welsh castle. Treasure and playing in the dirt. A ten-year-old's dream. He wouldn't miss me."

"He'd miss you." She kissed him again. "Just as I will. But I'm not ten, and I'd feel better if one of us is near him. So would you." Michael had become the center of their lives since the night he'd been born, but neither of them could deny that he was . . . unusual and always a challenge. "And you can never tell which way he's going to jump."

"Tell me about it," Joe said dryly. "You could come and work in London."

"And then you'd feel guilty about spending all those hours at the Yard." She gave him a quick kiss. "I'll tell you what I told Michael. Skype. Go finish packing. I need to clean up before I take you to the airport." She grimaced. "And I gave in and agreed to give an interview at one this afternoon. Annoying, but it was the only time the reporter could fit me into her schedule. I'll take her out on the porch and try to get rid of her as quickly as possible. But you guys are on your own until we leave here at two."

"We'll manage." He kissed the tip of her nose. "Reluctantly. Why the interview? Does it have anything to do with Nora? She's not even finished." He frowned, puzzled. "And you don't usually give interviews anyway. You say it's a waste of your time."

"It is a waste. They tend to focus on me and not the victim."

"Imagine that," he said mildly. "The foremost forensic sculptor in the world who is both charming and beautiful. How could you possibly compare to a hideous skull that's been buried for decades?"

"Not beautiful, interesting-looking. And I'm not charming, that would require effort. I always opt for kind and intelligent. You must already be missing me if you're resorting to flattery."

"You've got that right."

She cleared her throat. "Me too."

"So why the interview?"

"It's Jill Cassidy. I liked the story she did on that DFACS scandal. She never gave up and fought those politicians who were ignoring the child abuse and fraud claims all the way."

Joe nodded slowly. "I remember. She won a Pulitzer for it." He gently touched her hair. "I should have known it would have something to do with kids. She wants to do some kind of profile on you?"

She shrugged. "I guess she does. We didn't discuss it. I said I could give her an hour if she insisted on its being today. It seemed worthwhile. I don't think she'd waste my time on trivial junk."

"You mean like telling the public how brilliant and famous you are? Heaven forbid." He was heading down the hall. "Not only trivial, but totally boring..."

Eve shook her head as she watched him disappear into the bedroom. Wry, mocking, yet as full of mischief as their son. Nothing boring about Joe. She was already missing him. Their relationship had taken them through valleys and mountains, and they had come out of both with a closeness and love that no longer faltered no matter what strain was put upon it. She frowned as she had a sudden thought. Good Lord, what if that interview involved Joe and Michael? The last thing she needed was a journalist looking for a tell-all piece that violated her privacy. She could not permit it.

Don't jump to conclusions.

If she saw that was the way the interview was heading, she'd just end it immediately. She wasn't shy about protecting her family's privacy.

And she'd taken the interview because Jill Cassidy had shown herself to be a responsible journalist. Joe had been joking about Eve's being boring, but it was true that she was not someone whom social media would find particularly fascinating. She was not only a workaholic, she was too complicated... and very private.

She just had to hope she wasn't getting mixed signals from Jill Cassidy...

———◆———

"Hello. I'm Jill Cassidy." The young woman at the door was smiling warmly at Eve as she shook her hand. "Please call me Jill. I can't tell you how eager I've been to meet you, Eve Duncan. Thank you for agreeing to see me."

"Come in. I'm sorry I can't give you very long. I have to take my husband and son to catch a flight." Eve was studying the reporter and feeling distinctly relieved. Jill Cassidy must be late twenties or early thirties, a little on the thin side, with medium-length brown hair and wide-set blue eyes. Full lips that had a touch of sensitivity and humor and clear, glowing skin. But those eyes were steady and honest, and Eve felt the honesty was also very real. She was dressed in dark slacks and a simple white blouse that made her appear businesslike yet perfectly natural and unassuming. "I expected you to be older. You won that Pulitzer two years ago."

"I got lucky. Right story. Right timing." She was looking around the open living room and kitchen. "This is wonderful."

"It's home," Eve said simply.

"That's why it's wonderful. You can feel it. I'm traveling most of the time, so my home is usually the nearest hotel." She gestured to the smiling portrait of Eve dressed in her old blue work shirt on the wall beside the window. "That's terrific. Relaxed, but there's still a sense of purpose. Your daughter, Jane MacGuire, painted it?"

Eve's eyes widened. "Yes. You're right, Jane is terrific. Her career as an artist is zooming these days. How did you know about her?"

"I do my homework." Her gaze was wandering around the room. "You have a longtime relationship with Joe Quinn, a police detective whom you married eight years ago. You have a ten-year-old son, Michael; and besides Jane MacGuire, whom you adopted when she was about Michael's age, you and Joe Quinn took in another young girl, Cara Delaney, and made her your ward. She's not with you now either, since she's a promising violinist and she's on tour." Her gaze returned to Eve's face. "Now, I found her background to be very interesting indeed."

Eve stiffened, instantly on guard. That remark had been too full of meaning to miss. "Really? But you asked to interview *me*, didn't you? I don't consider my husband or children to be fodder for the press. I believe you'd better leave."

She shook her head. "Do you think I'd have mentioned Cara Delaney if I'd meant to cause you problems? I just had to make certain you knew that I could hurt you if I chose and had no intention of doing so. Otherwise, you'd be worried all the time I was talking to you that I was going to cause some kind of scandal by revealing that your ward is the granddaughter of Sergai Kaskov, a known figure in the Russian Mafia." She gestured impatiently. "I don't care about that. All I care about is that you're brilliant and have devoted most of your career to helping children who have been murdered and abused. Evidently, somewhere along the way, you've also been able to build a life for yourself and your family that I envy with all my heart. Good for you."

"You couldn't have hurt Cara." Jill Cassidy seemed to be sincere, but Eve was still wary. "She wouldn't give a damn about scandal. All she cares about is the music. Though you'd find the rest of the family very protective and might find yourself in an extremely uncomfortable situation." Eve stared at her. "You could have just not mentioned my family at all. This was all very deliberate."

She nodded. "Because as I said, I do my homework. You're sharp and very protective. You'd start questioning what I was asking of you the minute you realized I wasn't being totally honest with you."

Eve frowned. "That's not quite clear."

"And you like everything crystal clear," Jill said brusquely. "And you said we don't have much time. Can we sit down somewhere and talk?" She smiled crookedly. "Unless I've completely misread you, and you're going to throw me out?"

"I came close a few minutes ago," Eve said slowly. "I'm still not sure about you. I believe I might have to do a little homework on you, too."

"It's a good idea," Jill said soberly. "Don't trust me. I promise I'm not trying to hurt you or your family. But you don't know me." She smiled. "And all that honesty might be intended to disarm you. But can we still sit down and talk? That won't hurt you."

Eve hesitated. And that honesty *was* disarming her, she realized. Her first wariness was fading, and she was beginning to like Jill Cassidy. "We can talk." She gestured toward the porch. "I'll give you a cup of coffee on the porch. It's our only guarantee of privacy. Joe and Michael might be all over the place while they're packing."

"Great." Jill started to turn away; and then her attention was caught by the skull reconstruction on the worktable across the room. "You work here?" She moved across the room. "I thought you'd have a separate studio." She was reaching out and touching the skull. "May I?"

"It appears that you may," Eve said dryly. "And will."

Jill looked at her. "I just wanted to see your work. She's not finished?"

Eve shook her head. "Close. But Nora will take a few more days." She gazed at her curiously. "How did you know she was female?"

"The lips. The nose. Both very feminine. The rest is blurred and incomplete, but she's there, waiting to be born."

"No, she's not. Nora was born six years before a monster decided to snatch that life away from her. Now all I can do is help her to try to find someone who loved her as much as that monster hated her and send her home." She added grimly, "And hope I can find the monster and send him to the electric chair."

"Amen," Jill murmured. "I understand you've managed to do that a number of times."

"Not enough. Never enough." She gestured to the porch door. "There are too many monsters out there."

"Yes, there are." Jill was still staring at the reconstruction. "You called her Nora. You have some idea who she was?"

"No, I always name my reconstructions. It helps me to connect with them." She started for the door. "Now I have a question for you. You appear familiar with skulls and reconstructions. You not only have a good eye, you know what to look for. Have you been taught?"

Jill shook her head. "Heavens no. Self-taught on the Internet because it's both your profession and your passion. But the key word is familiarity. I only wanted to know what I was seeing."

"Are you planning a series of articles instead of just interviewing me?"

"No." She grinned. "And that's two questions." She opened the porch door. "I'll wait on the porch while you get me that cup of coffee. But I'll give you a teaser to make you want to hurry it along." She looked back at Eve. "I don't want to interview you at all. I want to offer you a job that I hope I can convince you to take. Gross misrepresentation. If you're too pissed off to even let me try, you can toss me in that beautiful lake. Okay?"

Jill didn't wait for an answer. She closed the door behind her.

———◆———

"I don't have time for this," Eve said as she handed Jill her coffee five minutes later. "You picked the wrong day, Ms. Cassidy."

"We've gone back to formality?" Jill asked. "At least you didn't choose the lake option."

"I considered it."

Jill tilted her head. "But you were curious. You have a certain amount of respect for me and were willing to risk being disappointed. But you also have an innate curiosity, which is natural considering your profession."

"That curiosity will be fading away if you don't satisfy it soon. You don't wish to interview me." She asked bluntly, "What the hell do you want with me?"

"Basically the same thing you've done during your entire career," she said quietly. "I want you to identify a number of skulls and bring resolution and peace to their families and loved ones." She paused. "I want you to bring them home."

"I already have a waiting list of cases," Eve said impatiently. "I don't need any more. There are other forensic sculptors you can hire."

"But they're not you." Jill leaned forward. "And they won't give those children the skill and dedication you would. They were murdered, and now they're already being forgotten."

"Children? Plural? How many children?"

"Twenty-seven."

Eve felt a ripple of shock. "A mass murderer?"

"Oh, yes. Though not what you might think."

Twenty-seven children. It made Eve sick to her stomach. "Then tell me what I should think."

"Maldara."

Eve went still. "My God."

Jill slowly nodded. "Though I haven't seen any sign of God in Maldara since the moment I stepped off the plane two years ago. What do you know about Maldara?"

"What everyone knows. Two warring groups in the depths of the Congo struggling for supremacy. Civil war. Blood. Gore." She swallowed. "Another Rwanda. So many deaths. The ruling party managed to triumph about eighteen months ago." She searched for a name. "The Kiyanis I think. Their president was able to persuade the U.N. to support her."

"Yes, Zahra Kiyani is very persuasive," Jill said. "Over six hundred thousand people died in Maldara during that conflict, and only fifty thousand were laid at her door. She was Teflon."

Only fifty thousand. Eve could only vaguely remember the details of that horror she had seen on TV and the Internet two years ago. "Men, women, and children. Butchered. I didn't want Michael to watch it." She lifted her head as a sudden thought occurred to her. "Children. You want me to do reconstructions on the children of that massacre?"

"Not all of them. You'd be there for decades." Jill's lips twisted.

"There are far too many. But there's a school in the village of Robaku, near Jokan on the northern border, where I've been doing volunteer work. Twenty-seven students were killed by a machete brigade led by Nils Varak, a mercenary who was hired by the Botzan faction because it was practically on the Kiyani doorstep. The children were chopped to pieces. Then the school was burned to the ground."

"Terrible," Eve said, sick. It wasn't difficult to envision the terror and pain that must have enveloped the children that day.

"Yes, every minute of it was terrible," Jill said jerkily. "Some of the children weren't dead when the fires were lit. Varak was too impatient to wait. He wanted to lure the people from the village to the school with the screams." She drew a shaky breath. "But you're in a hurry. I have to tell you why I need you. Almost half the villagers were killed that day, most of them parents. But some are left, and there are other relatives, grandparents, uncles, aunts, who also loved those children. But after the massacre, those relatives were devastated. They don't even know which of the children are their own. The damage was too great. The government of Kiyani offered a common grave, but they've refused the offer. They want to bury their own children in the village where they were born." She added softly, "It seems the feeling is universal. They want to bring their children home, Eve."

Eve nodded. The story had touched her unbearably. "Have they tried DNA?"

"It was a bloodbath. With the fires and scattered remains, only a few had enough quality DNA left to be matched. And even those parents wouldn't be satisfied. These are simple village people, Eve. They don't want to be given a piece of paper with a DNA result. They're willing to wait for the years it will take to DNA the bodies, but not the skulls. They want to see, to touch, to recognize." Her eyes were glittering with moisture. "They need *you*, Eve."

"Not necessarily me, Jill. I'm good, but I'm not the only one who could do this. Besides, it would be a massive undertaking to gather those remains and send them to me. The U.N. should hire several forensic sculptors and set up studios on-site at Robaku. That would be the quickest way to get it done."

"The quickest, not the best. Having you do it would be the best." Jill shrugged. "And U.N. funding isn't an option. They've already refused to approve anything but the least expensive methods of disposing of those children. Maldara has turned into one huge cemetery they don't want to face. If a mass grave wouldn't be such bad press, they'd probably even approve that over working with DNA."

Eve felt a ripple of shock. "That's pretty harsh."

"It's the way of the world," Jill said wearily. "The U.N. has too many fires to put out for sentimentality. They regard Maldara's fate as settled, so they want to put a period to it and move on in the most economical way possible. That's only good business. Zahra Kiyani would even like everyone to forget about that massacre and has been pushing to move the villagers to another location. I've been writing story after story about Robaku to keep the interest and sympathy high and not let the wishes of those relatives be forgotten."

"There are many charitable organizations not connected to the U.N.," Eve said. "I've worked with a few over the years. Ask for money and volunteers."

"I am," Jill said simply. "I'm asking you to volunteer. I can gather enough money together to pay you to come to Maldara and do the reconstructions on those children. You're the best one for this job, and they deserve the best."

"I'm sure they do, but there are other fine forensic sculptors." Eve had seen where this was going and had tried to offer alternatives to avoid having to refuse her. She could see that Jill Cassidy was passionately committed to helping those children. The story had touched and horrified Eve, and she could almost feel the agony of the parents who had lost their children to those butchers. "Not me, Jill," she said gently. "I have a career with commitments. I have a family who needs me. I can't go flying across the ocean to work in a country in the middle of Africa."

"I know I'm asking a lot." Jill's face was tense. "But they need help. If you could see..." She reached in her briefcase and pulled out a manila folder. "Here. You *can* see them." She thrust the folder at Eve. "You could put off your other commitments for a little while, couldn't you? These people have lost so much already. Someone should care enough to give them something to make—" She broke off, then said, "I can talk about your work, but there's nothing I can say that would make leaving your family any better. I don't even have a family any longer, but I know it would suck." She drew a deep breath. "But if you could give those kids just a few weeks, it would give me time to try to work something else out for them."

Eve shook her head. "I have a life, Jill. You're asking me for a major disruption. And I don't even know if it's the best thing for those village families. You're asking me to trust your judgment."

"Yes, I am. Or your own judgment after you look at the biographies and photos in that envelope." She reached out and grasped Eve's hand. "Look, I know it's a sacrifice. Who wants to go to a wild, underdeveloped country and set up shop in a jungle for those weeks? But if you agree to do it, I know you'll come back feeling good about it. And maybe it's not so underdeveloped any longer. It has a U.S. embassy, there's a temporary U.N. headquarters, and reps come in and out of Jokan, the capital city, on a regular basis." She grimaced. "It's practically civilized compared to when I first visited."

"You said that was two years ago." She frowned. "The fighting was still going on then. I'm surprised they let you in the country."

"They didn't. But I had a few friends in high places and even more in low places who managed to smuggle me under the radar. I had an idea it might be the story of the decade, and I wanted to be there." Her lips tightened. "I knew it was a second Rwanda, but I thought I was tough enough to take it. And I did take it, I just didn't realize I'd be caught up in the nightmare and start bleeding myself. You don't go through an experience like that without its changing your life."

"Changing?"

"I was first on the scene, and I told the stories." Her face was haunted. "But you can't do that in a place like Maldara without becoming part of the story."

"Yet you want me to go and tell stories of my own when I do those reconstructions," Eve said quietly. "And you know that it will probably hurt me to do them. Every single one I've ever done has hurt me, Jill. It goes with the territory. And this time, I wouldn't even have the comfort of doing it to try to find the butchers who murdered them. They had to have been killed or imprisoned by now."

"I know." She nodded jerkily. "So do it for their parents or grandparents. Nothing is perfect. Particularly in Maldara." Her hand tightened on Eve's. "Just *do* it. I promise I'll make it safe for you and as comfortable as I can."

"I know you would." Eve gently pulled away her hand. "And I admire you and what you're trying to do for these people. But I have my own commitments I have to think about. Maldara is half a world away from them. But I promise I'll try to find an organization that will be able to give you the help you need."

"Thank you." Jill's voice was unsteady. "I guess I couldn't expect anything else from you." There was desperation in her eyes as she held Eve's gaze. "But you're the help I need. *Please.* Will you promise to think about it?" She reached in her pocket and handed Eve her card. "Just call me, and I'll arrange everything."

"I'll think about it," Eve said. "But I'm afraid I'll disappoint you, Jill. I can't do—"

"Mom, we're ready to go!" Michael was standing in the doorway, his eyes shining with eagerness. "Dad's grabbing the suitcases and that present I made for Jane." His gaze was on Jill. "But if you're still busy, I'll help Dad take the suitcases down to the car and we'll wait for you there."

"No, I believe we're finished here." Eve got to her feet. "It took a little longer than I thought." She held out her hand to him. "This is my son, Michael, Jill. This is Jill Cassidy, Michael, come and shake hands with her. She's a very famous journalist, and you'll probably be seeing her stories in newspapers and on the Net."

"Really?" He was across the porch and smiling at Jill. "That will be neat. I'm very glad to meet you, Ms. Cassidy." He shook her hand and looked her straight in the eye. "I'll be watching for them. I think you must be very smart if you're this famous so young."

"Not so young." Jill smiled. "Compared to you, I'm ancient. I'm happy to meet you, Michael. I can see why your mother is so proud of her family."

"We're proud of her, too." He turned away and went back to Eve. "I think I'll go back inside and help Dad. He might need me." He leaned forward, and whispered to Eve as he passed her, "She's so *sad*, Mom. Be nice to her." Then he was through the door and talking to his father.

"Sweet kid." Jill was looking after him. "You're lucky."

"Yes, I am." She shouldn't have been surprised at Michael's instant insight, but she was. Jill had been hiding that vulnerability very well, even from Eve, until those last moments. But then Eve and Joe had known since the moment he was born that Michael saw deeper than other people. "But like all kids, he has a few issues." One of which was to make her feel guilty when she agreed with what he saw, she thought crossly. Gazing at Jill Cassidy right now, Eve was acutely aware of the scars that had been born of the emotional battles the woman had fought over the years. "He can be very demanding on occasion."

"I see absolutely nothing wrong with that," Jill said with a smile. "I can be demanding myself. I believe we'd get along fine." Her smile faded as she turned toward the porch steps. "But I'm in your way. You said you had to take your husband and son to the airport. Thank you for seeing me."

"You're welcome. I'm sorry I can't help you." She followed Jill to the steps. "I meant what I said, I'll get on the phone tomorrow and try to talk to several charities."

"I'm sure you will." Jill looked back at her, and Eve was once more aware of that hint of desperation in her expression. "Just look at the family photos and read my biographies of the children. That's all I ask. After meeting your son, I know that's a lot. But I have to ask it."

Eve gazed at the manila envelope on the cushions of the porch swing. "I'll look at them." She shook her hand. "But I can't let them change my mind. It was nice meeting you, Jill."

Jill nodded and made an effort to smile. "Yeah, I hope Nora turns out the way you want her."

"That depends on her," Eve said. "I never know until the last sculpting."

"Why doesn't that surprise me?" Jill waved and ran down the steps.

Eve stood there and watched her as she got into her dark blue Volvo and backed out of the driveway. Jill smiled again as she waved and drove down the lake road.

Smiles?

She's so sad, Michael had said.

"Hi." Michael was suddenly standing beside her, his gaze on the car. "Did we stay inside long enough? Did you have time to fix it?"

"No," Eve said. "Sometimes people have to fix their own problems. Though I'll make a few calls for her tomorrow." She gave him a little push to stop the protest she could see was coming. "But right now I want to spend time just being with you and your dad and not thinking of anyone else until you get on that jet. Go get your luggage."

Jill pulled onto a side road a few miles from the lake cottage and turned off the engine of the Volvo. She realized she was shaking. Stupid. Everything had gone well, and there was no reason for her to be this upset. Yet she had felt like she had to take a few moments before she got on the freeway. She had wanted to catch a final glimpse of Eve Duncan and her family before she took the next step that would send Eve spiraling into the coming nightmare.

Maybe it would not happen. She had tried to take precautions that might keep Eve safe.

Or might not.

Either way, Jill was committed, and all the regrets in the world wouldn't alter what she'd done. So stop this nonsense and make certain that the rest of the plan was set as well. She quickly dialed Jed Novak before she could change her mind. "It's okay," she said when he picked up. "They're on their way to the airport, and Eve Duncan isn't getting on that flight with them. The only worry I had was that she might change her mind. She's very close to her family, and that could have happened."

"But you said it wasn't likely," Novak said dryly. "And I built the entire scenario around your judgment. I'm glad you didn't disappoint me."

"You would have just made me come up with something else. You don't allow failure, Novak."

Silence. "No, I don't. Not once you were committed. The stakes are too high." He paused. "Is she going to do it?"

"I think she will. She turned me down, but she'll look at the photos and the children's stories. They'll be very effective. Then she won't be able to resist going back and finding out more about Maldara. She'll allow a little time to pass, then she'll find a way to do what I asked."

"You seem certain."

"I'm as certain as I can be considering how intelligent she is. As I told her, I did my homework." Jill added curtly, "She doesn't want to do it. She wants to keep her commitments with all those law-enforcement bodies she had on her agenda. And she has family responsibilities and knows that there's always a possibility of harm when you go to a country like Maldara. That's why you have to reassure her that the risk is minimal when she starts checking. Have you set it up?"

"Of course," he said dryly. "This isn't my first rodeo, Jill."

"No, you were probably there when they built the Colosseum. I'm the one who doesn't have the experience. But I have to do this right, Novak." Her hands tightened on the steering wheel. "And the risk has to be as minimal as we're letting her think. You have to keep her safe, Novak."

"It will go right if you've read Eve Duncan right. You've told me all the things that are con, what are the pros?"

"Only two things. I'm good at what I do. I made very sure the photos of the massacre and the families will shock and touch her. And I guarantee my stories in that envelope will do the rest. They're going to haunt her, she won't be able to forget them."

"And the other thing?"

"She likes me," she said simply. "And I know it's hard for her not to trust someone she likes." She drew a shaky breath. "Because I like her, too. So make sure we don't get her butchered, Novak."

"I'll work on it."

She braced herself. "And while you're doing that, I should tell you that on that last day before I left Maldara, I thought I was being followed."

"You were. Don't worry. I'm on it. I'll get back to you."

"That's comforting," she said dryly. "Kind of you to let me know." She cut the connection.

She didn't feel as if she could talk to Novak any more right now. He was a master at the games that all those covert organizations played, and she was a rank amateur. That was fine with her; she had never wanted to be anything but a journalist and tell the story.

But not this story.

She stiffened as she glimpsed Eve Duncan's Toyota driving down the lake road. She was at the wheel, and her son and husband were smiling and talking to her. She was also smiling and looked happy as if life was good and there was no Maldara in the world.

And Jill could make certain there would be no Maldara for Eve Duncan. She could step away and take the story in another direction.

But she knew she wasn't going to do it.

She was going to let it happen.

CHAPTER

2

I 'll call you from London as soon as we get in," Joe said. "Jane said that we'll be going out to breakfast after she picks us up, then drop by her apartment to rest until she and Michael leave for Wales tomorrow evening."

"And you'll be using her apartment while you're at the seminar," Eve said. "I told you it was meant to be. The timing was almost too good to be true."

"Not if you're not with us." His hand reached up to cup her cheek. "Change your mind?"

"I'm tempted." More than tempted. The idea of going back home while they flew off into the wild blue yonder was already causing her an aching sense of loss. "Maybe after I finish Nora. I'll see in a few days."

"Good." He kissed her. "I'll keep after you."

"If you have time," she said ruefully. "During that last seminar at the Yard, you were busy from dusk to dawn. And afterward, you and the guys were cementing international relations at every pub near Scotland Yard."

"Only the one on Whitehall. The others closed too early. But I might just have time for you." He grinned. "Try me." He slipped his arm around her waist, and they walked toward the jetway, where Michael was waiting, playing a game on his computer. "Though I'll have to think about it. I was a little insulted when you sent Michael in to tell me we had to sit down and wait until you finished that interview with Jill Cassidy."

"It wasn't exactly an interview. It turned out to be something different." That was an understatement. "And that wasn't me, that was Michael. He liked her. He was feeling sorry for her and thought I should help her."

"Why?"

"You know Michael. He just said she was sad." She shrugged. "And maybe she is. Journalists don't have tremendously happy lives. They see too much. Big-time stress. But I told him sometimes people have to fix their own problems." She turned and kissed him again, hard. "And the only problems I want to fix right now are yours and Michael's," she said fiercely. "You take care of yourself, and I'll expect at least one Skype a day. Even if it has to be from a pub on Whitehall Street."

"You'll get it." His hand gently caressed her cheek. "Don't work too hard. I don't want to come back to a haggard wife who will send me running back to that pub to drown my sorrows." He grinned. "Now go say good-bye to Michael. I'm sure he wants to lecture you about your mistreatment of Jill Cassidy."

"No, he won't. Not this close to the time he's going to have to leave me. I'll get a break." She was moving toward Michael. "But he might do it on our first Skype call!"

———◆———

Dammit.

Eve could feel her eyes sting with tears as she drove up the driveway to the lake cottage. The place seemed just as empty as she'd been afraid it would without Joe and Michael. It had been bad when she'd watched the plane take off, but this was worse. This was where there were a million memories, and she'd have to fight them every single day.

She wanted to run back to the airport and jump on the next plane.

Yeah, that would be mature and responsible. It would be good for Michael to spend time with his sister. He and Jane didn't get a chance to bond that often. And she'd be in Joe's way while he was networking. Just get busy and this month would fly by and they'd all be together again.

She ran up the porch steps and threw open the door. It was getting dark, and she flicked on the light. That was more cheerful. She threw down her purse and moved to her worktable in the studio across the room. "Hi, Nora." She looked down at the reconstruction. "It's just me and you, kid. But we'll get along just fine, won't we?" She touched the clay of her cheekbone with her index finger. "And after that, we'll find someone else to help."

Nora gazed up at her from blind eyes. Eve hadn't put the glass eyes in the eye orbits yet. That was always the last touch. Usually she didn't even notice that emptiness, but she did today. Probably because she was feeling so empty herself. "Maybe we won't work right away." She turned away. "No offense. I'll just have a cup of coffee, then call Jane and tell her they're on their way. We'll get together later tonight."

But the call to Jane went straight to voice mail. Jane was always busy, and she might even have a gallery showing. Later. Everything seemed to be later today.

She took her coffee to the porch and looked out at the lake. Beautiful as usual. But it wasn't as lit by sunlight as it had been earlier when she'd been out here with Jill Cassidy. The sun had gone down, and it was a little somber.

Jill Cassidy.

Promise you'll look at them.

Her gaze went to the manila envelope she'd left on the porch swing. She didn't want to look at those photos. She'd seen more than enough horror photos in her career in forensics. She was depressed enough today.

Promise me.

She could almost see Jill standing on those steps, pleading desperately.

She's so sad.

And Michael had ganged up on Eve.

Oh, well, just do it. She crossed to the swing, plopped down, and reached for the envelope. It might be better that her mood was as somber as that lake out there. She pulled out the photos and switched on the light. It couldn't be any worse than what she'd seen before . . .

———◆———

Wrong.

Two hours later, the tears were still running down Eve's cheeks. So much worse than anything she'd ever encountered in her career thus far. Not only the butchery and the burning of innocents, but Jill had researched and interviewed parents, relatives, friends, and siblings of each child in the village. Then she had written their stories from birth to the day of their horrible death. Each word simple but poignant until Eve had felt that every one of those children belonged to her.

She leaned her head back and closed her eyes, but the tears still flowed. She could still see that day, feel the darkness of terror as the militia had come and hacked and hacked with their machetes. Would she ever not see it? Jill Cassidy had made every moment come alive for her and anyone else who read those damnably beautiful, agonizingly human, stories.

Close it out.

Impossible.

Jill had known it would be impossible. That's why she had made Eve promise to look at them. Brilliant, wise, Jill Cassidy, who had done her homework and had no trouble reading her. She would have been resentful except for the fact that Jill could not have written those words if she hadn't been caught up in the same agony as Eve was feeling now. They were bound together by the pain of those helpless children butchered in that village.

But don't let Jill Cassidy manipulate her. Push it away. Don't give in to it. Six hundred thousand people had died in Maldara. These were only twenty-seven children.

But now, she knew every single one of them.

She opened her eyes. She would *not* cry again. Tears did no good. Find a solution or accept the pain. She reached for her computer and flipped open the lid.

Maldara . . .

———◆———

It wasn't Joe but Jane who called her four hours later. "I'm calling from the apartment. Michael and Joe are here and safe," she said. "But there's something missing. You. I thought I was going to be reasonable and not harass you, but then when you didn't show up at customs, I decided that was bullshit. Get on the next plane. I don't care if you smuggle that skull through customs and just work here at the apartment. Or if you decide to go with us to the dig. At least you'd be here. That's where you belong. Now do what I say, dammit."

Eve could almost see her toss her red hair as she said those last words. Jane was always passionate when it came to family, and this wasn't totally unexpected. "I'm thinking about it. Though we both know that you're all going to be so busy that you probably wouldn't know I was around."

"We'd know." She sighed. "I just thought that I'd add my two cents' worth to the guilt trip Joe has no doubt been bombarding you with. I guess I'll just have to leave it to him."

"You'll have enough on your plate with supervising Michael on that dig. He's so excited about it. I know it's going to be wonderful."

"I think it will. Most of the time, they only permit older students on these digs. I went on my first one when I was a teenager, remember? So when I ran across the information on this one in Wales that was allowing younger kids, I jumped on it." She chuckled. "And I'm not sure who's going to supervise whom. Michael is already making plans and reading all my literature on it. I'm expecting sunrise to sunset to be the time-frame agenda."

"See? You'd have to squeeze me in."

"I'm not handling this well. I'd better hand you over to Joe. He has more experience at bulldozing you. I love you."

The next moment, Joe came on the line. "As Jane said, we're here and already missing you. She insisted on trying her powers of persuasion one more time. We stopped for breakfast on the way from the airport. Did I wake you?"

"No, it's only a little after midnight here, and I've been busy," Eve said. "Good flight?"

"Passable. Michael and I played cards. He's decided that counting cards shouldn't really be considered illegal in the casinos, and he's perfecting his technique."

"Heaven help us. Don't you dare take him to a casino."

"I think he'll be content with Jane once they start working at the dig in Wales. Why weren't you sleeping? Nora?"

"No." She paused. "Just doing some research about some skulls found in Maldara. I didn't know much about it."

"Maldara? From what I remember from the news stories, you'd do better researching almost anything else. Nightmare stuff. I remember you were very careful to keep it away from Michael's eyes."

"Which meant I had to ignore a lot of it myself. I only knew it was a civil war between the Kiyanis and the Botzan factions in central Africa that tore the country and most of its people apart. It went on for almost two years before the U.N. sent in forces to stop it." Her hand tightened on the phone as she remembered the photos of what those troops had found when they'd crossed the border. "The Botzan had hired a mercenary, a guerilla leader, Nils Varak, to run rampant over the country and attack the Kiyanis. Most of the butchery and burning was done by him and his men. He used the Botzan militia machete troops on occasion, but mostly he liked the personal touch." She added harshly, "The news stories said he had more blood on his hands than Hitler before the U.N. forces managed to kill him."

"Not soon enough," Joe said grimly. "When he first started that bloodbath, every police department in the world was canvassed for information about him. When I read his rap sheet, I was tempted to volunteer to go after the son of a bitch myself. Varak was into everything from child trafficking to terrorism. Pay him enough, and he'd do anything."

Even kill twenty-seven small children who had done nothing to deserve it. "I agree, he wasn't killed soon enough. I don't remember your telling me about that query."

"It was hardly dinner conversation. Since I decided not to do anything about it, I didn't see why I should discuss it. I was just as glad you were in Michael-protecting mode. You didn't need any more darkness hanging over you." He paused. When he next spoke, his voice was curt. "And why were you researching skulls in Maldara? Whose skulls?"

She didn't want to get into this now, but she wouldn't lie to him. "Children. I don't really know. When do I ever know, Joe? I just heard about this massacre at a school in Robaku village from Jill Cassidy and felt I had to know more about it. But I couldn't find out much. In spite of the U.N. presence, that country seems to still be in chaos."

"I can believe it," Joe said grimly. "Which is why I don't like you even thinking about it."

"Maybe if someone had thought about Maldara before that chaos started, I wouldn't have had to hear about those children's skulls today." She drew a deep breath. "Go to bed, Joe. All I did was do a little research. No big deal. I'll talk to you tomorrow. Right now, I'm going to put in an hour or so on Nora. I've been neglecting her today."

Silence. "Yes, you have. And you were so anxious to get her finished. Now I'm anxious for you to do it, too, because I want you here, Eve." He paused. "I love you. Being without you sucks. I'll talk to you when I get back here to the apartment tomorrow night."

"I love you, too. Tell Michael I'll call him before it's time for him to leave for Wales this evening. Good night, Joe." She cut the connection.

She had worried Joe, and it might be for nothing. She should have just kept her mouth shut about Maldara. No, she shouldn't. She rejected the thought immediately. Their relationship was based on total honesty, and silence could also be dishonest. Besides, they were so close, he would probably have sensed her disturbance.

Just work on Nora for a few hours and go to bed and get to sleep. Maybe by the time she woke tomorrow, that aching unrest would have lessened.

She picked up her ruler to check Nora's mid-philtrum measurements one last time. That space between nose and lips was so small, so delicate, on a child. Six years old . . .

There had been six-year-olds in that classroom in Maldara, too. One girl and two little boys. Robaku had been a village school, and one teacher had taught various ages and grades. Jill Cassidy had spent a good deal of time and effort detailing the short lives of those six-year-olds.

Eve had to stop working and close her eyes for an instant as the wave of horror and heartbreaking sadness overcame her once more. Then she got control again and put the ruler down and started to fill in the clay around the mid-philtrum.

It might be a long night.

Damn you, Jill Cassidy.

———◆———

NEXT DAY
2:35 P.M.

Do it!

Eve stabbed in the phone number on the card that Jill had given her. She wasn't surprised when Jill answered the phone in two rings. "Get over here. I want to talk to you."

"I thought you might," Jill said quietly. "Actually, I thought it could be—"

"Get over here," Eve interrupted. "I'm angry, and on edge, and I want to see your face while I'm listening to what you say to me. You went to a hell of a lot of trouble to tear me apart, and I have an idea why. How quick can you be here?"

"Ten minutes. I'm in a motel just off the freeway."

"I thought you'd stay close," Eve said curtly. "I'm surprised you didn't camp out in your car."

"I thought about it."

"I'm sure you did. I'll expect you in ten minutes, and don't expect either coffee or politeness. We've gone past that now." She hung up.

She got to her feet and moved toward the door to the porch. She needed air and to calm down a little before she confronted Jill. She hadn't realized until she'd actually made contact with her how the anger had been building in the last few hours. Or perhaps it had started building earlier, during all the hours she'd been working on Nora last night.

She took a deep breath and gazed out at the lake, trying to steady herself.

Sunlight. Beauty. Peace.

Everything that she wanted to surround her while she was working on Nora and others like her who had been robbed of all three.

And this was Eve's life, her *home*.

The anger was growing again.

But now she had a target.

Jill was driving down the lake road and pulling into the driveway.

Eve met her at the top of the stairs. "You're early. You must be eager to see me."

"I broke a few speed laws. I figured that you needed to vent before you exploded," she said. "You don't get angry often, but when you do, it's supposed to be impressive."

"Of course you'd know that about me, too. Research."

"Yes." Jill's gaze was studying her face. "Circles. You didn't sleep last night. I'm sorry."

"Are you? I don't believe you. I think it was all part of your plan to manipulate me. You knew exactly how to do it. You knew which buttons to push and took time to coordinate them in the right order." Her lips tightened. "Those photos and biographies were a masterstroke. They brought me down as if I'd been run over by a fifty-ton truck. You knew they would, didn't you?"

"Yes. It was your principal weakness." She added, "And your greatest strength. I had to use it."

"You're not even denying it."

"Why should I? You'd know I was lying, and I wouldn't insult you." She paused. "Besides, I've won, haven't I?"

Eve stared at her in frustration. It was difficult to hold on to her anger as she gazed at the reporter. Jill wasn't boasting; there was only vulnerability and that sadness Michael had noticed. "Not yet. I *hate* being manipulated. Last night, I started thinking about every way you'd done that since you walked in here yesterday afternoon. It took me a little while to get it together because you were so clever and so good at what you do. Even those photos weren't close-ups of the children. Just loving family shots. Because you knew I never looked at facial photos of my reconstructions." Her lips tightened. "And then you hit me with the photos after the massacre."

"I didn't want to do it. But I had to convince you." She moistened her lips. "We need you, Eve. You don't realize how much. But I promise if you come, that you'll see how worthwhile it is."

"I can tell that you think it is. But you're asking me to put my life and career on hold while I do those reconstructions."

"Only for a few weeks. I told you, I wouldn't expect more from you."

"How generous of you," she said dryly. "It's what I expect of my-self that matters. You've been playing me to get what you want, but that's over." She was silent. "I'm the only one in charge of what I do, but there are things I have to know before I commit." She stared her straight in the eyes. "Is everything you told me the truth?"

Jill's gaze didn't waver. "Absolutely. Every word."

"Even those stories you wrote about the children at the school, *their* stories?"

Jill nodded. "I swear it. You can ask their parents and grandpar-ents. You believe me?"

Eve couldn't help but believe her. "You're so good at what you do. I had to be sure."

"I *am* good. I'm a fantastic storyteller. It's my primary talent. I have others, and I've always had to use whatever skills I have to sur-vive. But I try to be honest, Eve."

"I had to be sure about that, too. You told me not to take you at face value. I didn't. I spent a little time this morning finding out about you."

"I thought you might. Did you discover anything interesting?"

"You spent your entire life until you were eleven years old trailing around the world with your father, who was a photographer. When he was killed in Tibet, it took the U.S. consulate over a year to get you back to the States. But you had no relatives, so you were fostered out for the next five years. Then you worked your way through a community college and started freelancing. Your gift for languages helped you to get ahead, but the first couple years must have been hard."

"Not that bad. I liked traveling around on my own again. I was a little gypsy until my father was killed." She added, "But you didn't find anything incriminating, did you? Other than being a loner, I'm pretty much what I appear on the surface."

"I *wanted* to find something."

"I know you did. It would have been an excuse to close your eyes again." She paused. "Are you going to come with me?"

"I'm close," Eve said jerkily. "Not because you want me to do it. Whether it was for a good cause or not, you tried every weapon in your arsenal to make me do what you wanted. And I could see how you'd pried and researched into who I was to make that happen. That's probably what I resent most. Talk about violation of privacy? And you did such a damn good job." She gestured impatiently. "No, it's because last night I realized those stories were like a poison inside me. I couldn't forget them. And I knew the only way I might be able to was to do something to help, to heal, those children. But you probably knew that would be my reaction?"

"I thought it was likely. You're very caring."

"And I *can't* heal them, but I might be able to heal those closest to them."

Jill nodded silently.

"So when I decided that those stories might have trapped me into doing this, I decided I had to look the situation over and explore how bad it might be. First. My family. I have a husband and a son who need me. And I need them. From what I've been able to find out, Maldara is still too unstable to be considered safe on any level. Yet you said that I'd be safe while I did those reconstructions. How?"

"I have friends at the embassy. And the U.N. staff on-site think reporters have to be given special protection. No bad press. I'll just convince them to extend that protection to you."

"From what you said, they don't even want the work done at Robaku."

Jill grimaced. "But I've been a thorn in their diplomatic asses over the last year. They'll be glad to shut me up and get rid of my nagging as long as it doesn't affect their budget." She added, "But, you know, it might be a good idea for you to call one of those charities you mentioned and tell them you're volunteering to do the job. You have tremendous name recognition, so there's no question they'll jump at sponsoring you. Just ask them if they'll contact the U.N. and advise them you're operating at their request. That way you'd get the official protection and not raise any U.N. hackles by mentioning me." She shrugged. "And the charity would get credit in the international community that might translate to donations later. Everyone wins."

"And more manipulation," Eve said.

"Would you rather I do it? I'll do anything that will make you feel more comfortable." Jill was obviously being perfectly sincere.

"No, I'll take care of it." Eve ran her hand through her hair. "If it's even possible. I just remembered I don't have a visa, no documents. That could take—"

"Twenty-four hours," Jill said. "Give me your passport, and I'll have it processed. We can stop and have the necessary shots on the way to the airport."

"Twenty-four hours?"

She smiled. "I told you that I have friends in high and low places. This is a piece of cake." She turned and strode toward the door. "And while you're getting me your passport, I'll make *you* a cup of coffee." She glanced over her shoulder. "If I'm forgiven enough to be let back into your good graces?"

"Marginally." She followed her into the house. "I'll let you know when we get to Maldara."

"Then you might never forgive me. It's hot, humid, and the poverty will break your heart." She started pouring the water into the automatic coffeemaker. "How will your husband take your decision?"

Eve was not about to deal with that now. Later. "That's not your concern."

"It is if it's going to make you unhappy." Jill was frowning. "He's a detective. Let's see ... He'll be worried about your safety. I'll give you a couple of names of law-enforcement officials in the Kiyani government for him to contact. And I know a few agents with the CIA and MI6 who operate in Maldara who might reassure him."

"I wouldn't bet on it." Eve's brows rose. "Is there anyone you don't know in Maldara?"

"Not if they're useful." Jill handed her the cup of coffee. "Survival. You'll only have to be there for a few weeks. But I've been there for two years."

"Two years..." Her gaze narrowed on Jill's face. "Okay, I need to know what I'll be facing there that I couldn't find on Google. According to what I read, for decades Maldara has been torn by conflict between the Kiyanis to the north and Botzan to the south. The Kiyanis possessed most of the wealth in the country, which was based on rich farmlands and diamond mines. They even managed to develop a fairly stable republic in the last thirty years. The Botzans were poor by comparison, mostly mountain people, except for a decent fishing industry, and they changed rulers every couple years. The mountain population were principally made up of roving bands who made the majority of their living stealing from the Kiyanis, whom they hated. They'd been raiding the Kiyanis' properties for years before the Kiyanis suddenly decided to go on the attack. Civil war. The Botzan faction was finally defeated by the Kiyanis after the death of that mercenary, Nils Varak, and with the help of the U.N." She paused. "Is all of that correct? Is there anything else I should know? Is Botzan still a danger?"

Jill shook her head. "It's pretty well broken up now. The U.N. was getting too much static because of the Varak massacres, and they saw to it that the Kiyanis took over most of Maldara." She grimaced. "And Zahra Kiyani, their president, is taking full advantage. She's even charmed the U.N. into giving her the right to speak at the next General Assembly meeting."

"I think I read something about her. She's a modern-day Madame Chiang Kai-shek?"

"Yes, that's who they're comparing her to. But you'll hear a lot more about her now that she's been able to draw a breath and start taking stock. Her father, President Akil Kiyani, was assassinated six months after the conflict started, and she tearfully accepted the presidency to honor him."

"Sarcasm?"

"I'm not a fan. When I interviewed her, she reminded me of Eva Peron. She's quite beautiful and much more flamboyant, of course. But her grateful people had just erected a statue of her in the main square of the capital city of Jokan. I found that odd after a war that had almost destroyed the country." She shrugged. "But that's politicians. She seems to have everything under control. She's built a hospital and gives to charity. The army and police seem to do their jobs. Everyone is fairly safe as long as they stay in the capital and don't go running around the countryside. She might even invite you to tea. That village where the massacre occurred is just outside Jokan. She's visited it twice and had a splendid and tearful photo op. Unfortunately, I wasn't able to attend."

"I don't believe I would either." Eve could see how that political circus would have hurt Jill. "And I'd think you'd be ready to leave Maldara. Isn't your story almost finished?"

"It's finished when it's finished. I'll know when it's done. Like your reconstructions." She'd turned away and was gazing at the reconstruction of Nora on the worktable across the room. "You've made a lot of progress on her since yesterday. She looks close to completion."

"I had a lot of time to work on her. Thanks to you, I couldn't sleep last night." She took a sip of her coffee. "And looks can be deceiving. The final will probably take me another twenty-four hours or even longer. I'm going to need this caffeine."

"But I might be able to get you out before that."

"Wrong," Eve said flatly. "I don't leave until Nora's finished and sent off to Chicago. It's bad enough I'm having to put off other commitments, I won't push *her* aside."

Jill nodded. "Sorry. I knew that, I just didn't think. If you'll give me your passport, I'll get out of your way so you can get back to her."

"Fine." Eve went to the kitchen cabinet where she and Joe kept their documents in a lockbox. "You're being amazingly cooperative." She handed her the passport. "I'll call you when I'm available to leave."

"Cooperative?" Jill's brows rose as she slipped the passport in her pocket. "I know how lucky I am that I talked you into going. I'm not about to rock the boat. Anything you need, just let me know."

"I'll do that." Eve gave her a cool glance. "And neither of us should pretend that luck had anything to do with your persuading me to commit to several weeks doing the reconstructions on those children. You were clever. You made sure you knew what would push every button. And you played me."

"Yes, I did," Jill said quietly. "But I still consider myself lucky that you allowed me to do it. If I work hard enough to make this trip easy for you, I hope you'll forgive me." She smiled with an effort. "I'll be in touch soon if you don't mind. Just to see if there's anything you need." She turned and walked quickly toward the door. "In the meantime, I'll e-mail you those names and contacts I mentioned might be useful to you." She looked back over her shoulder. "I'm sure your Nora will turn out wonderfully. Good-bye, Eve." Then she was gone.

Eve stared after her for a moment. There was no reason to feel as if she had somehow hurt Jill and should try to heal the hurt. Eve was the one who had been maneuvered into throwing her life into chaos for the next few weeks. And Jill Cassidy had not even denied it was done deliberately. Yet the emotion she felt for those children had to be genuine, and where was the line drawn in the sand where brutality toward children was concerned? Eve had never found it.

Forget Jill Cassidy. Eve had made the decision. Now she had to cope with making the best of it.

She was still drinking her coffee as she crossed the room toward the skull on her worktable. As she'd told Jill, she'd need the caffeine.

"Okay, Nora." She stopped in front of the reconstruction. "We're almost there, but now you have to help me. You're going to have to tell me who you are, show me what to do..."

⎯⎯⎯◆⎯⎯⎯

Jill dialed Jed Novak as she walked toward her car. "It's done," she said jerkily. "She'll be ready to leave in twenty-four hours if she finishes the current reconstruction by then. I think she will. She's driven right now."

"Putty in your hands, Jill?" Novak asked mockingly.

"Don't *say* that," Jill said fiercely. "It's stupid. She's not putty in anyone's hands. I made a situation impossible for her, and she's just trying to survive it. She's a completely private person, and she knows I probed deep to get what I wanted from her."

"Easy," Novak said. "Bad joke?"

"Very bad joke." She stopped as she reached her car and drew a deep breath. "And a very bad meeting with a woman I admire, Novak. She's smart, and nothing really gets past her. So you need to prepare very carefully. I've given her your name and a few others to pave the way. She might call you. Make her feel comfortable." She paused. "Have you heard anything from Jokan?"

"Not yet. Only a few rumbles. We still have time."

She wasn't as sure about that as Novak. "Let me know if it changes. I'm not going to let Eve go near the place if it does."

"But you'd go yourself," Novak said softly. "Who's going to stop you, Jill?" He added wearily, "It probably wouldn't be me. Never mind. I'll let you know." He cut the connection.

No, it wouldn't be Novak, Jill thought. She had never known anyone as tough or more ruthlessly motivated than Novak. He would get the job done no matter who fell by the wayside.

Yet he hadn't been ruthless after he'd taken her to that hospital in Nairobi, she suddenly remembered. He'd swept her into the ER, giving orders and making everyone snap to attention. Then he'd stayed with her, guarding her, watching that she was given the best possible attention.

And he'd been there, moving shadowlike in the background, for the entire four days she'd been forced to spend at the damn place.

But there had been nothing shadowlike about those nights he'd sat beside her bed and fought off the dragons that attacked from the darkness. There had been moments when she had hated how strong and dominant he had been during that period when she had been so weak. But there had been other times that he had seemed her only path to survival...

———◆———

NAIROBI HOSPITAL

She screamed.

Darkness.

Pain.

She couldn't move!

She was smothering!

She sat bolt upright in the hospital bed, her hands tearing off the sheet.

"No." Novak was suddenly sitting on the bed beside her. "You're fine. Only another dream, Jill." He was holding her, rocking her back and forth. "I'm here with you. Nothing can hurt you."

She was clutching at him. Her heart was pounding so hard that she could hardly breathe. "I hate this." But she couldn't let him go yet. Another minute... Then she would be strong again.

No, she couldn't allow herself that time. It was another sign of weakness. She drew a deep breath and pushed him away from her. "Thank you. I'm okay now. I don't need you any longer." *Need. How she detested that word.* "In fact, I don't know why you're here anyway. As you said, it was only a nightmare. I'm not a child who can't deal with bogeymen." *She leaned back against the pillows and said impatiently,* "For that matter, I shouldn't even be in this hospital. It's been three days, Novak. I thought I'd be in and out of here in a matter of hours. Why won't they release me?"

"You know that besides severe bruising you had a cracked rib and a few other less obvious problems. I told them not to let you go until they could promise me that they'd done all they could for you." *He got off her bed and settled back in his chair.* "I guarantee they didn't want to break that promise. I tend to get a little testy. Now go back to sleep." *He paused.* "Same nightmare?"

"I don't want to talk about it." *She was glad of the darkness. His stare was always laser sharp, and she didn't want to face it right now. When he came to her at night, he was always only a deep, soothing voice, a strong hand that wove a barrier to keep out the weakness and the terror.* "Tell them to let me leave here, Novak. I would never have come if I'd known you'd make me a prisoner. You even have a shrink coming in to talk to me every day. I don't need all this. I'm not one of your agents. Give me a week or two on my own, and I'll work it out for myself."

"No harm in getting a little therapy. The doctor says what you're going through is PTSD. I think talking to the psychiatrist is doing you good. I've noticed that you're not as tense as you were that first day." *He added,* "And only one nightmare so far tonight."

"I can work it out for myself," *she repeated.* "That's the way it has to be. It's my story, and I have to tell it."

"What?"

She hadn't meant to say that, it had just tumbled out. What did it matter? He had learned more intimate things about her during these last days. "*When I was a kid, I had trouble understanding everything that was happening to me. But I loved books and reading, and the stories always made sense to me. There seemed to be a reason for everything, and I thought the writers had a kind of magic that could always make it that way if they tried hard enough.*" *She added,* "*And it still makes sense to me to think of myself as writing my own story, incomplete, a work in progress, but totally in control of who I am.*" *She shrugged.* "*Weird, huh?*"

"*Interesting. And totally logical for a premier storyteller.*"

"*And you're probably being polite and think that I'm nuts. That's okay, it works for me.*"

"*And that's all that's important.*"

"*See? You're being polite. Look, you're a busy man, you don't need to be wasting your time on me. I'm going to leave here tomorrow and go back to Maldara.*"

"*We'll see.*" *He leaned forward and took her hand.* "*Maybe if you don't have another nightmare tonight. So concentrate on keeping them all at bay.*"

"*I'm going to leave tomorrow.*" *But she found her hand instinctively tightening in his grasp. He had been her anchor in the storm, and she didn't want to let him go quite yet. She could go to sleep holding his hand as she'd done for the past three nights. She was nearly healed, but she could be with him for these next hours. She would be strong tomorrow.* "*No more nightmares, Novak...*"

And the next day Novak had taken her back to Maldara, and she had started to make the plans and do the research that had brought her here to Eve Duncan.

She looked back at the lake cottage as she got in her car. Eve was probably already working on that reconstruction. In a way, Eve reminded her of Novak as far as motivation and steely determination were concerned. But Eve lacked the kill gene that made Novak lethal. She didn't doubt that Eve would kill to protect family or friend, but that was different.

But she knew others who possessed that kill gene, too.

And she and Novak were sending Eve right into their target zone.

CHAPTER

3

Her hair was just right, Zahra Kiyani thought with satisfaction as she watched her maid, Dalai, straighten the strands at her temple. Her chignon was dark and sleek and shining, with just the right touch of sophistication. It accented her high cheekbones and slightly slanted eyes and made the deep gold of her skin glow. She'd wear it like this when she went to New York next week, she decided. Then everyone would realize that she was truly a woman of style and power.

"Send her away," Edward Wyatt said roughly from her bed across the room. "You've kept me waiting long enough."

"You'll spoil my hair." She met his eyes in the mirror. The Honorable Edward Wyatt might be considered important to his cronies at the U.N., but she knew exactly how to control him. "And then I'll have to have Dalai do it again. Such a waste." He was naked and fully aroused, she noticed. She'd kept him watching her and anticipating for the last thirty minutes, and he was ready and eager for the game to begin. But she was not, and she was annoyed that he should speak to her with so little respect. Make him wait. She turned to Dalai. "I think the ruby comb tonight. Did I tell you how much I enjoy wearing it? It has such meaning for me."

"Yes, madam, you told me." She met Zahra's eyes in the mirror as she hurriedly placed the ruby comb in the chignon. Her maid was probably remembering the details of the deadly story of the comb, Zahra thought with amusement. Dalai was so easy to frighten. "It will be beautiful."

"Yes, it will." Zahra glanced back at Wyatt. "Do you think I'll look beautiful when I give my speech at the U.N. General Assembly? Will you be proud of me?"

"Stop teasing and come over here."

"But you like me to tease you. You like everything I do to you." And she had found out early in their relationship that the thing he liked most was for her to dominate him. The twisted bastard went wild when he was forced into submission. She'd seen the signs on that first night she'd seduced him and had her agent, Lon Markel, check him out. Wyatt spent a good deal of money at several specialty houses when he was in London. That information was all Zahra needed. His particular addiction suited her very well. Domination could be used in many ways other than sex. She got to her feet and came toward him. "Do you think that your wife will think I'm beautiful? Perhaps we can have a threesome when I'm in New York. Shall I call her in London and tell her to join us?" She slipped off her robe and dropped it on the floor. "But perhaps she thinks a woman's duty is only to provide pleasure to a man . . . and whoever else he chooses. Haven't you taught her?" She slipped naked into bed. "I'll teach her for you."

He started to reach for her, and she pushed him away. "No, my rules. Always my rules."

"Bitch," he said through his teeth. "I'm going crazy. Let me *in* you."

"I told you, you'll mess my hair." She ran her fingers down his belly. "But I might allow you to persuade me. But you'll have to give me something that will please me to make up for it."

"What a whore you are."

"No, I'm a queen. I've told you that before."

"You keep saying that. Being president isn't enough for you?"

"No, presidents rely on elections. A queen has power because she is what she is. That's why it hurts my feelings that you don't believe me. You should feel honored that I let you have my body."

"Stop playing this game, Zahra. Just let me—" He gasped as her hand closed on him. "What...do you want?"

"I want you to tell me that you know I'm a queen, and you'll do everything you can to make sure that's how I'm treated in New York."

"You—know—I—will."

"How do I know it?" Her hand tightened around him. "Prove it to me. I haven't noticed you doing anything to make my position here in Maldara stronger lately."

"I do everything you ask." He gasped again as her nails dug into him. *"Shit."*

"I don't appreciate how unfriendly the newspapers have been to me. You have influence. Do something about it."

"I told you, interfering with the free press would be a mistake. It would shine too bright a light on me and my office here in Jokan. I can't do it."

"All I wish is for you to get rid of just one journalist. Jill Cassidy. That's not too much to ask."

"She's very well regarded, and it might cause a stir. You said you'd take care of it yourself."

And she would have, if only those fools had been a little rougher with the bitch that night in the jungle. She'd given explicit instructions, and it should have worked beautifully. But Jill had disappeared for only a few days after the attack; and then she was back in Jokan and still very much in the way. "It didn't work out. I want you to do it."

Wyatt was silent. "I'll do it. You know I'll do anything you wish. But you should know they will probably recall me. Is that what you want?"

No, it wasn't what she wanted. Wyatt was still useful, and it would take her time to develop a relationship with a replacement. "You know it's not," she said curtly. "Very well, I'll find another way. But you will be sure and block anything she tries to do here?"

"Of course." He looked relieved. "Whatever you want. That's a much better—"

He gasped. She was suddenly above him and he was deep inside her. *"Yes."*

She reached up and took the ruby comb from her hair and held it in front of his eyes. "Isn't it beautiful? Full of glitter and power. But there's always danger with power. What if I'd coated these prongs with a deadly poison?" She brought the prongs closer to his throat. "Then you'd really know how powerful I am, wouldn't you?"

He was staring in fear and fascination at the comb. "Yes."

"But it excites you, doesn't it?" She brought the comb still closer to his throat. "I can see it does." Then she was taking the comb away and putting it back in her hair. "Whatever I want?" She was moving fast, controlling him, not letting him touch her, totally dominating. "Stay still. Don't move. You have to be punished for not giving me everything I need tonight. I'll permit you to have this, but then I'll tell Dalai to use the quirt on you. You'll like that, won't you?"

His cheeks were flushed, his mouth open to take air. "Yes. But I— want you—to do it."

"Why should I care what you want? You're only my slave, and so is Dalai. I'll lie here as a queen should and watch the two of you perform for me." She leaned over him, her dark eyes glittering. Her sharp white teeth sank deep into his shoulder. "Say it."

"Whatever pleases you." He shuddered as the blood ran from the wound. "Yes... watch us... as a queen should..."

LAKE COTTAGE

"It's crazy," Joe said curtly when Eve finished telling him why she was going to Maldara. "I knew that there was something going on last night. I just didn't know I wasn't going to get a chance to talk you out of it."

"You have a chance now," Eve said. "I called you as soon as I was positive I was going. I won't be leaving until tomorrow afternoon at three." She added sarcastically, "It seems Jill has arranged with one of her friends in high places to lend her his jet and pilot to give us a lift to Maldara. For all I know, she might have even set it up before she came to see me. But at least that will eliminate a lot of red tape and give me more time to send Nora off and postpone my other commitments." She paused. "Please don't give me a hard time, Joe. It won't do you any good. I've decided I have to go."

"You *don't* have to go, dammit. You told me yourself that Jill Cassidy played you. Why should you let her have her way?"

"Because she made sure that I'd know her way was my way this time. I can't do anything else." She added wearily, "I'll e-mail those photos and biographies Jill gave me to you. Then I think you'll understand."

"Oh, I'll understand," Joe said. "But it won't make me want to keep from boiling her in oil at the earliest opportunity. I did a little more research after I hung up with you last night. I could see this coming. Granted, Maldara isn't the powder keg it was two years ago. But between Zahra Kiyani's power grab and all the other ex-mercenaries and crooks who are trying to line their pockets with what's left of that country, it could still be lethal. I don't want you there."

"Three weeks. A month tops. It's all I promised Jill." Then she realized what she'd just said. "No, to hell with Jill. It's what I promised myself. And I may not be able to do reconstructions on more than a portion of those children. I'll have to examine the skulls and make a decision. I may be done sooner. But if I'm successful with only a few, it will show what can be done and might encourage the U.N. to hire someone else to complete the job." She paused. "Remember when I said the timing was just right for you to go to Scotland Yard and Michael to take his trip with Jane? Well, maybe this timing is right, too. Maybe if I can help the relatives of those children, then it was meant to be."

"I'm not in the mood for you to bring up fate at this particular time." Joe was silent another moment. "I'm going with you."

Just what she'd expected. "No, you are not," she said firmly. "I wouldn't get anything done with you floating around like a drone ready to strike. You're going to stay at Scotland Yard, keep an eye on Michael, and call me on Skype as you'd planned to do. If I get nervous about anything, I'll let you know."

He didn't reply.

"Look, Joe, I gave you the names of those officials at the embassy and the U.N. that Jill sent me. She even supplied you with a CIA operative and someone from MI6 to call. Check them out. They should be able to tell you anything you need to know."

"Maybe. I recognized one of the names. I ran into Jed Novak two years ago when I was over here picking up a counterfeiter in Paris." He was silent again, thinking. "They'd given Novak a team and sent him to go after a terrorist ring in southern France. He has a reputation that's . . . impressive. I wonder what he's doing in Maldara . . ."

"Discuss it with him and find out." Jill had been right, Eve thought. A detective like Joe would feel more secure about her if he knew she was going to be surrounded by law enforcement he knew and understood. "I'll call you when I get there. I'm sure by that time, you'll have all the information you need."

"Are you trying to get rid of me, Eve?"

"Lord, no." The sound of his voice, the knowledge that he cared, was a comfort even when she had to argue with him. "I just have to get back to Nora if I'm going to finish her tonight. So just do all the things that will make you feel better about my going because it's going to happen."

He didn't speak for a moment. "I think it is, dammit. So by all means I'll do everything I can to prepare for it. Count on it. Good night, Eve."

Eve put down the phone after he'd disconnected. There had been a tinge of grimness in that last sentence. He was already planning what he could do, whom he could use to protect her. She wished she was like Joe and could prepare and make plans for the weeks ahead. There was no way she could do that this time. She just had to go with what she felt.

Because she couldn't see anything but the pitiful photos of those slain children and the siren call of the tales Jill had woven about each one of them.

JOKAN, MALDARA
THIRTY-SIX HOURS LATER

"We'll be landing at Jokan in forty-five minutes." Jill had come out of the cockpit and dropped into the passenger seat next to Eve. "I wanted to let you rest as long as possible, but now there are things I have to talk to you about." She grimaced. "You'll notice I've tried to stay out of your way during the flight."

"I could hardly miss it," Eve said dryly. From the moment the Gulf Stream had taken off, Jill had either been in her own luxurious leather seat across the aisle or in the cockpit with their pilot, Sam Gideon. She had been polite, seen that Eve had drinks and food, given her updates on their progress, but other than that, she had worked on her computer and allowed Eve total privacy. "I appreciate the effort, but you didn't have to treat me as if I had Ebola."

Jill smiled. "I didn't want to push my luck. I know you resent me.

No one has a better right. You'll meet a lot of people here who have problems with me, so you won't feel alone."

"You mentioned that the U.N. officials here weren't your fans. The Children for Peace charity had no problem dealing with them. They found the undersecretary, the Honorable Edward Wyatt, both charming and cooperative when they called him and told him they were sending me."

"Because I wasn't involved." Jill shrugged. "If they'd known I'd convinced you to come, they would have stonewalled you. Lately, it's been a solid wall whenever I need something from them." She made an impatient gesture. "And that's okay, I can work around them. I just have to warn you that I'm going to have to do that. It will be easier and safer for you if no one knows that I had anything to do with bringing you here."

She raised her brows. "You're abandoning me?"

"No, I'd never do that." She made a face. "Though you'd probably prefer if I did. But this is a country that's not like Main Street U.S.A. I know people, you might need me."

"If they don't hate you?"

She nodded wryly. "There is that to consider." She leaned forward, and said urgently, "You won't be alone. I'll surround you with people you can trust. And I'll be able to be on hand for you in a few days. I've had Sam Gideon set up an interview with the press on Thursday, to which I'll be invited. We'll have a nice meeting and find we have everything in common. Everyone knows I've been trying to convince the government to give the villagers what they want for their children. They just can't know that I brought you here."

"Why not?"

Jill hesitated. "Zahra Kiyani didn't like me any more than I did her. I told you, Robaku is a village practically on her doorstep. She was born and raised as Kiyani royalty, and now she's the president of the country. Her father gave up the throne to become president, which I don't believe pleased her. She also has more control than I'd like and is the prime mover in the effort to get the village moved to another location. I don't want her to influence anyone against what you're doing."

"You didn't mention that the deck was already stacked against me," Eve said dryly.

"It's not. I just have to deal around a possible bad hand," Jill said. "And I'm doing it. And I'm telling you about it."

"And letting me know the possibility that this Zahra Kiyani might get me ousted from the country before I can start doing one reconstruction. After a very long trip and a good deal of inconvenience." She shook her head. "And now you tell me?"

"You won't be ousted. We're working around it." She smiled. "And I thought this was the best time to tell you. You won't be likely to give up easily after traveling all this distance. And it's not as if I'll force you to stay. Gideon will take you directly to Robaku after you get off the plane, and you'll meet Hajif, the head of the village. He'll take you to the school and show you where you'll work if you choose to help them. President Zahra ordered the place be made into a sort of memorial, and you'll have to do the reconstructions on-site." She paused. "If you don't want to do it, just tell Gideon. He'll bring you back here, and you'll be on your way to your lake cottage within the hour."

"But you're confident that's not going to happen." Her eyes were narrowed on Jill's face. "You think you know me so well. I might surprise you."

Jill shook her head. "I'm not confident. I know you can surprise me. You're very complicated, and bad things can happen to any plan. I'm just hoping I'm not wrong about you in this instance." She got to her feet. "I'll go back to the cockpit. I'll stay on the plane until I'm sure I won't be seen getting off. After Gideon lands, he'll take care of you from then until we stage our meeting at the press interview."

"Gideon," Eve repeated. "You've dropped that name through the entire conversation. You're talking about Sam Gideon, our pilot, whom you introduced me to at the beginning of the trip?" She vaguely remembered a good-looking, dark-haired young man with a flashing smile. "I'm to put myself in his hands? I take it he's another friend of yours who is a bit more than a pilot?"

Jill nodded. "Well, he does own this Gulf Stream. And flying would be his career of choice if it were up to him." She made a face. "But he owns mega stocks and diamond mines and other boring stuff here in Maldara that tend to get in his way."

"Poor guy."

"Don't be sarcastic," she said quietly. "He's my friend, and he did me this favor. He's helped me before, and I trust him. The fact that he inherited a good portion of the entire wealth of this country made that a hell of a lot easier. I've known Sam Gideon ever since I first came to Maldara. He was born here and lived on a family plantation near Jokan before he graduated from Oxford and moved to London. He knows everybody who's anybody in the country. He won't let you get in trouble. And if he does, he has the man who can get you out of it on speed dial." She stopped at the door of the cockpit to look soberly back at her. "You might find him a little unusual, but you can trust him, too, Eve. I'd never turn you over to someone you couldn't trust." Then she was opening the cockpit door. "I'll see you Thursday if you're still here."

Eve watched the door shut behind Jill. That last sentence had probably been said to convince her that she wasn't being taken for granted. Yet every word Jill spoke sounded sincere. But the fact that she'd let her get here to Maldara before she'd told her that she happened to be having trouble with the ruling head of the damn country was both frustrating and suspicious. Trust her? Trust this Sam Gideon?

Eve shouldn't even get off the damn plane.

But she was already here in this place where savages had thought nothing of killing children as they studied in their classroom.

And she knew she was going to go to Robaku.

———◆———

"Jill says you're very important to her and I'm to be polite and respectful." Sam Gideon's dark eyes were twinkling with mischief as he came out of the cockpit after he'd landed the Gulf Stream. He had just a hint of an English accent that made the mockery in his tone take on an additional slyness. In his thirties, he was very good-looking, with olive skin, dark hair cut close to tame a tendency to curl, and that smile that was definitely reckless. "I told her that I'd been so polite to you when we were introduced that I'd never be able to do a repeat. So what you see is what you get." He shook her hand. "But I did promise her not to try to seduce you. Though it was a sacrifice since I do have a thing for intense, stormy women."

"Stormy?" Eve studied him. Jill had warned her that he was unusual, but it was clear there was much more to Gideon than what he seemed on the surface. He had chosen that remark deliberately because sex was blatantly inappropriate in this situation and definitely would have been forbidden by Jill. That opening could have been meant to either put her at ease or shock her. "Then it's lucky you're wrong about me. I have a very calm nature and avoid turbulence at all costs. Besides being married to a man who makes every effort to keep me from having to deal with the storms of life."

He chuckled. "And you've firmly put me in my place and given just a hint of a threat in case I step out of it. But I notice you don't deny the intensity, which means the storms probably come to you. Jill didn't really need to try to protect you from me, did she? But she tends to go the extra mile." He took her elbow and nudged her toward the door. "Now we've taken each other's measure and can get down to what's important to you." He threw open the door. "Welcome to Maldara, Eve."

A wild study of contrasts...

She stood on the steps, her gaze taking in the sleek commercial jets and military planes that occupied the hangars and runways of the small airport. Everything was new and modern and shining. In the distance, she could see a few skyscrapers on the horizon that contrasted sharply with the dense jungles surrounding the city. On either side of the road leading to Jokan, she could see ragged men, women, and children who had put up their booths of fruits and vegetables and brought their animals to sell at market.

"It's very . . . different," she murmured as she went down the steps. She was suddenly assaulted by heat, humidity, and the smell of gasoline from the planes on the tarmac. "Though I guess I expected more damage from the fighting."

"Jokan had less destruction than Botzan," Gideon said. "Amazing, since Varak's ghouls were hired by Botzan to decimate it. Our magnificent President Zahra claims her advisors and loyal people managed to hold them at bay by the grace of God." He was leading Eve toward the wire enclosure that she assumed was the parking lot. "The presidential palace wasn't touched. She was able to welcome all the diplomats with her usual grace and style when they liberated Maldara."

"Do I sense a little antagonism?" Eve glanced sideways at him as he opened the passenger door of a tan Land Rover for her. "Yet I don't believe Jill would refer to her as being magnificent in any sense of the word."

"Well, that's where we differ. I've had a closer relationship with Zahra than Jill has. I had an opportunity to assess her qualities." He tilted his head, considering. "I think she has a magnificent opinion of her own worth. I think she's not brilliant but has a magnificent talent for self-preservation." He paused, thinking. "Physically, she has magnificent breasts and possibly interesting, but not magnificent, sexual abilities. So Jill is not being entirely fair."

Her gaze narrowed on his face. "Yet you don't have any use for her."

"Not any more than I would have a use for a spitting mamba I ran across in the jungle." He smiled gently. "Except to sell the venom—

and then the snake would have to be alive to milk it. Much too much trouble." He was driving out of the airport onto the road. "But fair is fair. One has to be accurate. How else can you be allowed to make your own judgments?"

"I hope I won't even have to meet her," Eve said. "I intend to keep a low profile while I'm here."

"It will be difficult for you to do that. You're very famous, and you're in Zahra's kingdom. If she doesn't know that now, she will soon. And she's possessive of Robaku. Didn't Jill tell you?"

"Zahra's *kingdom*? But she's the president of Maldara."

"Zahra has a few bizarre ideas of her own regarding that." He shrugged. "Which are entirely in keeping with her opinion of her own magnificence. But I won't go into that since you're going to make the attempt to avoid her."

"You do know her very well, don't you?" Eve asked curiously.

"You mean, were we lovers? Oh yes. When I came back to spend the summer with my parents after graduating from Oxford, I was ready for a great passion. Zahra was the president's daughter, but she considered me deserving of her attention. I'm very rich, and she automatically associates wealth with royal entitlement. She thought she might be able to mold me into the prince she felt was her due. We had an interesting summer."

"A great passion?"

"No, but erotic and fascinating, until I saw the mamba raising its head. Then I left her and went back to London." His lips twisted. "She wasn't pleased. She'd thought she'd found someone who could survive her bite; and then she had to start over." He gestured to the curve of the road ahead. "Robaku is just ahead. I called from the cockpit and asked the headman, Hajif, to come to meet you at the school. Jill said you had a decision to make and to give you the information you needed to make it."

"And then you'll take me back to Atlanta immediately if I decide I don't want to stay?"

"Of course. Jill always keeps her word. Even if it means I have to bear the brunt of it." He gave her a keen glance. "But I think I'll probably get a good night's sleep tonight here in Maldara. I'd wager that intensity usually wins out when it comes to children. Why else are you here?"

"Your friend, Jill, conned me," she said flatly.

"Then she had her reasons," Gideon said. "And it probably hurt her more than it did you. Jill is one of those rare people who take honor seriously. She'd agonize over it." He paused. "And I bet she made it as painless for you as possible."

"The hell she did," Eve said curtly. "She wrote me a biography on each of those children that would tear your heart out."

Gideon gave a low whistle. "Ah, that pen of hers can be a lethal weapon. She's a great wordsmith. But she is usually responsible about how she wields it. Maybe you'll find that she was this time, too." He'd negotiated the turn in the road, and they'd suddenly left all semblance of the modern world and were in the jungle. He drove on a bumpy dirt road for another few minutes, then pulled to a stop and gestured to a large, square structure several yards away. "Robaku."

Eve stared in shock. Destruction. Chaos.

It was a burnt-out shell of a building. No roof. Only blackened, jagged openings that had once been windows. There was a wide, gaping opening that must have been a door, which vines and shrubs were trying to devour.

Eve could almost smell the acrid scent of the smoke from the flames that had destroyed the school. It had been a long time, but she could swear the smell lingered. She had thought it would at least have been cleaned up, perhaps flowers planted. Some attempt made to have the painfulness of the scene erased.

"Nothing...has been done." She got out of the Land Rover and stood looking at that gaping mouth of a door. "Jill said Zahra...some kind of memorial."

"This is Zahra's concept of a memorial. She ordered the villagers not to touch the school." Gideon got out of the car. "She said that everyone should see the horrible destruction that the war brought to her country so that they would never be tempted to repeat it. Unusual, but it sounded vaguely patriotic when she was quoted in the newspapers." He was striding toward the door. "Step into Robaku's pride and joy, Eve."

No hint of either pride or joy here, she thought, sick. She followed him slowly until she reached the doorway and stood staring into the half darkness. It was worse inside than it was outside.

The desks...

Most of them were blackened and destroyed, but a few of them had escaped the fires and sat there on the burnt-out floors as if they were waiting for the child who came to occupy them every day.

Eve could feel her eyes sting. "Oh, shit."

She moved into the huge room. The blackboard...broken and melted.

Something dark streaking the floor that was neither ash, nor dirt, nor burnt-out boards.

"Jill was told that's not blood on the floor," Gideon said. "That Zahra had given permission for the blood to be cleansed when the body parts were taken from here." His lips curled. "But since Zahra's own people extracted the bodies, I wouldn't give odds that they were careful about cleaning up the blood."

She couldn't take her eyes from those dark streaks.

He was looking at her face. "You don't look well. Maybe I'd better get you out of here."

She paid no attention to him. She was being bombarded by visions of what must have happened here that morning. The children at their desks...The teacher at the blackboard...probably chatter and smiles filling the room. Everything normal and right, as it should be for children in a classroom. As it was in her son Michael's classroom.

"Did...they have any warning? Why didn't they run away?"

"No warning. The school is located on this hill at the far end of the village. It's about a ten-minute walk to the village itself. Varak's militia struck the school first, then went on to burn the village. Hajif said they heard the screams from the children and ran toward the school to save them. But it had already been torched by the time they got there. A few of the bodies found inside were parents who ran into the flames to try to save their children. But most of the villagers were hacked to pieces by the militia, who were waiting for them. The children were only bait." He took her arm and was moving her toward the door. "And now I'm getting you out of here. Jill won't be pleased that I let you get this upset. You're done. You've seen it, you won't forget it."

No, she'd never forget it, Eve thought. It wasn't just the terrible ruins, it was as if the spirits of those children were still here ... still waiting.

She pulled her arm away. "It's not as if I'm going to break down or anything, Gideon." She concentrated on keeping her voice steady. "I've seen terrible things before in my career. It's just that this is ... overwhelming. I feel if I look over my shoulder, I might see them there." She did not look over her shoulder, but at him. "I thought this Hajif was going to meet us here."

"He always asks if he can meet us at the museum a little down the road. It's only a few yards away, and he finds this place pretty hard to take." He was leading her farther into the jungle. They were passing a beautiful brook surrounded by tall boulders. It seemed odd that anything beautiful could exist this close to that atrocity, Eve thought dully. And Gideon was saying quietly, "Hajif's grandson was killed in the massacre at the school."

Hajif. Eve thought for a moment, then made the connection with the biography Jill had written. "Hajif, grandfather of Amari, nine years old. Amari liked building model airplanes with his father. He wanted to be a pilot when he grew up ..."

"You have a good memory. His father was also killed in the massacre. Now there's just Hajif and his wife, Leta, left."

"It doesn't take a good memory to remember what Jill wrote about Robaku." She changed the subject. "Museum? Jill never mentioned a museum."

"It's part of Zahra's memorial. Not that there are many museum artifacts there. Just a few trinkets and photos. She just wanted a place to entertain dignitaries and news media that would show her off to advantage and keep her designer outfits from being contaminated by the soot of the schoolhouse." He lifted his head as a small black man with grizzled hair and lined face, dressed in flowing trousers and a loose white shirt, appeared, coming toward them. "Hajif." He moved quickly toward the man and bowed. Then he rattled off something in an African dialect and turned to Eve. "Eve Duncan, Hajif. She came to see Amari and his friends and hopes she can be of service."

"Jill Cassidy told me of her." The old man's English was broken but his expression was desperately eager as he turned to Eve. "It's we who should strive to serve you. Ask us, and it will be given."

"I don't know if I can help you," Eve said gently. "I'll have to examine the skulls and see if the damage will prevent me from being able to measure and do the sculpting. I understand there was considerable..." She hesitated. She didn't want to say that during fires, the brain often exploded and shattered the skull. "The fire might be a problem..."

"But Jill said you are wonderful and can work with such problems. Is that not true?"

"If there are no other elements that cannot be overcome."

Hajif was silent. "Please." His dark eyes were glittering with moisture. "We need to see him at least one more time as he was. My wife, Leta, keeps hoping that Amari escaped into the jungle and is afraid to come home to the village. She will not listen to me. She said that head in the box is not her Amari."

Eve frowned. "Head in the box?"

Gideon said quickly: "The remains of the children were sent to the American embassy to be kept at the medical lab there until they could be ID'd. But the villagers made such a fuss about the skulls being taken that they were allowed to keep them on-site until it was decided how to dispose of them."

"*She* kept them," Hajif said. "It should not be. They belong to us."

"Zahra stepped in and took over the preservation of the skulls until the decision could be made," Gideon said. "She put the skulls in her museum."

Eve stiffened. "What?"

"With all due respect, of course," he said ironically. "Blessed by the church. Properly preserved in specially crafted boxes." He gestured to a sleek, modern, one-story, gray-stucco building. "Would you like to see them?"

"Yes, I would." She was already striding toward the museum. "Now!"

The first thing she saw as she approached the building was the huge glass-enclosed gold-framed portrait of Zahra Kiyani beside the front door. Dressed in a white designer suit, she looked beautiful, sad, and dignified. Her arms were outstretched as if in welcome.

Eve ignored it, threw open the glass door, and went inside. Clean, bright, beautifully tiled green-and-beige floors. Several glass cases with very few artifacts, as Gideon had said. "Where are those boxes?"

Gideon nodded at a row of rust-colored leather boxes with elaborate gold lettering on the front. No names, just numerals. Not simple, dignified numerals, they were scrolled, then encircled with a fanciful design.

Hajif came to stand beside Eve. "Her soldiers told us that Amari is probably in the fourth box. And if we would consent to have the DNA test, Madam President's experts would be able to tell for certain."

And, until he consented, his grandson's skull would remain in that beautifully crafted box like a forgotten library book on a shelf only yards from their village. Or even worse, a macabre reminder of his death at the hands of Varak and his butchers. Jill had told Eve that the U.N. officials wanted those children to be buried and forgotten, and it was clear Zahra Kiyani was also systematically working to make that happen. Why? It could only be that as the surviving ruler of the conflict, she wanted everyone to forget the details of that brutal struggle to secure her new image. Children were so often used as pawns.

Eve could feel the anger begin to rise within her. It was all *wrong*. No one should forget those children. It was even worse than what had happened to Nora. At least the police were trying to find out what had happened to her. It didn't matter that those butchers who had killed the children of Robaku were known and probably ended up butchered themselves. Their victims needed to come home to the people who had loved them.

"Four?" Eve went behind the counter and looked at the glossy Roman numerals. "They said your grandson was numeral four?" She found the box and pulled it out. "And he was nine years old?" She laid the box on the counter and carefully opened it. The skull was blackened by fire but as carefully preserved as Gideon had said. "Let's take a look..."

"May I ask what you're doing, Eve?" Gideon was gazing over her shoulder with interest.

"Just checking to see how competent Zahra's experts are. It's not all that difficult to establish approximate age if you have the experience." She took the skull out of the box and set it on the glass counter. She carefully went over the skull, paying particular attention to the teeth. "It's a male, but the age is wrong. And the long bones of the face indicate he's at least twelve. One of the older boys in the class." She was trying to remember Jill's notes. "There were two older boys... one was... Maha?"

"Or Shaka," Hajif said eagerly. "Shaka was thirteen, Maha twelve."

"I'd have to examine him more closely to determine which one he is." Eve carefully replaced the skull in the box. "But he's *not* your grandson, and that 'expert' who said he was is no expert." She took the box to the back shelf and slipped it back in its place. "Your wife was right, Hajif. Your grandson might be in one of these boxes, but it's not that one."

"But you will find him?" Hajif asked. "You will bring him back to us?"

She stared helplessly at him. He wanted promises, and there were so many pitfalls that could get in the way of her giving him what he wanted. She wasn't even sure if these were the skulls from Robaku. That had been a stupidly careless mistake about Amari's age.

"My wife needs to know," Hajif said. "She . . . hurts."

And so was he hurting.

And, dammit, there should be some way to ease that pain. They had lost enough, they had a right to *know*.

She reached out and touched his shoulder. "Then we'd better do something to help her," she said gently. "But I'll need your help first, Hajif."

A brilliant smile lit his face. "You will do it? Anything. I will do anything."

"Will you get some men from the village to come here and take out all these display cases and shove them outside the building? Then I'll need a level table put in the center of the room. I'll show you how high it will have to be. And I'll need a stool of some sort."

"Right away." Hajif turned and moved quickly out of the museum.

"Any orders for me?" Gideon was smiling faintly. "Am I to assume that you're going to be delving into those boxes in the near future?"

"Yes," she said curtly. "Jill is going to feel very satisfied, isn't she? I don't give a damn. Those neat little boxes crafted of the finest leather with all those pretty gold letters made me go ballistic. They look like fashion accessories. I use boxes myself for transport. But this is pure showmanship, no dignity, no feeling. Zahra Kiyani made them part of her personal scenario. I want those kids out of those boxes."

"Obviously. You didn't answer me. What can I do?"

"Get me a cot to set up in here. I'll probably be spending most of my nights in this blasted museum."

"That's not necessary. And unless you're into communal bathing, the hygiene arrangements will be awkward for you in the village. I've made reservations for you at the one decent hotel in Jokan. I can run you back and forth."

"Keep the reservations. I'll need to use the room to shower occasionally. Otherwise, I can wash up in the bathroom here."

"How do you know there is one?"

"Of course there's a bathroom. You said that Zahra used this place to receive the media." She was looking around the room. "And I bet it has a lovely mirror for touching up her makeup." She saw a door across the room and strode toward it. She opened the door and glanced inside. "Yes, a great mirror with her traditional gold frame. I think I'm beginning to know Zahra Kiyani."

"Then heaven help you," Gideon said softly.

"I won't need divine intervention. I'll just stay out of her way and rely on Hajif and his people. I'll work hard and fast and get through this job as quickly as possible."

"Twenty-seven children, Eve," Gideon reminded her.

"I'll do as many as I can in the next month. I'll arrange for the others to be done by someone competent after I have to leave." She gave a last appraising glance at the bathroom and started to close the door. "Make certain I have towels, shampoo, and soap. That's all I need for the time being. Bring in my duffel from the car, will you? How many people in the village speak English?"

"Probably only a handful. But you have Hajif if you need a translator. He said he'd do anything as I recall." He paused. "And I'll stay within ten minutes' distance from you in case of emergencies."

"I'm not expecting any emergencies," Eve said. "This is what I do. I'm in control here. I can handle anything that comes along."

"I can see that." Gideon's gaze was on her flushed cheeks and glittering eyes. "And you can't wait, can you? Well, just know that I'm available." He turned toward the door. "I'll go get your duffel and find you a cot somewhere. You're really staying here tonight? Why don't you let me take you out to dinner and start tomorrow?"

"Because tonight I'll be going through all those skulls until I find one that fits Amari's age and description. Then I'll have to examine it and see if I can do what Hajif wants me to do."

"So Amari is going to be first?"

"He *has* to be first. His grandparents want it so much that I couldn't do anything else. After that, I'll be able to try to be more selective."

"Then I'll tell Jill that you have the initial process going at full speed." He looked back over his shoulder. "Anything else?"

"Bring in my computer and make sure I'll have no problem with Internet while I'm here. That's essential."

"You'll need it for your work?"

"Possibly for the final. But it's principally because I planned on using it to Skype. I prefer it to my smartphone to contact family, and I won't be stranded out here in the jungle and lose contact with my husband and son. That's *not* acceptable."

"Ah, yes, the protective husband in the background? Dedication and total devotion on both sides of the coin. You're an interesting woman, Eve Duncan. I believe I'm going to enjoy you."

"Interesting? You haven't seen anything, Gideon. And I couldn't care less if you enjoy me. Just get me what I tell you I need."

He chuckled. "I'll definitely get you what you need. It will be my goal in life while we're together." He mockingly flipped his hand to his head in a half salute. "I'll be back in a flash with the first installment."

He was gone.

Eve gazed after him with impatience and frustration. She still didn't know what to think of him after these hours in his company. He had smoothed her way seamlessly with Hajif and furnished her with both information and a subtle challenge. She hadn't the faintest doubt he would continue to do so until she could wrap up her work here. But he had almost casually admitted to having an affair with a woman about whom she was beginning to be very wary. And he was clearly loyal to Jill Cassidy and her agenda. And that agenda was aimed at using her to do whatever Jill wished here at Robaku.

Forget it. None of this is important right now, Eve thought impatiently. Jill Cassidy wanted to use her? Good luck to her. Since she had told Gideon that she was committed to doing these reconstructions, it meant that she automatically took charge of everything to do with those children. It was how she worked, and she would have it no other way. If Jill interfered, Eve would have to roll right over her if necessary. Jill had started this, but that didn't mean that Eve couldn't finish it...

CHAPTER

4

S he's a powerhouse," Gideon said when Jill picked up his call. "Eve listened. She questioned. She let me see the horror she felt. Then she took over. She's setting up shop even as we speak. She's even ordering *me* around. Doesn't she realize what a blow to my ego that is? You might have trouble with her."

Jill had known that from the beginning. The moment she had chosen Eve Duncan, she'd been aware that manipulation could only go so far and felt fortunate that she'd at least gotten Eve here. "Your ego will survive. I believe the only trouble we'll have right away is that she's a workaholic, and we'll have to keep her supplied with materials. Hajif is cooperating with helping her?"

"She's going to do the reconstruction of his grandson first. He thinks she's an angel from heaven." He paused. "She wanted to make certain that her computer and phone would operate at top efficiency. What do I do?"

The phone. Jill could see problems looming on the horizon. "Stall. It might be fine. I'll check with Novak. He's supposed to be here in five or ten minutes to smuggle me off this plane. I'll get back to you." She cut the connection.

She sat there staring out the window of the plane. It was starting.

The first step. Eve had now committed, and she'd be working on the skulls. Jill just hoped that they could move to the next step with more speed, and—

She tensed and whirled to the door as she heard the steps come down outside. She dived to press back against the wall as she saw a strong, brown hand open the door.

"Easy, Jill," Novak said dryly as he came into the cabin. He was hauling a broom and a large, stainless-steel waste-disposal container behind him. "I'd appreciate it if you'd neither shoot me nor hit me in the head with your object of choice." His skin was stained chocolate brown, his contact lenses were the same color, and he was dressed in red coveralls and hat with a cleaning-company logo on the brim. "It would spoil any chance of getting you out of here without being noticed. I'm supposed to tuck you in this waste-disposal container, and who would tote you out of here if you dispose of me instead?"

She let her breath out in relief. "I don't know why you're here anyway. I'm hardly important, and you could have sent one of your men to get me."

"Yes, I could have done that." He paused. "Just as you could have come back into the country alone without going near Eve Duncan and causing me this trouble."

"I had to make sure she'd get here safely. She's my responsibility." She held up her hand as he started to speak. "I know that Gideon could have taken care of her, but she's mine now. It was my plan, and I have to own it."

"That's right," he said mockingly. "She's an important figure in what you call 'your' story. It has to be as you dictate it."

Nairobi. She'd revealed too much to him that last night. "I'm surprised you remember I said that," she said lightly. "It must have been the sedatives."

"I could hardly forget it. I believe it defined your philosophy of life. I'm always on the lookout for clues to understand you."

"You're always on the lookout for clues, period. You take everything apart, then put it back together again." She dropped down in her chair again. "What about Eve's computer? She'll be Skyping her family and telling them everything that's going on. That means anyone who is hacking her will get a complete report via Joe Quinn."

He nodded. "I can't see that would be a problem right away. There's no reason why anyone would believe Eve's here for anything but the obvious. Besides, interfering would send up a red flag to Quinn. I'd rather not do that until the last minute. I've met him, and he'd be a son of a bitch to get rid of if he decided he had to step into the picture." He frowned thoughtfully. "And I've monitored her telephone conversations to him, and I think we'll let her take care of it. She's as protective of him as he is of her. She doesn't want him here either."

She gazed at him in surprise. She had never seen Novak this wary of anyone. He was always cool, always totally in control, and the smartest man she'd ever met. Even sitting here in those ridiculous red overalls and tennis shoes, he didn't appear anything but assured and able to conquer his particular world. She tried to smother the tingle of tension as she gazed at him. After their time together in Nairobi, she should have gotten over that edginess. But he'd always had that effect on her, a combination of wariness and fascination. The lean face, the intelligent, deep-set eyes that always seemed to see too much, the firm lips. There might be handsomer men than Jed Novak, but Jill had always found his super intelligence and quiet strength to be mesmerizing from the moment she had met him over a year ago. "I never actually got to meet Quinn. Have I missed something?" She smiled. "You're being very cautious."

"And so should you. Quinn respects her. He'll stay out of her business as long as he believes she's safe. The minute that changes, he'll go into overdrive."

"I would, too. That's why she has to stay safe." She tensed. "And when is that going to change, Novak? When do we get the skull?"

"Soon. I'm hoping not too soon. When I get word it's a go, we'll have to move fast." He met her eyes. "Whether or not you think Eve is ready for it. You'll have to go in and convince her."

"I know that," she said jerkily. "I'll do what I have to do. It might even be a relief." She got to her feet. "And now you should get me out of here. You've taken long enough to clean this plane. I need to get to the embassy, check in, and annoy the ambassador's secretary to give me any story that he has available on a dull news day."

Novak lifted a brow. "And make sure that no one makes the connection between Eve's arrival and you?"

"No one should if you've done your job. You said you'd arrange it so no one would realize I'd left Maldara."

"No one will. Your tail only caught glimpses of a look-alike as she moved through the streets or visited a friend or restaurant."

She smiled with an effort. "And now Eve appears here courtesy of a notable charity while I've been here all the time and obviously had nothing to do with it." She moistened her lips. "Did you, by any chance, manage to identify the man who's been following me?"

"Not 'by chance.' You insult me." His lips tightened. "We knew the day you showed up in Jokan a week after the attack. I had my own men on you, and he was spotted immediately. His name is Ken Bogani, and he's one of Zahra Kiyani's agents." He paused. "But I don't think he's one of the men who attacked you. We checked DNA, and there was no match for the specimen under your fingernails or the trace evidence on your clothes."

Not under her nails.

Think of the words, don't let the ugly pictures bombard you.

Novak's voice was cool and without expression, and she must be equally calm and composed. She'd already revealed too much to him when he had stayed with her while she was recovering in that hospital in Nairobi. She knew it was dangerous that she had become so dependent on him. But the situation was different now. She was a professional, and she mustn't show him any more weakness.

"But that doesn't mean he's not on the backup team, does it? It's odd you haven't been able to locate any of those men when you're so good at what you do. It's as if they dropped off the face of the earth."

"I'll find them, Jill."

"I know you will. But that shouldn't be a high priority anyway right now." Then she wearily shook her head. "And there's probably no connection between this Bogani and Hadfeld's death, or what happened to me. It wouldn't make sense. Zahra wouldn't have anything to do with Varak, a man who nearly destroyed her country. It has to be something as simple as the fact that I got in Zahra's way at the Robaku school, and I'm suddenly on her watch list."

"Not necessarily. I don't believe in simple answers when it comes to Zahra Kiyani."

Her gaze flew to his face. "You do think she's involved?"

"I didn't say that. You're right, it's not logical, considering who she is. It would be at odds with both Zahra's past and everything she stands for. I just don't discard the possibility because it might be complex."

"And she *is* complex." Jill was thinking quickly. "If you'd heard the bizarre stories Gideon told me about her...But if you think there's even a possibility, we need to pursue it. It's not that I'm afraid. It's not about me. We just have to look at everything, and—"

"It *is* about you." Novak's hands were suddenly hard on her shoulders. His eyes glittered down at her. He muttered a low oath. "I can see you thinking, trying to find a way to go after them. Are you crazy? It's *all* about you. They hurt you. Do you want it to happen again?"

"I believe you know the answer to that," she said unsteadily. "I didn't behave with a great amount of courage that night, did I? And I wasn't any better after you flew me to Nairobi. You had to...help me and I—" She broke off. "And now you're feeling guilty because you think it happened because you wouldn't give me what I asked you. I could see it coming that night you picked me up on that road. *I* made the decision. It was a big story, and I went after it. You had nothing to do with it."

"The hell I didn't."

"Okay, you want to feel guilty, go ahead." She pulled away from his grasp. "Though you don't have that reputation, and I don't know why on earth you're focused on me."

"Neither do I." He gave her a push toward the stainless-steel disposal cart. His voice was rough, but his hands were gentle as he lifted her into the cart and closed the lid. "Now shut up until I get you out of here and into the work van."

The waste container was hot, small, stuffy, and she had to curl pretzel-like inside. She could hear him open the door, and the sunlight pouring on the stainless steel made it even hotter. She knew she should be silent now. But he had been angry with her, and she had to make sure it wouldn't make a difference. She whispered, "You made me a promise. I won't let you break it, Novak."

"Don't you ever give up?" His voice was no longer angry but weary. "I can't break it. We're too close, and you have Eve Duncan, the only wild card in the deck." He started to maneuver the cart down the steps. "Let's hope I can keep her alive for you."

———◆———

"It's about time," Joe said as he answered Eve's Skype. "I know you asked me to wait until you called me, but you didn't say it would be at three in the morning."

"Sorry." She leaned back on her stool and took a swallow of coffee. Bless caffeine, she just might make it through the night. "It took me longer than I thought to set up my lab; and then I had to go through the skulls to see if I could find Amari."

"Amari?"

"Hajif's grandson. He has to be the first reconstruction." She started to go into the reasons for the selection, but he cut her off.

"Later," he said grimly. "All I want to know right now is that you've definitely decided to do the reconstructions. You said it wouldn't be a done deal until you got there and looked the situation over. If you've set up your lab, it means that you're committed. Right?"

"I have to do it, Joe," she said quietly. "I'll get them finished as quickly as I can."

"I know you will. I'll admit I was hoping it would go the other way." He paused. "You look tired. Don't work yourself into a nervous breakdown because you think I'm pressuring you. I'm behind you whatever you do."

"You're not the only one who's pressuring me," she said ruefully.

"Jill Cassidy? Tell her to go to hell."

"She's being very subtle. It's hard to have a confrontation when she dumped me on this Sam Gideon the minute the plane's wheels hit the tarmac here. I think she's designated him to do the pressuring for the time being."

"Sam Gideon?"

"Our pilot. I imagine he's several other interesting things as well. He mentioned casually that he'd been Zahra Kiyani's lover at one time. But Jill said I could trust him."

"Providing you can trust her."

"Neither really matters. I'm back at work. I'm the only one I have to trust now."

"Wrong. You have to trust me. You might have gone into your cocoon, but I have to make certain that no one messes around and tries to break into it."

"From long-distance," she said pointedly.

"For the time being."

She tried to change the subject. "Tell me what you're doing. Do you like the guest instructors at the Yard?"

"They're superb. I'll tell you all about them after you finish telling me about Robaku." He paused. "I want every detail, Eve. Every impression."

She laughed. "Joe, are you debriefing me?"

"In a way. Partly. But I've already been away from you too long.

I *need* you. It will help if you just let everything flow out and share with me."

"It's been quite a day. I don't even know if I'll remember everything. It's sad here. Some things will hurt talking about..." But she suddenly knew she needed to share them anyway. She always needed to share with Joe. It kept the bond firm, doubts at a minimum, and the love shiny and new. Do as he asked and let it flow. "I guess it started on the plane when Jill came to tell me that everything wasn't quite as I thought it was going to be..."

An hour later, Eve turned off the computer, sat there, and gazed around the room. For that short hour she'd been with Joe, it had faded away, and she wanted to keep it at a distance. She didn't want to face that schoolroom only yards away, nor the memory of those children who had died so terribly. She wanted Joe and Michael and the life she'd had only days before. She wanted to close her eyes and forget about anything else.

But there was always a price to pay if you allowed yourself to forget the madness and the horror.

It could come again.

She took a deep breath and pushed her computer aside. Then she took the skull she'd mounted on the dais and started to examine it. First, she'd have to repair the damage. Next, she'd start to measure. She was very tired, and she'd probably have to catch a nap on that cot before she actually started. Her hands tended to shake if she was too exhausted.

But she needed a little time with this young boy now that they had come together.

She looked down at the hideous, blackened skull and gently touched the cheekbone. "Hi. You've been through a nightmare, but you're not the nightmare," she whispered. "I think you probably know that by now, but we have to make certain everyone else does, too. We're going to make you as handsome as you were before that day, and that will make your grandmother very happy. Okay? And I usually give my sculptures names, but I believe I know yours, Amari. So we'll go from there. Are you ready?" She began to check for breaks in the orbital socket. "Let's clean you up a bit, then we'll get you started on your road home..."

"You're a fool, Wyatt," Zahra said savagely. "I don't *want* Eve Duncan at Robaku. Why would you permit her to come to my city and work on those children? I've worked hard to try to filter all publicity about them through me, and now you let some charity send a world-class forensic sculptor here? She's bound to attract attention."

"They went through the London office. I was told to accommodate them. What could I do?"

"What I want you to do." She drew a deep breath and tried to smother her anger. This was not the time to alienate Wyatt when everything must go smoothly over the next few weeks. "You said Duncan has already arrived? Did Jill Cassidy have anything to do with bringing her here?"

"The home office didn't mention her. But you know that her stories about the massacre did stir up a good deal of sympathy. It might have influenced the charity to act."

"Tell me about it. That's why you should have gotten rid of her. But she had no direct connection with Duncan?"

"No, I believe Duncan called the charity and volunteered her services. Though I was told she arrived on Sam Gideon's plane. Perhaps he had something to do with it."

Gideon. Zahra's hand tightened on the phone. Son of a *bitch*. Yes, he could have done it, just to annoy her. She'd made no secret of her views about Robaku. He was constantly getting in her way, and it was dangerous for her to do anything to put a stop to it. His plantation might have been burned to the ground during the conflict, but he still had enormous economic influence in Maldara. She wished he'd been burned up with the damn place, she thought savagely. "That doesn't mean she isn't involved." But her temporary chief agent, Bogani, had told her that Jill Cassidy had been in Jokan for the weeks since the attack. If she was involved, it had not been directly, and Gideon was quite capable of raising enough hell on his own. "I'm going to meet this Eve Duncan. I'll be able to tell if she's just a do-gooder or if she'll get in my way."

"Let it go, Zahra," Wyatt said. "What harm can she do? I'll keep an eye on her, and in a few weeks she'll be gone. She's probably doing it for the publicity and working on a few of those burnt-out skulls will be enough to discourage her."

"I want her gone now. Robaku is mine, and it's time all these arguments about the DNA ended." She was done talking to him. "Let me know if you find out anything else." She cut the connection.

She sat there for a moment. She didn't like this. She needed to talk to Lon Markel, her primary agent, and discuss how far she could go to discourage it happening. She started to dial her cell again, then stopped. Markel had been involved in the attack on the Cassidy woman, and she'd been told not to call on him again unless it was an emergency.

Screw it. No one could tell her what to do. Markel was *her* agent, her employee, and she trusted him more than she did the others in her service. He'd been with her for years before he'd been yanked away from her these past months. She'd only tolerated Bogani since she'd been told she couldn't have Lon Markel for the time being. But she would *not* have him hijacked and permanently taken away from her. She paid his salary, and she would do what she liked with him. She began to dial again.

She stopped and put the phone down.

It wasn't fear, she told herself. She was never afraid. It was just that perhaps it wasn't wise to use Markel again so soon. There was a slight chance he might have been recognized by Jill Cassidy that night. Of course, it was entirely her own decision. It would be better to handle this herself.

It was entirely her own decision . . .

———————◆———————

"How is it going?"

Eve looked up from her reconstruction to see Sam Gideon standing in the doorway. "Well enough." She arched her back to ease the stiffness. "Amari isn't easy. Just reconstructing the damaged bones of the right temple took me almost a day. It must have been a machete blow to be that shattered. But the measuring isn't causing me too much trouble. I'm almost done with it." She tilted her head. "I haven't seen you for two days. Weren't you supposed to stay around and be at my beck and call?"

"I was around. I peeked in a couple times, but you were so absorbed that I decided to let Hajif handle everything. He seemed to be doing a good job, and I'm always tempted to ask questions." He was looking at the reconstruction. "What are those red flags all over his face?"

"Depth-measurement markers."

"Not flattering. But the rest of him is looking a hell of a lot better than that first night, when you pulled him out of his box."

"Thank you for your critique. Now go away, Gideon. I'm busy."

"Presently. I just thought I'd drop by and give you fair warning. I just got word that Zahra Kiyani is on her way to pay you a visit. I thought you'd want to be prepared."

Eve frowned with annoyance. "I don't need this. Can't you get rid of her?"

"No, you'll have to do it. Zahra doesn't listen to me. She'd prefer that I didn't exist. I actually thought she'd be here before this. She obviously took a long time to make up her mind whether you were worthy of her personal attention." He paused. "It would be best if you didn't mention Jill. Zahra can't hurt me, but she'll try her best to hurt Jill. And Zahra has enough power in Jokan to make it . . . uncomfortable for her."

"You want me to lie?"

"That's up to you." He smiled. "No one is going to stop you from saying anything you wish to say. If you think what you're doing here isn't worth doing and that Jill should be punished for being involved, by all means have a chat with Zahra about it." He turned and headed for the door. "I'll just hang around outside until her entourage shows up and greet her." His smile was a combination of both mischief and malice. "That should make her day . . ."

She gazed after him with exasperation. She didn't want to deal with Zahra Kiyani, and she didn't want to have Gideon telling her how to handle the woman. She just wanted to go back to work and finish Amari.

But it was too late. She heard the roar of several automobiles exiting the road, then the slam of car doors as they reached the museum. Eve got to her feet and wiped her hands on her work towel. Then the door was being opened ceremoniously by a uniformed soldier, and Zahra Kiyani was sweeping into the museum. She did not look pleased, Eve thought. Evidently, seeing Gideon had definitely *not* made her day.

She was dressed in a designer gold-paisley suit and was just as beautiful as she appeared in her photos. Her frown disappeared, and she gave Eve a flashing smile. "How happy I am that you're here in my country." Her English was faultless, with just a hint of an accent. "And doing such good work. I thought I'd drop by and personally welcome you." She looked Eve up and down. "But I should have let you know. You're obviously working so hard that I might be in the way . . . " She trailed off and shrugged. "You do look so tired. I hope you'll forgive me."

The needle was faint but definitely there. Eve was annoyed enough about the interruption not to let it get a pass. "I'm not at all tired. When I become this involved in my work, I forget everything else. I'm looking forward to many engrossing hours spent here at Robaku," she said. "Thank you for coming to welcome me. But I know how busy you must be, so I won't keep you." She gestured to the skull. "And I'm busy as well. He's one of your own people, so I know you'll want me to finish as soon as possible."

"Yes, of course." She gazed at the skull. "One of the children..." Her glance shifted back to Eve. "I understand you have a child. Aren't you worried about leaving him to take care of my problems here? Children can be so very fragile."

Eve went still as she looked at her. Zahra's voice had been soft, and her expression was serene, but Eve had felt a chill. Could that have been a threat? "My son is always safe even when I'm not with him. And my work is too important to leave it undone when a charity says I'm needed."

Zahra nodded. "You appear to be very talented." She forced a smile. "Though I do prefer the certainty of DNA over a pretty sculpture. I suppose Jill Cassidy told you that we disagreed on that score?"

"Jill Cassidy? Isn't she a reporter or something? I believe I've heard of her. But it was Sam Gideon who told me about you."

She stiffened. "Really?" she said warily. "What did he say?"

"He used the word 'magnificent' quite a bit. I can see why he thought it applied to you." She inclined her head. "Now if you'll excuse me?"

But Zahra Kiyani was still looking around the room. "I can't say I like what you've done to my beautiful museum. It's in shambles. I'll tolerate it for now because I don't wish to be unfair. However, if I find that your work isn't what it should be, I'll have to ask you to leave. I'll be back next week to see if that charity that sent you has made a mistake." She moved toward the door. "I'll see you then, Ms. Duncan."

Then she was gone. A few minutes later, Eve heard the low roar of the cars as they departed Robaku.

Gideon came back into the museum a moment later. "That was very short. She didn't waste much time on you."

"No, *I* didn't waste much time on *her*," she corrected. "She only came to threaten and find out who had sent me here. I said enough to satisfy her so that she'd get out and let me work."

"Satisfy?" he repeated. "She looked almost triumphant when she glanced at me when she left."

"That's because I told her you thought she was magnificent. She probably thinks that if she made the effort, she could have you worshipping at her feet again."

He flinched. "That was wicked of you, Eve. When she has time to think it over, she'll realize I must have been lying to you." He tilted his head. "But you must have been doing a little prevaricating yourself if you let her believe it."

"I didn't lie. She asked what you'd told me about her, and I told her the truth. I just didn't elaborate."

"And were you equally truthful when she asked you about Jill?"

"I might have been a little less open. She had a perfectly good target in you, and bringing in Jill would have confused things and wasted more time."

"And you wouldn't have wanted that to happen," he said softly. "It was all for the benefit of Amari and friends."

She was silent. "I didn't like her." She was remembering that instant when Zahra had mentioned her son. She was still feeling that chill. "I've met women before who are antagonistic toward other women. I've never understood it. She was trying to be subtle, but underneath, she was practically bristling."

"She believes she has no need for them, and they might prove competitive. Not that she'd admit the latter." He smiled. "After all, she is magnificent."

Eve smiled back at him. "You left out one descriptive noun.

Magnificently arrogant." She waved her hand. "Now get out of here and let me work. If I'm lucky, I'll get Amari finished tonight or early morning and reward myself by letting you take me to that hotel so I can shower."

"And sleep in a real bed?"

"That's too much luxury. The cot is fine. I'm usually so tired I have no trouble sleeping. Out, Gideon."

"I'm going." He hesitated at the door. "But I should tell you that Zahra wanted to leave one of her soldiers on guard here. I'm sure she'd say it was for your protection, but I still sent him on his way."

"Does she think that I'm going to steal one of these skulls?"

"No, I'm sure she's checked you out thoroughly. She just likes to be in control, and you didn't fall into line. It probably wouldn't have done any harm to let the guard stay as long as I knew he was around. I just didn't want you to stumble over him if you went to get a breath of air." He grimaced. "As if you would bother." He lifted his hand in a wave. "I'll be back around midnight to see Amari in all his glory."

"No glory." Eve was already sitting back down on her stool. "Just a little boy spruced up and ready to go home to see his grand-parents..."

Then she closed everything out as she settled down to spend the next hours working on completing and checking the measuring. It was undeniably the most important if least satisfying part of the sculpting process. It was the precise building block of features and contours that made Amari who he was. But it was only the final stage of sculpting that revealed the details that gave him the person-ality and presence that brought him to life for Eve.

So do the hard, gritty work and make sure that she made no mis-takes. Then she'd do the initial smoothing and make ready for that final step. She felt her fingers tingling at the thought.

Stop it. Not yet. This boy deserved care and certainty.

The measuring...

It had not gone as well as she'd hoped with Eve Duncan, Zahra thought impatiently as she gazed out the window of her limo. She'd hoped to impress her enough so that she would be able to oust her during the next visit. But Eve Duncan was one of those women who thought so much of themselves that they didn't realize how far above them she was. Station and beauty meant nothing to them because they had some idiotic skill and thought they could compete. It was not only laughable, it was an annoyance. Now she would have to spend more time than she'd planned on getting rid of her. It would probably mean trying to influence that charity to—"

Her phone was buzzing.

She stiffened as she saw there was no ID.

Dammit! She had been afraid of this.

She punched in the access code and typed rapidly.

IT DIDN'T GO WELL. DUNCAN IS STUPID AND I CAN SEE SHE WON'T COOPERATE. IT WILL TAKE ME A LITTLE LONGER THAN I PLANNED.

A pause, then the answer.

WE BOTH KNOW THAT'S NOT ACCEPTABLE. I TOLD YOU I NEED HER GONE. MAKE IT HAPPEN.

Orders? She tried to smother the bolt of sheer rage that shot through her.

I'LL DO IT AS QUICKLY AS I CAN. HOW DARE YOU TELL ME WHAT TO DO. YOU HAVE NO IDEA HOW COMPLICATED IT IS TO KEEP ALL THE BALLS IN THE AIR.

Another pause.

HOW DO I DARE? YOU KNOW HOW I DARE, ZAHRA. NOW STOP STALLING AND GIVE ME WHAT I WANT.

She should have been more cautious. She might have made a mistake. She typed in quickly. AS SOON AS POSSIBLE.

The answer came back instantly.

MAKE IT HAPPEN!

———◆———

Eve finished the initial smoothing of the clay just after midnight.

She leaned back and gazed at the reconstruction as she wiped her hands. Everything was there, and smooth, and presumably correct. But he was like a baby asleep in the cradle, waiting to be roused. It was time to wake him up and bring him back to those who loved him.

Her hands were tingling again. But that was okay now. The blood flow usually helped the process and kept her from becoming exhausted.

"It's time for you to get to work, Amari," she said softly. "We're almost at the end, and I need a little help here. I'll be with you all the way, but there are so many tiny things I could miss that would make them sad if I didn't catch them. We don't want that to happen, so let's make sure it doesn't. Okay?"

She reached out and delicately touched the place on his skull that she'd repaired. "Let's do this, first. Let's make it go away forever..."

Smooth.

Careful.

Delicacy.

Don't hurry. It has to be perfect.

Don't let anyone know the pain that caused that wound.

See? It's gone now, Amari.

Perfect.

Smooth.

Mold.

Go on to the cheekbone.

It's going faster now.

Smooth.

Mold.

Hollow the left cheekbone a little more.

The clay was cool beneath her fingers.

Ears. Make them generic. Hajif could tell her if she'd gotten it right.

Smooth.

Mold.

Fill in.

The clay felt warmer now as her fingers moved faster.

Eyes.

No, not yet. There was something troubling about the eyes...

Go on to the nose.

Pay attention to the measurements of the space between the nose and upper lip.

Smooth.

Fill in.

Mouth.

So difficult.

Just go with what seemed right.

Eyes?

No, not yet. What was wrong with the eyes?

Go back to the cheekbones.

Not full enough, he'd not reached puberty and was still a child.

Smooth.

Mold.

Fill in.

Her fingers were flying now.

What's wrong with the eyes?

Check the measurements.

Measurements correct.

But something was wrong.

Not with the right eye, she realized.

Left eye. Outer corner of the left eye.

Too smooth.

Indent.

No, build up.

It didn't matter if she didn't know the reason.

Just do it.

Now it was right.

Go on to the curve of the lips.

Something was missing.

Mold.

A deeper crease.

Her fingers were hot, fast, mindless.

Let it all come together.

Smooth.

Fill in.

Mold...

CHAPTER

5

inished?" Gideon said behind her from the doorway. "It's almost three. I gave you an extra—"

"Almost," she interrupted. "I just need to put in his eyes. Go get Hajif and his wife."

"It's three in the morning. You want me to wake them up?"

"Yes, by the time they throw on some clothes, I'll be finished. And they're not going to care if it's three in the morning. They deserve to be the first to see him. Go!"

"You're continuing to order me about," he complained. "I can't say I'm accustomed to such treatment . . ."

He was gone.

And she was reaching for her eye case. There was no question about the color, they would be the same rich brown as Hajif's. She carefully inserted the glass eyes in the orbital sockets and sat back to look at him.

Yes.

Only Hajif and his wife, Leta, could tell her if this was Amari, but the skull had come alive as she'd wanted it to. She'd put the hint of a smile at the corners of his lips, and the shining brown of his eyes appeared oddly eager as he stared up at her. She'd engraved gentle curves that mimicked short curls or waves framing that face. It had just seemed right.

"Are you ready for them?" she whispered. "They're ready for you, Amari."

She stood up as she heard them coming. She stood to one side as she saw Gideon open the door and Hajif and his wife appear in the doorway. "I thought you wouldn't mind getting up a bit early, Hajif." She gestured to the reconstruction. "Is this what you wanted from me?"

Hajif stood stock-still in shock.

He was silent, staring dazedly at the sculpture. "I . . . did not expect this. It . . . is magic." He drew his wife, Leta, toward the worktable. His eyes were shimmering with moisture as he slipped his arm around her waist. "You see, Leta, he has returned to us." He reached out, and his index finger gingerly touched the raised scar at the corner of his left eye. "Remember how upset you were when the propeller flew off his toy plane? You kept saying one more inch, and he would have been blind. But he was fine, wasn't he?" He looked at Eve. "How did you know?"

"I didn't. Some things just seem right. Is it Amari, Hajif?"

He nodded. "It is my grandson." He turned to his wife, whose eyes had never left the face of the reconstruction. "Is it Amari, Leta?" he asked gently. "Has she brought our Amari back to us?"

"Yes." The tears were suddenly running down her cheeks. "He is not alive. He's not hiding in the jungle waiting to come home to us because he's afraid. They killed him, Hajif." She was sobbing. "They *killed* him."

"You knew that." He pulled her into his arms. "But does he look sad and afraid now? He is our Amari, and there is no fear."

"No fear," his wife said brokenly. "I have nightmares about how afraid he was when those butchers came."

"I know. I know." He held her close. He looked over her head at Eve. "Words cannot—I thank you. May we come and visit him here in the museum?"

She shook her head. "I don't believe he'd like staying here. Why don't you take him home?"

His eyes widened. "But he belongs to—"

"He belongs to you now." She grimaced. "As long as you promise not to ever put him in that box again." She took a step closer to Leta. "Leave him here for the time being," she told her gently. "Go home and make a place for him. No fancy shelves. Just a place where he'll be safe, and you can see him every day. Use his favorite colors, put things he loved around him. If you see something you think he'd like, give that to him, too. See him as he is now and let him become part of your life." She paused. "And maybe that will make the night-mares go away."

"I hope that is true." Leta suddenly launched herself into Eve's arms and was embracing her. "But if it's not, when I wake, I will have him with me." She awkwardly backed away, embarrassed. "Come along, Hajif. We must go home and find this place for him. It will not be as easy as she makes it out to be."

"But I'm sure you will be back in just a few hours with the perfect place." Hajif smiled again at Eve as his wife pushed him toward the door. "There is nothing I will not do for you," he said quietly, "You have only to ask."

"Oh, I'll ask," Eve said. "I have twenty-six other skulls to deal with after this. I'll need help."

"Skulls," he murmured, his wondering gaze on Amari. "It does not seem possible. He is . . . alive." He smiled brilliantly. "Magic."

"No, skill and experience," she called after him, as Leta pulled him from the room. She made a face, and said to Gideon, who was still leaning against the wall beside the door, "I don't think Hajif believes in witch doctors, but this is Africa. You can never tell."

"He may not be far wrong." Gideon straightened and strolled across the room toward the reconstruction. "This is pretty incredible."

"It's hard work and making sure every measurement is correct." She moved toward her duffel beside her cot. "And now you can take

me to that hotel and let me spend the next hour under a hot shower."
She slipped the strap of the duffel over her shoulder. "I need it."

"Give me a minute." Gideon was closely examining the reconstruction. "You're selling yourself short. Probably intentionally. I've
never seen anything like this. It's superb."

"Yes, I'm very good. I want to go, Gideon."

"Hmm." His index finger was tracing the scar at the corner of
Amari's left eye. "I just wanted to get a closer look at this. Hajif was
impressed. I agree." Then he gave her a slanting glance that held pure
mischief. "Magic . . ."

She ignored him, already on her way toward the door. "Bullshit.
Haven't you ever heard of inspiration? Get me to that hotel."

She heard him laugh as he followed her from the museum.

———◆———

The Soran Hotel was one of the few skyscrapers in Jokan, and it
looked like a luxurious Ritz-Carlton, Eve thought. It even had a
uniformed doorman who rushed to open her door. "You said it was
a decent hotel," she said to Gideon. "This is several steps up from
that. Zahra's intervention?"

"No, my father had it built when he still thought Zahra's father
could make a difference here in Maldara. Once Zahra took power,
she couldn't bear to give up a quality hotel when she could use it
to her advantage. Though it irritates her that I prevented her from
nationalizing it and still have major control. She tries to exert her
influence whenever she gets the chance." He walked with Eve into
the lobby and handed her a key. "Suite 735. It's the room I keep on
reserve for myself. You'll find it comfortable. Enjoy your shower. I'll
give you an hour, then have them bring you your meal. I'd guess you
haven't eaten for hours."

She couldn't remember when she'd grabbed that bowl of soup yesterday. "No, but I think I'm getting hungry."

"Then I'll call Pierre Gaillon, the chef, and get him out of bed. I hired him from the George V in Paris, and he does miracles with coq au vin. You won't be disappointed."

"I'm sure I won't. But I'm not accustomed to gourmet cuisine, Gideon. I'd be satisfied with a sandwich."

"I wouldn't. I told you that I'd take care of you." He walked her to the elevator. "I'm tempted to join you for dinner, but this is the time for you to relax, and I'm much too stimulating."

"I didn't notice," she murmured.

"Of course you did." He punched the elevator button. "You're just dedicated to keeping me humble. So I'll stay here in the lobby and talk to the manager and wait for you to call me and tell me how much you enjoyed that coq au vin. Try to get a nap if you can afterward. Call me if you need me."

"No nap." The doors of the elevator opened, and she stepped inside. "And I'll be ready to go back to Robaku as soon as I've eaten. I need to start the next reconstruction. I think I'm going to do one of the six-year-olds. But I'll call you as soon as I've finished that gourmet meal you're ordering for me." She said quietly, "Thanks, Gideon. I appreciate your making everything easier for me."

"My pleasure." He smiled. "It's been an interesting few days. If you don't mind, while I'm waiting around, I'll give Jill a call and tell her about Amari. She'll want to know."

"I don't mind." Being able to help Hajif had caused her resentment toward Jill to lessen, she found. There was no doubt that so far her work here had been worthwhile and caused a major difference in Hajif's and Leta's lives. "Tell her if she wants to see it, she should visit Hajif's home."

"And not get in your way?"

She found herself smiling as the elevator door started to close. "And not get in my way."

———◆———

"I won't get in her way," Jill said. "In fact, I'll wait until the press meeting day after tomorrow to even show up at Robaku. Do I detect a little softening?"

"A little." He paused. "She's got a different mind-set. Doing that reconstruction meant something to her. She's pretty fantastic, you know, Jill. You chose the right person."

"I'm well aware of that, Gideon. There wasn't a choice when I realized how amazing she was."

"But I like her," Gideon said. "And I'm not cut out for all this secretive bullshit." He returned to Eve. "And she covered for you with Zahra. But that isn't because she was fond of you but because she didn't like Zahra or the way she'd used the kids as a display for her museum."

"I thought that would push her buttons," Jill said. "It did mine. I deliberately left it as a surprise." She'd be glad when all this manipulation ended, she thought wearily. "But if she's so involved with the kids, it might make it more difficult when I try to move her away from them."

"No word about the skull?"

"Anytime now," Jill said. She was as impatient as Gideon. "Novak said he'd let me know as soon as he does. It has to happen, Gideon." She changed the subject to Eve. "Take care of her. I don't like that Zahra wanted a guard stationed at Robaku."

"She didn't get it. I'll be there for Eve," he said quietly. "The worst thing that will happen is that she'll drop from exhaustion. I don't seem to be able to control that possibility. Now let me go and order her dinner. The other possibility is that she might forget to eat and starve to death." He cut the connection.

Gideon seemed almost big brotherly, Jill thought as she hung up, and that was never Gideon's style. He was cool, sometimes amusing, sometimes sensual, and always wary these days. He tended to keep everyone at a distance. But he had said he liked Eve, and that might have made the difference.

They had both developed feelings for Eve since they had brought her to Maldara. It was becoming more and more difficult to face drawing her even deeper into the quagmire.

Novak, get that damn skull!

———◆———

"I'm clean at last." Eve stopped drying her hair and tossed aside the towel as she grinned at Joe on the Skype. "Sorry you have to put up with my soggy hair, but I wanted to catch you before you went to the Yard. I didn't get a chance to call you yesterday. Did you get my message that I was finishing Amari?"

"I got it," he said dryly. "Or I would have been on the next plane to Jokan. I take it that it went well? You're practically floating."

"I am floating. It was so *different*, Joe. You know I usually have to just send the reconstructions back to a police department and they do the follow-up to find who the child is and the killer. This time I was able to see that boy go home to the people who loved him five minutes after I finished. I got to see their *faces*, Joe."

"And it meant the world to you," he said gently. "That's wonderful, Eve."

"Everything's wonderful tonight." She chuckled. "I sent Amari home, Gideon brought me to this five-star hotel so that I could dine in style and shower, and I got to share it all with you. It can't get any better."

"Until next time." He smiled. "I'm not going to be able to get you away from that place, am I?"

"I'm needed here, Joe. But I'll leave when you and Michael are finished there. I promised you. Besides, I couldn't stand being away from you any longer than that." She heard a knock on the door. "That must be my room service. Gideon said that the chef was preparing me coq au vin, and it was guaranteed to be delicious."

"Evidently, I'll have to trust your opinion of this Gideon," Joe said.

"Though I'm not certain how I feel about his being able to whisk you to five-star hotels and ply you with gourmet meals. I'll have to tell you when I meet him. But as long as you're not sharing that meal with him, soggy hair and all, I guess I'll be able to tolerate it."

"You're joking," she said as she got to her feet. "I have to answer the door. I'll tell you tonight if it's as good as Gideon said. I love you. Have a good day."

"Only half joking. My humor is suffering drastically since I've been limited to Skype to see you. You'll remember I don't like sharing you. But I'm glad you've already had a wonderful day. I love you, too. Be safe."

Eve headed for the door as she disconnected the call. Those last remarks had had an edge, she thought. Joe had been very patient, but she knew he was worried. She had to be careful to reassure him that though everything was strange, and there were annoying elements like Zahra Kiyani, there had not been anything obviously threatening during these days.

A smiling waiter wheeling a white-draped cart with several silver-domed serving dishes bowed as she opened the door. "The chef sends his regards and hopes his offering will please you."

"I'm sure it will." She was suddenly ravenously hungry. She stood aside as he rolled the cart into the room. She would have to tell Joe about the elegant presentation when she talked to him tonight. It would amuse him. Or maybe it wouldn't. She'd have to think about it. But it would certainly emphasize that everything surrounding her at the moment was ultracivilized and completely without threat...

———◆———

Eve pushed back her chair and sighed with contentment.

The meal had been as fantastic as the presentation, and this coffee she was drinking was excellent as well. She was tempted to call Gideon to tell him how well he'd done, but she decided against it.

She'd call him after she got dressed and was ready to leave. That would be time enough. She was eager to get back to Robaku and start the new reconstruction.

She quickly dressed in slacks and a work shirt and brushed her hair. She did feel fresher and able to cope now. She'd been right to take this little break between reconstructions. She'd be able to attack the new work with a clear head, and that would make it go faster than—

Pain!

She bent double as agony knifed through her stomach.

She felt so sick.

Then her stomach was suddenly heaving.

She had to hold on to the vanity to make it to the toilet.

Then she was throwing up...

Time after time, trying to hold herself upright, fighting the violence of the vomiting.

Her head was throbbing, pounding...

And then the cramping attacked her stomach.

Hideous cramping.

Her legs gave way, and she fell to the floor.

Her head was on fire.

Her phone... She had to get to her phone. She reached blindly toward the vanity where she'd laid it.

No strength...

Only the pain and the terrible nausea.

She felt as if she must be dying.

Because everything was going dark...

———◆———

"I don't have much time, Jill," Gideon said curtly when Jill picked up his call. "I'm in an ambulance heading to the embassy hospital. I found Eve unconscious in her suite, and I couldn't bring her around. I have to get her to the ER right away."

Jill stiffened. "Gideon, what happened? You said she was fine when I talked to you before."

"I don't know what happened, dammit. No obvious wounds. She'd obviously been throwing up, but I don't know if it was drug-induced. All I know is she's damn sick."

Panic seared through her. "I'll meet you at the hospital."

"No, I'll call you when I know more. You can't do anything I can't do. Novak doesn't want you near her."

"That's too bad. I don't *care*. I figure all bets are off now. She could *die*, Gideon. She wasn't supposed to get hurt. There's no reason. Not for what she's doing at Robaku."

"Evidently, someone disagreed. And she might not be that sick. Let me find out." As she started to protest, he cut in harshly: "I told you I'd be responsible for her, and I screwed up. Do you know how that makes me feel? Now let me take care of her. I won't let you blow everything we've worked for because you're panicking. There's too much at stake. Now call Novak and tell him to check her suite and see if he can find out who or what brought her down. I ordered dinner for her, and she'd finished it. But you stay away from the hospital unless I call you, Jill." He cut the connection.

Jill *was* panicking. She was terrified. And there was no way she wasn't going to go to the hospital to see Eve. Gideon said he was responsible, but he was wrong. She was the one who was responsible for everything that had happened to Eve. She had chosen her, then done everything possible to make her come here.

Yet if she did show up at the hospital, it would make Eve more of a target than ever. Any association with Jill might draw attention to Eve. But this couldn't go on. She had to *do* something.

One step at a time.

First, do as Gideon suggested and phone Novak.

She quickly dialed Novak's number. "I suppose you already know what happened," she said unevenly. "Gideon asked me to call you. But you always know what's going on before anyone else does."

"I know an ambulance just took Eve to the embassy hospital," Novak said. "Stay away from there, Jill."

"I've already heard that song, and I'm trying to do it. Because if Eve manages to live through this, I don't want to make it any more dangerous for her than it is already."

"I know you're upset, Jill. But we don't know what her condition is right now. We'll do everything we can to—"

"Upset?" Her voice was shaking. "You bet I'm upset. I can't take this any longer. You go find out exactly what happened to her. And you make certain that Gideon lets me know as soon as possible whether I've killed her or not."

"It isn't your fault that—"

"Don't tell me that," she said fiercely. "I am to blame. I'm going to pray that I didn't hurt her too badly, but I won't try to escape the fact that if I did, the fault was mine." She drew a deep, shaky breath. "But it's not going to happen again. We thought she was safe, but she wasn't. And we let her walk right into it. It's got to change."

"I don't like the sound of that."

"And I didn't like it when Gideon said he couldn't wake Eve up." Those words were still chilling her. "It's got to change, Novak."

She hung up the phone.

———◆———

EMBASSY HOSPITAL
12:40 P.M.

"Eve? Open your eyes. I have to talk to you."

Gideon, Eve realized dazedly. It was good he was here...She'd been trying to phone him when she'd been so sick.

"Eve. Open your eyes, dammit. This might be my only chance to talk to you."

He sounded so urgent that she forced herself to open her lids. His face above her was as strained and urgent as his voice had been. He was frowning, and Gideon seldom frowned. Then he was smiling at her. "That's right. Now stay awake. These hospitals suck, and I have to try to get you out of here."

Hospitals? Green walls. The smell of antiseptics and cleanliness. Definitely a hospital. Eve had been around enough of them to recognize one when she saw it.

And Gideon's face above her was sober again. A hospital face...

"I was sick..." she whispered. Her throat was sore, and she could barely speak. She was sore all over, she realized vaguely. "Fast...it happened so fast. What happened to me, Gideon?"

"I don't know. They're calling it food poisoning." He was putting a straw between her lips, and she was sipping ice water. "But it was a damn violent strain if that was what it was. Besides the nausea, it caused unconsciousness. When you didn't answer your phone, I went up to your suite and found you crumpled on the floor. I couldn't wake you." He took her hand. "It scared me. So I called the American hospital that the embassy uses and had them send an ambulance. You still weren't awake when you got to their ER. They diagnosed it as food poisoning and pumped your stomach."

That was why the muscles of her stomach felt this sore..."Food poisoning...not such good coq au vin after all."

"Maybe. But I'll swear that chef would never give you anything contaminated. I know him."

"I might argue with you about that." She swallowed to ease the soreness of her throat. "I felt so sick. But I'm going to be okay?"

He nodded. "Very nasty case, and it's going to leave you weak for a few days. They say you'll have to rest. But you'll be fine eventually."

"That's good." She closed her eyes again. Then they flew open. "No, it's not. I can't stay here in the hospital. I have too much to do. I have to get back to Robaku."

"I thought that would be your reaction. That's why I wanted to

get to you before anyone else had a chance to try to brainwash you."
He smiled. "I prefer to do it myself."

"Go to hell, Gideon." She lifted her hand to her aching head. "Just
tell me what you want, and I'll see if I want the same thing."

"I want you out of this hospital. I want you back at Robaku. I'll
pull all the strings I have to in order to get you there. But you'll have
to put up a fight to do it. All those nice kind people who want only
what's best for you are going to go on the attack in about fifteen
minutes. And then, if you don't cave, they'll bring in the big guns."

"Don't be ridiculous. No one can keep me here if I want to walk
out of this place. I'm already feeling better. I'll just take a couple more
hours to rest, then I'll leave." Not totally the truth. She was still feeling terribly weak, and her head was throbbing again. "I can't just lie
around. It would drive me crazy. I always feel better if I'm working."

"I'm not arguing with you. I'm on your side. But I can't be the
one to force the issue this time. I'll just tell you that when I get you
to Robaku, I'll take care of you, and you'll be better off." He got to
his feet. "Now the first one to see you will be Dr. Jeremy Santiago.
He'll be comforting and reassuring but will tell you that you should
rest here for a few days and let the ambassador send you home to
the U.S. for a longer rest. When you refuse, you may even get a visit
from Ambassador Sandow himself. The message will be the same.
And that may only be the beginning. Your phone is on that night-
stand. When you get through running the gauntlet they set for you,
give me a call, and I'll whisk you out of here." He touched her hand
gently. "I'm sorry, Eve. I wish I could do more for you, but that's
not possible right now."

"It's okay." She only wanted to close her eyes and rest. "You didn't
cook that damn coq au vin. But you should really hire a different
chef for that fancy hotel."

"I'll try to do that." He was on his way toward the door. "As soon
as I locate him. He seems to have disappeared..."

Disappeared. That sounded all wrong, she thought wearily. But she was too tired to work out why right now. She'd get a little rest, then she'd think about it.

"Ms. Duncan, how glad I am that we were able to help you. I'm Dr. Santiago." A tall, plump man in a white coat was entering the room. "You were a very sick woman." He was beaming at her. "But you're going to be fine, and we're going to make you comfortable for the rest of the time you're in Maldara. But we do have to talk about plans for your recovery . . ."

———◆———

"Get me *out* of here, Gideon," Eve said in exasperation when he answered the phone two hours later. "I can't take much more of this. I've talked to two doctors, the head nurse, and I just had a telephone call from the ambassador. They want to keep me in this hospital for another week, then send me back to Atlanta."

"Told you so," Gideon said. "I'm just surprised the ambassador didn't visit you in person. Did you feel slighted?"

"Stop it. No one is listening to me. I tried to explain that I'm fine and need to get back to work, but they said they don't want to take the responsibility for my recovery since the attack was so severe."

"It was very bad, Eve," he said soberly. "You have to know that was true."

"*Get me out of here.*" She pronounced every word with emphasis. "Everyone agrees I'm not on the critical list. There's no reason why I can't go back to work."

"You're certain that's what you want to do? I don't mind persuading you, but I won't coerce you."

"You listen to me, Gideon. The last thing the ambassador said when I turned him down was that he thought it might be a good idea if I talk to President Kiyani, who had expressed concern I'd become this ill in her country. My head is already aching. I won't sit here and get a migraine from having to deal with her."

"I'll be there in thirty minutes." He cut the connection.

Eve put down her phone, leaned back on her pillows, and closed her eyes. She felt totally exhausted. She should probably have told him to bring her something to wear, she thought wearily. The clothes she had worn when the ambulance had brought her here must have been a total disaster. Oh, well, let Gideon worry about it. She had found him quite capable of producing anything she wanted while she was here in Maldara. Except maybe that coq au vin, she thought wryly. He hadn't done such a great job at that particular—

There was some sort of bustle in the hall...

Oh, shit.

Her door was being ceremoniously opened by the same uniformed guard she had seen at Robaku yesterday.

Zahra Kiyani entered the next moment. "What a terrible thing to have happened to you," she said sweetly. She motioned to the leather chair beside Eve's bed. "Dalai, do something with that chair. You know how careful I have to be to avoid germs in places like this." A young, pretty maid in an ankle-length tan sarong scurried forward and put a gold-silk shawl on the chair before fading into the background. "This hospital is truly deplorable," Zahra said. "You should have been brought to my hospital when you were taken ill. I had it built this year." She gracefully sat down on the silk-draped chair. She wore an exquisitely draped scarlet dress that contrasted boldly with the gold shawl. "It's like a wonderful palace but with all the modern facilities."

"This hospital seems entirely adequate," Eve said. "And I'm not certain patients who are as ill as I was would appreciate being treated in a palace. It's a little over the top."

"It's all what you become accustomed to." Zahra studied Eve. "And you still appear to be quite pale. Would you like me to have Dalai do a makeover to give you a bit of color? She's quite clever about all sorts of different things."

And one of them was evidently how to please Zahra at any cost,

Eve thought. The girl had seemed almost frightened as she'd scurried around at her command. "No, thank you. All I need now is a
nap. I'm planning on checking out of this hospital soon."

"So I've been told. I've come to try to dissuade you. We don't
want someone of your stature to take any chances with your health.
What if you had a terrible relapse? It would look very bad for my
government when I'm trying so hard to show the world that we
are not savages after that terrible war." She smiled. "Why don't you
transfer to my hospital, and we'll take great care of you? Then when
you're well, I'll either send you home or you can return to Robaku."

"I intend to return to Robaku today," Eve said. "And I don't need
to remain in your hospital or any other. My work is going very well."

Zahra's flashing smile remained, but it was now fixed. "As I said,
I'll have to visit you again and make that judgment. It would be un-
fortunate for you to go through so much when we might have to
send you home anyway."

"I'll take my chances," Eve said. "You'd have to have cause, and,
as I said, I have proof that my work is going very well. And I'll have
more proof when I finish the new reconstruction."

Zahra's smile was now a mere baring of teeth. "I hate the idea of
your being so stubborn. Look what's already happened to you. That
horrible bout of food poisoning. Did they tell you there was a possibility you might die? Wouldn't that have been terrible? It's really too
bad they don't have food tasters in this day and age."

Eve's eyes widened in shock. There had been a thread of intimi-
dation in those words, and that last remark had been totally bizarre.
"Food taster? I'm sure that my food poisoning was accidental, and
I'm glad we have no use for food tasters."

"Yes, of course. But I admit that I've often thought that they did
have their uses. When one is of a certain importance, naturally there
are people who wish to take that stature away from them in any way
possible." She met Eve's gaze with defiance. "I'm sure my own ancestors must have felt bound to protect themselves by such means.

After all, the food tasters at court were only slaves and considered of no importance. The royal line had to be preserved."

"Why? The idea is totally barbaric." Then something Zahra had said caught her attention. "Court? I don't know anything about your family background except that your father was the president of Maldara before you, and it was a republic." She added dryly, "But I doubt if he appointed any food tasters to his cabinet."

"No, of course not." She was smiling again. "But we're a very old family, and our traditions go back over two thousand years. Did you think that we'd emerged from the same jungle as those crude Botzans?" Her lips curled. "When he was president, it suited my father to pretend that we were one with all these people, but I would never be so stupid as to give up my heritage. We did not make the Great Journey from the north and struggle all through the years to keep our lineage pure just to sacrifice it to those uncivilized barbarians. I told my father that he couldn't do it." She drew a deep breath. "And I was right, the Botzans killed him. So you can see why I believe that one must protect oneself in any way possible. When death comes near, you should take it as a sign to stop and consider all the consequences."

There was that hint of a threat again. "I don't believe in signs and portents," Eve said. "And I do believe in doing what I think is right in spite of consequences."

"Too bad." Zahra shrugged as she rose to her feet. "I do hope you'll change your mind. Let me know, and I'll send someone to make accommodations for you." She snapped her fingers at the servant girl. "Dalai!"

The young woman jumped forward and snatched up the gold shawl on the chair. Her subservience annoyed Eve. In that moment, she could imagine Zahra indulging herself in any cruel arrogance she chose with those she considered beneath her. She found she wanted to strike out. "Thank you for coming." She paused. "Oh dear, I just had a thought. How do you know that all those stories about your so-called pure lineage weren't a fairy tale? You said yourself that it was a long time ago that your family came to Maldara." She smiled gently. "Who knows? Maybe the Botzans were really your first cousins."

Zahra stopped and whirled to face her. "You insult me," she hissed. "It was no fairy tale. *Look* at me." Her eyes were blazing. "I am everything she was and more." Her voice was shaking with anger. "She made mistakes I will never make. And someday, I will have the world she lost to her own stupidity."

She turned on her heel and left the room.

What was that all about? Eve wondered. She had clearly opened up a nasty can of worms when she had taken that potshot at Zahra's august family tree. And who the hell was *she*?

Later. Gideon should be arriving at any moment, and she needed these few moments to pull herself together. At least she had gotten rid of Zahra before she had to confront Gideon. She was in no mood to referee the explosiveness she sensed between them. She glanced at the clock on the night table. It was almost five in the evening. It seemed like days had passed since she'd talked to Joe early this morning. She'd promised him she'd call him back tonight and what was she going to say to him? He'd be worried and immediately on the attack.

Think about it on the way back to Robaku.

Too many questions. Too many decisions.

And where the hell is Gideon?

———◆———

"That bitch!" Zahra's lips were tight with rage as the chauffeur opened the door of her limousine outside the hospital. "How dare she? Did you hear her, Dalai?"

Dalai knew that Zahra didn't want an answer, only an audience, but she nodded as she slipped into the backseat beside her. One could never tell what would offend Zahra and cause her to take that rage out on the nearest target. Her anger with Eve Duncan was so intense that Dalai had to be extremely careful.

"She *insulted* me." Zahra leaned back in the seat, fuming. "And she doesn't even realize how lucky she is to be alive. Stupid. Incredibly stupid."

Agree. Then try to distract her. "Yes, madam," Dalai said. "And very rude. She doesn't have any idea how wrong she is. She's just a peasant, and you're a queen. You should pay no attention to her."

"Are you telling me what to do?" Zahra asked sharply. "You were stupid, too, today. You weren't quick enough when I told you to fetch that shawl."

The distraction hadn't worked. It had only served to transfer the anger from Eve Duncan to Dalai. She had been expecting it. Eve Duncan could not be touched right now. But Dalai was always available as an outlet. Be humble. Show Zahra fear. She liked the fear. "I know, madam. Forgive me."

"Why should I?" Zahra's smile was malicious. "You should be punished. You're obviously getting lazy. I'll think about it on the way back to the palace."

So that Dalai would have time to anticipate what was to come, she thought wearily. It was all part of the fear Zahra liked to make her feel. Dalai would almost certainly be beaten if she didn't think of some other way to distract Zahra once she got back to the palace. But it would be easier to distract her there, where Zahra had decisions to make and Dalai could make herself useful in helping her. If she was beaten, it would probably not be severely.

"What are you thinking about?" Zahra asked suspiciously. "You're very quiet."

"Nothing, madam." Dalai's eyes widened with fear. "Nothing at all."

It was a lie. She was thinking that it was worth a beating to have seen Eve Duncan cause that look of outrage and indignation on Zahra Kiyani's face.

And that someone should warn the woman what a dangerous thing it was to do.

CHAPTER

6

Gideon arrived ten minutes later, and he was a whirlwind of activity for the next hour. Somehow he managed to persuade one of the nurses to help Eve dress in the slacks and shirt he'd brought with him. Then he ignored all the protests of the doctors and nurses, negotiated a miraculously fast exit, and whisked her to his Land Rover, parked in front of the hospital.

"Now lean back and relax. I'll have you at Robaku in forty-five minutes." He buckled her seat belt. "You did good, Eve."

"So did you." She closed her eyes and took a deep breath. "I wasn't sure that they wouldn't call security. They were very determined, weren't they?"

"Very." He started the Land Rover. "I could see it on the horizon once they got you settled in that room. It seemed to be a concerted effort."

"It was annoying, but it's hard to be angry. After all, it's the job of a hospital staff to do whatever they think best to get their patients well. The only one I had problems with was Madam President. But then, that was a given."

"Sorry I didn't get there in time to spare you."

"So am I. You might have been able to keep me from insulting her." She shook her head. "No, I doubt it. I rather enjoyed it. She was so ugly to that young maid, and all that arrogant bullshit about royal tasters and such..."

Gideon went still. "Tasters?"

"It was almost a threat." She looked at him. "Some nonsense about her family having had poison tasters in the past and that it wasn't a bad idea. I found it peculiar she'd mention it in the same breath as telling me how sad she was that I'd become so ill. Is there any reason why I should consider it a threat?"

"There's always a reason to suspect Zahra of any effort at intimidation. She doesn't want you here, and she'd take advantage of any opportunity to make you feel afraid and uncertain."

"But there's no reason to think that my food poisoning was anything but an accident?"

Gideon was silent. "Not as far as I know. The food was examined, and it contained mushrooms that could have made you very ill. And we haven't been able to talk to the chef yet. We're still trying to locate him."

"And it would have been crazy for Zahra to slip me anything that would make me that ill just because I wouldn't get on the next plane and take off for home," Eve said. "She's the president of the damn country. She must have more important things to worry about." She made a face. "Though tonight I wasn't sure if she wasn't a little off base when she started talking about her Kiyani ancestors. That's when I lost it and told her that her ancient history could all be bullshit."

"What?" Gideon burst out laughing. "You do like to live dangerously. You couldn't have said anything to make her more angry."

"It didn't seem to matter at the time. She was talking something about the Great Journey and how much better she was than *her*. Whoever that was." She rubbed her temple. "It got pretty confusing."

"Not for Zahra," he said quietly. "It means everything to her. And I guarantee she doesn't think it's bullshit."

She nodded as she looked at him. "That's right, you'd know, wouldn't you? You were...intimate."

"Not exactly. But we had sex, and that was entirely different from intimacy." His lips twisted. "But she enjoyed me enough to consider me a candidate. It was amusing to watch her. If I'd stuck around, I might have gone from candidate to consort. Pity I didn't find her that exciting."

"Consort?"

"Yes, Zahra always considered herself a queen, and naturally, she needed a consort. Her ancestress had taken many important men as consorts, and she eagerly followed in her footsteps. I had enough power in Maldara to be fairly impressive, and she thought I'd be a good enough match."

Eve frowned. "Ancestress?"

"Oh, you didn't get that much in depth? Zahra only acknowledges two of her ancestresses, and only one earns her reluctant respect. One is Kiya, the founder of the Kiyani family. The other is Kiya's mother." He smiled. "But to get to the answers, you have to travel on the Great Journey. I can't tell you how often Zahra bored me with looking at her map of that journey." He took out his phone and pulled up a Google map of Maldara and the rest of northern Africa. "We sit right here above the Congo and directly northeast is Ethiopia, then South Sudan, Sudan, and Egypt." His index finger touched a destination on the Mediterranean coast of Egypt. "And here is the city of splendor that is no more. At least in its original state. Don't you think it's a fine birthplace for our Queen Zahra's ancestors?" He smiled. "Now reverse it, and we have the Great Journey that's now Kiyani history, whether or not it's true."

Eve looked at the city. "Alexandria? Zahra is claiming Egyptian heritage?"

"She will be soon. It serves her purpose right now to please the nationalists here in Maldara, but there's a certain glamour to the stories connected to the Great Journey, and Zahra will want to take advantage of them. Maldara is a small fish compared to Egypt. I'd bet Zahra will start climbing as soon as she makes her position unassailable here."

"The Great Journey." Eve was frowning. "I don't understand any of this, and you're making my headache worse. Tell me what you're talking about."

"I'm getting there. I told you that you'd have to go back to Zahra's favorite ancestress for clarity. Work it out for yourself. Who would Zahra accept as an acceptable predecessor?"

"I'm not ready to play games. You're enjoying this too much." But she was intrigued and thinking in spite of herself. "An ancestress who started her journey in Alexandria and traveled south to the jungle country of Maldara."

"Go on."

"Why would she do that? Alexandria was a queen city for thousands of years. It had the greatest library in the civilized world and the Pharos lighthouse, which was one of the seven wonders of the world. It had famous scholars and scientists."

"Which Zahra would not appreciate as you do, Eve. What would make that city acceptable as a place of origin for her? You said it in that first sentence."

Her eyes widened. "Queen city. The Pharaohs had their palaces on the bank of the Mediterranean." She took the next giant step. "And the most famous queen was Cleopatra. Zahra actually thinks she's related to Cleopatra?"

"By George, I believe you've got it. Not thinks, knows. She couldn't be more certain."

"She's got to be nuts," Eve said flatly.

"Perhaps. But you have to accept that she believes it, so you'll understand who she is. All her life, she's identified with the royalty of Egypt and particularly with Cleopatra VII. You can either call it bullshit or you can use it to manipulate her."

"Which did you do?"

He smiled. "I did what I had to do at any given moment. But I'm afraid you're too honest to follow my lead. Jill had problems doing it. Though she did become interested in the literary aspects of Zahra's fantasy. But then, Jill's a storyteller."

"So I've discovered," Eve said dryly. But she couldn't deny that her curiosity had been aroused. "What literary aspects?"

"The Great Journey wasn't only a map, it was a journal. It was passed down from generation to generation in the Kiyani family."

Her gaze flew to his face. "Whose journal?"

He chuckled. "Not Cleopatra. Gotcha."

"No, you didn't. I'm not that gullible. Everyone knows how Cleopatra died. And it wasn't on a Great Journey to this steaming jungle in the middle of Africa. Whose journal?"

"Does everyone know how she died? Zahra would disagree."

"Gideon."

"Just a little food for thought." He grinned. "And a warning not to take anything for granted in this world. You're right, it isn't Cleopatra's journal. But it was written by an ancestor of Zahra's whom she viewed with a certain respect and tolerance. Her name was Kiya."

"Kiya? That's right, you mentioned Zahra respected her. You're saying a woman made her way from Alexandria to Maldara and founded the Kiyani dynasty?"

"I didn't say she was alone. She had slaves and at least one consort. That was in a day when a woman had to be able to use a man to get what she wanted. That was why Zahra had respect for her in spite of her many flaws. But Kiya was powerful enough to pull things together and set up her household and family to suit herself." He paused. "And it was her name that remained on all the record books from the time she crossed the Maldara border." He smiled. "Kiya, beloved daughter of Cleopatra VII."

"What? It was actually true?"

"Perhaps. If it wasn't, Kiya told a good story."

"You said record books. Not just her journal?"

"Come on, what do you think? It was over two thousand years ago. The records were only vague references other than Kiya's accounts. And the Kiyanis became almost as savage as the natives who attacked them when they invaded their territory. But they were smarter, and they had more civilized methods of torture and murder than the tribes had seen before. So they beat them back and started to build their empire."

"Which evidently was no Alexandria. It's pretty much as undeveloped now as when they came here."

"They had several obstacles to overcome. A few Zahras and similar male counterparts appeared over the centuries. They were low on family values and high on world domination." He was driving off the highway and onto the bumpy dirt road that led to Robaku. "Like most families, good and bad. But with the Kiyanis, it just seems to be exaggerated. They go up and down like a roller coaster." He pulled up to the museum and shut off the car. "Here you are." He got out and ran around to open the door for her. "See? What else could you want? Chauffeur service, and I even provided you with entertainment to keep you amused." He was unlocking the door to the museum. "Now I'll get you settled and make sure that it's okay to leave you."

"Of course it's okay." She got out of the car and joined him as he opened the door. "I only have a little headache now." And her knees were still damnably weak. But she ignored both because she was still fascinated by the story with which Gideon had been regaling her. "Did Zahra ever show you this journal?"

"Of course." He nodded. "Not the original. But it had been copied multiple times over the centuries." He smiled mockingly. "It was at a time when she was still enthralled with the idea of me as a consort and wanted to impress me."

"And were you impressed?"

"It was . . . interesting. But her take on it was even more interesting."

He stepped aside for her to enter. "Now story time is over. Sit down. You're not as steady on your feet as I'd like."

"I'll get a cup of coffee and an aspirin and I'll be fine."

"I'm sure you will." He turned on the lights. "Go sit down," he said again. "I'll make the coffee. I could use one myself. I seem to have been telling you tales like some male Scheherazade all the way from Jokan. Do you suppose Scheherazade got hoarse from talking all night?"

"She had motivation. She was under a death sentence if she didn't keep the sultan entertained." She dropped down on her stool. "And you're no Scheherazade, Gideon." She suddenly chuckled. "Sorry, I just had a vision of you dressed up in a veil and harem outfit. I may never be able to look at you again without seeing it."

He flinched. "You really know how to hurt a guy." He was pouring water into the coffeemaker. "Oh, well, I have enough confidence in my manly vigor to be able to suffer through it." His gaze went to the reconstruction of Amari, which was still on the dais on her worktable. "He's still here. It seems a long time since I brought Hajif and Leta here last night."

"It was a long time." Her gaze shifted to Amari. "A lot happened..." She suddenly straightened on the stool. "And Hajif must have wanted to get in here to get Amari. They were so eager to take him home. But the door was locked, and we weren't here. I thought I'd be back before they were ready for him."

"And then you were so rude as to develop food poisoning and kept them out. I believe they'll forgive you."

"But I'm back now, and there's no reason why they have to wait any longer." She got to her feet and steadied herself on the worktable for a minute as that blasted weakness swept over her. "I'll go down and tell them that they can—"

"No," Gideon said firmly. "I'll go down and get them if you don't think they can make it through the night." He pushed her back down on the stool. "Rest."

He was out the door before she could protest.

Gideon was being a little too protective, she thought with exasperation. It wasn't as if she were tottering on the edge of death. She might as well have had Joe here. No, Joe would not have been that obvious. He would have been subtle and warm and...Joe.

Damn she missed him.

She looked at the clock. Eight-ten. No, it wasn't time to call him yet. She usually waited until she was sure he wasn't at an evening session at the Yard. That was about ten or eleven Maldara time.

And she needed that coffee if she was going to keep alert until it was time for her to make that call. She got to her feet and went to the cabinet where the coffee was brewing.

She'd just poured herself a coffee when Gideon came back into the museum.

"Caught you," he said. "What didn't you understand about the word *rest*?"

She was frowning. "Where are Hajif and Leta?"

"They weren't quite ready for him. They said they'd see you in the morning." He came to the coffeemaker and poured himself a cup of coffee. "So sit down. You don't have to be hostess to me. We're way beyond that, aren't we?"

"Yes." She was still staring at Amari. "I don't understand. They were so eager and Leta said only a few hours..." She shifted her gaze back to Gideon. "Unless you gave them the impression they wouldn't be welcome?"

He grimaced. "I wouldn't do that when I know you'd have my head. I was charming and caring, I just explained that the reason we didn't show up earlier was that you'd been very ill and had to go to the hospital." He held up his hands. "All very truthful."

"And you knew Hajif and his family probably wouldn't go to a hospital unless they were dying."

"It did occur to me that might be the effect."

"But you knew I wanted them to come."

He nodded. "People make their own decisions, Eve. I just gave them the facts."

And he was so clever that he knew just how to shade them. "I could go down to the village and bring them back with me," she said coolly. "I don't appreciate manipulation, Gideon."

"I know. Even if I didn't realize it, Jill told me. She was afraid that it might be the one thing that would keep you from coming here." He said quietly, "But I told you that if you left the hospital and came back to Robaku, I'd take care of you and you wouldn't suffer for it. I was acting instinctively with Hajif to keep that promise."

"Because you want me to rest?"

"Partly." He smiled. "I imagine it's difficult for the people around you to take care of you without a little manipulation and sleight of hand. Admit it. Doesn't your family have to resort to it on occasion? What about your husband?"

"Joe and I are honest with each other. Besides, that's different."

"Which means that you *try* to be honest with each other."

"Which means that you don't have the same rights and privileges."

"Unfortunately." He chuckled as her eyes widened. "I told you I liked intense women." He shook his head. "I'll back down now. You left yourself open, and I couldn't resist. I know you're as faithful as Penelope was to Odysseus."

He was impossible. "Now you're delving into *The Odyssey*? First, it was that wild tale about Kiyani, and now you're into mythology?"

"Well, I did minor in English Lit when I was at Oxford. And there was a two-headed female monster in *The Odyssey*. When you think about it, there might be some connection with Zahra Kiyani." His smile faded and he added soberly, "But I'm really still trying to distract you as I've been attempting to do since we left the hospital. That's not being fair. You've had a rough day, and some of it was my fault. You like honesty, and I should give it to you."

Eve frowned. "Distract me?" She didn't understand any of this, and it was beginning to frustrate her. "Distract me from what?"

"Any number of things." His lips twisted. "That's been my main duty since Jill called me into this with you. Protect and distract. I'm very good at both though you'd never know it by today. But Jill says she can't take any more, so evidently there's a change coming. I might as well begin again now. Yes, I did want you to rest, but only because you're going to have enough with which to contend when Jill gets here. That should be in about ten minutes. You're going to get all the honesty and absence of manipulation you can stand." He grimaced. "Which is completely wrong for the situation. I'm surprised Novak is letting her do it. I guess he thinks she deserves it. She paid the price."

"Who is Novak?" Then she remembered. "CIA. Jill gave me his name to pass on to Joe. What has he got to do with this?"

"You can ask Jill. I don't know how honest she's going to be. If she tells you about Novak, then you'll probably have the entire picture." He moved toward the door. "Now it's time I went into protection mode again. This time for Jill. She wants to make sure that Robaku isn't being watched. She doesn't want anyone to know that she's coming to see you tonight. I'll see you later, Eve."

He left the museum.

What the hell?

Eve put her coffee cup down and leaned back against the cabinet. Her knees were still shaky, and she hadn't needed those enigmatic words from Gideon to make her any dizzier. She hadn't understood what he was talking about, but she didn't like the sound of it.

Well, she would soon find out and handle it. She just wished that Jill Cassidy hadn't picked a night when she was feeling this weak and vulnerable to spring something of which even Gideon seemed to disapprove.

Forget it. Stop dwelling on something she couldn't change until she was confronted with it. She went back to her stool and began to prepare Amari for his final trip to Hajif and Leta tomorrow.

Then she stopped as she realized what she was doing. Not

questioning, just accepting what was happening to her no matter how strange she thought it. Meekly going back to this work she had chosen to do.

Or that had been chosen for her to do.

And Jill would be coming in that door soon, and, in spite of what Gideon had said, the reporter might try to manipulate her once again.

No way.

Clear your head and get ready for her, dammit.

"It's wonderful," Jill said quietly from the doorway behind Eve, her gaze on the Amari reconstruction. "Or should I say *he's* wonderful. Your Amari seems almost alive again."

Eve looked over her shoulder. "That's what you wanted, isn't it? You wanted him to come alive so that Hajif and Leta would have something besides a DNA report to file away? That's what I wanted, too." She turned on the stool to face her. "And I did it. But that isn't all you wanted, is it, Jill? That isn't why Gideon is outside cruising around in his 'protective mode' to be sure no one will know you're here. By the way, you're twenty minutes late. He must have been worried. Or maybe he isn't as efficient as he told me he was." She added coolly, "But what can you expect when you choose an errand boy who was born with a silver spoon in his mouth?"

Jill went still as she studied Eve's expression. "Gideon did his job. It was my fault. I had to make sure I wasn't followed." She crossed the room toward her. "I didn't want to ruin everything because I was having an attack of conscience. There was still a possibility that I could salvage bits and pieces even if you socked me, then threw up your hands and took the next flight out."

"You seem to think that a possibility. I probably will, too. Particularly since Gideon was talking about honesty, which was clearly lacking, and manipulation, which was obviously present. Though I'm not surprised he brought them up. I've known since the day I met you that you were very good at luring people into doing what you wish." Her lips tightened. "And yet I didn't realize that you were lying to me. I consider myself a good judge of character, and when you answered my questions, I would have sworn that you were telling me the truth."

"I was telling you the truth. I just couldn't tell you everything." Jill shook her head. "Otherwise, you wouldn't have come, and we had to have you here." She continued in a desperate rush: "And I thought it would be okay. I was sure we could keep you safe. I didn't expect this to happen. There was no reason."

"You mean that the food poisoning was no accident? I tried to tell myself that it didn't make sense that anyone would want to hurt me. But I've been sitting here waiting for you and trying to put everything together from what Gideon said, and that stuck out in living color. He was very tentative, but he didn't really deny it. I might have been too woozy to figure out the whys and wherefores, but the fact that it was intentional became crystal clear as I thought about it. Evidently someone believed they had reason not to want me here. Zahra?"

"I'm not...sure. I knew Zahra wouldn't want you here, but I didn't believe she'd feel strongly enough to actually strike out at you. She just wants control of Robaku. She's very careful of her image, and there's no way she'd want even a suspicion touching her."

"Yet Zahra Kiyani was in my hospital room this afternoon expressing her sympathy and her opinion that I should get the hell out of Dodge. Diplomatically, of course. Well, as diplomatically as she was capable of. But I was having trouble appreciating anything but the fact that she'd come running when there was a chance to get rid of me." Now Eve was having trouble suppressing her anger. "I was so sick, and I was told I could have died. When I woke up, the entire world seemed only to want to get rid of me. It pissed me off, and I didn't even know then that it had been a deliberate attempt. Then I got Gideon's 'distractions' laid on me and his irritation that you weren't behaving as everyone wanted you to." She glared at Jill. "That about topped off my day. If you hadn't come tonight, I was going to go after you. I'm mad as hell. I want answers, Jill."

"That's why I'm here." She looked for a place to sit down, saw only the cot across the room. She shrugged, dropped to the floor, and crossed her legs tailor-fashion. "That's what I've been trying to tell you. There are still things I don't know, but you'll know what I know."

"How refreshing. You're not denying that someone tried to kill me?"

"I'm not denying it could have happened. But Novak said that the poisoning was done by an expert, and you weren't meant to die. The mushrooms were blended with an additive from Egypt that altered the toxicity. They just meant to discourage you, just like they did me. It was meant to make you a little ill to encourage you to leave. That's the only reason why I think there was even a possibility that Zahra might have anything to do with it. This was more of a threat than an attempt on your life. She'd use every threat before she'd endanger her position."

"That threat was very painful. I thought I was dying. I couldn't tell the difference at the time." Eve went on to the next item on her agenda. "Novak. Jed Novak is the name of the CIA operative you gave me to reassure Joe. Gideon said he didn't think Novak would let you talk to me. Do you work for the CIA?"

"No." She grimaced. "Though Novak did do his best to keep me from coming here tonight. I told him I couldn't do anything else, and we'd have to make other plans if you blew up. I've only known Novak since I came here to Maldara, but I'd heard enough about him to reach out when I needed him."

"One of your friends in high places?"

"Novak operates on both levels. That's why he's so valuable." She added wearily, "He's gone to a lot of trouble and expense to set up the switch. He's got a right to be angry with me. But I'm not like him, and I can't go by his rules. Please believe me. I knew there might be some danger to you, but I thought we could get you out of here before it—"

"Became fatal?" Eve interrupted. "You're not making your position any more sympathetic. And you're certainly not making this situation less muddled. Now, I'm going to ask you questions, and you're going to answer me clearly and concisely."

"Whatever you say," Jill said quietly.

"You said that doing these reconstructions was important to you, but that's not the real reason why you put all your time and effort into luring me here. What was that reason?"

"I needed the best forensic sculptor in the world to come here to Maldara. I had a job that had to be done by the very best."

"What job? Not the children?"

She shook her head. "But I knew that would bring you. I hoped that once you were here, I could persuade you to do the other reconstruction."

"The honorable thing to do when offering a job is to give terms and let me decide."

"I couldn't take a chance. It was too important. We didn't even have the skull, and to get it might have made you—" She stopped.

"Made me what?" Eve said impatiently.

"An accomplice." Jill didn't let her absorb that but went on quickly: "We wanted to switch a skull that's being held in the vault at the U.N. headquarters in Jokan for a counterfeit so that you could do a reconstruction to verify the identity."

Eve stared at her, openmouthed. "What?"

"I know. It's not the kind of . . . You would never have done it."

"That's quite correct."

"That's why I wanted you to be here. I wanted you to see that schoolroom." Her voice was shaking. "I wanted you to see what he'd done to this village. I wanted you to see what he'd done to this *country*."

She stiffened. "He? Who are you talking about?"

"Nils Varak. You know it was his men who butchered those children."

"Of course I do. He was a monster. What does that have to do with anything? Varak was killed right after the U.N. forces invaded Maldara. Some kind of helicopter explosion."

Jill was shaking her head. "That's what I thought." Her voice was unsteady. "And, after what I'd seen while I traveled around the country writing my stories, I wanted to send up fireworks when I heard it had happened. I'd interviewed people who told *hideous* stories about him that I couldn't write about, that I didn't even want to remember." Her voice was jerky. "Robaku wasn't the first school he'd destroyed. He *liked* to kill the children. He told his men that it made their parents more likely to cave when they saw the remains of their children. Besides, it brought him a particular pleasure to take their lives before they'd barely started to live. And he didn't want to make it quick…he liked the machetes…"

"Stop," Eve said. Jill's face was tense, pale, her words hoarse and feverish. Eve could see that she was reliving those stories, and she suddenly couldn't stand for it to go on. "Okay, so he was a monster. Monsters should be destroyed, and that's what they did. The French forces said there was absolute proof that they'd cut the head off the snake."

Jill nodded. "Absolute. That's what they said."

Eve's eyes narrowed on her face. "You're saying it's not true?"

"I'm saying that I hope it's true. But I'm afraid it's not." She moistened her lips. "And what if it's not true, Eve? What if he's out there somewhere, waiting until all the smoke clears so that he can come out and start all over again? If not here, then somewhere else. Six hundred thousand people dead, and he killed a hell of a lot of them. And he'd do it again, he wouldn't stop. He liked it too much."

"I can't believe this. Why do you think Varak might still be alive?" She was trying to remember all the details of the account she'd read on Google. "He was killed in a helicopter explosion in the mountains in the south Botzan area. The French blew him out of the sky as he was trying to escape. But they immediately retrieved his skull from the wreckage, and he'd been positively identified by DNA." She went still, her eyes widening. "The skull? I can't believe you'd want me to do a reconstruction on Varak. Are you crazy? Absolute DNA ID. Everyone knows it."

"That doesn't mean it's true."

"It means that it will be accepted in any court in the world. And any reconstruction I do would not have a chance over DNA results. Even if I showed the skull didn't resemble Varak, it wouldn't make a difference. DNA rules."

"But it would insert an element of doubt with people who would go after Varak full throttle if they thought he was still alive." She paused. "One of them is Novak. The director of the CIA accepted the proof that Varak was dead. Novak would have to have some credible reason for them to reopen the investigation. But regardless, he'd never stop if he was sure that Varak was still alive. He almost caught him twice while he was on the hunt for him in the mountains. He was the one who notified the French he'd be on that helicopter."

"And he thinks that Varak slipped away?"

"He doesn't know, but he wouldn't put it past Varak. But he has to be sure. When I came to him, he promised me he wouldn't stop until he was certain Varak hadn't played him and everyone else for fools."

"*You* came to him? And he believed you with no proof?"

"No. Novak is a cynical bastard who doesn't believe in much of anything but himself. But I had a shred of information that caught his attention . . . as it caught mine."

"What information?"

"I had an informant with the Botzan faction, Ralph Hadfeld, a mercenary. After the war ended, he wanted to get out of Maldara with enough money to start again in another country before he ended up being caught and tried. He called me and tried to sell me the story of the century. He said that he had been in the hills with Varak that last day, and Varak didn't get on that helicopter. The last Hadfeld had seen of him he was in a jeep heading north."

"How reliable was this informant?"

"He'd never steered me wrong." She paused. "He said he'd taken a photo of Varak in the jeep when the helicopter was taking off. And the price he asked for the story and the photo was over a million dollars. I think he knew I'd put that info under a microscope. He said he'd give me two weeks but no longer. He wasn't sure if any of Varak's men had seen him take that photo, and he wanted out of the country."

"And you went to Novak for the money?"

She nodded. "I knew the CIA would authorize any amount to Novak. He's their golden boy." She drew a deep breath. "But he wouldn't give it to me. He listened, then he said that Hadfeld could be playing me. He said he'd go after him himself, and he even had an idea how the info could be verified. He said that I should keep out of it."

"And you didn't do it."

"It was *my* story, my informant, and I had to know if it was the truth. But if Novak wouldn't give me the money, I had to go somewhere else. So I called Sam Gideon. I knew I had a chance with him. There was no way he'd want Varak to slip away after what he'd done here. Gideon agreed to make the buy, and I called Hadfeld."

"You got the story and the photo?"

"No, he said he'd call me later with arrangements. And he did call me one night a few weeks ago and set up a place in the jungle to meet him." She looked away. "Emphasis on *set up*. It was a trap. When I got there, Hadfeld was dead, a very bloody death. He'd been tortured. Evidently, Varak's men had been tracking him and forced him to make the call. They wanted to make sure that I saw what they'd done to him."

"But you got away?"

There was the faintest hesitation. "Yes, I got away." She looked back at Eve. "But if they did that to Hadfeld, I didn't need much more to convince me that what he was going to sell me was the real McCoy and that Varak was still out there. Wouldn't you feel the same?"

Varak *alive*? Eve felt a ripple of shock. She had been so involved with listening to the horrific details of Jill's story that the idea that Varak had not been killed in that helicopter crash had not actually gotten through to her. But as she stared at Jill, a chill went through her. How could she not consider it? Because Jill Cassidy thought it was true and had gone to this extreme to prove it. "I might feel there was a chance except for the DNA."

"Novak says that DNA can be faked if you know the right experts. Particularly in an explosion, when only minute amounts can be extracted."

"I've never heard of its being done with complete success. Particularly not in a circumstance where the scrutiny is so intense."

"Novak says it can be done. I believe him. But he wants to be sure that skull isn't Varak's before he goes to the people who matter. It's a scenario that will have everyone from politicians, to noted scientists, to Novak's own CIA director, ready to tear it apart. And in the furor, Varak could disappear."

"And you want me to be caught in the middle."

"No. But you might be anyway," Jill said. "I don't know what's happening. No one should have targeted you just for doing these children's reconstructions. I could see it if they thought you were working on trying to prove Varak is still alive."

"Which you want me to do at the earliest possible opportunity." Eve shook her head. "I can almost see why you decided to set up this elaborate charade. You needed to hold all the cards possible to even think I might do it."

"And even then I knew you might tell me to go to hell," she said soberly. "I only hoped that you'd remember that Varak had created all this carnage. He should pay for it, Eve. And he shouldn't get a chance to do it again." She looked at the reconstruction of Amari. "Those villages were helpless before his militia. They were savage. Varak even hung some of the body parts in the trees…"

Eve flinched. "Shock value, Jill?"

"Anything I can do." She got to her feet. "I'm sorry I wasn't completely honest with you. You know everything now. I'm praying that you won't let my duplicity affect your decision. Let me know what you're going to do, and I'll make it easy for you." She grimaced. "Unless a miracle happens, and you decide to help us. Then I can't promise it will be easy, only that we'll try to keep you safe." She headed for the door, then stopped before she opened it. "No, I still wasn't totally honest. I'd better tell you all of it. Even though it's going to make you even angrier. After I decided it had to be you who did Varak's reconstruction, I told Novak what he had to do. We had to get rid of Joe Quinn, so Novak pulled strings with some bigwigs in London and got the Scotland Yard seminar pushed up so that it would fit in with our plans."

"What?" Eve's eyes widened. "You went to those lengths?"

"You love Quinn," she said soberly. "You were right when you said I'd probed every facet of your life. That was a very big part. The chances were very slim that you'd leave him unless the circumstances were right."

"You're damn right."

"Your Michael was easier. Novak just had to find a conveniently located dig in the U.K. and send Jane MacGuire folders that described it with glowing references to how healthy and fun it was for children. Jane doesn't see your son that often. She grabbed at the chance to give him a treat like that."

"And you did your research and knew that Jane had gone on digs before."

She nodded jerkily. "I had to make sure that if I took you away, it would be worthwhile for them. You had to be certain they were safe and happy."

"How very kind," Eve said sarcastically.

"No, completely selfish. I interfered in your life. I had to do it in the most painless way possible. You have a right to be furious about that, too." She paused. "I'm sorry," she whispered. "I wouldn't have done it if I hadn't thought that it was necessary. We can't let a Robaku happen ever again."

Then she was gone.

Leaving Eve alone with her confusion and anger . . . and terror. She didn't know how long she sat there just trying to comprehend all that she had been told. At least ten, fifteen minutes passed while she struggled to understand both the horror of the possibility Jill had shown her and this feeling of betrayal and being used.

She closed her eyes and let the emotions flow over her, not trying to sort them out yet. She could still see Jill's face before her. She'd looked like a little girl sitting on the floor at Eve's feet, her blue eyes big and so full of fear yet terribly earnest as she tried to do what she'd thought was honorable and right.

She would *not* feel sorry for her, Eve thought fiercely. Jill had been totally manipulative and moved them all around like chess pieces to get what she wanted. It didn't matter that she'd thought she was doing it to keep that monster from getting away to strike again.

But how could it not matter? It was what Eve did every day of her life. Bring the children home so that monsters would be punished and not be free to kill again.

But she did not lie or cheat or use anyone else to do what had to be done. There was no question what she should do now that she knew why Jill had brought her here.

"Are you okay?"

Her eyes flew open, and she saw a tall man wearing a black-leather jacket standing in the doorway. She had never seen him before. "Who are you?"

"Jed Novak." He held up his hand. "Sorry to startle you. I'm no threat."

That was a lie. Novak might not be a threat to her at this moment, but she had been around dangerous men for most of her life. She was married to one. She knew she was facing one now. "You're CIA. Jill told me about you. Did she send you to try to convince me that everything she did was fine and for the greater good? Go away, Novak."

"No, she didn't send me. She told me not to come." He smiled faintly. "She was afraid I might attempt to intimidate you. She wanted to be sure to be fair to you. She's having a major guilt trip. She was scared to death when she thought you might die this morning."

"She should feel guilty. I can see you're not similarly prone to it. What a surprise."

"I have my moments. But I've learned that guilt has no place once I've made a decision. I'd end up in a psych ward with all the blame that can be laid at my door. Jill, on the other hand, has a conscience that constantly gets in her way."

"Not so I'd notice."

"You should have noticed. Jill fought me and Gideon and herself to come to you tonight. She knew it was the wrong thing to do."

"Then why are you here, too?"

"Because I need to try to save the mission." His lips tightened. "If you won't help us, Jill will go off in another direction and might get herself killed. She's vulnerable, they know her name, they know her face." He paused. "And they know she'll never stop. So that's why I'm here to repair the damage and ask you to forget everything but why she did it. I know that it was a shock, but you're tough. I can see you're okay."

"No, I'm not okay." Her voice was cold. "I'm angry, and I feel as if I've been treated like a marionette in a puppet show. How did you think I'd feel?"

"Just like that." He walked toward her. "That's why Gideon and I both tried to talk her out of it. She knew it was a risk, too. She told you everything?"

"Yes," she said tersely. "Even down to how she pulled the strings with Joe and Michael."

"I was hoping she'd leave that out." He made a face. "That must have struck a little too close to home."

"It was an invasion," she said harshly. "And I can't believe that she'd be able to talk Gideon into helping her do this. He's not even CIA. It's crazy."

He nodded. "And it was crazy that his home was burned to the ground and his parents butchered by Varak. Did he mention that?"

"No," she said, shocked. "And neither did Jill."

"He doesn't like to talk about it." His lips tightened. "I was with him in the mountains when he heard about it. He knew those mountains like the back of his hand, and he was trying to help the farmers who had fled their villages to find safe havens. The killing of his parents was particularly brutal even for Varak. It was clear that Gideon had been targeted to discourage him from throwing in more help and money to fight that son of a bitch." He added softly, "And then to find out that we might not have killed him after all? He has to know, Eve."

"Well, I don't. Not if it means risking my freedom and my life with my family because I became involved with this madness. Stealing a skull, doing a reconstruction, when it could mean absolutely nothing?"

"You wouldn't have to steal the skull. The skull is being held in the main vault at the U.N. headquarters in Jokan. I've arranged a bribe to one of the guards to switch the skulls. It would be brought to you, and you'd do the work in total privacy here at the museum. Then, when we have an answer, you document it, and your work is over. If the skull is really Varak's, then we return the skull to the U.N. headquarters and make another switch. And that would be the end of it."

"No, it wouldn't. I'd have to undo the reconstruction and bring it back to the way I started. And what if it's not Varak?"

"Yes," Novak said softly. "What if it's not, Eve?"

Eve couldn't answer. It was a question that frightened her more than anything else. What if her work uncovered a horrible truth about the man who had killed those children here at Robaku and all those other children slain in this bloody land?

"It's something to think about," Novak said. "I promised Jill that I wouldn't reveal you as a source, but there would probably be suspicions."

"Of course there would be," she said impatiently. "She brought me here because I have a reputation. I'd be the first one anyone would suspect. There would be so much uproar, I could lose that reputation, and the entire world would think I'm some kind of radical crackpot."

"Or a brave woman out to save that world," he said quietly. "It could go either way, but in the end it would depend on how much it means to you. No matter how we try to protect you, you'll probably go through a firestorm. I'll try to move fast enough to get my hands on Varak right away, but no guarantees."

"There are too many ifs and mights in this scenario. And I seem to be the one who's bearing the brunt of all this violence and ugliness that's going on. I was *poisoned* today," she said through set teeth. "It's easy for Jill to wring her hands and talk about how Varak has to be stopped when she's not taking the punishment."

"None of it's easy for Jill," he said roughly. His coolness had suddenly become ice. "You don't know what you're talking about. I gave her every chance to get out of this, and she still went after them. And if you bail on us, she'll still do it. No matter what they do to her. And there are worse things than a bout of food poisoning, Eve."

His violence had caught Eve off guard. All the smoothness and persuasiveness had disappeared in a heartbeat when she'd attacked Jill. And it had been triggered by that one comment Eve had made. Why? Then she was suddenly remembering two sentences that Jill had spoken that had been lost in the bombardment of information she had been throwing at Eve.

They meant to hurt you and discourage you as they did me.

And that tiny hesitation, *Yes, I got away.*

She met his eyes across the room. "She said she got away after she found Hadfeld. It wasn't true?"

"Oh, they let her get away afterward. They wanted to teach her a lesson first. There were four of them. They beat her and they raped her and left her to crawl out of that jungle to find her way back to the road. So don't tell me about her not paying her dues. The only thing she asked me when I found her on that road was to let her be the one to go after them."

"And you agreed?"

His lips twisted. "At that point I would have given her anything she asked. She believed that Hadfeld was telling the truth, and she'd paid the price. I could have negotiated that payment and handled the transaction. I didn't do it. I wanted to go after him my way. So she did it on her own."

And Jed Novak was not as cynical as Jill had said, Eve thought as she gazed at him. She didn't know what he felt for Jill, but she could tell that what had happened to her that night had struck a deep chord. And it had struck a deep chord in Eve as well. The mere fact that Jill had not tried to arouse Eve's sympathy by letting her know about the attack made the feeling even more poignant.

But that didn't change the situation. It merely made it more painful. "Do you believe that skull is Varak's, Novak?"

"Maybe. I was convinced he was dead at the time, and I tend toward doubting everything that comes my way. The attack on Jill made it seem less likely. I do believe that skull could be a phony.

I've been sending agents into the mountains asking questions of the people who were there the day of the explosion. There are a few who have doubts that Varak was on that helicopter. The others are afraid to admit to anything that would disturb the status quo." He shrugged. "And I've already started to trace a few scientists who could possibly fake that DNA. But I can't make a move on them until I'm sure I know what I'm doing. Varak would be quick to get rid of any witness."

"If he hasn't done it already," Eve said. "You're not being at all reassuring."

"Jill made me promise not to lie to you. The decision is yours. I'd appreciate it if you'd make it quickly. The switch is supposed to be made tomorrow night. It would be foolish for me to spend a fortune in bribe money if I have no forensic sculptor of your caliber to do the work. By the way, I'll have to ask you not to talk to Quinn on your Skype about any of this. It was safe to let you contact him before, but not now. There's the possibility that you might be hacked." He met her eyes. "This would take only a few days, and you might be able to keep a monster from coming back out of the shadows. Jill thinks that it's worth it. Let me know if you agree."

He turned on his heel and left the museum.

CHAPTER

7

There was no decision to be made, Eve thought. Particularly after that last remark about her not talking to Joe about it.

She shouldn't even think of doing that reconstruction. There were so many reasons why it was a bad idea.

And there was only one reason why she should do it.

To stop a monster from coming out of the shadows and striking again.

Someone had killed Hadfeld to keep Jill from getting evidence that the monster was still out there, waiting.

And that violence and horror done to Jill. Eve's own pain and sickness. Maybe Varak was no longer hiding but was on the move.

Her gaze went to Amari on the dais in front of her.

"I don't know what to do," she murmured. "But that was a terrible thing he did to you. We have to be sure that he paid for it, don't we?"

He gazed back at her with those big brown eyes and the eager expectancy that she had unknowingly sculpted in his expression. Eagerness to go home, to end the sadness of that final parting.

But could that sadness be ended if those shadows remained?

"In my court?" Eve nodded slowly. "Yeah, I know. You've had enough to deal with." She got to her feet. "Okay. I'll think about it and get back to you." But not here, where she was surrounded by those lavishly trimmed boxes, and Amari, who was both her triumph and despair. She headed for the door. She needed *air.*

She stood outside and breathed deep, her gaze on the night sky. There was moonlight, the bright orb barely visible over the canopy of trees. Just stand here and look and listen to the night sounds and don't think about anything that Jill had told her earlier.

She had come here for a specific purpose, to help Amari and all the other children who had been so terribly mutilated and destroyed. It wasn't right to put that aside and go on a wild-goose chase that could be a senseless waste of time.

It wasn't right.

Then why was she walking through the overgrown brush down the path toward that schoolroom she'd never wanted to see again?

Go back.

There's no one there.

No way she could help what had happened in that room.

Those lonely desks, the dark streaks on the floor...

She stood in the gaping opening and gazed at that broken blackboard. Had the teacher been standing there when the school had been overrun? Had the children had time to scream before the machetes began to tear into them? They must have been so afraid...

"Eve." It was Gideon standing beside her. He asked gently, "What are you doing here?"

"I don't know." That desk couldn't have been Amari's. It was too small. Maybe one of the six-year-olds... "I'm just... They were used to kindness... They wouldn't have known why..."

"No, they wouldn't." He touched her wet cheek. "We have to hope it was very quick. Come on, I'll take you back to the museum." He was propelling her away from the schoolroom and down the path. "It's been a bad day for you. You need to get some rest. We all ganged up on you, didn't we? We should have waited until you'd had time to heal at least."

"Yes, you should." Now that she was no longer looking at the schoolhouse, she was beginning to function again. Though she was unutterably sad and weary. "And you'll hear from me about it later. Right now, I have to take it all in and start thinking instead of feeling." They had reached the museum, and she turned to face him. "How did you know I was down there?"

"Jill told me to keep an eye on you." He smiled. "Though I would have done it anyway. I care about you, Eve. You may think that we all just wanted to use you, but it's not true. Yes, we had to do what we had to do, but that didn't change how we feel, who we are."

"And what you had to do dominated your life," she said soberly. "You didn't tell me about your parents, Gideon."

His smile vanished. "They were good people. I loved them. What else was there to say? Except that I have to be certain Varak died in that helicopter." He held the door open for her. "So many people died here in Maldara. After I went back to our plantation, which Varak had burned to the ground, I thought it was only one more graveyard out of thousands."

She shook her head. "I'm so sorry that you lost them, Gideon."

His brows rose. "But not sorry enough to forgive me?"

"No. I have to understand it first, and I'm not nearly there yet." She grimaced. "Particularly since I'm feeling so alone right now. Your friend, Novak, asked me not to call and talk to Joe about this. Do you know how difficult that is for me?"

He nodded. "But you're not as angry as you were, or you'd want to do it anyway and to hell with whether or not your phone was being tapped."

"No, that isn't an option, whatever I decide." She moistened her lips. "Because I can't be sure you're not right. I told you before that I felt that if I looked over my shoulder, I'd see one of those children? What if I looked over my shoulder and saw Varak in that classroom? What if he's out there somewhere?"

"Welcome to our nightmare," he said quietly.

"I have enough of my own." She turned and went into the museum. "Good night, Gideon. I'll see you in the morning."

"Night. Try to sleep."

She might actually manage to sleep, she thought as she locked the door. She had thought she might start to work, but she was too exhausted. Tomorrow would have to do.

She went to the bathroom, washed, then brushed her teeth. Then she went to her cot and sat down with her computer.

How she wanted to Skype Joe, to see his face, to release all the tension and share everything with him. But Novak had said there might be someone listening, spying, and even the idea of that intrusion made her angry. It was as if she were being robbed. Hell, she *was* being robbed.

Don't think about it now.

Just make sure that Joe wouldn't worry without totally lying to him.

And she hated the idea of that half-truth, too.

She texted.

WILL CALL YOU TOMORROW EVENING. HAD A BIT OF FOOD POISONING AND I'M HITTING THE SACK EARLY. I'M FINE, BUT YOU KNOW HOW THAT KIND OF THING TAKES IT OUT OF YOU. A GOOD NIGHT'S SLEEP WILL FIX ME RIGHT UP. I LOVE YOU.

EVE

LONDON

Son of a bitch!

Joe clicked off Eve's text message and leaned back in his chair. He didn't like this at all. Knowing Eve was ill was bad enough. But the fact that she'd played down the severity of her illness and hadn't Skyped tonight made it worse. She either didn't want to answer questions, or she didn't want him to see the toll that food poisoning had taken. Or it could be both.

She had been so happy when she'd called him from that hotel early this morning. He'd even felt a little of the uneasiness he'd had about her being in Maldara fade.

Now it was back in full force.

He wasn't going to be able to take much more of this.

Eve did not like him hovering, but then she shouldn't have taken off for a country like Maldara. Even food poisoning could be dangerous if not properly treated, and he wasn't sure what kind of medical facilities were available. And how had she gotten food poisoning anyway? She knew all the rules about not eating fresh products in foreign countries.

It wouldn't be a bad idea if he took a flight to Jokan and checked out what—

His phone was ringing.

Michael.

"Shouldn't you be in bed by this time?" Joe asked when he answered Michael's call. "Jane was telling me that you were up before daylight, and they were working you like slaves at that old castle."

"Yeah, but it's fun. Every time I find something, I go look in Jane's archaeology book and see if it's anything that could be interesting." He paused. "But I was wondering if maybe it would be more fun if we went over to that Maldara place where Mom is right now. You said that it was in the middle of the jungle, where there are all kinds of wild animals and stuff. What do you think?"

Joe stiffened. This coming out of the blue from Michael was weird as hell. Particularly since he'd been raving enthusiastically about his work on the dig since he'd arrived there. "I think that your mom would tell you that she's not there to have fun and that she wouldn't have time for either one of us. She's doing the same kind of work she does at home, and it has nothing to do with jungles or wild animals." He paused. "But I believe you knew that, Michael. I don't remember discussing the wild animals when I was telling you about Maldara."

"No, you just said it had jungles. I looked the rest up on the Internet."

And what else had he found on the Internet about that war-torn country that would have sent up red flares? "Well, you don't have to worry about your mom hiking around the jungle and getting eaten by tigers. She's working in a museum doing her work, and you know how boring museums can be."

"Not all museums are boring," Michael said. "Remember that movie *Night at the Museum*? That was cool, wasn't it?"

"In a crazy kind of way." Michael was being entirely too persistent, Joe thought. Which meant he was genuinely worried. Time to cut to the chase and get to the bottom of this. "So why are you calling me now when you should be sleeping? Did your mom say something the last time she phoned you?"

"No, she's only called me a couple times, and she was asking about what Jane and I were doing. She seemed okay." He was frowning. "But I was just thinking today that maybe we should go be with her. I don't like her there alone."

"She's not alone. She was very careful to give me an entire list of people she could call on if she ran into trouble."

"But they're not us."

"No, they're not us." And Joe felt exactly the same as his son about that. He wanted to be the one who was there for her. But something Michael had just said was making him uneasy. Michael had always had an almost psychic bond with Eve, even before he was born. She might not have said anything to him, but that didn't mean he hadn't sensed something. "Today? Why would you suddenly feel like that today, Michael?"

Silence. Then Michael said simply, "Something was wrong. I got scared."

"Why?"

"I don't know. It was really bad, then it was gone. She's okay now. I just don't want her to be alone anymore."

"Neither do I," he said gruffly. "I'm working on it." He had to try to reassure Michael even though his son's words had done the opposite to him. "It might be nothing. Your mom had a touch of food poisoning today. But, as you said, she's fine now."

He shook his head. "It was . . . really bad, Dad. Can we go, please?"

"Not right now. You know your mom, she wouldn't like it if we showed up on her doorstep without an invitation. I'll work it out." He added brusquely. "In the meantime, stop worrying. Enjoy the dig and take care of Jane. She went to a lot of trouble to give you a good time."

"I know she did." He paused. "You probably won't take me with you if you go, and that's okay. I know you'll take care of her. She'll be safe." He paused. "She's *got* to be safe."

"I believe I know how to do that," Joe said dryly. "I've been taking care of your mom for a long time, since long before you were born. Now get to bed. Let me keep an eye on her for both of us."

Michael was silent. "Sometimes it seems to be easier for me to keep an eye on her. But, okay, whatever you say. Good night, Dad." He cut the connection.

She's got to be safe.

And Michael had been very worried that Eve *wasn't* safe.

So was Joe supposed to rush out and take the next plane to Jokan because his son was getting some kind of psychic vibes that all was not well with Eve's world?

Why not? It was what Joe wanted to do anyway, and Michael's instincts had been almost a hundred percent correct in the past.

But that meant trusting Michael's instincts over Eve's explanation. Which would definitely not please her.

Okay, he didn't like it, but he'd give Eve the twenty-four hours she'd requested and talk to her tomorrow night. She'd be honest with him. If something was wrong, she'd tell him then.

Or he'd be able to know just by looking at her face. As he would have tonight if she hadn't sent him that damn text instead of Skyping.

It was really bad, Dad.

———◆———

ROBAKU
3:40 A.M.

Machete!

Varak liked killing children, Jill had said.

And he was there in the schoolroom waiting for Eve to come so that he could show her that bloody machete.

She didn't have to look over her shoulder, she could see him now, smiling, waiting . . .

But she couldn't see him clearly because she didn't know his face. She could see the evil, but how could she stop him if she didn't know his face?

And he was raising that machete . . .

———◆———

Eve jerked wide-awake, her heart pounding. She was panting, unable to get her breath. She sat upright on her cot.

Only a nightmare. Only? She felt as if she'd been there that day and been helpless to stop that carnage. She got sluggishly out of bed and went to the bathroom. She drank a glass of water and stood there looking in the mirror. She was pale, and the hand holding the glass was shaking. She looked as helpless as she'd felt when she'd faced Varak in that nightmare.

She *wasn't* helpless. She couldn't be helpless. She steadied her hand as she put the glass down on the vanity. And she wouldn't let herself spend her life looking over her shoulder, wondering if he was still there, waiting with that bloody machete.

Eve grabbed her phone and punched in Jill's number the minute she left the bathroom. "I want you over here. I want Novak, too. Right now. If I can't sleep, I'm not going to let either one of you sleep, either."

"Twenty minutes," Jill said. "And I'll find a way to get Novak there."

"I know you will. I'll make the coffee."

Silence. "That sounds promising."

"Not necessarily. I desperately need the caffeine, and I want both of you to be awake enough to give me answers." She cut the connection.

———◆———

Jill arrived fifteen minutes later. "Novak is right behind me." She went over to the cot and pulled it into the center of the room. "If you don't mind, I'll try to avoid sitting on the floor at your feet this time. I don't mind being humbled, but I have an idea I might need all the dignity I can gather together for this session. You really should have Hajif find you a few more chairs."

"You do it." She gave Jill her coffee. "I like the idea of your being humble, considering what you've put me through." Her lips twisted. "Though I can't see Novak being humbled in any situation."

"He pretends well." Jill sat down on the cot. "But you're right, he knows what he wants and goes after it." She glanced at Novak as he walked into the room. "I've saved you from groveling, Novak. Come and share my cot."

"How can I resist? I've never had that invitation from you, Jill." He strolled toward Eve. "But I think we should get down to business before pleasure. Since you summoned both of us, I assume you do mean business?"

"*My* business," Eve said. "I had one hell of a night. I have to be sure that Varak won't ever come back. And the only way I can do that is to do a reconstruction and see for myself that I don't have to worry about it." She added, "Which could get me into all kinds of trouble. You're going to go after that skull tonight?"

"That's the plan," Novak said. "We'll try to keep you from being hurt by this. All you'll have to do is perform the reconstruction and the computer measurements and photos. We'll keep your identity confidential."

"Which will be fine if this skull is Varak's. It will be bullshit if it's not," Eve said. "We all know that my identity will be secret only if we return that skull to the U.N. vault before the switch is discovered. You won't do that if you think that I've proved Varak is alive. You'll want to take the next step and find the person who falsified the DNA." She looked him in the eye. "And then you'll try to hunt down Varak and trap or kill him. Isn't that right?"

He nodded slowly. "I've told you that I would."

"And that's why it's a miracle she's even considering doing it," Jill said.

"More than considering," Novak said softly, his gaze studying Eve's face. "She's going for it. She only wants us to tell her the best way to do it."

"Wrong. I want to tell you how *I'm* going to do it," Eve said. "When you leave here, I'm going to start on the reconstruction of the six-year-old girl who's next on my list. I'll get as much done as possible today and tonight before you give me the Varak skull. I hope to get past the measuring to the initial sculpting. At that stage, a layman can't tell how much is being accomplished. Then I'll start work on Varak. That will be slower; depending on condition, it may take me up to three days. If I'm interrupted or have to leave the museum for any reason, I'll hide Varak away and put the six-year-old on the dais in his place."

"Only three days?" Jill leaned forward, tense. "Are you certain?"

"No, not if the damage from the explosion is more extensive than I think. But they would have had to have found some kind of basic bone structure to even begin to identify Varak and start to search for DNA. You said there were five passengers on that helicopter?"

"Including the pilot," Novak said. "But according to my inter-rogation of Varak's men we captured after the explosion, Varak was wearing a leather jacket that day. There was melted leather in the rubble near the remains of the body." He grimaced. "Which was ba-sically the skull."

"And the jacket led you to the right victim," Eve said. "How con-venient that they didn't have to waste time beginning their search for the DNA. Particularly since the whole world was so very eager to know that Varak was dead."

"Do you think that didn't occur to me?" Novak asked. "But the French forces had made the kill and were in charge of the investiga-tion. The U.N. told us to back off. Why do you think I even listened to Jill when she came to me with that story about Hadfeld?"

"Because you're not an idiot," Jill said. "Though you should have—" She broke off and turned back to Eve. "If the skull isn't too degraded, it will only be three days. That would be enough time. Novak said that the safe is only opened for a visual check every five days."

"Only? You appear to like that word. I'm glad you think it's going to be so easy," Eve said dryly. "It doesn't seem like that much time to me to do the reconstruction, determine if it's Varak, then erase all signs I'd even done the work so that you can slip it back into the safe as if it had never been touched." She added grimly, "And, if it's *not* Varak, then everything will probably blow up in my face."

"Our faces," Jill said quietly. "You're not alone in this. Anything that happens to you happens to me from now on." She smiled faintly. "If you get tossed into jail, they'll have to give me the next cell."

"I'd prefer to avoid that possibility," Eve said. "I have a son to raise, and I don't want to leave it up to Joe." She glanced at Novak. "Which brings me to what I have to do to keep Joe from going bal-listic about this. Joe told me that you'd met him. Did you actually think you could keep him out of it?"

"I was hopeful. But I was considering options. Unfortunately, developments are escalating."

"You mean because I was poisoned yesterday? You mean because no one told me what had happened to Jill before she drew me into this nightmare? Yes, I think either one of those events might have caused Joe to believe the situation here had escalated out of control." She added, "And I haven't told Joe any of the details about either one, but I'm going to have to do it. Jill gave me your name to reassure Joe, but he's not going to be reassured by the fact that I almost died and you can't find the chef who was responsible for the poison. Has that changed?"

"No, Gaillon hasn't shown up back at the hotel. I suspect he might have taken a bribe and skipped the country, or he might have proved embarrassing to whoever hired him and was taken out. I'm exploring both possibilities. I'll let you know as soon as I know."

Eve was shaken for a moment by Novak's coolness and complete lack of expression. But then she should have expected it. Jill had told her he was ruthless, but she found she wanted to disturb that coolness. "How nice of you. But you can see how Joe wouldn't believe you're particularly efficient." She glanced at Jill. "Look what you let happen to her."

His lips tightened, but there was only a flicker of expression in his eyes. "That's true. So what's your remedy for the situation? How do we keep him out of this?"

"We can't. It's too late. If there were any way that I thought I could keep him in London, I'd do it. But the minute I ended up in that hospital yesterday morning, I knew it was the end. Even if I left this place, he'd be back here checking out that hotel and why it happened to me. Joe never lets go, it's not his nature."

"I repeat, do you have a remedy?"

"I can't keep him out, so I tell him the truth." She paused. "And we invite him to help clean up this mess. He'll be here anyway the minute he hears what's been happening." She shrugged. "And he can be a great help, he's a superb detective. Give him all the facts and turn him loose. You'll be surprised how good he is."

"I don't doubt it. He has that reputation. I would have ordinarily welcomed his help. But I remembered that when I met him, I thought he'd probably be a difficult man to control, that he'd always go his own path." He was searching her face. "And you don't want him here, do you?"

"You're damn right I don't. But I can't go away until I know about Varak. And Joe will come regardless when he knows I was targeted." She added curtly, "And I might still be targeted. You can't deny that, can you?"

"Not as long as you're working on the skull. After that, you might be safe."

"Might?" She shook her head. "Then your job is to keep Joe so busy that he's nowhere near me while I'm working on that reconstruction. Otherwise, you can forget about my doing it. I won't risk him. Do you understand?"

"I understand. Anything else?"

"Evidently you don't trust me to Skype him. Get me a satellite smartphone that's virtually impossible to hack. And make sure my security is good enough that Joe will feel comfortable about leaving me alone here."

"I would have done that regardless."

"I had to be certain. Joe would notice."

"I imagine he would," he said. "But you should know that Gideon is fully capable. After his parents were killed, he came to me and asked to be sent to a training camp the CIA runs in Afghanistan. He did very well."

"You mean he's fairly lethal." She nodded. "I can see he'd be motivated. But he just doesn't give off those vibes."

"He's complicated," Jill said. "He adapts to the situation. I think you've found that out."

"Yes, I have." She added, "But then so do you, Jill. But I don't think you persuaded Novak to send you to a training camp to increase your kill quotient."

"I was tempted to blackmail her into it at one time," Novak said grimly. "I still might decide to do it. She's damn vulnerable."

"Back off, Novak," Jill said. "I'm not that vulnerable. I made one mistake. You keep coming back to it."

"Because I can't forget it," he said grimly. "Though you appear to have managed."

"Do I?" Jill asked. "No, I haven't forgotten. Though I try very hard."

Novak muttered a curse as he turned back to Eve. "I'm supposed to take possession of the skull at eleven tonight. Can you put off talking to Joe Quinn until I'm certain the switch has gone through? You might not have to bring him here. That guard, Swanson, is very edgy, and even the prospect of retiring with a fortune may not overcome his nerves. I might have to start all over if he panics."

"I can't believe you'd let that happen," she said caustically. "Joe said you were the CIA's go-to man."

"Which only means in situations like this I can't delegate, I'll have to be there tonight when the switch is made."

"Then you won't let this Swanson change his mind." She shrugged. "I'll wait, but the result will probably be the same. Once I let Joe know how sick I was, it will be all over. If I don't tell him I'm on my way to him, he'll be coming here." She stared him in the eye. "So handle it, Novak. Having Joe hovering over me while I complete that reconstruction would be suspicious to say the least. Joe's reputation is remarkable, and no one would believe he'd fly here from Scotland Yard just for a conjugal visit."

"I'll handle it," Novak said. "Just stall him. Okay?"

"No, it's not okay. And it won't work for long. Get me that phone so I can talk freely to him, or it won't work at all." She made an impatient gesture with her hand. "Now both of you get out of here. I have to start to work." She got to her feet and strode over to the row of leather boxes on the shelf. "Did I tell you how much I hate these boxes? But no more than I hate everything else that happened here." She took down the box with the skull of the six-year-old girl that she'd set aside in preparation. "Her name is Mila. She has a right to expect my full attention, but instead I'm making her part of this charade."

"You'll make it up to her," Jill said quietly as she got to her feet. "And I believe she wouldn't mind that she has a role in catching the man who did this to her and her friends. Do you, Eve?"

"No." Eve opened the box and gazed down at the small, blackened skull. "Very clever, Jill. Just the right thing to say."

"Not clever. It's what I feel. From now on, that's what you'll get from me." She headed for the door. "Now I have to get back to my apartment and change. I'm supposed to be back here for that press interview Gideon has set up for this morning." She smiled as she stopped at the door. "It's good that you'll be in the midst of working on a new reconstruction. I'll be able to be admiring and ask dozens of questions."

"Not dozens." Eve was frowning with exasperation. "And I completely forgot about that damn press interview." Too much had been going on that was more important. "I have to *work*. Tell Gideon to get everyone in and out within an hour."

"Don't worry. It will be just long enough to make me appear to be only another journalist out to get a feature story. Along with trying to convince Zahra that it was Gideon and not me who was behind bringing you here."

"Zahra's going to be at the interview?"

"It would surprise me if she wasn't," Novak said as he joined Jill at the door. "She seems to be ever present. She'll want to take some of the media attention away from you and focus it on herself." He glanced at Jill. "And her agent, Bogani, is still following Jill everywhere she goes."

"She's being followed?" Eve frowned. "Why? Just because she's trying to keep Zahra from swallowing up this village?"

"Interesting question," Novak said. "I'm looking into it. I'll see you this evening, Eve."

Eve turned to Jill as he left the museum. "Why?" she repeated. "Novak may be 'looking' into Zahra Kiyani, but I think she's weird as hell, and I want more than a look. I wouldn't put anything past her and her 'food tasters.'"

"Gideon told me about that conversation." Jill shrugged. "Novak's 'looks' are very thorough. But I agree she's a piece of work. It seems to run in the family. Remind me to tell you about Kiya and her journal. It's enlightening." She lifted her hand in farewell. "I'll see you at the press interview. You won't have to suffer through it for too long. Gideon is a master at this kind of bullshit. He was trained from childhood to be head of the Gideon financial empire. This is nothing."

"No wonder Zahra wanted him as prince consort," Eve murmured. "Well, all I want is for him to get those reporters and Zahra out of here and let me keep on working."

"He'll do it." Jill turned to leave. "One hour. No more."

One hour.

Jill had kept her word, Eve realized, as she watched Gideon whisk the six reporters he'd invited out the door. He'd managed to get them all individual interviews with her that were at least five minutes long, and he hadn't allowed them to take control or ask her any awkward questions. More important, he'd made Jill just one of the crowd with no special privileges, and Jill had played her part to perfection. She'd been eager, intelligent, and no one would have been able to guess she'd ever met Eve before today.

Then he'd turned the spotlight on Zahra Kiyani and switched the reporters' focus to her. Thirty minutes of Zahra's exuding charm, and he'd started herding the reporters toward the exit.

"He's very good, isn't he?" Zahra was suddenly at Eve's elbow. Then she frowned. "Though I could have used a few more minutes with the media before he decided to get rid of them. But it's difficult to control Gideon."

"I thought the timing was just right," Eve said. "I have to get back to work. It was kind of you to take the time to come."

"I couldn't do anything else." Zahra's flashing smile illuminated her beautiful face. "I had to make sure that you were all right after that horrible food poisoning yesterday. You're a little pale, but better than I thought. But, of course, you'll have to worry about a relapse. These things do happen." She didn't wait for a reply but gestured at Jill, who was now being ushered out the door by Gideon. "What did you think of Jill Cassidy? She and Gideon know each other, but I notice he didn't give her any more time for her interview than the other reporters. I was expecting...more."

"That wouldn't have been fair, would it? What did I think of her? She seems very competent and appears to know quite a bit about the village. She said I could ask her anything I needed to know, but I don't believe it will be necessary. I'm only interested in working."

"And besides, you can ask me," Zahra said softly. "I'm the only one you should consult. Robaku is really my property. My father allowed these villagers to live here, but now it's time for them to settle somewhere else. Keeping this village alive only keeps the memories of the war fresh to everyone. I've been trying to make that clear to you. It's just as well you stay away from busybodies like Jill Cassidy, who can only cause trouble."

"I'll keep it in mind." But she found she was too annoyed to leave it at that and be diplomatic with Zahra at the moment. The woman always managed to push her buttons. That comment about evicting the villagers from their homes had been a jab too deep to ignore. "But I did enjoy reading her stories. Now that I think of it, I might want to discuss them with her. It's always wise to get a few viewpoints." She turned and moved toward her worktable. "Thank you for coming, but you really didn't have to check on me. I'm doing very well. Not a hint of a relapse."

"It's early days," Zahra said. "Dalai!" Before she swept toward the door, Zahra gestured imperiously to the young servant girl who had been hovering in the background. "You might keep that in mind as well." She brushed past Gideon as if he weren't there. "And you might have given those reporters their story for the day, but you saw how eagerly they turned to me. You mustn't feel bad about that. In the end, they'll always come back to me. I have a certain glamour that you'll never possess." She lifted her chin. "I'm a Kiyani."

Then she was gone.

Gideon gave a low whistle as he gazed after her. "Her ego is flying high today." He turned to Eve. "Did she do you any damage?"

"Only a not-so-subtle hint that I could have a relapse if I wasn't careful." Now that Zahra was gone, Eve found she felt chilled. "I don't like it. There's something very savage about Zahra Kiyani. And I'm tired of threats, subtle or not. She might have had something to do with my getting ill, right?"

"It's possible."

"Then I want to know if it's more than possible. I want to know why. I want to know everything about her."

"Then we'll have to accommodate you. But I assume that's not first on your list? You appear to have a full agenda."

"Yes." And her agenda tonight included looking at a skull that might be that of Nils Varak.

Another chill.

"You might say that." She quickly looked down at the measurements she'd started on Mila. "Not first, but Zahra is definitely on the list."

———◆———

Zahra braced herself as soon as she got in her limousine. She'd like to wait until she got back to the palace, but she'd found that wasn't an option. Now she seldom had a choice, and nothing she did was private any longer.

Not from him.

She typed the text.

DUNCAN'S WORKING ON ANOTHER DAMN SKULL. SHE'S NOT PAYING ANY ATTENTION TO ME. IT'S NOT MY FAULT.

The return text came immediately.

OF COURSE IT'S YOUR FAULT. I TOLD YOU TO GET RID OF HER. YOU DIDN'T DO IT. YOU WERE TOO FRIGHTENED. NOW I MIGHT HAVE TO HANDLE IT.

She'd known she'd get the blame. It made her furious.

YOU DON'T UNDERSTAND. I WON'T GIVE UP WHAT I'VE WORKED FOR ALL MY LIFE BECAUSE YOU'RE IMPATIENT. IT COULD HAVE WORKED. FEAR AND PAIN ARE WEAPONS TOO. THEY JUST DIDN'T WORK ON DUNCAN. I'LL TRY SOMETHING ELSE.

The reply came explosively:

YOU'RE RIGHT, I AM IMPATIENT. YOU MADE ME PROMISES. YOU'RE NOT KEEPING THEM.

She couldn't let him get away with that bullshit.

YOU MADE ME A PROMISE TOO. YOU SAID YOU'D GET IT BACK FOR ME AND YOU DIDN'T DO IT. IT'S MINE. I WANT IT BACK.

He didn't answer, and Zahra began to get nervous. It was all very well to defend herself, but the result could be unpredictable.

STOP WHINING. IT'S ALREADY IN THE WORKS. BUT THAT HAS NOTHING TO DO WITH YOUR NOT GETTING RID OF DUNCAN. I'LL GIVE YOU A FEW DAYS BUT AFTER THAT I'LL TAKE OVER. DO YOU WANT THAT TO HAPPEN, ZAHRA?

The threat terrified her.

I'LL MAKE IT WORK. I'LL GET HER OUT OF THERE. JUST A LITTLE MORE TIME.

She had to wait for a full moment.

FOUR DAYS. SHOW ME YOU'RE NOT A COWARD AND WE'LL COME TO TERMS. OTHERWISE IT WILL BE MY TERMS.

The text conversation was clearly ended.

She drew a deep breath and tried to keep control. She had expected anger, not an ultimatum. But she could work with it. She would try to fix Duncan her way, but if necessary, she'd do whatever she had to do. The alternative was too dangerous to accept.

Four days . . .

CHAPTER

8

I've brought you dinner," Jill announced from the doorway of the museum. Her arms were full of take-out sacks. "I'd bet you haven't eaten today."

"You'd lose," Eve said. "I had a sandwich before that ghastly interview. I know I have to take care of myself when I'm working."

"Well, this Chinese takeout is much better. It's the only restaurant in Jokan that I'd trust to have genuine ingredients that have nothing to do with monkeys or reptiles." She was taking cartons out of the bag and putting them on the worktable. "Sweet and sour soup and a bland beef lo mein. I figured your stomach might still be tender."

"Good guess." Eve was looking at the cartons. "But this isn't necessary. I shouldn't take the time."

"Yes, you should. There's no telling when you'll allow yourself to eat after Novak dumps that skull in your lap. You know that's true." She smiled. "Besides, I hate to eat alone." She set her own cartons on the desk. "So eat, and if you want an excuse while you're doing it, so you won't feel you're wasting your time, ask me any questions you wish about Zahra Kiyani. Gideon told me that you were becoming very wary about Madam President. Since he let me read the Kiya journal, he thought that I'd be less likely to be biased."

Eve gazed at her for a moment and reached for a carton and utensils. "You're sure about the reptiles and monkeys?"

"I have a friend in their kitchen. He wouldn't steer me wrong. Trust me." Then she made a face. "You really can trust me, Eve. About everything."

"Really?" Eve said noncommittally. Then she changed the subject. "Why didn't you bring another meal for Gideon? Isn't he still drifting around the village?"

"I didn't see him. I think Novak sent him off to do something or other after he finished staging that interview." She handed her a handful of paper napkins. "But don't worry, Novak would have sent a man here to replace him."

"I'm not worried. Though I'm sure Gideon would say that no one could replace him." She tried the soup. "Excellent. Now tell me about Zahra. Gideon said that there was a possibility that she was to blame for my very painful morning yesterday. Do you agree?"

"I agree it's a possibility. Zahra is capable of anything. How far would she go? I'd judge to the limit if she thought it safe. But she's cautious, and she'd make certain that the end result would be worth any action she takes." She was gazing thoughtfully down into her soup. "She's into power, and she believes it's her due. It's all part of that royal bullshit she's embraced since childhood." She looked up at Eve. "Gideon told you she believes that she's descended from Cleopatra?"

"Are we back to this Kiya again?" Eve asked impatiently. "I ask about Zahra, and I get a tall tale about Cleopatra's daughter."

"Because when I first came to Maldara and was trying to get a handle on how to keep Zahra from kicking all those villagers out of their homes, I had to understand her. I didn't even come close until Gideon told me about Kiya. Then it started to come together. In many ways, Zahra *is* Kiya. With a generous sprinkling of Cleopatra thrown in."

"How?"

"You take a psychotic personality and throw in the idea that noth-ing is forbidden and everything is your right to take. The final result you come up with is a very dangerous woman. Zahra really admires Cleopatra, you know. If you look deeper into who Cleopatra really was, you can see the similarities. She wasn't the gorgeous, tragic queen that the movies portrayed. Intelligent, yes. And she possessed a kind of glamour that had its own attraction. But she killed her brother and sister. There were even rumors that she might have killed her own father. No one counts how many of her slaves bit the dust. Food tasters were a way of life, and any cruel indulgence was allowed with slaves. According to Kiya's journal, Cleopatra even threatened her with death and torture innumerable times when she was angry with her. It didn't matter that Kiya was her daughter."

"Gideon said that you appreciated the literary aspects of her jour-nal," Eve said. "Do you think it was fact or fiction?"

"It . . . was persuasive."

"But Cleopatra only had one daughter, Selene, who later became Queen of Mauretania."

"Only one acknowledged daughter," Jill said. "According to Kiya, she was the result of a sexual liaison between Cleopatra and a soldier in her army while Caesar was away. She gave Kiya to her slaves to raise, and later, Kiya herself served as a slave to Cleopatra. Evidently, she wasn't treated too badly. Cleopatra ordered her named Kiya after Queen Kiya, who was a queen to Akhenaten during the Eighteenth Dynasty. She was one of Cleopatra's favorite ancestors because she was known as the Beloved Wife. Other of his queens were called royal and powerful, and Nefertiti was famous for her beauty, but Cleopatra thought Akhenaten probably loved Kiya more. Wherever her name was inscribed, it was followed by Beloved Wife. Anyway, maybe Cleopatra wanted to tell her daughter she loved her even though she'd made her a slave. At times, Cleopatra actually did show her affection." She added ironically, "Providing Kiya kept in mind her lowly place in the scheme of things."

"Which would have been very painful considering that she knew she was Cleopatra's daughter."

"True. But she seemed to have inherited Cleopatra's toughness because she adapted and played her mother's game while she waited for her chance."

"Chance?"

"To be a queen herself." Jill finished her lo mein and pushed the carton away. "I wonder if she actually managed to outthink Cleopatra, or if she took advantage of circumstances."

"What are you talking about?"

"The Great Journey." Jill leaned back. "What do you know about how Cleopatra died?"

"What everyone knows. When she knew Octavian was on his way to capture her, she locked herself in her mausoleum and committed suicide by letting an asp bite her."

Jill nodded. "Partially right, according to what Kiya related in her journal. Not complete enough. No one gives more than a mention to the slaves she took with her into the mausoleum to die with her. They were the maids Eiras and Charmion. But there was one more slave who went with her."

Eve stiffened. "Kiya?"

"According to Kiya's journal, she went there with her mother by her own choice. She makes a point of saying she felt it her duty to do whatever her mother wished her to do. Or whatever seemed wisest." She paused. "Do you know what else is seldom mentioned? Cleopatra's burial treasure that was in the mausoleum. One of the greatest treasures ever compiled. That was why Octavian was rushing to reach her—he needed that treasure."

Eve stared at Jill, guessing where this was going. "And did he get it?"

"Oh, yes, it was a vast treasure, and he was very pleased with it." She smiled. "And, according to Kiya's journal, there was so much that Octavian never even missed the wagonload of treasure that was taken out of the mausoleum during the time before Cleopatra actually got around to committing suicide."

"My, my," Eve murmured. "Kiya, again?"

Jill nodded. "Remember her line about whatever was wisest to do? It seems that what was wisest for Kiya to do was not to kill herself with Cleopatra. Her mother had sent Caesarion, her son and heir, away to hide from Octavian. Kiya convinced Cleopatra that she should spare a little of her treasure to make certain her heir was safe and had enough funds to fight Rome. Then Kiya magnanimously volunteered to risk her own life to take the treasure to Caesarion." She sighed. "But unfortunately, Octavian found Caesarion and murdered him before she was able to get to him. What a pity. The only good thing was that Cleopatra had already killed herself and didn't have to hear the sad news." She shook her head. "But what could Kiya do with this huge fortune in the back of her wagon? What a conundrum."

"The Great Journey," Eve said.

"Well, she obviously had to leave Alexandria or Octavian would kill her. The only solution was to go somewhere far away, a wild, mysterious place that she had been hearing about in the market." She nodded. "The Great Journey."

Eve chuckled. "You're a much better Scheherazade than Gideon. How much do we believe?"

"As much as you like. It's a great story, so I prefer to believe it all. Particularly since Kiya was such a scheming bitch that she reminds me of Zahra. If she was that clever, couldn't she have found a way out for Cleopatra? Was this her master plan from the beginning, or was she making it up as she went along?"

"Probably a little of both."

"I believe you're right." Jill got to her feet and went over to the coffeemaker. "She had been waiting for a long time, but when the opportunity came, she was ready. She even knew where she was going." She made the coffee and leaned back against the cabinet. "But after that first journal about the Great Journey, the treasure isn't mentioned. I found that interesting."

"Dispersed by her heirs through the centuries?"

"Not much to buy in primitive Maldara. It seemed to disappear when they reached the border." She shrugged. "A mystery to solve. But, then, the entire story is something of a mystery all bound up in True or False." She suddenly smiled. "And, speaking of True or False, that story about the way Cleopatra died wasn't entirely true, according to Kiya. She didn't die of the poisonous bite of an asp though she wanted everyone to think she did. The snake was a symbol for royalty, and Cleopatra liked the idea for that reason. But she wanted her death to be as perfect as her life, so she wasn't going to take any chances. Kiya said that she did extensive research by having several slaves bitten by asps so that she could study the effects before she made her decision."

"Charming."

"Entirely practical from Cleopatra's viewpoint. When a goddess dies, it must be with glory and dignity. But she found when an asp bites, it causes swelling and ugly discharge and intense pain that lasts up to six hours or longer. It's a horrible death. There was no way she was going to put up with that agony and loss of dignity. So she opted to have the snake brought to the mausoleum for effect, but she arranged to have her jeweled hair comb coated with a fast-acting poison. She pressed the prongs of the comb into her arm when the time was right."

Eve's brows rose skeptically. "Definitely another True or False."

"But think about it. Consider what we know about the era and Cleopatra herself. It's possible." Jill shrugged. "And, if you believe in Kiya, then it's more than possible." She smiled quizzically. "Anyway, did I manage to help you to get a glimpse of Zahra's character by studying Kiya?"

"With a few major differences. Kiya was a survivor. Everything she did was because she had to fight or die. Zahra doesn't have that excuse. It's pure ambition."

"How very perceptive." Jill poured coffee into a cup and took it back to Eve. She mockingly inclined her head. "Your after-dinner coffee, madam." She looked at the scant remains of the food. "And you managed to get most of your dinner down. That's good." She took the sacks, plastic plates and utensils and tossed them into the trash can in the corner. "That should hold you until I get back. I have to go now. I'll see you about midnight."

Eve stiffened, her eyes widening. "You're going with Novak? Neither of you mentioned it."

"It's my story," she said simply. "In more ways than one. Novak would have just argued with me. It's better if I just present him with a fait accompli." She headed for the door. "Get back to work on Mila. With any luck, we'll have a replacement for her within a few hours."

If they weren't caught and killed by those guards at the U.N., Eve thought. The soldiers guarding that vault might shoot first and ask questions later. This would be considered robbery on an international scale. She was sure Varak's skull must be the principal prize being held there. Villains on the mega scale of Varak were rare, and proof of his demise was even more rare. Trying to steal Varak's skull would have been like trying to steal Bin Laden's corpse. Eve had not been worried about Novak. He was a professional, and Joe said a good one. But Jill was different. Novak had said she was vulnerable, and she'd already been terribly hurt. She said impulsively, "Jill."

Jill looked back over her shoulder and grinned. "What's the matter? Going soft on me? I'm the bad guy, remember? I'm the one who got you into this mess."

"I remember." But she still had to say it. "But it won't hurt you to be careful, Jill. You're ... valuable." She turned back to Mila's reconstruction, and said lightly, "Who else knows where to get Chinese food with no serpents or monkeys?"

———◆———

U.N. HEADQUARTERS
JOKAN

No Novak.

And it was only fifteen minutes until he had to meet with Swanson, Jill thought tensely. She'd gotten here twenty minutes ago and expected to see some sign of him before this.

Her gaze narrowed on the huge mansion on Wabona Street that had formerly belonged to the owner of a diamond mine before it was taken over by the U.N. The house and grounds were enclosed by a twelve-foot stone fence that the U.N. said was necessary for their employees' security. Though she knew most of the employees had been given quarters in the city after Edward Wyatt had taken residence in the mansion. The house itself was dark now, and there was only one uniformed guard at the gate.

And there was a camera mounted on that gate.

Jill's hands tensed on the steering wheel of her Volvo. She was parked some distance down the street from that front gate, but she'd be in view of that camera the minute she walked within several yards of it.

But Novak would have taken care of that camera, wouldn't he?

And how had he been planning to get rid of the guard?

No way to be sure without checking. She would have had to call him anyway, but now the need was imperative. It was getting very close to that eleven o'clock deadline.

She dialed his number. "Where are you, Novak?" she asked when he picked up. "I need to know if you've taken out this damned camera."

He muttered a curse. "I knew it. I was hoping that you wouldn't do this. Why couldn't you leave it up to me?"

"Where are you?" she repeated.

"In the garden behind the building. Swanson is going to meet me here with the skull."

"How do I get back there?"

"You don't. Stay where you are, and I'll call you after I've left the garden."

"That won't work for me. I started this, I need to take my share of the risk. Tell me a safe way I can get to you."

Silence. "There's an unlocked gate on the north side of the block. No guard. Camera is disabled. Get here quick. I only have five minutes to make the switch and get out after Swanson shows." He cut the connection.

Yes!

Jill was out of the Volvo and running down the street.

North side of the block...

Where was the gate?

There!

She was inside.

She paused for a minute, breathing hard, leaning against the gate, her gaze searching the darkness.

A large fountain. A courtyard... Paths leading toward the main house. The windows were dark here, too.

Where the hell was Novak?

"Keep quiet and follow me." She hadn't heard him approach and could barely make him out in his dark garb. He was carrying one of the gaudy paper totes sold in the marketplace. He added curtly, "The courtyard."

She had to almost run to keep up with him as he moved toward the courtyard. She skidded to a stop as he put out his arm when they reached it. No one was there. "Shouldn't he be here by now?" she whispered.

"If he hasn't gotten nervous." He glanced at his watch. "And turned me over to his captain. Be quiet, Jill. I need to—" He stopped, his gaze on the doors at the far end of the courtyard. "Okay..."

A young soldier in a British private's uniform was hurrying toward them. He was pale, obviously nervous, and carrying a medium-size brown-leather suitcase. It had to be Swanson, Jill thought with relief.

He stopped short as he reached Novak, his gaze fixed warily on Jill. "Who is she? You were supposed to be alone."

"Yes, I was," Novak said dryly. "Plans changed. You're not compromised. She's just an expert to make sure that you're not trying to pass off bogus merchandise."

"I couldn't do that. The imprint of the ID on the skull can't be counterfeited."

"She'll verify it." He handed Swanson an envelope, then the shopping bag. "The replacement. And if anything is wrong, I'll be back for you."

"Nothing will be wrong." Swanson stuffed the envelope in his jacket pocket. "But you have to have it back by Monday. When the inspectors come, I can't cover for you."

"I know that. Get out of here and get that replacement skull in the vault."

Swanson turned away. "I'm going. You have only three minutes before that guard will be back at the gate after his smoke. You'd better hope he doesn't come back early."

He was gone.

And Novak was grasping Jill's arm and running with her toward the gate. He pushed her through it and was locking the gate behind them. "Run! South to the end of the block and around the corner."

Jill ran.

She didn't look back.

Three minutes.

But it must be less than that now . . .

Then Novak was passing her, and the next moment pulling her around the corner.

She pressed back against the high stone wall, breathing hard.

"Don't stop. Keep moving." Novak jerked her back into motion. He was still running, holding tight to the suitcase. "My jeep's a half block down."

She saw it, the black jeep he usually drove. She dived into the passenger seat as soon as he pressed the lock release.

Novak shoved the suitcase onto her lap and slammed the driver's door. The next instant he was starting the car and pulling away from the curb.

Jill's heartbeat didn't slow until they were three blocks away from the U.N. headquarters. "So I'm an expert?" she asked after she got her breath.

"What else was I supposed to say? It was as good a lie as any. I would have been ready with a better one if I'd known you'd do this to me."

He was angry, she realized. It wasn't unexpected. He liked to be in control. He probably thought he had a right to be angry with her for interfering with his plans. Too bad. She hadn't been about to let him do this without her.

"I think you did know. You even said it when I called you. So stop growling about it. You know I had to be here."

"The hell I did. If I hadn't thought that you might do something to blow the switch if I didn't monitor you, I'd have hung up when you called."

"I would have been careful. I wouldn't have done anything to put you in danger. That's what this was about." Why couldn't he understand that? "We've been together since the beginning. I wasn't going to let you be alone. You might be CIA's golden boy, but stealing this skull could cause you big trouble if anything went wrong."

"I can take care of myself." He was gazing at her incredulously. "What could you have done to save my ass anyway?"

She shrugged. "I'd just say that I was the one who was going after the skull because of the story potential. Everyone would believe me. Reporters have the reputation of doing anything for a story." She added quietly, "And I'd tell them that you were trying to stop me. But I had to be there at the switch tonight or it wouldn't have worked. Swanson had to see me."

Silence. "Oh, he saw you all right." He looked straight ahead. "And he'll remember you. You're crazy, you know."

"Maybe. And it might have all been for nothing. Everything seems to have gone smoothly. But I had to do it."

"Why, dammit?"

"I owed you," she said jerkily. "The night I was ... hurt, you came after me. You didn't have to do it. You'd already told me to stay out of it. But you found me, and you took care of me." She moistened her lips. "It was a bad time for me. I've been alone most of my life. I wasn't alone that night."

"Your thinking is wonky as hell," he said hoarsely. "That's not how I remember it."

She shook her head. "And then you did everything you could to let me help, to let me find them. I *need* to do that." Her hand touched the suitcase he had thrown on her lap. "And it's brought us to this. One step closer." She had a strange, tingling feeling in her palm. The skull was here, separated from her only by the sleek hardcover leather of the case. Was it the head of the monster? "How could I not be here, Novak?"

His glance shifted back to her face. "*You* couldn't," he said. "Because you don't see things like other people. But do me a favor and don't try to save me again. Okay?"

"You didn't listen to me." She changed the subject. "Swanson was nervous tonight. Do you think he'll be able to hold himself together until we can get the skull back to him on Monday? What's to keep him from going on the run before that? That would trigger instant suspicion."

"I only gave him half of his money. He'll be motivated to keep cool and do everything right until he gets the other half Monday. After that, I don't care what he does. One way or the other, we'll have our answer by then." He paused. "Provided Eve comes through for us."

"Yes." Her hand tightened on the case. "After tonight it will all be up to Eve."

"Everything went well?" Eve carefully moved her reconstruction of Mila to the cabinet she'd cleared in readiness. "No problem?"

"It depends on how you look at it," Novak said as he placed the case on her worktable and opened the snaps. "And also how you look at this skull. I don't think Swanson had the guts to double-cross me, but you'll have to tell me." He opened the lid of the suitcase. "Check the ID number on the skull interior below the left-ear cavity before you go any further. It should be 1066." He gave her a small vial. "One drop should bring it out."

She carefully took out the skull and put it on the dais. "This is like something from a James Bond movie," she grumbled. "Ridiculous, Novak."

"The CIA is much more advanced than 007 these days," he said dryly. "But the Brits did work out a way to guarantee the authenticity of this skull. It's foolproof." He watched as Eve put a minute drop of liquid on the back of the ear bone. It fizzed, and four tiny numbers appeared—1066.

"Though it's a bit showy," Novak said. "I could have done without the sound effects."

"But you're always understated." Jill took a step closer. "This is the skull they took from the helicopter? We're certain?"

"The Brits would be insulted. The skull had almost a guard of honor before the French forces turned it over to the scientists the Brits flew in to tag it," Novak said. "And I was there in the lab watching as they did it. I'm naturally suspicious, and I wanted to be sure. I stayed with it through the entire ID process until they put the skull in the vault." He turned to Eve. "This is the skull taken out of that helicopter. Now can you find out if it's Varak's?"

"I can find out what this man looks like. If it's a strong resemblance to Varak, then it should be fairly simple," Eve said. "If it's not, you'll have to prove whether or not he's Varak to your satisfaction.

But I told you, the DNA specimen taken from that back molar was judged absolute proof." She frowned as she examined the skull. It was badly burned, and it was no wonder that other DNA was not available. It was going to be very difficult to do the reconstruction. "I can't promise anything else."

"We can't expect you to do anything but your best," Jill said. "I'm grateful you're going to do it at all." She grimaced. "Particularly since you have a perfect right to tell me to go to hell."

"Yes, I do." Eve was securing the skull to the dais. "But then I'd never know if Varak is down there ready to greet you." She shrugged. "So I guess I'll have to forgive and forget until I find out for sure. After that, we'll go into it again."

"Works for me," Jill said. "I suppose you're going to start on him tonight? A little rest would do you good."

"I'll get some sleep tonight. I'm going to need it. But I'll work on repairs for a few hours before I go to bed." She turned to Novak. "But now I talk to Joe. Did you get my phone?"

"Yes." He took a sleek, small gray phone out of his jacket pocket and handed it to her. "Very safe."

"I'm glad something is safe around here," Eve said. "I guarantee Joe isn't going to be impressed by it. Alarms are going to go off the minute the call doesn't come in on my computer Skype." Her gaze shifted back to the blackened skull. It seemed to be staring malevolently back at her. Foolishness. Those stories that Jill had told her about Varak were causing her imagination to run riot. "Why don't you both get out of here? You've done your part. Don't worry. Nothing Joe says will change my mind. I've agreed to do this. Now I'm committed."

"I'm not quite finished here." Jill put up her hand as Eve started to speak. "I'm not hanging out to eavesdrop on your conversation. It's time we trusted each other." She glanced at Novak. "I speak for myself. Novak has been playing in the shadows for so long it comes natural to him. Most of the time, he can't help himself. But he won't do anything to hurt you."

Novak's eyes narrowed on her. "What are you up to?"

"I'm just trying to tell her that she has to put up with having me bunk here at the museum from now on until the reconstruction is finished."

"What!" Eve said. "No way."

"My thought exactly," Novak said to Jill. "After all you've gone through to make sure that no one was aware of the connection between you?"

"The press interview already established that, and you'll just have to make certain there's no one snooping around here. You'll do that anyway."

"Why?" Eve's lips twisted. "Because we trust each other so much?"

"I want you to have someone here to protect you. I think that has to be me."

"I have her guarded, Jill," Novak said. "You know that."

Jill shook her head. "How quickly could they get to her? It might not be soon enough." She turned back to Eve. "I won't bother you. You won't know I'm here. Unless you need me."

"I don't want you here."

"I'm sorry," Jill said sincerely. "It has to be this way. I got you into this, and I have to be responsible for you."

"The hell you do."

Jill smiled slightly. "Then we'll have to be responsible for each other. Earlier today, I told Hajif to have a cot ready for me. I'll go down and tell him to bring it up now." She headed for the door. "It will be fine, Eve."

"It's not *necessary*, Jill," Novak said.

"Yes, it is." Jill looked at him over her shoulder. "I don't want her to be alone."

"That seems to be her mantra these days," Novak said to Eve between set teeth, as they watched her walk out of the museum.

Eve repeated, "I don't want her here, Novak. I can take care of myself."

"I'm sure you can. Quinn would make sure that you would never be helpless. It doesn't seem to make any difference to Jill." He looked back at Eve. "Oh, she can take care of herself, too. She survived here in Maldara for two years. And she might not have gone to one of our training camps like Gideon, but she knows karate and is an excellent shot."

"You said she was vulnerable."

"Because she does things like this," he said harshly, his eyes glittering in his taut face. "Because she knows that no matter how good anyone is, there's always a situation where being good isn't enough. She was hurt in one of those damned situations recently. She doesn't want anyone else to be hurt." He gestured impatiently. "You might as well give in to her. You're not going to win. She'll make it work for you. But she won't let you go through this alone." He turned and headed for the door. "I'll go help her. First I have to send someone to pick up her car at the U.N. building, then talk to the guards so that we can get her settled. Go ahead and call Quinn."

Eve shook her head ruefully. So much for privacy and being in total control of the reconstruction process. She supposed it didn't really matter if Jill stayed. If Jill annoyed her, then she would just toss her out.

She doesn't want anyone else to be hurt.

Those poignant words had touched Eve in spite of her resistance to this invasion of her privacy. That memory of Jill's attack must be a constant battle to overcome. But she was dealing with it and not trying to hide away.

Courage...

And, dammit, Eve's own admiration for the blasted woman that had flowed in and out like a tide was back again.

Until Jill did something else to infuriate her.

She looked back at the skull.

She shivered again.

It might not be entirely unwelcome to have someone else in this place while she worked on the skull.

Think about it later.

Joe.

She reached for the phone Novak had given her.

———◆———

"What the hell is happening?" Joe said the instant he picked up the call. "Why aren't you using your computer? I want to *see* you."

"Well, I don't want to see you right now. Later we'll arrange face time on this smartphone," she said wearily. "But now you're going to be pissed off, and it's enough that I'll have to hear you. But I would have bitten the bullet and continued on the Skype if Novak hadn't said this phone he gave me was guaranteed not to be hacked. That was important."

Silence. "Why? No, don't answer that. First I want to know exactly how ill you were yesterday. That's what's important and was driving me crazy. What the hell happened to you?"

"And that will go back to why the new phone is necessary. I'll tell you everything. Just don't say anything until I've finished. Okay?"

"I'm listening," he said grimly. "But I don't think there's going to be anything okay about it."

And it wouldn't get any better, she thought. *Just go for it.* She dived in, and started, "It was right after I hung up from talking to you when I was at the hotel..."

He was ominously quiet as she related the entire story of the last twenty-four hours. When she stopped, he only asked, "That's all? Nothing else?"

"That's not enough? Say something."

"Give me a minute. Right now, anything I'd say would be obscene."

"I went down that road, too. But here I am, sitting here staring at this ugly skull that I hope is Nils Varak's." She added quietly, "Because I don't think I could bear it if I find out that it's not, and he's still out there. Yes, I was drawn into this by deceit and subterfuge, but in the end, that's the bottom line. I can't let a monster who almost butchered an entire nation walk away."

"You told me that you could have died," he said harshly. "I can't think of anything else right now."

"But I didn't." She had to batter through that protective side of him, which was always present and paramount and make him start looking at the entire picture. "But the fact that I came close makes me wonder if Hadfeld wasn't telling the truth as Jill thought. Even Jill can't figure out why anyone would try to hurt me just for doing those children's reconstructions here at Robaku. It was the perfect red herring."

"It certainly lured you," he said curtly. He didn't speak for a moment. Eve could almost hear the volatile storminess in that silence. "I want you out of there. But I'm not going to be able to persuade you to come, am I?"

"Not now. I have to be certain."

"Eve."

"I know. But I can't leave until I know the man who killed those children is dead, Joe." She said with sudden passion, "You told me yourself what a monster he was. Since I've been here, I've seen it with my own eyes. If you could have seen that schoolroom, you'd understand."

"Yes, he was a monster, and that monster is making you go through hell even now that he's dead."

"*If* he's dead."

"You wouldn't question those DNA results if Jill Cassidy hadn't conned you."

"She conned me to get me here. She's not conning me about her belief that Varak is still alive. Neither is Gideon or Novak. They're all very smart and taking big risks because they think Varak might not have been on that helicopter."

"They *should* be the ones to take the risks and not drag you into it."

"All I'm doing is the reconstruction, Joe."

"And you won't give that up," he said. "Okay. Then do the damn reconstruction. But I'm not going to trust anyone else to keep the heat off you while you're working on it. I'll take the next plane out."

"I didn't expect anything else," she said. "But it's not what I want, Joe. I believe that Novak will see that I'm safe. I don't want you involved in this."

"And I don't want you working on that reconstruction that could either get you thrown into jail or murdered. It's a standoff." He paused. "I'm involved in everything you do. It will always be that way. And prepare to see me involved up to my neck in this fiasco. I'll make a few preparations, call Jane and Michael, then I'll be leaving."

"Michael," Eve repeated. "Don't say anything to him that would worry—"

"He's already ahead of you. He called me yesterday and wanted us to take a trip to Maldara. I stalled him, but he won't be surprised that I'm leaving. It was almost a direct order that I go and take care of you."

"Shit."

"Exactly. That's why I have to call Jane and make sure she'll see that he won't try to find a way to join me."

"Heaven forbid."

"And why I have to wrap this up as quickly as possible. No doubts, no strings. Finished. I'll call you when I know when I'll arrive in Jokan. Bye, Eve." He cut the connection.

Michael.

Eve had realized that he might be a problem since they'd always had that special sensitivity to each other. But recently he had also been reaching out to Joe in a similar manner. She should have been just as worried about that as Joe's reaction. The mere idea of Michael's being here in Maldara frightened her. Her gaze flew back to the skull on the dais in front of her.

He liked to kill children.

She didn't want Michael anywhere *near* this place where so many children had died. Even if there proved to be no physical danger, he might sense that overpowering aura of death.

"How did it go with Quinn?" Novak had come in and was standing behind her. "As expected?"

She nodded. "He'll be on his way soon. He's not happy with any of us. He says this has to be wrapped up quickly. No doubts. No strings. Finished. That's the way Joe always works his cases." She stared into the skull's gaping, empty eyes. Evil. Death. Terror. Had those eyes looked out with pleasure at the bloody savagery he had created? That's what Jill had said, that's what Eve had felt, when she had stared into the darkness of that schoolroom. "Joe's right, Novak," she whispered. "No matter what I find, I can't stop until it's finished."

CHAPTER

9

LONDON

Two hours later, Joe left Jane's apartment and headed for the taxi stand on the corner of the block.

"Could I give you a lift, Quinn?"

Joe tensed, then he whirled to see a dark-haired man standing beside the door of the apartment building. Joe's gaze raked his features with one quick glance. "You're Sam Gideon. What the hell are you doing here?"

"Easy." Gideon put up his hands. "Just offering you a lift as I said. I expected you to be a bit edgy but not on the attack. And how did you know who I was, anyway?"

"Did you think I wouldn't find out every detail about everyone Eve was connected with at Robaku?" he asked coldly. "I could tell that she was beginning to trust you. That made you dangerous. And now she tells me that you were responsible for getting her poisoned. That might make you dead."

"I don't blame you," Gideon said. "I screwed up. I was supposed to take care of her, and I didn't do it. I thought she was safe." He made a face. "I really don't want you to attack and make me defend myself. I'm pretty good these days, but you were a SEAL and can probably cause me intense bodily pain or death. Besides, I think Eve has forgiven me and might get pissed off if I end up seriously damaged. Wouldn't it be better to just put up with me and let me help you to get to her as soon as possible?"

"I'd have to think about it," Joe said. "The other option is much more tempting."

"I was afraid of that." Gideon sighed. "Novak warned me that you'd probably be major pissed off. But he also said you were smart and that might make a difference. How long is it going to take for you to think about it before I prepare for personal Armageddon?"

"I repeat, what are you doing here? The last thing I heard from Eve was that you were in Maldara." He was quickly processing the information he'd acquired about Sam Gideon. "You're the rich guy who was banging Zahra Kiyani. Not a good recommendation. I don't like what I hear about her." He added, "But you also pilot a Gulf Stream, and I assume the lift you offered wasn't just to the airport. How quickly can you get me to Maldara?"

"Shall I go down the list? One, yes, I am rich, and I did have an interlude with Zahra that might prove beneficial to us. Two, the reason I'm here is that Novak knew that when Eve agreed to do the reconstruction, it wasn't going to work unless we brought you into the mix ASAP. So he immediately sent me here to put myself at your disposal. Three, it took me seven hours and thirty minutes to get here from Maldara today, and I believe I can guarantee to get you back in the same time. Anything else?"

"Novak sent you? Then he owns you?"

"Was that meant to insult me?" Gideon smiled. "I have many talents, but I'm new to this game Novak knows so well. Yes, I let Novak own me because he's an expert at what he does. I'd let you own me if you show me you're better than Novak." His smile faded. "I'd let the devil himself own me if it meant that he could deliver Varak to me. Is that clear?"

Joe studied him. "It seems to be. I'll have to give it time to verify whether you're being honest or just telling me what I'd consider acceptable." He turned on his heel. "In the meantime, get me to Maldara. And seven hours and thirty minutes is not what I wanted to hear. So be prepared to spend that time filling me in on every phase of what you and Novak have been doing regarding that damn skull. Eve might be a major part of this, but I know Novak isn't waiting for verification or permission from his director. He's already on the move, isn't he?"

"You'd have to ask him."

"No, I'm asking you." Joe's smile was tiger bright. "And by the time we reach Maldara, I'll have answers. I believe we'll start with the DNA..."

ROBAKU

"Hey, you said you were going to nap for a while. Isn't it time you stopped working?"

Eve looked up from the reconstruction to see Jill standing beside her. She realized she hadn't heard her leave her cot on the other side of the room. But then she had been so absorbed that she hadn't been aware of anything but the reconstruction in front of her. "Soon." She stretched her stiff neck around in a circle. "I got carried away with doing Varak's repairs. It took awhile. But I have a clean slate now. I can start with the measuring."

"He doesn't look clean to me." Jill was gazing at the blackened skull. "He still looks like something from a horror film." Her glance shifted to Eve. "And you're calling him Varak. I know you told me that you always have to name your reconstructions so that you can connect, but this is different, isn't it? You're assuming he *is* Varak?"

"No." Eve shrugged. "I didn't know what to name him, so I decided to give him the benefit of the doubt. If he is Varak, then I'll have it right; if he's not, then I still might be close." Her lips tightened. "Because it would be almost certain that he's a Varak victim, maybe even one of his butchers who was on that helicopter. Either way, this is a Varak entity."

"Complicated. Sort of a reconstruction with a split personality. But what else could we expect from Varak?" She asked curiously, "How does that affect you in making a connection with him?"

Eve felt herself stiffening. She quickly looked back at the skull. "I won't have to worry about that yet. There's a lot to do first. The measuring, the initial sculpting."

"And you'd prefer not to dwell on it," Jill said softly, reading her expression. "Have you ever done a reconstruction before on someone...like Varak?"

"You mean an evil son of a bitch who scared the hell out of me?" She moistened her lips. "Once. Several years ago. I hoped I'd never have to do it again. Call me crazy. But when a soul is that evil...it seems to linger...And I imagine Varak would be a million times worse." She straightened her shoulders. "I'll face that when it comes. Now I have work to do."

"After you sleep a few hours," Jill said. "You said soon."

"This isn't soon," Eve said flatly. "I let you stay with me, but I won't have you ordering me around."

"I'll back off. I just didn't want you to get too tired." Jill paused. "I was wondering after Joe Quinn called back and told you that he was on his way whether you might be waiting up for him. It will be a few hours yet before he gets here."

"I know that, Jill." She found her lips curving with amusement. "It's not as if I'm pining away and burning a candle to light his way."

"I wasn't certain," Jill said quietly. "You love him. I wasn't sure how that worked. I've heard it's different for different people."

Eve's brows lifted. "You've heard?"

She shrugged. "I had a major crush on a guy in college, but that went away fairly soon. And, though I'm usually too busy, I do love sex. But I've been around long enough to realize that it's more than that to some people. It would be for you."

"Yes, it is," Eve said. "But Joe and I have been together long enough that we don't need burning beacons to find each other in the darkness. We know who we are and where we are, and there's no question that we would ever lose each other. Burning beacons are fine, but they tend to be a little wistful." She chuckled. "We just go straight for the heart of the flames."

"Which is very difficult to research," Jill said. "Sorry that I misunderstood. But you have to admit I've been very good about keeping out of your way. You didn't even know I was here all night."

Eve couldn't deny it. Once Jill had set up her cot on the far side of the room and settled down, she had been totally silent. "The reality might have been better."

"Maybe. But you wouldn't have had anyone to keep you company in warding off the monster." She smiled. "I know about monsters, too, Eve. Company can be a help." She turned away. "Could I get you a cup of coffee?"

Yes, Jill knew about monsters, Eve thought. They were unlike in so many ways, but in that one way, they were sisters. Sisters... That thought had come out of nowhere. They had both grown up fending for themselves and fighting for survival. It would have been nice to have someone like Jill there to share that struggle. She felt a sudden rush of warmth. "Coffee? No thanks. I've had too much caffeine tonight as it is." She leaned back on her stool. "For that matter, I've had more coffee since I met you than I've had in the last six months. I seem to need it to survive. Does that tell you anything?"

"Sorry. But you can't blame me entirely. You're a workaholic, and you do like your coffee. Can I get you a water?" She was going over to the ice chest. "If you're going back to work, I'll stay with you in case you need a reminder that you promised you'd nap. Is it okay if I drag up one of those chairs I got Hajif to bring up and sit and watch you? I promise I'll be quiet and won't ask questions." She took out two bottles of water from the chest and brought them back to the worktable. "Though it will be torture." She wrinkled her nose. "You know how curious I am."

Eve shrugged as she took the bottle of water. "I don't mind questions while I'm doing the basic measuring. It's almost automatic since I've done it so many times. And it's so important that I recheck it several times anyway. It's when I get into the layers that I have to concentrate."

"Good." Jill was dragging a chair over to the worktable. "I only had time for an overview of your work process while I was researching you, and I've been frustrated ever since. When I'm interested, I have to know everything." She plopped down on the chair. "Now tell me where we're going with this."

Eve laughed. "We? I wish it could be a joint operation. I could use a little help on this one." She paused. "Okay, I'll answer your questions, but then at some point you have to answer mine. You're not the only one who is curious. All I got was a thumbnail sketch about Jill Cassidy." She added mockingly, "And I have to know *everything.*"

Jill was silent, wary. "That's not... easy."

"Take it or leave it."

"I'll take it. You have a right. But maybe not tonight." She smiled with an effort. "Now tell me why you have to concentrate on 'layers.'"

"Because it tells me what I need to know." She started to measure. "There are more than twenty points of the skull for which there are known tissue depths. Facial-tissue depth has been found to be fairly consistent in people the same age, race, sex, and weight. There are anthropological charts that give specific measurements for each point. For instance, in a Caucasian male like Varak, the tissue-depth thickness between the mid-philtrum point, which is the space between the nose and the top lip, is ten millimeters. The architecture of the bone beneath the tissue determines whether he has bulging eyes or jutting chin or whatever."

"What happens next?"

"I insert the depth markers and take strips of plasticine and apply them between the markers, then build up all of the tissue-depth points. Kind of like a connect the dots game in three dimensions."

"Only that's an enormous simplification," Jill said quietly.

Eve glanced at her. "Enormous," she agreed. "But that's the basic step. Then you worry about being absolutely true to your measurements and keeping track of the placement of facial muscles and how they influence the facial contour. And so on and so forth. Are you bored yet?"

"No way. I want to know about noses and mouths." Her gaze was narrowed on Eve's face. "But you're getting tired. You're fading. I can see it. I don't want to be an extra stress on you. I'll just sit here and watch quietly until you give up and go to bed."

She was right, Eve realized. She was suddenly feeling drained. She had thought she'd be fine for another hour or so, but if she wanted to finish these basic measurements, she needed to gather her strength and concentration. "Whatever." She shrugged. "Later."

She closed Jill out and focused entirely on the hideous skull before her. Strange, she never considered skulls hideous. It must be the thought of Varak...

Whatever it was, she wanted to be done with him for a while.

But the last measurements, which should have taken her another thirty minutes, stretched out to an hour. She was totally exhausted when she pushed back her chair. "Enough," she told Jill as she headed for her cot. "Now I need a nap."

"At last," Jill murmured as she flicked off the overhead light and followed Eve. "Can I get you anything? Another glass of water?"

"No...too tired." She crawled onto the cot. She was yawning as she pulled up the sheet. "You wanted to know about mouths and noses? They can be difficult. I'll tell you about it some other time..."

"You do that. Don't worry about it. That's another story. I can wait."

"Another story...Sounds like you. But sometimes the story turns out to be a mystery and has to be guesswork that you have..."

———

Eve was asleep.

Jill shook her head as she gazed down at her before she gently tucked the sheet higher around Eve's shoulders. She was glad that Eve had finally given in, but she wished it had been before she was this exhausted. Yet she'd known it had to be Eve who made the call. She turned and glided away from Eve's cot.

She should probably go back to her own cot across the room and try to get a few hours sleep herself, but she knew she was too wired to relax. Too much had been going on in the last twenty-four hours, and she hadn't had Eve's nonstop work to burn off adrenaline and energy.

And these nights, she had to be as exhausted as Eve had been before she could sleep without the nightmares coming.

Don't think about them. It was only a matter of time before she'd overcome that damn weakness.

Fresh air.

Clear her head and listen to the soothing night sounds.

She quickly moved past the worktable, avoiding looking at the Varak reconstruction as she headed for the door. Not now. She'd face that battle again later. He was part of this village's nightmare as well as her own personal nightmare. She needed to get away from him for a little while.

She drew a deep breath as the cool night air hit her face.

Bright moonlight.

Night sounds. Jungle sounds. Birds. Animals . . . Was that a monkey?

That was better. She could feel some of the tension leaving her. She sank down and leaned back against the stucco wall of the museum. Twenty minutes, and she'd be ready to go back inside and try to sleep . . .

"Is everything okay?"

She jumped.

Novak was a dark silhouette a few yards away.

"It would be if you didn't move like a damn panther," she said wryly. "I didn't hear you. What are you doing here?"

"Making phone calls. Checking on the sentries I set up. Waiting for Quinn to show up and raise hell. According to Gideon, he's as pissed off as we thought he'd be." He dropped down beside her. "I didn't think that you should be the only one to take the flak."

"I was prepared for it." She leaned her head back against the wall and gazed up at the night sky. "After all, it was my plan. When will Quinn be here?"

"Three or four hours. He would have gotten here sooner, but he's having Gideon drop him off at our private airfield at Baldar and will make his way here on his own."

She frowned. "Why?"

He shrugged. "He was a SEAL. His instincts are to go in and make that first strike before anyone knows he's hit the ground running. He'll want to slip in and look the situation over. Particularly where Eve is concerned, and he trusts no one in Jokan." He grimaced. "And that includes us."

She studied his expression. "And you'd do the same?"

"Certainly. I have a few problems with trust myself." He was suddenly bending toward her, his eyes narrowed on her face. "You didn't answer me. Is everything okay? I saw the lights go out in the museum, and I thought you'd both be going to sleep."

"Eve's asleep. I thought I'd get some air before I tried to settle down."

His gaze was still searching her face. "Why?"

She was suddenly aware of something different about him tonight, a tension, a recklessness, and that tough ruthlessness that was such a part of him seemed more obvious than usual. It was making her uneasy. "For goodness sake, because I wanted some air. Stop interrogating me, Novak."

"But I do it so well," he said mockingly. "Check my credentials. Though I'm better with Al-Qaeda and Isis. You're really not worth my expertise." He changed the subject. "You didn't think Quinn would go easy on you?"

"Why should he? I think Eve is beginning to forgive me, but I knew her family might never do that. I can take any flak Quinn hands out."

"Yeah, you're just collateral damage," Novak said bitterly. "How could I forget?"

"I don't know. I guess because it seems to bother you." She was trying to keep her tone light. "We've discussed this before. In your job, you usually accept it as a fact of life. Yet you seem to be making some kind of exception for me." Her gaze shifted to his face. "You were even kind to me those days in Nairobi. Extraordinarily kind."

"Imagine that," he said dryly. "Since I'm sure you didn't deserve it. You've caused me nothing but trouble since the day you came to me with that wild tale about Hadfeld. And when you showed up at the U.N., I was ready to break your neck."

"I know." She moistened her lips. "But I had to do it."

"You made that clear. No debt left unpaid." He added harshly, "What did you say? You'd been alone all your life, but I hadn't left you alone when you needed someone that night. So I had to have my payoff, too."

"I was grateful. I don't understand why it upset you."

"Then you should have thought about it," he said curtly. "I *know* you, Jill. You forget that I was there with you after those therapy sessions that shrink put you through in Nairobi before he'd release you. I know what kind of life you've led." His words were suddenly spitting like bullets. "Talk about collateral damage. You trailed all over the world behind your father from the time you were four, and he paid more attention to his camera than he did to you. It's no wonder that you were so confused you had to develop your own concept of who you are and how to survive. You had to fend for yourself."

"I never said that," she said quickly.

"No, but you made a few slips, and after I left Nairobi, I did a check to fill in the blanks. Your father never even made provisions for you if anything happened to him. When he was killed in Tibet, you ended up in an orphanage in Hong Kong for over a year until you managed to convince the local U.S. ambassador that you were a U.S. citizen. You were only eleven years old, and you had to do it yourself."

"My father never intentionally hurt me," she said quietly. "I just wasn't high on his list of priorities. Some men aren't meant to be parents. I'm not a victim, Novak."

"No, you didn't let yourself be a victim even when you were bouncing through five foster homes, who accepted you only for the paycheck and treated you less decently than that orphanage in Hong Kong."

Novak was really on the attack, she realized in bewilderment. His intensity was overpowering, and she could almost feel the electricity he was generating. What was happening with him? Suddenly, she didn't care. He had no right to bring back the memories she kept firmly tucked away. She sat up straight. "You're damned right I didn't let myself be a victim," she said fiercely. "You're only a victim if you don't learn from a bad experience. It was one of the first things I found out when I was a kid. Do you know how I won that Pulitzer?"

"You wrote a series on the corruptions in the DFAC system," Novak said. "I made the connection. But it wasn't enough. Not unless it ended with your own foster parents ending up in jail."

"Maybe they did. I don't know. I wrote the series years later. I was past any desire to punish individuals. I just wanted to punish the system, so it couldn't happen again to someone else."

"I wouldn't be so forgiving." His smile was suddenly savage. "As a matter of fact, I have to admit to taking down their names for future reference."

"What?" she said, shocked. "You're joking?"

"If you want jokes, call on Gideon. As you've said, I don't tend to

be soft and easy. I grew up on the streets of Detroit, and I guarantee
that everyone who ever caused me problems ended up regretting it."

"I can believe it. But these are *my* problems, Novak."

He shrugged. "I've decided you're entirely too philosophical and
I should take over the handling of this type of difficulty myself."

She gazed at him in disbelief. "Are you crazy? Not if it's my business."

"It's all how you view it. That doesn't seem to make any difference
to me." He added through set teeth, "Which really is beginning to
piss me off."

"I'm the one who should be pissed off. You're not making sense.
Why are you being like this?"

"It was bound to come out sooner or later. I've been holding it in
too long." His lips twisted. "I don't *want* this. I want it to be like it
was when I first met you over a year ago." His light eyes were glittering. "You were smart and gutsy, and I wanted to go to bed with you
three minutes after I met you. That was all I wanted, very simple and
clean, with no complications. That's what should have happened."

"What?" She inhaled sharply. "You never said anything. You never
made a move."

"We were both busy and at opposite ends of the country most of
the time." He smiled sardonically. "But tell me you didn't know it
was there waiting to happen."

She was silent. The words had shocked her, but she couldn't deny
that what he'd said was true. Yes, she had known, but she had refused
to acknowledge it. She had instinctively blocked even thinking about
him sexually. She was still doing it. Because along with that instant
explosive sexual attraction had come the realization that he would
demand too much of her. She had a career she was passionate about,
and he wasn't like anyone else she had ever met. He . . . disturbed her.
Novak was too difficult, and she had not wanted to have to deal with
him. She swallowed. "Well, then it was a good thing that it never got
past that first three minutes."

"The hell it is," he said roughly. "If we'd just gone to bed together, then it might have been over by this time. It wouldn't be like this. I don't like feeling what I'm feeling now. It's too damn complicated. And I don't have any way to control it."

"I don't know what you're talking about. All I'm getting out of it is that you're angry and it's somehow my fault that we didn't jump into the sack together. That's not complicated, it's plain nuts. And it's bullshit that you're not in control. You're always in control of yourself and everyone around you."

"If I were in control, we wouldn't even be having this conversation. After Nairobi, I swore to myself that it wasn't going to happen, that you were off-limits, that you were walking wounded, and that's how I had to treat you."

She stiffened. "Walking wounded?"

"What do you think? It *killed* me to see you like that. I didn't expect to feel that way."

"Walking wounded," she repeated. "You son of a bitch. How do you have the nerve to say that?"

"With extreme trepidation. You don't want anyone to know you're not invulnerable. It doesn't go along with the story you've created to always keep your personal world in order. But I was there with you when you woke from those nightmares. You're still having them, aren't you? I think I might have held on if you hadn't lied to me tonight." His eyes were blazing. "That's why you came out here, not because you wanted a breath of air."

She didn't answer him. "I'm *not* walking wounded. So you can stuff your pity, Novak."

"You're not listening. Don't worry. There wasn't pity even when I was there with you in that hospital. I don't know what it was. I was just...aching and wanting to kill someone, anyone." He added fiercely: "And there's sure as hell no pity now, or I wouldn't have decided to toss out all that crap about going through this by myself. I don't know what I was thinking. So I'm going to be my usual selfish self and take what I want any way I can get it."

"Going through what by yourself?"

"I *feel* something for you, dammit." He added fiercely, "It's that same sexual attraction multiplied about a thousand times, all mixed up with what I felt in that hospital and what I've learned to feel about you since then. You don't want pity? Great. Because sex was my first choice anyway. Though I doubt if we can go back to square one. It probably wouldn't be enough for me." He was suddenly on his feet, looking down at her. "I just had to give you warning that if you really are walking wounded, you should get away from me. Run, not walk. Because these days, whenever I look at you, I want to take you to bed. If I can talk you into it, that's where we'll end up. And I don't know where we'll go from there because I'm not sure I'll be able to let you go after that." He reached out his hand and pulled her to her feet. "And now you'd better go in and get to bed. You shouldn't have to worry about having nightmares unless they're about me. I've given you enough to think about to distract you." His voice was suddenly low and intense. "But remember that I'd never hurt you, and it would always be your choice."

Electricity. Intimacy. His hand grasping hers was warm, vital, and she could feel her pulse pounding in her wrist. He must feel it, too, because his thumb was rubbing back and forth on the pulse point. She was shaking, her breasts firming, tightening. He was too close ... No, he wasn't close enough.

She needed to pull away from him. Why didn't she do it? Because her emotions were in such a shambles that her responses were purely physical. She couldn't think, she could only feel. Don't let him see it. She had sworn she'd never be weak again, and no one was more dominant than Novak. She nodded jerkily. "Of course it's my choice. And you won't hurt me because if you did, I'd pull out the Beretta in my jacket pocket and shoot your nuts off."

He blinked. "Point taken." Then he threw back his head and laughed. "And that side of you is another reason why I'm finding handling you so complicated."

"Then don't try to handle me." She turned toward the door. She had to get away from him. Because she wanted his hands on her again, dammit. He had only touched her hand and wrist, yet her pulse was still pounding crazily. "I was right, the first time. It was good that it never really started. It would never have worked out."

"Maybe." Then he was smiling recklessly. "But this is a new game with new rules. And we can change those rules as we go along. Anything you want to do." He reached out and gently touched her cheek with his index finger. "Go to sleep. I had to be honest with you, but I'm not going to let it get in the way of what we have to do. Good night, Jill. If I can deter Quinn, I'll try to do it."

Her skin was warming, throbbing beneath that gossamer-light touch. She moved her head to avoid it. She had an idea that "honesty" couldn't help but get in the way. It was as if he had ripped down a safe, sheltering barrier between them and left only heat, electricity, and vibrant awareness. "I told you I didn't need your help." She opened the door. "Good night, Novak."

"Jill."

She looked over her shoulder.

He was standing there, lean, muscular, infinitely male. "I just wanted to tell you that you've convinced me." His smile was both intimate and knowing. "After careful observation, I can see you're no victim and definitely not walking wounded. What a relief." He turned away. "Let the games begin..."

Games? Jill's pulse was pounding, and her breath was uneven as she closed the door behind her. This wasn't any game she wanted to play. No, that was a lie. It was obviously one that she wanted passionately to play in every single physical way possible. She just couldn't permit it to happen.

If she could stop it. Because Novak had decided that wasn't the way he wanted it. Screw it. It was only sex, dammit. Why didn't she just go back outside to him and find somewhere to make it happen?

Because it was never only sex to her, and she couldn't risk its being anything more to her with Novak.

I wanted to go to bed with you three minutes after I met you.

That had been an exaggeration. He'd been too angry with her during those first three minutes on that mountain in Botzan. And she'd only been concerned with persuading him to get out of her way so that she could get to that bandit, Abdi Zolak, and keep him from getting killed...

———◆———

BOTZAN MOUNTAINS
ELEVEN MONTHS AGO

"What the hell are you doing here?" Jed Novak was skidding down the hill toward Jill. His blue eyes were glittering with fury in his taut face as he pulled her down behind a banyan tree. "Do you want to get killed? There's a band of roving bandits camped up on that hill. I gave orders that this area was to be cleared."

"I know you did, Novak," Jill said impatiently. "You didn't make any secret about it in any of the villages I had to go through to get here." She jerked her arm away from him. "You wanted to send a message to Zolak that the big, bad CIA were on their way and that he'd better not throw in his lot with those Botzan mercenaries. He was just to meekly give up his weapons and let you take him down." Her eyes went back to the top of the hill. No movement. But there probably wasn't much time before Zolak would get edgy that she hadn't shown up yet. "Only he won't do that, and you're stupid if you think he will. He's too scared of not dying a brave death that will make his sons proud of him." But Jill knew that Novak's reputation was that he was far from stupid. She had only seen him from a distance since he'd arrived in Maldara, but she'd made it her business to research him. He was superintelligent, and the word was that he'd been sent here to Maldara by Langley to try to find a way to stop this hideous war. So reason with him. Persuade

him. It was her only hope to get Abdi Zolak home to his village. Her gaze shifted back to Novak's face. "He'll fight you. He has fifty-two men in this band he's gathered. There would be deaths on both sides." She leaned forward, her voice urgent. "But I can keep that from happening, Novak. The only reason he's here at all is that he agreed to come down from his hideout and meet with me. Wouldn't it be better to let me go up there and talk to him?" She wasn't getting a response. Okay, try harder. "Look, I'm Jill Cassidy, and I'm a reporter, not some missionary out to save Zolak's soul. I know he's been a thief and a bandit most of his adult life. But he's always taken care of his family and his village. And he's not a murderer... yet. But if he joins those mercenaries, he'll become what they want him to be. Here in Maldara, that means butchery. And the only people who can stop him are his wife and family. He cares about them. I might be able to talk him into going back to them so they'll have a chance to do it."

"I know exactly who you are, Jill Cassidy." Novak's eyes were fixed on her face. "I had reports on you from my men watching that village down the road. I'm used to handling reporters getting in my way, but I didn't think I'd have to deal with one who seems ready to get herself killed for the damn story." He looked up at the hill, then turned back to her. "I have credible info that Zolak is up there, and I'm going to go get him. I have orders to find any way I can to keep those mercenaries from recruiting any more local people to add fuel to the fire that's burning up this country. Zolak's an experienced fighter, he's exactly what they're looking for." His voice hardened. "And I don't give a damn about Zolak's soul or the story you're hoping to get from him. I'd prefer you stay alive, but that's up to you."

"I'm not going to get myself killed. Not if you stay out of my way." She had to get through to him. In spite of his coldness, she could tell that Novak was listening, his face was very intent. She had an idea he always listened, was always thinking, trying to put everything together. "Zolak only became involved in this war because he thought that it would be just like the raids he'd been doing most of his life here in the mountains. From the time he was a young boy, that was what he was taught. But he didn't count on all the deaths, and the slaughter of children all around him when this country exploded. He told his wife it made him sick. There's no way he wants to join those cutthroat mercenaries Botzan hired. He wants out if we can find a way to bring him home honorably." She reached out, and her hand closed on his arm. "Help me to do that, Novak. I've heard you're smart and have enough influence to pull it off. Or just let me do it on my own."

He was silent, gazing down at her hand on his arm. Then he looked up at the top of the hill. "You said he agreed to meet with you?"

She drew a relieved breath. "Yes, but he said I'd have to come alone. I've been writing my stories from his home village for the last month. I've grown to know his wife and children. They're the ones who told me how he felt about the war. I talked to him on the phone myself last week. He wants to go home to protect his own village from all the Varaks of the world. I believe him." She added: "But he's very proud, he could be forced to go the other way if we don't let him keep his dignity."

Novak's eyes were narrowed on her face. "You think you know him that well?"

"Some stories are easier than others to read. Will you stay here and let me go up there?"

His lips indented in the faintest smile. "What would you do if I didn't?"

"Find a way to go around you. But I don't think I'll have to do that. You have a job to do, and you'll do it. What do you care if some egotistical reporter thinks she can do it better?" She paused. "As long as you think I'll get Zolak to go home, you're going to let me go up that hill." She took her gun from her pocket and handed it to him. "Will you keep this until I get back? Zolak said I can't be armed."

Novak looked down at the gun for an instant. "Then of course you have to obey his rules." He put the Beretta in his jacket pocket. "Go on. You don't want Zolak to get nervous. You can tell him that I'll work out something for him once he's back at his village if you think it will help."

"It will help."

"Good." Then he reached for his automatic rifle and settled down on his stomach, sighting down the scope before lifting his head to look at her. "But you'll have to put up with me covering you for the entire time you're up there with Zolak. I'd find explaining away the death of a reporter much too awkward."

"Don't interfere, Novak."

"Did I say I'd interfere? I'll give you your chance. But we've just met, and how do I know whether or not I'd regret it if Zolak decided to kill you? I do hate regrets." He smiled. "But you'll learn what I hate most is to lose an opportunity."

She inhaled sharply. She wasn't sure what he meant. Yet she found she couldn't look away from him. The intensity, the force, the intelligence that was far more interesting than just good looks. She wanted to stay and see what else was there . . .

He nodded at the hill. "Get going. It will be fine. I've got your back."

She hesitated for only a second, then she was turning and swiftly climbing the hill. She could see the bushes move as Zolak's sentries spotted her. She felt she was safe from Zolak, but she didn't know how nervous those sentries would be.

Forget it. Think of what she had to say to Zolak. How to persuade him to save his life and that of his family. How to keep him from joining those butchers. She couldn't worry about anything else right now.

Not even that strange, intimate moment before she had left Novak.

Besides, she found that anxiety was ebbing away. She could almost feel Novak down there, watching her, aiming that rifle, protecting her. With every step she took, she was beginning to have a feeling that everything was going to be okay. She was going to pull this off. She was going to be able to convince Zolak to change his story or start a new one.

And somehow it all had something to do with the fact that this time she wasn't alone and that Novak had been there for her. Strange. When she was almost always alone.

You'll learn what I hate most is to lose an opportunity, Novak had said.

Well, so do I.

But at this moment, my opportunity is with Zolak waiting for me on that hill. I don't have time for you.

But I do admit it does feel good that right now you have my back, Novak.

———◆———

And that day Jill had talked Abdi Zolak out of going to join the mercenaries and gone with him back to his village to get him settled with his family. But the next week she'd been sent to Jokan to cover an attack. Novak was right, they'd been at opposite ends of the country for almost a year, only seeing each other casually.

But there had been nothing casual about him tonight, nor the way she was feeling. Which was an indication she should regard it as even more dangerous. Damn right, they couldn't let it affect the work they had to do.

So forget everything but getting rid of the monster who might already be knocking on their door.

———◆———

DAWN

The first pearl shading of dawn was lighting the sky as Joe punched in Jed Novak's number. He'd just done an initial reconnoitering of Robaku. "Your security sucks, Novak," he said curtly. "Two sentries? And they were deaf and blind. I could have taken them down in my sleep. Is this how you're supposedly keeping Eve safe?"

"No," Novak said. "There's another sentry nearer to the museum that you didn't see who informed me that you were near the village. Plus there's another guard down the road furnishing surveillance on anyone approaching from Jokan. I'm also using a drone that's equipped with an infrared monitor to make a pass over the village every ten minutes. It just identified you as an unknown object and will notify those three sentries immediately."

"Two of whom would already be dead," Joe said. "But the drone is a decent idea if you increase the number of flyovers."

"I'll consider it." He paused. "And those sentries are good men, you're just better. If you're through critiquing my arrangements, would you like to come and have a civilized discussion? Where are you?"

"In the palmettos behind you." Joe moved out of the trees. "And I'm not feeling particularly civilized at the moment." He swiftly covered the yards that separated him from Novak. "But we might as well get this over with before I go to see Eve." His gaze went to the stucco building behind Novak. "That's the museum?"

"Yes, but you probably already know that. I imagine you had Gideon draw you a map of the village or you wouldn't have been so familiar with it. And you have plenty of time. Eve's asleep, and Jill said she's been pushing too hard and really needs it."

"That should make you both very happy," Joe said bitterly.

"It doesn't. We don't want to drive her to exhaustion," Novak said. "But the sooner we get this over with and have an answer, the better for all of us. We can't do that without Eve." He met Joe's eyes. "I realize you want her out of here, but you don't have a chance until she finds out if that skull she's working on is Varak's. I believe you know that."

"Oh, I do. Because you have her caught in your net. So by all means let's move fast. Tell me what else you're doing other than depending on my wife. You wouldn't be able to stand in the background any more than I would. You'd go straight to find the scientist who could have created the DNA evidence. Gideon said he knew you'd been investigating, but no details." His lips twisted. "He said you were a very secretive man. Imagine that."

"Wouldn't it only be practical to wait for Eve to give us some evidence of proof?"

"But that's not your style. I'm surprised you didn't ask for the money to pay off Hadfeld in the beginning. Politics in the director's office?"

Novak nodded. "The U.N. was being difficult. And I'd already been accused of being something of a fanatic about Varak." His lips tightened. "But Jill wouldn't wait. She went for it herself. Which ended with her going after Eve."

"Big mistake," Joe said. "I still haven't decided what I'm going to do about that. But I do know that if that reconstruction is not Varak, I'm not going to stand around and wait for politicians to decide what to do. I've got to be ready. So go back to the DNA evidence. Who do you believe to be responsible?"

Novak gazed speculatively at him. "No questions about the possibility of even being able to defeat the mighty DNA? What do you know about falsifying DNA evidence?"

"Enough," Joe said curtly. "I had a murder case two years ago in which I was positive I knew who the murderer was but couldn't prove it. I *knew* that Richard Sander had killed his wife. But the DNA blood evidence seemed infallible. So I assumed that it was a big lie and went out to prove it."

"And you did it? Interesting. How?"

"Followed the money. I traced a bank draft from Sander to Tel Aviv to a dummy company. Then, when I started digging, I found out that one of the scientists, Sol Goldfarb, who had set up the company, had previously worked for an Israeli think tank that created a way of proving whether or not DNA evidence had been falsified." He shrugged. "And if you know how to prove that, then it's the next step to be able to create a better way to do it yourself."

"And did you get your killer convicted?"

"No, I had an extradition problem getting Goldfarb out of Israel. But I'm still watching him. I'll do it someday." His expression became more serious. "And then I'll hang them both out to dry."

"I'm sure you will," Novak said. "And Israel did do some groundbreaking work in that direction. You must have learned a lot while you were trying to gather in Goldfarb. But I don't think that the person who falsified the DNA on Varak is in Israel. I'm betting on Egypt."

"Why?"

"Because Yusef Dobran is the most talented scientist I've ever run across in that line of work. His execution is nearly foolproof. He's also the most expensive, and it would take big money to hire him. He's got money to burn these days, and he can afford to be picky. Besides, anyone undertaking a replication of Varak's DNA would think twice about doing it. Not only would it be dangerous because of the consequences of being caught, but the first thing Varak would do is eliminate the witnesses."

"Then why would Dobran do it?"

"I have no idea. Fear? Blackmail? A staggering amount of money that he just couldn't refuse? We'll have to find out."

"If he's still alive."

Novak nodded. "He's alive. He's rich enough to be able to afford excellent protection and lives in an exclusive area just outside Cairo, with a bevy of bodyguards." He paused. "But everyone has an Achilles heel. He has an assistant, Hassan Sebak, who's willing to co-operate for the right price."

"And he's already told you Dobran did the job?"

"No, he's very cautious. But he did tell us that Dobran had recently done a very big job. For a price, he's willing to find a way to bypass Dobran's guards and get me in to see him. After that, it's up to me to find out if he did the job and who hired him." He paused. "Or up to you, Quinn."

"You'd rather risk my neck than your own?"

"Any day of the week." He smiled faintly. "But I realize it's your decision. We'll play it your way. My highest priority is keeping Eve working, and I'll do that any way I can. I don't want you to persuade her to do anything else."

"You must realize that's bullshit," Joe said impatiently. "Jill Cassidy researched her, and you know exactly what Eve will do. I've done all the persuading I can, and now I have to jump in and help her try to stay afloat."

"She thought that would be your plan, so I'm offering you the opportunity. I'll send Gideon with you to Cairo along with any backup you need. Find out what you can about Dobran and everything he knows. It's not many men I'd trust to go after him, but you'll be able to do it. I'll stay with Eve and protect her while she's finishing the reconstruction." He paused. "Or you can stay here and hold her hand, and I'll go to Cairo."

"And that remark is obviously aimed at sending me down the road. I'll think about it." He started toward the museum. "But right now, I want to see Eve."

"Not yet." Novak was suddenly moving past him. "Give me ten minutes. Jill insisted on staying with Eve to protect her, and I don't want her shooting you. I'll go and get her out of there." He disappeared into the museum.

Joe muttered a curse. Patience. But he was not feeling patient. Ten minutes? He didn't want to stand here twiddling his thumbs. He wanted to see Eve *now*. He wanted to talk to her, see her face, and he wanted to know why she was willing to risk everything for this madness.

If you could have seen that schoolroom, you'd understand.

The schoolroom. The place that had horrified and captured Eve in a way that Novak and Jill Cassidy would never have been able to do.

The schoolroom...

He turned on his heel and started down the path.

———◆———

"Joe..."

He was near her. The familiar scent of him surrounded her. Eve could feel his warmth, sense the strength...

"Shh," he said softly. "It's not time to wake up yet. Just let me hold you..."

He was here, gently sliding onto the cot and turning her into his arms. Safety...Love...Home...

Her arms slid around him, and she nestled closer. "Not much room on this...cot, Joe."

"We'll manage." His lips brushed her temple. "We always manage. Though I agree it's not conducive to doing what I've been wanting to do since I left you in Atlanta. So just rest a little longer and let me hold you. That will be good, too."

Yes, they always managed to be together. And it was wonderful just having him here beside her.

She relaxed against him and lay still, listening to his heartbeat. "Jill was...here. Where is she?"

"I have no idea. Nor do I care." He kissed her ear. "I believe Novak removed her from the premises to avoid conflict."

"She meant well."

"And she's won you over," he said grimly. "She won't find me that easy."

"I wasn't easy. She just proved to me that I wouldn't be able to live with myself if I didn't do the reconstruction." She rubbed her cheek against his shoulder. "I have to do it, Joe."

"I know." He was silent a moment. "I saw the schoolhouse. I could see the effect it would have on you." Then he burst out, "Hell, it tore *me* apart."

"It's the children," she whispered. "I keep thinking about Michael. Outside of the home, a schoolroom is where a child feels safest. What if Michael had been in that classroom facing Varak with those other children? You wouldn't be able to keep from trying to stand between them either, Joe."

"No, I wouldn't." Joe was silent again. "Then let's get moving and make sure no one else will ever have to face him." He brushed a strand of hair away from her forehead and gave her a kiss on the tip of her nose. "So much for you getting a little extra rest." He carefully released her and moved off the cot. "That wasn't going to happen, was it? Lights?"

"Wall switch beside the door." She was already missing the *feel* of him. She saw him silhouetted against the faint light pouring into the glass of the windows as he lithely crossed the room. It must be almost dawn. "I slept longer than I intended anyway." She sat up and swung her legs to the floor. "I've got to get back to work."

The lights flashed on, and Joe's gaze immediately zeroed in on the skull on her dais. "This is him?" He went to the workbench and examined the reconstruction. "You've only done the basic measuring..." he murmured. "You have a long way to go."

"Not so long," she said defensively. "I had repairs. It will go faster now."

"I'm not on the attack," he said. "I'm just trying to gauge the time frame I have to work with." He paused. "Novak wants me to go and check out a scientist who might have been capable of doing the DNA substitution. Did you know anything about that?"

"Not about the DNA." She had to be honest with him. "But I told him I didn't want you hovering over me while I did the reconstruction. I would have trouble concentrating. Is what he wants you to do something that would be helpful?"

He nodded slowly. "It would have been my first move anyway. I just don't like leaving you again." He was still looking down at the skull, thinking. "But Novak seems to have your security well in hand." His lips twisted. "And your friend, Jill, is apparently ready to stand guard over you. Which is only right considering that she got you into this."

"I don't think I could call her a friend, but she will protect me as much as she's able." She met his gaze. "I'll be okay here, Joe. Don't worry about me."

"Of course I'll worry about you," he said roughly. "You're barely recovered from being poisoned. You look exhausted and pale, and you'll drive yourself until you get this finished." He tapped the skull. "But I can't help you do it, so I'll have to go and find another way to reach the same goal. I suppose I'll head for Cairo."

"Cairo?" Eve repeated. "Egypt? That's where you're going to find this scientist?"

He nodded. "Yusef Dobran. Why the surprise?"

"Not surprise really. But Egypt has been turning up in the conversation ever since I got here. Zahra Kiyani has a passion for it. But it had nothing to do with Cairo."

"One can never tell where a passion will take you." He turned away from the reconstruction. "I'll go tell Novak I'll head to Cairo to talk to his scientist. I'll be back before I leave."

"You'd better. Otherwise, I'll track you down."

"Promises. Promises." He smiled at her over his shoulder. "It's going to be okay, Eve. And that's another promise."

She watched him walk out the door. She wanted to go running after him, to touch him again...Instead, she got to her feet and headed for the bathroom to wash up and change her clothes. They both had their jobs to do, and the sooner they were done, the sooner they could be together.

It was best that Joe was leaving, she told herself. Best that he wasn't going to stay here in the center of the hurricane, where she had to be with the reconstruction. After all, it was what she had wanted.

But Joe never stayed out of the eye of the hurricane for long. How did she know there wasn't a worse storm waiting for him in Cairo?

CHAPTER

10

Joe saw Novak standing by the path the moment he left the museum. "I'm going to Cairo."

"I thought you might. I'll call Gideon unless you prefer someone else to accompany you. He's been involved with investigating Dobran from the beginning. He's very good, and he has advantages that my other men don't have."

"Money and contacts?"

Novak nodded. "Those, too. But I was thinking that he learns from every situation and adapts to find a way to win the next one. Didn't you find that to be true?"

Joe nodded. "Gideon will do." He looked him in the eye. "As long as you make it clear that he obeys my orders instead of yours. And as long as I find him valuable. The minute I find he fails me in either category, I'll send him back to you and work on my own." He paused. "He wouldn't tell me anything on the way here. He lies very well, but he's obviously clever, and I realized he'd know more about you than what he told me."

"I'm glad you didn't force the issue with him. I like Gideon, I might have had to address it with you." He added, "Yes, he knew. As you say, he's clever, and I needed him. But he's his own man, and I'll let him know that he can trust you. You'll have to forge your own relationship with him."

Joe nodded. "Whatever. And I'll need to know everything there is to know about Yusef Dobran and his assistant, Hassan Sebak. Right away."

"What Gideon doesn't know, he'll find out for you. When do you leave?"

"In the next hour or so."

"I'll assign someone to take you back to the airport and let Gideon know you're coming. Backup?"

"Get someone local to Cairo that Gideon can call if needed. I'll let him know when I think—"

"Hello. You're Joe Quinn?" It was a woman's voice from the path behind him. "I'm Jill Cassidy. We've never officially met." She was coming out of the brush from the direction of the village. She slanted a cool look at Novak. "You lied to me, Novak. Hajif didn't need to see me. I told you I wasn't going to hide from Quinn." She turned back to Joe. "You deserve to meet the person who hurt Eve and manipulated your family." She lifted her chin. "Is there anything you'd like to say to me? Whatever it is, I'll listen and agree with every word. There's no apology I can make that will make what I did any better." She held his gaze, and said quietly, "But I owe you, and I promise I'll find a way to make it right."

"Believe me, she will, Quinn," Novak said dryly. "Which isn't always a good thing."

"You're right." Joe was gazing straight in her eyes. "Your apology sucks. What you did to Eve is unforgiveable. Eve may have come up with some way to find excuses for you, but I won't. If you need to kill a snake, then cut its head off. Don't make Eve do it for you. You could have gotten her killed."

"I know that," Jill said steadily. "It's all my fault. And even if I wanted to stop her now, I couldn't do it. It's too late. All I can promise is that I'll take care of her."

"Yes, you will," Joe said fiercely. His hands clenched into fists as the rage tore through him. His gaze went from her to Novak and back again. "Because you're right, it is too late. So Eve is going to do what you asked her, and I'm going to find where the snake is hiding. And you will both make certain that nothing happens to Eve. Not a scratch, do you hear? If anything does, then I'll come after you, and I'll never stop until I kill you." He whirled back toward the museum. "Call Gideon, Novak. I need to get out of here."

Eve was coming out of the bathroom when Joe walked into the museum. "That was quick," she said warily as she studied his expression. "What's wrong?"

"Nothing. It's just time that I left." He took her into his arms. "No, that's a lie. I just ran into Jill Cassidy and blew my cool." He held her close. "And uttered dire threats if she and Novak didn't take care of you." His arms tightened. "And meant every one of them."

"I'm sure you did." She looked up at him. "They both want to keep me safe, Joe. Just take care of yourself."

"Always." He kissed her. "I'll call you when I can. Try not to work too hard." He cupped her face in his two hands. "Yeah, that's not likely. I'll see you soon, love."

She nodded and blinked to keep back the tears. "I'm sorry that I pulled you into this, Joe."

"I'm not. I just wish it had happened sooner." He pulled her close again for a long moment, then he was turning away. "I'll call Michael on the way to Cairo and reassure him that you're doing well."

"I'll have to call him again myself soon. It was just difficult..." She made a face. "He'd see right through me and worry."

He nodded. "He does that anyway even long-distance." He suddenly whirled back and was across the room again. He kissed her, long, hot, passionately, then he let her go. "Change your mind. Let me take you out of here. I'll find another way to do this."

Her arms tightened around him. "What if you can't? I have that skull here, now. Give me the time, and I can do this. You know I can."

He muttered a curse and pushed her away from him. "Yes, you can do it. I thought I'd try one more time." He turned away again. "Hell, I would have tried sex if it wasn't for that damn cot and a whole roomful of skulls glaring down at us."

Eve shook her head with a smile. "The cot was a problem, but the kids wouldn't have been glaring; children usually think sex is funny." Her smile faded as her gaze fell on the Varak reconstruction on the dais. She suddenly shivered. "But I think he might have been a challenge."

"No, he wouldn't. We wouldn't let him," Joe said. "But I prefer you not have the distraction. He bothers you. So get rid of him, and when I come back, we'll discuss the other hurdles to overcome." He paused at the door and looked back at the reconstruction. He smiled, then deliberately gave the Varak skull the finger. "Get rid of him," he repeated. "He's no threat to you. Alive or dead, we won't let him touch you."

Then he was gone.

———————◆———————

Jill opened the door of the museum ten minutes later. "Quinn is on his way," she said. "Novak got him out of the village as soon as he could. I think he was afraid he'd have to protect me from him and that would have caused all kinds of trouble with you." She hadn't moved from the doorway. "Am I allowed to come in? I have to do it anyway because I have to be near you. But I hope that you'll still permit me to do it. I know that Quinn was terribly angry with me."

"For heaven's sake, come in." Eve shook her head with exasperation. "And you should have expected him to be angry. Your research should have told you that Joe can be very cool most of the time, but he has his limits."

"And you're definitely one of those limits." Jill shook her head. "No, you're the supreme limit. I did realize it, I just hadn't experienced it." She came into the room. "It's going to take me a long time to find a way to get him to forgive me."

"No question." She sat down at her worktable. "Does it matter?"

"Yes. Making amends is always important. I'll just have to do something very good that will make up for the bad. It's all a question of balance. The monks taught me that when I was a kid."

"Monks?"

"In Tibet. They were cool dudes." She looked at Eve with a frown. "You haven't had breakfast yet, have you?"

"I'll eat later."

She shook her head. "You'll get involved and put it off. I'll go down and get some fruit from Hajif, then send someone to Jokan for something more substantial." She frowned. "Tea or coffee? I can make you decaf."

"Tea will be fine. And now isn't the time for decaf."

"No, it isn't." She started to turn away. "Thank you for not letting him turn you against me. I know that I'm nothing to you, and he's everything. But you won't be sorry. I'll keep you safe."

"Just don't let anyone disturb me until Varak is finished. That's all I need from you." She grimaced. "And that's all Joe will want also. To have this over."

Jill shook her head. "But he wants something else more. He told Novak and me he'd kill both of us if you got even a scratch while we were taking care of you." She smiled. "So I have to make certain to pay attention to his priorities even if they conflict with yours." She headed for the door. "I'll be right back. Please don't acquire any scratches while I'm gone."

Eve shook her head ruefully as Jill disappeared. She had known Joe was in a fury when he'd come back to the museum, but she'd hoped he'd been exaggerating when he'd said he'd been threatening dire things. She should have known better. Well, Novak and Jill would have to learn to accept Joe as he was and be damn glad to have him on their side.

She forced herself to turn back to the Varak reconstruction. Blank gaping holes for eyes stared at her from that scorched, blackened face. Joe had realized that she had been nervous about doing this reconstruction. And though he hadn't wanted her to do it, he had offered her his support in typical Joe fashion. She smiled as she remembered that scornful, insulting finger Joe had given Varak before he left.

Lord, she loved him.

"He's right, I can do this," she murmured as she gazed into those gaping eyes. "Screw you, Varak."

She leaned closer, her gaze intent, as she started to measure again.

———◆———

Gideon was standing beside the steps of the plane when Joe was dropped off at the airfield. "I hear we're going to Cairo," he said as he turned and went up the steps. "I thought that's where we'd end up after you talked to Novak."

"But you still didn't tell me anything about Yusef Dobran on the way here," Joe said as he followed him into the plane. "That could have been dangerous. I was frustrated as hell."

He shrugged. "It was the chance I took. You were an unknown quantity." He grinned. "And what I did know was explosive. I had orders to bring you here. I wasn't certain that you wouldn't make a detour to Cairo on your way if you thought you had a chance to bring this to a close a bit faster." He headed for the cockpit. "And after all the effort I put in setting up Hassan Sebak, I wasn't going to let it all go down the tubes because you were in a hurry."

"You set up the deal with Sebak?"

"Novak can't do everything." He dropped down in the pilot's seat. "Though he'd prefer to try. But I convinced him that I could handle this better than he could. It was quite an accomplishment, since Novak thinks very highly of himself." He was doing the checklist.

"Rightly, of course. But I'm a bit impatient. He has too much on his plate, and I *want* Varak." He looked at Joe. "So sit down, buckle up, and we'll get out of here. I'll tell you everything I know about Cairo on the way."

Joe slowly sat down in the copilot's seat. "You think Dobran did the DNA. You believe Varak is alive? Why?"

"Because Jill does, and I trust her. Nothing has changed that since the day she came to me and asked for the money to give to Hadfeld." His lips twisted. "Besides, I can't do anything else. It's a puzzle I have to solve. I'll use you or anyone else to help me do that." He started the Gulf Stream checkdown. "But I'll let you use me as well, Quinn. When I get this baby in the air, I'll be at your disposal."

"Yes, you will," Joe said grimly as he buckled his seat belt. "And I'm pretty good at puzzles, Gideon, but I don't intend to spend much time on this one. I want an answer before Eve gets finished with that damn reconstruction." He leaned back in his seat as Gideon started to taxi. "And you don't know what impatient means yet."

"Five minutes," Gideon said, as the plane left the ground. "Just five minutes..."

It was only four minutes before he gained the altitude he needed and turned to face Joe. "What do you want to know?"

"Dobran. Everything."

"He was born in Cairo to an upper-middle-class family, his parents were both prestigious professors of arts and antiquities at the Cairo University. But Yusef chose to go for a medical degree at the Sorbonne in Paris and went on to get both a medical and chemistry degree there. He was totally brilliant, but when he was at the Sorbonne, he developed a drug habit that required he make more money than he could earn in medicine. That led him to explore other alternatives that took him into the DNA netherworld, and he found his niche. He spent six years in Paris, and by the time he returned to open his own lab in Cairo, he had developed a stellar reputation among the criminal underworld. For the last fifteen years, he's built on that reputation, and I'm sure Novak told you that Dobran is probably our man."

"And what do you think?"

"That Dobran is an arrogant asshole who will do anything to prove how clever he is. He likes money, but he also considers himself one of the elite intelligentsia like his parents. Unfortunately, both his parents and his social set don't agree and have ostracized him."

"What a pity. Does he have a wife? A mistress?"

"He changes mistresses every few months, but he always visits them in town and never permits them to come to his Asarti estate." He glanced at Joe. "He's very careful. Only his guards and his drug dealer and Hassan Sebak are permitted on the property. That's all."

"And what does Sebak do for him? What kind of assistant? Does he help in the lab?"

"Sometimes. But he's more of a gofer. He runs interference and errands for Dobran." He smiled faintly. "And he makes sure that all is secure and well in his gallery. That may be his most important task as far as Dobran is concerned."

"Gallery?"

"Dobran is a collector. Paintings, sculptures, antiquities. He has a fabulous collection that he's acquired since he came back to Cairo. It's what he spends those fat fees that he gets for his work on." He shrugged. "It's almost as much an addiction as his drug habit. Though it could be that he just wants to stick it to his father and all those other people who don't recognize how superior he is."

Joe's gaze narrowed on his face. "But you don't believe that."

"No, but I'm giving you both sides of the coin. Though it could be a little of both. He was exposed to fine art and antiquities from childhood, so the appreciation has to be bred into him. But he's shown himself to be vengeful and selfish all of his adult life. I'm certain that adds to the pleasure enormously. Hence, the addiction."

Sharp. Very sharp, Joe thought. Gideon was impressive. "Two addictions. Drugs and his art collection. Which can we use?"

"That's up to you," Gideon said solemnly. "Novak said that I'm to let you lead the way. I gave you possible weapons, so now I'll meekly let you take charge."

"Meekly?" Joe's brows rose. "Is that supposed to be amusing? You're like a chameleon adapting to your surroundings to get what you want. That's a dangerous talent."

"Only if you don't want the same thing." He handed his phone to Joe. "Check out the photos of Dobran and Sebak. You'll want to know them on sight."

"That goes without saying." Joe glanced at the two photos. Dobran was in his early forties, hollow-cheeked, thick, dark eyebrows. Sebak, older, receding hairline, a little plump. "What else do you have?"

"Shots of his estate, Asarti, outside Cairo. It's a château he bought from a French businessman five years ago and had renovated. You'll notice the placement of his exterior sentries are clearly indicated." He gave Joe a glance. "Just in case you don't want to rely on Hassan Sebak to get us in to see Dobran. I dangled the money, and he snapped at it, but he's a little too comfortable with Dobran. He tends to be nervous. He's still tempted, but it's possible he could change his mind before the deal is struck. He might decide that trapping us is a safer option for him."

Joe flipped through the photos. "No interior shots?"

"No, but you'll find a copy of the original renovation plans filed by his architect when he bought the château. That should do it."

Joe examined the plans. "Yes, that should do it."

"So do we ignore Sebak and go for his boss?"

Joe thought about it. "Not immediately. There are things Sebak can tell us that might help us. And you've already proved that he can be tapped." He held up his hand as Gideon opened his lips to protest. "You haven't set the deal in place, so he won't have a decision to make that will impact us. Where are Sebak's quarters? Is he in the house?"

Gideon nodded. "Dobran assigned him quarters near the gallery. I told you that was his main duty to Dobran. Care and security for his treasures."

"Yes, you did." His gaze was raking the house plans. "And yet there's something missing..."

"What?"

Joe didn't answer, his gaze still on the plans. "You can get us to the house, but after that, we're on our own?"

"I can do better than that. I hijacked the Internet info of the company who installed his security system and got one of Novak's experts to figure out the codes to both the exterior and interior. I can disable the alarms, video cameras, and the motion sensors to everything but the gallery. That's on a separate circuit and code. The security there is foolproof against fire, theft, earthquake, and acts of God or Satan. Dobran doesn't want anyone touching his treasures."

"But we can get to Sebak's quarters?"

"If we can get past the guard stationed near the French doors in the library." Gideon's eyes were narrowed with interest on Joe's face. "Look, we can have Herb Nassem, the operator Novak set up as backup, drop us off and pick us up at the château. And I can manage to get us into the place. But all this would be difficult. If you still want Sebak, why not let me set up a meeting with him in the city instead?"

"I don't want to waste the time," Joe said curtly. "I want it all. I want Sebak. I want Dobran. I want answers. And I want it all to go down tonight." His lips tightened. "And since you've done such good prep work, we might be able to pull it off."

Gideon blinked. "If we don't get killed. You were right, I don't understand the word impatience as you define it." Then he smiled slowly. "Go for the entire jackpot? It's very appealing. Providing you have a plan?" When Joe just looked at him, he said, "You don't have a plan."

"Not yet." Joe went back to flipping through the photos on

Gideon's phone. He added absently, "I'll get there. We have all day. But the first order of business is that we've both got to memorize this floor plan. Now tell me about Dobran and his drug addiction. He obviously has to keep it under control, or he wouldn't be this successful. What does he use?"

"Opium pipe. He started off on pills, but after he came back to Cairo, he found himself an antique pipe that I'm sure made him feel like a caliph. But you're right, he keeps control. He likes money too much to do anything else. Sebak said he locks himself in his suite at night and goes into never-never land. But during business hours, he's not a user."

"That could be bad or good. Do you know his typical schedule? We need him coherent but not troublesome..."

———◆———

ROBAKU
2:45 P.M.

"You've got your red voodoo markers in place," Jill said as she handed Eve a bottle of water. "Don't argue. Drink it and take a deep breath. You've been racing nonstop all day." She tilted her head critically as she gazed back at the reconstruction. "Now he looks more like a ghoul than ever. Does it bother you?"

"No." Eve took a drink of water and leaned back. "That's a necessary process that leads to a successful conclusion. Why should it bother me?"

"You said you weren't looking forward to working on a man like Varak. Just checking." She made a face. "And I suppose I shouldn't have even mentioned it. It's my damned curiosity again. I'm glad that he's not putting his mojo on you."

"If he were, it would be because I let him. If evil lingers, it could be because we invite it into our minds." She took another drink of water and looked directly into the skull's gaping eyes. She hadn't realized until this moment that she had not done that since she had started working. Well, why should she? she thought defensively. She'd been doing depth measurements. It wasn't because she'd been afraid. "The trick is to concentrate on the work and not give in to imagination." She was speaking as much to herself as to Jill. "I've probably blown Varak's mystique out of all proportion because of what I've learned from reading and hearing about him." And the horrible nightmares. The machete glittering in the darkness of the schoolroom. She forced herself to keep her gaze on the skull. "Do you realize I don't even know what he looks like? That's not a bad thing since I avoid it anyway. But I only saw a couple photos of him on Google, and none of them were close-ups. I wasn't inter-ested in him, only the children. I just got a vague impression that he was very big and had dark hair. Then when I came here and saw what he'd done in that schoolroom, I didn't want to look at him. He's not even a human being to me any longer. He's a Hitler or Bin Laden."

"Close," Jill said. "But you have to add a little Jeffrey Dahmer to be exact."

"You should know." She tore her gaze from the skull. "I'm sure you've researched him ad nauseam, just as you did me."

"As much as I could. He was a big part of the story of what hap-pened here in Maldara, and I had to try to understand him." Her lips twisted. "I never succeeded. I felt like one of those FBI profilers trying to see into the mind of a serial killer. There has to come a time when there is no answer but the fact that Varak was a monster." She paused. "But I think you should know about Varak. Because he didn't look like a monster. He was quite good-looking in a Slavic kind of way, and he's over six-five and very powerfully built. Strong. Exceptionally strong, and he liked to break things…and people." She moistened her lips. "And everyone around him sensed that he did, and it gave him power over them. He loved power from the day he was born. He searched for it in violence, sex, money, or anything else that gave him the same thrill."

"You seem to know him better than you thought you did," Eve said slowly.

"Maybe I wanted to be like you and close my eyes to the monster. But I'm not allowed to do that because I have to tell the story. And now you don't get to do it either because I brought you into this. You have to get to know him. I'll try to make it as brief as possible." She paused. "Varak grew up in the slums of Johannesburg and was the first of three children born to Marta Varak, a worker in a local clothing factory. His father was a soldier who deserted Marta after eight years, and she became a whore to support her children. She treated them all well enough, but she was besotted with Nils. She spoiled him rotten, and he might have been the reason her husband deserted her. Nils didn't like the competition, and there's no telling what he did to push his father out the door. There was no doubt he was the perfect sociopath and was as smart as he had to be in every category. He had temper tantrums until he learned it didn't get him what he wanted, then he became devious. But he had all the signs of a psychopath from the time he was a toddler. There were rumors that were never proved that he killed small neighborhood animals. Then, when he was nine years old, his eleven-month-old baby sister suffocated in her crib when he was supposed to be taking care of her. It was said to be accidental. His mother said the poor boy was devastated even though he always complained about her crying. The only family member Nils got along with was his younger brother, Oscar, because he let Nils totally dominate him. When he was fifteen, he took Oscar with him to Venezuela when he joined a rebel group as a mercenary. But when Nils formed his own army two years later, Oscar took off and went back to Johannesburg. He was evidently tired of being his brother's punching bag." Jill paused a moment. "You know the rest. Varak has been building his reputation country by country and one massacre at a time. Only the massacres and the butchery kept getting worse and worse. Maldara was just the last in the line of his bloodbaths."

Eve looked back at the skull. "I hope this *is* Varak. Somehow we have to put an end to him, Jill."

Jill nodded, her gaze on the reconstruction. "You're working very quickly, aren't you? As I said, you're on fire. But you said three days..."

"I said *maybe* three days, he's going very fast." She took another drink of water. "But it may slow down as I do the fill-in. I have to be very careful."

Jill was studying her expression. "But you don't believe it will slow down, do you?"

Eve didn't answer for a moment. "No, sometimes a work just takes off and leaves me far behind. I can't seem to do anything wrong. This could be one of them."

"So how long?"

Eve shook her head. "I have no idea. Right now it's a fever. But sometimes a fever breaks." She finished her water. "And I won't know if I don't get back to work."

"I'm dismissed?" Jill asked. "When am I allowed to disturb you again?"

Eve started to put on another depth marker.

"When?" Jill persisted. "Next on my list is a cup of beef soup. I have to keep you strong. Give in, and the interruption will go faster. Tell me when it will be convenient."

Jill obviously wasn't going to surrender, Eve thought resignedly. "Before I begin the final sculpting."

Jill's eyes widened. "Shit. You're going to finish tonight."

"I didn't say that."

"But you are, aren't you?"

"Perhaps. More likely tomorrow."

"I think...tonight." Jill's gaze went to the reconstruction. "What did you say about sometimes a work's just taking off?" She murmured, "Maybe we're not the only ones who are impatient..."

—————◆—————

ASARTI
1:40 A.M.

"You're sure the kitchen entrance is the safest?" Joe asked as he went down the path after Gideon. "I've always found less obvious—"

"Have I been wrong yet?" Gideon interrupted. "Face it, I've been bloody perfect. After Nassem dropped us off down the road, I led us right past those sentries, didn't I? You shouldn't mess with perfection, Quinn." He'd reached the kitchen alcove, and his fingers were racing over the security panel. "Particularly since I'm not at all sure that I'm not the only perfect thing about this venture."

"Perfection is overrated," Joe said. "It doesn't leave room for innovation." Yet he couldn't argue that Gideon had fulfilled every need. He had been a constant surprise to Joe. And this door was opening silently with no alarm. "Okay, you're awe-inspiring. Meet me at Sebak's quarters. I'll go take out the guard in the library."

"I'll do it," Gideon said as he moved down the hall. "The guard will be easy. I'll let you handle Sebak. You want him alive, and my impression is that he's very edgy. I bet he has a gun in his bedside table."

He probably knew Sebak did, Joe thought as he turned in the opposite direction and made his way through the darkness toward Sebak's suite.

Sebak's door was locked. Definitely edgy.

It took Joe two minutes to silently pick the lock. Then he was inside.

More darkness.

But Joe's eyes were accustomed to it now, and he could make out a bed across the large room.

Joe moved silently toward it.

Movement!

The bedcovers were suddenly thrown aside, and the man who had done it was lunging toward the bedside table.

Joe was across the room in seconds, and his hand came down in a karate chop on Sebak's wrist as he fumbled to get the drawer open.

Sebak cursed in pain as he turned and launched himself upward at Joe. "Son of a bitch. What are you doing? One scream, and I'll have guards all over the place." He struck out blindly and hit Joe in the chin. "They'll *kill* you."

Enough.

Joe's hand cut down on Sebak's neck in a karate chop and put him out.

He went limp.

Three or four minutes maximum before he'd regain consciousness, Joe thought. Get ready.

He flicked on the bedside light, checked to make sure the man was indeed Sebak, and removed the .38 revolver from the drawer of the bedside table. Then he took out his handcuffs and snapped them on Sebak's wrists.

"No trouble at all?" Gideon was at the doorway, his gaze on Sebak. "I admit I'm disappointed. I wasn't aiming for serious, but a few minor problems would have made me feel better about having to be so wary around you. I don't like not feeling totally in control of the situation."

"Then you shouldn't have told me that he'd go for that gun." Joe took a small roll of duct tape out of his jacket pocket. "Did you take down the guard?"

Gideon nodded as he watched him tape Sebak's mouth. "Complete with the duct tape. I did a neater job than you." He closed the door and walked toward him. "I think he's coming around. Maybe you'd better be the first one he sees. You're more threatening. I concentrated on being intelligent and charming when I was trying to lure him to our side. That's not the impression we need right now." He stepped out of Sebak's field of vision. "So be intimidating, Quinn."

"I will," Joe said grimly as he moved forward and jerked Sebak's head back. Sebak's eyes flew open, and he gazed up at Joe in alarm. He tried desperately to open his lips and speak.

"I'll let you talk soon," Joe said harshly, "when I'm sure you understand what will happen to you if you scream or cause me any trouble. Nod if you understand."

Sebak nodded but then tried to lift his arms and strike out. When he saw the handcuffs, he began to struggle frantically.

"Helpless," Joe said. "I can do anything I wish to you, and you won't be able to stop me. And you might be able to get out of this alive if you don't make me angry." His voice lowered. "But it's going to be very easy to make me angry. I need information, and you've been playing games with my friend. Do you know there's a pressure point I can press here on your neck that can make you very sorry that you did that?" He reached down, and his thumb and forefinger found the exact place. "Ah, there it is."

Sebak opened his lips, trying to scream as pain jagged through him.

"But I never play games, Sebak. I just make certain the pain keeps coming and coming until I get what I want. I want this information very much because without it, someone I care about is going to suffer." He pressed the cord again and watched Sebak's face as it twisted in agony. "I won't permit that to happen. I'll do anything I have to do to keep it from happening. But I don't care if you suffer at all. I believe you understand that now, don't you?"

Sebak nodded frantically.

"Good. Then you won't try to escape, and you'll cooperate with everything I ask of you. Is that true?"

Sebak nodded again.

Joe leaned forward. "Then I'm going to take off the tape, and we'll begin." He stared deep into his eyes. "But you'll have to remember that if I see any sign of trickery, I won't hesitate. You're expendable, Sebak. And, if I don't get what I want, then I'll have no hesitation about showing you that." His fingers moved gently on Sebak's neck, and he could feel the muscles tense. "You're in my way. It's up to you to prove that I should keep you alive." He suddenly reached up and ripped off the tape with one motion. "Are you going to scream, Sebak?"

"No!" His gaze was holding Joe's. "I promise. I won't—" He stopped. "I want to live. Tell me how I can do that."

"I fully intend to do that." He said over his shoulder to Gideon, "It's over. Come out, come out, wherever you are. Sebak isn't going to have any trouble believing that I'll do anything I have to do now."

"I can see that." Gideon moved forward. "Intimidating, indeed. Is that how you treat the prisoners at your precinct when you're inter-rogating them?"

"No, that's my job, and there are rules. This is Eve, and there are no rules." He looked back at Sebak and gestured to Gideon. "You'll remember him, he was going to give you a great deal of money. But now you've decided that's not necessary, haven't you?"

"I remember him." Sebak's tone was surly. "We can still deal. I'll get you in to see Dobran. You didn't have to hurt me."

"Yes, I did," Joe said. "I don't have time to do anything else tonight. But I could learn to enjoy it if you don't cooperate." He took a step closer to Sebak. "And we will pay a visit to your boss, but I think you know a good deal, and that will save me time. Gideon tells me that he indulges in his favorite opium pipe in the evening and might be a bit bleary when I wake him."

Sebak hesitated. "Gideon said that he wanted info about some DNA project Dobran was doing. I don't know anything about his business." He looked suddenly alarmed as he met Joe's eyes. "Well, maybe a little. But you'd do better to talk to him."

"I think you'd know about this," Joe said softly. "It was a very big job, perhaps the biggest Dobran has ever done. It would have been very difficult for him not to call in all the help he could get to keep himself safe and the work secret. You're his errand boy, and he trusts you. You might not know anything about the lab work, but you'd be drawn into the job itself."

"He doesn't trust anyone that much."

"I thought we had an understanding," Joe said. "Now I'm going to ask questions, and you're going to answer quickly and fully. Or we go back to the moment before I ripped off that tape. Do you want that, Sebak?"

"No! I just—" He was breathing hard. "He knows bad people. He could have them kill me."

"That's your problem, but you have a bigger one with me." Joe smiled. "Don't you?"

"Yes."

"Then we go forward. What do you know about that DNA job Dobran took on several months ago?"

He was silent, then said reluctantly, "He didn't want to do it. From what I overheard when he was talking on the phone, the money was more than he'd ever been offered before, but he said it was too dangerous. He said that he had plenty of money and didn't need to run that kind of risk to get more."

"And who was on the phone?"

Sebak shrugged. "I don't know. Somebody important. Dobran said something about not caring how big they were, it was nothing to him. He had enough business, and he wasn't going to run the risk."

"But evidently he did run it."

Sebak's lips twisted as he nodded. "Dobran was offered a price he couldn't refuse. A box was delivered here a few days later, and he sent me to take it to Caladon that same day."

"Caladon?"

"Kalid Caladon. He's Dobran's favorite art expert. He's expert *and* discreet. Dobran has all his artifacts appraised by him."

"And this was an artifact that Dobran sent to him for appraisal? What kind?"

"A gold statue. Dobran was excited about it. He was even more excited when I brought the report back from Caladon. He had me set up a special glass case in the gallery for the statue and arranged maximum security for it." He added, "And he started work on the new DNA project the next day."

"How? Did he meet with someone? Did he go to the lab?"

"He didn't go to the lab. But he must have met with the client because he flew out that morning." He added quickly, "And that's all I know. I did what Dobran told me to do, then I was out of it. Dobran spent the next three weeks at the lab before the job was finished."

"You know nothing else?" Joe asked.

"Only that Dobran is crazy about that statue and spends time with it every day." He thought of something else. "Oh, and he told me to put two more guards on the property." He added sourly, "But they didn't keep you out, did they?"

"Names," Joe said. "I need client names."

"I don't have any names. I've told you all I know." Sebak's voice was shaking. "You'll have to get it from Dobran."

Joe was afraid that was true. Sebak was still too frightened not to tell him if there was anything left to confess. "Then that's what we'll do." He pulled Sebak to his feet. "Let's go."

"And am I to be allowed to interrogate Dobran?" Gideon asked. "I'm getting very bored, Quinn."

"Maybe." He pushed Sebak across the room and out the door. "But we're going to make a stop before we go to see him. I want to take a look at that statue."

"I told you that I don't have the code for the gallery. You'll have to rely on Sebak."

"I'm certain he'll cooperate," Joe said as he nudged Sebak toward the gallery. "Isn't that right?"

"I don't know why you want to see it," Sebak said. "It's just a statue."

"Maybe I'm an art lover. Besides, I want to see what Dobran sees

in it and why he wanted it so badly." He stopped before the ornate carved doors of the gallery and gestured to the panel. "Do your
thing. If you set off an alarm, I don't have to tell you that you'll regret it."

"No." Sebak was quickly putting in the code. "I wouldn't do that.
Haven't I done everything you've told me to do?" The carved door
opened to reveal steel panels that slid silently to each side. "You see?"

"Yes," Joe said. "You've made a good start. But it's all in the
follow-up. Where's the statue?"

"At the end of the second row." He hurried on ahead. "I'll show
you."

Gideon gave a low whistle as he fell into step with Joe. "I've seen
rooms at the Louvre that don't have this many treasures." His gaze
was on the rows of glass cases on either side of them containing
Egyptian artifacts of every description. "No mummies? I half expect
to see King Tut in one of those cases. I bet there are artifacts in here
that the government would never permit to be owned in a private
collection."

"No bet." The gallery was very heavy on Egyptian artifacts, but
there were also priceless originals on the walls by Cezanne, Rem-
brandt, Titian... "It's clear he sometimes took his fee in fine art.
That Titian is worth far more than this château."

"You have a good eye," Gideon said. "And whoever sent Dobran
that artifact must have known that it would be irresistible to him."

"Here it is." Sebak had stopped before a softly lit case at the end
of the row. He gestured impatiently. "I told you, it's just a statue."

Joe inhaled sharply as he gazed at the superb artistry of the work.
It was no more than eighteen inches but was made of pure gold, and
every complicated detail of the slim Egyptian woman it represented
was done to perfection, from her crown headpiece to her sandals.
"Yes, you did. Only a statue." He bent closer. "Take it out of the
case. I want to examine it."

"I'm not allowed to do—" He met Joe's eyes and reached out to press the coded release on the top of the case. "Be careful. He'll kill me if it's damaged."

"It's gold. I'm sure it's already very old, and gold isn't that fragile." He took the statue and looked at it. It was just as magnificent as he'd first thought. "But I can see why he was impressed by her."

"I can't," Sebak said sourly. "I don't know why he wanted it. He has others, you know." Sebak nodded at the row of cases across the room. "Probably older than this one. Age is everything to value according to Caladon. This one is only 44 B.C. But Dobran couldn't wait to get his hands on it."

"Why?" Joe murmured. "It's exquisite, but why would it mean that much to him?"

Sebak shrugged. "He told me to make sure Caladon cleaned the base carefully so that every engraved hieroglyph was clear. I think he hoped it would be a name, but it wasn't. Yet he didn't seem disappointed. When he got the statue back from Caladon, he even had a gold plaque made for the case itself with the same words inscribed." He gestured to the small rectangular gold plaque inside the case. "And that wasn't even done in hieroglyphics."

"No." Gideon was suddenly pushing forward to shine the beam of his flashlight down on the gold plaque. "It's ordinary, modern Egyptian script, and it only shows that Dobran is a true collector. He wanted to see the proof, know what he had, every time he came to see her. It was his way of claiming her as his property, bringing her into his world where she didn't belong." His gaze was narrowed, focused on the delicate script. Then he abruptly went still. "Shit." He muttered an oath beneath his breath. "Let's get to Dobran fast, Quinn. No wonder he put on extra guards. I'm surprised that he's still alive. We have to get the hell out of here. I think we've found out all we need to know."

"In a minute. I don't want Sebak around when I'm talking to Dobran." He pushed Sebak down on the floor and fastened his manacles to the leg of the case. When Sebak started to protest, Joe taped his lips shut again. "And you might have found out all you want, Gideon. But evidently I haven't," he said. "I don't speak Egyptian, much less read it. What does it say? Is it a name?"

"No, Sebak is right, no name." Gideon turned toward the door. "Just a kind of title."

"What title?"

"Three words." He threw open the door. *"Great Beloved Wife."*

CHAPTER

11

"Take it away." Eve pushed the bowl of beef soup to one side. "I can't eat any more, Jill. And if you argue with me, I'll throw this bowl at you."

"I'm not arguing." Jill took the bowl and turned away. "I'm lucky I got that much down you. But you had to eat something, you've been on fire all day." She glanced over her shoulder at the skull. "I can tell he's waiting for you. Or that you're waiting for him. Or something..." She shook her head. "He's blurred. I look at him, and I can't tell anything about him. Can you?"

Eve nodded. "Like you, I can tell he's ready and waiting."

"Are you nervous?" Jill asked.

"No. Yes. I'm a little sick to my stomach, but I need this. I have to know." She drew a deep breath. "Now be still and let me get back to work. I don't want to hear from you until I've finished."

"You won't." Jill sat down in a chair across the room. "Promise. I won't even watch what you're doing. But I do have to be here to watch your back. Okay?"

"Okay," Eve said absently, as her fingers reached out to tentatively touch the brow bone on the reconstruction. "You have that photo of Varak?"

"In my briefcase under my cot. It's waiting for you, Eve."

Waiting.

She sat there gazing at the smooth clay before her. Everything had been waiting for this moment. The measurements had been taken and checked. The initial sculpting done, the part that told her basically nothing but laid the groundwork. Now it was time to make him come alive.

She shuddered. No, she couldn't think of it like she did other reconstructions. She didn't want him to come alive. Ever since she'd put that skull on the dais, she had been fighting not to think of the person he could be, so that she could block out all the evil and think only of the work itself.

But now she could no longer do that, she had to accept who and what he was so that she could sculpt that face. Was it her imagination, or did she feel something dark and angry stirring?

She moved her shoulders to release the tension, her gaze never leaving the skull. "Okay, are you ready?" she whispered. "I'm not afraid of you. Be as angry and ugly as you like. I'll still get what I want from you. You took so much from so many. Now you have to give at least some of it back."

Her fingers moved down to his right cheek.

Come to me.

Smooth.

Mold.

Fill in.

Darkness.

Anger.

Pay no attention to it. Keep working.

Go to the ears. That should be easier. They had to be generic. She had no idea whether they stuck out or had longer lobes. Just let it flow and do what seemed right.

Anger.

I don't *care.* I'm doing this.

She could no longer even attempt to block him out, but she could keep to the flow and work through that anger and do what she had to do.

Smooth.

Mold.

Fill in.

Hatred.

Work faster. Go to the mouth.

Generic again. She knew the width but not the shape. Better to make the lips closed and without expression. Because the only expression she'd be able to put would be anger and hatred.

Concentrate.

Her fingers were flying now, hot and facile on the clay.

She could do this.

Lips done.

She was moving too fast.

Check the measurements. They were still important.

Nose width, 31 mm. Correct

Nose projection, 18 mm. Okay.

Now concentrate and do the job.

Anger.

Go away!

More shaping to the nostrils.

Mold.

Smooth.

Creasing on either side of the nose.

Good.

Smooth.

Mold.

Fill in.

It was better now. She could still feel the darkness dragging at her like a huge lodestone, but it was only exhausting, not frightening.

She was working feverishly.

Start the creases beneath the orbital cavities.

Fill in.

Mold.

Smooth...

———◆———

ASARTI

"Great Beloved Wife?" Joe repeated as he followed Gideon down the hall toward Dobran's suite. "What the hell is that supposed to mean?"

"Trouble." He glanced over his shoulder at the statue Joe was still carrying. "And very revealing. Plus as dangerous as a flesh-eating parasite for Dobran to possess. That's why we've got to get out of here ASAP. There's no way that Zahra would let that statue out of her hands if she hadn't intended to get it back. She probably has her own version of a SWAT team watching the house, ready to take Dobran out."

"Zahra Kiyani?" Joe said. "You're saying she hired Dobran. Why would she want to fake Varak's death? He worked for the Botzans, her enemy. She had every reason to want him dead. He almost destroyed her country."

"You'll have to ask Dobran. All I know for sure is that she almost certainly did the hiring."

"Because of the statue." Joe looked down at the statue. "It belonged to her? You've seen it before?"

"No, but it's a statue of Kiya, one of Akhenaten's queens during his reign in the Eighteenth Dynasty. On every artifact bearing her name, it was followed or preceded by *The Great Beloved Wife*. That's what's engraved on that statue you're holding. Zahra has always had an obsession about her. Kiya, Zahra's ancestor who founded the Kiyanis, was named for Akhenaten's wife by her mother, Cleopatra. Even in Kiya's journal, she mentioned that the reason that Cleopatra gave her the same name was because of the stories, passed down through the centuries, of how Queen Kiya was so loved by Akhenaten. Didn't Eve mention any of this to you?"

"Probably. It's vaguely familiar. But I guarantee I wasn't paying much attention to any tall tales about Cleopatra. I had other things to think about. As I do right now." He added grimly, "And there could have been other people who had access to a statue of Akhenaten's queen."

"But maybe not one sculpted between 50 and 30 B.C., when Cleopatra and her daughter were alive. That's unusual in itself when Akhenaten and his wives died back in the Eighteenth Dynasty." He slowed and gestured ahead. "Dobran's suite is the second door on the left. Let's see if he can give us a few answers, provided he can focus through his usual haze. Though it might not be possible. Either way, we have to get out of here. Agreed?"

"Agreed." Joe moved quickly down the hall and unlocked the door.

The heavy scent of opium.

A man dressed in loose trousers and an open white shirt was lying sprawled on the couch with an opium pipe in his lips. He appeared to be asleep.

Shit.

"Not much chance of getting answers," Gideon said. "Still want to try?"

"Hell, yes," Joe said. "I don't like the alternative of having to take him with us and get answers later."

"You didn't mention that alternative," Gideon said. "I don't like it either."

"Hold this." Joe thrust the statue at Gideon. Then he was across the room and yanking the pipe out of Dobran's mouth.

No response.

He shook him. "Wake up, Dobran."

Dobran opened his eyes. "Go away." His voice was slurred. "You have no...right to be here. Son of a bitch...I'll have you...castrated."

"Oh, now that does make me mad. Wake up." Joe slapped him. No response. Once again. "Keep your eyes open, dammit."

"Tired..."

"Give me the statue, Gideon." He dug his hand in Dobran's hair and jerked his head back. He held the statue squarely in front of his face. "If you don't keep your eyes open, I'm going to hammer this statue into a pile of rubble."

"No!" Dobran's lids flew open. "Mine. I'll kill you..."

"Is it yours? Who gave it to you?"

"Bitch. Arrogant bitch...Only a down payment. She promised she'd give me more. She said she had lots more..."

"Who?"

"But she never gave me anything else...and she even wanted that statue back. Bitch." He reached out and tried to grasp the statue. "So beautiful...Mine."

"Who?" Joe repeated.

"Did I tell you I was going to castrate you?"

"Who?"

"Maldara...Kiyani..."

"Why?"

"How do I know? She wanted it done..." His eyes closed. "They pay me, I do it. But he was too dangerous. She shouldn't have cheated me."

"Who was he?"

"You know who he is. Everyone knows him..." He was dozing off to sleep again. "But she shouldn't have tried to take the statue back..."

And no matter how Joe shook him, he only got mumbles and complaints. Joe was cursing low and vehemently beneath his breath as he released Dobran's hair and let his head fall back on the pillow of the couch. "Dammit, it's not *enough*."

"What do you mean? You know it was Zahra. He said as much."

"Yes, but I'm going to have to squeeze more out of him. I can't risk his going on the run or ending up a corpse if Zahra decides he has to be taken out." He put the statue in his backpack. "And Eve may need him to testify if all this shit comes tumbling down around her." He slipped on the backpack. "Come on. Help me. We've got to take him with us."

"That was the scenario I wasn't looking forward to facing." Gideon helped him get Dobran onto his feet, and they half carried, half pulled him toward the door. "How do you intend we do it? Go right through all those sentries, lugging him along behind us?"

"No, we go back to the gallery, pick up Sebak again, and let him show us the other way out."

"What other way out? We have the house-renovation plans. Every exit leads out front or to the side gardens protected by sentries."

"But there was something missing." They'd reached the grand staircase and were having to balance Dobran's weight to keep him from falling down the stairs. "I told you that it wasn't right."

"But you didn't tell me why."

"The gallery. You said everything was built around keeping the gallery safe. But there was only one door, and it led to the hall and the front doors. Dobran would have wanted another way to get his treasures out of the château in an emergency. Only he wouldn't have wanted it put in the house plans for everyone to see."

"You're guessing."

"Of course." They were on the staircase landing. "But it's a good guess, and I'm banking on it. It's better than trying to yank Dobran through that garden and having to deal with—"

An explosion rocked the house.

Fire!

Flames were suddenly ripping through the foyer below them.

Then another explosion.

"The gallery." Joe and Gideon were dragging Dobran down the rest of the steps. "Get him to the gallery."

Smoke.

Another explosion. This time from the kitchen.

It was hard to see now.

It took them twice as long as it should have to reach the gallery.

A minute more to punch in the code he'd watched Sebak enter.

Then they were inside.

The heavy steel door slid closed behind them.

Joe released his hold on Dobran and pressed the lock on the door. "Bring him. I've got to get to Sebak." He was running down the aisle. "We've got to get out of here before the local fire department shows up with the police and an antiterrorist unit. And those grounds out front will be teeming with Dobran's sentries by now." He'd reached Sebak and knelt to free him from the handcuffs and rip off his tape.

"What did you do?" Sebak screeched. Tears were streaming down his chalk-white face. "I heard the explosions. Are you trying to kill me? I did everything you told me to do." Then he saw Gideon and Dobran. "I thought you were only going to question him. He's the one who will kill me."

"Not if you get us out of here," Joe said as he jerked him to his feet. "You'll never see Dobran again if you help me get him away from here before anyone breaks in and tosses another bomb. I didn't set off those explosions."

"You're lying," he said uncertainly.

"Have it your way. I don't have time to argue. I have to find a way out." He pushed him down to his knees again. "I'll put the manacles back on you and you can wait for someone to come ... or not."

"No." He struggled back to his feet. "I'll show you. But then you'll let me go?"

"We'll talk about it. I'm still not sure you don't know more. But we're not going to let Dobran go, I need him. So he won't be around to go looking for you. Move!" He was gazing around the gallery. "No doors. But there's another way out, right? Show me. Hurry!"

"I will. I'm hurrying." Sebak was running toward the back of the gallery. "The mummy..."

"Mummy?" Joe was helping Gideon move faster with Dobran. "What are you talking about?"

Sebak was standing before an upright ornate mummy sarcophagus whose top was a huge, carved hawk. "It's a passageway that leads out of the back of the house and down a tunnel toward the road." He was opening the lid, then swinging the five-foot shelf containing the wrapped mummy to one side. "Dobran liked the idea of using the mummy to hide the door." He ducked inside. "Follow me."

"Wait a minute." Joe had a thought. "Gideon said that everything in the gallery was on a separate control. Does that include video cameras?"

"Of course," Sebak said. "Everything."

"Then where can I pull the tapes?"

"They have a special code to release each section of the display areas. There are six kiosks."

"Six!"

"Sirens, Quinn," Gideon said quietly.

Joe heard them, too.

"Shit." *No time to stay and grab the videos. Worry about it later.* "Get going, Sebak."

Sebak disappeared into the darkness.

"Macabre," Gideon said dryly as he dragged Dobran farther into the sarcophagus. "This decision must have been made during one of his more bizarre narcotic episodes."

"Whatever." Joe was negotiating the entrance to the tunnel while still trying to help Gideon with Dobran. "Pull that lid shut behind you, then call Nassem and tell him to meet us at the road in back of the château."

"I'm sure it's bad luck to close the lid of a coffin on oneself." Gideon slammed the lid behind him. "Oh, well, I look to you to protect me."

"Don't count on it."

"But I most certainly do, Quinn. Otherwise, I'll drop Dobran and let you lug him out yourself." Gideon reached for his phone. "And I think those sirens are closer..."

———

ROBAKU

It was done.

Eve was breathing heavily, as if she'd been running.

She was shaking from exhaustion.

But you didn't beat me, you son of a bitch.

No, he wasn't quite done. But only the eyes were left to insert. The eyes were always the last step in completing a reconstruction.

Her hands were trembling as she reached for her eye case.

"Eve?" Jill was beside her. "Can I help you now? You don't look so good."

"Tired..." Eye case. "I have to get the eye case. We can't look at him until I put in the eyes."

"I won't look at him. I know this choice is as important to you as the sculpting itself." She gave Eve the eye case and opened the lid. "Which ones?"

"Brown. We'll try brown first. Brown eyes always predominate." She took out the right eye and carefully put it into the socket. She didn't look at the face, her gaze fixed only on that dark, shiny eye. "I think it's time you got that photo, Jill."

"I do, too." Jill squeezed Eve's shoulder. "I'll be right back. Put in the other eye."

Eve was already doing it. She carefully inserted the left eye.

Anger.

Screw you. I've *done* it.

"Here it is." Jill handed her the blown-up photo. "May I look now? I don't need the photo. I know what the son of a bitch looks like."

"Go ahead." She forced herself to look down at the features of the man in the photo. She felt a ripple of shock as she gazed into those dark eyes so much like the ones she'd just inserted. The shape of the orbital cavities were identical to the ones she had just created. Varak? It must be Varak. What other features were the same? She identified the curve of the cheekbone immediately. She remembered those bold, Slavic cheekbones. She couldn't take her eyes from the photo, caught by the sheer power of that face. Dominance. Power. Intensity. And darkness, so much darkness.

"Eve," Jill said gently.

Eve glanced up from the photo. "You should be relieved. It has to be him. It was lucky that I was able to repair those orbital—"

"Eve. Look at him."

Eve's gaze followed Jill's to the reconstruction.

She stiffened. Her hand was shaking as she reached for her phone. "I've got to call Joe."

———◆———

ASARTI

Joe's phone was vibrating in his pocket.

Not now. Later.

He couldn't answer it. He was almost at the end of the tunnel. He could see Sebak ahead, rolling aside a large boulder.

"No!" Joe called. "Don't go out there yet. We don't know what's happening. This might be too easy. It doesn't take a mental giant to figure out that there might be a back way out of that gallery. Explosives. Fire. Then someone waits to see who goes running. Let me take a look." He pushed Dobran at Gideon and strode to the opening. Shrubs. A thin stand of trees. A stretch of lawn that led to the road several yards away. As he watched, he saw their driver, Nassem, pull to a stop at the curb of that road.

No sentries. No police. No fire trucks. They all seemed to be at the front of the house, where he could hear sirens, shouts, breaking windows.

"Safe?" Gideon was beside him.

"How the hell do I know? Probably not." Joe's gaze was scanning the trees. "But it's safer than any other option."

"What are you doing to me?" Dobran had raised his head and was staring blearily at Joe. His voice was slurred. "You won't get away with this." He saw Sebak a few feet away. "Call the guards. Why are you just standing there?"

"You said you'd keep him away from me," Sebak said to Joe. "He saw me with you. Knock him out or something."

"Sorry," Gideon said. "With the drugs, he's handicapped enough. Yes or no, Quinn?"

"Yes. But you head for the car and let me follow. Zigzag. Don't give anyone a good shot. I'll cover you." He unlocked Sebak's manacles, then pulled out his gun and pointed it at him. "Help him get Dobran to the road. If you cause us any trouble, I'll put a bullet in you, Sebak." His gaze was scanning the trees. "Go!"

Gideon moved. Joe stood in the shadows for an instant, letting his vision become accustomed to the dark as Gideon and Sebak streaked toward the car. No one on the grounds or behind the trees. What about those upper branches? If he were a sniper, that's where he would be.

But a sniper would now have to change positions because he had a prey constantly moving in a zigzag pattern.

Watch.

Look for any motion.

Which tree?

A rustle in the leaves of the oak tree.

Joe swung his gun to cover it.

An owl flew out of the branches.

But something nearby might have startled it.

The pine next to the oak.

A rifle barrel aiming, then leveling.

Shit!

Joe was aiming even as he ran toward the tree.

His shot was only a second behind that of the sniper.

That second was enough, dammit. He heard Sebak scream with terror as he watched the sniper plummet from the tree to the ground.

Joe barely glanced at the man's bloody skull as he tore across the grass toward Gideon, who was kneeling beside Dobran.

Gideon looked up at him and shook his head. "Head shot. Dead. Either the shooter was good, or I wasn't zigzagging at my top potential."

Joe muttered a curse. "He was good, and there's no doubt Dobran was the target. It was no random shot. He was being slow and careful, or I would have seen him before I did. And I went for the head. So I can't even question him."

"Then may I suggest we get out of here?" Gideon asked. "With all that noise going on in the front, I doubt if anyone heard the shots, but it's best not to risk it." He glanced at Sebak, who was curled up, frozen, a few yards away. "What do we do with him?"

"Take him with us," Joe said curtly as he turned and ran toward the car. "You're right, we have to get back to Robaku. We came up almost empty with Dobran. I'll let Novak question Sebak and see what else he can drag out of him. And as soon as we get back to the plane, I want you to call Novak and tell him to find a way to get those security videos out of the gallery museum before the police yank them and get around to scanning them. The last thing we need is for anyone to know we were here if they didn't know already. There has to be a reason why there was only one sniper waiting here for the rats to run out of the trap. We've got to have time to put everything together."

"You're calling me a rat?" Gideon jerked Sebak to his feet and pushed him toward the car. "Most unkind and inaccurate, Quinn. I've been more a beast of burden tonight..."

———◆———

Joe glanced at his phone the moment they were a few miles away from Asarti.

Eve.

He muttered a curse as he punched in the return. "What's wrong?"

"That's what I was about to ask you. Why didn't you answer me?"

"I was involved. Things didn't go as expected. Are you all right?"

"No." She went on quickly: "I'm okay. It just doesn't seem as if anything is all right at the moment. I just finished the reconstruction. I thought it was going to be fine, that we'd gotten lucky." She paused, then said shakily, "I was wrong. It isn't Varak."

"No, it isn't," Joe said. "Look, I have to get off the line, you stay where you are until I get back there. We'll be boarding Gideon's plane in another fifteen minutes. Let me talk to Jill."

"Why?"

"Because I don't want to relay a message through you. I have a few orders to give, and you might phrase them as requests. They are *not* requests."

Silence.

"You weren't surprised about Varak, were you? Why not?"

"Not now. You'll know everything I do as soon as I get back there. Until then, all I want is to make certain you're safe. Let me talk to Jill."

Silence.

Then Jill's voice on the line. "What's happening? Eve is upset enough without having you worry her."

"Does Novak know about the reconstruction yet?"

"No, Eve wanted you to know first. I'll call him when she hangs up from you."

"No, you will not. Novak doesn't know until I'm there to control him."

"Control? Novak? And he deserves to know. He's been in this from the beginning."

"The only one who deserves to know is Eve. But I'll probably need the two of you to get her out of this nightmare, so you'll both know as much as I do once I'm certain that I can trust Novak. He's entirely too accustomed to running the entire show, and I won't risk Eve because he has some plan I don't know about."

"He wouldn't risk her."

"And I don't trust either of you, so how would I know? We'll discuss it when I get back. Until then, no one finds out that the reconstruction is done. Eve is still working on it. As long as no one knows there's a weapon to be wielded, then no choices will be made that might put a bull's-eye on her chest."

"I won't lie to him."

"That's up to you, but if you ever want me to trust you as Eve appears to do, you'll handle it so that only you will have the responsibility. You *will* do this, Jill."

Silence. "I'll consider it."

"No, you'll keep her *safe,* and when I get there, we'll let Novak join the party. I'll see you in a couple hours, Jill." He cut the connection.

He glanced at Gideon. "Any comment?"

He shrugged. "Not unless you expect a vote of approval. I'm playing this straight down the middle. From your point of view, you might even be right about Novak. He does have an obsession about Varak that might lead him to be a little impetuous." Gideon looked him in the eye. "But then so do I. That doesn't mean I'd do anything that would hurt Eve. I don't believe he would either. But you'll have to make up your own mind. I won't get in your way as long as you don't put obstacles in my path." He smiled faintly. "It was an interesting evening. You do keep things moving, Quinn..."

———◆———

"He knew that it wasn't Varak," Eve said, as Jill handed her phone back to her. "Something happened there tonight."

"Well, we obviously won't know what it was until he gets here," Jill said sharply. "He could have spent the time he used trying to intimidate me on telling us. But evidently he didn't want to do that. And something pretty important happened tonight with us, too." She shook her head. "Sorry. I'm a little annoyed with him."

"He told you that you couldn't tell Novak," Eve said.

"Novak has a right to know. He's not going to run out and start some kind of bizarre offensive just because we're certain."

"We might be certain, but proving it is a different matter. We always knew that would be true, Jill." She looked at the reconstruction. Why could she still not shake this feeling of darkness and hate as she gazed at the skull? "And I can see why Joe might not want to jeopardize either my life or freedom."

"Do you think I can't?" Jill grimaced. "But he's put me on the spot by not letting me tell Novak. We've been on the same team, and now I'm not supposed to trust him? At least he said that it would only be until he got back here."

"You're going to do it?" Eve gazed at her in disbelief. Then she smiled faintly. "I don't believe it. You're angry with him. Why are you doing it?"

"He offered me a price I couldn't refuse. The bastard said it would help him to trust me." She got to her feet. "But I don't intend to lie to Novak. It will only take Gideon a couple hours to get Quinn here, and you're not going to be finished with this reconstruction until he walks in that door." She took out Eve's computer and opened it. "You said there were all kinds of computer details and comparisons to complete a reconstruction job. Sit down and start doing them."

Eve slowly dropped back down on her stool. To her amazement, she couldn't smother her smile. Only moments before, she had been swirling downward through confusion and terror, yet now she was feeling an instant of welcome humor. "And what if I finish before Joe shows up?"

"I've got it covered. I'll be nagging you and asking questions to make certain that computer reconstruction will have so many minute details that it will take you twice as long as it usually does." She opened her own computer. "Though I might annoy you a little."

Eve brought up her forensic programming. "And all to keep from lying to Novak?"

"And to stop your idiotically stubborn husband from saying I didn't obey his damn orders. He said to keep you safe and not tell Novak." She was focusing on the photo. "It's up to me if I do it in a way that may please both of them . . . " She suddenly looked up at Eve. "Do you think I'm being manipulative again?"

"Perhaps. But I can see it's sheer self-defense." And it would keep Eve busier until Joe did walk in that door. She had been frightened when he hadn't called her back, and she didn't want to think about what he'd been doing during those minutes. "I'll permit myself to be manipulated as long as I'm aware it's happening."

"It just seemed easier."

"You sound like my son, Michael. He's always certain everything would be easier if he did it."

"I'll take that. You love the kid." Jill looked down at the photo again. "Now I'll get back to doing a facial analysis, while you get busy with the victim."

Victim.

Eve felt a ripple of shock at the word.

All the time she had been working on this reconstruction, she had never consciously thought of this skull as that of a victim. The possibility had always been there, of course. But she had only felt the darkness, the antagonism, the hate. Even now, it was difficult to feel sympathy for this man who had died in Varak's place. Split personality, Jill had called it, when Eve had given the name Varak to the reconstruction. Was it the reason that lingering darkness remained?

Or was it the ferocious anger that his identity had been stolen as well as his life taken from him in this horrible way?

Either way, she had to change how she thought about him.

Not a monster but a victim.

CHAPTER

12

Joe and Gideon walked into the museum two hours and fifteen minutes later, followed closely by a very grim Novak.

"Surprise. Surprise," Novak said sarcastically as he glanced at the completed reconstruction, then at Jill. "At least a surprise for me until Quinn showed up here fifteen minutes ago and told me. But I appear to be the only one who wasn't on the need-to-know list."

"I really just finished his computer input ten minutes ago," Eve found herself saying quickly. "Stop glaring at Jill, Novak."

"But you knew two hours ago it wasn't Varak." He made an impatient gesture. "I'll deal with that later."

"No, you won't," Eve said. "My job. My decision." She turned to Joe. "How are you? I was worried. What happened in Cairo?"

"Not much that was good," Joe said. "Except that we might have acquired some valuable information to coordinate with what you found out about the ID of the reconstruction."

"But you got Dobran killed," Novak said bitterly. "He's the only witness we knew about, and he's dead. And we needed his information. I'll interrogate Sebak, but from what Gideon told me, I doubt if I'll get anything. By all means, tell them what happened at Asarti. It will be interesting to have all the cards on the table for a change."

"I'm sure it would be a great change for you," Joe said coolly. "That's why I didn't want you to know anything before I could be here to keep an eye on what you were doing." He turned to Eve. "I did get Dobran killed. As I said, there was as much bad as good that happened at Asarti." He spent the next minutes filling her in on the events of the last twenty-four hours, and ended with, "And I don't give a damn about Dobran's death, we can work around it. What I'm worried about is that whoever staged those explosions and the sniper attack will probably know in a matter of hours who was taking Dobran out of that château tonight."

"What?"

"Dobran had to be the target. We were careful, and no one knew we were in the château. It had to be a random accident that we were there at the same time as the attack. But I killed that sniper, and once they find him, they'll look for more answers."

"And who are 'they'?" Jill asked.

Joe's gaze returned to the reconstruction. "You tell me. Someone who wanted to eliminate Dobran as a witness but also wanted something Dobran had in his possession that could be plucked from his gallery in the confusion of the fire."

"But why will they know you were there?" Eve asked.

"Sebak said there was video surveillance in the gallery. Gideon was able to eliminate the cameras everywhere else but not in the gallery. And we were in too much of a hurry to get out of there with Dobran to stop and disable them."

"Amateurs," Novak said sourly.

"Walk in our shoes," Joe said curtly. "I needed Dobran. You'd do the same."

Novak was silent. "Maybe."

Joe turned back to Eve. "And once I'm identified, it will only be a short time before they'll make the connection to you. The first thing we've got to do is get you out of here."

"Do we?" Eve had known this was coming. It was Joe's protective instinct at work again. "I don't think so. Not the first thing, Joe. The first thing we have to do is figure out what happened and why. I'm not going to run away and hide from being arrested by the U.N., or whoever killed Dobran, until I know what I'm facing."

"I can take care of that once I know you're safe."

"No, Joe," she said quietly.

"Dammit, Eve." His eyes were blazing. "Dobran was a witness, and he's dead. Tonight, you proved with that reconstruction that Varak's death was a big lie. Do you think they'll let you live?"

"I haven't proved anything as long as the courts believe in the DNA. Dobran is dead, and I'd bet any lab evidence has been destroyed by now." She held up her hand as he opened his lips. "I'm just saying that we might have time to figure this out because they'll have to figure out what we know, too. I have no intention of getting myself killed." She smiled at him. "So back off and stop pushing. Now show me that statue. That could be very interesting." She looked at Gideon. "You really think it had to belong to Zahra Kiyani?"

He nodded. "Everything Dobran said indicated that it had to be her." His lips twisted. "Particularly the part where he called her a bitch. That definitely struck home." He watched as Joe dug into his backpack and pulled out the gold statue. "And it's the statue of the first Kiya. Who else would have it?"

"Who, indeed?" Jill came closer as Eve took the statue from Joe. Her gaze was lit with eagerness and curiosity as she stared down at it. "And why would she have it?" she murmured. "It's beautiful, isn't it? It must have nearly killed Zahra to have to give it up." She reached down and traced the script. "Great Beloved Wife..." She glanced at Gideon. "She never mentioned this statue to you?"

"There were things that she didn't confide. I imagine a multimillion-dollar artifact might be included in that range since she wasn't sure I was totally besotted with her." He glanced at the statue. "She should have told me about it. The fact that she had it would have definitely sparked my interest."

"She told Dobran that she had a lot of other artifacts. That it wasn't going to be the only payment," Joe said.

"I remember you said that." Eve was still looking down at the statue. Exquisite. And the idea that it might have been created in the court of Cleopatra VII added to the mystique. "Which leads us to the distinct possibility that the treasure that Kiya mentioned in her journal did exist, might still exist, and Zahra has it in her possession." She frowned. "And she still gave him this one artifact, which must have meant a good deal to her, to get him to falsify that Varak DNA."

"And in the end, that's the only thing of real importance," Novak said curtly. "All this talk of artifacts and Zahra Kiyani's obsession with them is bullshit. If Zahra is guilty of being an accomplice to Varak, then it doesn't matter whether she did a payoff at a bank in the Grand Caymans or with these artifacts. It means she's as guilty as that son of a bitch, and we have to go after her."

"No one is denying that," Jill said. "I just find it interesting as a storyteller that the story appears to be growing in scope." She met his eyes. "And I don't agree that it's not important. The fact that Zahra has a secret treasure cache worth millions, possibly billions, that she can tap at any time, automatically furnishes her with weapons. For one thing, it could have lured Varak into her camp. And since everything to do with Kiya is important to Zahra, it has also somehow become woven into this terrible connection to Varak. That makes it very important, Novak. You're just still pissed off that I didn't let you know the reconstruction was finished."

Silence. "Yes, I am." He turned to Joe. "When Gideon called me from the plane, I arranged for a couple agents to go to Asarti and blend in and see what was going on out there." He paused. "And how we can manage to cover your tracks. I should get a report soon."

"It better be very soon. Or everything may come crashing down on us." He looked at the reconstruction. "Do we agree that Zahra Kiyani has to be working hand in glove with Varak to maintain the lie that he's dead? The question is why, and how far it goes." He paused. "And how far it went while the war was still going on. If Varak was allowing her to use him as a double agent to defeat Botzan, it would make sense why her casualties were so slim."

Gideon gave a low whistle. "Oh, I can see that happening."

"But where is Varak right now?" Jill asked quietly. "Would he run the risk of staying in Maldara?"

"Questions," Eve said wearily. "So many questions." She looked at Joe. "But we still have time to get the *answers*. Let's just take a deep breath, then go after them."

"We'll see," Joe said. "As long as I don't see any sign of your becoming a target while you're doing deep-breathing exercises." He glanced at Novak. "And as long as I get that report from your people at Asarti right away."

"You'll get it," Novak said. "And now I'm going to go interrogate Sebak. I'll let you know if I find out anything more from him. It's not professional to hide information from people with the same goals." He turned and headed for the door. "You might keep that in mind, Quinn."

"I will," Joe said. "As long as you set the example." He turned to Gideon as Novak left the room. "One more thing. I want to know everything Zahra Kiyani does from now on. I need to know it all. You're familiar with the palace and know her routine better than anyone else, so you're the best one to do it."

"Lucky me. You do realize that my face is also on those videotapes? It's only a matter of time before Zahra realizes I'm not only an inconvenience but a threat." He shrugged. "So I guess I'd better get busy doing the advance prep work we need before she decides to target me." He strolled toward the door. "But you're right, I still have a few contacts in her personal entourage, and I'm very familiar with the gardens and every room in that overdone monstrosity of a presidential palace."

"Not only the bedroom?" Jill asked dryly.

"You underestimate me. I never limit myself when it comes to keeping a relationship fresh." He paused at the door, and said soberly, "Zahra's very complicated, but you can count on her striking fast and hard when she decides she's being threatened." His gaze went to the statue in Eve's hands. "And that's a threat, Eve."

The next moment, he was gone.

Eve drew a shaky breath as she shook her head. "Well, that appears clear enough." Her hands tightened on the statue for an instant before she handed it back to Joe. Why was her hand shaking? The statue wasn't that heavy. But it seemed heavy. "But I can't let myself worry about Zahra Kiyani. I created that reconstruction for only one reason, and that was to find out if Varak was still out there." She wearily rubbed her temple. "And he's alive, Joe. I haven't been able to really comprehend that yet. He's out there . . . waiting."

"Because you're so exhausted that you can scarcely sit on that stool," Joe said roughly, his gaze raking her face. "You've pushed yourself until you're ready to collapse." He turned to Jill. "Get out of here. Leave us alone."

"Joe, she didn't do anything," Eve said quickly.

"I know that. Not this time," Joe said. "And no one would have been able to stop you. I've been there. But now all the adrenaline is gone, and you're crashing." He glanced at Jill. "You did as good as you could under the circumstances. I just want you out so that she can draw a breath without looking or thinking about Varak for the next few hours." He stepped toward Eve and pulled her to her feet. "Come on. I promise you that we're on our way to getting the son of a bitch." He slipped his arm around her waist. "We'll just take a little time together now, okay?"

"Do I have a choice?" His arm felt strong and warm around her, and she felt secure for the first time since he'd left her so many hours ago. "I guess I do, and I choose you, Joe." He was leading her toward her cot. "I'll always choose you."

"Because you're very smart." His lips brushed her temple. "Smarter than Varak or Zahra and sometimes even me. That's why you're going to rest now." He glanced over his shoulder at Jill, who was on her way out the door. "See to it. You understand?"

Jill nodded, gazing thoughtfully at Joe, then Eve. "I believe I'm beginning to understand quite a bit." She turned back and opened the door. "Don't worry. She won't be disturbed. I'll take care of it."

———————

KIYANI PRESIDENTIAL PALACE

He wasn't answering her!

Zahra gazed furiously down at her blank screen. She'd texted him twice, and he was ignoring her. Arrogant bastard.

She texted again.

DID YOU GET IT? WHEN CAN I PICK IT UP?

No answer.

YOU SAID I COULD HAVE IT BACK TONIGHT. WHERE IS IT?

At last an answer.

THERE'S A PROBLEM. I'LL TEXT YOU LATER.

She stiffened. No, this couldn't be happening. He had promised her!

I WON'T TOLERATE THIS. I'VE BEEN WAITING TOO LONG. I WANT IT NOW.

The answer came with swift brutality.

YOU'LL GET WHAT I CHOOSE TO GIVE YOU WHEN I CHOOSE TO DO IT.

The screen went blank.

Rage.

She closed her eyes, trying to subdue the anger. This was her fault, she had allowed him to intimidate her until he thought she was just another one of his cowed whores. And it had come down to this indignity.

It was over. She would not let it go on!

"Dalai!" She got to her feet as the maid came running out of the anteroom. "Come with me. We're going out."

———◆———

Over an hour later, Dalai was driving Zahra off the main road and through the thick foliage of the jungle that surrounded and hid the armed compound and large house.

Zahra phoned as she got closer. "I'll be there in a few minutes. Call off your men, Varak."

"I've known exactly where you were since you got off the road. What a fool you are. I'm tempted to sit here and watch them blow you to bits."

"You won't do that. I'm too valuable to you. I'm not afraid of you." That was a lie. There were moments when she was afraid, but not of physical abuse. She was afraid of his reckless egotism and his power to send all her plans toppling. "So threaten all those idiots around you who can't see through you. I'm done with bowing down at your altar to feed that ego." She hung up.

Five minutes later, Dalai drove her up to the gates of the stockade, where Lon Markel was standing guard. Zahra leaned forward and nodded curtly at him. "Open those gates. I have to see him, Markel."

"Did he give you permission?" Markel asked with the hint of a sneer. "You know that he—"

"Open those gates!" Markel was *her* agent, only on loan to Varak, and he was daring to question her! It just showed how much respect had been stolen from her by that son of a bitch. "Now!"

He shrugged, opened the gates, and stood aside.

Two minutes later, Dalai screeched to a stop before the long porch of the house.

"Do you wish me to come in, madam?" Dalai asked. She was tense with nervousness as she watched the door open and Varak come out on the porch.

She was actually trembling, Zahra noticed impatiently. You'd think she'd have learned to control herself by now. But just one glimpse of Varak, and she was falling apart. "I haven't decided." She got out of the car. "Stay here, I'll let you know." She strode up the steps, her gaze on Varak. He was staring straight at her, and she could see why a weakling like Dalai might be afraid of him. The expensive plastic surgery for which Zahra had paid an enormous fee might disguise his features, but those dark eyes were piercing, and the power and ferocity were unmistakable. His black hair had been dyed to a pale sandy shade and allowed to grow longer than his usual cropped cut because she had thought it might soften his appearance. Perhaps it did at first glance, but that was also a failure in Zahra's opinion. All these temporary measures were only safe as long as everyone was certain Varak was dead.

"What do you think you're doing?" Varak said harshly. "I told you not to come here again. You could have led them right to me. People are always watching you."

"And I'm supposed to pay any attention to what you tell me to do?" She stopped before him, glaring. "And I'm no fool. I went out the secret panel, and I leave a car parked in a garage down the street. No one saw me."

"I know they didn't, or I wouldn't have let you come near here. Do you think I didn't know you'd do something like this?" He turned and walked back into the house. "Come in. I don't want my men seeing your tantrum." His lips twisted. "Or I'd have to either beat you or cut your throat. I don't allow myself to show weakness to them as I've demonstrated to you on many occasions." He poured himself a drink from the bar just inside the door. "You like that about me, don't you, Zahra?"

"I like to see power at work. It amused me to watch them grovel." She added through set teeth, "But I'm not amused now, Varak, and I won't grovel to you. What are you trying to do? Give me my statue."

"I'm trying to give it to you, bitch," he said. "I told you that there was a problem. I'm not playing mind games with you." He drank down his whiskey. "And I have more to worry about than your fancy statue. Something weird happened at Asarti last night that might be more important to both of us."

"Nothing is more important. Give me my statue."

"I'd have to find it first. Because it wasn't at Asarti."

She went still. "What?"

"Interested now?" Varak asked. "You weren't interested in anything about the way I was going to get the statue back. You just snapped your fingers and said you wanted it."

"You said you'd get it back from Dobran a few days after the skull was identified as you. You *promised* me. But he still has it."

"He has nothing. Dobran is dead. I had a sniper set up to take him out last night."

"Good. Then why don't I have my statue?"

"You were going to have it," he said harshly. "I was tired of hearing you nag me. I thought I'd get you off my back about the statue in case I had to go to Robaku and take out that Duncan woman in the next couple days. I knew I couldn't trust you to do it."

"My statue," she reminded him.

"I was going to eliminate Dobran as a witness and take the statue at the same time. I sent in a team to bomb the place and start fires that would block all the entrances and force them to use the one through the gallery. Dobran liked that statue, too, and I knew he and Sebak would go after it and out the gallery exit if they were forced to run. Then all I had to do was put several of my men with the fire and police departments who answered the alarm. They'd only have to break into the gallery and find a way to grab the statue and smuggle it out of the château. Not a difficult job in all the confusion that would be going on." He poured himself another drink. "It should have worked. I should have rid myself of Dobran, and you would have had your statue."

"Should?"

"I got Dobran." He lifted his glass to his lips. "Unfortunately, Nolan, my sniper, was also taken out by someone equally efficient." He sipped his whiskey. "And I just heard from the team who went into the gallery to get your damn statue that it had already been stolen. No sign of other thefts, just that one artifact. Unless Dobran decided to sell it."

"Not *my* statue." Her eyes were blazing. "Stolen? What really happened to it? Dobran loved it, he wouldn't have let it be stolen, and certainly not purchased."

"Maybe not. I'm leaning toward agreeing with you. We have the murder of my very talented sniper to consider. As I said, something weird happened up there last night. We might not have been the only ones who were after Dobran, and that's much more threatening than anyone's taking your statue."

"Then you should have gotten all this taken care of before anyone else had a chance to go after Dobran or my statue. I told you enough times that I wanted it done."

"Forget the statue!" He suddenly hurled his glass across the room to crash against the wall. Then his hands were around her throat. "You listen to me," he hissed. "You're not stupid. I wouldn't have gotten on your merry-go-round if I'd thought you were. Now stop acting as if you're an imbecile. I might have saved us both by taking out Dobran last night, but it might be too late if someone is onto us and got to him first. We've got to think about saving our asses."

His grip was bruising her throat. For an instant, she was feeling panic mixed with her fury. He always liked to hurt her. She knew how brutal he could be. "Let me go, Varak. How dare you speak to me this way. Stupid? I'm the one who had you brought to me when you were only one of Botzan's dirty mercenaries. I gave you the chance to come out of this war alive and richer than you ever dreamed." She stared him in the eye. "I've protected you, hidden you. I've done everything for you, and I've only asked you to do a few small things to keep our heads above water during a difficult time."

"A few 'small' things?" His thumbs pressed harder into her neck. "Play a double game and attack when and where you told me? Help you to set up your fancy image with the U.N., so they'd choose you to run this son of a bitch of a country?" He bent his head and his tongue touched the hollow of her throat. He whispered, "And make certain that papa dearest was killed in a timely manner so that you could take over the presidency?"

She inhaled sharply. "I did what was necessary. He wouldn't listen to me. He wanted to negotiate peace with them. You made no objection at the time." She went on the attack. "And as long as you continue to cooperate, I'll protect you...provided you protect me. But I won't let you destroy what I'm building. I'll get you out of Maldara as soon as it's safe. Then all you'll have to do is arrange to move my treasure safely out of Maldara for me, and I'll give you the share I promised."

"If it even exists; you've never let me see it." His fingers pressed harder. "I'm beginning to doubt you, Zahra. You don't want that to happen."

"Don't be foolish. It would be dangerous to take you there. I showed you the Great Beloved Wife, didn't I? Dobran jumped at getting it. You could see how valuable it is." She met his eyes. "I promise that as soon as I have the treasure secure, I'll buy you an island somewhere, and you can set up your own little kingdom."

"You have it all planned." He dropped his hands from around her throat. "But it's my decision, and an island sounds boring. I liked the life I was living before you dropped into my world. When we split that treasure, I'll look at my options."

That was what she was beginning to fear. She reached up and massaged the bruised flesh of her throat. The prick had hurt her this time. "I just want to keep you safe."

"I'm touched, Zahra." His lips twisted. "But you'd do better to think about keeping us both safe by helping me find out what happened at Asarti."

"You said you'd take care of that." She paused. "You really think that it might be more than just a theft? That someone knew that Dobran did the DNA?" She was getting more nervous as she thought about it. "It might not be so bad. No one could trace the statue to me. I took it from the treasure."

"You're back to covering your ass."

She made an impatient gesture. "What are you going to do?"

"My team at Asarti who slipped in with the firemen haven't been able to get the security videotapes of the gallery yet. They'll go back later and try again. That might tell us something. But that's not all. Hassan Sebak has disappeared. We need to track him down."

"Sebak didn't know about you. I made it a condition that the DNA remain absolutely confidential." She shrugged. "But, by all means, go after him. He might have stolen my statue, and all this worry might be for nothing. Besides, we have to remain safe."

"I notice which one you put first," he said sarcastically. "How nice of you to give me permission. But I've already set it in motion." He turned away and stripped off his shirt. "Now take off your clothes and lie down on that couch."

She had half expected it. Her resistance always aroused a sexual response in Varak. On occasion, she had actually used it to stir the passion hotter. But that was when she had attempted to use sex to bind them tighter together, when she'd had hopes that Varak might be someone she could control as she hadn't been able to control Gideon. But lately she had realized that Varak would not be controlled either, and the sex was only to subdue her.

He snapped his fingers and repeated mockingly, "Take off your clothes, Zahra."

Arrogant bastard. She shook her head. "I have to get back to the palace."

"But our agreement is that I'm never to be without amusement out here in the wilds. Have you forgotten?"

"I send you women to amuse you all the time."

"But I'm bored with them. They're whores, and nothing is new or exciting. No matter what I do to them, they just accept it." He smiled. "While you accept nothing without a battle. I want you to scream for me."

For a minute, she was tempted to pit her skill against his. But it was a struggle she was never sure she could win with him. She couldn't afford to lose when so much was at stake. "Not now." She turned to go. "But you enjoyed Dalai the last few times you had her. Fear is also exciting for you. I brought her with me in case I needed to negotiate." She looked at him over her shoulder. "I imagine you have no trouble making *her* scream?"

He smiled. "No trouble at all. She's like a startled doe most of the time. But you've trained her well, she never says no. Though I always prefer your services."

"She'll have to do. Don't damage her too badly. She's valuable to me. And I'll need her back by tomorrow."

She opened the door and motioned for Dalai to come into the house.

The girl was already tensing as she got out of the car, Zahra noticed. She had gone pale and was looking beyond Zahra at the open door.

Panic.

No, Varak would have no problem making her scream.

———◆———

ROBAKU

Jill called Novak the moment she walked out of the museum.

He didn't answer.

She called again.

No answer.

And then again.

He answered curtly, "What do you want, Jill?"

"I need to talk to you. Quinn just kicked me out of the museum, and I can't just sit and do nothing. Where are you?"

"In the village. Hajif set me up with a vacant hut to use as an office, and I'm trying to coordinate the men I sent to Asarti to gather information."

"Can I help?"

"No."

Time to eat crow. "I realize you're pissed off at me, and you have a right to be."

"Damn straight."

"Quinn doesn't trust you. Not me either, but I'm working on it." She paused. "And I knew it would only be a couple hours delay. It didn't seem too bad. What can I do to make it right with you?"

He didn't answer.

"What can I do?" she repeated.

"The eternal question with you." He was suddenly walking toward her out of the brush and turning off his phone. "You should have stuck with Quinn. As you said, I'm more pissed off with you than he is right now."

"It wasn't really Quinn, it was Eve. I had to balance what she—" He had put his fingers over her lips, and she looked up at him, startled.

"Hush," he said. "I'm trying very hard not to confuse this anger with anything more emotional or sexual. But since it's always there, it's a factor. Along with the fact that I find myself oddly hurt that you didn't trust me to handle this situation. That's very weird in itself. But it will help if you don't make excuses or tell me you owe me anything." He took his fingers away. "Now why did Quinn kick you out?"

Her lips still felt warm and tingling even though his touch was gone. "He wanted her to rest." She moistened her lips. "I was just another disturbance."

"Yes, you are." His lips twisted. "So he tossed you to me?"

"No, he wouldn't care where I went. She's the only thing important to him. It's kind of nice. Warm..." She met his gaze. "It was my choice to come to you, Novak. Because I do trust you." She added simply, "How could I do anything else after what you've done for me? No matter how much you want your own way, you'd never do anything to hurt me. I'll always come to you if you'll let me."

He was silent. "Oh, shit." He took a step toward her. Then he stopped abruptly. "You leave yourself wide open, dammit. You haven't been paying any attention to what I've been saying to you, have you?"

"Sure I have." She smiled with an effort. "Some of it sort of scared me. I'm really not the kind of person anyone would obsess about. I don't know what I'd do with you if I didn't believe you'd probably change your mind before all this is over."

"I can offer suggestions," he said thickly. "And you must be wrong because the obsession is definitely there." He paused. "But there's nothing I'd do to you that should scare you."

"You're back to walking wounded again?" She shook her head in exasperation. "For Pete's sake, it's not about sex." Though that was patently untrue. She couldn't get near him without this feeling of heat and electricity. She drew a deep breath. "Is it okay if we don't talk about this? I just wanted you to know that I do trust you. And it's important that you not shut me out of anything when everything seems to be exploding around us."

"Heaven forbid that you miss one single minute of any combustion coming our way," he said dryly.

She nodded. "Heaven forbid," she echoed quietly. "It's my story, my responsibility, and if I don't tell it, then it might not get told. And I brought Eve into this, and now Quinn is involved." She made a face. "You might say I even brought you into this, Novak."

"The hell you did."

"I came to you. Just as I'm coming to you now. You turned me down then. Don't turn me down this time."

He swore under his breath. "Low blow, Jill."

She nodded. "Yes. But I speak fluent Egyptian and Arabic. Can't you use me to find out what's happening in Cairo?"

"Possibly."

"Novak."

"Hell, yes, I'll use you," he said roughly. "Haven't I done that from the beginning? Quinn's right, we've got to either eliminate or delay anyone's finding out who killed that sniper and was in the château tonight. And we need time to get a plan together. Which means we have to get our hands on those gallery videotapes. I'll see if I can patch you into the local Cairo police from the Museum of Egyptian Antiquities, and you can express concern that some of the antiquities on loan to Dobran might have also been stolen. In short, lie through your teeth and work your magic."

She nodded, frowning thoughtfully. "I can do that. But it might be better if I contact a friend of mine, Matt Kimbro, who's a reporter for the *Cairo Messenger* and also does freelance. He knows most of the players in the government and police department. I worked with him during the nine months when I was covering riots in Cairo. He's been there for years, and he knows where all the bodies are buried." She grimaced. "And believe me, in Cairo, that's a hell of a lot of bodies. He owes me a favor, and I could ask him to call a few people and maybe follow up with the police and security company." She shrugged. "Or I could do both."

"Yes, you could." His lips were quirking. "And probably will." His smile faded. "And I'm glad there's someone who owes you a favor instead of your being obsessed with payback."

"I'm not obsessed, there just has to be a code, or nothing makes sense." She was taking out her phone and checking the directory. "And in my profession, I've found it's always more valuable to have someone owe me. It just didn't turn out that way with you."

"And why does this Kimbro owe you?"

"I'll never tell." She grinned as she started to punch in Kimbro's number. "Because that would be breaking the code."

"I'll find out, you know," he said softly. "I can always find out whatever I need to find out. And there's nothing I'm not going to know about you, Jill."

"The CIA showing all its black hat–white hat power. You have a tendency to surround and conquer." She met his eyes. "Did it occur to you that might be why you scare me? Who wants anyone to know everything about them? I'd feel smothered. Stay out of my private life, Novak."

He was silent. "I don't know if I can." He paused. "I'll have to see how it works out." He turned and headed back toward the village. "When you finish setting up Kimbro, come and let me know, and I'll give you something else to do. I wouldn't want to waste your talents."

———◆———

The long facial bones . . .

Not right. But so close.

Eve could see them before her even though her eyes were still shut. She moved restlessly on the cot as she realized how close . . . Just like the shape of those orbital cavities . . .

Too close.

It seemed impossible that all those details could be that identical and not actually be Varak. It didn't make sense, Eve thought frantically. Had she done something wrong? They all thought she was perfect. But she wasn't perfect, she could make mistakes. And what if Varak was the biggest mistake of her life? She had told them the reconstruction wasn't Varak, but the resemblance was too close. It didn't make sense. But what had she done wrong? Why had she made that mistake? Why were those orbital cavities—

"The brother!" Eve's lids flew open, and she sat bolt upright on the cot. "He has to be the brother."

"Shh, go back to sleep," Joe said. "Nightmare?"

"Only the same one that I've been living with while I've been doing this reconstruction. And I can't go back to sleep. The minute I woke up, I started to worry about the shape of his damn eyes." She threw aside the sheet and swung her feet to the floor. "When I was first looking at the photo of Varak, I thought that the reconstruction I had made had to be him. There were so many similarities. It was only when I actually compared them that I realized that I hadn't been working on Varak's skull." She was moving across the museum to her worktable. "But I got caught up in the computer verification; and then Jill was upset with what you were forcing her to do about Novak. Things kept getting in my way." She was dropping down on her stool and looking at the reconstruction. "And I didn't make the connection. I should have made the connection, Joe. It was stupid of me not to realize who he was."

"And it only took five hours of sleep to send the stupidity packing." Joe was on his feet and strolling toward her. "Before you start working again, don't you think you should put on some clothes?"

"I'm not going to work," she said absently. "I just wanted to take one more look at him. I was so scared, I'd made a mistake. There was all that darkness and anger... And the bone-structure similarities. If you compare it with the photo, you can see it."

"I'll accept your word for it." He put his hands on her shoulders as he stood behind her, gazing down at the reconstruction. "The brother? You think this was Varak's brother? He's never been mentioned. I don't remember his even having a brother."

"I didn't know either until Jill told me about him. He had no part in Varak's life after he was a teenager. He was Varak's younger brother, Oscar, and, as far as I know, they hadn't seen each other for years. He was afraid of him because he'd been bullied all his life." She shivered as she gazed at the reconstruction. "He had good reason to be afraid. There's nothing more cold-blooded than choosing your own brother to die in your place." She reached out and touched the orbital bone of the left eye with her finger. "But it was a clever choice. Not only was the bone structure similar, but even the DNA would have been similar if the minutest trace was found outside of Dobran's work. Insurance, Joe."

"You're fairly certain?"

"It's a very good bet." She looked up at him. "And that's going to help us, isn't it? We needed to find out who he was before we could claim he wasn't Varak. He was a murder victim, Joe. There's a chance that there might have been a witness to it. Or at least someone might have seen Varak with Oscar during the period right before his supposed death." She was trying to think of everything Jill had told her. "Johannesburg. His brother was supposed to have gone back home to Johannesburg after he split with Nils Varak. Can we trace him that way?"

"I'll trace him, you'll stay out of it." Joe held up his hand. "Look, you've done what you set out to do. No one is more dangerous than you to Varak now. You've shot holes in the fancy scenario he rigged up with Zahra Kiyani." He shook his head as she started to speak. "And don't tell me it doesn't mean anything if the courts accept the DNA over your work. It does mean something because you're so well respected. Why do you think Novak wanted you on his team? Jill might have wanted your expertise, but Novak knew that you could influence people and change minds. You'll stir up a hornet's nest, and Varak will come out and try to squash you before you do damage."

"But that's a good thing," she said quietly. "We want to bring him out, don't we? It will be easier for us."

"To use you as bait?" Joe shook his head. "Forget it. I want you out of Maldara. I'm going to send you to London and pull strings to surround you with every man from the Yard that I can beg or steal."

"I notice you say you're going to send me, not take me. Because you told me this had to be finished, didn't you? There's no way you're going to let Varak get away now that you know he's alive. You'll stay here and do what I should be doing while I'm palling around with all your buddies from Scotland Yard."

"It's the reasonable thing to do. You don't have to be here, Eve."

"No? I don't see it that way. I brought you here, Joe." She looked back at the reconstruction. "And *he* brought me. Jill thinks she's responsible for involving everyone in this nightmare, but it was Varak. Because he's alive, we're all swirling around him, drowning in what he is and what he's done. I won't go away and take a chance on letting him pull anyone else into that whirlpool." She smiled with an effort. "But you've convinced me how important I am, so I'll stay here at Robaku, where Novak and you can protect me." She paused. "Unless we can think of a way to use me with more efficiency."

"Eve."

"No, it's not done. *I'm* not done. I can't stir up any hornet's nest right now because if Varak doesn't go after me, he'll go on the run. We can't afford to have him do that, Joe. So I'll stay here and work on Mila, be a thorn in both Varak's and Zahra's asses, and we'll try to think of a better way to build a rat trap to catch them." She drew a deep breath and had to stop. This had been too painful. She always hated conflict with Joe when she knew it was pain and worry driving him. She had to get away from him and recover. She got to her feet. "And now I'll go get dressed. You're right, nudity lacks a certain dignity when I'll probably have to argue about this with Jill and Novak, too."

A muscle jerked in Joe's cheek. "Not Novak."

"We'll see." She headed for the bathroom. "I've been getting a different viewpoint about him lately. Jill trusts him."

"Eve," Joe said. "Don't do this."

She stopped at the door of the bathroom. "I know you're unhappy about it. But I can't do anything else." She opened the door, and added simply, "Because whenever I close my eyes, I see that schoolroom, Joe."

CHAPTER

13

Jill was waiting when Eve came out of the bathroom forty-five minutes later. She was staring at the reconstruction and looked up as Eve crossed the room toward her. "You really think it's the brother?"

"I do. I'm surprised you didn't think of it before I did. You're the storyteller. It's definitely a macabre twist on the story of Varak."

"It probably would have come to me eventually. I was just upset and a bit scattered at the time. But it does make sense."

"Now we have to find proof that Varak murdered his brother or try to discover when and where he disappeared. Hopefully, it will be about the time that helicopter exploded in the mountains."

"Quinn and Novak are already working on it. Dobran took a flight somewhere the day after he accepted that statue. It would be logical if it was to Johannesburg to examine and accept the body of Oscar Varak and prepare it for the DNA implant," Jill said. "Why do you think I'm here? Quinn came storming down to the village and told Novak that he had to put a trace on Varak's brother and determine if this is really him." She nodded at the reconstruction. "He wants all the puzzle pieces we have to be in place before anyone discovers that the skull is gone from that U.N. headquarters." She grimaced. "I got the impression he was trying desperately to stave off having you tossed in jail. I told him I wouldn't allow that to happen."

"If I remember correctly, you didn't give me the same promise," Eve said dryly. "You just said you'd be in the cell next to mine."

"Well, I didn't think that would go over well with him. He's still very tentative with me. Instead, I decided I'd come here and let Novak deal with him and see if you need any help."

"Only with information. What's been happening? It seems as if I slept for a long time."

"Not for a normal person." She shrugged. "I managed to get a reporter friend, Matt Kimbro, to go and squeeze information out of the local Cairo police. The police did collect all the security videos in the château, but they hadn't gotten around to viewing them yet. They're still in the evidence room."

Eve stiffened. "But they will view them. It's only a matter of time. And they'll find out it was Joe in that gallery."

"Maybe." She paused. "I told Kimbro it was important to me that I get hold of those gallery tapes. The evidence room might not be a problem for him if his contact is on duty. It's like the rest of the police department in Cairo. Bad and good. It's not that unusual for things to go missing...if the price is right. He said he'd let me know."

"A very good friend," Eve said. "To risk getting arrested."

"Yes. But he's smart, and I told him if it gets down to taking any serious chances, he's to call me, and I'll get him help. I'll go myself if necessary. Together, we'll be able to do it."

"And get yourself arrested, too?"

"We have to get those security tapes. It could hurt Quinn *and* you."

"Then let Novak go help your friend Kimbro."

"I will if it's more efficient. But Kimbro trusts me, and he was more likely to be accommodating if I was in the background. He's *my* friend, and he owes *me,* not Novak." She smiled. "And Kimbro might not need help. I told you, he's smart." She changed the subject. "Now, what other information do you need? Oh, Gideon has

already gone to the presidential palace in Jokan to see what information he can gather about Zahra Kiyani. That's all I know right now.
Sorry, more later."

"Nothing to be sorry about. It's fairly substantial." She was rifling
through her cabinet and pulling out the reconstruction she'd begun
on Mila. She carefully put the Varak reconstruction in the cabinet in
its place. "And certainly more productive than what I'll be doing."

"I can't believe that."

"Believe it," Eve said curtly. "Sitting here and working is the only
way I'll be able to keep Joe from going ballistic. He wanted me to fly
back to London to cozy up with Scotland Yard."

"He told us." She hesitated. "Not a bad idea, Eve."

"You should have thought of that when you brought me here,"
she said curtly. "There's no way I can go back and forget everything
I've seen and learned in Robaku." She glanced at her. "And you
knew that would happen, so don't let me hear that again from you."

"Just a comment," Jill said. "Maybe because I wish I could take it
all back."

"I know you do." She began to put in the depth markers. "Too
late." She added, "So make amends and work with me to find that
son of a bitch who killed these kids."

"You know I will." She turned away. "I'll go down to the village
and get you something to eat. You've lit a fire under Quinn, and I
doubt if he'll be here anytime soon. Maybe by the time I come back,
I'll be able to give you another report. Anything else I can do?"

"Not unless you've taken up forensic sculpting." Eve waved her
hand. "Out with you. Let me get into Mila."

"On my way." Jill headed for the door. "I guess I'm used to staying
close and watching out for you. No need of that now. Quinn and
Novak have arranged a virtual army to guard you."

I don't doubt that, Eve thought. The knowledge tended to smother
her. But she shouldn't complain, it was all part of the surveillance
which she'd told Joe she'd accept.

And she wasn't complaining; it was just difficult.

Mila. This little girl deserved her attention. Think of Mila.

———◆———

"Fruit. And a salad creation that Leta made for you from Hajif's garden. The dressing is spicy but good," Jill said as she came back into the museum two hours later. She set the tray down on Eve's worktable. "No protein. But I'll work on that for your supper." She glanced at Mila as she went to the cooler to get Eve a water. "How's it coming?"

"Fine." She pushed back and started to eat the salad. "You're right, this dressing is good. What's Joe doing? I take it not making salad. Did he find out anything from Scotland Yard?"

"Only the brother's background. After Oscar went back to Johannesburg, he was into everything from petty thievery to gunrunning. No connection with his big brother during that time. It's pretty clear he wanted the break to be permanent. For the last seven years, he was involved with piracy in the Indian Ocean. He was first mate on a schooner that raided corporate ships and held executives for ransom. At least two of the prisoners were executed during those years. Oscar definitely was not a pleasant man. He learned a lot from big brother."

"But he was an amateur compared to Varak," Eve said. "And the last lesson he learned evidently was a horror story. Was he definitely back in Johannesburg at the time Dobran flew down for a visit?"

"Novak is checking that out." She shook her head. "It seems Quinn and Novak are working in tandem. Pretty scary, huh?"

"Intimidating. But it probably won't—"

Jill's phone was ringing. "Hold that thought." She glanced at the ID. "Cairo. It's Kimbro." She answered. "What's the word, Kimbro? Can you get the tapes?"

He sighed. "I'm afraid not. It's impossible." Then he chuckled.

"Because I've already got them. You persist in underestimating me, Jill. They're tucked in my camera bag right now. Piece of cake."

Jill breathed a sigh of relief. "No trouble?"

"Just a return of favors. I slipped in and slipped out of that evidence room with my customary grace and style, leaving a hefty bribe behind. Which you will return to me with interest."

"Why should I? You owed me." She added teasingly, "And it was a piece of cake."

"So that I won't consider you in my debt now. I know you, Jill." He paused. "But to make sure, I'll accept another bribe. I want to know why you were ready to let me run that risk to get these tapes. You're usually boringly protective." He added, "And I want in on the story."

Jill's smile faded. "No, you don't. Not this story. Not now, Kimbro."

"It must be one hell of a scoop," he said softly. "If not now, when?"

"Soon. Don't push me, Kimbro. I won't shut you out. I promised you that you'd get the story of a lifetime. Just don't go probing into anything concerning Asarti. Okay?"

He sighed. "Okay. I guess you want these tapes right away? Where can I drop them off?"

"Where are you now?"

"Having breakfast at a sidewalk café about six blocks from the police station."

"Cocky."

"Why not? I told you it was a piece of cake. No problem at all. Really simple. You'd have been proud of me."

"Yeah." But she was beginning to be distinctly uneasy. "But sometimes things can be too simple. We've both gotten in hot water when we least expected it. Look around you, is there anyone there in the restaurant who looks familiar?"

"Not really. You're too suspicious." Silence. "Maybe that guy in the gray suit with no tie who's reading the newspaper. But I can't be sure."

"Then pretend you *are* sure and do me a favor. Get up and walk out of that restaurant. Don't look as if you're in a hurry. Stroll, don't run. Take a taxi and go back to your apartment and lock the door. I'll send someone to meet you and pick up those tapes."

Silence. "What is this, Jill?"

"Just do it, okay? I'm not sure if it's necessary. But it will make me feel better. Don't play games. Be careful. Call me when you get to your apartment." She hesitated. "And I think perhaps it might be a good idea if you go with the person who comes to get the tapes. I'll let you know when you call me."

Silence. "You're nervous about me. This must be nasty."

"Very nasty. I told you that in the beginning."

"You're going to feel very foolish about this if you're wrong. I'll rub it in, you know."

"I can take it. Are you leaving the restaurant?"

"I just threw some cash down on the table. I'm strolling, not running. There's a taxi down the street. You'll owe me for cab fare, too."

"Fine. Has the man in the gray suit moved?"

"No, he's still reading his newspaper. Looks like you're wrong."

"Good. Thanks, Kimbro. Call me as soon as you get to your apartment."

"You can bet I will. I didn't finish my breakfast. I'll use it as a guilt trip to make you tell me why you wanted these tapes. See you, Jill." He cut the connection.

"What's happening?" Eve asked.

"Maybe nothing." Jill was dialing Novak. "But Kimbro managed to get hold of those tapes, and I'd really like Novak to have them picked up right away."

"And your friend, Kimbro, too?"

"It might be a good idea to have Novak's men look over the situation and see if it's a good idea." She was biting her lower lip. "I don't have a good reason. I guess I'm allergic to having everything go just as it should. It's not been happening much since I came to Maldara. It makes me nervous." Novak picked up, and she said quickly, "We've got the security tapes. Kimbro is on his way to his apartment now." She rattled off the address. "Send someone to pick them up right away." She paused. "And make certain whoever you send knows what he's doing. Okay?"

"Why?"

"Because Kimbro is my friend, and I'm not taking chances. Don't argue with me, Novak. I've got what we needed. Now you do your part."

He was silent. "Orders? I'll send Nassem." He hung up the phone.

"Mission accomplished?" Eve asked as she watched Jill slip her phone in her pocket. "You were pretty sharp. You don't usually speak to Novak like that."

"He'll survive. I wanted him to get off the phone and do what I needed." She shrugged. "I know it was overkill, and he'll make me pay for it later. It seemed the thing to do at the time." She looked at the food on the tray in front of Eve. "You've scarcely touched your salad. Can I get you anything else?"

"No, I'll finish this. I've been a little busy listening to you." She made a face. "Stop hovering over me. I know you want to go back down to the village and make sure Novak is doing what you want him to do. Go!"

Jill smiled. "As you command." She headed for the door. "It's ridiculous, you know. I'm overreacting."

"Or it might be instinct," Eve said soberly as she gazed back at her Mila reconstruction. "I believe in instinct. I hope that you *are* overreacting. Let me know when Novak's agent actually has those security tapes in his hands."

"You'll be the first to know."

"I'd better be," she said wryly. "It appears that I'm the only one who is out of the loop."

Five minutes later, Jill had reached the hut where Joe and Novak had set up shop. Joe was no longer there, but Novak appeared to be just as busy as when she'd left. She hesitated at the door.

"Stop dithering," Novak said without looking up from his computer. "Yes, I did contact Nassem, and he'll be at Kimbro's apartment in thirty minutes. Satisfied?"

"Yes, you did the best you could." She came into the hut. Hajif had only managed to produce the one small bench where Novak was sitting for the makeshift office, but there were colorful blankets placed around the hut against the walls. Jill dropped down on one of the blankets and leaned back against the wall. "And it might not even be necessary. He was pretty sure he wasn't followed."

"But he's your friend." Novak's voice was without expression. "And with you, that means commitment and, therefore, possible inconvenience for me. I'm beginning to become accustomed to it."

"Poor you." She grinned. "Where's Quinn?"

"He received a call from his son. He wanted privacy."

"And probably to ensure that he not reveal a softer side to you," she said. "That's reserved for Eve and company." She took out her phone. "What other calls do you want me to make now that we've nailed down the security tapes?"

"You can call Gideon and see if he's made any contacts in Zahra Kiyani's august household yet."

"Busywork?"

"Maybe. You seem to be a little edgy. But useful busywork. Gideon sometimes gets carried away and goes in depth with any project. He needs structure."

"He's brilliant. You're lucky to have him."

"But I don't have him, that's my point. No one has him. He might go off in any direction if it pleases him. But he might be less likely to stray from the path if you're around."

"I'm not his guardian." She added slyly, "If that's what you want, then I should have gone with him."

"That's not what I want," he said flatly. "And you know it. Stay away from Zahra. Just check on Gideon. If nothing else, it will keep your mind off Kimbro."

"Busywork," she repeated. But she still dialed Gideon's number. No answer. She tried it again. In the middle of the ring, she got another call.

Kimbro.

She quickly pressed accept. "Are you in your apartment?"

"Locking the door now. Happy?"

"Moderately. Herb Nassem, a CIA operative, will be picking up the security tapes in about twenty minutes. Don't give them to anyone else."

"Can I ply him with liquor and see if I can talk him into telling me why those tapes are so important?"

"No, he has no idea. You weren't followed?"

"No. Not even that guy in the restaurant. He never stirred from that table when I got in the cab." He paused. "All kidding aside, you're not getting into anything over your head? I'm here for you if you are. Iron Man is my middle name. You don't need to get involved with these CIA guys. They can be trouble."

"Tell me about it," she said dryly. He might still want the story, but she was touched anyway. "I'll call you if I need to ditch them. But I hear Nassem is reliable. If he wants to pull you out of there, go with him."

"If you insist . . . and promise to keep in touch."

"Absolutely. When Nassem gets there, let me know. Thanks, Kimbro." She cut the connection and looked up to see Novak gazing at her. "He says he wasn't followed and that CIA can be trouble. I agree. But I'll give them the benefit of the doubt if this Nassem comes through." She grinned. "Probably not you. You're too far gone."

"Definitely." He tilted his head. "You're relieved."

"So far. I'll feel better once Kimbro gives the tapes to your guy. He should be there in another twenty minutes. I want this over."

Novak nodded and turned back to his calls. "It sounds as if you've got it covered."

"I hope I do." She started to dial Gideon again. "I couldn't reach Gideon before. While I'm waiting for Kimbro's call, I'll try him again..."

———

But it wasn't over in twenty minutes.

No call from Kimbro.

It didn't mean anything, Jill told herself. Nassem could have been stuck in traffic or something. Cairo was always a traffic nightmare...

Another fifteen minutes.

No call.

She started to dial Kimbro.

It went to voice mail.

Shit.

Her hand was shaking as she started to punch in the number again.

"I've already tried him twice," Novak said quietly.

She went still. "What?"

"Nassem always has orders to call his superior, Karim Absar, when he makes contact with the subject. He was on his way up in the elevator after he reached the apartment building when he checked in twenty minutes ago. But he didn't call back after contacting Kimbro." He paused. "And he didn't answer when Absar called."

"So you called Kimbro," she said shakily.

"Twice."

"You said that." She moistened her lips. "Something must have happened. We should call the police or an emergency number." She rubbed her temple. "No, not the police. Stupid. We just robbed the damn police. The medical-emergency number. I think it's 123 in Cairo."

"My people will be faster. When they couldn't contact Nassem, I told them to get over to Kimbro's apartment right away. They should be arriving any minute."

"Efficient. You're always so efficient, Novak." She was having trouble concentrating on what she was saying. All she could think about was Kimbro. "You called him. Why didn't you tell me?"

"You were already worried. There was no use making it worse until I was sure that it was necessary. It could have been anything. It didn't have to be—" He stopped. "We're still not sure what problem they might have run into. We won't know until Absar's team gets there."

"But you have an idea, don't you?" She drew a deep breath. "Of course, we both do. But he didn't think he was followed, Novak."

"And he might not have been. If they had an ID on him after he took the tapes, they might have just gotten his address and been there waiting for him to show. Or his tail might have been very, very good."

"He might not have had to be that good. Kimbro was cocky. Piece of cake." She could feel her eyes stinging. "He said it was a piece of cake."

He muttered a curse. "We don't *know*, Jill."

She nodded. "We have to wait. You're right, we should find out soon." *Keep control.* Novak was being his usual professional self, and she had to follow his lead. But it was so hard. She linked her arms around her drawn-up knees and held them tight. "I told him to hold off, and I'd get him help, but he thought he could do it without any help. Cocky. He's always so cocky. And he had the deal made before I even knew it. I should have known he'd do something like that. I should have expected it."

"Shut up," he said roughly. "I can see where this is going, and I'm not letting you take either one of us there. It could be okay, Jill. I'll get a report from Nassem or Absar any minute, and we'll—"

His phone rang. "It's Absar."

She stiffened, her eyes flying to Novak's face as he answered the call. Whoever Absar was, he was spitting out words as soon as Novak answered, not giving him a chance to reply. Her gaze was focused desperately on Novak's face as he listened, but his expression told her nothing. "The tapes?" he asked once.

Still no expression.

Then, evidently, he was asked a question because he did answer. "No, don't wait. Take care of it. It has to be clean." He cut the connection.

She sat up straight, her gaze on his face. "Not good," she said jerkily. "Though I don't know how I can tell. I never know what you're thinking. Kimbro?"

"Dead."

She couldn't breathe. She felt as if she'd been kicked in the stomach.

"Dammit!" Suddenly Novak was on his knees beside her. His face contorted, his hands grasping her shoulders. "I had to say it fast and hard and get it over with. I *know* you. I couldn't play around with it when you knew it was coming."

"Yes, I knew it was coming," she said stiltedly. "I was just hoping I was wrong."

"Well, you weren't wrong." She was suddenly pulled into his arms, his hand on the back of her head, her face buried in his chest. "Kimbro's dead. Nassem's dead. Both found in Kimbro's apartment. Stop shaking. I can't take it."

Jill couldn't take it either. She was clutching desperately at him. He seemed to be the only warmth in her world right now. "How?"

"Will you let me tell you later?"

"No. Now."

"The attack was probably made when Kimbro opened the door for Nassem. It appeared to be an assault from the rear. Absar thinks they might have been waiting in a vacant apartment down the hall for their chance to go after Kimbro. Nassem was almost decapitated by a knife blow to the back of his neck." He paused. "Or possibly a machete."

Machete...

"Kimbro?"

"Same weapon. Two blows to the chest and abdomen, one kill blow to the throat. It had to be fast, he would have bled out very quickly."

She closed her eyes tightly. "Is that supposed to be comforting?"

"The only comfort I can give you."

"It sucks, Novak." But she was still holding tightly to him. "The tapes?"

"Gone."

"And machetes are a strange weapon of choice for a thug in Cairo." She added unsteadily, "But it was Varak's favorite weapon."

"Varak wouldn't have been the one who did this, Jill."

"But he had an entire troop of machete killers in his personal army. Who knows what kind of force he has now? He could have sent one of them to take care of this small job. Nothing much, just killing a reporter who got in his way. A reporter who *I* put in his way." She couldn't stop talking, couldn't stop the tears from flowing down her cheeks as she lifted her head to look up at him. "That's why I was afraid. All those deaths...I thought: What if Varak is still alive and comes back to do it again? And he *is* back, Novak. I brought him back. I set out bait for the tiger."

"The hell you did." His hands were cupping her face as he glared down at her. He said fiercely, "You know that's not true. Stop feeling sorry for yourself. I won't *have* it."

"I don't feel sorry for myself. I feel sorry for Kimbro, dammit. And I have to accept responsibility for the—"

"I gave you the assignment. You didn't even realize that anyone but you knew what Kimbro was up to. And you told me yourself he not only wanted to repay a debt, he wanted the story. If he hadn't moved too quickly, we could have had someone to protect him from the moment he left that police station. He was careless and overconfident, and it got him killed."

"It's not that easy. I drew him into the web because I was worried about what those tapes would do to Eve and Quinn. You can't absolve me of blame, Novak."

"Then let me share it. Because I sure as hell can't take watching you like this."

He meant it. All the fierceness and the almost brutal intensity that electrified him were naked in his face. It shocked her. She instinctively pushed him away. "You can't do that, Novak. You have your own problems." She shook her head to clear it. "And you shouldn't have to deal with all this angst I'm going through either. You had a man killed today also. Did you know Nassem?"

For an instant, his face still retained that shockingly fierce intensity. Then it was gone, and he said without expression, "I'd met Nassem a couple times. He was a good operator and supposed to be a good guy."

"Very vague. Is your life usually that vague?"

"It's safer to keep it that way in my job."

But there had been nothing safe or vague about him only a moment ago. Forget it. She shouldn't have even asked the question. Keep away from anything personal with Novak. "I can't do that." She got to her feet. "I used to try, but it doesn't work for me. People pop up, and suddenly there's a Kimbro or a Hajif or a Gideon." She was wiping her cheeks with the sleeve of her shirt. "Or even a Novak."

"And you get hurt."

"It depends on how the story goes. Sometimes I can make it come out right. I'm not sure about this one. I'm beginning to doubt it." She said unsteadily, "I suppose I should take care of arrangements for Kimbro. He doesn't have a wife or kid, but he used to talk about his mother in Toronto."

"Later perhaps. Not now."

Her gaze flew to his face. "Why not?"

"It's better if the bodies just disappear for a while. We don't want

the police or Egyptian government involved in this yet. I told Absar
to do a cleanup."

"What about the evidence? I don't want it cleaned up. I want the
people who killed Kimbro to be caught."

"We'll send in a forensic team. Absar's already on the job. We'll
find the murderers and take care of it. I promise you."

"He was my *friend*."

"Then be a friend to him. Don't go after the errand boy, go after
Varak. They have those tapes now, and all hell may break loose." He
met her eyes. "It's starting, Jill."

She stared at him for a long moment.

It was starting.

It had already started when Eve completed that reconstruction.
But Kimbro's death had marked the beginning of the battle to come.
There was no turning their backs on the struggle now. Those secu-
rity tapes would light a fire that could cause a gigantic bonfire.

Accept it. Stop this clinging and weeping and wailing that wasn't
going to help.

But Kimbro . . .

"All right. Then let's find Varak." She turned and headed for the
door. She added fiercely, "But you keep your promise, Novak. I'm
holding you to it." She paused at the door. "How quickly can we
expect those tapes to explode in our faces?"

"Not long. I wouldn't say that either Zahra or Varak have a great
degree of patience, and their underlings will know it. It's possible
they could be seeing them in the next few hours."

"And then we wait for the explosion."

"Or attempt to cause one of our own." His gaze was scanning her
face. "Are you okay now?"

Her lips indented in a ghost of a smile. "No, but I'll be better
when we figure out how to cause that explosion. I don't like to feel
this defeated. It's got to change."

"Michael just called, Eve," Joe said grimly when he came into the museum. "He was phoning from the dig site in the middle of the day. I believe that constitutes big-time worry on his part." He shook his head. "Though I managed to stave off any action, Jane might have to face problems later."

"Dammit." Eve frowned as she turned to face him. "How did he sound?"

"Calm. Reasonable. Just trying to talk me into bringing him here to see you. He's worried, not panicking. Being Michael."

"And even when he panics, we wouldn't know it," Eve murmured. "He'd just do what he thinks he should do. Which scares me to death." Her lips twisted. "And he has perfect timing, doesn't he? You want me to go to London. He's putting pressure from his end. I'm caught in the middle."

"No conspiracy, Eve."

"I know." She sighed. "I'll call him back and try to reassure him. But he can read me like a book. Honesty is great except when you have to deal with someone like Michael."

"It will help if he just hears your voice," Joe said. "The vibes are always there between you, but just talk to him." He moved over to stand beside her. "It always helps me." His hand reached out to caress her cheek. "Even if you say the wrong thing."

"And even the times when you turn a deaf ear." She held his hand to her cheek for a moment. "But you must be more concerned about him than you're letting on if you ran here right after you talked to him." She looked up at him. "Or did you consider it an opportunity?"

He shook his head. "I wouldn't use Michael as a pawn, no matter how much I want my own way."

"I didn't think you would, but you really wanted me to get out of Dodge." Her gaze was searching his face. "What else, Joe? How bad?"

"Not good. Right after I hung up from Michael, I got a call from

Jill. It seems that her friend Kimbro is dead, and the gallery tapes were taken."

"She must feel terrible," Eve said, sick. "I know she was worried."

"She should be worried," he said. "We should all be worried about those tapes."

"Are you blaming Jill?"

"Why should I blame her?" he said impatiently. "She was only trying to help. I'm the one who left those tapes in the gallery. I should have found a way to get them out of there myself."

"Sure, you had so much time, and nothing at all was happening around you," Eve said. Joe's first instinct was always to shoulder the burdens. "Forget it. How can we make it right?"

"It might be too late. As soon as they view those tapes, they'll go after me, and that will lead to you. The only thing we can do is brace ourselves for the impact. We're already doing all that's possible to go after Varak at top speed."

Brace for the impact. Eve shuddered at the words. Brace for Varak's striking out at them like a vicious rattler. Brace for Zahra's moving forward, sleek and dangerous and totally without conscience. "At the moment, it doesn't seem like top speed to me."

Varak wielding his glittering machete in that schoolroom.

Varak striking out at those helpless children.

He likes to kill the children.

She inhaled sharply as she remembered Jill's words.

"No!" Her hands closed into fists. "I don't have to wonder what else the son of a bitch might do. He uses children, Joe. That's why he staged the massacre at the schoolroom. He wanted to lure their parents to the school from the village, so he attacked the children. He knew it would be the one sure way to trap them." She met his eyes. "Because there's nothing a parent wouldn't do for their child." She paused. "There's nothing we wouldn't do for Michael. We have to be prepared that one of Varak's moves might be to go after our child." Even as she said the words, she could feel the fear and panic rising. "You were so worried about me, Joe. But forget about me. We should be worried about Michael. We should concentrate on keeping him safe."

"Slow down. You or Michael? That's no choice at all."

"But it's always been the right choice for us." She drew a shaky breath. "First, we have to keep Michael away from Maldara and away from me. We don't want to draw Varak's attention to him. Particularly not in connection to me. But we can't be sure he's safe at the dig either. Varak probably has all Zahra's power behind him, and judging by the appearance of that sniper at Asarti and Kimbro's death in Cairo, he must still have his own scumbags at his command. He could send someone to find him."

"I'll tell Jane to disappear with him until this is over."

"You know that would only make Michael more determined to go his own way. It's better to keep him busy. Besides, Jane should be protected, too. And while we're at it, even Cara's probably not safe. You'll have to make sure he can't touch anyone in the family. But I'm most worried about Michael and Jane. I'll call Jane and tell her what we're facing." She got to her feet and went into his arms. "I believe it's time for you to call those buddies of yours at Scotland Yard and persuade them to assign him that army of detectives you were going to surround me with." She laid her head on his shoulder, and said softly, "It was a good idea, just not the right person."

"Exactly the right person." His arms tightened around her. "I don't suppose I can talk you into going to be with Michael?"

She shook her head. "I have to stay away from him. Haven't you been paying attention?"

"I wish I could tell you that you're all wrong about this." He paused. "I might, if I hadn't gone down and looked at that school-room for myself." Joe's lips twisted. "Okay, then I suppose I'd better get on the phone again with the Yard. I just spent half the morning harassing them about Oscar Varak." He gave her a quick kiss before he turned away. "We'd better get ready to defend the gates."

"And brace for the impact," she repeated somberly as she reached for her phone to call Jane.

———————

"Why didn't you tell me all this before?" Jane asked quietly. "All Joe has been saying is that I should keep an eye on Michael because he might decide to take off and go to see you. That was worry enough, but now you're telling me that he might actually be in danger on this dig? Not fair, Eve."

"I know it wasn't. I was so grateful to you for giving Michael such a great time, and I guess I was hoping that what was happening here wouldn't get in the way. I just wanted to keep you out of it as long as I could. That time just ran out."

"I'd say it did," she said dryly. "And you had no business keeping me out of it. I'm supposed to be merrily playing in the dirt with Michael while you're being hunted down by this Varak. I should be with you."

"No, you shouldn't," Eve said firmly. "You should be exactly where you are right now. Joe has arranged to give you and Michael all kinds of protection, but those Scotland Yard people don't know Michael as you do." She paused. "And Michael would never be anything but honest with you even if he thought you were getting in his way. We both know he wouldn't be quite as honest with anyone else. This might be a bad time for him. He's going to need you."

"Now you're scaring me."

"I just mean he's going to be worried about me, and there aren't many people who can handle a kid like Michael when he's determined to do something." She made a face. "I wish I had ten of you at that dig."

"Do you?" Jane shook her head. "I can see why you're concerned, but I still want to come there and—" She stopped. "Okay, I'll do what you want. But no more trying to keep me out of this. Be honest with me. And be honest with Michael. Though he probably knows what's going on anyway. But it might be making him uneasy for you not to be perfectly open with him."

"You could be right," Eve said. "Sometimes it's hard to know what to do. First instinct is always to protect. Very well, honesty all the way. Thanks, Jane."

"And that's not all. If I'm responsible for taking care of Michael, then I'll do it my way." She added, "You're right, Joe's friends at the Yard might not cut it as far as Michael's concerned. And I can't furnish ten of me who could handle him. But I'll make a call, and I'll have at least one person who's capable of doing it here at the dig tomorrow."

"Who?"

"Seth Caleb's at his estate in Scotland." Her lips twisted. "I don't think you'd argue that Michael would be no problem for him. Michael adores him, and they're soul mates. Half the time, I don't even understand what's going on between them."

Jane was talking about Michael's relationship with Caleb, but she wasn't mentioning the off and on, tumultuous and passionate relationship she'd had with Caleb in the past. Eve hesitated. "The last thing I heard from you was that you weren't seeing Seth Caleb any longer. Has that changed?"

"No, I'm not seeing him, but Caleb has no qualms about dropping in on me whenever he pleases. And it will please him that I need him to come and guard Michael."

"I don't want to make things difficult for you, Jane."

"Things are always difficult when Caleb is around. We might as well make use of him. You and Joe will feel safer that Caleb is with Michael, won't you?"

Eve couldn't deny it. "He's totally remarkable."

"And that's all that's important." Jane smiled. "If I can't be with you, then you'll know that you've nothing to worry about as far as Michael is concerned." Her smile faded. "But you'll have me to worry about if you don't call me every day to tell me what's happening. This can't happen again, Eve."

"It won't. Never again. Good-bye, Jane." She ended the call. She knew Jane too well not to realize that having Caleb at that dig might be a strain considering the volatility of her relationship with him, but she also knew she wouldn't be able to talk her out of it. Jane would make any sacrifice, do everything she could to safeguard Michael and the entire family. It was her nature.

"Everything all right?" Joe was studying her expression.

"Great." She smiled with an effort. "Jane is in fine form. Michael couldn't be in safer hands. And that dig will definitely be braced for impact."

———◆———

"Get over here!" Varak's voice was crackling with fury as Zahra picked up the phone. "Right now, Zahra. Or I'll come to that fancy palace of yours." His disconnect was a crash in her ear.

He was clearly in a rage, Zahra thought, but he had no right to speak to her like this. She had already been out there to see him earlier today, and she wouldn't be at his beck and call. Then she stifled her own anger. She couldn't take a chance with Varak's volatile temperament right now.

And he must not come here. How many times had she told him that they must not take any chances? She would have to go, but he would hear from her about this when she got to his damn compound.

She tore out of the palace and, a little over an hour later, screeched to a stop in front of his house. She jumped out of the car and was climbing the steps when the door flew open and Varak came out on the porch.

"I won't take your rudeness, Varak," she said. "Next time, I'll tell you to go to hell."

"You'll take whatever I give you." He grabbed her wrist and was pulling her inside the house. "You've put me at risk for the last time. You promised me that you'd make certain I'd be safe if I played your game. Now everything is falling apart, and it's your fault."

"Nothing is falling apart except that I don't have my statue."

"The hell it's not." Varak's face was livid, twisted with anger. "I told you that you had to get rid of Duncan. But you were so frightened that all those diplomats who suck up to you would turn their backs and walk away. Now look what you've done."

"I *tried* to get rid of her. I even had Bogani drown that chef to protect us. I haven't done anything else but put up with your arrogance and insults." She glared at him. "And I've reached the end of my patience with you. What's supposed to be my fault, Varak?"

"It *is* your fault." He strode across the room toward the desk. "Do you want to see why you don't have your precious statue? I just got the security tapes from the gallery at Asarti." He pressed the button on his computer. "And guess who was dragging Dobran through that gallery."

She was looking over his shoulder at the computer screen. "How should I know who—" She stopped. "Gideon? It was Gideon at Asarti?"

"You told me he was once your lover. He seems to have forgotten old loyalties and formed others. He wasn't alone." He fast-forwarded the tape. "Do you recognize this man, Zahra?"

"No, I've never seen him before."

"Neither have I. So I ran a check through a database I use. Actually, he's very well known in some circles. He's Joe Quinn, a detective with the Atlanta Police Department." He took a step closer to her, his eyes glittering. "And he's married to Eve Duncan. Now what would he be doing at Asarti, Zahra?"

She inhaled sharply. "How should I know? None of this is my fault."

"And it's not your fault that he was obviously trying to extract

Dobran from that château when my sniper shot him? Not your fault that the one man who could tell the world that I'm still alive was being snatched away by the husband of the woman who is the premier forensic sculptor in the world? You don't see the connection?"

Zahra was afraid that she did, but she'd have to be wary about admitting it to Varak while he was in this foul mood. "Perhaps. But I don't know how the connection would be made. Duncan was working on reconstructions of those children. I saw them when I went to the museum for the press conference. Nothing to do with you. There was no threat."

"And was there no threat from bringing an expert forensic sculptor within a stone's throw of the U.N. headquarters where the skull was placed? Why do you think Quinn wanted Dobran? He already knew that Eve Duncan had been working on that skull and was certain it wasn't me. She fooled you. Can't you see it? Gideon brought her to Maldara, and everyone knows he and Jill Cassidy are friends. They all fooled you."

"I asked Wyatt, and he told me that Cassidy had no connection with the Children for Peace charity that contacted the London office."

"Just as she had nothing to do with trying to skewer me by paying Hadfeld for that story about my still being alive? I wanted to kill her then, but you persuaded me that I should only hurt and scare her. You should have realized that she wouldn't give up. She just went in another direction. So don't tell me that she had nothing to do with Eve Duncan's coming here." His voice was low and thick with rage. "Or that Duncan wasn't pretty damn sure of what Quinn would find at Asarti. Joe Quinn wouldn't have risked his reputation if Duncan hadn't thought she had proof that the skull in the U.N. vault wasn't mine."

"How could she know that?"

"That's what we're going to find out." He whirled to face her. "And I know you're ready and willing to help, aren't you?"

"Of course, I gave you my word." *Keep him calm. And this might affect both of us.* "Tell me what I can do."

He reached in her handbag and took out her phone. "You're going to call Edward Wyatt and tell him that you're in the mood for something different and are coming to see him at the U.N. residence tonight for your fun and games. You'll tell him to send everyone away so that no one will recognize you. You'll make it sound erotic enough that he'll be panting to do anything you want him to do."

He grinned. "But then he does that anyway. Right?"

She ignored the question. "What are you planning, Varak?"

"You'll get me and my men into that vault room, where I can check out that skull. Wyatt's already given you the code ID imprinted on it. If that code's not on that skull at the U.N. vault, then we'll know what Eve Duncan has been working on at that museum at Robaku."

"And what good will that do?"

"Then we start covering our bases and nullifying any gains Duncan and those others might believe they've made. The minute I know for sure that she has the skull, the game changes." His eyes were flickering, blazing with intensity. "I have a plan ready. Do you think I spent all these months cooped up in this compound without thinking of ways to protect myself and end up back on top, where I belong?" He nodded at the phone. "Make that call."

She was still glancing down at the video. "They do have my statue."

"I don't want to hear about that statue again," Varak said between clenched teeth. "*Listen* to me. You're going to do as I wish, or I'll blow all your plans to hell and take what I want in my own way. I'm sick of your stalling about giving me my share of that gold. Do you understand? I'm done with taking orders from you. From now on, you'll do what I tell you to do. Make the call."

"You will hear about it again," she said fiercely. "Because I will get it back. Don't give me orders, Varak." She was thinking, trying to figure out which way to go. She couldn't let him see that he'd intimidated her, but she could tell he was ready to do exactly what he threatened. The blowup she'd feared all these months was very close. Play along. Give him what he wanted now and see how she could turn it around. "I'll do this because it seems the best way to be certain that we're in as bad a situation as you're telling me. You do have your uses, and you might even be able to point a way out of it." She had a sudden thought. "But Wyatt is accustomed to having Dalai join us. I'll need her to come with us tonight, and I gave her to you earlier today. I have to have her back. Where is she?"

"Bedroom." He shrugged. "If she'll be any good to you."

She didn't like the sound of that. "I told you not to damage her." She was heading for the bedroom. "Now what have you done?"

"I enjoyed myself." He followed her into the bedroom. "You promised me more time than just these few hours, but I made them count. But you can have her now. If you think that it won't turn him off."

Zahra was gazing critically at the young girl. Dalai's wrists and ankles were tied to the four posts of the bed. Her naked body was bruised, her nipples bloody. Tears were running down her cheeks, her eyes were desperate, pleading, as she looked at Zahra. "Please..."

"She's not too bad," Zahra decided. "I'll tell Wyatt I did it, and it might even excite him." She went over to the bed and untied the ropes. "Though if I'd left her with you until tomorrow, it would have taken me weeks to repair her." She tossed a sheet to Dalai. "Wrap up and go get in the car. And stop crying, it's not as if it hasn't happened to you before. You should be accustomed to it by now. You're making me angry."

"I'm...sorry." The girl was frantically trying to get to her feet. "Don't leave me, madam. I'll do anything you want me to do."

"Yes, don't leave her, madam," Varak said mockingly. "She was a complete bore."

Zahra ignored him. "Just get out of here, Dalai. You'll have to make yourself presentable when I get you back to the palace." Zahra heard Varak laugh behind her as she began punching in Wyatt's number.

She drew a deep breath when Wyatt picked up the call. "I've been thinking about you. I've been amusing myself with Dalai today, but she's not enough for me right now. I'm coming to you tonight, and I want you to send everyone away and be prepared to entertain me . . ."

CHAPTER

14

Now what had Zahra been up to? Gideon wondered.

He drew farther back in the shadows of the old coach house as he watched Zahra drag Dalai out of the maze bordering the street and into the far end of the coach house.

He knew exactly where they were going. He had used the secret passage hidden in that last stall many times to get into Zahra's quarters during the summer when their affair had been red-hot.

Whatever it was that was causing Zahra to have reason to creep around in the dark and use those passages at a time like this was probably worth exploring...

What the hell? More than probably. He hadn't had much luck so far today.

He had spent most of the day moving around the exterior of the palace and refreshing himself on any changes that might have occurred in the years since he'd broken with Zahra. Most of the new guards were unknown to him, but there was one he remembered who might be willing to deal if the money was high enough. He'd been holding off going inside the palace to explore and had only just verified that the secret passage leading to Zahra's wing was still available and intact. Then, when he'd seen Zahra and Dalai moving from the maze into the coach house, his curiosity had flared.

Dalai... The girl was draped only in a sheet, and she looked very much the worse for wear. Not good for her, but it might be an opportunity...

What a bastard I am, he thought bitterly. The girl was like a frightened rabbit around Zahra, and he was thinking about using her? Rabbit... He vaguely remembered Zahra scornfully calling her that in those days when she'd first come to the palace all those years ago. He scarcely remembered Dalai Sadar from the old days. She had been a new servant in Zahra's entourage then and not even into her teens, still a child. She had been brought from one of the Kiyani farms in the north when Zahra had said she needed a new maidservant. He only recalled Zahra's being impatient with her and telling him that she scurried around like a frightened rabbit and that it was going to be boring having to train her.

He recalled feeling sorry for the girl at the time and had often tried to ease the sting of Zahra's scathing words. But he had already been trying to edge away from Zahra, and a few months later, he'd made the break and was on his way to London.

And Dalai had grown up under Zahra's less than tender care and become the pretty, well-trained rabbit that Zahra had intended.

Had there been blood on that sheet?

His phone was vibrating in his pocket.

Jill. He took the call.

"I've been trying to call you for the last few hours, Gideon," Jill said in exasperation. "Why didn't you pick up?"

"I was busy. Granted, I'm very familiar with this palace, but when your aim is to spy on the enemy, you don't want to draw attention to yourself by chatting on the phone as you stroll around the property. It defeats the purpose. You caught me this time in the old coach house, where I could talk."

"Coach house? Zahra has a coach—Never mind. I've reached you now. Have you talked to Novak?"

"Would I answer his calls when I refused to answer yours? That would be rude."

"Stop it, Gideon. I have to tell you something." She paused. "We weren't able to get the security tapes back. Novak's agent, Nassem, was killed, and so was my friend, Kimbro. Kimbro actually had the tapes in his possession, but we have to assume that when he was killed, the tapes were taken by one of Varak's men."

"Shit. Nassem?" Gideon repeated. "He was a good guy, Jill."

"That's what Novak said." She cleared her throat. "So was Kimbro. But the reason I was trying desperately to get in touch with you is those tapes. If Zahra and Varak don't know that you were involved in that break-in already, they will soon. You shouldn't be there, Gideon. We don't know what they'll do if they think we might be getting close."

"I'm careful." He added grimly, "And all the more reason why we should find out what's going on with Zahra. I remember she has an office that adjoins her suite. I thought that I might rifle through her desk and see what I can find out. There are too many blanks that need to be filled in."

"It sounds too risky to do it alone. Come back here, and we'll find a way to work on it together. Haven't you been there long enough?"

"Maybe. I spent most of the time finding out that I knew practically none of Zahra's personal guards any longer. There's one I might approach if necessary." He paused. "But I did have what you might call an encounter with Dalai Sadar this evening. Do you remember her?"

"The young girl that runs around at Zahra's beck and call? There's not much to remember. She obviously tries to fade into the background. I feel sorry for her, and Eve was really irritated at the way Zahra treated her. Was she around when you were playing your sex games with Zahra?"

"Barely. She was just a kid, not even in her teens yet. I remember trying to get Zahra to be easier on her. But I wasn't around that long. Our ship had sailed."

"But you met Dalai this evening?"

"As I said, more of an encounter." He changed the subject. "I'm going to stick around for a little while. Quinn would say that would be a waste of time coming back to Robaku for help when I'm already here at the palace. He's all for conquering by combining tasks." He paused. "I'll see how I feel about that office when I get within striking distance. If I decide against going for it, I still have one other path I can try before I come back to Robaku."

"What?"

"Never mind. It's a long shot, but you can never tell what will work. I'll call you when I leave here. Don't phone me again. I won't be able to answer you." He ended the call.

A long shot. He stood for a moment in the darkness, staring at the wall passage into which Zahra and Dalai had disappeared. He had to admit he was curious... So go for the long shot?

And perhaps... reparation?

Gideon had no trouble remembering the layout of the rooms once he reached Zahra's wing. The maid's room was two doors down from Zahra's suite. She always wanted privacy but also to have instant service when she required it.

He moved silently down the hall, listening for activity from Zahra's suite or the guards on the floor below. He had waited almost an hour before he'd entered the passage. If it had been blood on that sheet, Zahra would probably have needed time to take care of Dalai's wounds.

He hesitated. Time to make the decision. Go to Zahra's office? Or go to Dalai?

Either would be a risk.

He stopped outside the maid's room.

No decision. That blood... He'd known this would be the choice.

He listened.

No sound of activity.

He silently opened the door and slipped into the bedroom. The room was so plain and without color, it appeared almost sterile. A bed. A pine washstand. A chair against the far wall.

He could see Dalai sitting on the edge of the bed, still wrapped in the sheet, her eyes fixed dully on the floor.

"Dalai," he said gently.

She stiffened, her gaze wide with alarm as she saw him.

Oh, shit. She was going to scream.

This was turning out to be a stupid idea, he thought. "Shh. Please don't scream. I'm Sam Gideon. Do you remember me? I'm not going to hurt you."

She didn't scream. She just sat on the bed, panting, looking at him with those wide, dark eyes. "Of course . . . I know you. What do you want with me? Did Madam Zahra send you? I wouldn't think she'd choose to permit you to have me."

"All I want is to talk to you. Zahra didn't send me." He grimaced. "In fact, she would be very angry with me if she knew I was here. I'm surprised you remember me. You'd just come to the palace when I first met you, and I didn't stay around for long. Your Madam Zahra and I were once what you might term an item, but that was long ago. She can't stand me now."

"I remember everything about you." She was still stiff and unrelaxed. "But you're right, now Madam feels differently. You have to leave here. I didn't think she'd send you to me. But she'll still punish me if she finds you here." Her voice was trembling. "She does hate you. I can tell every time she sees you or talks about you. You make her angry. She *must* not get angry."

"Because she'll punish you?" He came toward her, his gaze on the sheet. "You're bleeding. Did she do that to you? And those bruises on your shoulders?"

"Go away."

"I thought I knew what a bitch she was, but I might have been way off." His lips tightened. "You don't have to take this, Dalai."

"Go *away*."

"Did she do it?"

"No. Yes. Go away. You'll make things worse if she comes in and sees you."

"Then we'll keep our voices down, and she won't come in. Unless she decides to come in and clean you up. I was thinking I'd given her time to have done that already."

"Take care of me?" She gazed at him in bewilderment. "Why would she do that? She told me to take care of it myself because she had to take me out again later tonight." Her hands clenched on the sheet. "You have to leave. She'll be angry with me. She'll think it's my fault. She'll give me to him again."

"Him?"

She was shaking her head. "You have to go. She'll hurt you, too." She was beginning to tremble. "And I can't take any more right now."

"I'll leave soon." He was having trouble keeping his temper. She might be a rabbit, but she had clearly been mistreated, and she was displaying a courage that touched him. "Maybe you shouldn't have to put up with any more of this. That's what I want to talk about. But first things first; it annoys me that Zahra didn't take care of you." He went to the washstand and poured water in the basin. "So I believe I'll do it myself." He grabbed a towel and washcloth and came back to the bed. "You looked like you could use a little help when I came into the room. You were just sitting, frozen."

"I'm just...tired. I was...resting." Her hand clutched at the sheet. "Go away. I'll do it."

"But I'm not in the mood for Zahra to get her own way right now. I'm very irritated with her. So sit very still." He was pulling the sheet down as he spoke. "And I'll take care of—" He went still, staring at her breasts. "You look as if you've been savaged by a wild animal."

She had gone still. "It doesn't hurt much anymore. I don't believe she'd like you to see it."

"No?" The anger and pity were growing more by the second. "Who did this?"

She didn't answer.

"Maybe later?" He dipped the washcloth in the water. "Sit still. I'll try not to hurt you." His lips tightened. "Though I don't know how I'm going to do that. You look...raw." He was dabbing carefully at her breasts. "You should probably go to a doctor. I'm tempted to take you with me when I go."

"No!" She was frantically shaking her head. "I'm fine. She'd be angry. It won't matter. She said it wouldn't. Some men aren't like you. Some men like to see—" She broke off. "Why don't you just go away?"

"Easy." He lifted his eyes to her face. "I went away a long time ago and that's why I don't want to do it now. I was thinking about that when I saw you downstairs. I was such a selfish bastard, just out of college, and I didn't care about anyone but myself. I thought you'd be okay, but what did I know? I broke with her and went my merry way. Hell, I've hardly thought of you all these years."

"Why should you?" She was looking at him with bewilderment again.

"That's right, you don't expect anyone to think about you or watch out for you." He held up his hand as she opened her lips. "But I'm not going to make it difficult for you. I can see this isn't the time. Do you have any salves you can use on these wounds?"

She nodded jerkily.

"Why doesn't that surprise me?" His lips twisted. "Then I'll let you do it so that Zahra won't be angry with you. Just let me finish this bit to make sure you won't get rabies from the son of a bitch."

She nodded slowly, her gaze fixed on his face. She sat very still while he finished washing and drying her upper body. Then, when he sat back on his heels, she asked quietly, "Is that all? I can see you're angry. Have you changed your mind? Do you wish anything else of me?"

It was clear what she meant, and he felt another ripple of rage mixed with pity. He shook his head. "Just get your damn salve."

He watched as she dropped the sheet, got to her feet, and walked naked across the room to a drawer beneath the washstand. Her body was exquisitely fragile, and he realized that there were more bruises than he had thought. That delicate gold skin had to have been brutally beaten. She took a small round tube of salve from a drawer and rubbed it over her wounds. Then she turned to face him. "It's done. But it might be a waste if she wishes me to bathe later to prepare myself again."

"Prepare for what?"

She didn't answer.

"Or should I say whom?"

She didn't answer. "What do you want with me? Why did you come?" She moistened her lips. "I'm very confused, and I'm so tired. I'm forbidden to complain. But, if it pleases you, I would like you to go so that I can rest."

"What would please me is if I knew what else you were going to have to face tonight from Zahra." He took a cotton throw from her bed and wrapped it around her. "Sit down. Rest. I'll be out of here soon. I didn't mean to stay this long. You threw me a curveball I didn't expect. I just have a few things to say, and I'll be gone."

Where to start? She was looking at him with those doe eyes that were making him feel as if he were aiming a rifle at her. *Start at the beginning. Start with honesty.*

"I didn't come here to cause you any trouble. But I'm going to ask you to help me. There's no reason why you should because it's clear no one has helped you all these years. Certainly not me." He shook his head. "And it might even be dangerous for you. If Zahra can treat you like this, there's no telling what else she'll do to you."

He paused. "But I have to ask it because it's very important, and you may be our only hope."

"Help you?" She was frowning. "I don't understand. I can do *nothing*. She hates you and wouldn't permit me to help you. She would punish me."

"Permit? Punish?" He paused. "You're not a slave, Dalai. Even in Maldara, slavery is forbidden. I won't tell you that there wouldn't be danger, but I will tell you that I'll protect you if you help me." He added, "And I promise Zahra will never be able to punish you again."

"You lie to me." She shook her head. "I belong to her. My father sent me to her and told me I must always do as she commands."

"You belong to no one but yourself. He was mistaken." He wasn't getting through to her. How could he expect to overcome the brainwashing Zahra had been giving her all these years? But every word she spoke was tearing him apart, and he had to keep trying. "You've lived here in the palace and heard all the speeches the diplomats made about freedom. You know that Zahra wasn't telling you the truth. You're free to do as you wish."

She shook her head. "I've heard all that, but I'm different. She said that I belong to her, like the slaves that Kiya brought from Egypt on the Great Journey belonged to Kiya. That I have to do everything she wants me to do." She added wearily, "And she *can* punish me. So that's another lie, too. Will you go now?"

"Not yet. I have to tell you what I need. Then I'll let you kick me out."

"Kick you out?" she asked in horror. "I could not do that."

He smiled. "Yes, you could. You just need the practice, and it would come naturally to you. But you might need my friend, Jill, to help you get over the first hesitation."

"Jill," she repeated tentatively. Then she said slowly after a moment's thought, "Jill Cassidy. I've heard Madam speak of her. She does not like her either."

"No, Jill has gotten in her way, and she doesn't like it." His eyes narrowed on Dalai's face. "But you probably knew that, didn't you? That's why I need your help, Dalai. You know everything that goes on with Zahra. You've been with her for years, and she obviously treats you like wallpaper when she's not mistreating you. You see and hear everything. She'd never think that you'd betray her."

"Because I would not. You do not know what she would do to me."

His lips tightened. "I can imagine, judging by what I've seen tonight. But I'm asking you anyway. Terrible things have happened here in Maldara, and Zahra is part of a plan to start it all again. There were so many deaths. My friends and I are trying to keep it from happening, but we're working in the dark. We need names and faces." He paused. "Particularly the name and face of one man who Zahra might be protecting. I believe you probably have information that might shine a light on that darkness. Information that can save lives. I *need* it, Dalai." He paused. "And in return, I'll promise to take care of you, and protect you, and give you a life that will give you all the choices you could wish. Is it a deal? Will you trust me?"

"You want *me*?" She was gazing at him in horror. "She would kill me. She would let him hurt me."

"If you helped us, we'd keep you safe. Just furnish us with what we need to stop Zahra...and anyone else with whom she's dealing. We'd protect you and even send you far away if you wish."

"I cannot answer questions." Her voice was shaking. "She said she would treat me as Kiya would someone who betrayed her. She even showed me the place with no air."

"What place?"

"Go away!"

"I'm going." He moved quickly to the door. "I understand why you're upset. But I had to do it. If you help us, it could save lives. I know you think of me as an enemy, I've never done anything for you. But getting rid of Zahra might even save your life someday."

"You don't understand *anything*." Her eyes were glittering, blazing. "I don't want to die like a Kiya slave. I don't want to die at all." Her voice was no longer shaking but very strong and hard with determination. "I won't let you or her or anyone do that to me."

That sudden change of demeanor from meekness to ferocity had startled him. "I'm trying to understand, Dalai." Gideon looked over his shoulder as he reached the door. Ferocity? He must have just frightened her. Except for those huge, blazing eyes, she looked infinitely fragile, and he couldn't leave her like that. "Don't let anyone else hurt you the way you were hurt tonight. Do you have a phone?"

"Of course, Madam might need me. I must always be available to her."

"Of course," he repeated. He strode back across the room and threw his card on the bed. "I'll leave. But if you change your mind or get in trouble, call me, and I'll come and get you. And you won't have to tell me anything if you're afraid to do it."

Her eyes widened. "Why would you do that?"

"I told you. Because I didn't do it when I should have done it all those years ago. When I got bored with her, I just took off. I didn't give a thought to you."

Her eyes were still bewildered. "Of course, you didn't. Why should you?"

"I can't explain it if you don't know. Anyway, deal or no deal, call me if you need help."

"I cannot do that," Dalai said jerkily. She was silent another moment. "I think you are trying to be kind to me. But if I'm not very good, she said he will punish me again, and I can't risk it." Her voice was shaking again. "I could not *stand* it."

His eyes narrowed. "Zahra's not always truthful. She might not keep her word. If she changes her mind, you might remember that I'm offering you your own choices." He added with sudden urgency, "No strings, dammit. Just use the card and call me."

"I'm going to tear it up and throw it away. She might find it," she said unsteadily. "But I'll remember your number. I have a very good memory. But don't expect me to use it."

It was a small victory, but he'd take it. "I never expect anything. I hope for everything." But she was still so damn defenseless. He impulsively reached into his pocket and pulled out his pearl-handled switchblade knife and threw it on the bed beside the card. "Take this in case you need it. My father gave it to me when I came home from Oxford. I think he'd want you to have it." He smiled. "Now you can't tear that to pieces. It's a keepsake."

"No, but I can never use it." She reached down and gingerly touched the pearl handle. "I'll have to hide it away so that no one will ever see it." She shook her head. "Why don't you understand? I can't resist, or it makes it a thousand times worse for me."

"No, I don't understand. Because if you'd let me help, we could beat this." He turned and moved back toward the door. "Just trust me." He carefully opened the door and cautiously looked up and down the hall. "Take care of yourself, Dalai," he said. "Since you won't let me do it. And no one else seems—"

"I've never thought of you as my enemy."

He stiffened at the words and looked over his shoulder. "What?"

"I never blamed you for leaving me," she burst out suddenly. "Why should I? Everybody leaves. And I never thought I was important enough for you to worry about." She stared him in the eye. "And I liked it when you were with her. You smiled at me and joked. It was different than it was later. You were nice to me."

He was silent. "You have a very limited experience in that area. And that makes me feel like even more of a bastard than I did before. But *call* me. Let me help you."

She shook her head. "Go away."

He had to go, he thought in frustration. But she was sitting there, fragile, helpless, and he wanted to scoop her up and take her somewhere safe. Another casualty in this damn war that had taken so much from so many. But a casualty that he thought he might have prevented.

"Call me!" He closed the door and moved swiftly down the hall.

———————◆———————

ROBAKU

"It's about time you got here." Jill came down the path toward Gideon when he arrived at Robaku an hour later. "Would it have hurt to have phoned me as soon as you could? Did you find out anything when you were going through Zahra's personal quarters?"

"I didn't get that far," Gideon said. "I was checking out something else, and I got involved." He held up his hand. "Don't ask. I came up with zeros all around."

"And you're upset." Jill was reading his expression. "You didn't by any chance run into Zahra while you were 'involved.'"

"If I had, I would have probably broken her neck," he said grimly. "I was ready to do it tonight."

"Why?"

"A poisonous combination of personal guilt and a few revelations that were particularly infuriating." He stopped, then said, "Okay, I was thinking about using her maid, Dalai, to help us. I thought she could be a fount of information. But I blew it. And besides, she's been used enough." He made a face. "At one point, I believe I even offered your services, Jill. Be prepared if I drop her on your lap if I change my mind. Why should I be any different? Do you know Zahra even used the Kiya card on Dalai to convince her that she was only a slave and didn't have any right to argue about how she was treated?"

"Kiya," Jill repeated. "It doesn't surprise me. After all, a queen must have her slaves. It was clear she seemed to consider Dalai her special property."

"Exactly."

"That sounded bitter." She was thinking. "I did feel sorry for her. And I remember that Eve was angry about the way she was treated." She nodded suddenly, and said recklessly, "Go ahead. By all means, hand her over to us. We're so frustrated that we'll be glad to find a way to get some of our own back."

"Easier said than done. I'd have to fight Dalai as well as Zahra." He changed the subject. "No word about whether the security tapes were delivered to Zahra or Varak yet?"

"Not as far as we've heard. I was hoping you'd know something when you got back from the palace."

"Well, Zahra was definitely on the move this evening, and she had plans for later tonight." His lips twisted. "I was tempted to follow them, but it sounded as if it might concern Dalai more than any connection to Asarti."

"Novak is monitoring the chatter, but nothing yet," Jill said. "Other than that, we're just trying to think of a way to make certain Eve's safe and find proof that it's Oscar's skull that we have in that museum. We'll probably hear about what Varak plans to do about those tapes soon enough." She shrugged. "But I don't think anyone is going to sleep well tonight."

"Then I might as well go have a drink with Novak and confess that I had an utterly worthless day. I don't dare go to Quinn. He won't accept any report that won't contribute to keeping Eve safe and out of jail."

"By all means go get a drink. You look like you need it. I might join both of you later before I go to Hajif's to turn in. He offered me a mat in his hut, and I'm trying to give Eve and Quinn their privacy." She turned and strolled toward the museum. "But first I'll go tell Eve that you're back and that we might have to adopt Dalai before this is over..."

U.N. HEADQUARTERS
10:32 P.M.

"You look beautiful tonight." Edward Wyatt stood at the top of the grand staircase and watched Zahra walk up the curving stairs to-ward him. Her dark hair shone as she passed beneath the huge crystal chandelier. His eyes lingered on her breasts, spilling out of the low neckline of her nude-colored silk gown. "Fantastic. Do you know how many times I've imagined you walking up to my bedroom to-ward me here in my own place? This is my domain, everyone has to kowtow and fawn to me. But all I could do was wonder what you would do to me if I could ever get you here."

"But I'm the one who arranged this. I'm always the one in charge," Zahra said coldly. "And if you didn't do as I told you to do, I will not stay. You've sent everyone away? I mustn't be seen here or I'll be known as your whore when I go to New York for my speech, and all those diplomats will not give me the respect I deserve. I'll be angry if you've made this visit difficult for me, Wyatt. I've been looking forward to it since I called you."

"Do you think I haven't?" he asked hoarsely. "I couldn't think of anything else. Of course I sent them away. I told my private secre-tary that I was having a confidential meeting with a member of the Botzan secret service who wanted to speak to me about a possible terrorist threat he might need our help to solve. That's what you wanted, right?"

"That's exactly what I wanted. We'll see if you can please me in other ways tonight." She had to get Wyatt out of the hall and into his bedroom right away. Varak had said he wanted the way clear to bring his men down to the vault ten minutes after she and Dalai arrived. She turned and said to Dalai behind her, "Come along. I want to see him perform. He's sure to be better than you were today. Where's your bedroom, Wyatt?"

"Third door." He gestured as she swept by him but paused to

watch Dalai hurry after Zahra. "Hello, Dalai." He smiled maliciously. "How are you? You appear to be moving a bit stiffly. I hear she gave you a hard time today. I hope you're not going to spoil things for me tonight."

She quickly shook her head. "I'm fine, sir."

"You wouldn't lie to me?"

"Of course she wouldn't lie," Zahra said impatiently. "I'll allow you to strip her down so that you can see the bruises. I thought you might enjoy it. Providing you don't waste my time with this chatter."

"I'm sorry." Wyatt moved down the hall and flung open the door for her. "I promise I won't waste your time."

"We'll see. Dalai, come and help him undress. I find I'm eager to see just how much he's been anticipating this." She gave him a cat-like glance over her shoulder. "And judge what kind of torment it will take to make it worth my while to have come here tonight."

———

Varak carefully drew the heavy bronze box out of the vault and laid it on the desk. "Get me the liquid, Markel."

Markel had it ready. "You're sure this will work?"

"Don't question me." Varak flipped open the lid and stared down at the blackened skull. "Hello, Oscar. How nice to see you again," he murmured. "It seems okay, Markel. He's as ugly a son of a bitch as the day I burned him to a crisp." He took the skull out of the container and turned it over. "Did I tell you that I'd been wanting to do that since the prick took off and ran back to Johannesburg, Markel? Well, actually since he annoyed me when he was a kid. I just hadn't gotten around to it yet."

"You told me," Markel said nervously. "Why don't you check the number so that we can get out of here?"

"There's no hurry now. Zahra will keep Wyatt busy." He was opening the vial. "And who knows, this might actually be Oscar. It could be that Duncan didn't go this route. If she did, then I'll act accordingly. I've got my plan in place." He put a drop of liquid on the bone near the ear. "And I'm actually looking forward to showing that bitch, Duncan, there's no way she can beat me." He added with sudden harshness, "I'm tired of hiding away when all I want to do is break out and let them all see what I can do."

"You said that the gold would be worth it." Markel's gaze was focused on the skull. "Did you make a mistake?"

Varak's head swung around like a striking cobra. "I don't make mistakes."

Markel backed away. "I only thought maybe circumstances had changed," he said quickly. "Is there anything I can do to help you with that skull?"

Varak didn't speak for a moment, and Markel tensed. Then Varak said, "No, I've got it." He looked back down at the skull. "Just be still and let me see how this is going to play out. Whatever goes down, I'll get what I want." He added, "Because I don't make mistakes, Markel."

He waited as the liquid did its work.

"Anything?" Markel asked.

Varak didn't answer. His eyes were on the skull.

Son of a bitch!

No numbers appeared. Nothing.

It was *not* Oscar.

And the rage was beginning to sear through Varak.

It was an insult that Eve Duncan had thought she could do this to him. Of course, she was only a woman, and Joe Quinn might have manipulated her. But she had to have been the one to do the actual reconstruction to prove that skull wasn't Varak's. He was suddenly furious with everyone connected to this defeat. Gideon, Joe Quinn, Eve Duncan, Jill Cassidy. He wanted them all *dead*.

No, he wouldn't accept that they had defeated him.

"Varak?" Markel said tentatively.

"Shut up," Varak hissed. He took the skull and hurled it across the room to smash against the wall. "The bitch thinks she fooled me." His hands clenched into fists as the white-hot rage tore through him. "Let's show them how wrong they are. Set the C-4."

"Where?"

"Everywhere, you fool. Everywhere."

Markel hurried out of the vault room.

Varak strode across the room and jammed an explosive in the empty eye socket of the skull lying on the floor.

Markel was back in the room and setting the charges.

"When you finish, get the other charges set throughout the house," Varak said. "Then tell the men to do the other blocks. Be ready to detonate when I call you." Then Varak was running out of the vault, down the hall, and up the staircase. Where the hell was she? Then he heard voices behind a door down the hall. A second later, he was throwing open the door of Wyatt's suite.

Wyatt was naked and kneeling before an equally naked Zahra. His head swiveled, and he stared in shock at Varak. "No one is supposed to be here. What are you—doing—"

"Blowing your brains out." Varak shot him directly between the eyes.

Then he glared at Zahra as Wyatt fell to the floor. "It's the wrong damn skull. It had to have been switched by that bitch, Duncan. You should have gotten rid of her. You should have gotten rid of all of them." His eyes were blazing. "That's why she sent Quinn to Asarti. You're to blame for this. Now I have to protect myself."

"And you call killing a U.N. diplomat protecting yourself?" She was staring in horror at Wyatt's shattered head. "How am I supposed to handle this?"

"I don't give a damn. I've already made plans to get rid of all the evidence. You just find a way to keep them from coming after me. Fix it. Put your clothes on and get out of here. This place is going to blow in another seven minutes. I won't wait for you."

"You're blowing it up?" She shook her head dazedly. "You are in-sane. Do you know what kind of nightmare you're going to—" She was gasping, choking as his hands closed on her throat.

"Listen to me," he hissed. "And keep listening. From now on, you're going to do exactly as I say. I'm done playing with you. Do you know how much I want to squeeze just a little harder and break your damn neck? I won't tolerate your ordering me about. I'm in charge now. Do you understand?"

She couldn't speak, so she nodded.

He released her, and she backed away, holding her throat. His smile was savage. "Yes, you do understand. Now get out of here and do what I told you. You're always telling me how clever you are. Now prove it. It's my game now, my orders, Zahra." He whirled and strode toward the door. "Fix it!"

———◆———

Zahra gazed after Varak for an instant as anger and shock struggled within her. Fix it? How was she supposed to fix this catastrophe? She looked down at the blood spattered over her naked body. It was like him to barge in and make things as difficult and horrible as possi-ble for her, she thought bitterly. And this time it had been far worse. She was trying to swallow. She reached up and touched her bruised throat. This time she'd thought he was going to kill her. She knew he'd been very close.

"What do we do?" Dalai whispered from the bed across the room as she scrambled to sit up. "Do we have to do what he says?"

Zahra had forgotten she was there. She whirled on her as she grabbed her gown. "You do what you always do. You obey my or-ders." She slipped the gown over her head. "And my orders are that you do whatever he says until I tell you differently. I don't want you causing me any trouble while I work this out. I might have to do some delicate negotiations with him before I get what I want." She headed for the door. "Now get dressed and go down and get in the car."

"Negotiations," Dalai repeated numbly as she threw on her top and sarong skirt. "Then I'll have to do what he wants. That's what you mean?"

"That's what I said, isn't it? Hurry. We have to get out of here. He's a little crazy right now. He *hurt* me. The bastard almost killed me. I have no idea what he's going to do next."

"Yes." Dalai's voice was trembling as she hurriedly stumbled after Zahra down the grand staircase. "He's very angry. I can see there's no telling what he'll decide to do now..."

ROBAKU

"Wake up, Jill!"

Novak, she realized sleepily. He was shaking her, and he sounded really—

Then she was wide-awake. Her eyes flew open.

Darkness, but Novak was kneeling above her with a flashlight. "What's wrong? What are you doing here?" She sat bolt upright on her mat. "Is Eve—"

"Eve is fine as far as I know," he said roughly. "You can check yourself as soon as we get to the museum. I've called Quinn, and they're waiting for us. Put on your shoes, and we'll get over there." He pulled her to her feet. "Because there's a hell of a lot wrong. I just got a call from my agent, Palmon, in Jokan to tell me to check my computer."

"Jokan?" She was slipping on her tennis shoes. "What happened in Jokan?"

"What didn't happen in Jokan?" He was pulling her toward the door of the hut. "I don't believe there's any doubt now that Zahra and Varak believe they know why Eve sent Quinn to Asarti to get corroborating evidence from Dobran."

"Stop talking in riddles. Just tell me." She tried to stop at the door of the hut. "And give me just a second to tell Hajif and his wife I'm leaving. I don't want to frighten them."

"I'll send someone." He was pulling her down the path toward the museum. "As for telling you, it's not really necessary. That should give you a hint." He gestured to the night sky to the north. "What do you think, Jill?"

She halted, frozen, her gaze on the baleful red glow that lit the entire horizon.

"Screw your hints," she whispered. "What happened, Novak?"

"The entire block that the U.N. occupied was blown to kingdom come. Along with two of the side streets on either side. Pretty clear that whoever set those charges didn't give a damn if they blew up the entire city to make certain of that U.N. building."

"Casualties?"

He shook his head. "It only happened forty-five minutes ago. But my agent says that no one could have lived through the primary explosions at the U.N. site. Initial information from Wyatt's staff is that he was the only one there tonight. But it's a total inferno, and the soldiers and police can't even get near it to try to recover bodies. The neighboring streets are even worse. There were definitely multiple deaths in those shops and houses. I'll be given updates as soon as they're available."

"Why?" she asked dazedly. She swallowed to ease the tightness of her throat. "Why would they do it? An attack on a U.N. facility would cause an uproar. Zahra wouldn't want to be associated with anything like that."

"Unless it wasn't her call," Novak said grimly. "Unless she's lost control of the agenda. We'll probably know soon enough. This is her city, she'll have to be involved in explaining and mopping up this disaster."

"And soon," Jill murmured. She couldn't take her eyes off that glowing red horror in the distance. "I don't see how she could possibly talk her way out of this holocaust."

They had reached the museum, and Jill saw that it was ablaze with lights. Joe was throwing open the door. "What the hell?" His eyes were glittering, his lips tight. "What's happening there, Novak? You've got to know something."

"You know as much as I do right now," Novak said curtly. "I'll find out all I can when I get to Jokan. I sent Gideon on ahead when I got word, and I'm on my way. I only wanted to bring Jill to you before I left." He turned away. "Take care of her. There's no telling what's going to happen next."

"You're leaving?" Jill asked, startled. Then she recovered. "Of course you are. This is a disaster, and you're CIA. I should be going also. I have contacts, I might be able to—"

"No," Novak said. "You'd get in my way. I don't want you seen there. Eve may be the prime target, but you've got to be high on their list by now. It's not as if I won't let you know right away. For once, just do as I say for—" His phone rang. "Gideon." He answered and listened for another minute. "When?" he asked. "Find out and get back to me. I'll be there as soon as I can."

"What is it?" Eve asked as she joined them at the door.

"President Zahra Kiyani has just requested TV time to address the nation in response to this national disaster. Gideon believes that she'll be speaking in the next hour or so. He'll give me a definite time in the next fifteen minutes." His lips twisted. "It probably won't be immediately. She'll want to give every news agency on the planet time to chime in and give her maximum exposure. I imagine the palace newsroom is already packed."

"Of course, it is," Jill said. "It's a great story. I should be there." She stared him in the eye. "I *will* be there, Novak."

"You'll have to pass," he said coolly. "You have another story to cover. Anything Zahra has to say will almost certainly have a direct influence on Eve. You're the one who chose Eve to be the one to put her neck on the line. Hell, you've been in agony about your responsibility for getting her poisoned." His voice became crisp and cold. "So suck it up and forget about that story luring you to the palace. You haven't finished this one yet. Stay here and make sure she lives to read it." He turned and strode down the path.

Jill stared after him, stricken.

"Pretty rough," Eve said quietly. "He probably didn't mean it all."

"Yes, he did." She shivered. "He always means what he says. You can always count on that." She drew a deep breath. "And the bastard is so damn smart that he's usually right. He sees right through you and cuts out all the bullshit like he has a scalpel." She turned to Joe. "You can see that, can't you? You know he's right about my being to blame for Eve's being in this position."

He nodded. "He's right. You had plenty of help, but you're the one who worked and made it happen."

"And yet I was ready to run back to Jokan as soon as I saw another story beckoning, another way to go after Zahra and Varak. It was fresh and new, and all I could think about was that maybe this was the direction I should go."

He was silent. Then he said, "Do you think that wasn't my first thought?" He made a face. "I've been frustrated as hell, and I don't respond well to it. But it's second thoughts that matter, and I knew it was impossible."

"But I had to have that second thought drummed into me." She turned to Eve. "Forgive me. It won't happen again."

"Stop talking as if this is all about me," Eve said, disgusted. "Joe is bad enough. But I have to put up with him." She turned and went over to the computer on her worktable. "I'll stand only so much from you, Jill." She turned on the computer. "Now let's see if we can find out what's happening in Jokan."

CHAPTER

15

The local Jokan television station switched from the shots of the U.N. disaster to the newsroom at the presidential palace two hours later.

Zahra Kiyani walked slowly up to the stage from a carved door opened by two uniformed soldiers. She was wearing an elegant white suit, and every glossy hair in her chignon was in place. She looked absolutely stunning as she turned to face the audience.

But her expression was tense and sober, and she paused a moment before she started to speak. "I grieve with you, both my own people and the loved ones of those friends from foreign lands who died tonight in that terrible massacre." Her voice was shaking, and her eyes were suddenly shining with tears. "You will notice I wear white instead of black for mourning. For those who are not familiar with Kiyanis, this is the custom of my family to honor our dead." Her voice broke. "And everyone who died tonight I regard as a member of my own family." She stopped a moment, struggling. "This is a monstrous thing that happened, and there are no words I can say that will explain or give comfort to you. All I can do is give what answers I can and grieve with you. First, I have to express my heartfelt condolences to the family of the Honorable Edward Wyatt, whom I've been told almost certainly perished in that explosion tonight. We had become friends during these last months. His Herculean efforts to help me bring health and happiness back to my countrymen after the devastation they had suffered will live in my heart and memory forever." Another emotional pause. "Unfortunately, that bravery and dedication very likely caused him to be targeted. The police are still investigating, but we suspect Botzan terrorism. They have informed me after questioning the wife of Edward's private secretary, Peter Greville, that Edward had scheduled a confidential meeting tonight with a Botzan secret agent who was attempting to capture a radical, terrorist group who were trying to revive the terrible war that killed so many of us." She swallowed. "Including my own father. I had received reports and threats to my life from this group for the last few months, but my own secret service had not succeeded in apprehending them. I can only believe that Edward thought the force of the U.N. might bring them to justice and risked his own life in order that the peace would not be broken." She cleared her throat. "Because that was the kind of noble, giving man the Honorable Edward Wyatt has been since the moment I first met him. May God bless his family and my eternal thanks to Great Britain for sending him to my country so that I could learn from him." She lowered her head and was silent a long moment, struggling. "Forgive me. This is as difficult for me as it is for you all. I know I promised you information, and I will give it. Naturally, because this hideous disaster has just occurred, that information may be sketchy, and I beg you to understand. I can only tell you what I've been told. The consensus of those around me is that the terrorist group got wind of the meeting with Edward and wished to set an example. It was easy for them because he had sent all of his guards and employees away for the night in order to satisfy the demands of the Botzan secret agent. That was like the Edward I have come to know, risking everything..." She went on: "But in the last hour we've found out that he was not the only target. The terrorists weren't satisfied with only killing him. His private secretary, Peter Greville, and several of the guards were attacked and shot in their residences in the early hours of the morning. The police told me that there's reason to believe that they wanted to make certain everyone connected with the death of Nils Varak paid the same price. You might remember that Varak's skull was being held at the U.N. headquarters." She shuddered. "It shouldn't surprise us that the monster who almost destroyed my country should be worshipped by those murdering terrorists." The tears that had been brimming were suddenly running down her cheeks. "But it does surprise me. I can't understand anything about people like this. Shouldn't the deaths stop sometime?" She looked directly in the camera. "But we all have to understand it because we have to stop it. It can't go on any longer. Together we *can* stop it. Help me, and I will help you. I will let you know whatever I find out about this atrocity so that we can share knowledge as well as our sorrow. I will set my own agencies and soldiers to seek out those answers. I'm going to cancel my trip to New York to speak at the U.N. in order to devote myself to keeping those beasts from devouring my country." Her voice was suddenly ringing with resolve. "That is my duty, and I will give every minute of every day to it. I ask for your prayers and your support." She stepped back. "Good night and God bless."

She turned and walked away.

———◆———

Jill gave a low whistle as she looked up from the computer screen. "She aced it. I bet every reporter in that room is giving her a standing ovation. Hell, I'd probably do it, too, if I didn't know she was lying through her teeth."

"But you do know," Eve said. "Gideon told me once that she was magnificent in a number of ways. This is apparently one of them." She leaned back, and added thoughtfully, "Do you know what I was thinking about when she speaking? She was totally beautiful, totally persuasive, and able to move everyone with whom she came in contact. Mesmerizing. She reminded me of her favorite ancestress."

"Kiya?" Joe asked.

"No, she tolerated Kiya, but she identified with Cleopatra. Cleopatra had the power, and Zahra adores power. Pity. Because Kiya was probably more intelligent." She shook her head. "But Zahra definitely covered all the bases with that speech. She produced a logical villain based on recent history. She glorified Wyatt and Great Britain and the entire civilized world. She even gave a reason why those guards were killed when they weren't even at the U.N. headquarters tonight and why the place was chosen to be targeted. You can bet that Swanson and anyone connected to that skull was on the hit list. All very logical and acceptable." She grimaced. "And then she sealed the deal by setting herself up as a combination Joan of Arc and Mother Teresa with all the glamour of Cleopatra. That YouTube video is going to get millions of hits, and the Zahra Kiyani legend is going to grow and grow."

Jill nodded. "Hell, she might decide to bypass using Egypt as a stepping-stone and go straight to Washington. After that speech, it's going to be nearly impossible to make her out to be anything but a heroine. It's like Jackie Kennedy in that bloody pink suit."

"That's what she intended," Joe said harshly. "What they both intended. What the world believes to be Varak's skull is now totally destroyed, and if we brought up the skull on which Eve just did the reconstruction, it would be an uphill battle to prove it wasn't a complete forgery. It throws everything into confusion. Very smart. Zahra and Varak make a formidable team."

"Murderers," Eve said with a shiver. "Another massacre, and she managed to sugarcoat it."

"Yes." Joe met her eyes. "It just goes to show how determined they are to protect themselves. They assassinated Dobran and killed your friend Kimbro, Jill. That explosion tonight was just another safety measure. They're going down the list and checking off the hazards to eliminate." He paused. "And you're probably next on the list, Eve. You have a spotless reputation, and that's dangerous to them." His tone was suddenly urgent. "The game's changed. *Now* will you let me take you out of here?"

"Do it, Eve," Jill said. "As he said, it's going to be an uphill battle from now on. If you stay, you'll be vulnerable to anything they decide to do to you."

"What am I supposed to do? Let Joe bury me in the mountains somewhere and hope Varak won't dig me up?" Eve shook her head. "I won't live like that. I won't let Varak believe he can roam the earth and get away with all this slaughter. There has to be a better way to handle this. We just have to find it." She was thinking, trying to see some way out. "We have to take advantage of any weakness they might have. Zahra has to have a different agenda than Varak. Jill says she's always been cautious, and she must feel as if she has a tiger by the tail."

"This is all guesswork," Joe said impatiently. "And all it means is that I'm not getting what I want and that Eve is still in danger as long as she's here." He drew a deep breath. "Because who's to know if Zahra won't think of some clever reason to blow up this village as well? I wouldn't put it past her." He strode toward the door. "I need some air. Then I'm going to call Novak. I'm having problems with your 'logic,' and I want solutions."

———◆———

OUTSIDE U.N. HEADQUARTERS
JOKAN

Gideon's eyes were stinging from smoke as he closed his computer after watching Zahra's speech. "Interesting. She's either amazingly improved from the time when we were an item or she was inspired. What do you think?"

"I have no idea." Novak added, "But Jill would say she told the

story with incredible conviction and that she came across as a combination of Angelina Jolie and Mother Teresa."

"I believe she was inspired...maybe by Varak," Gideon said absently as he gazed at the ambulances still racing from the homes and
shops on the streets surrounding the U.N. toward the hospital. He
was realizing that some of the smoke he was breathing was carrying
the scent of the burnt flesh of those victims caught in the flames. It
was too damn familiar. "But I don't think even Mother Teresa could
inspire any mercy for the people who did this. What's the count?"

"More than fifty. If the staff of the U.N. hadn't been sent home, it
would have almost doubled."

"She mentioned that some of the guards who took care of the
vault had also been assassinated. Swanson?"

Novak nodded. "They wanted to get anyone connected to the
skull. It was a well-planned raid."

"Varak can be brilliant." Gideon's lips twisted. "The smell of this
smoke reminds me of the day I came back home to bury my parents. He was very thorough. Everything stank for weeks of smoke
and flesh. He burned every living soul on the property."

"You never told me that."

"It was over," he said. "Until it wasn't." He looked away from
the ambulances. "Do you need me any more tonight? I think I
should—" His phone rang, and he glanced down at the ID. Presidential palace. No designated name.

He quickly turned away from Novak. "Excuse me. I've got to take
this."

Novak's brows rose. "Confidential?"

Gideon didn't answer as he moved a few more steps away. He
punched the access key. "Gideon."

"I've got to see you right away." Dalai's voice was shaking. "You
said you'd help me. Will you still do it?"

He stiffened. "Yes. But I'm a little busy right now. I'm sure you
can hear the sirens."

"I've been hearing them ever since I got back to the palace. I think I'll hear them forever."

"Then I imagine you heard more than the sirens. How close were you to the explosion?"

She didn't answer. "I need to see you. I'll be at the coach house in thirty minutes. Please come."

"How can you get away? I'm standing here watching the U.N. headquarters burn to ashes. And I just heard Zahra give a speech to rock the ages."

"She's surrounded by all those reporters. She doesn't want me around to get in her way. She told me to stay in my quarters."

"She never did like to share the spotlight."

"Will you come?"

"I'll come." He cut the connection. He turned back to Novak. "I'll see you later. I have something to do."

"Curious. Or someone to see?"

He smiled. "Perhaps."

Novak's narrowed eyes were studying his face. "It's that young maid of Zahra Kiyani."

Gideon's smile never wavered. "Perhaps."

"Be careful. It could be a trap. It's odd that you'd hear from her after Zahra probably blew up a good bit of the city. She could be dangerous. Are you sure it's worth it?"

"No. But it's promising." He lifted his hand. "I'll call you later and let you know."

———◆———

Dalai wasn't in the coach house when Gideon slipped inside the back entrance twenty minutes later. But the entire palace seemed to be teeming with activity, he noticed. He'd been lucky not to be seen coming here.

It could be a trap.

Yes, it could. He was taking a chance that Dalai had not gone to Zahra and told her that he had been to see her. Or more likely, she might have lost her nerve and was still cowering in her bedroom.

Then, suddenly, the door of the passage opened, and she was there, running toward him. "I was afraid you'd leave. Madam called me down to the press office to redo her hair. She said it wouldn't photograph well if she—" She broke off and drew a deep breath. "But you didn't leave. So it's all right."

"Yes, it's all right," he said gently. "Why did you call me? Did someone hurt you again?"

"No, not like that. Usually it's only him. It was the blood...he shot Mr. Wyatt in the head. There was so much blood." She was biting her lower lip. "But he *will* hurt me again. I know it. She's too afraid of him. She'll do anything to keep him from hurting her. But I don't matter to her. She'll use me again and again to please him." She was gazing desperately up at him. "But I can't *bear* it. I can stand most things, but not that. I'll tell you whatever you want to know. It's a kind of bargain, isn't it? But you don't have to promise to keep me safe, or send me away somewhere. Just keep me away from him."

"Hush." He reached out to stroke her hair. "I will promise to keep you safe. But I can't do that unless you help yourself. You're still not telling me names. Give me his name, Dalai."

She was silent. "It's very...hard. She said no one is supposed to know it. She said she would send me to—" She swallowed. "Varak. His name is Nils Varak." She was looking searchingly at his face. "But I think you knew it, didn't you?"

"But I had to be absolutely certain. Now I am." He added grimly, "I believe you're aware that Varak's presence here in Maldara is a huge secret. There aren't many people who would be brave enough to say his name."

"Yes, I knew it was a secret. That's why Madam spent all that money for that plastic surgeon to change his face. And I'm *not* brave. I had to do it. After I came back tonight, I was lying in bed and shaking. Because I knew I was going to have to do it. I knew I had to ask you to help." She braced herself, and, suddenly, she was no longer trembling. "Because I'm not strong enough. I don't know any of the ways that you would. I'll have to learn them. You were always so strong when you were with her. You were never afraid. You even laughed at her when she tried to order you about. If I do what you wish, you'll keep her from giving me to him again." She paused, then said quietly, "Or because I believe you hate him, you will kill him. That would be much better."

Gideon felt a ripple of shock. He had not expected those last words. Dalai had spoken with no passion, only simplicity and determination. But who could blame her after all she had been through? "I'll never let you go back to him." He smiled grimly. "And, if you can tell me where to find the bastard, I have friends who will be glad to go with me and see that Varak will never live to see another day."

She closed her eyes for a moment. "I'm sorry to make you do this. I know it should be me." She opened her eyes. "But I will repay you."

"Just tell me where I can find him."

She nodded. "He has a compound deep in the rain forest over an hour from here. It's off Nagali Highway, and the roads going to and from the property are patrolled by Madam's soldiers. And he has his own soldiers at the compound. Many soldiers. I don't know how many." She paused, thinking. "He likes explosives. I've seen them in the warehouse there."

"Yes, I'm aware that he likes explosives," Gideon said harshly. "Anything else?"

She shook her head. "I'm sorry. I was always in the bedroom."

He felt another bolt of rage and pity. "Nothing to be sorry about. You've told me a great deal. We don't have to talk about him anymore. Let's talk about Zahra. She's very important, too."

"She can't help you get to the compound," Dalai said quickly. "Varak doesn't like her to come there. He's afraid she'll be followed."

"No, forget about the compound for a moment. I need to know

everything about her relationship with Varak. We might be able to use it. Are they lovers?"

She shook her head. "She used to sleep with him. But she doesn't anymore. She sends him whores...or me."

"That doesn't surprise me. Well, why does she put up with him? What binds them together?"

"I don't know what you mean." She was backing away from him. "I have to go now. I've been here too long."

She was suddenly on edge, he realized. She had started to shake again. The minute he had started to question her about Zahra...He was thinking back to the conversation in her room. "You're frightened. You said something about Zahra's sending you to the place where there was no air. What did you mean?"

"It's not important to you. I've told you about Varak. He's the only one you have to worry about." She started to back toward the stable.

"Wait. I could try to take you out of here now."

"No, you couldn't. Not while Varak is still alive. You might not be able to do it if you did." She glanced back over her shoulder. "And then she would know. It would be worse for me."

"I'll make sure that we're very careful when we go after him, so that won't happen. But I can't just leave you here." He reached in his pocket and scrawled numbers on a card. "This is my friend Jill's phone number." He came toward her and put the card in her hand. "If you don't hear from me, if something happens, call her, and she'll take care of you."

"No," she said fiercely. "Nothing is going to happen to you. You're strong. No one can hurt you. Do you think I'd send you to him if I thought—" She broke off and whirled away from him. "I will call you if I hear of something that might hurt you."

Then she was gone.

Gideon gazed helplessly after her for a moment before he turned toward the maze that led to the street. After this night of fire and death, he hadn't dreamed that Dalai would furnish them with the weapon that might bring Varak down. He should be happy and full of hope. But that vulnerable young girl who had been a victim all her life was still here, and he had no real grasp of what she was facing.

Stop thinking about her. He could only help Dalai by eliminating the threat that was terrifying her the most. So they'd have to go over what she had said about the compound and start planning.

He reached for his phone to call Novak.

———◆———

ROBAKU

"Varak," Jill murmured. "It seems too good to be true. I thought everything was going down the tubes when Zahra came out with that save earlier tonight." She was gazing at the night sky over Jokan, which was still glowing malevolently. "I was afraid to hope."

"And it might be too good to be true," Novak said. "We won't know until we check out that compound where Dalai said we could find Varak." He looked at Gideon. "I told you it could be a trap. You said the girl seemed almost as terrified of Zahra Kiyani as she was of Varak. Zahra has been brainwashing her since childhood."

"It wasn't the same," Gideon said. "She's scared of Zahra. But she thinks she'll only be safe from Varak if he's dead. There's a distinction."

"One of which I approve," Joe Quinn said, turning to Eve, Jill, Novak, and Gideon, who were standing in front of the museum. "It's the first break we've had. Let's go for it. You can check out the terrain and make sure it's as safe as it can be for us, Novak."

"I appreciate your faith in me," Novak said dryly. "I definitely want to check out everything connected with the girl. Gideon is being a little too trusting."

"Only because he's feeling guilty about not having helped Dalai when he had the chance," Eve said. "He was trying to persuade us to adopt her."

"Maybe," Gideon said. "But now we might owe her." He turned back to Novak. "How do we verify the information?"

"I'll send a team to the property to take a good look as soon as it gets light. In the meantime, I'll order a couple infrared drones to scan the area." He cocked a brow as he glanced at Joe. "Providing that meets with your approval?"

"It does." He added, "As long as I'm heading the team that goes in at daybreak."

"No!" Gideon was adamantly shaking his head. "You head the team, Novak. Keep Quinn out of it."

"That's not going to happen," Joe said curtly. "What the hell is wrong with you, Gideon?"

"I've seen how you operate," Gideon said. "It's half instinct and half intellect and all exactly how you want it to go. It might be effective, but I don't want to rely on your decisions when I promised Dalai that we'd be careful not to tip our hand and get her in trouble with Zahra. I wouldn't want Zahra to cut her throat if she thinks she's been betrayed."

"You shouldn't have made her promises," Novak said slowly.

"Well, I did." He met Novak's eyes. "I knew there was a possibility you'd want to move fast. But we've known each other a long time, and I didn't believe that you'd let her get killed if there was any way to keep it from happening. I don't care if you send me or someone else to pull her out of that palace if you make a decision to go for it. I just don't want any action taken without warning." He paused. "And I trust you not to do it."

Novak stared at him for a moment. Then he shrugged and turned away. "I'll do whatever is possible. No promises." He glanced at Joe. "It appears that I'll be heading that team. No offense. I'd trust you implicitly. You're just a little too volatile for Gideon at present." His gaze shifted to Eve. "I wonder why?"

"Joe wouldn't let anything happen to Dalai," Eve said quietly.

"Unless he thought there was reason to think your safety was on the line," Novak said. "Then no one else would have a chance. But hopefully that won't happen today." He looked back at Joe. "Right, Quinn?"

"Hopefully." Joe added impatiently, "It doesn't matter. I'd rather be checking the area for land mines anyway. The girl mentioned explosives."

"Whew." Gideon smiled. "That was close. Defusing land mines seems an ideal job for you. Sorry, Quinn."

"You might be very sorry if you pull that shit again." He turned to Novak. "What time do we leave?"

"Six."

"Then we'd better get some sleep." Joe took Eve's arm. "If you don't mind sharing a bed with a callous bastard like me."

"Ouch," Gideon murmured as he watched them leave. "I knew that was a mistake. But I wasn't able to do anything else for that poor kid."

"I knew it was a mistake, too," Novak said. "You're lucky you didn't piss him off." He turned and headed down the path. "And now I'll go back to the village and do a check to see if Dalai is telling us the truth about the location of Varak's compound and find out everything I can about it. I'll encode and send out two of the X-4 drones. Gideon, I want you to go to the airport and see that there's no slip-up. Got it?"

"Got it."

"Make sure they're functioning properly with the codes I enter. I want accurate information before we start out. In the past, Varak's hideouts have always been almost impregnable. I have to know what to expect, or I'll have to make adjustments." He added, "And try to get a couple hours sleep."

"All those goals might not coincide," Gideon said dryly as he disappeared down the path.

Jill stood hesitantly, gazing after him. She felt totally useless, when she should have had a hand in helping to make this plan work.

"What are you waiting for?" Novak was looking over his shoulder. "An invitation?"

She went still. Then she was running after him. "I'm glad you re-membered your manners," she said lightly as she fell into step with him. "I was wondering if I was going to have to barge in on you."

"I knew that would be your next step. You wouldn't have been able to go back to Hajif's hut and try to go back to sleep. That would have been far too sensible and normal."

Yes, Novak had developed an almost paranormal ability to read her, Jill thought. It should have made her uneasy, but she was finding it oddly comforting to have him there, understanding who and what she was. Not always approving, often frustrated, volatile, and disturb-ing, but an undeniable part of the fabric of her life.

"I wouldn't have been able to sleep," she said. "I'm excited. Can I do something to help you get those drones programmed?"

"Perhaps." He saw her frown and grinned. "Okay, I'll put you to work. Why not?"

"Right." She nodded. "You can never tell when I'll run across a time when I'll need information like that. Drones seem to be an es-sential part of my life these days." She ducked through the opening of the hut. "How long will it take?"

"Not that long if all goes well. We have Gideon on the other end double-checking." He lit the lantern. "He'll be very careful about not making any mistakes. He knows I'm not pleased with him."

"He was doing what he thought was right," she said quietly. "And you must have thought he was right, too, or you wouldn't have let him talk you into doing what he wanted."

"I hadn't decided one way or the other when Quinn stepped in. It would have been more diplomatic to let him take the reins." He shrugged. "But Gideon didn't allow me the choice. I don't like to be put in that position."

"Joe Quinn is almost a stranger to Gideon, he had to go with the man he trusted. It was important to him." She stared him in the eyes. "I'd be the same. I trust you. If it was important, I'd go to you, Novak."

He went still. "Don't trust me too much, Jill. That's what I told

Gideon. I only do what I can." His lips twisted. "And since I'm such a selfish bastard, what I can do sometimes alters from minute to minute."

She shook her head. "I don't believe you."

"No?" He gazed at her for a long moment. Heat. It came lightning fast out of nowhere. Taking her breath away. She couldn't look away from him. "Well, I did warn you," he said as he took out his computer. "Let's get to work. I'll show you how to look up the address and directions and coordinate it into the drone's memory."

She was relieved that electric moment had passed. Or was she? She was feeling a strange sense of loss. Of course she was. "It sounds complicated." She came closer to look down at the screen. Then she was beginning to get excited again at the challenge before her. "You're sure it won't take more than an hour or so?"

It took an hour and five minutes to program the two drones.

It was not nearly as complicated as she had thought to learn the codes and keep them straight. She had followed Novak's lead, and it was like learning a new game that was as absorbing as it was exciting. She found she was disappointed when she had put in the last equation. "Is that all?"

Novak was grinning. "Unless you want to teach it something else. We're supposed to be gathering information, but I suppose we could rig up a bomb or two to drop on that compound."

"No, that would be breaking your word to Gideon." She was still looking at the computer screen. "It's very sophisticated, isn't it?"

"State of the art." He held up his hand. "But I can see you already creating a story about it. Don't do it. Drones are constantly being upgraded, but this one is very special."

"Okay." She sighed. "But it was great fun. Thank you for letting me play with it."

"My pleasure. It was fun watching you. Your cheeks are still flushed, and your eyes are shining like those of a kid opening a Christmas present." He chuckled. "Next time I'll show you how to set the bomb capability."

"It was fascinating." Her smile suddenly faded. "And dangerous. Bombs and all those technical spy devices... I shouldn't be this excited. I just got caught up in the moment. It's not a game."

"It's whatever you make it." He signed out of the program. "And for you it was a game and a story unfolding and excitement."

"But not for you."

"No. Much darker," he said. "But it was good stepping into your world for a little while." He turned to look at her. "Maybe I'll remember it when it gets a little too dark in mine." He reached down and pulled her to her feet. "Now go to Hajif's and get to sleep. You should still have a few hours."

Heat, again. Out of nowhere. Tingling through her body, causing her breasts to swell. She quickly pulled her hand away. "Hardly seems worth it."

"I don't suppose I could talk you into not getting up when we take off? There's no reason why you should."

Other than the fact that she should be going with him. The darkness of which he'd spoken was suddenly overwhelming her. This was her fight as well as his, and now he was going to face the monster while she was supposed to stay here and snooze. "There's a reason," she said tightly. "You know there's a reason." She turned on her heel. "I'll see you at six."

A few minutes later, she had reached Hajif's hut. She stood outside the door, breathing hard. She couldn't go in right now, she was too upset. She sank down on the ground and leaned back against the wall. Her hands clenched into fists.

She *hated* it. She felt helpless, and it shouldn't be like this. She was the one who had gone to Novak in the beginning and asked him to help her go after Varak. Now he was going to leave her behind when she was responsible for everything that had happened since that night? Reason told her that she would not be an asset if she insisted on going with Novak. She had no military experience and might even be a danger to the team. He had a right to expect her to stay out of it.

But she wanted to go. She *needed* to go with him. Varak was a devil from the depths of hell. He had reached out and killed thousands of people. Who knew what kind of force he still had at his command? It might be intended to be an exploratory foray into that jungle, but that didn't mean it would stay that way. The panic was rising as the thought stabbed through her. How many stories had she written about good plans gone wrong?

They could all die.

Novak could die.

No!

She jumped to her feet. She tore across the short distance that separated her from Novak's hut in seconds. The next instant she was inside. "This is all wrong!" she said fiercely. "I can't have it like this."

He whirled to face her. "What's wrong?" He was instantly on the attack. "What happened?"

"I won't be cheated." She hurled herself at him. She was in his arms. She was kissing him. "I won't have *you* cheated. Varak has already taken too much. Take off your clothes."

"What?" He pushed her away from him to look down at her. "What the hell are you doing, Jill?"

"Nothing that's in the least thought-out, or probably even sane. And you have a perfect right to say you've changed your mind and don't want me. But I think it's still there, or I wouldn't be feeling—"

"Shut up," he said hoarsely. "You're damn right it's not sane. And every word is making me rock-hard. Get out of here."

She shook her head. "You want it. You want me. You've told me you do." She broke free of him and pulled her tee shirt over her head and threw it aside. "And I wish you'd take your clothes off so that

I won't feel as if I'm some kind of sex maniac. I'm not very good at this seduction bullshit. I've always thought that kind of thing was phony." She was trying to undo her bra. "But if that's what you want, then I'll try to—"

"Stop it." He grabbed her wrists and held her still. "You're killing me." He drew a deep breath. "Talk to me. Tell me what brought this on before I throw you out."

"That's just like you. You tell me what you want, then all of a sudden you're worrying and pushing me away because you think that I'm so damn vulnerable." She glared up at him. "I'm not weak. Sometimes bad things happen to me, but I can handle them. I'll always be able to handle them without you taking care of me. So back off, Novak."

"You're not answering me."

"Because when you come into the room I tense up because I know your just being here will change everything. It shouldn't be that way. I write my own story, dammit. But not when you're around. Why do you think I've been fighting you? But now Gideon pulls this thing with Varak out of his hat, and suddenly it doesn't matter." She repeated through set teeth, "It doesn't *matter*. So take off your clothes, Novak."

"Not quite yet." His gaze was narrowed on her face. "Why did it make a difference?"

"Don't be stupid. I can't go with you, dammit. I'd be a liability. What if something happens to you? What if you die? Then Varak would win because we'd both be cheated by him. We wouldn't be able to have this." She was trying to steady her voice. "I won't have that, Novak. I want you to have everything you want. And I want to have everything I want. And we both know what we've wanted since the day we met." She swallowed. "So will you please let go of my wrists and take me down on those blankets over there and do something about it?"

"So I'm to thank that bastard, Varak, for you?" His hands tightened on her wrists. "I don't think so, Jill. I don't find that prospect appealing." His lips twisted. "What am I saying? I'm going crazy at the thought of dragging you down on those blankets. I just can't stomach the idea that he'd have anything to do with it." He suddenly smiled recklessly. "So I'll have to make sure that it's only between you and me. Because I'm not going to be fool enough to walk away from you no matter what brought you here." He dropped her wrists and started to unbutton his shirt. "Though I admit I had a crazy idea that I should be noble and all that crap. But I'm way past that. I've been wanting you too long."

"I never asked you to be noble. You're the one who called me walking wounded." She watched him drop his shirt on the floor. His body was so lean and sleek and muscular, like a panther's. She couldn't take her eyes off the corded muscles of his stomach. "And I just didn't want you to think I wasn't strong. I've never shown anyone as much weakness as I've shown you."

"That's supposed to be weakness?" Two movements, and he pulled her into his arms. He was rocking her gently back and forth. "Just be quiet, will you? You're making me crazy. I don't want to feel like this about you right now. All I want to think about is how much I *need* you." Then she realized her bra was gone and he was rubbing her breasts back and forth against his chest. She gasped as she felt the warmth of his flesh against her, the faint abrasiveness of his chest hair against her nipples, which was causing her to tighten and swell. "That's right," he murmured. "This is what I want...But it's not enough. I want my mouth on you."

And the next moment, his mouth closed on her nipple.

Suction.

His tongue...

His teeth...

Her back arched as she felt the pressure.

"Wait," she gasped. She was wildly shedding her clothes as his mouth never left her. "I can't take—"

"Yes, you can. You can take everything. This is how strong you are." He pulled her down on the blankets. "So don't tell me you're not strong." He was shedding his clothes as he spoke. "I'll show you what you can take." He stopped suddenly as he looked down at her. "I'm going wild. I'll try to let you set the pace, but I can't promise. The last thing I want to do is hurt you. Don't let me do that. Just tell me."

She was panting, moving against him. The feel of his hips against her... "Will you stop worrying? I *know* you, Novak. Just *touch* me." Then she suddenly lunged upward and took him instead. "Yes!"

He froze. His face contorting. "Well. That ends that, doesn't it?" he said hoarsely. "It's up to you from now on. I'm gone..." He started to move.

Fast.

Hard.

Heat.

Hot. So hot.

She heard herself gasping, crying, as she met him, tried to take more of him.

Crazy.

It went on and on. He was moving her, positioning her, so many positions... until she thought she couldn't take any more; and then she found there were no limits.

His face over her, tense, almost in pain.

Then it was going faster, harder.

"Novak..."

Darkness.

Light.

Pressure.

Impossible that it could go on.

But it had to go on, she couldn't let him leave her...

Then he was gathering her close, lifting her. "Jill?"

But he wasn't leaving her she realized out of the haze of madness. He was taking her with him.

Her fingers dug into his shoulders.

She thought she screamed. But there was no sound, she realized. Because she had no breath and was clinging helplessly to him as wave after wave was overwhelming her.

"Okay?" His chest was moving in and out with the force of his breathing. "I didn't do—"

"Don't you dare," she gasped. "I'm quite sure you wouldn't ask that of any other woman at a time like this. I'm fine, better than fine."

"You're not any other woman." His voice was low against her throat. "I'm not sure I'll ever be able to compare you to other women." He lifted his head to look down at her. "So don't expect it."

She met his gaze. She wanted to pull him down and return to the hot, erotic intimacy that had gone before. She couldn't read his expression and it was making her uneasy. Sensuality. Intensity. Something else . . .

"That's fine with me." She smiled with an effort. "I don't mind being unique. As long as you understand who I am and realize you can't change me."

"Ah, yes, I mustn't try to influence your story." His lips twisted. "I'll try to keep that in mind." He kissed the hollow of her throat. "But you evidently don't mind me taking action on this level. You came to me."

"Yes."

He licked her lower lip. "And you didn't once think of Varak, did you?"

He knew she hadn't. She still wasn't sure what he was thinking. "Novak, what are you doing?" She paused. "Are you angry?"

"I wouldn't be so ungrateful. I don't really know what I am at this moment. I'm having problems sorting out what I'm feeling about this particular chapter in your story." His lips moved down to her breast, and his tongue flicked lazily at her nipple. "But I do know that we're both in complete agreement that this was entirely successful." He moved over her. "And we want more. You're ready for me. Am I wrong?"

She was more than ready. It had been such a short time, but she was burning. Dangerous. It was so dangerous to feel that sexual intensity for him. She wasn't even certain that it was only sex. She had always been confused about her emotions regarding him. Admiration, respect, gratitude were all mixed with that wariness. It would be even more dangerous if it was more than sex.

Worry about it later. She bit her lower lip as the waves of heat moved through her. She couldn't think now that his hands were moving, teasing, entering. Just take what he was offering. "No, you're not wrong." She pulled him down to her, and whispered, "There's nothing I want more than this now, Novak."

———————◆———————

Voices.

Novak was on the phone, Jill realized drowsily.

Then she was wide-awake. Her eyes flew open, and she saw Novak sitting at the bench across the hut. He was fully dressed and gazing at his computer.

"What is it?" Then she shook her head as she realized what it must be. "What time is it? Did you get the drone results?"

He nodded. "About ten minutes ago. They came in a little after five. I've been going over the results with Gideon."

"What were they?" She was quickly throwing on her clothes. "Why didn't you wake me?"

"No need. You didn't get much sleep," he said absently, his gaze on the computer. "It's not as if you could do anything about it."

That was true enough, Jill thought. She had probably drifted off to sleep only minutes before he'd received those results. And it only heightened her frustration that he was perfectly right about her not being able to help him in any way. That was what had started the sexual marathon that had caused her to still be here when those results had come in. "You're probably right," she said curtly. "Call it curiosity. I'd like to know."

He turned to face her. "I'm sorry. I didn't think." He tapped the screen. "Very heavy foliage and tree cover. Glimpses of what could be a residence and four bunkhouses. Several possible vehicles. Farther back on the property, a concrete pad that could be used for a helicopter." He looked up at her. "And the infrared showed at least forty or fifty figures under that heavy canopy of foliage."

"Then it could be true." She inhaled sharply as excitement gripped her. "Dalai must have told Gideon the truth. It could be Varak."

"It could be Varak," he agreed. "Particularly since the drone also detected the presence of explosives throughout the area. Varak has always been fond of his land mines. But that foliage is like a thick blanket, we won't know until we get there. And several of those figures were probably sentries moving around the property. One false step, and we could get ourselves killed, or tip Varak off that we're on the property. We've got to be careful."

"Then you won't be able to go in and get him right away." She tried not to sound as relieved as she felt. "You'll have to mount surveillance until you're certain?"

"Probably. I want to know everything about the place, and I want a visual on Varak."

"Dalai told Gideon that Zahra had paid for plastic surgery."

"I've been on the hunt for Varak ever since he showed up in Maldara. I studied him for years after he started his killing sprees here. He might change his face, but he's a big bastard, and he won't have been able to change the way he moves. I'll know him." His lips tightened. "And then I'll find a way to go in and get him."

"Unless you find an opportunity to get your hands on him today," she said bitterly.

He nodded. "Maybe."

"That's what I thought." She turned and headed for the door. "Do let me know when you make a decision."

"Jill."

"Look, I know you have to do this," she said jerkily. "But next time, I want to be there when it happens, so you find a way to not get yourself killed today."

"I'm not going to get myself killed," he said quietly. "What happened between us blew my mind. I have no intention of cutting what we have short. Will you come back here tonight, and we'll do it all over again? Plus more erotic embellishments?" He added mockingly, "Provided that Varak doesn't kill me."

He was actually joking? "You bastard."

"I admit I'm a little raw about your having to use such a sleazy excuse as Varak to come to me. Particularly since I've discovered that you've become an obsession." He added softly, "I'll come to you with no excuse at all. From now on, I won't be able to leave you alone. Expect me."

"The hell I will." She left the hut and strode toward Hajif's place. She'd wanted to *hit* Novak. The news that the possible strike on Varak might be temporarily averted had thrown her from despair to relief, then to anger. He was annoyed that it was Varak that had been the impetus to bring her to him? Screw him. She had been in a turmoil of emotion all night. Scared to death that he might get killed, then having probably the most erotic sexual encounter she'd ever experienced.

She had reached Hajif's hut, and she stopped to get a breath and calm down. It wasn't sunrise yet, but she knew that it was almost time for Novak to go to the museum to meet with Joe Quinn. She couldn't hide away here. She would wash, change her clothes, and be on her way there, too. Eve would expect her, and it wasn't professional to do anything else. Though she knew Novak would have made certain Eve was guarded, if Joe was going with Novak, Jill should be there to protect and support Eve.

Screw Novak.

But please keep him safe today, dammit, she added quickly

CHAPTER

16

I'll call you as soon as we know anything," Joe said. He kissed Eve and headed for the door, where Novak was waiting. "Don't worry. I checked Novak's security arrangements, and you'll be fine."

"Yes, I'm really worried about that," Eve said dryly. "I'm not the one who's going to be checking out land mines."

"I know what I'm doing, Eve," he said quietly as he glanced over his shoulder. "You know that's true."

"I know, but that doesn't help much." She gestured impatiently. "Get out of here. The sooner you leave, the sooner you'll get back. Keep safe."

He nodded, and his glance shifted to Jill. "Make yourself useful. Watch over her."

"I will," Jill said. "Why do you think I'm here? I realize she's my responsibility." She was trying not to look at Novak. The anger she had felt was dissipating, lost in the panic, and she tried to hold on to it. "Good luck." Her gaze shifted to Novak. "You, too, Novak. Don't do anything stupid. You promised Gideon."

He smiled mockingly. "I'll keep that in mind. I'll definitely see you later, Jill."

Then they were both gone.

And Jill found herself going to the door to watch them go down the path. Her hands clenched into fists. "Look at them. They can't wait to get out there and play their war games. They could get themselves blown up."

"Yes, they could." Eve came over to stand beside her. "And it's really getting to you." Her eyes were on Jill's face. "Maybe more than I would have thought."

"And it's not bothering you?" Jill shook her head. "I know better than that. I've never seen anyone as crazy about a man as you are about Joe Quinn. I didn't expect you to be this controlled."

"I have to be controlled," Eve said quietly. "Joe is a detective, and he's in danger every day. I face this too often to let myself fall apart every time he walks out the door in the morning. It's his job, and it wouldn't be fair to him. And he's fantastically efficient at that job, and that helps."

"Is he really that good with land mines?"

"Yes, trained by the SEALs, and he kept up with advances. He's done work on cases where he had to defuse them. And once when we were in Scotland, he got rid of a number of them planted on the road bordering a lake we were exploring. He knows what he's doing. So I trust him with those damn bombs as well as everything else." Her lips twisted. "Even though at times like this it nearly kills me. Particularly since this time I'm to blame for his being here."

"No, you aren't. I am," Jill said in frustration. "Joe knows that, everyone knows that. Which is why I should be going with them today." She raised her hand. "Mistake. You don't have to tell me it would be a mistake. I know it would be a mistake. I'd be a liability. I don't have the training." She added gloomily, "I think I should get Novak to send me to that same CIA training camp in Afghanistan where he sent Gideon."

"What? I don't believe you'd stand a chance in persuading him," Eve said. "And he'd probably be right. That's not where you make a real difference in life. You don't shoot people. You use your brain and figure out how to change the way they think so that they'll do what you want. It's part of your ability as a storyteller. That's where you make the difference. That's your talent, and who should know better than I how good you are at it?" She grimaced. "Though considering the kind of situations in which you become embroiled, it might not be a bad idea to keep that training camp on the back burner as an alternate plan. But I'd find another way to reach the same goal."

"Easy to say. Right now I feel like one of those medieval women who were left home to tend the castle while the men rode off to save the world. It's driving me crazy." Her gaze suddenly narrowed on Eve's face. "And I bet it's driving you crazy, too. You'd hate it as much as I do. How do you cope?"

"Like you, I try to be reasonable about the greater good. I have a son to think about, and that has a tremendous influence." She suddenly smiled recklessly. "And when I can't stand it any longer, I go for it, get on my trusty steed, and ride hell for leather and leave that safe, boring castle behind."

Jill smiled back at her. "I thought as much." Her smile faded. "But what are you going to do today?"

"I'm going to work on Mila." Eve went over to her worktable. "Because that's where *my* expertise lies. And I'll try to get lost in my work and forget that Varak might have a more sophisticated land mine than we've seen yet. I'm going to trust Joe and Gideon and Novak. I'm going to wait for Joe's call. If I have to stay in the castle, I'll be as productive and inventive as I possibly can. So that next time, I might be the one to save the world." She glanced over her shoulder. "Sound like a plan?"

"It sounds like you," Jill said. She turned away. "I'll have to think about it. I'm having trouble adjusting at the moment. Thanks for letting me vent. I needed it."

"I could see that. No problem." She smiled. "It was good talking just to remind myself of all the things I knew were important. Sometimes emotions get in the way." She paused. "I'm scared, too, Jill.

Varak seems like the ultimate bogeyman. He's escaped so many times during these last years. No one has been able to touch him. And now he's got Zahra Kiyani in his corner. When Gideon told us about the compound, I thought that it was going to be okay. But what if it isn't? Novak's drones uncovered some nasty surprises."

"They'll find a way to get around them. It might just take a little while."

"Yeah, I know." Eve forced her gaze to shift back to her reconstruction. "Definitely time for me to get to work."

Jill watched Eve's hands flying over the clay. Eve was focusing, her determination unquestionable as usual. It was a quality Jill envied at this moment.

Then do something about it, she thought impatiently. She turned and went out the door. The morning sunlight was getting stronger, and it was warm on her arms as she sat down beside the door. She had promised to watch over Eve, but she needed a little distance now.

Because Eve's words had struck a strong, resounding chord. She had to think about them, examine them, let them begin to come alive. She knew about words. They were a part of her mind, part of who she was. And these words might be some of the most important of her life.

You don't shoot people. You use your brain to figure out how to change the way they think so that they'll do what you want. It's part of your ability as a storyteller.

That's where you make the difference.

That was true. All her life that was what had made the difference. Yet from the time she had brought Eve to Maldara, she had stepped back because of guilt and uncertainty. She had relied on Novak, Gideon, Joe Quinn, and Eve herself to make most of the moves forward. She'd been content to merely sit on the sidelines and watch over Eve.

And Kimbro had died. Eve had been poisoned. There was no

telling how much blame Jill had to shoulder about the bombing of that U.N. building because she hadn't been more aggressive.

She had to close her eyes for an instant. She couldn't be sure that everything would have been different if she'd been more true to herself. But what if it had been? When you wrote a story, every chapter, every paragraph, every plot point made a difference.

She opened her eyes and drew a long breath. Okay, don't look back. Look forward. Do what Eve said she could do, use her primary talent. Figure out a way to change the way the story would go. Pray that trip to Varak's encampment would yield dividends but don't count on it. Rely only on yourself.

Look at the principal characters and how they would behave. Explore weakness, strength.

Varak was a sociopath, almost impossible to judge.

But Zahra...

What had Eve said about Zahra?

And now he's got Zahra Kiyani in his corner.

But did he really have her in his corner? Could her character be moved, shifted?

Think about that...

And who else had moved into the spotlight?

Dalai.

Strange to think of that slender, vulnerable girl in anything as bold as a spotlight. She had fluttered in and out around Gideon, then had run away. But there had been no doubt that she had been honest and helpful about Varak. Jill hadn't realized until now that something about her encounter with Gideon had made her uneasy...

Put the thought aside. Let it simmer.

Go back to the beginning, when she'd first gotten that offer from Hadfeld.

That was really the start of the story...

NAGALI RAIN FOREST
2:35 P.M.

"Quinn's not back yet?" Gideon murmured to Novak as he crawled back from checking on the other men on the team. "It's been almost an hour. I don't like it. He stopped us four times before we got half a mile into the property to disarm land mines. I have an idea this whole jungle is one big time bomb."

"So does Quinn," Novak said grimly. "That's why he wanted to explore ahead to make sure that it would be minimally safe for us to go forward without blowing ourselves up. The sentries are the least of our worries."

"Well, they may not be the least of Quinn's worries. I didn't hear any explosions, but one of the sentries might have gotten him." Then he shook his head. "No, Quinn's too sharp. Forget I said that. I just want to get moving. So do the rest of your team, Novak."

"Do you think I don't?" He paused, struggling with his own impatience. "Quinn knows what he's doing." He added, "I hope."

"That didn't appear to be a sincere vote of confidence." Joe Quinn was suddenly moving out of the palmetto bushes next to them. "But I can see why. I thought I'd be back before this."

"Why weren't you?"

"I knew after a half hour that I wasn't going to be able to bring any of the team much farther than this point. I've never seen an area so heavily seeded with land mines. Varak must be truly paranoid. I watched one of his sentries, who obviously had a defined path, and he was very careful about not going off that path. He probably didn't know where all those land mines were either."

"And that surprises you?" Novak asked. "Varak would have been amused if one of his men was careless enough to get himself blown up." He asked, "Where were you for the rest of that hour?"

"Taking photos. Trying to determine sentry placement. I found the helicopter pad." He looked at Novak. "And I located the main house and bunkhouses."

Novak tensed. "Varak?"

"I didn't see him. And that area is so heavily fortified, there's no way we'd be able to get into his house or get a shot at Varak without being blown away ourselves." His lips twisted. "I thought I'd better get back instead of staking him out. After all, you are heading this team."

"Not so that anyone would notice," he said. "You said that the team wouldn't be able to go any farther, but you managed to flit all around the damn encampment."

"I knew what I was doing. One man with experience. An entire team tramping through there would end up in pieces. The odds are someone would make a mistake." He looked at Gideon. "And that young girl you were so concerned about would pay for it when Varak got spooked. Do you want that?"

"No. But I *do* want Varak." He turned to Novak. "What do we do?"

Novak thought about it. Dammit, he couldn't see any options at the moment. He muttered a curse, then said to Gideon, "Go back to the men and get them out of here and back to Robaku." He whirled back to Quinn. "You said one man could do it. How about two? Can you take me back to that house so that I can verify that bastard is Nils Varak?"

Quinn gazed thoughtfully at him. "Maybe. You want to stake him out?"

"I want to see him *move*. And maybe there's some way we can get in that house for DNA. If we can't, I want to get a video to send to our lab for facial analysis and verification. They'd be able to determine if his basic facial structure would support that plastic surgery Zahra paid for. It's not much, but I don't want this all to be for nothing. Can you do it?"

Quinn was thinking about it. "You do know that it gets dark very early in rain forests like these. Those tree canopies block out all light. You'd have only a limited amount of time to stake him out. We'd have maybe three or four hours." He added grimly, "And it's hard as hell to avoid those land mines when I can see. Even at dusk, it would be a risk. I can't use a flashlight because of the sentries."

"Stop telling me about the problems. Will you do it?"

"Shit," Gideon said. "Novak!"

"Answer me, Quinn." Novak held his eyes. "Can you get me there?"

Quinn suddenly smiled. "Sure, no problem. I know the way now. Providing you can follow in my steps without a single deviation. Not even an inch." He added dryly, "That would be nearly impossible for you considering that you don't like to go any way but your own."

"But not quite impossible," he said curtly. "I'd have the comfort of knowing you'd be blown up before I would." He turned away. "Let's go, Quinn."

Quinn nodded. "By all means. I was pissed off about having to stop and come back to you anyway." He moved back into the palmetto bushes. "Stay close, Novak. I'm going to be moving very fast."

ROBAKU
5:50 P.M.

"What do you mean they went back into that jungle?" Jill stared at Gideon in horror. "Gideon. Why did you just leave them there?"

"I had orders, dammit," Gideon said. "I couldn't go with them, but I could get the team safely back. That's what I did."

"Since when did you ever obey orders," Jill's voice was shaking. "You do what you like."

"Not when it comes down to sacrificing thirty-two men by not obeying two men who have a hell of a lot more experience than I do."

"No, you'd rather sacrifice—"

"Easy, Jill," Eve said. "It's not his fault. Would you like to go up against Novak or Joe?"

"Yes, I'd like to knock their heads together." But she realized Eve was right. It was just the shock that had caused her to attack Gideon. Shock and sickening fear. But she had to control it. Eve was just as frightened as she was, and she mustn't make it worse for her. She forced herself to nod at Gideon. "You did what you could. I'm just scared."

"Me too." He made a face. "I nearly flipped when Novak wanted to go back with Quinn to stake out Varak. I would have done anything I could to stop them. I was worried about Quinn's being a wild card, but Novak was just as bad today."

"Or just as good," Eve said quietly. "They're both professionals, and they wanted to get the job done. What can we do to help them, Gideon?"

He shook his head. "Not much of anything. Just wait. I left two men on the road that borders the property to send me word if anything . . . unusual occurred."

"You mean if one of those land mines blew up," Jill said.

Gideon nodded. "That was what Quinn was worried about. I told you that he told Novak he wanted to get out of that jungle before it got dark."

"Yes, you did." Eve was looking out the window at the fading light. "It should be dark soon."

Gideon didn't say anything.

Jill's gaze flew to his face. "Gideon?"

"Not in that rain forest," he said. "It's probably been pitch-dark for the last thirty minutes."

She inhaled sharply. She felt as if she'd been kicked in the stomach.

Gideon said quickly, "You know they'll call as soon as they get to a safe area."

"Whenever that is," Eve said numbly. She straightened her shoulders. "Yes, Joe will call me as soon as he can. I know that."

"Of course you do. Let's go outside and get some air." Jill strode toward the door and opened it for Eve. "Like you said, they're both professionals."

She watched Eve go out the door before she turned to Gideon. "How bad was it out there?"

"Deadly. What you'd expect from Varak," he said soberly. "It's set up to be a killing field, between the land mines and the multiple snipers. If the team had gone in, the chances are we'd have never come out. Novak knew that, but he was desperate."

"So he took the chance himself." Her lips twisted. "And he'll do it again." She started out the door toward Eve. "If Varak didn't kill them both this time." Her hands clenched into fists at her sides. "We'll have to see if Eve gets that call."

———

The call didn't come until almost an hour later.

Jill's heart jumped, and she whirled to face Eve.

Eve nodded and quickly checked the ID. "Joe."

Relief so great it made Jill dizzy. "Thank God."

Eve answered the phone. "You're an idiot, Joe," she said huskily. "Are you both all right?" She nodded at Jill at his answer. "You don't deserve it. When will you be here so that I can tell you in person?" A moment later she hung up the phone. "Another forty-five minutes. They didn't leave the stakeout until it was almost fully dark, and it took them longer to get back through the jungle."

"I would think it would. Was the risk worth it? Did they get what they needed?"

Eve made a face. "Joe said partially successful. But partially is never enough for Joe."

"Nor for Novak." Jill tried to keep her voice steady. "I'll go inside and tell Gideon that they evidently didn't get blown up. Coming?"

Eve shook her head. "I'll wait out here. I'm too edgy to be cooped up right now."

"And you want to see Joe the minute he walks down that path."

"You might say that," she said lightly. She leaned back against the wall. "Though I do intend to be very stern with him."

"Yeah, sure." Jill opened the door and went into the museum.

Gideon immediately looked up. "Eve heard?"

Jill nodded. "Both okay. They'll be here in about forty-five minutes. You'll probably hear from Novak soon."

Gideon gave a low whistle. "I'll call the airport and let the team know."

"Do that." She was silent a moment. "They didn't get everything they needed. They'll probably go back, won't they?"

He hesitated. "It depends on how successful they were."

"The only results they'd consider successful enough to stop them from going after Varak would be if they'd managed to kill him or had gotten some scrap of DNA material that would prove his identity. Neither of those things was likely to happen according to Joe. Right?"

"That's what he said," Gideon said warily.

"Then no way should they run the risk of going after him again," she said flatly. "We need to leave him alone and try another direction."

"It's Varak, Jill," he said gently. "He's out there waiting for us to scoop him up."

"It's the wrong thing to do. I sat here all day, going over everything that has happened since I got that first message from Hadfeld, until the moment you showed up with the location of that compound from Dalai. It's like a story with huge gaps missing, but nothing I

thought of or tried to put together made going after Varak in that
jungle the right thing to do." She held up her hand as he started to
protest. "And I'm not going to argue with you. I know where you're
coming from. I'll talk to you later." She turned and headed for the
door. "Will you stay here with Eve until Joe and Novak get here?
I'm tired, and I think I'll go down to Hajif's hut and rest for a while."

His eyes widened in surprise. "You don't want to wait until they
get here?"

She shook her head. "So I can hear about how they avoided the
killing fields? Maybe later. Right now, it doesn't appeal to me. It
makes me feel sick to my stomach." She headed down the hill toward
the village.

She needed to be alone. She didn't know what her attitude would
be when she saw Novak again. The day had been fraught with tension and worry and attempts to forget that he might not be coming
back. That first moment when she had realized he was safe had been
dizzy and shocking and put her on an emotional roller coaster. What
they had between them was only sex and passion and the strange
bond of fascination that had formed these past months, she told herself. Last night, she had been swept away, and today had been so
emotional that she couldn't regain her equilibrium. It was better if
she took a step back until she was more cool and able to analyze her
responses.

And there was no way that would have been true if she'd been
there when he'd walked into the museum tonight. No, she needed
to go to see Hajif and Lcta, have a light meal, then go to bed.

She would deal with Novak tomorrow.

———◆———

Her phone rang three hours later.

She tensed, then rolled over on her sleeping mat and reached for it.

Novak.

Bite the bullet. He wouldn't stop calling until she answered. "Hello, Novak."

"Get out of there and come to me. I need to see you."

"I'm already in bed."

"I don't care. Come to me, or I'll come and get you. You don't want Hajif and Leta to be upset." He cut the connection.

No, she didn't want Hajif to be drawn into this. She rolled off the mat and threw on her clothes. A moment later, she'd stalked out of Hajif's hut. She saw Novak in the doorway of his hut, framed against the lantern light behind him, and strode toward him. "What do you want, Novak? That was completely rude, and I don't appreciate you—"

"Shut up." He pulled her into the hut and jerked her into his arms. "I'm having a very bad day." He kissed her. "And I didn't need to have you hiding out and avoiding me at the end of it. Particularly after Gideon was telling me how weird and stiff you were being." He kissed her again. "That's not going to happen. If you don't want to screw me, that's your decision, but you're going to be with me. I need you." He pushed her down on the blankets. "Do you want a drink? I could use one right now. A glass of wine?"

"How polite." She sat up, trying to get her breath. What had started out as anger was transforming into that same electricity she had felt last night. Her breasts were swelling, her lower body tingling, readying. "And you can't force me to be here. What's wrong with you, dammit?"

"Wine," he answered himself. "You like wine." He poured a merlot from a bottle into a glass. He poured himself a whiskey and sat down cross-legged in front of her. He handed her the goblet. "No force. I merely made a suggestion."

"Bullshit."

He grinned. "Okay, I wanted to catch your attention."

"I almost decked you."

"And I wanted a little sympathy after a hard day."

"Not the way to get it. And since when have you ever come to anyone after something goes wrong? I've never seen anyone so self-sufficient."

"It's a new era." He took a sip of his whiskey. "Maybe I've never found anyone with whom I wanted to share my very rare failures. Or maybe I just wanted to see you sitting here and know that there was someone I cared about whom Varak hadn't been able to touch. Anyway, I was frustrated as hell when you weren't there when I got back to that museum. I needed you."

He had said that before, and suddenly Jill's impatience was dwindling before it disappeared entirely. It would take a lot for a self-assured man like Novak to admit to needing anyone. "Gideon said that it was bad out there." She took a sip of her wine. "A setup for a killing field." She added with sudden fierceness, "So why did you go back with Quinn and try to get yourself slaughtered? Varak's killed close to six hundred thousand people in that war, and he clearly built that compound as a trap. You knew it, and you still talked Joe Quinn into staking out that house."

"I didn't have to talk very hard. Quinn wanted him as much as I did. I only had to let him control how he got me through that land-mine tangle. Quinn likes control."

"And you don't?" She shook her head in frustration. "The two of you together are a complete disaster."

"Actually, I found we worked very well together today."

"And that could be an even bigger disaster." She drew a deep breath. "Would you like to tell me why you waited until after dark to start trying to get back out of that jungle when Quinn told you how dangerous it would be?"

He shrugged. "It wasn't that bad. Quinn had the route pretty well memorized, including land-mine placement. And we had no choice. We didn't get even a glimpse of Varak until almost twilight. I was afraid we might have to give it up for the day." His lips twisted. "But then Varak's true nature came to the rescue. He evidently hadn't had his quota of blood recently. He had one of his soldiers dragged to that dirt yard before the front porch to be punished for some infraction at the attack on the U.N. headquarters. At least that was the excuse. I think he probably just wanted his men to witness how all-powerful he was." He paused. "He used a machete. He took a long time. I had no problem getting the videos."

Jill felt sick. "You said that you'd know him just by the way he moved. Was it really Varak?"

He nodded. "I'd swear to it. But that wouldn't be enough, of course. Not now that Zahra has convinced everyone that Varak's skull was destroyed at the U.N. headquarters. Probably the videos won't be enough either, but we can send them through our photo techno unit at Langley to establish what he could have looked like before surgery. But we'll have to go back and break into that house in the compound and get a DNA specimen so that I can get the director to let me stage a raid powerful enough to bring Varak down."

"That means you're determined to go back there," Jill said tightly.

"It's our only option if we want to grab the bastard before he decides to leave the country. We're lucky to get the chance."

"I don't believe there's any luck connected to Varak unless it's bad luck. He definitely couldn't be recognized?"

He shook his head. "His face has been changed, his hair is sandy-blond, not black. The only thing that's the same is that muscular, powerful body and the way he walks. The arrogant bastard strides around as if he owns the world..."

Muscular and powerful... As arrogant as if he owned the world.

Jill went still. "His hair is dyed blond now? I only remember Dalai telling Gideon that he'd had plastic surgery."

"Very good plastic surgery. But his hair is kind of dirty blond now."

Fair hair. Suddenly, her chest was tight, and she was having trouble breathing. It couldn't be the same man, could it? Varak wouldn't take the risk of exposing himself just to inflict that act of terror on her. And she hadn't been able to see what shade her attacker's hair was in the darkness, only that it was light, fair. But she had felt the straw-like texture beneath her fingers when she'd been fighting him.

But it had done her no good to fight him, she remembered in a panic. She'd felt so weak, and he'd been brutally strong...

As if he'd owned the world.

"Jill?" Novak's gaze was narrowed on her face.

"You said you took a video." She moistened her lips as she put her glass of wine carefully on the floor beside her. "I want to see it."

"No, you don't," he said flatly. "You don't want to ever see that bloodbath."

"You took it. I want to see it."

"Why?" he asked roughly. "So that you can add it to your collection of nightmares? There's no need for you to see it."

"That's up to me, isn't it?" She had to keep her voice steady. "You thought it important enough to risk getting yourself killed. Show it to me."

"I tell you, it's the stuff of nightmares. You don't want to—" He suddenly broke off. "Nightmares..." His gaze was searching her face. "Don't make me show you this, Jill."

"I want to see it."

He muttered a curse. "And it seems I'm going to let you see it." He got to his feet, went to the phone lying on the bench, and brought it to her. "Do me a favor and don't watch more than the first five minutes. He does a lot of strutting during that period and doesn't get into the carnage until you see him take his machete."

She was bracing herself to press the PLAY button. "He loves that machete." She swallowed. "That's how he killed those children."

"Press the button," he said roughly. "Just watch it and get it over with."

She pressed the button.

Fair hair. Eyes glittering as Varak strode out on the porch and looked down at the man kneeling in the yard.

Ferocity.

His lips pulled away from his teeth like that of a feral animal.

Malicious pleasure.

Anticipating the pain to come.

He was speaking, hurling threats at the man on his knees.

Then he was walking down the steps.

Power. Arrogance. As if he owned the world...

She couldn't take her eyes off him. She was staring in helpless fascination.

Even when one of Varak's men handed him his machete.

"No, dammit!" Novak was there beside Jill, jerking his phone away from her. "No more."

"No more," she repeated dully. She didn't need any more. She'd seen enough. "Thank you. I...couldn't seem to stop. He was like a snake that was weaving back and forth and hypnotizing me. Not letting me move." She hadn't been able to move that night in the jungle either. "I couldn't move at all. Only snakes aren't that strong..."

"Shh." She was suddenly in his arms. "No, they're not that strong. And I'll be chopping the head off this particular snake very soon. He's just jumped even higher on my kill list." His hand cupped the back of her head, his lips at her temple. "It was him?" he asked softly. "He was one of those sons of bitches who raped you that night?"

She shook her head. "No, he was the one who was telling the rest of them how to do it." Her voice was shaking. "He kept saying they weren't hurting me enough. That it wouldn't do any good unless they broke me. He seemed angry about it. He was the one who kept beating me and beating me..." She had to take a deep breath. "It was him. I recognized the eyes." She added, "And the voice. I didn't realize I'd remember so much. It was such a hideous blur. Or maybe I just tried to block him out." She recalled something else. "And that laugh. I'll always remember him laughing when he leaned over me and asked how I liked it—" Her fingers bit into his shoulders. "But he never actually raped me, and I didn't get a chance to scratch him. He must have been very careful about DNA. He'd know how dangerous it was to him...Maybe that was why he was so angry. He'd hate it that he couldn't make me suffer as much as he wanted." She buried her face in his chest. "But you were right—arrogant. As if he owned the world."

"He won't own more than six feet of it when I get my hands on him," Novak said harshly. "I knew you thought he was one of them when you kept insisting on seeing the video. I couldn't stop you when you had a right to know." His lips tightened. "And I had a right to know, too. I've been wanting to kill those bastards from the night it happened."

"It never occurred to me it could be him," Jill said. "I just thought it was a few thugs hired by the people who killed Hadfeld to make certain I left Maldara. Why would Varak become involved in . . . that . . . when it would automatically put him in danger?"

"Why would he use a machete on that man today? The idea probably amused him. I'll have to ask him before I gut him."

His voice was colder than she'd ever heard it, and Jill was beginning to be afraid she'd made a terrible mistake. Novak had already been determined enough to go after Varak in that hellish jungle, and she might have tipped the scales even more. She rushed to repair the damage. "Don't use me as an excuse. I've told you time after time that none of that was your fault. I wasn't your responsibility. Do you hear me?"

He didn't answer.

"And what if you're wrong about making another run at Varak?" she said harshly. "I've been thinking about it today, and it seems too dangerous. He's sitting there with his land mines and his damn machete ready to strike. I know you believe it's the logical way to go, but it could get you—"

"Hush." He pulled her down and fitted her spoon fashion against him. "Just lie here and let me hold you. We'll talk later. You're upset, and I didn't handle any of this right."

"No, you didn't. You should believe me when I tell you something. I know it's partly my fault. I got upset when I realized Varak—" She stopped and started again: "How can I persuade you not to go back into that jungle after Varak?"

"You can't." His lips were brushing her ear. "I can make this work, Jill. All I have to do is figure out the best way to do it."

"You mean to keep him from using that machete on you. It's the *wrong* thing to do," she said passionately. "We can go at it another way."

He didn't answer.

And he wouldn't answer, she thought. "Stubborn jackass."

"Only when I know I'm right. Relax. We'll talk later."

But he wouldn't listen then either. "No, we won't. You're already making plans, and they don't include me. You're scared that I'll break apart. It's been like that from the beginning." She added, "So you shouldn't be upset if I make plans that don't include you."

He stiffened against her. "What's that supposed to mean?"

"It means that this is *my* story, and I'll do anything I can to make it come out right. You're about to mess it up."

"I don't like the sound of that."

"Ditto. Do you want it more clear? It seems I'm going to have to take events into my own hands." She tried to relax her muscles and took a deep breath. "So I'm going to do as you suggest and lie here and take a little while to pull myself together. Because you were right, that video shook me up. But it probably shook you more than it did me because I promised myself that I'd never let any of those men hurt me again. They're no more than a passing memory to me now, and soon, they won't even be that. And it doesn't change anything that one of them was Varak. It will just take a little longer to forget him." She closed her eyes. "I'm going to try to sleep. When I wake up, I hope you'll make love to me because l found it wonderful, and I'm not at all sure that we'll ever do it again."

"Are you finished?" Novak kissed her ear again. "I don't know what's happening with you, but I'm very good at working through problems. That all sounded very final. But I assure you it is not." He held her closer. "By all means rest. Because once we start, we'll be doing it again and again and again . . ."

CHAPTER

17

J ill moved silently across the dimness of the hut.

"Come back," Novak murmured, as she reached the door. "There's still plenty of time."

She glanced over her shoulder. Novak was only a glimmer of strength and sensuality in the half darkness, but she still felt a hot tingle of sensation run through her. Ignore it. The hours with him that had gone before had made her body too accustomed to the sheer sexual eroticism of what they were together. Her breasts still felt heavy. Her skin felt satin-smooth and pliant. "You're wrong. We're out of time. Maybe I'll see you later, Novak."

The next moment, she was out of the hut. She drew a deep breath of the moist, humid air and started up the path toward the museum. It was only a little after six, and she'd been tempted to go to Hajif's, but she'd be too close and available to Novak there. Last night, he had shown her that he would have no qualms about bursting into Hajif's home if he wished.

And she did not wish to see Novak anytime soon. The sex had been too hot, and there had been that element of domination of which she was always aware with Novak. He hadn't liked it that she'd refused to communicate with him in any other way than the one that had driven both of them to the edge and beyond. If she'd stayed any longer, she would not have been able to fend off either arguments or conversation.

Conversation? They were so far apart, it was a totally foreign concept. He just wanted her to say that he was right, and he wasn't listening to her. And she was so frightened that Varak would kill him that she was desperate to try anything that would leave Varak out of the equation.

And that meant leaving Novak out of the equation as far as she was concerned.

Okay, then, start as she intended to continue.

Check in with Eve, then explore the path that had been beckoning to her since yesterday afternoon . . .

———◆———

"You've been very restless this morning." Eve looked up from her Mila reconstruction as Jill put coffee in front of her. "Everything okay?"

"As okay as it can be." Then Jill was silent. But she couldn't leave it at that. "Did Joe mention when they'd be going back to Varak's compound?"

Eve shook her head. "Just that they want it to be right. They were frustrated as hell yesterday." She added soberly, "I don't like it either, Jill. But I can't convince him that we have any other option. Joe doesn't like it that they found that helicopter pad. It would be too easy for Varak to get a helicopter pickup and fly out of there if he took the notion."

"And that means they probably won't wait longer than tomorrow or the next day." Jill forced a smile. "And that's not long to come up with another solution. But miracles happen, don't they?" She tilted her head. "Now I should let you get back to work. Is there anything else I can get for you?"

"No. How many times do I have to tell you that you don't have to wait on me, Jill?"

"It's no trouble. I don't have anything else to do now that Joe is here. He's eliminated my primary job of making sure that you're safe. He's so good at it that I feel useless. You don't really need me any longer." She lifted her hand as she headed for the door. "If you think of anything you want, give me a call. Till then, I'll stay out of your way."

"You've made sure never to be in my way," Eve said quietly. "And no one could ever call you useless."

"That's good to hear." She smiled as she opened the door. "See you later."

Jill moved quickly down the path and into the jungle several yards from the museum. She wanted complete privacy, and this area had seemed the best way to ensure it.

She sat down beneath a kapok tree and took out her phone. She paused, looking down at it. She could still change her mind. She might be wrong. But she had to go with her instincts. She drew a deep breath, took out the slip of paper with the phone number Gideon had given her when he'd come back from the palace the night before last.

This is how you make a difference.

She hesitated, then dialed the telephone number.

It rang once.

No answer.

It rang again.

Nothing.

On the third ring, it was quickly picked up.

"This is Jill Cassidy, Dalai," she said quickly. "Is it safe for you to talk? If it isn't, hang up on me."

Silence. "Is he dead?" Dalai's voice was a mere agonized breath of sound. "Gideon said you would only come to help me if he couldn't. Did I kill him?"

"No," Jill said quickly. "He's still alive. Can you talk? Where is Zahra?"

"The British prime minister is here. She took them to the hospital to visit the victims." She brushed the question aside. "Tell me. Is Gideon *hurt*?"

"No." Jill added deliberately, "But he could have been. It was very close."

Dalai struggled to get control. "Thank God. How I prayed that he would be safe."

"That's very kind." The girl was obviously sincere, but Jill had to harden her heart against the impulse to soften. Difficult to do since all she could think about was how much Dalai must have gone through over the years. "But you still sent him out to that compound."

"He *wanted* to go. You all wanted to go. You all knew how evil Varak is. I told you everything I could to help you."

"We realize that. It wasn't enough. Though Gideon was still grateful. And he did what he could to protect you before he went into that jungle to go after Varak." She added, "But that compound was one huge trap. It was a miracle they got out alive." She paused. "And they're going to go back if you don't stop them. Help me to stop them, Dalai."

Dalai was silent. "You know *nothing*. How can I do that?" She paused, her voice edged with panic. "Varak has to die, and I cannot do it. Do you think I haven't thought about it? But when I'm with him, it's as if he devours me."

"It's the fear that devours you," Jill said. "Do you think I don't know how that feels?" But she couldn't be too sympathetic or Dalai wouldn't take that final step they needed her to take. The girl had come so far against tremendous odds. Just from listening to Gideon about their encounters, Jill could read between the lines. Dalai was clearly a fighter but not a trusting one. She had even been afraid to trust Gideon. So give her something to fight against, someone to fight beside. "But don't expect me to let you cover your head and send people I care about to do what you should be doing. This is your battle, too. What you gave us didn't work. As I said, every step at that compound is a trap. We need more from you." She paused. "Gideon told me about the way you handed him Varak on a platter but dodged talking about Zahra. He accepted it because he felt sorry for you." Her voice became flat and uncompromising. "I don't feel sorry for you. I can't afford to do that. It's too dangerous for all of us. I won't pity you, but I'll respect you and work with you. Because I believe you can do anything you have to do to help us, Dalai. I thought a long time about how you fit into the picture, everything that you'd discussed with Gideon, your background, what you must have felt, what you wanted out of life. What your story really was . . . And then I realized that Gideon was letting his guilty feelings blind him to the fact that you aren't quite the victim he thinks you to be. Yes, you've been mistreated and threatened and terrorized. Who could deny that's true?" She paused. "But I believe you've managed to survive it because you're very, very strong. You had to be strong to live with Zahra Kiyani since you were a child. She's a powerhouse and as evil as they come. Gideon believes you've been brainwashed, but I think you've just done and said the things you had to in order to survive. I did the same thing when I was living in all those foster homes when I was a kid. But you had it even rougher than me. It took someone very smart and patient to fight that silent battle with Zahra all these years. I imagine most of the time she doesn't realize you're doing it. You're still fighting, but I'd bet somewhere down deep you've been waiting for your chance to get away from her. You might even have a plan? I think that first night that Gideon came to you, the reason you were so upset was that you were afraid he'd get in the way of any plan you might have to free yourself from Zahra. Is that true?"

Dalai didn't reply.

It was pure guesswork and instinct, but Jill had to go with it once she'd started. "But then Varak showed up on the scene, and it was a horrible scenario that you couldn't tolerate. You had to do something, anything, to get rid of him. You're frightened of Zahra, but in the end you didn't see her as the prime immediate threat. You thought you'd have time later to find a way to escape from her. So you distracted Gideon from discussing anything about her so that he'd concentrate on Nils Varak. Varak had hurt you terribly and would hurt you again if given the opportunity. It was to your advantage to have us go after him with full force right away and prevent him from doing that." She smiled sadly. "So you called Gideon and delivered the message you wanted to send. When you left him, Gideon had a mission."

Dalai was silent. Then she finally said, "You're . . . very clever. Madam said you were." Another silence. "That's the reason she hated you. She tried to get that Wyatt man from the U.N. to stop you. But he couldn't do it, so she had to go to Varak."

It wasn't that frank admission that surprised Jill but the fact that Dalai's voice and manner had altered in the space of that silence. Both were no longer trembling or fearful, only troubled.

"Gideon is clever, too," Jill said quietly. "He would have realized what you were doing if he hadn't been so conscience-stricken about how he treated you when you first came to the palace. He has a great heart, and it tends to get in his way."

"There's no reason for him to feel badly," she said jerkily. "He treated me very well. Everyone else was afraid of her." Then the words tumbled out. "I didn't *want* to do this. But he was always so smart and strong. It's what I most remembered about him. I thought he'd be all right. I didn't mean not to tell him the whole truth." Then she stopped. "No, I guess I did. But I gave him Varak, someone I knew he wanted very much. And, yes, I knew it would also keep me from being hurt again. There's nothing wrong with that. I thought I could tell him all the rest about Madam later, when it would be safer for me."

"No, there's nothing wrong with that," Jill said. "I can understand how you might feel you had to protect yourself any way you could." She paused. "As long as it didn't hurt anyone. Because I realize what you went through. We're alike in many ways. We've both been victims." She added, "I believe you know that, don't you? You said Zahra had to go to Varak to help her. You heard exactly what Zahra asked Varak to do to me when she couldn't get what she wanted from Wyatt."

Silence. "She was very angry with you. He told her it would be better to kill you, but she said that would be... awkward, and that they should just hurt you." Another silence. "I knew what that meant. I was very sad. You should have done what she wanted."

"No, that would have been the wrong thing to do." Jill hesitated, then said deliberately, "Because that would have made me the slave she's tried to make you, Dalai. You know that if you don't fight, that's what happens. I was hurt, but I healed, got to my feet, and started to fight again. I'm fighting now. And that's what you've got to do."

"Do I? Even though she said she's like Kiya, and I was meant to be her slave?" Jill realized there was actually a trace of sarcasm in Dalai's words, and it only showed how far they had come toward honesty in these last minutes.

"Bullshit. How do you know that you're not the one who's like Kiya? You can be whatever you want to be. Look at you. You've already started to fight." She added dryly, "Though definitely in a manipulative manner. I'm afraid we're also alike in that quality, and lately, I've become very aware how destructive it can be. I've sworn off it myself unless it's an emergency." She changed the subject. "But it's time to admit that the only way you're going to get rid of Varak is through using everything you know about Zahra. Zahra's the key. It's too deadly going after Varak. There are too many traps. So you'll have to give me a way to use Zahra to bring Varak to us."

"There's no way to do that," she said quickly.

"I believe we'll think of a way. We'll talk, and something will come to us. It probably won't be as slick and efficient as what you were planning to have Gideon do. But we'll get there."

"You don't *know* her." Her voice was suddenly harsh. "Stay out of this. Let me handle her. I know how she thinks, how she reacts. You could spoil everything. You don't know what she'd do."

"No, but you do. You know everything about her." It was time to stop pushing. She had to step back and let the decision come from Dalai. "If you're ready to help us, then find a way to call me. I don't want to put you at risk again. Let me know, and I'll somehow find a way to get you out of there so that we can talk more freely." Her voice took on an urgency that could not have been more genuine. "But we don't have much time. People will die." Now add the single plea that might change the story. "Gideon will die."

She cut the connection.

Jill drew a deep breath. It was done.

Now all she could do was sit here and wait for a call that might not come.

The call came three hours later, when the sun had just started to go down.

Her heart jumped as she saw the presidential palace ID on her phone. *Yes.*

"I will help you." Dalai's voice was intense and angry when she came on the phone. "I have no choice. Though you'll probably be like all the rest of them who care only about themselves. But you mustn't be stupid or careless. Do you hear me? I won't be put in that...place again."

"Hopefully, I won't be either of those things," Jill said. "How can I help you? Should I send someone to the palace to get you?"

"You're already being stupid. You'd spoil everything if you did that." Dalai drew a deep breath. "Besides, I'm already here."

Jill stiffened in shock. "What? Where?"

"Robaku. I knew that's where you were. Madam was angry enough about it. I decided there was no sense my trying to tell you anything on the phone. I'd have to come there anyway."

Jill was stunned. "Just like that? You walked out of the palace and just decided to come here to see me. How?"

"Madam leaves a car in a garage two blocks from the palace that we use when she goes to see Varak. Most of the time, she likes me to drive, so I have the keys."

Jill shook her head in bewilderment. "Then you could have escaped whenever you chose."

"No, I couldn't. She would have chased me down and caught me. It wasn't the right time. Neither is this, and you keep on asking questions," she said, exasperated. "I only have a few hours before she'll be back from that meeting with the British prime minister. I've parked down by this brook with the boulders. I've come this far. Now you come to me."

"I'll be right there." Jill was jarred out of the shock as she realized what the consequences were of Dalai's decision. "How long have you been here? No, you had to have just gotten here, or they would have been all over you. Look, you might have visitors before I get there. Don't run away. Just wait for me."

"Visitors?" Dalai repeated, alarmed. "Not Gideon. I don't want to see Gideon. I came to see you."

"Fine. Just wait for me." She hung up and called Novak. "Did you get the drone intruder report?"

"It just came in. How the hell did you know?"

"She's no threat. Don't do anything. Don't tell anyone you got it." Dalai had mentioned Gideon, she remembered. "Don't tell Gideon. She particularly doesn't want Gideon."

"Who is no threat?" he said sharply. "What are you doing, Jill?"

"Dalai. And I'm trying to get off this phone so that she won't run away." She was already striding down the path toward the brook.

"But I can see that's not going to happen unless I let you come. Okay, meet me at the brook. And don't you let anyone hurt her." She cut the connection as she rounded the bend and saw Dalai standing beside the brook. She was wearing a black cloak over her top and sarong skirt, and she looked as if she were going to fly away any minute. Jill drew a breath of relief. "I was afraid you'd be gone. It would have been wise of you to give me a little warning." Jill skidded to a stop before her. "I'm sure you must have picked up information from Zahra and Varak that this place is a virtual armed camp."

"No, they've never mentioned it." She was frowning. "Varak doesn't like having Eve Duncan here, but Madam told him to stay away from Robaku. She didn't want to cause an incident if—" Dalai broke off, then said impatiently, "And I wasn't sure I was coming here, so how could I give you warning? I didn't know if I'd change my mind. But no one saw me."

"Except the spy in the sky. Which means Novak saw you." She looked down the path. "Don't get spooked. Here he comes. It was easier to bring him here than argue."

Dalai froze, her gaze on Novak. "I have to go."

"No, you don't. This is Jed Novak. I trust him. Gideon trusts him." She turned to Novak. "Don't you do anything intimidating. She's here to help us. She's already literally gone the extra mile. So let me handle it."

Novak stopped, staring at Dalai. "She doesn't appear to be a threat. Though her coming here automatically makes her suspect." He took a step closer. "And she doesn't seem to be intimidated, only wary." He smiled at Dalai. "Maybe we should have a truce to see if either one of us has cause for concern." His smile faded. "Though I didn't like it that she didn't want Gideon here."

"I was...ashamed," Dalai said. "He was kind, and I knew he pitied me." She looked him straight in the eye. "I used it."

"Not good." He glanced at Jill. "Why is she here?"

"Because I don't want to see anyone get blown up by that homicidal maniac. She might be able to tell us how to work around it. She knows Zahra, inside and out."

Dalai was still holding Novak's eyes. "And she says Zahra is the key. Do you believe that, too?"

"Jill and I are at odds on that score. But I'm always willing to listen to differing opinions." He was gazing at her searchingly. "Do you think she's right?"

"She might be. That's why I'm here." She shivered. "Though I don't want to be. I *hate* this place."

"Because of the children," Jill said. "I understand."

"Yes. No." She shook her head. "It always frightens me. I want to leave here." She said impatiently, "But I'm here, so what do you want to know?"

"Everything," Jill said. "But you told me when you first got here that you couldn't tell me anything on the phone. You said you would have had to come here anyway. Why?"

"Because you think you understand, but you can't. I knew I'd have to show you." She whirled on her heel and strode along the bank toward the tall boulders that bordered the north side of the brook. "Let's get it over with."

Jill was running after her. "Where are you going?"

"The boulders." Dalai was hurrying down the path. "Now don't talk to me. I'm nervous about this, and I'm afraid I'm doing the wrong thing. I've never trusted anyone but myself before. I still don't." A moment later, they'd reached the edge of the creek, and she was skirting around it until she reached a group of tall boulders that bordered it to the south. "The third one..."

Then she fell to her knees and was digging at the dirt at the base of the boulder. *"Yes."* She had revealed a nine-inch-square keypad. Then she froze, gazing down at it. "Give me a minute. I'll be all right in just a minute."

"What the hell is this?" Jill fell to her knees beside her. The girl was clearly terrified. She reached out to take her hand. "What's wrong? Let me help you, Dalai."

"No one can help me." Dalai was staring down at the keypad. "That's what she said. No one can help you, Dalai."

"Zahra?" Jill was frowning in confusion. "She was the one who said that to you?" Then she stiffened. "Zahra was *here*?"

Dalai drew a deep breath. "Of course she was here. She's always been here. She regards Robaku as her special place. She brought me here several times a year from the time my father sent me to her. Usually at night, when she considered it safe." She pulled her hand away from Jill's. "And she hated it when you got in her way."

"You mean when she built the museum?"

"No, she thought that was a triumph. It was all your stories and keeping those villagers from being moved." She was looking down at the panel, bracing herself. "There's a code." She was punching in a four-letter code. "She gave it to me when she first started training me to help her take care of this place. She waited almost a year before she trusted me with it." Her lips twisted. "When she thought that I'd been taught to obey every rule she'd set out for me as a slave should." She paused. "And the consequences if I failed in any way."

"Dalai, what are you talking about?" Jill asked quietly.

"You wanted to know about Zahra Kiyani. I'm telling you about her." She met Jill's eyes as she punched in the final letter. "This is who she is. Shall I tell you what the four letters of the code are?"

Jill was beginning to make a wild guess.

Then she heard a click, and the rocky ground around the boulder appeared to shift. The next instant, it slid open to reveal a trapdoor with a metal ladder.

She heard Novak mutter a soft oath behind her.

"The ladder is very sturdy and safe," Dalai said. "So is the cavern below. It was built by Zahra Kiyani's great-grandfather, but the Kiyani family kept it updated and repaired through the years. You can understand why she didn't want the village disturbed in any way."

Jill was gazing down into that darkness. "You've known about this for years?"

"She needed someone to come with her to check and make certain all was in order. She trusted me. She made certain I could be trusted." She reached in her cloak and pulled out a flashlight and thrust it at Jill. She made an impatient gesture toward the ladder. "Go and see for yourself. I can't go down there yet."

"Stay here, Jill," Novak said. "It could be a trap."

"She's still shaking. Just look at her," Jill said. "For heaven's sake, it's no trap. I'm going down, Novak." She turned on the flashlight. "You can keep an eye on her if you want—" Novak was already climbing down the ladder. "It's okay, Dalai. You can wait for us here." Jill headed for the trapdoor and started down the ladder.

There were over twenty steps, and she saw Novak standing on the ground beside the ladder. She jumped from the fourth rung and caught hold of him to steady herself. The earth was soft and mushy beneath her feet, and the smell was a blend of earth scents and rotten vegetation. And something else that was causing Jill's stomach to tense. She moved the beam of the flashlight to pierce the darkness. Stone walls, a path leading south, away from the creek.

"I think we know what that code is." Novak had pulled out his pen flashlight and was looking around at the stone walls. "She gave us enough clues."

And he'd already figured it out, she thought. He'd probably done it before she had. That intelligence and the amazing ability to put puzzles together... "I need to be sure." Jill started down the narrow, rocky path.

"I don't suppose you'll let me go ahead, Jill," Novak said.

"No. My story." She gave him a smile over her shoulder as she moved faster. "I brought you here. Are you trying to cheat me?"

"Perish the thought. I just wanted to be sure there weren't any snakes down here."

"Keep an eye out. But I don't think Zahra would permit that. I'm sure she always sent Dalai down to check it out."

Then she made the turn in the stone path.

She stopped and inhaled sharply.

"It's true . . . " She had to gather her composure before she glanced over her shoulder at Novak again. "Now you can tell me what four-letter code Dalai punched in at that boulder."

"Kiya," he said softly. His gaze was traveling around the sizeable room and all the treasures it held.

"Too easy." She was dazzled as the beam of her flashlight fell on wonderful vases, trunks overflowing with gold and precious jewelry. And several truly superb gold statues. "If Zahra hadn't been so arrogant, any security expert would have told her that was the least safe password she could have chosen." She crossed the room and touched one of the statues. "Well, we found where Zahra grabbed that wonderful statue she gave to Dobran. But none of those statues are as fantastic as the Great Beloved Wife."

"Amazing." Novak was examining one of the engraved gold coffers. "There's so much here. I know that it was supposed to be a wagonload of treasure. But that was a long time ago. You would have thought the family would have gradually let some of it go."

"Family tradition," Jill said. "Gideon said that Zahra was an absolute fanatic about family history and tradition. Evidently, it was a trait passed down through the ages." She drew a deep breath, then wished she hadn't. That sickeningly familiar scent . . .

"Jill?" Novak's gaze was on her face.

"I'm fine. I just want to get out of here. We should get back to Dalai."

"I'm here." Dalai was standing behind them. Her face was chalk pale. "I told you I'd only be a minute." She pulled the cloak closer about her as if to ward off a chill. "Have you seen enough?" She was gazing searchingly at Jill's face. "Maybe more than enough. You're very clever, Jill. I believe you see things that others wouldn't see."

"I see that you look ill." Jill moistened her lips. "And frightened.

Why are you so frightened to be down here?" She was thinking back, trying to put together everything she knew about Dalai. "Gideon said that you were terribly afraid of Zahra." She was trying to remember. "He said you said something about the place with no air." Her gaze flew to Dalai's face. "Is that this place, Dalai?"

Dalai nodded. "I can't breathe down here." She swallowed. "I know it's my imagination, but it doesn't make any difference. My heart starts to pound, and I want to scream."

"Just being underground?"

"What?" Dalai looked at her as if she were crazy. "No, it's the cage." She moved jerkily across the room to a row of large, gold, bejeweled chests against the far wall. "That's what Madam called it, the night she made me get into it." She paused beside an elaborate gold chest whose top was thickly patterned with a beautiful, closely woven, openwork design. She threw open the chest, and Jill saw that it was empty. "It was that first year she brought me here, and she had to make sure I was broken enough that I'd never betray her." Her voice was trembling. "So one night she made me climb into this chest, and she locked it. It wasn't quite airtight, but I thought it was. It was dark and I couldn't breathe and I thought my heart was going to jump out of my chest. I screamed, and I couldn't stop screaming. I heard her laughing. She said she was sure Kiya had punished her slaves this way, and I had to learn that every time I failed her, she would put me in this cage. If I was lucky, she'd remember to take me out." She was looking down at the coffin-like interior. "She remembered in thirty-two hours."

Dalai couldn't have been much more than a child, Jill thought in horror. An experience like that would have scarred anyone, much less a vulnerable girl totally dependent on that monster. It was a wonder that she had not been totally crushed. "I don't know what to say," she said gently. "You'll never be able to keep from remembering that time, and I can't help what happened to you." She added with sudden harshness, "But I'll be there to lend a hand when you're ready to throw that bitch into her own cage."

Dalai looked at her in surprise. "I didn't tell you that to make you feel sorry for me. I just had to make you understand." She turned away from the chest. "She only put me in that chest one more time, and I knew what to expect, so it wasn't as bad. But I couldn't stop remembering that first night whenever she made me come down here."

"I can understand why," Novak said grimly. "But I don't understand why you even came down today. We saw what you wanted us to see. You were right, we had to experience it for ourselves."

Dalai shook her head and turned to Jill. "No, I had to make sure that you knew everything that happened here." Her gaze was searching Jill's face. "I think you do. You figured it all out. When I first saw your expression after I came down, I could tell." She met her eyes. "Do you want me to put it into words?"

Jill couldn't look away from her. That scent was surrounding her... The panic was rising. "No." She whirled away from her. She couldn't go yet, she knew there was one more thing to check. "I'll be right back, Novak. Take care of her."

Then she was out of the treasure room and stumbling down another short path. The pungent scent was stronger now, and she could see broken boards on the ceiling up ahead. She had to stop as she saw the dim light piercing the cracks in that wood.

Sickness.

Horror.

"Jill." Novak was holding her. "Come on. Let's go back."

"I had to be sure," she said numbly. "I couldn't believe what Dalai was trying to tell me." She was clinging to him. "That's the schoolroom, Novak. It's only a few yards away from Kiya's treasure. The Kiyanis allowed that schoolroom to be built practically on top of their precious treasury. Dalai said Zahra's great-grandfather moved the treasury here, and that was very smart, wasn't it? I'm surprised it wasn't Zahra. Because no one would disturb a village school or suspect what was below it." She swallowed. "But I could smell the scent of that schoolroom the minute I came down here. The chalk, the burnt walls and floorboards... All that death... I know it so well."

"I know you do." He'd turned her and was leading her back toward the treasure room. "And it's going to hit you harder any minute, so I want to get you out of here. That's why I left your Dalai and ran after you."

"She's not my Dalai, she doesn't belong to anyone. But someone should help—" She stopped and closed her eyes. "There's more... She was trying to tell me, but I didn't want to listen. I didn't want to hear the end of the story." Her eyes opened. "But I have to hear it now." She pulled away from him and strode back into the treasure room. Dalai was still standing where she'd left her beside the golden cage. Jill crossed the room toward her. "The schoolroom." Her hands clenched into fists at her sides. "It was all coming together before, but I need the words now. It wasn't just a random attack, was it? Tell me."

Dalai shook her head and said unevenly, "Zahra didn't have enough cash to keep paying Varak, and she was afraid the Botzan army might take Robaku."

"Go on," Jill said.

Dalai was shivering. "So she told Varak about the treasure and promised him a share if he stayed, kept working for her, and found a way to keep her treasure safe until the war ended."

"And he took the deal," Jill said hoarsely.

"Yes, he wants that gold. It's still all he talks about."

"The gold," Jill repeated jerkily. She had to get the words out. "And his solution to get it was to stage a massacre that killed all those children and half their parents and made that schoolroom a memorial site that no one would want to desecrate."

Dalai nodded.

"One more question. Did Zahra approve of his 'solution'?"

"Not right away. She said that it appeared to be a practical plan, but he would have to lower his fee since she was going to have to do a good deal of the publicity and diplomatic work herself."

"Yes, that would enter into any negotiations," Jill said unsteadily. "Couldn't you tell someone?"

"I wanted to live," Dalai said simply. "I was afraid. I'd only heard bits and pieces of the plan, and I didn't know about the schoolroom. But I know that I will go to hell forever for being such a coward." Her voice broke. "When I heard about the children…"

"Yes, the children…" Jill said dully. The children who had died only yards from where she was standing. She couldn't stand here, thinking about it. She had to get out of here. She turned and headed for the ladder.

A few minutes later, they had all surfaced by the boulders. It was only twilight, Jill realized. It had seemed a very long time ago that she had descended that ladder. She looked at Dalai as she got to her feet. "Yes, you're sorry," she said jerkily. "I can see it. But now you have a chance to change your story. To not let a massacre like that ever happen again. Can we count on you?"

Dalai looked away from her. "I'm here, aren't I? I've told you things that would get me killed…or worse." She lifted her chin as she turned to face her. "I'll do whatever I can. But I'm still a coward. Don't expect me to be something I'm not."

"All I want now is for you to listen and call us if there's anything we should know." She added, "And I'll do the same. We'll do the rest together, Dalai."

Dalai gazed at her for a moment before she turned and went toward her car. Then she suddenly looked back at them. "You're going to do it, aren't you? You're actually going to take them both down?"

Jill nodded. "I promise you. And you're going to be there when we do it. No one deserves it more."

"I…believe you." Her dark eyes were filled with wonder. "And I think I might be able to…trust you."

"Good." Then Jill had a sudden thought. "Have you been here too long? What if Zahra's missed you?"

"Then I'll lie to her. I've learned how to do that very well. I'll make her believe me." She shrugged. "Then Madam will beat me, and I'll weep and be very contrite and afraid. She's too busy right now to do anything else to me."

"I wish you wouldn't call her Madam," Jill said bitterly. "It sounds so subservient. It reminds me of the way she's treated you all these years."

"It's what she wants me to call her. If I stopped, she would think it odd and punish me. But someday I will not care what she thinks." She got into the car. "Because she won't be able to use her fine, golden cage if Robaku is no longer available to her. Isn't that sad?" She didn't wait for an answer but drove away from the brook area and headed for the road.

"She's certainly not the rabbit Gideon said Zahra called her." Novak's thoughtful gaze was following her. "And she might say she's a coward, but I don't see that either. It's as if she was opening, changing, revealing new facets, every moment she was here."

"She's a survivor," Jill said. She turned and headed for the museum. "And what she's done today may make us survivors, too." She glanced at Novak, and said fiercely, "Because we know how to fight Zahra and Varak now. We know what holds them together. You know damn well we have a weapon if we use it right. And it's got nothing to do with Varak's compound. So don't tell me that you're going back there."

"I wouldn't dare," he said dryly. "You're so savage, you might throw me in that golden cage."

She shuddered. "Don't even talk about it. I don't understand how Dalai was able to go through what she did." She looked back at the tall boulders, which suddenly appeared threatening in the gathering darkness. "I made her a promise, Novak. Now you have to call everyone up to the museum and get a plan together to make sure that I didn't lie to her."

CHAPTER

18

K iya?" Gideon shook his head. "It seems impossible that treasure has been here in Robaku all this time. You'd think Hajif or someone else would have stumbled over it at some time or other."

"Dalai said Zahra was careful," Jill said. "And who would believe that it was right under their feet for all those decades." She smiled bitterly. "And after the massacre, no one wanted to go near that schoolroom. Just what Varak thought would happen." She turned to Eve, who had been very quiet since Jill and Novak had returned to the museum over an hour ago. "I couldn't believe it when I saw it. Don't go down there, Eve. It...hurts."

"I have no intention of looking at that treasure," Eve said. "It would make me ill." She leaned back against the cabinet. "All I want to do is find a way to use it to get our hands on Varak." She crossed her arms tightly across her chest. "Soon."

Joe nodded. "That's the aim," he told her quietly. "If Varak has been sitting there in that compound waiting to get his hands on that gold, all he'll need is a push. He set up his compound as a trap, and we can do the same thing with Robaku. Dalai said that they had no idea how we were fortified. We can just make sure that it appears to be a simple, sleepy village with only a minimum number of guards

to give Varak trouble. And we'll have to find a way to get the villagers out of the line of fire. We just have to make sure it's all handled
right."

"So that no one gets a machete in their throat," Eve said wryly.

Jill had heard enough. "But first we have to get him here." She
was on edge. Yes, both Joe and Novak had plans that would probably
work once Varak was lured to Robaku. They were already thinking
of strategy, and that was fine. But that wasn't her priority. "Zahra."
She got to her feet. "We have to make her be the one to spur him
to leave that compound. That's what I told Dalai, and that hasn't
changed. And I should be the one who does it." She smiled faintly.
"I'll weave her a fine story and make her believe it's her own. As
Eve said, it's what I do well. The rest of you can think and scheme
and spend your time making Robaku the most splendid trap on the
planet. Just let me get him within your range."

Novak was shaking his head. "And let yourself be within the range
of a woman who would have no compunction about tossing you
into the deepest dungeon if she can get away with it. Even Dalai said
she hates your guts."

"Then as Joe said, it's my job to handle it right. I'm going to call
my publisher when I get back to Hajif's hut and ask him to set up an
interview for me tomorrow with Zahra Kiyani. That's the first foot
in the door." She met his eyes. "I'm going to do it, Novak. Don't
get in my way."

"No promises," he said curtly.

"If you do, I'll just work around you. I'm going to do what I do
best." She headed for the door. "Now you all do what you do best,
so mine won't be for nothing."

Then she was out the door and moving down the path toward the
village. She carefully didn't look at the path that led to the sparkling
brook and those tall boulders. The horror and sadness were still too
close to her. She just wanted to get away from them for these next
few moments.

"Jill."

She stopped and looked behind her.

Eve was coming down the path after her.

"It's going to be okay, Eve," Jill said quickly. "Don't try to talk me out of it. It's the only way that makes—"

"Hush," Eve said, still coming toward her. "Stop talking and start listening. I have something I have to say to you."

———◆———

THE NEXT DAY
10:40 A.M.
KIYANI PRESIDENTIAL PALACE

"What a pleasure to see you, Ms. Cassidy." Zahra's tone was almost a purr as Jill walked into the small, elegant office where she'd been escorted by both a uniformed soldier and a bespectacled young clerk. Zahra was sitting in an elaborately carved chair behind an equally graceful desk. She was dressed in a deep teal-colored maxidress and looked stunning as usual. "But then it's always a delight to have you visit the palace. We have such a long-standing relationship. Of course, it's not always been harmonious, but I believe we'll be able to iron that out now. I'm sorry you weren't among the journalists here the other evening to hear my speech. I was truly spectacular."

"I was a little busy, but that's what I understand." Jill paused. "It was superbly done. But then, you're always ingenious." She glanced around the office. "I assume this office is totally secure? You wouldn't have had me brought here if it wasn't. And your clerk gave me the equivalent of a strip search before they let me in to see you." She smiled. "As you said, you can't count on my being either reasonable or harmonious. You've always considered me a troublemaker."

"And so you are." The purr had suddenly vanished. "I thought I could discourage you, but you were too stupid. You kept insisting and getting in my way. Robaku is *mine*. You had no business writing all those stories objecting to my moving those peasant families out of the village."

"Actually, I *was* stupid," Jill said. "I agree with you on that score. Because I thought our battle was entirely about Robaku and those children. I had no idea you had another agenda entirely on the back burner." She paused. "Or that you'd gotten yourself involved in something that was more ugly than I could ever dream. Not until Joe Quinn went to Asarti that night and came back with this." She pulled a photograph out of her bag and pushed it across the desk at Zahra. "She's very beautiful, but you should have known that Gideon would recognize it as the first Kiya."

Zahra stiffened, her hand clenching the photo. "I don't know what you mean." But her gaze was almost hungry as she stared at the statue. "I've never seen it before."

Bingo. Jill realized she had hit a nerve. Move the needle a little farther. "What a pity. It's extraordinary. Joe Quinn gave it to his wife as soon as he got back from that fishing expedition. Because she's an artist, too, he thought Eve would appreciate it."

"He gave it to *her*?" Zahra couldn't seem to take her gaze from the photo, and her lips were tightening viciously. Then she forced herself to look away. "It doesn't make any difference. It's just a statue. It has nothing to do with me."

"But the fact that that crook, Dobran, had it in his possession, and did the DNA falsification on Nils Varak, might be very awkward for you if it came to light."

"No proof," Zahra said. "I know nothing about Nils Varak other than he's a monster who almost destroyed my country. We've taken whatever weapon you thought you had away from you." Her eyes narrowed on Jill's face. "See what response you'll get if you take that nonsense to the media or anyone else. You should have seen how that British prime minister was bowing and scraping to me yesterday. I'm a heroine, haven't you heard?"

"Yes, and you won't be easy to topple," Jill said. "But you've made me very angry, Madam President. I'm going to try exceptionally hard to see that happen. I've found political figures aren't that difficult to bring down once you find their Achilles heel. I won a Pulitzer doing that a few years ago."

Zahra's lips curled. "Threats?"

"Not yet. First, I'll tell you what I'd do to win another Pulitzer. I won that first one totally on my own. This time I'd have help. I'll bring Eve Duncan in to give interviews and tell her story. It won't have quite as much weight after you and Varak destroyed the skull at the U.N., but she has an amazing amount of respect and credibility. It would stir up a good deal of talk and cause people to start asking questions." She smiled. "And I'd be there to answer those questions. You thought my stories were troublesome before? I'd never stop. Eve has already been speaking to the U.S. embassy and asking them to intercede with the U.N. to grant extended permission to continue her work at Robaku. She can be very persuasive."

She leaned forward across the desk, her eyes shining, her words firing like bullets. "We're planning to set up permanently at Robaku, and you'll never get rid of us. Before we're through, you'll never say that Robaku is yours again. It will be *mine* and Eve Duncan's. We've already drafted plans for tearing down that hideous schoolroom and building a fine chapel where families can come and pray for their slain children. I'll be taking pictures of the schoolroom and showing what it could be with public support. I'll spend a lot of time describing the children who died there. You'll remember how much sympathy my stories have aroused in the past year? Well, before we're through, anyone who reads those stories about Robaku will want to get in there with a jackhammer and tear that schoolroom down themselves." Jill could see the shock in Zahra's face at the picture she'd drawn. Okay, hit her with another one from a different direction. "And you might be interested to know that in another fifteen minutes, Eve Duncan will make an announcement on your

local television station that she's invited several top news agencies to
Robaku for a press interview tomorrow afternoon. She's promised
to divulge a startling revelation regarding the tragedy." She added
mockingly, "They were all very eager to accept the invitation. I'm
afraid you're old news now, Zahra. And Eve Duncan gives so few interviews."

Her eyes were suddenly wary. "Revelation?"

"It's a good way to intrigue and start the buzz going, don't you
think?"

"That sounds like a threat to me," Zahra hissed. "You'd both blow
your credibility. No one would believe you. You wouldn't take the
chance."

"I admit I hesitated, but Eve is an idealist. Once she finished the
reconstruction of that skull, she said she couldn't live with herself if
she kept silent. What could I do but throw my support behind her?"
Jill paused. "And it's not a threat but a warning. Or perhaps an opportunity. I don't really want you if I can have Varak. He's the big
story. You're small potatoes."

"What?" Jill could see her eyes flash. She'd thought that bruising
Zahra's vanity would be the way to hit home. Then Zahra recovered
quickly. "Varak is *dead*. There is no story where he's concerned."

"I think there might be. I've studied Varak for years, and I know
what a complete sociopath he is." She tilted her head. "I have no idea
why you're doing this, Zahra. I wonder if you realize what you've
gotten yourself into by dealing with him. You're a strong, dominant
woman, and he won't put up with it. It's only a matter of time before
he kills you." She smiled faintly. "You've probably already had to talk
yourself out of situations you found dangerous."

"I don't know what you're talking about," Zahra said through set
teeth. "Varak is dead."

"No, he isn't. Not yet. But you'd be much better off if he was." Jill
added bluntly, "Because I'll never stop going after him, and you'll be
caught in the cross fire. Pity, since you've been doing so well lately.

But they'll burn you at the stake once they find out how you've been coddling Nils Varak." She paused. "But if you find a way to deliver him to me, I won't care if he's accidentally shot by you or one of your soldiers. Maybe you could set it up so that you'll truly be a heroine. All I want is the monster dead and the story finished. I might even be able to persuade Eve that Varak dead is the primary goal, and we don't want to spend years in courts just to tangle with your lawyers. As I said, you're ingenious, and I'm sure you could figure out how to come out of a scenario like that in fantastic shape. Consider it a challenge."

"I consider this insanity." Zahra got to her feet, her cheeks flushed. "And I'll have to ask you to go." Then she suddenly burst out, "You think you can do this to me? You'll lose. I always win." Her eyes were glittering with malice. "Just as I won from you before." She took a step toward her. "Did what they did to you hurt, bitch? I told them it had to hurt."

"Then they did what you told them to do," Jill said steadily. "I've already figured out that had to be Varak. Why do you think I want him so much? Give him to me, and he'll never bother either of us again. Take the challenge, Zahra."

She turned and strode out of the office.

Her phone. Jill had to have her phone.

She quickly stopped at the clerk's desk and picked up her belongings from the security basket.

Don't look to see if anyone is following.

Just hope that Zahra was now turning on the TV in that office to watch Eve Duncan and make sure Jill hadn't lied to her.

Eyes straight ahead.

Jill called Gideon as she walked out of the palace. "The Kiya statue. It has to be in full view, somewhere close to Eve, while the TV broadcast is going on."

Gideon cursed. "We don't have time, Jill."

"Make time."

Bitch! Bitch! Bitch!

Zahra's hands clenched into fists as she watched Eve Duncan's face on the TV across the office. Eve was sitting at her worktable, and Zahra's statue of Kiya was resting on the dais like a favorite ornament. Like it belonged to her. Zahra wanted to throw something at that image, which had no hint of the glamour or fascination that Zahra possessed. The only thing she could see in that woman was boring sincerity.

Maybe no one was watching her damned announcement.

But they probably were, and they'd probably watch her TV interview tomorrow, too. Jill Cassidy was right. Those news reporters were like hungry vultures.

She felt a rush of panic. Things had been going so well. She'd thought she had everything under control. Now she had to deal with the scandal that might come if Eve Duncan came forward, with Jill Cassidy standing beside her. That was going to be a media and diplomatic nightmare to straighten out. How was she going to handle it?

Her phone was ringing.

Varak. She hoped he hadn't seen that TV announcement. But the bastard always knew what was going on.

She answered the phone. "Don't blame me for this. It's not my fault. I just found out about it."

"It *is* your fault. I told you to fix it. What's that announcement the whore is going to make tomorrow?"

"What do you think? According to Cassidy, they're going to cause big-time trouble. I told her that no one would believe them, but she was raving about setting up permanent shop at Robaku to call attention to Eve Duncan and her reconstruction work." She added the one threat that had frightened her the most: "And getting permission from the U.N. to tear down the schoolroom and build some kind of chapel. There's no doubt that they'd find the treasure."

Varak was cursing. "If you'd gotten rid of them earlier, this would never have happened. You've stalled me and stalled me until we're down to this. I can't afford for even one person to believe them. It's my neck on the line, you stupid cunt."

Zahra felt the fury surge through her. It was too much. He was talking to her as if she were one of the whores she provided for him. As if she didn't have enough to worry about without these insults. "Then if you think I've done so badly, why don't you take care of it yourself?" she spat out. "Maybe I was wrong to keep you from being reckless enough to take us both down. Get rid of all of them for all I care. Do what you like!"

She cut the connection.

She was breathing hard, panting, as her anger continued to rise. She should probably call him back and try to pacify him, but she couldn't do it. It had gone on too long. The son of a bitch had actually almost strangled her the last time she'd seen him. Hadn't Jill Cassidy said something about how dangerous it was to deal with him? As if she didn't know that for herself. But she was smarter than Cassidy ever dreamed of being, and she could handle him.

If she wanted to do it.

Think. She slowly leaned back in her chair. The situation had turned critical. She could either face a nightmare of explanations and suspicions if Eve Duncan gave her interview tomorrow, or she could accept that in the end, Varak's solution was best. Eliminate those troublesome people at Robaku who were a threat to her and Varak. And who'd had the nerve to steal *her* Kiya statue, she thought angrily.

Or she could handle the problem in a way that was infinitely more pleasing and satisfying in her eyes. A little more difficult, but it would eliminate giving that son of a bitch anything he wanted.

Take the challenge, Jill Cassidy had said.

Zahra could meet any challenge.

She just had to decide which way she wanted to meet it.

But regardless, it would have to involve Varak. She reached for her phone to call him back.

"I was angry," she said the moment he answered the phone. "I'm still angry. But it's clear something has to be done. You've been nagging me about your share of the treasure? Well, I'm ready to talk about it. But not until you give me everything I need before you fly out of here."

———◆———

ROBAKU

"You could have called me when you were on your way back here," Novak said curtly when he met Jill as she parked her car. "Would that have been too much bother?"

"No, but I knew that you'd have someone monitoring the front gates of the palace and would know when I left." She was walking quickly toward the museum. "And I didn't know what kind of high-tech listening devices Zahra's people might have. I took a risk even calling Gideon. I didn't want her listening in when I chatted with anyone."

"It wouldn't have been a 'chat,'" Novak said. "And they don't have anything that high-tech. Strictly low-grade stuff."

"I didn't know." She added wearily, "And I didn't want to talk to you anyway. Zahra is never easy, and she was particularly difficult today. I had to concentrate on doing what I had to do." She glanced at him, and said deliberately, "What I told you that I could do. Pressure, Novak."

"And did you do it?"

"I believe I did. I won't know until I see signs later. I lined up choices for her. I suggested she could kill Varak, which I'm sure she'd like to do. And I told her that schoolroom would be threatened by

Eve and me, so she might order Varak out of his rat hole to attack us. She'll be terrified that her precious treasury might be discovered. Or there's the possibility she's so besotted with the statue that she might get careless and go after it herself. But even then, she'd probably pull Varak into it in some way. Zahra might take one choice or none at all. But it might lead her to make her own choices, which might suit us as well. All we care about is getting Varak here." They had reached the museum, and she put her hand on his arm. "How did Eve's TV announcement go?"

"Fine. She was warm, concerned, businesslike, appealing." He grimaced. "And hating every minute of it. She doesn't care for the media."

"I know. But this time it wasn't my fault. It was her idea to get Gideon to set it up." She paused. "I did everything I could to talk her out of it. It paints a big bull's-eye on her chest."

"And you don't have one? Be serious."

He was right. After that conversation with Zahra, she'd put everyone here at Robaku at risk. "We knew what we were getting into from the beginning. Eve didn't."

"She knows now. She thinks you're doing the right thing. She's right." He was standing looking at her. "Though I hate to admit it." He suddenly kissed her, hard. "And I know you pulled it off with Zahra. We're going to find out before this day is over that you changed the story to suit yourself." Then he was releasing her and turning away. "I've got to get back to the village and make sure we've made Robaku look like a peaceful, helpless place that Attila the Hun would lust to get his hands on."

"Not too helpless," she called after him.

"Be quiet, Jill," he said over his shoulder. "You told us to do our job and let you do yours. You're officially on the sidelines now." He disappeared around the curve of the path.

But she didn't want to be on the sidelines. She was still on edge and needed to know what was happening. She opened the door and went into the museum to see Eve.

"I'm glad you're back." Eve looked up from working on the Mila reconstruction. "I wanted to get rid of Novak. He was pacing the floor in here after I threw out that TV crew. That was the last thing I needed."

"But he said you did very well."

She shrugged. "As good as can be expected." She smiled. "We had to scramble to get that Kiya statue displayed. Why did you want us to do it?"

"I'm not sure. Instinct. The sight of it might be the final thing that pushes her over the edge. It seemed right."

"And your instincts have proved to be very good as far as getting people to make that final commitment. I'm evidence of that." Her eyes narrowed on Jill's face. "How did you do this time?"

She smiled. "As well as can be expected." No, Eve deserved more than that. "I wish I knew. It might have worked. Everything seemed solid. I appeared to be striking the right notes. We'll have to see." She looked around the museum. "All those skulls in their pretty boxes are gone. Where are they?"

"I thought it would be better if we hid them somewhere in the jungle. Zahra knows they're here and wanted to get rid of them. She could have Varak target them."

"Target," Jill repeated. "That's what I told Novak you were now."

"Of course I am. Now stop talking about it." She looked back at Mila. "I want to finish this bit, then I want to call Michael and talk to him for a while. It will relax both of us."

"You told me that he . . . knew things. Won't he realize that something is wrong?"

"More than likely. But he'd realize it anyway. I'm not going to cheat either one of us today because I want to pretend everything is fine. I'll just tell him I don't want to discuss it, and he'll accept it."

"That's good." The bond between mother and son must be as intricate as it was strong, but Jill knew that this call might not have been made if Eve hadn't been aware how precarious was their position. "He's a wonderful boy."

"Yes, he is." Eve looked up and made a face. "Now stop fretting about us. I have no intention of dying today. I just don't want Michael not to have heard my voice when he's going to be worrying. Joe can't call him right now, so it's up to me."

"Where is Joe?"

"Varak," she said simply. "He went to keep an eye on the compound to see if there's any indication that Varak might be going to take action. He promised to report back to Novak as soon as he saw any signs." She met Jill's eyes. "And that should tell us if your talk with Zahra worked. I really hope it did because Joe was not at all pleased about my little TV show today."

"I hope so, too." That was a massive understatement. Jill dropped down in a chair and tried to relax her tense muscles. "I guess all we can do is wait to hear from Joe."

The call came from Joe two hours later.

Jill straightened in her chair as Eve took the call. Her gaze flew to Eve's face, trying desperately to read her expression.

But Eve was listening and only said one sentence before she ended the call. "Then I'll expect you."

She put down the phone, and her eyes met Jill's. "Joe's on his way back. You did it, Jill." Her eyes were shining, and the excitement and triumph were all there in her face. "Varak's on the move!"

———◆———

KIYANI PRESIDENTIAL PALACE
10:40 P.M.

Where the hell was Dalai?

Zahra strode into her quarters and tore off her dress and threw it on the bench. "Dalai, get in here. I need you!"

Dalai was suddenly in the room, her eyes wide with alarm. "I'm sorry, madam. I thought you'd be downstairs longer."

"You're not supposed to think. Just be here when I want you here. I need to change and be ready to get out of this place. Get me that scarlet pantsuit and the black boots."

"Right away, madam." Dalai flew toward the closet room.

This wasn't the time for the idiot girl to be this careless, Zahra thought. Everything tonight had to go precisely as she had planned. Dalai must not hesitate with performing even one order.

And Dalai wasn't the only one who had to perform faultlessly to Zahra's orders. She dropped down on her vanity stool, reached for her phone, and punched in Varak's number.

"I don't have time to talk to you now," Varak said impatiently when he picked up. "The team I sent to reconnoiter Robaku just got back. I've been getting their report."

"What was it?"

"It's going to be a snap. We'll be in and out in a heartbeat."

"Then you'll take time to talk to me. I agreed to this madness, but I won't go into an attack on Robaku blindly. I have to know what I have to deal with when all the smoke clears. It's got to look like the attack was made by the same terrorist group that blew up the U.N. headquarters. You can't be careless or messy, or I'll never be able to justify the deaths. Duncan is too famous."

"I thought that you'd agreed never to give me orders," he said softly. "When this is over, you might need another lesson."

Bastard. He couldn't resist the threat even in a situation where he might be getting everything he wanted. Zahra instinctively raised her hand to her throat. "When this is over, I'm never going to see you again. You can take your share of the gold and go straight to hell."

"So brave now that you're back in that fine palace. Perhaps I'll get a palace of my own now that you're doing the smart thing and giving me what you promised." His voice lowered. "But how do I know that your Kiya's treasure is worth my time? Maybe you've been lying to me. You've never actually let me go down there to see it."

And she wouldn't this time if there was any other choice. "I told you that I'll let you go down there tonight before you attack Robaku. You can check it out yourself."

"I wouldn't have it any other way. It had better live up to expectations."

"You said you were in a hurry. I'm trying to give you an update on what I've done to protect us. Do you want to hear it, or would you rather threaten me?"

"Both. But I'll listen as long as it includes the release of that damn gold you've been promising me all this time."

"I have no choice. I can't be careful any longer. And I have to get rid of you before someone finds out that Duncan is telling the truth at that press conference."

"How awkward. It would be a disaster for me, bitch."

"Don't worry, I'll get you safely out of the country. I've arranged to have an army transport truck be driven to Robaku and parked a few miles down the highway. You can have your men drive the truck to pick up your share of the treasure after you've eliminated the problem at the village. And I want you out of Robaku and on your way to the airport within an hour."

"But you claim there's such a lot of gold," he said mockingly. "And it would go faster if I didn't have to divide it. Perhaps I'll arrange to get a second truck."

She stiffened. "Don't even think about it. I have a private jet waiting at Jokan airport for you to get out of the country. If the pilot sees more than one truck driving up to be unloaded, then he has orders to take off and leave you to find your way through the jungle and out of Maldara on your own."

Silence. "You wouldn't do that. I'd still be a risk for you."

"I won't let you steal my share of Kiya's treasure," she said fiercely. "You caused me to lose the Great Beloved Wife statue. I won't be cheated of anything else. You deliver my Kiya statue back to me and clean up that village. Then you get out of my country."

Another silence. "I'll let it go for now. I can always come back."

"That would be madness. Even you wouldn't run that risk again."

"Wouldn't I? But I run through money so quickly, and the idea of your looking over your shoulder is so pleasant. I can just see—" He broke off, and said impatiently, "But I have no more time. I have to make certain I'll have no problem with Robaku tonight. Give me the code to that treasure room."

"So you can steal it all and go on the run? You'll get the treasure when I know that you've given me what I need."

"And how will you know that?" he asked sarcastically. "I can't see you risking your neck and dodging bullets to come and check."

"Of course not. I'll send Dalai to report back to me and open it for you. You've always found her accommodating." She saw that Dalai had come back in the room and was frozen in place at the door. "And if you do everything I've told you to do, then I might allow you a bonus. You can take her with you." She smiled maliciously as she saw the young girl go pale. "Plane flights can be so boring."

"I'll decide later. Just have her there ready to open that door when I'll need her."

"At two in the morning?"

"Two. If everything goes as planned." He cut the connection.

She set her phone on the vanity and looked at Dalai. "You kept me waiting. How many times have I told you that mistakes have consequences?"

"It won't happen again, madam." Her voice was trembling. "Please don't send me to him."

"What you wish isn't important. But you might be lucky. I'm not certain how things will work out tonight."

"But you're sending me to Robaku alone? You told him you aren't going with me."

"But I seldom tell the truth to Varak. That would be the height of foolishness. Eve Duncan still has Kiya's Great Beloved Wife. I saw it on that television broadcast. Varak knows how valuable it is. He said he'd get it back for me as part of our deal." Her lips twisted. "Oh, he'll go after it, but he'll also try to steal it from me. How could I trust a little rabbit like you to keep him from doing it? No, I'll have to be there in case he tries to steal it after he rids me of Duncan. That statue is *mine*." She met Dalai's eyes in the vanity mirror. "And you'd better not make any mistakes tonight, Dalai," she said coldly. "I won't tolerate them."

"I promise I won't make any mistakes." Dalai nodded at the clothes on the bed. "May I help you dress? Is that what you're wearing?"

"Why else would I tell you to bring them?" She gazed at her image in the mirror and was abruptly dissatisfied. "I have to look spectacular tonight. Do you understand? I have to look like the queen I am. Whenever anyone looks at me, they have to be impressed. It's going to be a special night."

She could see that Dalai was staring at her, puzzled. But she wasn't about to make explanations. She was the only one who counted, and everyone would realize that after this was all over. Whichever choice she made, she would make it a success. "Hurry. It's almost eleven. Do my hair..." She added, "And I want to use the ruby comb in it tonight."

Dalai's gaze flew to her face.

Zahra caught the glance. "That always alarms you, doesn't it? Why? You've never seen me actually use it in the way it should be used."

"It doesn't alarm me. Whatever you wish." She was heading for the closet room again. "I'll go get the comb out of its special container. I'll be right back."

———◆———

Dalai had to steady her hands as she dialed Jill. She had to hurry. Zahra seldom followed her into the closet room for any reason, but this was a strange night. She kept her voice to almost a whisper when Jill answered. "It will be two or shortly before. They're going after Kiya's treasure."

"It's been taken care of," Jill said. "Anything else?"

"Only to watch Eve Duncan. Zahra's angry about the statue. She won't stop until she gets it." She cut the connection and thrust her phone in her pocket. Don't stop. Keep moving. Nothing must look suspicious. Every motion, every word, must seem totally natural. She knelt at the mahogany jewelry box that held the special container and drew out the jeweled comb. So beautiful. But Zahra had never cared about the beauty. She had just wanted to play her deadly game when she had taught Dalai to make the poisonous liquid with which the prongs were usually coated.

She put the shimmering ruby comb on its tray and took a deep breath. Then she started for the closet door to go back into the bedroom.

Be natural. Don't let her see anything.

She could do this.

But Zahra was right.

This was going to be a very special night.

<hr/>

"Two," Jill said as she turned back to Eve and Joe. "And we might have gone overboard about luring Zahra with that statue. Dalai is worried about Eve." She looked at Joe. "Can you persuade her to get out of here? If the statue is the bait for the trap, I could take her place here."

"It's not only the statue," Joe said grimly. "The two of you set Eve up, and now they want her dead." He turned to Eve. "Are you happy now?"

"No, but I will be if you stop growling and get out of here," Eve said. "You've arranged all kind of surveillance around this museum, Joe. You said Varak will reconnoiter before he strikes and will know exactly where I am. But he won't risk coming after me if he thinks it's a trap. He's got to feel as if he's in charge." She looked him in the eye. "Well, if I'm a target, let them come and try to take me. That way we'll know Varak won't skip out on us. That's what this is all about. Then you can whisk down and save me like Superman."

"Get out, Eve," Jill urged. "Sometimes things don't turn out as planned. He's right, we did this together. But you wouldn't have even been on this continent if it wasn't for me. Do you think I could stand the thought of—"

"Out." She turned her back on them and went to her worktable. "I don't care about what you think you can stand, Jill. I won't let Varak have even a chance of escaping tonight." She looked down at the half-finished reconstruction of Mila staring up at her from the dais. "He's never going to be able to do this to a child again." She sat down on her stool and began to smooth the clay beneath Mila's cheekbone. "So both of you clear out, and do whatever you have to do to make that bastard think that I'm as helpless as those kids were when he took his machete to them. Let's get this over with."

———◆———

"I'm going to stay here." Jill stopped abruptly only a short distance from the museum. "It's not as if I can do anything down at the village, Joe."

"You can keep me from pissing off Novak," Joe said curtly. "Not that I'd ordinarily care, but most of the action will probably be aimed at the village, and I'm leaving him in the lurch. He knows that there's no way I'll be anywhere but with Eve."

"And you shouldn't be. What does that have to do with keeping Novak from being pissed off?"

"He asked me to send you down to Hajif at the caves, where the villagers are sheltering. He wants the old man to keep his eye on you." His lips twisted wryly. "Which he knew would be a near-impossible task. If Eve hadn't wanted to get rid of you also, I wouldn't have even been able to get you out of that museum."

"You didn't get me out. There's no reason why I can't stay here. I might be needed."

"No, you won't," he said bluntly. "You'd probably only get in my way. I have no desire to watch over anyone but Eve, and you might distract me. Go down and let Hajif find you something to do."

She silently shook her head.

He muttered a curse. "I can take care of her myself. I don't need you. Shall I show you?" He took her wrist and pulled her off the path and into the jungle. He pointed at a large banyan tree a few feet away. "That's where I'll be situated. From the second branch I'll have a clear shot at anyone approaching the front of the museum. No one could get past me." His tone was low, intense. "And I'm a dead shot, Jill. Do you want to hear about my qualifications in the SEALs? What's more, I wouldn't hesitate for a second. All Varak has to do is show himself, and he's history."

"I know that."

"And there are two more of Novak's men who have sharpshooter credentials who will be stationed within signaling distance. You're not needed here, Jill. We can take him down."

She might not be needed, but she desperately wanted to be here.

Joe nodded slowly as he read her expression. "But it's not smart, you could get in our way."

She gave one last glance at the museum, then turned on her heel. "Heaven forbid I do that. By all means, go climb up your damn banyan tree and do all that SEAL stuff. Just don't let her get hurt while you're flexing your muscles."

She took off down the hill toward the village.

CHAPTER

19

"Hurry, Dalai!" Zahra was running past the brook toward the tall boulders. "Can't you see that I don't need to have him angry with me right now? Tonight is going to be difficult enough for me."

"I'm right behind you," Dalai said. "I don't see him. He hasn't gotten here yet. You don't have to—" She inhaled sharply as Varak stepped from behind the boulders. He was dressed in camouflage and had an ammunition belt across his body, a gun on his shoulder, and a holstered machete at his waist. He was carrying a large backpack. He looked angry and impatient, and Dalai could feel the fear tighten her throat. No matter how often she told herself that she must not be afraid of him, it didn't help.

He barely glanced at her as he turned to Zahra. "I thought you weren't going to be here." He smiled mockingly. "Don't you trust me?"

"No." Zahra took a step toward him. "I want my statue. Dalai is nothing. I decided you'd have no trouble refusing to give it to her after you took it from Duncan." She met his gaze. "But you'll have a lot of trouble if you try to cheat me."

"You flatter yourself." His lips twisted. "The only problem I've ever had with you was surviving your vanity and stupidity. Now show me how to get into that treasury room, then get out of here. The only thing I want to do is take a look down there and make sure you aren't cheating me. After that, I don't have much time. I've got to give Markel the signal to start the attack on the village while I take care of the museum."

"By yourself?" She frowned. "I told you not to be careless."

"There are half a dozen men here on the hill who will be on hand if I need them. But I won't need them. I have a few special surprises that I've planned for her, including the one you offered me." His gaze went to the museum in the distance. "Duncan's like you, a stupid woman who doesn't realize who she's dealing with. It will be a pleasure to teach her."

"I don't care how you do it as long as I get everything you promised me." She knelt before the third boulder and quickly entered the code. "Go down, take a look around to make sure that I didn't lie to you. Then come up and get rid of every single trace of anyone who might be a difficulty to me."

He started to move toward the ladder, then stopped. "I think you'd better come with me." He gestured down into the darkness. "I don't like the idea that you've changed your mind about sending pretty little Dalai here alone. I don't care for abrupt changes of plans."

She shrugged. "I'll go if you like. Do you think I have someone down there ready to knock you out and toss you in a trunk as I did Dalai one time?" She laughed. "You would have been amused. But I'd never try that with you." She'd pulled out her flashlight and was climbing down the ladder as she spoke. "Come along, Dalai, he's afraid of us."

Dalai turned on her own flashlight, took a deep breath, and followed her. It was worse than it had ever been, she thought. This place of horror and Varak, who was the giver of pain and terror. It would be all right. She could get through this. No one was really paying attention to her. Be the rabbit Zahra thought she was.

Varak stood and watched them both go down before he turned on his flashlight and ran down the ladder.

The beam of his flashlight illuminated the hallway; and then he was striding down the hall and into the treasury.

He stopped short. "Holy shit!"

"I told you I didn't lie." Zahra was behind him. "This is *mine*. Kiya meant it for someone like me, who was strong enough to use it as it should be used."

"You mean by giving it to me?" His beam was going from treasure to treasure, examining the jewels and the gold. "Yes, I'm sure she knew exactly what she was doing." He turned back to Zahra. "And there's so much. No wonder you were willing to give me half. But it would be very hard to choose." He paused. "Almost impossible."

She stiffened. "Then I'll make it easy. I'll stay down here with Dalai, and I'll choose the items I want while I'm waiting for you to bring me the Great Beloved Wife. You will come back, have your men quickly load the treasure I will give you, and get out. I will keep my share safely here at Robaku as I've always done." Her voice hardened. "And you will not betray me. Did I forget to mention that I told my Minister of Police that I feared for my life from those terrible terrorists? He insisted on having me monitored so that I would be able to be immediately traced in an emergency. If I don't call in every hour, they'll come after me," she said fiercely. "You said you'd have no trouble with an attack on this sleepy little village. You won't find my personal guard quite as easy to handle. You might end up with nothing."

He was silent. Then he shrugged. "Just commenting." He smiled. "I believe I can tolerate our arrangement." He suddenly turned to look at Dalai. "Did you really toss her in a trunk down here?" He watched as Dalai froze, her gaze fixed on him. "I believe you did," he said softly. "When you start choosing your half, save the trunk for me."

"If I get my statue," Zahra said. "And you make sure I'll have no more trouble with Robaku. Then you'll get everything I promised."

"I've already paid my dues to you. I did it the day I destroyed that schoolroom for you. Consider everything else as a bonus." He met her eyes. "And you know I'll do it well. You've watched me do it before. There won't be anyone left alive when I've finished here."

"And how you enjoy it." She chuckled. "You should pay me."

"Not amusing." He glanced around the room overflowing with treasure. "And if I don't get what I consider my fair share, I'll have to take it. Now show me how I get to that tunnel you said would take me to the museum from here."

The tunnel! Dalai froze. Why was he asking that? Dalai's eyes widened in panic as she whirled to Zahra. "The tunnel you had started when you had the museum built? But remember, you decided not to finish it. You said you liked the idea of linking them to have a way to get the treasure out, but then you realized thieves could also get into the treasure room through the museum."

"Of course, I remember," Zahra said coldly. "But necessities change. Varak said he needed a way to get into the museum undetected. The tunnel was over two-thirds done, and Varak said that he'll have no problem setting off an explosion that will allow him to blow the rest of it. He said one blast, and he'd be inside the museum." She smiled. "Won't that be an interesting surprise for Eve Duncan?" She turned to Varak. "I don't mind your blowing her up, but you bring me my statue intact. I'm making it easy enough for you."

"You forget that there's more than this little surprise to think about," Varak said sarcastically. "It's only a way to get in without being seen. I also have to worry about what happens once I hit that area with the second round of explosives. Where's that tunnel?"

"Behind that granite rock to the left of the ladder. Show him, Dalai."

Dalai was already moving toward the ladder. This was all going wrong, she thought desperately. Who would have thought Zahra would remember this old tunnel? But Dalai should have thought about it. Eve Duncan might die because she hadn't considered the possibility it might be used.

"Get out of my way." Varak was striding out of the treasure room and heading toward the ladder. "You're shaking. Why are you scared? It's no wonder I find you such a bore." He was working at loosening the rock behind the ladder with the pick he'd yanked from his backpack. "Maybe I should take you with me and show you something to be really afraid about." The rock came free, and he rolled it aside and peered into the damp darkness. "Stinking mess." He put on his backpack. "I'm going to have to crawl most of the way. You'd better not have lied to me, Zahra." He disappeared into the darkness.

Dalai watched for a moment before she whirled around and turned back to Zahra. "Did you lie to him? Can he get through?"

She shrugged. "He thinks he can. I wouldn't lie when it means my statue. I want him to get to the museum."

"But you lied to him about the Minister of Police. I wasn't sure he'd believe you."

"Neither was I. But it worked, didn't it? Not bad for a 'stupid' woman."

"Do you think that he'll actually get you the statue?"

She shrugged. "I believe he'll kill Duncan and take the statue from her. Whether he intends to give it to me won't be clear until it happens. But at least he will have done what I needed him to do as far as Duncan is concerned. Once he gets back here, I'll know what I need to do about him." She tilted her head as she gazed critically around the treasure room. "Pity. I might actually have to give him some of Kiya's treasures if he does everything he promised he'd do here. As he said, he's quite lethal, and he could succeed." She added cheerfully, "But I can always arrange to get all of them back later. All I'd have to do would be to hire someone like Varak to help me. As long as Varak stays away from Maldara and isn't causing me any problems, I could live with his having a moderate share ... for a short time."

"There's no one 'like' Varak. He would take more than a moderate share."

Zahra's smile deepened. "Then I would have to make an adjustment."

"You mean, you would kill him," Dalai said quietly. "That's why you wore the ruby comb tonight."

She shrugged. "It's another alternative, another way to get rid of him. It would be easy enough. The bastard is so big and strong. Yet all I'd have to do would be to get close enough to him to just run those prongs over his throat." She reached out and stroked a gold-rimmed vase next to her. "Not quite as safe, but I could use this attack on Robaku to my political advantage. I've been considering—" She broke off, frowning as something struck her. "You don't sound like yourself, Dalai. Why are you asking me all these questions?" She started to turn to face her. "Haven't I told you that—" She stopped as she saw that Dalai had crossed the room and was staring down at the golden trunk. "What are you doing?" Then she thought she realized what was happening. "He frightened you." She shrugged. "It might not happen. The idea just intrigued him."

"As it intrigued you." Dalai's gaze hadn't shifted from the trunk. "It must have made you feel very strong and powerful." She lifted the lid and gazed down inside it. "Because being that afraid made me even weaker and more dependent on you than ever."

"You had to be taught your place." Zahra was frowning again. "And you're sounding very disrespectful. I won't permit that, Dalai. You know what I'll do to you."

"My place," Dalai repeated. "I've let you tell me what that is all these years. I believe I've learned it very well." She paused. "But not from what you told me. It was because I had to teach myself who I really am to survive you."

"What's *wrong* with you?" Zahra hissed. "I won't take this from you. Have you forgotten who I am? I'm the leader of this country. Your father sent you to serve me. I let you live in my palace. You're nothing, Dalai."

"So you tell me," Dalai said. "Nothing. Or rabbit." She paused. "Or slave. But I'm none of those things, Zahra."

"Zahra?" Her lips tightened, her expression incredulous. "Insolence. You do not address me in that fashion."

"No, I won't address you at all," Dalai said. "After I've finished with you, I will go away and not see you again. I will try not to ever think of you." She met her eyes. "And I believe I will succeed because I'm stronger than you think I am."

"Go away? Do you think I'd let you leave me?" Zahra's dark eyes were glittering, her lips curled. "Perhaps I will, but only to go to Varak. I'll let him teach you manners, you little slut. You shake when he looks at you."

"Yes, I do. But how will you send me to him when you said you might kill him? You must make up your mind, Zahra." Her smile had a tinge of mockery. "Because threats won't work anymore. I'm afraid of Varak, but I'm not afraid of you. I haven't been afraid of you for a long time."

"Of course, you are. You know what I can do to you. You jump when I snap my fingers."

"Because I knew it pleased you, and it kept me safe. Pretense. Only a game. You had to believe I would never betray you. You had all the power, and I had to wait until it was my time." She met her eyes. "I realized when I was lying in that trunk that I wasn't going to live if I didn't change and become as strong as you are. I'm afraid your punishment backfired, Zahra."

"And you think this is your time?" She laughed. "What a fool you are. I've never been more strong."

"And I've never had a time when I wasn't alone. It makes a difference." She shined the beam of her flashlight around the room. "Kiya's treasure. I've always hated it. But only because of what you did to me here. You said she was like you, but I think she stood on her own."

"Not alone?" Zahra's voice was suddenly suspicious. "Why aren't you alone? Why are you saying all this now?"

"Because you're not going to get your statue. You're not going to get to make a choice of alternatives. Varak is going to die, and everyone is going to know what you've done." She was looking down at the trunk again. "I could tell them, couldn't I? You've shared so much with me."

"You? No one will believe you," Zahra burst out. "Why would anyone pay attention to a little servant girl when she's muttering lies against me?"

"Perhaps when they hear from your own lips that they're not lies." She reached down into the trunk and pulled out a disk lodged against the ornate side of the gold interior. "Your voice is very well-known, Zahra. Jill Cassidy thought that there would be no problem having it identified by experts." Her smile was bittersweet. "It was her idea to put the recording device in this golden trunk. I wouldn't have chosen it because the fear is still with me. But she's kind, and she was upset when she heard about my hours in this cage."

"You and that bitch *bugged* my conversation with Varak?" Zahra's eyes were blazing. "It won't do you any good." She was moving toward Dalai, every step sleek, catlike. "Because you're going to give it to me. Who knows? I might forgive this madness if you don't make me more angry."

"No, you won't." Dalai was backing away, slipping the disk into her jacket pocket. "I've gone too far. We both know it. You'll have to stop me any way you can."

"I want that disk," Zahra said between clenched teeth. "Give it to me."

Zahra jumped toward her.

Dalai threw her flashlight at her, and it hit Zahra in the mouth. Then Dalai dived behind a huge urn as the flashlight rolled across the floor.

"Hiding, little rabbit?" Zahra was half kneeling as she moved across the dim room. "How stupid to throw that flashlight at me. How are you going to see me? But I still have my flashlight, and I'm catching glimpses of you. Frightened? Look at you, dodging behind all those trunks and statues in the dark. I'm closer to you now. I can hear you breathing. And you said you weren't afraid of me. Liar."

Dalai froze behind a carved chaise. She could hear Zahra breathing. But Zahra sounded excited, and Dalai realized that she was excited, too. She wasn't frightened as Zahra assumed. The blood was pumping through her veins, and there was no fear, only the rush of adrenaline. She felt... eager, her gaze on every move Zahra made.

She could see Zahra's shadow behind the glare of her flashlight. She was reaching up to her chignon.

The ruby comb, Dalai thought. She had been expecting it.

She watched in fascination. Zahra was loosening the comb in her hair, getting it ready for the strike. "You're right. You've gone too far," Zahra said softly. "You went too far the moment you thought you could stand up and be anything but the slave you are. Slaves should always kneel, Dalai. You should have remembered that."

Then she leaped. She was on top of Dalai. She hit Dalai's head with the flashlight. Then she struck Dalai again.

Dalai rolled away from her, grasping the flashlight and using all her strength to pull it away from Zahra. Then she was frantically searching in her jacket pocket as she watched Zahra pull the ruby comb from her hair.

She was aiming the prongs at Dalai's face! Dalai felt the prongs break the skin at her chin as she fought to push Zahra's hand aside. Strong. Zahra had always been so strong...

"*Yes,*" Zahra said fiercely. Her eyes were gleaming down at Dalai. "That should be enough. You'll feel the poison any second. You're *dead*, Dalai. We both know it." But the comb was moving again, raking Dalai's throat, she could feel the blood flow... "But this is pure pleasure..." Zahra whispered: "I want more. I want to see you suffer. You thought you could hurt *me*? You betrayed me!"

Zahra was enjoying this too much, Dalai thought. If Dalai didn't move quickly, Zahra might decide to cut her throat. Dalai's hand closed on the switchblade knife in her pocket. Distract her. She gazed at Zahra frantically, pleadingly. "Please, don't do—"

She rolled to the side, taking Zahra by surprise. The switchblade was out and open.

Dalai reached out and plunged the pearl-handled knife into the hand holding the comb.

Zahra screamed.

"What are you doing?" Zahra was staring at her hand in disbelief. "Why did you—You fool! It's too late. You'll be dead in—"

"That's what you said." Dalai's heart was beating hard as she carefully edged away from the knife she'd plunged into Zahra's hand. She swallowed. Everything had gone so quickly, she was having trouble believing what she'd done. "And you might be right if you hadn't always let me prepare the poisons for the comb. But I couldn't take a chance that you would use the poison on Eve Duncan instead of Varak. I had to be in control." She stared into Zahra's eyes, then her glance shifted to the knife sticking upright in the hand clutching the comb. "You understand control, Zahra."

Zahra's eyes widened in horror as she realized what Dalai meant. "The comb had no poison? You switched the poison to that knife?"

"I had to be prepared. That's what I told myself. But it might have been a lie." She said wearily, "Maybe this was always how I intended it to end. I could have run. I could have hit you on the head. I could have just pretended that nothing had changed. But I let the words come. I let you go after me." She was slowly sitting up. "Because something *had* changed, and I couldn't ignore it."

"It *hurts*." Zahra was staring dazedly down at the wound in her hand. "It's burning, you bitch. You did it. It's really the poison." She was suddenly trying to move toward her. "I'll *kill* you."

Dalai shook her head. "You're already too weak. Remember how you described what the poison would do to frighten me? All you can do is lie there and hate me. It won't be long now."

"I *won't* die," Zahra panted. "Weak people like you die. I'll live through this. I'm like Kiya and Cleopatra, queens who ruled the world." Zahra's voice was frantic with fear and anger as she felt the poison sear inside her. "But I would have been greater than them. I have to be greater. I won't let you take that from me. I won't let anyone take—"

Dalai shook her head. "You're not great, Zahra." She leaned closer and looked into her eyes. "You're nothing. You should recognize that word. *Nothing.* And soon you'll be less than nothing."

Zahra's eyes were filled with outrage and horror. Her mouth fell open, and her eyes glazed. "*No!* Not me. I won't have it! This can't happen to—"

She was dead.

Dalai stared at her for a long moment. So many years of fear and torment... She should feel something, shouldn't she? She felt nothing but flatness and bewilderment. She got wearily to her feet. It didn't matter what she was feeling. Maybe she'd know later.

Now she had to do something to help Jill or Eve Duncan. Varak had seemed so confident that he could get through that tunnel. Dalai had to call Jill and let her know. She was helping no one staying down in this splendid golden treasury that Zahra had worshipped.

Hurry!

She reached for her phone as she started to run up the ladder.

She heard the explosions before she'd gone more than two rungs.

She climbed the rest of the rungs, panicked.

Then she was outside, staring desperately in the direction of the museum. But she couldn't see it! It had disappeared.

All she could see was the thick layer of rolling black smoke reaching for the sky.

———◆———

"Come back inside." Hajif was trying to draw Jill back into the cave. "You're not supposed to be out here. All is going well. Mr. Novak said that it should be over soon."

She could see that it was going well as she gazed down at the streets of the village. Varak's men had been sitting ducks for Novak's team waiting for them. But there was still violence and blood and all the hideous signs of war to which Jill had become accustomed.

The acrid scent of tear gas...

Gunshots.

Men running...

Explosions.

Men firing automatic rifles...

And men with machetes...

How she hated those machetes.

"Come back inside," Hajif said again. "Mr. Novak will not be—"

Kaboom.

The ground shook, throwing her to the ground.

Then another explosion.

Her eyes flew toward the hill.

Smoke. The entire hill was wreathed in thick, black, smoke.

"What is that smoke?" Hajif's gaze had followed Jill's to the top of the hill. "Was it a bomb? I don't see a fire."

Neither did Jill though she thought she could see a dull glow beyond those thick clouds of smoke. "I think...it's a military-grade smoke grenade. I've seen them before, in Pakistan. Varak must have launched it with a chemical explosive of some sort to keep feeding the smoke." She was struggling to get to her feet. "Probably oil or carbon base...I don't know why he—" She broke off as the reason came to her. "No one can see through that smoke. You'd be almost blind."

Smoke. Black. Impenetrable. Curling like thick shadow serpents into the sky from the hill.

From the museum.

That thick black smoke would completely obscure vision from only a few yards away.

And Joe's position in that banyan tree was more than twenty yards from the museum. He wouldn't be able to see anything.

Panic iced through her. "No!"

Then she was ripping off her tee shirt. "Keep everyone in the caves, Hajif." She wrapped the tee shirt over her mouth and nose as she tore away from him. She heard Hajif shouting behind her as she ran through the jungle and streaked up the path.

Through that impossibly thick smoke, she couldn't even see the banyan tree where, only hours earlier, Joe had shown her he'd set up to take his shot. She didn't know if he was still there in the jungle or heading toward that museum as she was doing.

She didn't care. She only knew what she had to do.

Get to Eve.

She reached the museum. The door had been thrown wide.

No fire. But smoke in every corner and pouring out the door.

And there was a gaping black hole where the back windows had been. A hole big enough for Varak to have been able to take Eve out of the museum and avoid that front entrance.

And no Eve.

Maybe Joe had already gotten her out...

But Mila's reconstruction was still on the worktable. Eve would never have left her there to be destroyed.

She grabbed the skull and took it with her as she tore back out of the museum.

Her eyes were stinging as she ran out into that thick cloud of smoke again. She shouted, "Eve!"

"Here she is!" It was a man's voice in the distance. "Come and get her, Jill. It *is* Jill Cassidy, isn't it? How could I ever forget your voice? I was hoping to see you here."

And how could she ever forget Varak's voice? Laughing as she struggled beneath the weight of his body as he beat her. Don't think of that moment of weakness. Make him speak again so she could locate him.

And so Joe could locate Eve.

"Say something, Eve," she called. "Has he hurt you? He's a coward and very good at hurting helpless women...or children." Her hand tightened on her gun. "Isn't that right, Varak?"

"Yes, because they're of no importance. Except when they're being stubborn. Your friend Duncan is proving to be very obstinate. She won't tell me where the Great Beloved Wife statue is hidden. Come and help me persuade her."

"Stay where you are, Jill," Eve called. "You know you can't do anything. Don't give him what he wants."

Jill was almost sure Eve's voice was coming from the dense jungle behind the museum. She started toward it. "You're alive. That means there has to be something we can do."

Are you listening, Joe? Do you hear us? All that training, all that intensity and boundless passion. Track him. Find him.

She was struggling to breathe. Her throat felt raw. But there was less smoke as she rounded the curve in the trail that led to the rear of the museum. She thought she could see darker figures among the haze. Eve?

"I see you, Jill," Varak said. "You're just a shadow in all this smoke, but I can make you out. And I don't see the gun in your hand, but I know it's there. Because you had one when we had our little party with you. It didn't do you any good then. It won't do you any good now. Because your friend, Eve, also had a gun, and I was forced to smash a few fingers and take it away from her. I admit I was tempted to use my machete on them. But perhaps later...right now all you have to know is that the barrel of the gun is pressed to her temple. That means you're going to come forward and toss your gun to me, or I'll press the trigger. I'll give you to the count of three. I want that statue, and I don't have time to play games. Unfortunately, I've had a call from Markel, and he says things aren't going as we hoped in the village. So it seems I've got to get out of here." His tone was suddenly harsh. "But I'm not going before I get that statue. It appears as if I'm going to need money. But I'd do it even if it weren't worth a fortune, just to keep it away from that bitch, Zahra. She worships it." He started the count. "One . . . Two . . ."

"Stop." She knew that the crazy bastard would do it. "I'm coming toward you. We can work this out. Don't hurt her."

Where are you, Joe?

He had to be close. He was a much better tracker than she was. There had to be a reason why he hadn't made his move, and it was probably that threat Varak had made.

She stopped a few yards from Varak. The smoke was still thick here, but she could see him. He had a scarf covering his mouth and nose, and it brought back the chilling memory of that night in the jungle. Forget it. Fear was her enemy, and it would only weaken her. She flinched as she saw that he hadn't been lying about the gun pressed to Eve's temple. She quickly tossed her gun on the ground beside him. "If things aren't going your way, you should let her go and run. If Eve Duncan dies, they'll never stop hunting you."

"I've been hunted for most of my life. I haven't been caught yet." He cocked his gun. "The statue, Eve," he said softly. "I know you have it. I saw it when you were bragging about that press conference on TV. Where is it?"

"I'm listening. I want to live," Eve said. "I have a family. I did hide that statue. But Jill might be right. Maybe we can make a deal."

She was playing for time, Jill knew. Banking on the belief that Joe was close. But Joe couldn't do anything as long as that gun was pressed to Eve's temple.

So get the barrel away from her.

Give Joe his chance. Give Eve her chance.

How?

Then, as she looked down at the reconstruction of Mila that she was still carrying, she realized she knew.

"But maybe we shouldn't give in to him, Eve. He's bound to be lying to us." Jill's voice deliberately rose hysterically. "I told you what he did to me. I can't let—" In midsentence, she hurled Mila's skull with full force at the hand in which Varak was holding the weapon and knocked his gun up in the air. The next instant, she dived to the ground next to him, reaching for the gun she'd just tossed to him.

She heard Varak swearing as he stomped on her hand and instinctively swung the weapon in his hand toward her to fire it.

Pain.

She gasped as the hot wave of agony spread through her side.

But he was turning away from her toward Eve again.

No!

But Eve was tearing away from him and dropping to the ground. "Now, Joe!"

A single shot from a Remington 700.

Varak's body whiplashed as the bullet struck him in the throat. His eyes bulged as he saw the blood spurting. "What the—" Then he started to fall to the ground.

But Joe's second bullet tore into Varak's left eye, jerking him backward.

And then the third bullet struck him in the center of his forehead, and his head exploded.

Jill saw him collapse a few yards away, the blood pouring from the wounds. So much blood...

Dead. Is that how monsters died?

Eve was kneeling beside Jill, her face pale. "Lie still." Her voice was shaking. "Why couldn't you have just waited? I could have stalled him. You're bleeding, dammit."

"Mila...I'm sorry about Mila. I couldn't think of anything else to do. All that...work..."

"What? Mila? Where did that come from? For heaven's sake, I think that she'd forgive you. I know I do." Her voice was suddenly fierce. "Providing you don't die on us. I won't have that, Jill."

"Of course, I...won't die." Jill's voice sounded strange, slurred, even to herself. "I'm just a little...tired..."

Darkness

There was light streaming through that window, Jill realized as her eyes opened. Strange. It had been dark only minutes ago, but now it was light...

She saw Novak's face above her. And that hospital smell...

"Nairobi?" she whispered drowsily.

"No, we're done with Nairobi." He leaned forward. "Embassy hospital. But we do keep meeting this way. It's got to stop, Jill. I don't think I can take much more."

Then she was wide-awake. "Eve!"

"She's fine," he said. "You took the bullet. But you're fine. It was a flesh wound in your left side, and you have a cracked rib." He grimaced. "Well, maybe Eve's not so fine. She was with you most of the night after the doctors patched you up. She wouldn't let anyone else get near you. She only left when Quinn said that her son was on the phone and needed to talk to her. Then she graciously allowed me to sit with you."

"No one needs to sit with me. You shouldn't be here anyway. I know you've got stuff you need to do." She had a vague memory of smoke and explosives and men running... "Your team probably needs you. It must be a major disaster scene at Robaku."

"It is, but we've got it under control. I've been back and forth to Robaku all night." He paused. "And I *should* be here." His hand covered hers on the bed. "Stop giving me orders. This isn't your story anymore until you get out of that hospital bed. It's mine."

His hand was warm and safe, and she didn't want to move it. "You said I was fine." She had a sudden thought. "Dalai. Is she okay?"

"Other than trying to fight everyone in the emergency room to make them release her. They insisted on keeping her overnight to make sure those cuts on her face and throat didn't contain the same poison that killed Zahra. Her room is down at the end of the hall." He shook his head as she tried to sit up. "No, you don't get out of that bed until the doctor says that you can. I'd say she's proved she can take of herself."

"That doesn't matter. I brought her into this. She deserves my support."

"And I can see that you're already planning on how to get down that hall as soon as I leave this room. Relax, Jill. It's not going to happen."

He wasn't going to budge. He was being his usual domineering self. She fell back against the pillows. It wasn't worth fighting him right now. Her throat still felt raw, her side was throbbing, and she had to figure things out anyway. "You'll have to leave here soon. You've programmed everyone not to be able to do without you. You said you had it under control. What does that mean? What did you do?"

"As soon as Varak's men were subdued, I had photos taken of the scene and Varak's body removed and flown to Nairobi for complete DNA and lab work. Then I brought U.S. Ambassador Sandow and his staff to Robaku and started the real battle." His lips twisted. "To keep us all from getting arrested. I had to call in my director to use all his political connections to try to smooth the way until I could get those DNA results. I'm lucky he didn't cut me loose. He still may decide to do it."

"Not likely. You're the golden boy, and he'll know that if anyone can clean up this mess, it will be you." She smiled. "And I might be persuaded to write a story or two to sanitize your spotty image."

"I'll pass. You're right, as long as I can manage to make this appear as a triumph for democracy and keep a civil war from erupting, I'll dodge the flak." He paused. "That's going to be the prime danger, Jill. The Kiyani legislature is already in an uproar about their president's being murdered. We gave them no details, but we're going to have to do it soon. They're making threats to everyone in Maldara, and Botzan is the main target. It doesn't help that Zahra had recently turned herself into a heroine." He met her eyes. "We're exploring options to keep them from turning this into a disaster."

It was clear there was meaning behind that last sentence. Options? What would keep this from becoming—

No! She immediately rejected the thought that had occurred to her. But she knew that it had occurred to Novak, too. She was silent a moment, trying to think of any other possible way to avoid it. But there wasn't any other option at this moment, dammit. "You know what you have to do," she said jerkily. "No more deaths. No more war. There can be no confusion or infighting. Zahra has to stay a heroine. She has to be the one who helped take down Varak in revenge for his attack on the U.N." Her lips twisted bitterly. "Varak killed her, and she died a martyr. You can stage that beautifully, Novak. You'll have to get a reputable journalist to break the story as soon as possible." She added fiercely, "But it won't be *me*. I won't lie and make Zahra Kiyani out to be anything but who she is. And when all this craziness is done, I'm going to be the one who discovers that disk that proves that a mistake has been made, and Zahra is actually a murdering bitch. Is that understood?"

"Understood," he said quietly. "It will save lives, Jill."

"Stop trying to soothe me. I know it's necessary. We can't let our trying to keep Varak from starting his slaughter all over again begin a war of its own. But it's a lie, and I hate it. So go away and do what you have to do. I'll look at it as one of those dark Grimms' fairy tales instead of a story that I can be proud of. I'll block it out and be fine with it in a few days."

"No, you won't," he said. "And I'm not fine about any of this. I don't want you to send me packing. You scared me to death," he said hoarsely. "I just want to sit here and make sure you're not going to fade away."

"Well, now you've had your time to do that," Eve said brusquely from where she was standing in the doorway. "Now get back to work, Novak. Joe said you know all those diplomats and politicians better than he does, and he needs you to keep them at bay until we get the results back on Varak's DNA. The situation is getting explosive. Right now, no one is sure that we didn't perform our very own coup."

"Maybe we did." He got to his feet. "My director said that it was only a question of semantics. However, you'll be comforted to know that Jill and I discussed a way we might avoid a civil war." He was heading for the door. "But there are a few more things that might be helpful. I think I'll give Gideon a call." He looked back at Jill, and said sharply, "Stay in that bed until you see the doctor."

Before she could answer, he was gone.

"If anyone can stop the tanks from rolling, he can," Eve said with a grin. "He might just roll back over them." She came across the room and dropped down in the chair Novak had vacated. "Joe says he's watched him, and he's incredible at pulling strings and manipulating situations. Rather like someone else I know."

Jill flinched. "Mine was a onetime effort. And I've tried to make up for it."

Eve's smile ebbed. "I'd say throwing yourself in front of a bullet for me might qualify. But it wasn't only a onetime effort. You pulled the strings that brought Varak to Robaku."

"And almost got you killed." She looked at Eve's bandaged hand. "Varak said he hurt your hand. Are you okay?"

"Just bruised. And don't be ridiculous. We all knew what the stakes were. We were all ready to pay them." She leaned forward. "I'm not going to thank you. That goes without saying. I just need to tell you that, in spite of the way we started out, I've been thinking of you as my friend for a long time now. I *keep* my friends, Jill. I have no intention of letting you slip away because you're still having guilt feelings. So get a grip and realize that we're in it for the long haul."

"I'll try to oblige." She found her throat tightening with emotion. "Though I'm not sure Joe wouldn't agree that the guilt is justified."

"You still have a cracked rib from the bullet you took for me. Joe might just think you walk on water right now."

Jill chuckled. "That won't last."

"You can never tell. Life has been nothing but surprises since I got to Maldara."

"But you'll be very glad to leave."

Eve nodded. "I want to go home." She paused. "But not quite yet. I'm going to take a quick trip to see Michael and Jane while Joe and Novak settle all the furor that happened at Robaku. Then I'm coming back to finish the reconstructions of those children. It shouldn't take me more than a few months, and I want to finish what I started."

"What *I* started."

"Whatever. You're doing it again, Jill. Stop it." She got to her feet. "Now I'm going to tell your doctor that you're awake. And then I'm going down the hall to see Dalai. I tried before, but she wasn't talking to me. She's kind of shut down. She seems very much alone."

"As soon as they let me up, I'll go and see what I can do," Jill said. Then she changed her mind and reached for her phone on the bedside table. "No, it's not me she needs."

CHAPTER

20

Y ou're putting me to a lot of trouble, Dalai." Gideon sighed as
he opened the door of her hospital room. "Particularly since it
seems I'm a busy man today, very much in demand. You could be a
little more accommodating."

She stiffened, her gaze flying to his face. "I didn't mean to cause
you trouble. I didn't ask to see you. Go away."

"That appears to be your theme song where I'm concerned." He
came into the room and strolled over to the bed. "But I can't go
away because Jill thinks that I have to make things right with you."
He shook his head. "Which is unreasonable because you've told
her that I was the injured party. But Jill has to make her stories end
the way she wants them to, so I guess we'll have to go along with
her." He gently touched her cut chin. "Zahra hurt you. I told you
to let me know if that happened again. You persist in not listening
to me."

She moved her head away from his touch. "It's nothing," she said
jerkily. "And it shouldn't matter to you anyway."

"Ah, yes, because you used me." He shook his head. "I'm an incredibly rich man, Dalai. Do you realize how many times I've been
used since that first time I saw you when you came to Zahra? The

two seem to go together. You become accustomed to it after a while. Sometimes it's even amusing watching the process."

"Amusing?" She looked at him in disbelief. "This was different. I could have killed you."

"Only if I was too stupid to protect myself."

"I could have killed you," she repeated.

"You appear to be stuck on that thought." He frowned. "So I guess I'm going to have to go at this from another angle. Yes, there was a slight possibility that you might have been to blame for getting me killed if everything had gone wrong. So you'll just have to do something to make up for it."

She tensed, her hands clenching on the sheet. Her eyes lifted to meet his own.

"No," he said quietly. "How could I do that to you when all I can see when I look at you is that big-eyed young girl who could have been my sister." He shrugged. "But I have no sister, and Varak killed my parents. We're both alone. But I believe we could manage to be friends. So I think we should stick together for a while until you become accustomed to life without Zahra."

She frowned suspiciously. "Are you pitying me again?"

"Perish the thought. I'm going to put you to work." He smiled. "Because it appears I'm going to be used again. This time by Novak, and I can't talk him out of it. He thinks he can quiet down all the uproar in the Kiyani government by arranging with the generals and bureaucrats to accept me as interim president until they can scramble and set up an election." His eyes were suddenly twinkling. "Since everyone would find me acceptable due to my charm, wit, and fat wallet. I told Novak to get me out of there fast, or they'd draft me for the duration."

"President..." She was looking at him in bewilderment. "Like Zahra?"

"Interim," he repeated. "And definitely not like Zahra. So will you come back to that place you must have hated, and we'll make the best of it for the time we have to be there? Then I think you might be ready to go to school or start a new life. Whatever you like."

"I have no money to start a new life. I have *nothing*."

"Not true. You have Kiya, the Great Beloved Wife. Novak is pulling strings to donate the Kiya treasury to the Kiyani people, but I bought the Great Beloved Wife in a separate deal at an enormous fee."

"And you think I would take that from you?"

"No, I'm not offering. I know better. But the interest on what the statue will bring in from tours and exhibits will be a tidy sum. You can consider it part of your salary."

"And what am I supposed to do for this salary?" she asked warily.

"Jill says that you've been very inventive surviving Zahra. I'm sure you'll find ways to make that hellish period in the palace bearable for me. You've listened and know everything that's going on in that government. You know where all the political bodies are buried. Maybe you'll even be able to get me out of that interim position sooner. Now that would earn a gigantic bonus."

"No, it would not," Dalai said flatly. But her eyes were shining with sudden interest. "No pity. But I could do this. I know these people. I've watched them all for Zahra and reported back to her. And I know their servants and every flaw in their lives." She frowned. "But it would be easier if you could make them accept me with respect. It made it more difficult for me when they saw the way Zahra treated me."

His lips tightened. "You mean as a slave."

"She did not say that word around anyone but me."

"But the implication was there."

"Always."

And it was incredible that she'd managed to rise above that stigma as well as all the other abuse Zahra had inflicted on her, Gideon thought. *But don't show sympathy or I'll never get her to accept help.*

He said lightly, "Then I guess we'll have to give you a fancy official title and your own staff to overcome it. What do you think?"

She stared at him for a long moment. "I think you're still trying to be kind to me." She was gazing directly into his eyes. "You cannot help yourself. It is your way, your character. And I need that kindness right now. But I will not need it for long." She lifted her chin. "Give me a little time, and you will see that I will get stronger and stronger. I don't know anything about this being friends. But you will learn to rely on me. It will be me who helps and lends *you* strength when you need it, Gideon."

Gideon nodded solemnly. "I don't have the slightest doubt that will be true." He turned to leave. "I'm already anticipating being deep in your debt."

"Wait." She moistened her lips. "I'm sorry I can't return your knife to you. You said it was a keepsake. Eve told me that Novak probably won't give it back because he thought Zahra's death shouldn't be connected to me."

"It was *your* knife, Dalai. I told you that I thought my father would want you to have it." He smiled. "I know he'd think it couldn't have been used for a better purpose. Neither do I."

She stared at him defiantly. "And neither do I."

He chuckled. "Then we won't worry about it, will we? Now I have to go and see Jill and tell her that we've come to an agreement. If that's all right with you?"

She nodded. "Yes, go talk to Jill." She suddenly smiled. "Because you're not at all sure about any of this except that you wish me to be safe and happy. But she will understand. When I told her that Zahra had told me once that she was like Kiya and I was only her slave, she said bullshit. She asked me how I didn't know that I wasn't the one who was like Kiya." She straightened, and her smile vanished. "Tell Jill that I've decided that she was right. I *am* like Kiya." She added quickly, "But I won't let that hurt you or anyone I care about. I just have to learn who she really was and how to control it."

"I'll tell Jill." He added gently, "And being like Kiya isn't all that bad. She changed the world for herself and generations after her. I'm looking forward to seeing what you can do." He lifted his hand. "I'll see you tomorrow, Dalai."

———

"She *is* like Kiya, Gideon," Jill said thoughtfully. "She's a survivor. Her story has been a nightmare so far, yet here she is on the road to her own Great Journey." She tilted her head. "But I didn't mean for you to practically adopt her, Gideon. I just wanted you to do something to make her feel better."

"And I did it," he said lightly. "But I'm warning you that she'd be insulted if you mention adopting her. She's having enough trouble understanding the friendship concept. If there's any adoption going on, I have an idea that she'd be the one in control." He leaned forward and brushed a kiss on Jill's forehead. "Don't worry about it, this is right. It's what I should have done a long time ago. We'll work it out together. Maybe I should be grateful that Novak is pulling me into that mess in the Kiyani government. It will give Dalai something to challenge her." He straightened and turned to leave. "What's next for you? Are you going to be at that news conference tomorrow? I need a friend in the media to glorify all my good points."

"The media loves you. That's another reason why Novak is bulldozing you through the legislative session. You're perfect, Gideon."

"True." His brows rose. "Does that mean you're deserting me?"

She shook her head. "It means I'm tired and need to move on," she said wearily. "It means I don't want to be around when all of Maldara is fawning over Zahra's memory. It means I've been fighting this battle for two years, and now that we're ending the story, I'm ready to skip the epilogue. I feel flat. I need something fresh and new to spark me."

"I'm fresh. I'm new. Just watch what I do to those stale old bureaucrats once I get my foot in the door." He added coaxingly, "It will be fun, Jill."

"I've been doing some research in my spare time on a project that will be fun, too. And you'll be too busy to miss me, Gideon. Maybe I'll come back for the coronation."

"Coronation was Zahra. I have no royal aspirations. Just a little fun for the shortest possible time, then I'm back in my plane and heading for the wild blue yonder." He grinned. "Don't lose touch, and I'll head your way."

She watched him walk out of the room before she turned and started packing up the few belongings Eve had brought to her. She was going to miss Gideon. He had been her friend and ally since this had begun. But it wasn't as if she was losing him entirely. People moved constantly in and out of her life. It was how she lived, how she worked. It didn't alter how she felt about them.

It wouldn't change how she felt about Novak.

Don't think about Novak right now.

It was hurting, and it wasn't as if she hadn't known that it was going to end like this. It was why she'd fought to keep it from beginning. It was too intense. He was too dominant. They'd both do far better alone.

Alone.

She wasn't really alone, she told herself. She had friends, she had her work, she didn't need a man like Novak, who would be a constant disturbance.

She didn't need Novak.

She would finish packing, check out of this hospital, and go say good-bye to Eve. Eve had said that their friendship was for the long haul, and she owed her that courtesy.

Then she would give Novak a call on her way to the airport. That would be the best way to handle it.

No, Novak would be furious. He would recognize it for the escape it was. She didn't care. It would be too easy to let herself delay the inevitable. She would take any way she could to avoid the pain of what had to be done.

She needed that escape, she thought wearily.

———◆———

"You're not going to get away with it," Eve said flatly when Jill walked into the museum two hours later. "Gideon blew the whistle on you with me. I squealed to Novak. He should be here any moment."

"So much for enduring friendship," Jill said. "I was going to call him. He's just...busy."

"Absolutely. Novak is doing a hell of a lot to keep this country stable. He doesn't deserve having to face you running out on him right now. Don't be a coward. It's not like you. At least you should stick around until he has a chance to get his breath." She crossed the room and gave her a quick hug. "Ordinarily, I'd stay out of your business. But you've never made it a practice to stay out of mine, so why should I worry? We've gone way past that." She smiled. "Whatever you choose is fine with me. But you never ran out on me, and it's not fair to do it with Novak."

"You're damn right it's not," Novak said grimly from the doorway. "But that doesn't mean you didn't try to do it." He was across the room and pulling Jill toward the door. "And I could see it coming when you woke up in that hospital room." They were outside now, and he slammed the door shut behind him. "You were worried and concerned and wanting to set everything in order."

"Of course I was. I'd just returned to consciousness, and I wanted to make sure everyone was alive and well, dammit."

"No, there was more to it than that. I know you very well now, Jill. There was an edge. You were relieved when I was called away by Quinn. If Eve hadn't phoned me today, I would still have been here with you anyway. I would have tracked you down. I wasn't about to let you walk away."

"It seemed to be a good time to do it." She moistened her lips. "We have our own lives to lead, and they would interfere with each other. We both know that what we had was purely sex, sparked by the adrenaline from what we were going through."

"Do we?" He jerked her into his arms and kissed her. "I don't know anything of the sort. I don't know what's happening with us, but I'm not afraid to stay around to find out. But it's clear that you *are* afraid." His hands closed on her shoulders. "Not that I blame you. You haven't had the most stable life since your father tossed you out into the world. But it still makes me mad as hell."

"I can tell." She tried to shrug away from him. "I'm not afraid. I'm just being reasonable."

"And keeping your own personal story close to you, private and untouched. I know you don't want to let anyone come in and add anything to your life. But I'm not going to let you get away with that." His eyes were boring into hers. "Because I'm too selfish, and I won't let you go. And I won't let you lie to yourself and cheat us both. Remember the night you were so afraid Varak was going to cheat us? It's the same thing, Jill." His grasp tightened. "You're smart, recognize it. You don't have to commit. Just admit to yourself what you're doing."

She couldn't look away from him. Was it true? She wouldn't be questioning herself if there wasn't an element of truth in his words. And she'd thought she knew herself so well. She smiled with an effort. "And admit you're right?"

He went still. "That would also help a hell of a lot."

"I won't do it." She paused. "But I might admit that I was running away, and that's neither honest nor intelligent. That would also mean I thought there was a reason to be afraid of you. But you've never done anything to make me afraid. You never will." She suddenly kissed him. "So that means this is my problem, and I refuse to be afraid of it. I'll have to examine why it exists and face it."

His arms tightened around her. "*Yes.*"

She smiled and shook her head. "Not that easy, Novak. I told Gideon the truth about being ready for something new and fresh. I'm still going to leave Maldara. You're going to be busy here for a long time straightening out Varak's identity and preventing those bureaucrats in Botzan and Kiyani from starting another civil war. After you finish, if you still think there's something besides sex between us, come and see me. And who knows, maybe the sex will be enough."

"I don't believe that will be true." His eyes were narrowed on her face. "And just where am I supposed to find you?"

"I'll let you know. My first stop is Cairo to do more research." She found herself drawing closer to him. She wanted to touch him. The excitement was growing. Why be afraid to take a chance? Why not have it all? Novak was the most exhilarating man she had ever met. Share the sex. Share that wonderful mind. There was time enough to see what else might be waiting for them. "After that, I could let you know where I'll go from there."

"Research?" He tilted his head. "Just what are you doing, Jill?"

"I've been thinking about Kiya. I thought I'd try to find out her story. Or at least where she was buried."

"In Egypt?" He shook his head. "She died in Maldara according to the journal."

Jill shook her head. "No, not Cleopatra's daughter. We already know a good deal about her. The *first* Kiya. Akhenaten's Great Beloved Wife from the Eighteenth Dynasty. She had such a powerful influence, yet no one knows that much about her. Her life is surrounded by mystery, and we're not even certain where her remains can be found."

"You've found yourself a deeper mystery to dig into?" He shook his head ruefully. "And you can't resist the story."

"No, why should I?" It was all clear to her now, all hesitation gone. "The world is filled with millions of incredible, wonderful stories. And each one is an adventure to explore. But I'm inviting you along on this one, Novak. Do you know why?" Her brilliant smile lit her face as she went back into his arms. "Because I'm beginning to believe that if we're lucky, if we don't screw this up, in the end, you might be my very favorite story of all time."

AUTHOR'S NOTE

Kiya, daughter of Cleopatra VII, never existed except in my imagination. However, Queen Kiya, the Great Beloved Wife of the Pharaoh Akhenaten, was real and one of the most mysterious and intriguing figures in Egyptian history. No one is sure where she came from before arriving at his court, though some scholars believe she might have been a Mitanni princess. But once she was established in Cairo, Kiya was evidently a source of boundless controversy and excitement. From the richness of her monuments, there was no doubt she had an exalted status, and, at one time, Egyptologists thought she might have even been the mother of Tutankhamun. This proved to be unlikely, but her title of Great Beloved Wife certainly must have made her position at court very competitive with Akhenaten's beautiful chief wife, Nefertiti.

But Kiya disappeared from history during the last third of Akhenaten's reign. Her name and images were erased from monuments and replaced by those of Akhenaten's daughters. Why?

Exile? Death? Disgrace?

Or did Kiya just become bored with the court and go away on her own Great Journey to a far land?

You know which one I would choose.

But it's a mystery...

ABOUT THE AUTHOR

Iris Johansen is the #1 *New York Times* bestselling author of more than 30 consecutive bestsellers. Her series featuring forensic sculptor Eve Duncan has sold over 20 million copies and counting and was the subject of the acclaimed Lifetime movie *The Killing Game*. Along with her son, Roy, Iris has also co-authored the *New York Times* bestselling series featuring Kendra Michaels. Iris Johansen lives near Atlanta, Georgia.